W9-CCE-947

 *Oracle Press*™

Oracle9*i* PL/SQL
Programming

About the Author

Scott Urman is a Senior Member of Technical Staff in the Diagnostics and Defect Resolution (DDR) team in Oracle's Server Technology division. He currently focuses on the internals of JSP and Oracle Text, and has worked with JDBC, PL/SQL, and OCI. Prior to joining DDR, he was a Senior Analyst in the Languages division of Oracle Worldwide Technical Support, focusing on all of Oracle's language tools. He has been with Oracle since 1989. He is also the best-selling author of *Oracle8i Advanced PL/SQL Programming* and *Oracle8 PL/SQL Programming*.

Oracle Press™

Oracle9i PL/SQL Programming

Scott Urman

McGraw-Hill/Osborne

New York Chicago San Francisco
Lisbon London Madrid Mexico City
Milan New Delhi San Juan
Seoul Singapore Sydney Toronto

McGraw-Hill/Osborne
2600 Tenth Street
Berkeley, California 94710
U.S.A.

To arrange bulk purchase discounts for sales promotions, premiums, or fund-raisers, please contact **McGraw-Hill/**Osborne at the above address. For information on translations or book distributors outside the U.S.A., please see the International Contact Information page immediately following the index of this book.

Oracle9*i* PL/SQL Programming

1234567890 CUS CUS 01987654321
Book p/n 0-07-219148-1 and CD p/n 0-07-219149-X
parts of
ISBN 0-07-219147-3

Publisher Brandon A. Nordin	**Proofreader** Susie Elkind
Vice President & Associate Publisher Scott Rogers	**Indexer** Jerilyn Sproston
Acquisitions Editor Lisa McClain	**Computer Designers** Carie Abrew, George Toma Charbak
Project Editor Laura Stone	**Illustrators** Michael Mueller, Lyssa Wald
Acquisitions Coordinator Athena Honore	**Series Design** Jani Beckwith
Technical Editors Simon Slack, Sharon Castledine	**Cover Series Design** Damore Johann Design, Inc.
Copy Editor Dennis Weaver	

This book was composed with Corel VENTURA ™ Publisher.

This book is dedicated to all of my readers and users of PL/SQL.

Contents at a Glance

PART IV
Appendixes

Contents

PART 1
Introduction and Development Environments

PART II
Basic PL/SQL Features

PART III
More PL/SQL Features

PART IV
Appendixes

Acknowledgments

project like this book takes quite a lot of time to do properly. There are several people who need to be acknowledged for their help with this project. First of all, thanks to my technical reviewers— Sharon Castledine and Simon Slack. Both of them have been with me for past editions, and no doubt will continue their efforts for future ones. I believe that we have found all of the technical errors, and any remaining errors are solely my fault. Thanks also to Lisa McClain, Laura Stone, and Scott Rogers from Osborne for keeping me (and this project) on track. And, of course, thanks to my family and friends (you know who you are) for their comments and advice.

I used a number of resources during the development of this book, including several Oracle manuals. These include the *PL/SQL User's Guide and Reference, Oracle Server Application Developer's Guide, Oracle Server Administrator's Guide, Oracle Server SQL Reference, Oracle Server Concepts Manual,* and the *Programmer's Guide to the Pro*C/C++ Precompiler.*

If you have any comments about this book, I can be reached via email at Scott.Urman@oracle.com. One of the best rewards of being an author is the comments and suggestions I have received from you on the first three editions, and I welcome your comments for this book as well. Please let me know what you think!

Introduction

racle is an extremely powerful and flexible relational database system. Along with this power and flexibility comes complexity, however. In order to design useful applications that are based on Oracle, it is necessary to understand how Oracle manipulates the data stored within the system. PL/SQL is an important tool that is designed for data manipulation, both internally within Oracle and externally in your own applications. PL/SQL is available in a variety of environments, each of which has different advantages.

The first of the PL/SQL books I wrote was *Oracle PL/SQL Programming*, published in 1996. This first edition covered up to PL/SQL version 2.3 with Oracle7 Release 7.3—at the time the most recent version of the database and PL/SQL. The second edition, *Oracle8 PL/SQL Programming*, published in 1997, expanded the material in the first edition and included information up to Oracle8 Release 8.0, the then current version. The third edition, *Oracle8i Advanced PL/SQL Programming*, was published in 2000. That edition focused on the advanced features, up to and including Oracle8*i*.

This book continues the updates, incorporating the features of Oracle9*i*. It complements the third edition by containing the introductory material that did not fit there. Together, this book and *Oracle8i Advanced PL/SQL Programming* provide complete coverage of the PL/SQL language.

What's New?

So what is new in this edition? The main differences, of course, focus on the features available with Oracle9*i*. The discussions of these new features have been integrated throughout the book, where appropriate. For example, Chapter 3 includes a discussion of the CASE statement (one of the Oracle9*i* features), along with the basic PL/SQL syntax. Continuing the tradition of including PL/SQL development environments, there are new versions of all of the development tools contained in the last edition, plus one additional IDE.

Accompanying CD-ROM

The CD-ROM included with this edition contains two different types of information:

1. As with the previous editions, electronic versions of all the examples used in the text are included.

2. Trial versions of six different development tools from five different vendors are included. This edition contains tools from Quest Software, Compuware Corporation, Embarcadero Technologies, BMC, and Allround Automations. We will discuss these tools in more detail in Chapter 2.

On Microsoft Windows systems, when you insert the CD-ROM a small application should automatically start that gives you more details about the CD-ROM, along with instructions on how to install each of the development tools. On other systems, or if the application does not start automatically, there is a `readme.html` file in the root directory that explains the CD-ROM's contents. I encourage you to try it out.

Intended Audience

This book is designed to be both a user's guide and a reference to PL/SQL. It is appropriate for all users, but especially those who have not used PL/SQL before. The advanced material is discussed in some detail in Chapter 12, but I encourage you to peruse *Oracle8i Advanced PL/SQL Programming* for the full story.

How to Use this Book

This book is divided into 12 chapters and 3 appendices. The chapters themselves are divided into three parts: Introduction and Development Environments, Basic PL/SQL Features, and More PL/SQL Features.

Part I: Introduction and Development Environments

The first part of the book introduces PL/SQL and the environments in which it runs. We also cover the PL/SQL development environments that are included on the CD-ROM in this section.

Chapter 1: Introduction to PL/SQL
This chapter introduces PL/SQL and describes some of the major features of the language. It also discusses the versions of PL/SQL and which database versions they correspond to. The chapter concludes with a description of the database schema used as an example throughout the book.

Chapter 2: Development and Execution Environments

PL/SQL can be run in many different types of environments, both on the client and the server. In this chapter, we discuss different locations for the PL/SQL engine and see the implications of communication between different engines. We also examine the development tools included on the CD-ROM, including screen shots.

Part II: Basic PL/SQL Features

This section discusses the relational features of PL/SQL, including the syntax of the language, datatypes, how to use SQL, built-in SQL functions, cursors, error handling, and collections.

Chapter 3: PL/SQL Basics

Any discussion of a programming language must start with the syntax of the language and the available datatypes. In this chapter, we see all of the types that PL/SQL offers and the control structures that are supported.

Chapter 4: SQL within PL/SQL

The procedural constructs of PL/SQL are only part of the story. It is availability of SQL that truly makes the language powerful and useful. In this chapter, we describe the uses of SQL queries and DML statements, as well as the transactional implications.

Chapter 5: Built-In SQL Functions

The SQL language has dozens of built-in functions that give extra functionality to the language. We see these functions in this chapter, including the versions in which each was introduced.

Chapter 6: Cursors

Cursors are used to handle multirow queries. They allow you to loop through a result set and process each row in turn. In this chapter, we examine the syntax of cursors and discuss the different types of fetch loops available. We also see how to use cursor variables.

Chapter 7: Error Handling

No program is complete without the ability to intelligently respond to runtime errors. PL/SQL supports the use of exceptions (similar to Java) that provide a concrete infrastructure to handle any runtime situation. We see how exceptions work in this chapter and discuss the semantics of exception propagation in detail.

Chapter 8: Collections

Collections are groups of PL/SQL objects, and include index-by tables, nested tables, and varrays. These datatypes are all similar to arrays in other languages. We discuss how to store nested tables and varrays in the database, along with collection methods.

Part III: More PL/SQL Features

The third section of the book covers the use of procedures, packages, functions, and triggers. We also briefly examine some of the more advanced features of PL/SQL in this section.

Chapter 9: Creating, Procedures, Functions, and Packages

In this chapter, we see how procedures and functions (collectively known as subprograms) are created and stored in the database. We examine the syntax for both subprogram and package creation, and discuss how parameters are passed.

Chapter 10: Using Procedures, Functions, and Packages

Chapter 10 extends the discussion in Chapter 9 to cover additional features of subprograms and packages, including how to call them from SQL statements and the dependencies between them. We also discuss how packages interact with the shared pool.

Chapter 11: Database Triggers

Triggers are a special type of PL/SQL block that are executed automatically whenever the triggering event occurs. This can be a DML operation such as an INSERT statement, a DDL statement, or a system event. Triggers can also be executed instead of a given DML statement. We discuss all of these trigger types in this chapter.

Chapter 12: Advanced Features

Chapter 12 briefly describes some of the advanced features of PL/SQL. These include object types, dynamic SQL, LOBs, and pipelined functions. We also see some of the more commonly used built-in packages, such as DBMS_ALERT, DBMS_JOB, DBMS_LOB, DBMS_PIPE, DBMS_SQL, and UTL_FILE. We also look at the new Oracle9*i* enhancements to the communications packages UTL_TCP, UTL_HTTP, UTL_SMTP, and UTL_INADDR.

Appendixes

The appendixes supply useful reference information about PL/SQL.

Appendix A: Guide to Supplied Packages
This appendix discusses the built-in packages available with Oracle. These packages greatly extend the capabilities of the language.

Appendix B: PL/SQL Reserved Words
This appendix lists all of the reserved words for PL/SQL. You should avoid using these words for variables and other PL/SQL objects.

Appendix C: The Data Dictionary
This appendix summarizes many of the data dictionary views, especially those that are most relevant to the PL/SQL programmer.

PART
I

Introduction and Development Environments

CHAPTER
1

Introduction to PL/SQL

L/SQL is a sophisticated programming language used to access an Oracle database from various environments. It is integrated with the database server so that the PL/SQL code can be processed quickly and efficiently. It is also available in some client-side Oracle tools. In this chapter, we will discuss the reasons for the development of PL/SQL, the major features of the language, and the importance of knowing the PL/SQL and database versions. We will also introduce the concepts that we will study in greater detail throughout the course of the book. The chapter concludes with descriptions of some conventions we will use and the database tables that are used as examples.

Why PL/SQL?

Oracle is a relational database. The language used to access a relational database is *Structured Query Language* (*SQL*—often pronounced *sequel*). SQL is a flexible, efficient language, with features designed to manipulate and examine relational data. For example, the following SQL statement will delete all students who are majoring in nutrition from the database:

```
DELETE FROM students
    WHERE major = 'Nutrition';
```

(The database tables used in this book, including the students table, are described at the end of this chapter.)

SQL is a *fourth-generation language.* This means that the language describes what should be done, but not how to do it. In the DELETE statement just shown, for example, we don't know how the database will actually determine which students are majoring in nutrition. Presumably, the server will loop through all the students in some order to determine the proper entries to delete. But the details of this are hidden from us.

Third-generation languages, such as C or COBOL, are more procedural in nature. A program in a third-generation language (3GL) implements a step-by-step algorithm to solve the problem. For example, we could accomplish the DELETE operation with something like this:

```
LOOP over each student record
    IF this record has major = 'Nutrition' THEN
        DELETE this record;
    END IF;
END LOOP;
```

Object-oriented languages, such as C++ or Java, are also third-generation. Although they incorporate the principles of object-oriented design, algorithms are still specified step by step.

Each type of language has advantages and disadvantages. Fourth-generation languages such as SQL are generally fairly simple (compared to third-generation languages) and have fewer commands. They also insulate the user from the underlying data structures and algorithms, which are implemented by the runtime system. In some cases, however, the procedural constructs available in 3GLs are useful to express a desired program. This is where PL/SQL comes in—it combines the power and flexibility of SQL (a 4GL) with the procedural constructs of a 3GL.

PL/SQL stands for Procedural Language/SQL. As its name implies, PL/SQL extends SQL by adding constructs found in other procedural languages, such as

- Variables and types (both predefined and user-defined)

- Control structures such as IF-THEN-ELSE statements and loops

- Procedures and functions

- Object types and methods (Oracle8 and higher)

Procedural constructs are integrated seamlessly with Oracle SQL, resulting in a structured, powerful language. For example, suppose we want to change the major for a student. If the student doesn't exist, we want to create a new record. We could do this with the following PL/SQL code:

```
-- Available online as 3gl_4gl.sql
DECLARE
  /* Declare variables which will be used in SQL statements */
  v_NewMajor VARCHAR2(10) := 'History';
  v_FirstName VARCHAR2(10) := 'Scott';
  v_LastName VARCHAR2(10) := 'Urman';
BEGIN
  /* Update the students table. */
  UPDATE students
    SET major = v_NewMajor
    WHERE first_name = v_FirstName
    AND last_name = v_LastName;
  /* Check to see if the record was found.  If not, then we need
     to insert this record. */
  IF SQL%NOTFOUND THEN
    INSERT INTO students (ID, first_name, last_name, major)
      VALUES (student_sequence.NEXTVAL, v_FirstName, v_LastName,
              v_NewMajor);
  END IF;
END;
```

This example contains two different SQL statements (UPDATE and INSERT), which are 4GL constructs, along with 3GL constructs (the variable declarations and the conditional IF statement).

NOTE
*In order to run the preceding example, you first
need to create the database objects referenced (the*
students *table and the* student_sequence
sequence). This can be done with the tables.sql
*script, provided as part of the online code. For more
information about creating these objects and the
online distribution, see "Example Locations" later in
this chapter.*

PL/SQL is unique in that it combines the flexibility of SQL with the power and
configurability of a 3GL. Both the necessary procedural constructs and the database
access are there, integrated with the language. This results in a robust, powerful
language well suited for designing complex applications.

PL/SQL and Network Traffic

Many database applications are built using either a client/server or three-tier model.
In the client/server model, the program itself resides on a client machine and sends
requests to a database server for information. The requests are done using SQL.
Typically, this results in many network trips, one for each SQL statement. This is
illustrated by the diagram on the left side of Figure 1-1. Compare this with the
situation on the right, however. Several SQL statements can be bundled together
into one PL/SQL block and sent to the server as a single unit. This results in less
network traffic and a faster application.

Even when the client and the server are both running on the same machine,
performance is increased. In this case, there isn't any network, but packaging SQL
statements still results in a simpler program that makes fewer calls to the database.

The benefits of packaging PL/SQL apply to a three-tier model as well. In this
case, the client (which is often running in an HTML browser) communicates with
an application server, which in turn communicates with the database. This latter
communication is where the PL/SQL benefits apply. We will examine this type of
environment more in Chapter 2.

Standards

Oracle supports the ANSI (American National Standards Institute) standard for the
SQL language, as defined in ANSI/ISO/IEC 9075-1:1999 "Database Language SQL."
This standard, commonly known as SQL99 (or SQL2), defines the SQL language
only. It does not define the 3GL extensions to the language that PL/SQL provides.
Oracle9*i* compiles with the majority of the features required by the CORE portion
of this standard. For more information, see the *Oracle SQL Reference*.

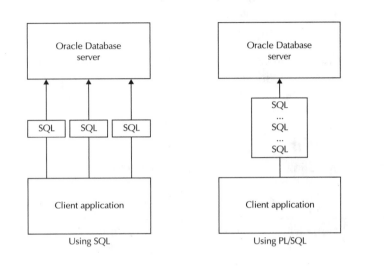

FIGURE 1-1.   *PL/SQL in a client/server environment*

Features of PL/SQL

PL/SQL's many different features and capabilities are best illustrated by example. The following sections describe some of the main features of the language. We will be examining these features in more detail throughout the course of this book.

Block Structure

The basic unit in PL/SQL is a *block.* All PL/SQL programs are made up of blocks, which can be nested within each other. Typically, each block performs a logical unit of work in the program, thus separating different tasks from each other. A block has the following structure:

```
DECLARE
    /* Declarative section - PL/SQL variables, types, cursors,
       and local subprograms go here. */
BEGIN
    /* Executable section - procedural and SQL statements go here.
       This is the main section of the block and the only one
       that is required. */
EXCEPTION
    /* Exception handling section - error-handling statements go
       here. */
END;
```

Only the executable section is required; the declarative and exception-handling sections are optional. The executable section must also contain at least one executable statement. The different sections of the block separate different functions of a PL/SQL program.

The design for PL/SQL is modeled after the Ada third-generation language. Many of the constructs available in Ada can also be found in PL/SQL, including the block structure. Other Ada features found in PL/SQL include exception handling, the syntax for declaring procedures and functions, and packages.

Error Handling

The exception-handling section of the block is used to respond to runtime errors encountered by your program. By separating the error-handling code from the main body of the program, the structure of the program itself is clear. For example, the following PL/SQL block demonstrates an exception-handling section that logs the error received along with the current time and the user who encountered the error:

```
-- Available online as Error.sql
DECLARE
  v_ErrorCode NUMBER;            -- Code for the error
  v_ErrorMsg  VARCHAR2(200);     -- Message text for the error
  v_CurrentUser VARCHAR2(8);     -- Current database user
  v_Information VARCHAR2(100);   -- Information about the error
BEGIN
  /* Code that processes some data here */
EXCEPTION
  WHEN OTHERS THEN
    -- Assign values to the log variables, using built-in
    -- functions.
    v_ErrorCode := SQLCODE;
    v_ErrorMsg := SQLERRM;
    v_CurrentUser := USER;
    v_Information := 'Error encountered on ' ||
      TO_CHAR(SYSDATE) || ' by database user ' || v_CurrentUser;
    -- Insert the log message into log_table.
    INSERT INTO log_table (code, message, info)
      VALUES (v_ErrorCode, v_ErrorMsg, v_Information);
END;
```

NOTE
The previous example, like many others in the book, can be found in the online distribution. For more information, see "Example Locations" at the end of this chapter.

Variables and Types

Information is transmitted between PL/SQL and the database with *variables.* A variable is a storage location that can be read from or assigned to by the program. In the previous example, v_CurrentUser, v_ErrorCode, and v_Information are all variables. Variables are declared in the declarative section of the block.

Every variable has a specific *type* associated with it. The type defines what kind of information the variable can hold. PL/SQL variables can be of the same type as database columns:

```
DECLARE
  v_StudentName   VARCHAR2(20);
  v_CurrentDate   DATE;
  v_NumberCredits NUMBER(3);
```

or they can be of additional types:

```
DECLARE
  v_LoopCounter BINARY_INTEGER;
  v_CurrentlyRegistered BOOLEAN;
```

PL/SQL also supports user-defined types: tables and records. User-defined types allow you to customize the structure of the data your program manipulates:

```
DECLARE
  TYPE t_StudentRecord IS RECORD (
    FirstName    VARCHAR2(10),
    LastName     VARCHAR2(10),
    CurrentCredits NUMBER(3)
  );
  v_Student t_StudentRecord;
```

Conditionals

A PL/SQL program can conditionally execute different portions of code depending on the result of a test. A statement like this is known as a *conditional* statement. The main construct for this is known as the IF statement. For example, the following block will query the database to determine the total number of students, and will insert different messages into temp_table accordingly:

```
-- Available online as Conditional.sql
DECLARE
  v_TotalStudents NUMBER;
BEGIN
  -- Retrieve the total number of students from the database.
```

```
SELECT COUNT(*)
  INTO v_TotalStudents
  FROM students;

-- Based on this value, insert the appropriate row into temp_table.
IF v_TotalStudents = 0 THEN
  INSERT INTO temp_table (char_col)
    VALUES ('There are no students registered');
ELSIF v_TotalStudents < 5 THEN
  INSERT INTO temp_table (char_col)
    VALUES ('There are only a few students registered');
ELSIF v_TotalStudents < 10 THEN
  INSERT INTO temp_table (char_col)
    VALUES ('There are a little more students registered');
ELSE
  INSERT INTO temp_table (char_col)
    VALUES ('There are many students registered');
END IF;
END;
```

Looping Constructs

PL/SQL supports different kinds of loops. A *loop* allows you to execute the same sequence of statements repeatedly. For example, the following block uses a *simple loop* to insert the numbers 1 through 50 into `temp_table`:

```
-- Available online as SimpleLoop.sql
DECLARE
  v_LoopCounter BINARY_INTEGER := 1;
BEGIN
  LOOP
    INSERT INTO temp_table (num_col)
      VALUES (v_LoopCounter);
    v_LoopCounter := v_LoopCounter + 1;
    EXIT WHEN v_LoopCounter > 50;
  END LOOP;
END;
```

Another type of loop, a *numeric FOR loop,* can be used as well. This looping construct provides a simpler syntax. We can accomplish the same thing as the preceding example with

```
-- Available online as NumericLoop.sql
BEGIN
  FOR v_LoopCounter IN 1..50 LOOP
    INSERT INTO temp_table (num_col)
      VALUES (v_LoopCounter);
```

```
    END LOOP;
END;
```

Cursors

A *cursor* is used to process multiple rows retrieved from the database (with a SELECT statement). Using a cursor, your program can step through the set of rows returned one at a time, processing each one. For example, the following block will retrieve the first and last names of all students in the database:

```
-- Available online as CursorLoop.sql
DECLARE
  v_FirstName VARCHAR2(20);
  v_LastName  VARCHAR2(20);
  -- Cursor declaration.  This defines the SQL statement to
  -- return the rows.
  CURSOR c_Students IS
    SELECT first_name, last_name
      FROM students;
BEGIN
  -- Begin cursor processing.
  OPEN c_Students;
  LOOP
    -- Retrieve one row.
    FETCH c_Students INTO v_FirstName, v_LastName;
    -- Exit the loop after all rows have been retrieved.
    EXIT WHEN c_Students%NOTFOUND;
    /* Process data here */
  END LOOP;
  -- End processing.
  CLOSE c_Students;
END;
```

Procedures and Functions

Procedures and functions (together known as *subprograms*) are a special type of PL/SQL block that can be stored in the database in compiled form, and then called from a subsequent block. For example, the following statement creates a procedure PrintStudents, which will echo the first and last name of all the students in the specified major to the screen, using the DBMS_OUTPUT package:

```
-- Available online as part of PrintStudents.sql
CREATE OR REPLACE PROCEDURE PrintStudents(
  p_Major IN students.major%TYPE) AS

  CURSOR c_Students IS
```

```
    SELECT first_name, last_name
      FROM students
      WHERE major = p_Major;
BEGIN
  FOR v_StudentRec IN c_Students LOOP
    DBMS_OUTPUT.PUT_LINE(v_StudentRec.first_name || ' ' ||
                         v_StudentRec.last_name);
  END LOOP;
END;
```

Once this procedure is created and stored in the database, we can call it with a
block similar to the following:

 `-- Available online as part of PrintStudents.sql`
```
SQL> BEGIN
  2      PrintStudents('Computer Science');
  3   END;
  4  /
Scott Smith
Joanne Junebug
Shay Shariatpanahy
```

NOTE
*The output from DBMS_OUTPUT.PUT_LINE
is available in SQL*Plus by using the* `set
serveroutput on` *command. For more
information, see Chapter 2.*

Packages

Subprograms, along with variables and types, can be grouped together into a
package. A package has two parts: the specification and body. Together, they allow
related objects to be stored together in the database. For example, the RoomsPkg
package contains procedures that insert a new room, and delete a room from the
rooms table:

 `-- Available online as RoomsPkg.sql`
```
CREATE OR REPLACE PACKAGE RoomsPkg AS
  PROCEDURE NewRoom(p_Building rooms.building%TYPE,
                    p_RoomNum rooms.room_number%TYPE,
                    p_NumSeats rooms.number_seats%TYPE,
                    p_Description rooms.description%TYPE);

  PROCEDURE DeleteRoom(p_RoomID IN rooms.room_id%TYPE);
END RoomsPkg;
```

```
CREATE OR REPLACE PACKAGE BODY RoomsPkg AS
  PROCEDURE NewRoom(p_Building rooms.building%TYPE,
                    p_RoomNum rooms.room_number%TYPE,
                    p_NumSeats rooms.number_seats%TYPE,
                    p_Description rooms.description%TYPE) IS
  BEGIN
    INSERT INTO rooms
      (room_id, building, room_number, number_seats, description)
      VALUES
      (room_sequence.NEXTVAL, p_Building, p_RoomNum, p_NumSeats,
       p_Description);
  END NewRoom;

  PROCEDURE DeleteRoom(p_RoomID IN rooms.room_id%TYPE) IS
  BEGIN
    DELETE FROM rooms
      WHERE room_id = p_RoomID;
  END DeleteRoom;
END RoomsPkg;
```

Collections

PL/SQL collections are similar to arrays in other 3GLs. PL/SQL provides three
different types of collections: index-by tables, nested tables (Oracle8 and higher),
and varrays (Oracle8 and higher). The following example illustrates various types
of collections:

```
-- Available online as Collections.sql
DECLARE
  TYPE t_IndexBy IS TABLE OF NUMBER
    INDEX BY BINARY_INTEGER;
  TYPE t_Nested IS TABLE OF NUMBER;
  TYPE t_Varray IS VARRAY(10) OF NUMBER;

  v_IndexBy t_IndexBy;
  v_Nested t_Nested;
  v_Varray t_Varray;
BEGIN
  v_IndexBy(1) := 1;
  v_IndexBy(2) := 2;
  v_Nested := t_Nested(1, 2, 3, 4, 5);
  v_Varray := t_Varray(1, 2);
END;
```

Conventions Used in This Book

I use several conventions throughout the remainder of the book, which are discussed here. These include the icons used to delineate differences between PL/SQL versions, the fonts used, how I refer to the Oracle documentation, and the location for the online examples.

PL/SQL and Oracle Versions

PL/SQL is contained within the Oracle server. The first version of PL/SQL, 1.0, was released with Oracle version 6. Oracle7 contained PL/SQL 2.x. With Oracle8, the PL/SQL version number was increased to 8 as well. Oracle8i (which corresponds to 8.1) consequently contains PL/SQL version 8.1, and Oracle9i contains PL/SQL version 9.0. Each subsequent release of the database contains an associated version of PL/SQL, as illustrated in Table 1-1. This table also describes the major new features incorporated in each release. This book discusses PL/SQL versions 2.0 through 9.1. Features available only in specific releases are highlighted by icons, as in:

| Oracle**8**
and higher | This paragraph discusses a feature available with PL/SQL 8.0 and higher, such as object types. |

| Oracle**8i**
and higher | This paragraph discusses a feature available with PL/SQL 8.1 and higher, such as native dynamic SQL. |

| Oracle**9i**
and higher | This paragraph discusses a feature available with PL/SQL 9.0 and higher, such as native compilation. |

Oracle Version	PL/SQL Version	Features Added or Changed
6	1.0	Initial version
7.0	2.0	CHAR datatype changed to fixed length Stored subprograms (procedures, functions, packages, and triggers) User-defined composite types—tables and records Intersession communication with the DBMS_PIPE and DBMS_ALERT packages Output in SQL*Plus or Server Manager with the DBMS_OUTPUT package
7.1	2.1	User-defined subtypes Ability to use user-defined functions in SQL statements Dynamic PL/SQL with the DBMS_SQL package

TABLE 1-1. *Oracle and PL/SQL Features by Version Number*

Oracle Version	PL/SQL Version	Features Added or Changed
7.2	2.2	Cursor variables User-defined constrained subtypes Ability to schedule PL/SQL batch processing with the DBMS_JOB package
7.3	2.3	Enhancements to cursor variables (allow fetch on server, and weakly typed) File I/O with the UTL_FILE package PL/SQL table attributes and tables of records Triggers stored in compiled form
8.0	8.0	Object types and methods Collection types—nested tables and varrays Advanced Queuing option External procedures LOB enhancements
8.1	8.1	Native dynamic SQL Java external routines Invoker's rights NOCOPY parameters Autonomous transactions Bulk operations
9.0	9.0	Native compilation CASE statement DATETIME and TIMESTAMP types Pipelined and table functions

TABLE 1-1. *Oracle and PL/SQL Features by Version Number* (continued)

It is important to be aware of the PL/SQL release you are using so you can take advantage of the appropriate features. When you connect to the database, the initial string will contain the database version. For example,

```
Connected to:
Oracle8 Enterprise Edition Release 8.0.6.0.0 - Production
With the Objects option
PL/SQL Release 8.0.6.0.0 - Production
```

and

```
Connected to:
Oracle8i Enterprise Edition Release 8.1.7.1.0 - Production
With the Partitioning and Java options
PL/SQL Release 8.1.7.1.0 - Production
```

and

```
Connected to:
Oracle9i Enterprise Edition Release 9.0.1.0.0 - Production
With the Partitioning option
JServer Release 9.0.1.0.0 - Production
```

are all valid initial strings. Note that the PL/SQL release corresponds to the database release. As of Oracle9*i*, the PL/SQL version is not printed as part of the version string. However, if you query the `v$version` data dictionary view, you will see the PL/SQL version along with the version of other Oracle components, as the following SQL*Plus session shows:

```
SQL> SELECT * FROM v$version;
BANNER
----------------------------------------------------------------
Oracle9i Enterprise Edition Release 9.0.1.0.0 - Production
PL/SQL Release 9.0.1.0.0 - Production
CORE    9.0.1.0.0       Production
TNS for Solaris: Version 9.0.1.0.0 - Production
NLSRTL Version 9.0.1.0.0 - Production
```

The majority of the examples in this book were done with Oracle 8.1.7, running on a Solaris system. The Oracle9*i* examples were written with Oracle9*i* version 9.0.1, also on Solaris. All of the screen shots were taken on a Windows NT system connecting to a database on a Solaris server.

Fonts

The main text for this book is in Optima font, whereas `Courier` is used for code examples, such as the select from `v$version` in the previous section. Within a paragraph, I also use `Courier` to refer to a database object or a variable used in a code example. Definitions and syntax diagrams are also in Optima. For example, the following is the syntax for declaring a variable:

variable_name type [CONSTANT] [NOT NULL] [:= *value*];

Keywords within a definition (and in body text, for that matter) are in UPPERCASE, whereas user-entered information is in *italics,* both in the definition and in the body text.

Oracle Documentation

In many sections of the book, I refer you to the Oracle documentation for more information. Because the names of the manuals change with versions, I generally use a shortened version. For example, the *Oracle Server Reference* refers to either the *Oracle8 Server Reference*, the *Oracle8i Server Reference*, or the *Oracle9i Server Reference*, depending upon which version of Oracle you are using.

Included CD-ROM

The CD-ROM accompanying this book has two main things on it:

■ The code for the examples used in the book. This code can also be found on McGraw-Hill/Osborne's Oracle Press Web page at **http://www.osborne.com**.

■ Trial versions of five PL/SQL development tools, from different vendors. These can be found in the `Development Tools` directory. For more information, see Chapter 2.

For more information on the CD-ROM contents, see the `readme.html` file in the root directory.

Example Locations

The examples included in the online distribution are identified by a comment on the first line indicating the filename. All of these examples are in the directory named code on the CD-ROM (and the Web page as well), in a subdirectory with the chapter number. For example, consider the following looping example, which we saw earlier in this chapter:

```
-- Available online as SimpleLoop.sql
DECLARE
  v_LoopCounter BINARY_INTEGER := 1;
BEGIN
  LOOP
    INSERT INTO temp_table (num_col)
      VALUES (v_LoopCounter);
    v_LoopCounter := v_LoopCounter + 1;
    EXIT WHEN v_LoopCounter > 50;
  END LOOP;
END;
```

This example can be found online in the file `code/ch01/SimpleLoop.sql`. The file `code/readme.html` describes all of the examples.

Example Tables

The examples used in this book operate on a common set of database tables that implement a registration system for a college. There are three main tables: students, classes, and rooms. These contain the main entities necessary for the system. In addition to these main tables, the registered_students table contains information about students who have signed up for classes. The following sections detail the structure of these tables, with the SQL necessary to create them.

NOTE
These tables can all be created using the
tables.sql script found in the online distribution
in the code subdirectory.

Sequences

The student_sequence sequence is used to generate unique values for the primary key of students, and the room_sequence sequence is used to generate unique values for the primary key of rooms.

```
CREATE SEQUENCE student_sequence
    START WITH 10000
    INCREMENT BY 1;

CREATE SEQUENCE room_sequence
    START WITH 20000
    INCREMENT BY 1;
```

students

The students table contains information about students attending the school.

```
CREATE TABLE students (
    id              NUMBER(5) PRIMARY KEY,
    first_name      VARCHAR2(20),
    last_name       VARCHAR2(20),
    major           VARCHAR2(30),
    current_credits NUMBER(3)
    );

INSERT INTO students (id, first_name, last_name, major,
                      current_credits)
    VALUES (student_sequence.NEXTVAL, 'Scott', 'Smith',
            'Computer Science', 11);
```

```
INSERT INTO students (id, first_name, last_name, major,
                      current_credits)
  VALUES (student_sequence.NEXTVAL, 'Margaret', 'Mason',
          'History', 4);

INSERT INTO students (id, first_name, last_name, major,
                      current_credits)
  VALUES (student_sequence.NEXTVAL, 'Joanne', 'Junebug',
          'Computer Science', 8);

INSERT INTO students (id, first_name, last_name, major,
                      current_credits)
  VALUES (student_sequence.NEXTVAL, 'Manish', 'Murgratroid',
          'Economics', 8);

INSERT INTO students(id, first_name, last_name, major,
                      current_credits)
  VALUES(student_sequence.NEXTVAL, 'Patrick', 'Poll',
          'History', 4);

INSERT INTO students(id, first_name, last_name, major,
                      current_credits)
  VALUES (student_sequence.NEXTVAL, 'Timothy', 'Taller',
          'History', 4);

INSERT INTO students(id, first_name, last_name, major,
                      current_credits)
  VALUES (student_sequence.NEXTVAL, 'Barbara', 'Blues',
          'Economics', 7);

INSERT INTO students(id, first_name, last_name, major,
                      current_credits)
  VALUES (student_sequence.NEXTVAL, 'David', 'Dinsmore',
          'Music', 4);

INSERT INTO students(id, first_name, last_name, major,
                      current_credits)
  VALUES (student_sequence.NEXTVAL, 'Ester', 'Elegant',
          'Nutrition', 8);

INSERT INTO students(id, first_name, last_name, major,
                      current_credits)
  VALUES (student_sequence.NEXTVAL, 'Rose', 'Riznit',
          'Music', 7);

INSERT INTO STUDENTS(id, first_name, last_name, major,
                      current_credits)
  VALUES (student_sequence.NEXTVAL, 'Rita', 'Razmataz',
```

```
                    'Nutrition', 8);

INSERT INTO students(id, first_name, last_name, major,
                     current_credits)
   VALUES (student_sequence.NEXTVAL, 'Shay', 'Shariatpanahy',
           'Computer Science', 3);
```

major_stats
The major_stats table holds statistics generated about different majors.

```
CREATE TABLE major_stats (
   major           VARCHAR2(30),
   total_credits   NUMBER,
   total_students  NUMBER);

INSERT INTO major_stats (major, total_credits, total_students)
   VALUES ('Computer Science', 22, 3);

INSERT INTO major_stats (major, total_credits, total_students)
   VALUES ('History', 12, 3);

INSERT INTO major_stats (major, total_credits, total_students)
   VALUES ('Economics', 15, 2);

INSERT INTO major_stats (major, total_credits, total_students)
   VALUES ('Music', 11, 2);

INSERT INTO major_stats (major, total_credits, total_students)
   VALUES ('Nutrition', 16, 2);
```

rooms
The rooms table holds information about the classrooms available.

```
CREATE TABLE rooms (
   room_id         NUMBER(5) PRIMARY KEY,
   building        VARCHAR2(15),
   room_number     NUMBER(4),
   number_seats    NUMBER(4),
   description     VARCHAR2(50)
   );

INSERT INTO rooms (room_id, building, room_number, number_seats,
                   description)
   VALUES (room_sequence.NEXTVAL, 'Building 7', 201, 1000,
           'Large Lecture Hall');

INSERT INTO rooms (room_id, building, room_number, number_seats,
```

```
                    description)
    VALUES (room_sequence.NEXTVAL, 'Building 6', 101, 500,
            'Small Lecture Hall');

INSERT INTO rooms (room_id, building, room_number, number_seats,
                    description)
    VALUES (room_sequence.NEXTVAL, 'Building 6', 150, 50,
            'Discussion Room A');

INSERT INTO rooms (room_id, building, room_number, number_seats,
                    description)
    VALUES (room_sequence.NEXTVAL, 'Building 6', 160, 50,
            'Discussion Room B');

INSERT INTO rooms (room_id, building, room_number, number_seats,
                    description)
    VALUES (room_sequence.NEXTVAL, 'Building 6', 170, 50,
            'Discussion Room C');

INSERT INTO rooms (room_id, building, room_number, number_seats,
                    description)
    VALUES (room_sequence.NEXTVAL, 'Music Building', 100, 10,
            'Music Practice Room');

INSERT INTO rooms (room_id, building, room_number, number_seats,
                    description)
    VALUES (room_sequence.NEXTVAL, 'Music Building', 200, 1000,
            'Concert Room');

INSERT INTO rooms (room_id, building, room_number, number_seats,
                    description)
    VALUES (room_sequence.NEXTVAL, 'Building 7', 300, 75,
            'Discussion Room D');

INSERT INTO rooms (room_id, building, room_number, number_seats,
                    description)
    VALUES (room_sequence.NEXTVAL, 'Building 7', 310, 50,
            'Discussion Room E');
```

classes

The classes table describes the classes available for students to take.

```
CREATE TABLE classes (
    department          CHAR(3),
    course              NUMBER(3),
    description         VARCHAR2(2000),
    max_students        NUMBER(3),
```

```
    current_students NUMBER(3),
    num_credits      NUMBER(1),
    room_id          NUMBER(5),
    CONSTRAINT classes_department_course
      PRIMARY KEY (department, course),
    CONSTRAINT classes_room_id
      FOREIGN KEY (room_id) REFERENCES rooms (room_id)
    );

INSERT INTO classes(department, course, description, max_students,
                current_students, num_credits, room_id)
  VALUES ('HIS', 101, 'History 101', 30, 11, 4, 20000);

INSERT INTO classes(department, course, description, max_students,
                current_students, num_credits, room_id)
  VALUES ('HIS', 301, 'History 301', 30, 0, 4, 20004);

INSERT INTO classes(department, course, description, max_students,
                current_students, num_credits, room_id)
  VALUES ('CS', 101, 'Computer Science 101', 50, 0, 4, 20001);

INSERT INTO classes(department, course, description, max_students,
                current_students, num_credits, room_id)
  VALUES ('ECN', 203, 'Economics 203', 15, 0, 3, 20002);

INSERT INTO classes(department, course, description, max_students,
                current_students, num_credits, room_id)
  VALUES ('CS', 102, 'Computer Science 102', 35, 3, 4, 20003);

INSERT INTO classes(department, course, description, max_students,
                current_students, num_credits, room_id)
  VALUES ('MUS', 410, 'Music 410', 5, 4, 3, 20005);

INSERT INTO classes(department, course, description, max_students,
                current_students, num_credits, room_id)
  VALUES ('ECN', 101, 'Economics 101', 50, 0, 4, 20007);

INSERT INTO classes(department, course, description, max_students,
                current_students, num_credits, room_id)
  VALUES ('NUT', 307, 'Nutrition 307', 20, 2, 4, 20008);

INSERT INTO classes(department, course, description, max_students,
                current_students, num_credits, room_id)
  VALUES ('MUS', 100, 'Music 100', 100, 0, 3, NULL);
```

registered_students

The `registered_students` table contains information about the classes that students are currently taking.

```
CREATE TABLE registered_students (
    student_id NUMBER(5) NOT NULL,
    department CHAR(3)   NOT NULL,
    course     NUMBER(3) NOT NULL,
    grade      CHAR(1),
    CONSTRAINT rs_grade
      CHECK (grade IN ('A', 'B', 'C', 'D', 'E')),
    CONSTRAINT rs_student_id
      FOREIGN KEY (student_id) REFERENCES students (id),
    CONSTRAINT rs_department_course
      FOREIGN KEY (department, course)
      REFERENCES classes (department, course)
    );

INSERT INTO registered_students (student_id, department, course,
                                 grade)
  VALUES (10000, 'CS', 102, 'A');

INSERT INTO registered_students (student_id, department, course,
                                 grade)
  VALUES (10002, 'CS', 102, 'B');

INSERT INTO registered_students (student_id, department, course,
                                 grade)
  VALUES (10003, 'CS', 102, 'C');

INSERT INTO registered_students (student_id, department, course,
                                 grade)
  VALUES (10000, 'HIS', 101, 'A');

INSERT INTO registered_students (student_id, department, course,
                                 grade)
  VALUES (10001, 'HIS', 101, 'B');

INSERT INTO registered_students (student_id, department, course,
                                 grade)
  VALUES (10002, 'HIS', 101, 'B');

INSERT INTO registered_students (student_id, department, course,
                                 grade)
  VALUES (10003, 'HIS', 101, 'A');

INSERT INTO registered_students (student_id, department, course,
                                 grade)
  VALUES (10004, 'HIS', 101, 'C');

INSERT INTO registered_students (student_id, department, course,
                                 grade)
  VALUES (10005, 'HIS', 101, 'C');
```

```
INSERT INTO registered_students (student_id, department, course,
                                 grade)
   VALUES (10006, 'HIS', 101, 'E');

INSERT INTO registered_students (student_id, department, course,
                                 grade)
   VALUES (10007, 'HIS', 101, 'B');

INSERT INTO registered_students (student_id, department, course,
                                 grade)
   VALUES (10008, 'HIS', 101, 'A');

INSERT INTO registered_students (student_id, department, course,
                                 grade)
   VALUES (10009, 'HIS', 101, 'D');

INSERT INTO registered_students (student_id, department, course,
                                 grade)
   VALUES (10010, 'HIS', 101, 'A');

INSERT INTO registered_students (student_id, department, course,
                                 grade)
   VALUES (10008, 'NUT', 307, 'A');

INSERT INTO registered_students (student_id, department, course,
                                 grade)
   VALUES (10010, 'NUT', 307, 'A');

INSERT INTO registered_students (student_id, department, course,
                                 grade)
   VALUES (10009, 'MUS', 410, 'B');

INSERT INTO registered_students (student_id, department, course,
                                 grade)
   VALUES (10006, 'MUS', 410, 'E');

INSERT INTO registered_students (student_id, department, course,
                                 grade)
   VALUES (10011, 'MUS', 410, 'B');

INSERT INTO registered_students (student_id, department, course,
                                 grade)
   VALUES (10000, 'MUS', 410, 'B');
```

RS_audit

The RS_audit table is used to record changes made to registered_students.

```
CREATE TABLE RS_audit (
    change_type     CHAR(1)     NOT NULL,
    changed_by      VARCHAR2(8) NOT NULL,
    timestamp       DATE        NOT NULL,
    old_student_id NUMBER(5),
    old_department CHAR(3),
    old_course      NUMBER(3),
    old_grade       CHAR(1),
    new_student_id NUMBER(5),
    new_department CHAR(3),
    new_course      NUMBER(3),
    new_grade       CHAR(1)
    );
```

log_table

The log_table table is used to record Oracle errors.

```
CREATE TABLE log_table (
    code            NUMBER,
    message         VARCHAR2(200),
    info            VARCHAR2(100)
    );
```

temp_table

The temp_table table is used to store temporary data that is not necessarily relevant to the other information.

```
CREATE TABLE temp_table (
    num_col     NUMBER,
    char_col    VARCHAR2(60)
    );
```

books, class_material, & library_catalog

The books, class_material, and library_catalog tables are used to represent the library used by the students. They are used to demonstrate collections, and are described in Chapter 8.

Summary

In this chapter, we saw a broad overview of PL/SQL, including the purpose of the language and the major features. We also discussed the importance of PL/SQL and database versions and how they correspond. The chapter concluded with a description of the accompanying CD-ROM and the example tables used in this book. In the next chapter, we will discuss PL/SQL development and execution environments, including the development tools available on the CD-ROM. We will start our discussion of the PL/SQL language itself in Chapter 3.

CHAPTER
2

Development and Execution Environments

L/SQL blocks can be run from various environments, each of which has different properties and capabilities. In this chapter, we will discuss the locations where a PL/SQL engine can be found. We will also discuss different environments available for developing PL/SQL applications, including both Oracle tools and tools available from third parties.

Application Models and PL/SQL

A database application can be divided into three parts:

- **The user interface**   Responsible for the application's look and feel. This layer handles the input from the user and displays the application output.

- **The application logic**   Controls the work done by the application.

- **The database**   Stores the application data persistently and reliably.

There are two different models for designing an application, which apportion the above parts into different locations.

In order to compile and run a PL/SQL block, you need to submit it to the PL/SQL engine. Similar to a Java virtual machine, the *PL/SQL engine* consists of both the compiler and runtime system. With development tools available from Oracle and other vendors, PL/SQL can be used at any of the application layers, and PL/SQL engines can exist in different places.

The Two-Tier Model

The two-tier, or client/server, model is a traditional one for application design. Here, there are two portions of the application—the client and the server. The client handles the user interface, while the server contains the database. The application logic is split between the client and the server. There is a PL/SQL engine on the server, and in some cases, on the client as well.

PL/SQL in the Server

PL/SQL has been available in the database server since version 6 of Oracle, and the server is the original location for a PL/SQL engine. Because the database server also processes SQL statements, this means that both SQL statements and PL/SQL blocks can be sent to the database and processed. A client application, written using either Oracle's development tools or tools by another vendor, can issue both SQL statements and PL/SQL blocks to the server. SQL*Plus is an example of such a client application in which SQL statements and PL/SQL blocks entered interactively at the SQL prompt are sent to the server for execution.

The following example shows an interactive SQL*Plus session. Text is entered by the user at the SQL> prompt, and SQL*Plus then sends the statement to the server for execution and displays the result. In the example, the lines in bold show the result displayed by SQL*Plus. We will examine in detail the syntax of PL/SQL blocks and SQL statements, such as the CREATE OR REPLACE PROCEDURE statement, throughout the course of this book.

```
-- Available online as SQL_PLSQL.sql
SQL> CREATE OR REPLACE PROCEDURE ServerProcedure AS
  2  BEGIN
  3    NULL;
  4  END ServerProcedure;
  5  /
Procedure created.

SQL> DECLARE
  2    v_StudentRecord students%ROWTYPE;
  3    v_Counter BINARY_INTEGER;
  4  BEGIN
  5    v_Counter := 7;
  6
  7    SELECT *
  8      INTO v_StudentRecord
  9      FROM students
 10      WHERE id = 10001;
 11
 12    ServerProcedure;
 13
 14  END;
 15  /
PL/SQL procedure successfully completed.

SQL> UPDATE classes
  2    SET max_students = 70
  3    WHERE department = 'HIS'
  4    AND course = 101;
1 row updated.
```

NOTE
The above example, like many in this book, can be found on the included CD-ROM. Examples that are on the CD-ROM are indicated with a comment like `-- Available online as xxx.sql`, *where* `xxx.sql` *is the filename on the CD-ROM. For more information, including a description of all the online files, see the* `readme.html` *file in the* `code` *directory.*

Figure 2-1 illustrates this scenario. The client application (in this case, SQL*Plus) issues both a PL/SQL block (which contains both procedural and SQL statements, including a call to a server-side stored procedure), and a separate SQL statement to the server. Both the PL/SQL block and the SQL statement are sent over the network to the server. Once there, the SQL statement is sent directly to the SQL statement executor contained in the server, while the PL/SQL block is sent to the PL/SQL engine, which parses the entire block. During execution of the block, the PL/SQL engine executes the procedural statements (such as the assignment and the stored procedure call). But it sends any SQL statements inside the block (such as the SELECT statement) to the same SQL statement executor.

The vast majority of applications that use PL/SQL will use the PL/SQL engine on the server, rather than a client-side engine. Typically, an application (which can be

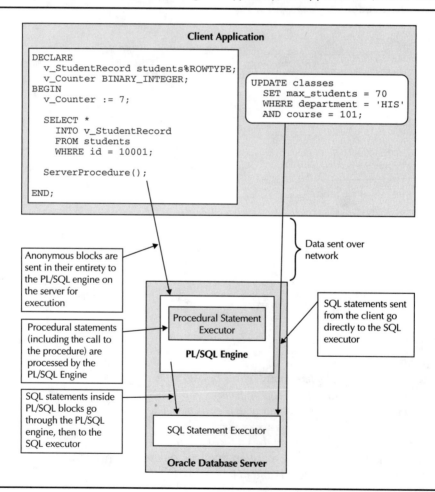

FIGURE 2-1. *PL/SQL engine on the server*

written in Pro*C, JDBC, OCI, or other languages) resides on the client, and sends both SQL statements and PL/SQL blocks to the server. Generally, PL/SQL blocks are sent the same way as SQL statements, with the addition of processing to retrieve the values of output variables. For information on how to submit PL/SQL blocks from a particular client-side tool, see the Oracle documentation.

PL/SQL on the Client

In addition to the PL/SQL engine on the server, two of Oracle's development tools (Forms and Reports) contain a PL/SQL engine. The development tool itself runs on the client, not the server. The PL/SQL engine also runs on the client. With client-side PL/SQL, procedural statements within PL/SQL blocks are run on the client and not sent to the server. This client-side engine is different from the PL/SQL on the server. PL/SQL blocks are contained within a client-side application written using these tools. An Oracle Forms application, for example, contains triggers and procedures. These are executed on the client, and only the SQL statements within them, and calls to server-side stored subprograms, are sent to the server for processing. The local PL/SQL engine on the client processes the procedural statements, as illustrated in Figure 2-2.

Stand-alone SQL statements issued by the application (the UPDATE statement) are sent directly over the network to the SQL statement executor on the server, as before. However, the client processes PL/SQL blocks locally. Any procedural statements (such as the assignment) can be processed without network traffic. SQL statements within PL/SQL blocks (such as the SELECT statement) are sent to the SQL executor, and calls to server-side stored subprograms are sent to the server-side PL/SQL engine.

Oracle Precompilers   You can use the Oracle precompilers such as Pro*C/C++ and Pro*COBOL to create applications that execute PL/SQL in the server. The resultant applications do not contain a PL/SQL engine. Thus, both SQL and PL/SQL statements issued by the application are sent to the server for processing.

The precompilers themselves, however, do contain a PL/SQL engine within them. This is used during precompilation to verify the syntax and semantics of anonymous blocks within the application code. The precompilers are unique among Oracle's development tools in this respect.

Communication Between Engines

In the scenario illustrated in Figure 2-2, there are two separate PL/SQL engines that communicate with each other. For example, a trigger within a form (running in client-side PL/SQL) can call a stored procedure within the database (running in server-side PL/SQL). Communications such as these take place through remote procedure calls. A similar mechanism is used to communicate between PL/SQL engines in two different servers, through database links.

In this situation, PL/SQL objects in different engines can depend on each other. This type of relationship works the same way as PL/SQL objects in the same database, with some caveats. For more information, see Chapter 10.

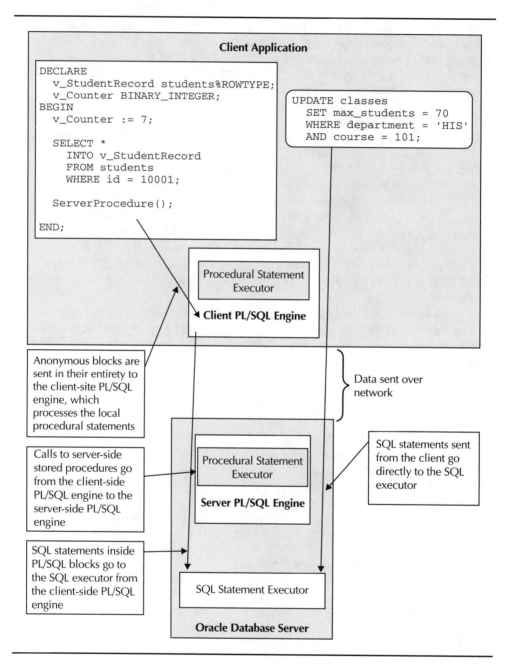

FIGURE 2-2. *PL/SQL engine on the client*

The Three-Tier Model

In a three-tier model, the user interface, application logic, and database storage are split into three separate parts. The client in this model is typically thin, such as a browser. The application logic is entirely contained within one layer, known as the application server. In this environment, the PL/SQL engine is generally found in the server only. Applications written using this model are typically more scalable, and support a larger number of users, than applications using the two-tier model. Modifications to the application are generally easier as well, because only the application server needs to be changed, rather than all of the clients.

The Oracle Internet Application Server (IAS) is a complete application server. Through the PL/SQL cartridge, you can execute stored procedures on the server and return the results as HTML pages. This is facilitated by the PL/SQL Web Toolkit, which is part of IAS. This situation is illustrated by Figure 2-3. For more information on the PL/SQL cartridge and the Web Toolkit, see the Oracle documentation.

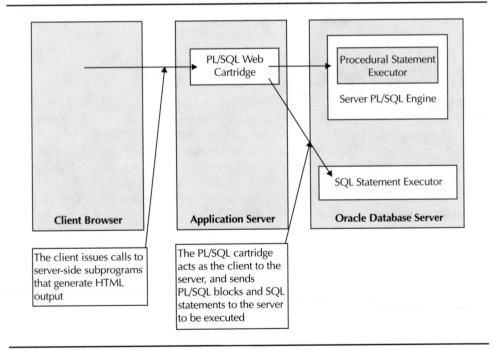

FIGURE 2-3.   *The three-tier model*

NOTE
With Oracle9i, Forms and Reports applications now run solely as part of a three-tier system, and not in a traditional client/server environment.

Connecting to the Database

In the previous sections, we have seen that PL/SQL (and SQL) statements are generally sent to the server to be executed. In order to do this, you must first connect to the database and establish a database session. This requires the database to authenticate you, usually in the form of a userid and password.

PL/SQL itself contains no syntax for connecting to the database or establishing a database session. Rather, this is done by the environment that issues the PL/SQL commands. For example, in SQL*Plus this is done by the `connect` command. Other tools have their own method of establishing a database connection, as we will see in later sections.

This applies for client-side PL/SQL engines as well. Although there may not be authentication in the form of a userid and password, the client-side environment (such as Oracle Forms) is responsible for sending the PL/SQL block to the engine for processing, after authenticating in some fashion.

PL/SQL Development Tools

There are many different PL/SQL development tools available, both from Oracle and from third parties. In this section, we will briefly introduce and discuss the development environments found in Table 2-1. As the table indicates, SQL*Plus is provided by Oracle Corporation with the database itself, and the remainder of the tools are available from third-party vendors. Trial versions of these third-party tools are included on the CD-ROM packaged with this book. We will introduce these tools in the following sections. For a more complete introduction to the tools, I recommend installing them on your system and consulting the documentation for each.

NOTE
The tools that are included on the CD-ROM can be found in the `Development Tools` *directory. For more information, see the* `readme.html` *file at the root level of the CD-ROM.*

For consistency, all of the screen shots in the following sections take place in a schema with the same set of sample objects. In all cases, the development tool is running on a Windows NT machine, connecting to an Oracle9i database on a Solaris server. In addition to the tables and types used throughout this book (described in

Tool	Vendor	Web Site	Included on CD-ROM?
SQL*Plus™	Oracle Corporation	www.oracle.com	No
Rapid SQL™	Embarcadero Technologies	www.embarcadero.com	Yes
DBPartner™	Compuware	www.compuware.com	Yes
SQL Navigator™	Quest Software	www.quest.com	Yes
TOAD™	Quest Software	www.toadsoft.com or www.quest.com	Yes
SQL-Programmer™	BMC Software	www.bmc.com	Yes
PL/SQL Developer™	Allround Automations	www.allroundautomations.nl	Yes

TABLE 2-1. *PL/SQL Development Environments*

detail in Chapter 1), there are examples of other PL/SQL and Java types. The following table lists the sample objects used in this chapter. The online file setup.sql can be used to create all of them at once.

Object Name	Object Type	Script to Run
Sample tables and types	Sequences, tables, types	tables.sql
AddNewStudent	Procedure	ch09\AddNewStudent.sql
AlmostFull	Function	ch09\AlmostFull.sql
ModeTest	Procedure	ch09\ModeTest.sql
ClassPackage	Package	ch09\ClassPackage.sql
Point	Object Type	ch12\Point.sql
SimpleClass	Java source	ch02\SimpleClass

SQL*Plus

SQL*Plus is perhaps the simplest of the PL/SQL development tools. It allows the user to enter SQL statements and PL/SQL blocks interactively from a prompt. These statements are sent directly to the database, and the results are returned to the screen. It is a character mode environment, and there is no local PL/SQL engine.

Generally, SQL*Plus is shipped along with the Oracle server, and is available as part of a standard Oracle installation. For more information on SQL*Plus and its commands not covered in this section, see the *SQL*Plus User's Guide and Reference*.

SQL*Plus commands are not case sensitive. For example, all of the following commands declare bind variables:

```
SQL> VARIABLE v_Num NUMBER
SQL> variable v_Char char(3)
SQL> vaRIAbLe v_Varchar VarCHAR2(5)
```

Although SQL*Plus is a character-mode environment, the Windows version does include some GUI operations. These are mainly to connect to the database and set the various SQL*Plus options, which are also available through character-mode commands. On UNIX systems, there is no GUI version of SQL*Plus.

Oracle**9i** and higher | Similarly, Oracle9i provides a version of SQL*Plus that is designed to run from a browser. This version, known as iSQL*Plus, provides a SQL> prompt for character-mode input within a browser, with any output displayed below. iSQL*Plus, similar to the Windows version, provides some GUI operations (such as connecting to the database and reading from files), but is essentially character mode. See the Oracle documentation for more information on installing and using iSQL*Plus.

Connecting to the Database

Before you can issue any SQL or PL/SQL statements in SQL*Plus, you must connect to the server. This can be done in one of the following ways:

- By passing a userid and password (and optionally a connect string) on the SQL*Plus command line

- By using the `connect` statement once you are in SQL*Plus

- (Windows and iSQL*Plus only) By specifying the username, password, and optionally the connect string in the initial Log On dialog box

As the following example illustrates, if you do not specify a password, SQL*Plus will prompt you for it and will not echo the input to the screen. Figure 2-4 shows the Windows Log On dialog box.

```
$ sqlplus example/example
SQL*Plus: Release 9.0.1.0.0 - Production on Tue Oct 9 16:32:22 2001
(c) Copyright 2001 Oracle Corporation.  All rights reserved.

Connected to:
Oracle9i Enterprise Edition Release 9.0.1.0.0 - Production
With the Partitioning option
JServer Release 9.0.1.0.0 - Production

SQL> exit
Disconnected from Oracle9i Enterprise Edition Release 9.0.1.0.0 - Production
With the Partitioning option
```

```
JServer Release 9.0.1.0.0 - Production
$ sqlplus example
SQL*Plus: Release 9.0.1.0.0 - Production on Tue Oct 9 16:33:23 2001
(c) Copyright 2001 Oracle Corporation.  All rights reserved.

Enter password:

Connected to:
Oracle9i Enterprise Edition Release 9.0.1.0.0 - Production
With the Partitioning option
JServer Release 9.0.1.0.0 - Production

SQL> connect example/example
Connected.
SQL> connect example/example@V806_tcp
Connected.
```

Executing SQL and PL/SQL

Once SQL*Plus is started, it presents you with a SQL> prompt. From here, you enter a SQL or PL/SQL command to be sent to the server. You can also enter commands to SQL*Plus itself (such as the set serveroutput on command, described in the section "The DBMS_OUTPUT Package" later in this chapter). When you execute a SQL statement, it must be terminated by a semicolon (or a forward slash). This semicolon is not part of the statement itself—it is the statement terminator. When SQL*Plus reads the semicolon, it knows that the statement is complete and sends it to the database. On the other hand, with a PL/SQL block, the semicolon is a syntactic part of the block itself—it is not a statement terminator. When you enter the DECLARE or BEGIN keyword (which start a PL/SQL block), SQL*Plus detects this and knows that you are running a PL/SQL block rather than a SQL statement. But SQL*Plus still needs to know when the block has ended.

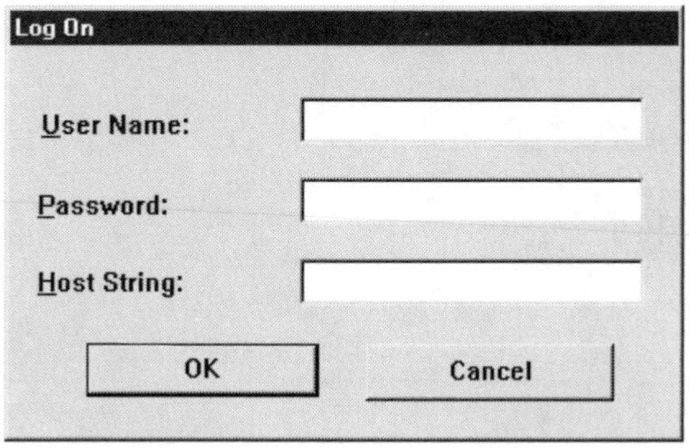

FIGURE 2-4.   *SQL*Plus Log On dialog box*

This is done with a forward slash, which is short for the SQL*Plus RUN command. SQL*Plus also allows you to terminate a PL/SQL block with a period, after which you can enter `run` or another SQL*Plus command.

Figure 2-5 illustrates both a PL/SQL block and a SQL statement. Note the slash after the PL/SQL block which updates the `registered_students` table. The SELECT statement after the block does not need the slash because the semicolon is present. (You can use a slash instead of the semicolon for SQL statements as well, if desired.) This figure also illustrates the results of the block (the message saying "successfully completed") and the results from the SELECT statement (the data from the table).

Using Files

SQL*Plus can save the current PL/SQL block or SQL statement to a file, and this file can then be read back in and executed. This useful feature is valuable both during development of a PL/SQL program and later execution of it. For example, you can store a CREATE OR REPLACE command in a file, and modify the procedure in the file. In order to save the changes in the database, you can simply read the file into SQL*Plus. Files can contain more than one command as well.

```
Oracle SQL*Plus                                                    _ □ ×
File  Edit  Search  Options  Help
SQL> DECLARE
  2     CURSOR c_Music410Students IS
  3       SELECT *
  4         FROM registered_students
  5         WHERE department = 'MUS' AND course = 410
  6         FOR UPDATE OF grade;
  7   BEGIN
  8     FOR c_Student IN c_Music410Students LOOP
  9       UPDATE registered_students
 10         SET grade = 'A'
 11         WHERE CURRENT OF c_Music410Students;
 12     END LOOP;
 13   END;
 14   /

PL/SQL procedure successfully completed.

SQL> SELECT *
  2     FROM registered_students
  3     WHERE department = 'MUS' AND course = 410;

STUDENT_ID DEP    COURSE G
---------- ---    ------ -
     10009 MUS       410 A
     10006 MUS       410 A
     10011 MUS       410 A
     10000 MUS       410 A

SQL>
```

FIGURE 2-5.   *PL/SQL in SQL*Plus*

The SQL*Plus `start` command reads a file (either on disk, or with Oracle9*i*, on the Web through a URL). Whatever text is in the file will be executed as if it had been entered at the prompt. The at sign (@) is a shortcut for the `start` command. For example, assume that the file `File.sql` contains the following lines:

```
-- Available online as File.sql
BEGIN
  FOR v_Count IN 1..10 LOOP
    INSERT INTO temp_Table (num_col, char_col)
      VALUES (v_Count, 'Hello World!');
  END LOOP;
END;
/

SELECT * FROM temp_table;
```

We can now execute this file from the SQL prompt with

```
SQL> @File
```

The output from this is shown in Figure 2-6. The `set echo on` command (the first command in the figure) tells SQL*Plus to echo the contents of the file to the screen as they are read from the file.

TIP
You can use this technique to execute the samples found throughout this book.

The DBMS_OUTPUT Package

PL/SQL has no input or output functionality built directly into the language. The UTL_FILE package (described in Chapter 12) does provide the ability to read and write from files, but this is not the same as printing to the screen. To rectify this, SQL*Plus, in combination with the DBMS_OUTPUT package, provides the ability to output messages to the screen. This is done in two steps:

1. Enable output in SQL*Plus with the `set serveroutput` command. This command has the format

   SET SERVEROUTPUT {ON | OFF} [SIZE *n*]

   where *n* is the size of the output buffer. If *n* is not specified, it defaults to 2,000 bytes. The maximum size is 1,000,000 bytes. The ON or OFF keyword turns the output on or off, respectively.

2. Within your PL/SQL program, use the DBMS_OUTPUT.PUT_LINE procedure. This procedure will add its argument to the output buffer.

```
± Oracle SQL*Plus                                                    _ □ ×
File  Edit  Search  Options  Help
SQL> set echo on
SQL> @ch02\File
SQL> BEGIN
  2    FOR v_Count IN 1..10 LOOP
  3      INSERT INTO temp_table (num_col, char_col)
  4        VALUES (v_Count, 'Hello World!');
  5    END LOOP;
  6  END;
  7  /

PL/SQL procedure successfully completed.

SQL>
SQL> SELECT * FROM temp_table;

   NUM_COL CHAR_COL
---------- ------------------------------------------------------
         1 Hello World!
         2 Hello World!
         3 Hello World!
         4 Hello World!
         5 Hello World!
         6 Hello World!
         7 Hello World!
         8 Hello World!
         9 Hello World!
        10 Hello World!

10 rows selected.

SQL>
```

FIGURE 2-6.   *Reading from a file*

With these steps complete, the output will be printed on the screen by SQL*Plus *after* the block completes. During execution, the buffer is filled by the DBMS_OUTPUT.PUT_LINE calls. SQL*Plus does not retrieve the contents of the buffer and print them until control returns to SQL*Plus, after the block has finished execution.

NOTE
DBMS_OUTPUT and UTL_FILE are packages. See Chapters 9 and 10 for more information on creating and using packages, and Appendix A for descriptions of many of the packages supplied with the database.

Figure 2-7 illustrates some calls to DBMS_OUTPUT.PUT_LINE.

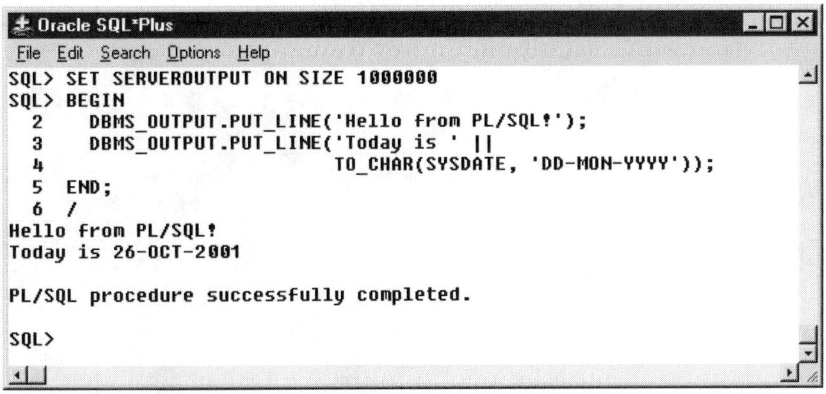

```
Oracle SQL*Plus                                          _ □ ✗
File  Edit  Search  Options  Help
SQL> SET SERVEROUTPUT ON SIZE 1000000
SQL> BEGIN
  2      DBMS_OUTPUT.PUT_LINE('Hello from PL/SQL!');
  3      DBMS_OUTPUT.PUT_LINE('Today is ' ||
  4                          TO_CHAR(SYSDATE, 'DD-MON-YYYY'));
  5  END;
  6  /
Hello from PL/SQL!
Today is 26-OCT-2001

PL/SQL procedure successfully completed.

SQL>
```

FIGURE 2-7.   *Using DBMS_OUTPUT*

Rapid SQL

Rapid SQL, produced by Embarcadero Technologies, is a GUI development environment that has the following features, among others:

- ■ Autoformatting of PL/SQL and SQL statements
- ■ Support for debugging server-side PL/SQL procedures
- ■ Support for Oracle8*i* Java classes and sources
- ■ Access to PL/SQL profiler data
- ■ SQL job scheduling
- ■ Project management
- ■ Support for Windows Active Scripting
- ■ Support for third-party version control systems

For more information on installing and using Rapid SQL, see the online help.

Connecting to the Database

When you first start Rapid SQL, you will get a window similar to Figure 2-8. The pane on the left allows you to explore database objects, sorted by datasource. The pane on the right is the working pane, which can show different types of objects as you work with them. A *datasource* records all pertinent information about a

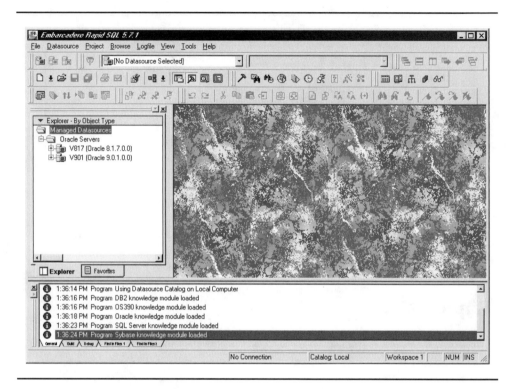

FIGURE 2-8. *Rapid SQL main window*

remote database, such as the type of database, userid, password, and connect information. The first time Rapid SQL is run, it will automatically discover available datasources for you by searching the SQL*Net configuration for your machine. Double-clicking on a particular datasource will bring up a dialog box allowing you to enter a userid and password for that connection, as shown in Figure 2-9. You can add new datasources and modify existing ones through the Datasource menu.

If you choose, Rapid SQL will remember the userid and password, and will not prompt you again for that datasource. You can have multiple connections open at one time.

Executing SQL and PL/SQL

SQL and PL/SQL blocks can be executed through a SQL editor. SQL editors are created by selecting File | New | SQL from the menu. A SQL editor can contain both PL/SQL blocks (ending with a /) and SQL statements. All of the statements and blocks within one editor can be executed by clicking on the Execute button, as shown in Figure 2-10. The output results from the editor can be seen by clicking on the Results tab, shown in Figure 2-11. The results output contains PL/SQL results

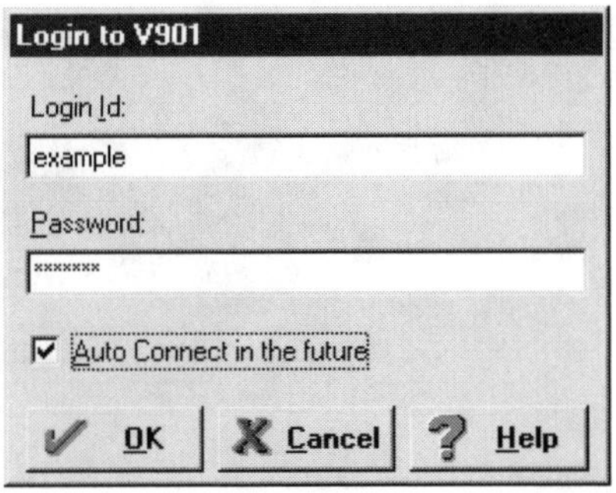

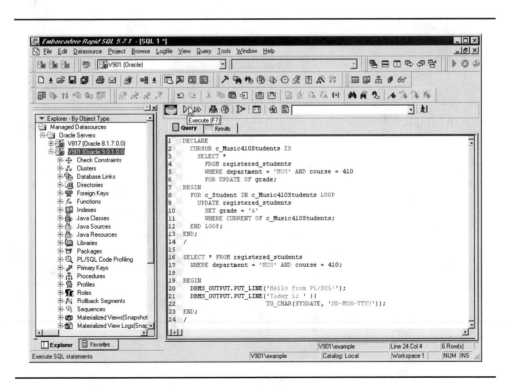

FIGURE 2-9. *Database Connection dialog box*

FIGURE 2-10. *A SQL editor*

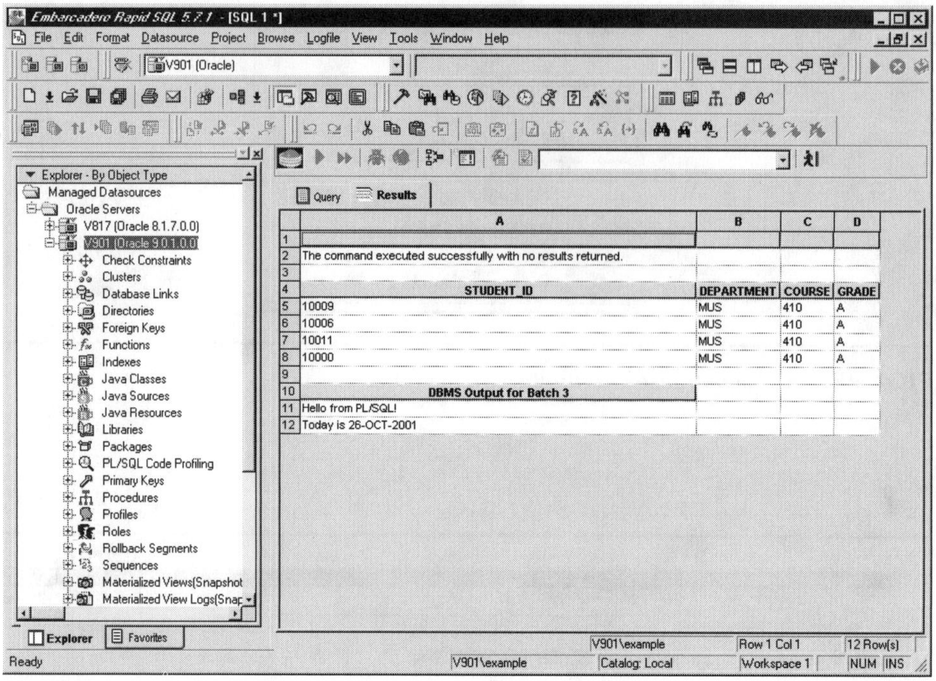

FIGURE 2-11. *Results tab*

(such as successful completion) and SQL query output. Any output from DBMS_
OUTPUT.PUT_LINE is also shown in the results output.

Debugging Features
Rapid SQL has the ability to debug PL/SQL stored procedures, functions, and
triggers. Anonymous blocks can be debugged as well, but Rapid SQL will
automatically create a server-side procedure containing the code of the anonymous
block to debug it. The debugger allows you to step through a procedure and view
the values of the variables currently in scope. You can also see the current call stack
and dependencies at any point. A sample debugging session of the AlmostFull
function is shown in Figure 2-12.

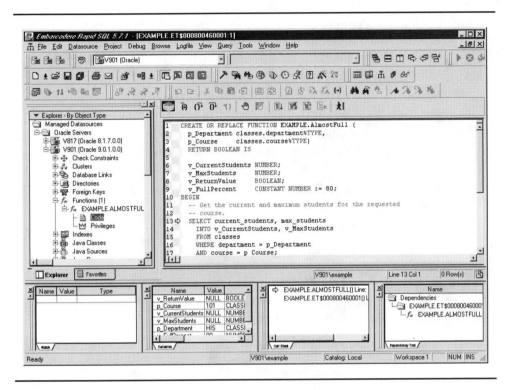

FIGURE 2-12. *Rapid SQL debugging session*

Other Rapid SQL Features

In addition to the features we have already discussed, Rapid SQL has the following features:

- **Object browser** Allows you to see all the objects in a given datasource. The objects can be sorted by owner or by type, and you can choose to see only the objects owned by the current user.

- **PL/SQL compilation errors** Any errors resulting from a submitted PL/SQL block are automatically shown, along with the line and column number reported by the server. Clicking on an error will take you to the source line that caused the error.

- **PL/SQL Profiler access**   Allows you to use the PL/SQL Profiler (found in Oracle8*i* and higher) to analyze a running PL/SQL program. Rapid SQL provides a GUI interface for setting up the profiler tables, starting and stopping the profiler, and analyzing the output.

- **Scheduling options**   Provides the ability to run files and execute jobs automatically at specified times. The results can be saved in a file, or emailed.

- **Types of editing windows**   Allows you to create and modify different types of objects, both on the client and the server. These include general SQL and PL/SQL files, HTML files, and Java files.

- **Code-generation facilities**   Automatically generates code to perform DDL operations and other SQL statements based on user input.

- **Version control**   Integrates with third-party version control tools to monitor changes to your files.

DBPartner Debugger

DBPartner Debugger is published by Compuware Corporation. It is a GUI development environment that has the following features, among others:

- Autoformatting of PL/SQL and SQL statements

- Support for debugging server-side PL/SQL and Java procedures

- Support for Oracle8*i* Java types

- Project management

- Support for debugging and tracing of any application

- Support for third-party version control systems

DBPartner Debugger is one component of the DBPartner Suite of products. Other components include the SQL Tuner and Viewer. For more information on installing and using DBPartner Debugger, see the online help.

Connecting to the Database

When you first start DBPartner Debugger, it will prompt you for a database connection. You can store profiles for different connections, each of which records the userid and connect string. By specifying the userid as "userid/password," the password can be stored as well. This dialog box is illustrated by Figure 2-13. More than one connection can be active at one time.

In order to use DBPartner Debugger properly, a server-side setup is necessary. This will create a database user that contains tables that store information necessary to DBPartner Debugger. This can be done during installation, or it can be done after the program is installed through use of the Database Setup Wizard, the first screen

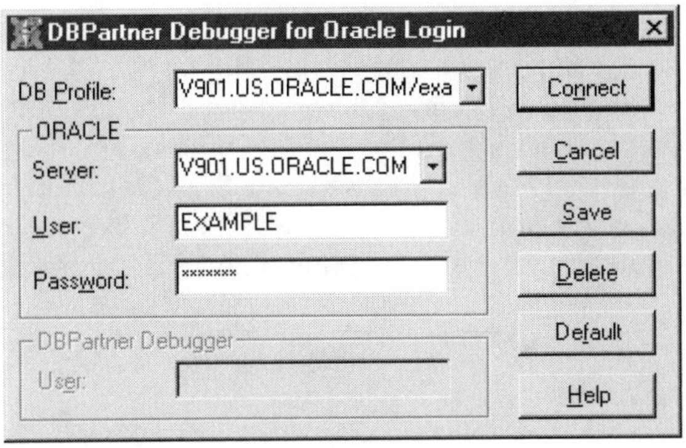

FIGURE 2-13. *DBPartner Debugger Connect dialog box*

of which is shown in Figure 2-14. The wizard allows you to install, de-install, or upgrade the server-side objects for multiple databases. It can be run using the Database | Setup Wizard command. A DBA connection is required for the server-side install, as it is necessary to create a database user. A DBA connection is not required for other tasks.

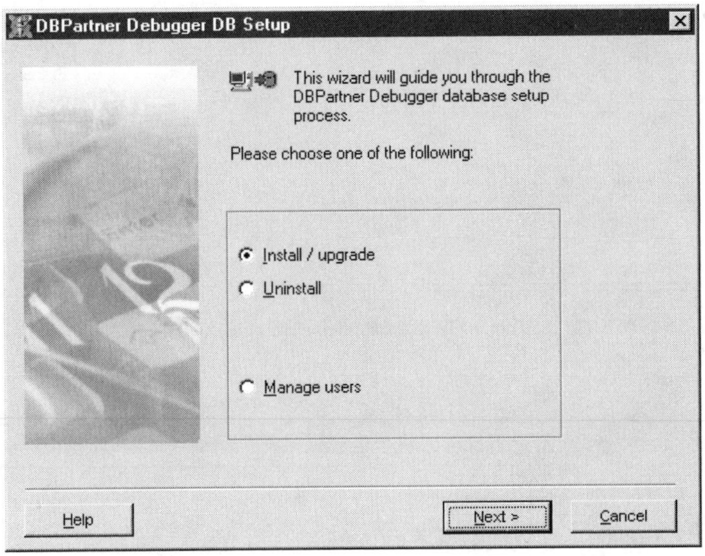

FIGURE 2-14. *Initial screen of Database Setup Wizard*

Executing SQL and PL/SQL

SQL and PL/SQL statements are executed through a SQL Notepad window, created by choosing File | New SQL Notepad from the menu. A SQL Notepad can contain both PL/SQL blocks (ended by /) and SQL statements. The contents of a SQL Notepad are sent to the server by clicking on the Execute button, as shown by Figure 2-15. Output from SQL queries is shown in a separate SQL Output window, also shown in Figure 2-15. Any output from DBMS_OUTPUT.PUT_LINE can be seen by clicking on the DBMS Output tab in the bottom pane of the SQL Notepad, and this is shown in Figure 2-16.

Debugging Features

DBPartner Debugger has the ability to step through server-side PL/SQL programs and anonymous blocks. You can start a debugging session by either selecting File | New Debugger from the menu, or by right-clicking on an object in the browser and

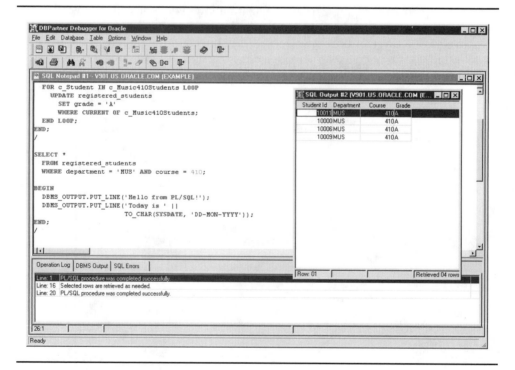

FIGURE 2-15.   *A SQL Notepad window*

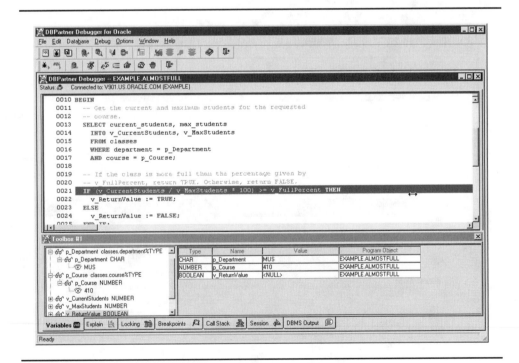

FIGURE 2-16. *DBMS Output tab*

selecting Debug. If the object you are debugging takes input parameters, DBPartner Debugger will prompt you for the input values and automatically construct an anonymous block with those values to call the object. A sample debugging session is shown in Figure 2-17.

FIGURE 2-17. *PL/SQL debugging*

In addition to debugging server-side PL/SQL procedures, DBPartner Debugger can debug server-side Java procedures (Oracle8*i* and higher). The debugger will automatically step into a Java procedure called from a PL/SQL procedure, and vice versa. This feature is unique to DBPartner Debugger. A sample Java debugging session is shown in Figure 2-18.

DBPartner Debugger also has the ability to automatically start a debugging session when a given procedure is executed by any session in a database. This allows you to debug applications started from other machines, such as an application server. A debugging session can also be started automatically whenever a SQL statement or PL/SQL block is issued by an application running on the same machine as DBPartner Debugger.

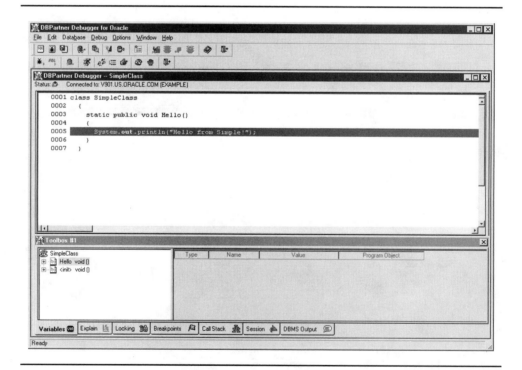

FIGURE 2-18. *Java debugging*

Other DBPartner Debugger Features

In addition to the features we have already discussed, DBPartner Debugger has the following features:

- **Object browser**   Allows you to view objects in the database, sorted by object type. You can also see the data dictionary tables to which you have access. Double-clicking on a given object will open it for editing.

- **Types of editing windows**   Allows you to see and edit information appropriate to the type of object being modified. DBPartner Debugger supports SQL and table/view editing widows. A SQL editing window can modify SQL statements, PL/SQL blocks, or Java source.

- **PL/SQL compilation errors**   Any errors resulting from a submitted PL/SQL block are automatically shown, along with the line and column number reported by the server. Clicking on an error will take you to the source line that caused the error.

- **Version control**   Integrates with third-party version control tools to monitor changes to your files.

- **Explain plan**   Automatically generates explain plan output for SQL statements.

- **Other products**   The DBPartner suite includes two other utilities as well: the SQL Tuner, which can analyze and tune SQL statements issued by any application; and the SQL Viewer, which can trap individual SQL statements and PL/SQL blocks and route them to the debugger or viewer.

SQL Navigator

SQL Navigator is published by Quest Software. It is a GUI development environment that offers the following features:

- Autoformatting of PL/SQL and SQL statements

- Support for PL/SQL debugging

- Database browser

- Support for Oracle8 object types and Oracle8*i* types

- Code templates

- Support for third-party version control systems

Connecting to the Database

Like DBPartner Debugger, SQL Navigator asks for a database connection when it is first started. Connection profiles are stored automatically for later use, but the password is not stored. The window used to establish the connection is shown in Figure 2-19. If you don't connect to a database upon startup, you will be prompted with this same dialog box upon opening an editing or browsing window. SQL Navigator supports multiple connections to different databases simultaneously.

Many of the options within SQL Navigator require that a user SQLNAV be created on the server. The Server Side Installation Wizard aids in creating the necessary user and objects. This wizard can be run as part of the installation, and also after installation by selecting Tools | Server Side Installation Wizard. Server-side installation is necessary to explain plan support, team programming, third-party version control, and support for SQL Navigator Tuner. Figure 2-20 shows the initial screen of the wizard.

Executing SQL and PL/SQL

SQL and PL/SQL statements are executed from a SQL editor window. A given window can execute either a single statement or an entire script. PL/SQL blocks

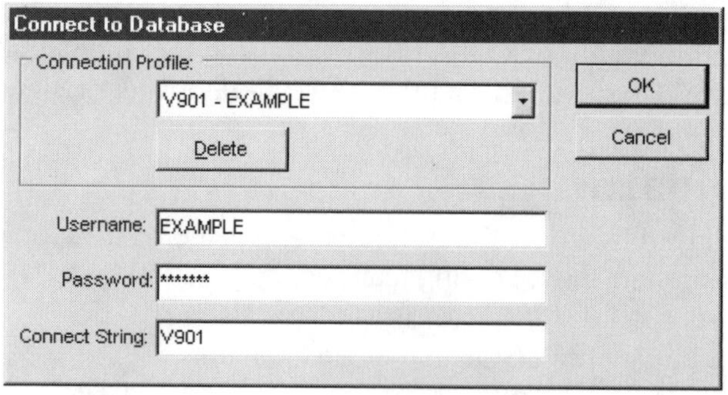

FIGURE 2-19. *SQL Navigator Connection dialog box*

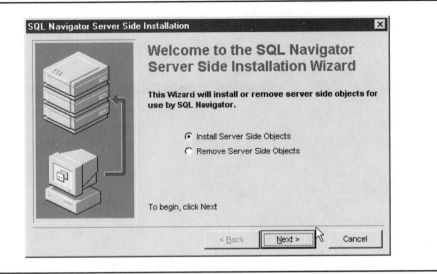

FIGURE 2-20. *The Server Side Installation Wizard*

should end in a / when contained in a script. Substitution variables (in the sense of SQL*Plus) are also supported by scripts. You can execute an individual statement within a script or a portion of a script. Figure 2-21 shows a SQL editor window, with the output window docked below it. The output window will contain the results of each statement (if a query, then the data is shown), and optionally will echo the SQL or PL/SQL command as well.

If you want to see DBMS_OUTPUT.PUT_LINE output as well, you can enable it by clicking on the Server Output ON button, or by selecting Tools | Server Output from the menu. If this is enabled, then the output from DBMS_OUTPUT.PUT_LINE will be intermixed with the other output in the output window, as shown in Figure 2-22.

Debugging Features
In order to step through a PL/SQL program, Debug mode must be turned on by either clicking the Debug ON button or by selecting Debug | PL/SQL Debugging from the menu. Once enabled, running a given block will enter the debugger, where you can examine variables, set watchpoints, and step through the code. A sample debugging session is shown in Figure 2-23.

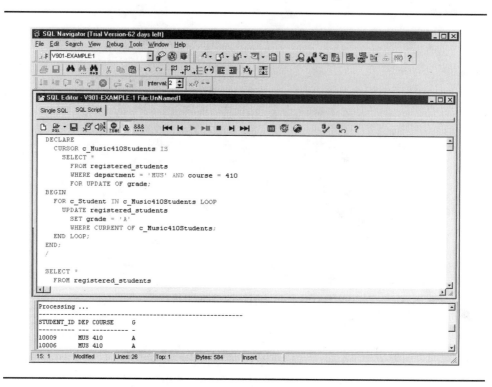

FIGURE 2-21. *A SQL Editor window*

SQL Navigator also has the ability to attach to a separate session and the debug PL/SQL commands that are issued by it. This requires a separate session to call DBMS_DEBUG with a given session name, which is then used by SQL Navigator to identify the session.

Other SQL Navigator Features

In addition to the features we have already discussed, SQL Navigator has the following features:

- **PL/SQL Profiler** Allows you to turn profiling on and off for a given program and view the profiling data. Profiling support is not built directly into SQL Navigator; rather, there is a separate executable that must be installed for the profiling support. See the installation program for details.

- **Database Navigator** Allows you to browse objects in the database. The DB Navigator has various filters, which can be used to restrict the objects shown (by current user, for example). Double-clicking on an object will

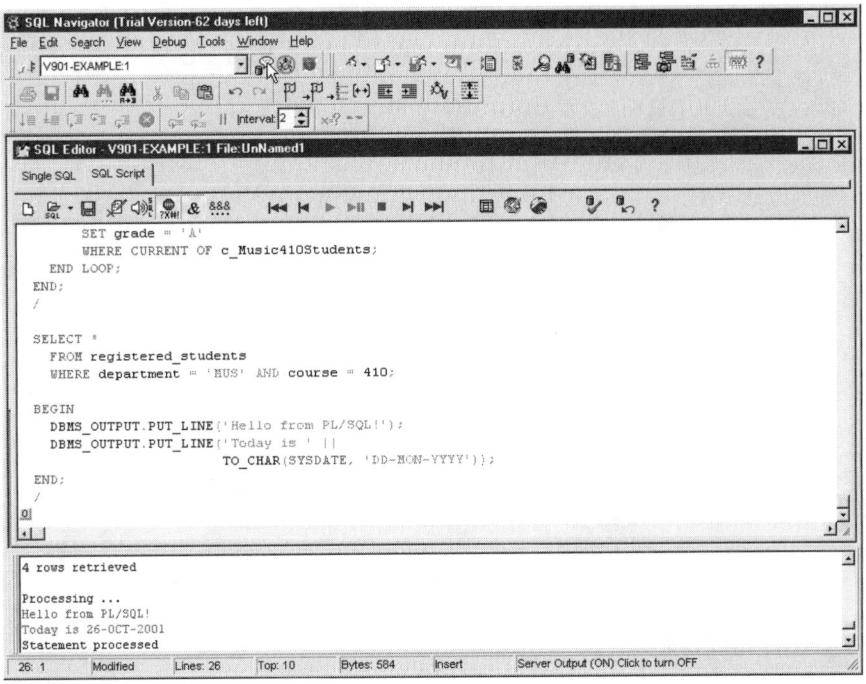

FIGURE 2-22. *Output from DBMS_OUTPUT.PUT_LINE*

bring it up for editing. Editing Java objects is not supported with this version of SQL Navigator, although they can be compiled and dropped through the DB Navigator.

■ **Individual editing windows**   Contains a separate type of editing window for database objects, including tables, views, SQL scripts, PL/SQL blocks, stored procedures, triggers, and roles. These windows present a graphical interface that automatically generates the correct SQL command based on user input.

■ **Query builder**   Allows you to graphically select tables and columns to query, including entering the WHERE and other clauses of the SELECT statement. The query builder tool can also be used to automatically generate DML statements.

■ **PL/SQL errors**   If a submitted PL/SQL block has compilation errors, they will be shown when you compile the object from a stored program editor. Clicking on an error highlights the source line, and double-clicking on an

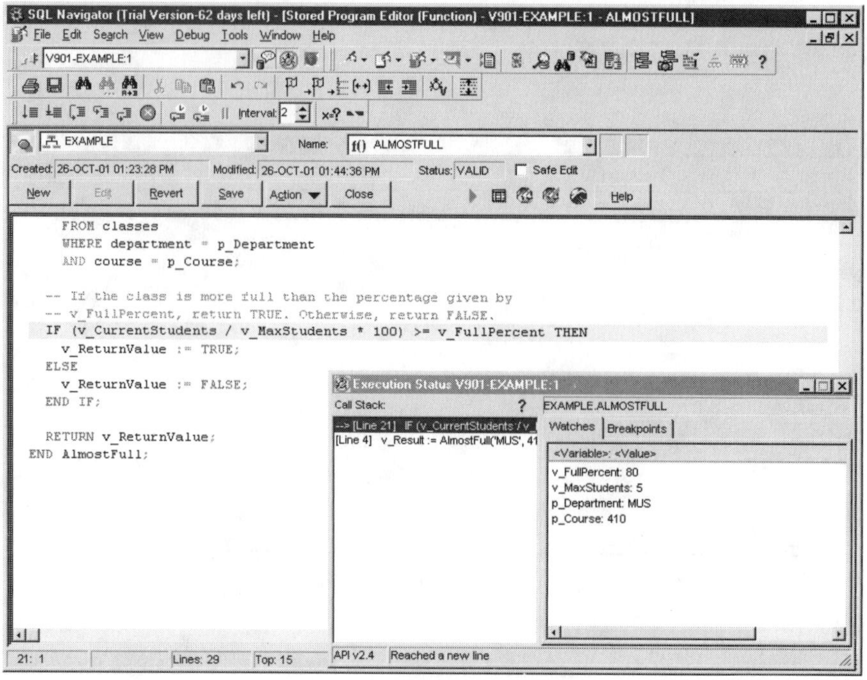

FIGURE 2-23. *A debugging session*

error will bring up a window with the cause and action from the Oracle documentation.

■ **Code templates**   The Code Assistant, available on the Tools menu, provides a library of commonly used PL/SQL and SQL constructs. Highlighting a particular construct will bring up a description in the Code Assistant Information window, and double-clicking will copy it to an available editing window, where it can be customized.

■ **Explain plan tool**   Allows you to capture and analyze the explain plan information for a given SQL statement.

TOAD

TOAD (Tool for Oracle Application Developers) was originally developed separately from SQL Navigator, but is now produced by Quest Software along with SQL

Navigator. Consequently, the two tools share some features, including the licensing mechanism. However, there are differences, as we will see. TOAD has the following features:

- Autoformatting of PL/SQL and SQL statements

- Support for debugging PL/SQL procedures

- Database browser

- Support for Oracle8 object types and Oracle8*i* types

- Code templates

- Support for third-party version control systems

TOAD is designed to be a lightweight, but still powerful, development environment. It has much smaller disk and memory requirements than the other tools.

Connecting to the Database

TOAD can support multiple database connections at any point. When you first start the application, it prompts you to connect with the dialog box shown in Figure 2-24. Further connections can be made from the File | New Connection command. Once a connection is established, it will remain active until you explicitly close it by selecting File | Close Connection. Passwords are not stored in the connection profiles.

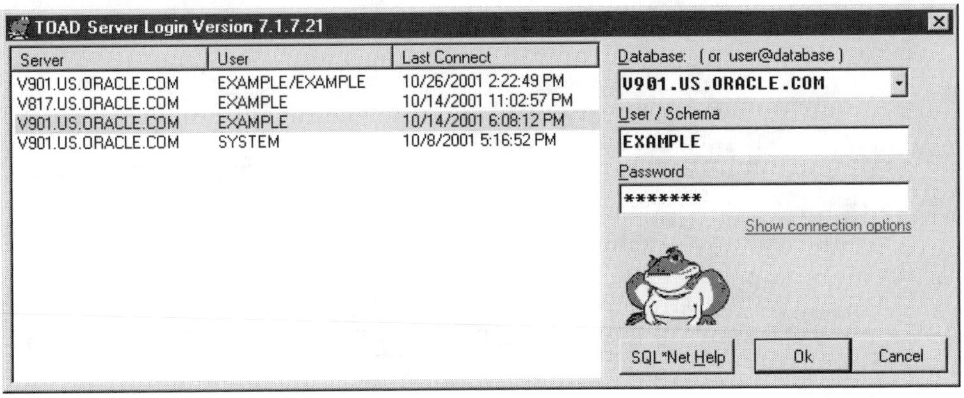

FIGURE 2-24. *TOAD Connect dialog box*

One unique feature of the way that TOAD manages connections is that the connection associated with any window can be changed dynamically. This allows you to work with multiple servers at the same time, while keeping the number of windows to a minimum. A given work window can be associated with only one session at a time, however.

Executing SQL and PL/SQL

SQL and PL/SQL statements are executed from within a SQL edit window. A given SQL window can contain one or more SQL statements or PL/SQL blocks, which can be executed individually or as a script. If the statement is a query, the output is displayed in the bottom pane of the window, as shown in Figure 2-25. The Script Output tab on the bottom pane shows the output from running the entire script. Individual statements and blocks within the window can be run as well, by clicking on the appropriate button at the top of the window.

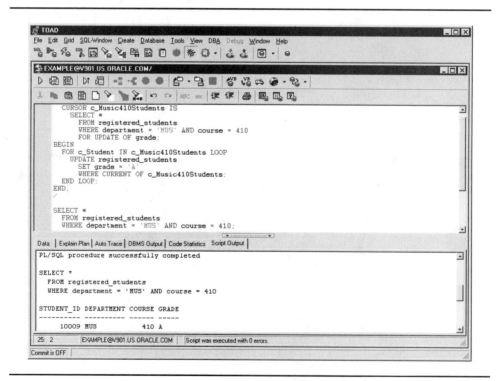

FIGURE 2-25. *SQL output*

SQL edit windows can also be used to show any output from DBMS_OUTPUT.PUT_LINE, as well as statistics and explain plan output. Similar to the SQL*Plus SET SERVEROUTPUT ON command, output from DBMS_OUTPUT.PUT_LINE must be turned on first by clicking the button on the DBMS Output tab. Sample output is shown in Figure 2-26.

Debugging Features

A stored procedure can be debugged by clicking on the Step Into button, or by selecting Debug | Step Into from the menu. Any parameters to the procedure must be set by the Set Parameters dialog box first. If necessary, the procedure and any dependent objects will be compiled with debug first, and then the debugging session will begin. While debugging, you can set breakpoints and watchpoints, and examine the values of local variables. A debugging session is shown in Figure 2-27.

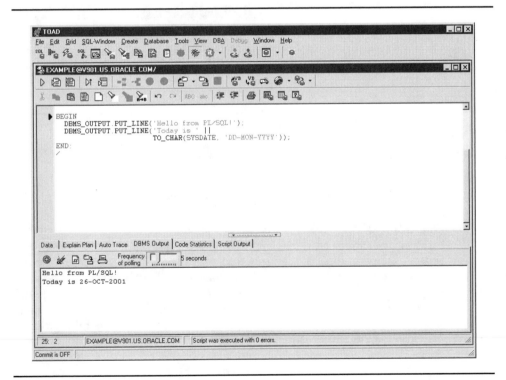

FIGURE 2-26. *Output from DBMS_OUTPUT.PUT_LINE*

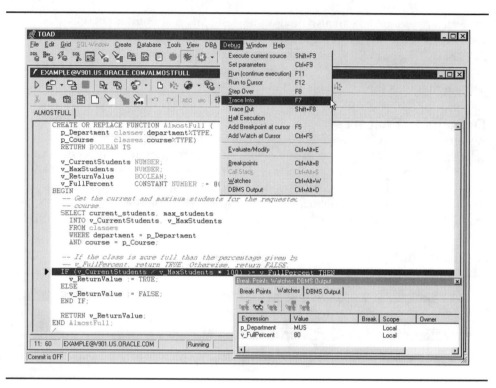

FIGURE 2-27. *A TOAD debugging session*

Other TOAD Features
In addition to the features we have discussed, TOAD has the following features:

- **Object browsing**   TOAD has two types of database browsers: the schema browser and object browser. The schema browser allows you to select objects such as tables, procedures, and packages. Instead of a tree structure like the browsers in the other tools we have examined, the schema browser has tabs to select the type of objects, which are then shown in the pane on the left. The right pane shows details about the object. You can also compile or drop objects from this browser. The object browser, on the other hand, is used solely to examine Oracle8 object types and type bodies.

■ **Editing windows**   TOAD has two types of editing windows: a SQL edit window, which we have already seen, and a stored procedure edit window. As their names suggest, SQL edit windows are used to edit single SQL statements or SQL scripts, while stored procedure edit windows are used to edit stored procedures, functions, packages, and triggers. From a stored procedure edit window you can compile, run, or debug the procedure shown in the database. Stored procedure edit windows can be loaded from database objects or files, or can be used to create new objects.

■ **Code templates**   TOAD can automatically enter PL/SQL and SQL constructs based on keyboard shortcuts.

■ **DBA features**   TOAD has a number of features valuable to a DBA, such as viewing database initialization parameters, and an import/export utility.

SQL-Programmer

The next GUI development tool that we will examine is SQL-Programmer, by BMC. It supports the following features:

■ Autoformatting of PL/SQL and SQL statements

■ Support for PL/SQL debugging

■ Database browser

■ Support for Oracle8 object types and Oracle8*i* objects

■ Code templates

■ Support for third-party version control systems

■ Scripting of database objects

Connecting to the Database

SQL-Programmer supports multiple simultaneous connections to different databases. The Connection dialog box is shown in Figure 2-28. Passwords are not stored in connection profiles, but you can store different profiles for different servers. This dialog box also shows the current connections that are open.

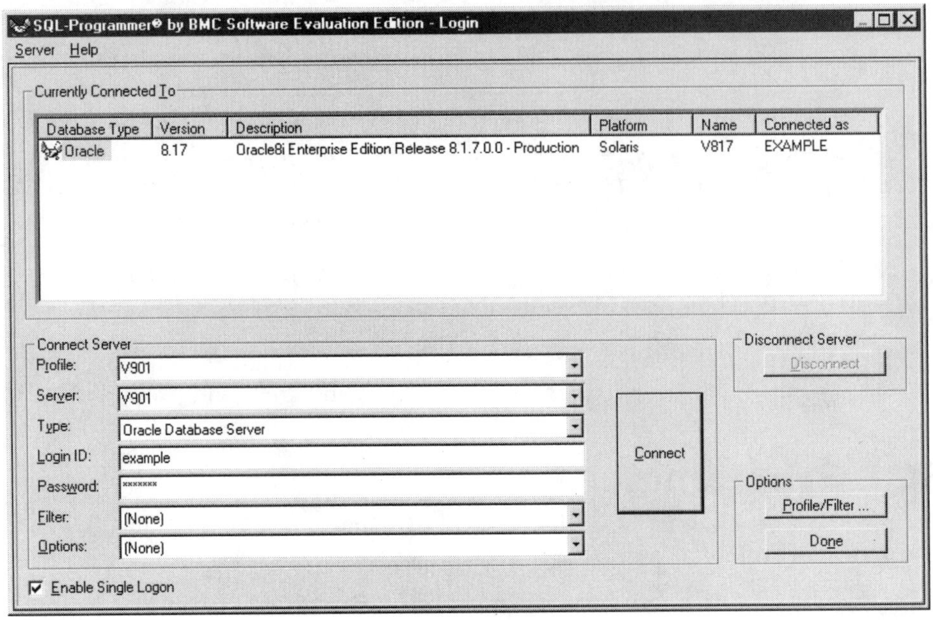

FIGURE 2-28. *SQL-Programmer Connect dialog box*

Executing SQL and PL/SQL

The main window of SQL-Programmer is designed to work with individual PL/SQL objects, as opposed to scripts. Clicking on a particular object will open it in an SPDW (SQL-Programmer development window). Different SPDWs have different features, depending on the type of object being manipulated. For example, Figure 2-29 shows the AddNewStudent procedure in an SPDW. Because of this, you cannot run arbitrary SQL and PL/SQL commands directly. You can, however, create a batch object, which consists of several commands to be run in sequence. Batch objects can be stored on the server, if desired.

In order to run a procedure from an SPDW, you must first fill in the arguments to be passed to the procedure, if any. SQL-Programmer will then construct an anonymous

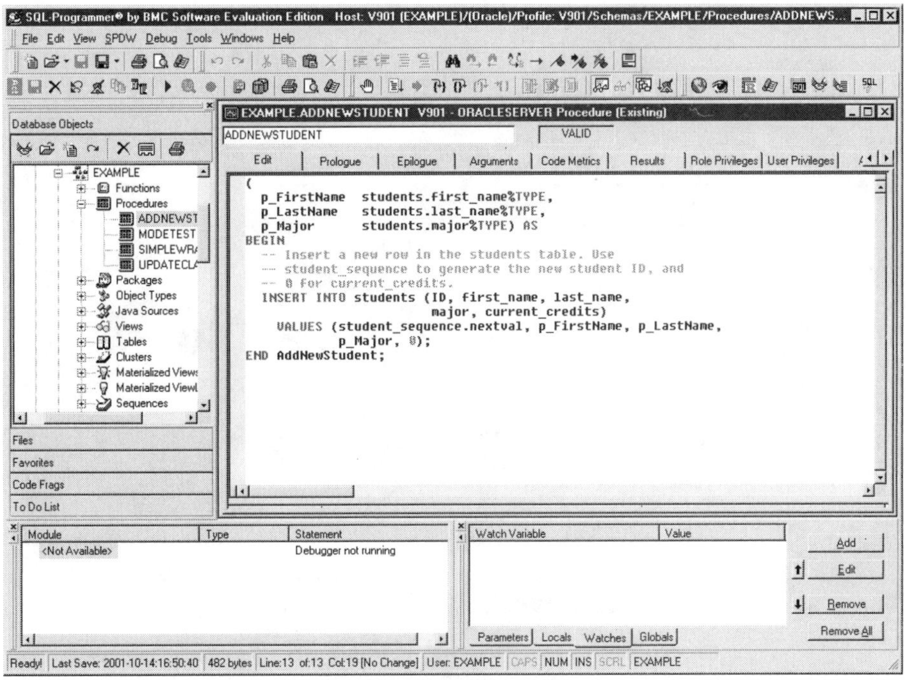

FIGURE 2-29. *An SPDW*

block to call the procedure. The arguments for AddNewStudent are shown in Figure 2-30. If the procedure uses DBMS_OUTPUT.PUT_LINE, the output can be seen by first enabling the output (by clicking on the appropriate button), and then running the procedure. The output is available under the Results tab of the SPDW.

Debugging Features

A given procedure can be debugged by clicking the Step In button, or by choosing Debug | Step In from the menu. This will start a debugging session. Variables can be dragged from the code into the watch window to set new watch variables,

| Edit | Prologue | Epilogue | Arguments | Code Metrics | Results | User Privileges | Auditing | S ◄ ► |

Name	Type	In/Out	Execute Value	Has Value
p_FirstName	students.first_n	IN	Chuck	True
p_LastName	students.last_na	IN	Choouly	True
p_Major	students.major%T	IN	Computer Science	True

FIGURE 2-30. *AddNewStudents arguments*

and the current stack can be seen in the bottom left pane. Figure 2-31 shows a debugging session.

Other SQL-Programmer Features

In addition to the features we have already discussed, SQL-Programmer has the following capabilities:

- **Object browser**   The SQL-Explorer window allows you to browse through the database objects, sorted by schema and object type. If there is more than one connection active, a single SQL-Explorer can view objects from both connections.

- **Compile errors**   If a procedure has compile errors, then the SPDW will show the errors in an error pane below the text. Double-clicking on a particular error will highlight the relevant section of the code in the pane above it.

- **Code templates**   When you create a new object from the SQL-Explorer, it will automatically be filled in with the appropriate template. The available templates can be specified from the Options menu.

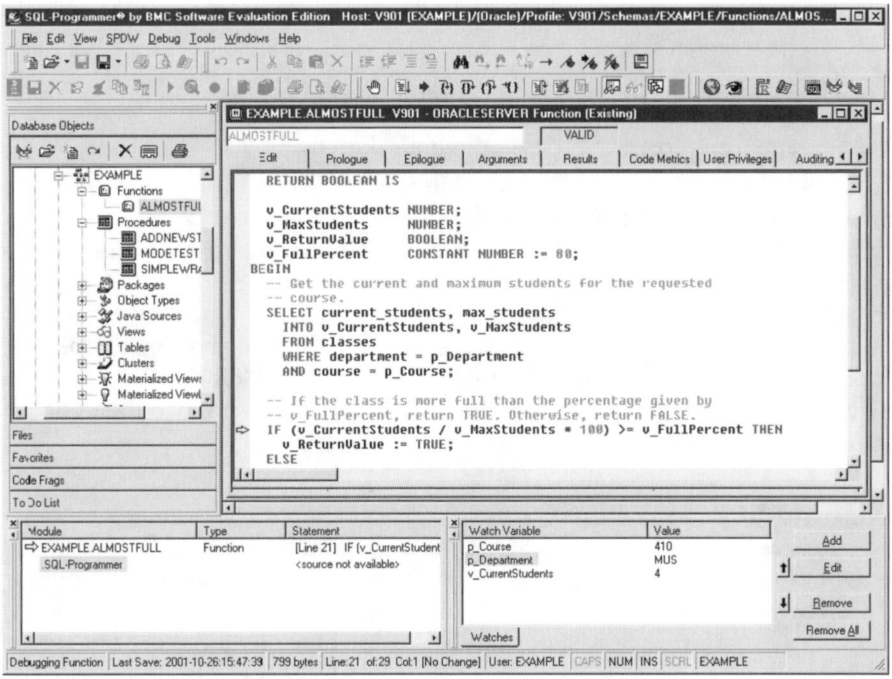

FIGURE 2-31. *A debugging session*

■ **Scripting** The scripting interface allows you to create a script for any combination of database objects. This script will contain code to automatically re-create the objects on any other server. Thus, scripts provide a good mechanism to copy individual objects, or entire schemas, between databases.

PL/SQL Developer

The final GUI development tool that we will examine is PL/SQL Developer, by Allround Automations. It supports the following features:

■ Autoformatting of PL/SQL and SQL statements

■ Support for PL/SQL debugging

■ Database browser

- Support for Oracle8 object types and Oracle8i objects

- Code templates

- Support for third-party version control systems (through an external plug-in)

- Support for most SQL*Plus commands directly

Connecting to the Database

PL/SQL Developer's Connection dialog box is shown in Figure 2-32. Connection profiles are saved, but the passwords are not. More than one connection can be open at a time, but a given window can only support one connection. This includes the object browser itself. A new connection can be established by choosing Session | Log on from the menu. The main window for PL/SQL Developer is shown in Figure 2-33. The object browser is the left pane, and the space to the right is used for the various development windows.

Executing SQL and PL/SQL

There are several ways to execute SQL or PL/SQL commands in PL/SQL Developer. In order to modify an existing procedure, you choose it from the object browser and select edit, which will bring it up in a program window. You can use the SQL window to enter a single SQL statement or PL/SQL block (without the final slash). Finally, the command window presents you with a SQL> prompt, just like

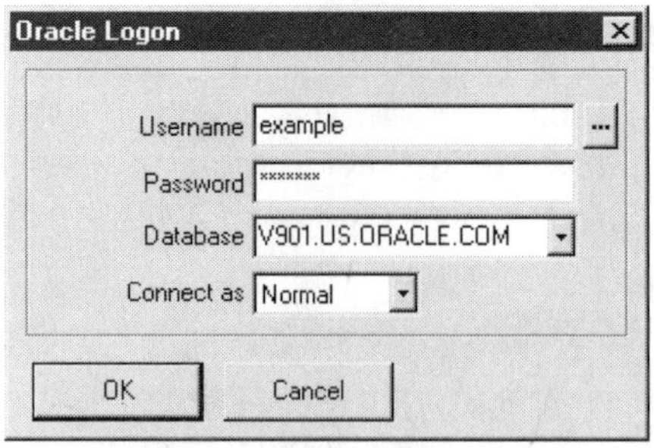

FIGURE 2-32. *PL/SQL Developer's Connection dialog box*

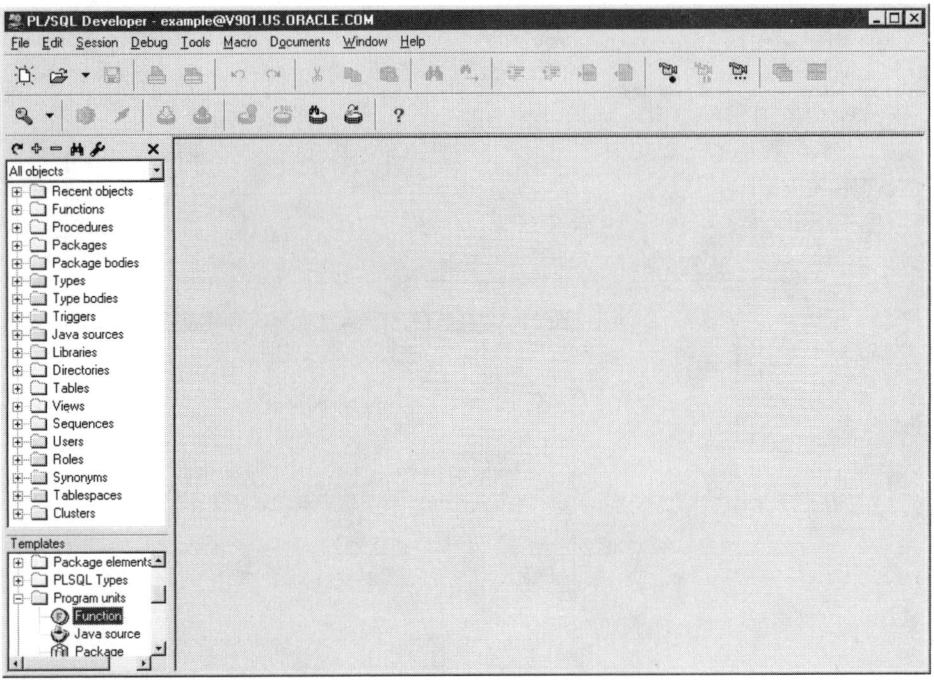

FIGURE 2-33.   *The main window*

SQL*Plus. It accepts many of the SQL*Plus commands, in addition to several PL/SQL Developer commands. Figure 2-34 shows both a SQL and command window.

The results from DBMS_OUTPUT.PUT_LINE can be seen by clicking on the Output tab in a SQL window, or inline in a command window.

Debugging Features

Debugging a stored procedure is done from a test window. This window allows you to specify the parameters to the procedure. Once this is done, you begin debugging by clicking the Start Debugging button. From here, you can step through the program, set breakpoints, see the call stack, and establish watched variables. Figure 2-35 shows a debugging session.

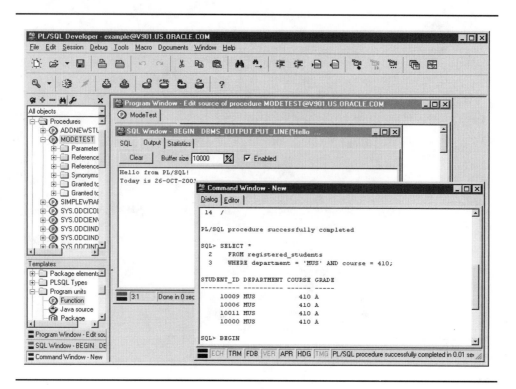

FIGURE 2-34. *Execution windows*

Other PL/SQL Developer Features

In addition to the features we have already discussed, PL/SQL Developer supports the following:

- **Object browser** The object browser allows you to see all the accessible database objects, subject to user-defined filters. A given object can be edited, dropped, or recompiled from within the browser.

- **Code templates** The object browser also contains templates for automatically generating new database objects, both PL/SQL types and SQL types. A template will prompt you for the various options for the object in a GUI, and then create the object.

- **Support for add-ins** PL/SQL Developer provides support for various plug-ins, which add functionality. Several plug-ins are available from Allround Automations' Web site, including one for source control support.

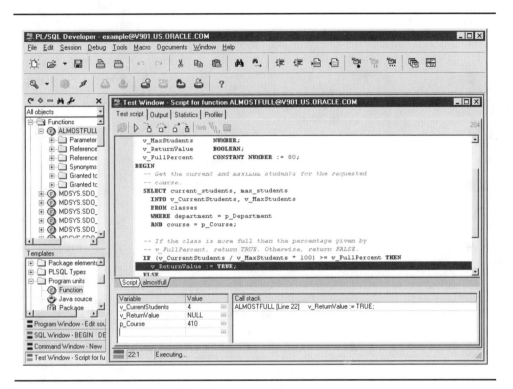

FIGURE 2-35.   *A debugging session*

- **PL/SQL Profiler access**   Test windows also allow you to enable profiling. After a test run is complete, the Profiler tab of a test window allows you to examine the profile output.

- **Macro recording**   You can record macros for commonly executed commands, which will be run in sequence when the macro is executed.

- **PL/SQL errors**   Compiling a PL/SQL block with an error will automatically highlight the error in the source text. Double clicking on the error will bring up the appropriate error text from the Oracle documentation.

Summary of Development Tools

Table 2-2 summarizes the features of the different PL/SQL development environments. I recommend that you try each of them to see which best suits your needs. For more information about any of the tools, see the online help for each.

Feature	SQL*Plus	Rapid SQL	DBPartner	SQL Navigator	TOAD	SQL-Programmer	PL/SQL Developer
Availability	Shipped with the server	Sold separately	Sold separately	Sold separately	Sold separately	Sold separately	Sold separately
GUI environment	No	Yes	Yes	Yes	Yes	Yes	Yes
Object browser	No	Yes	Yes	Yes	Yes	Yes	Yes
Code templates	No	Yes	Yes	Yes	Yes	Yes	Yes
Project management	No	Yes	Yes	No	No	No	No
Code formatting	No	Yes	Yes	Yes	Yes	Yes	Yes
Job scheduling	No	Yes	No	No	No	No	No
Version control	No	Yes	Yes	Yes	Yes	Yes	Available with extra plug-ins
Support for Oracle8i Java types	Yes	Yes	Yes	Limited	Limited	Yes	Yes
Server-side setup required	No	No	Yes	Yes	No	No	No
Simultaneous connections	No	Yes	No	Yes	Yes	Yes	No
Support for PL/SQL debugging	No	Yes	Yes	Yes	Yes	Yes	Yes
Support for Java debugging	No	No	Yes	No	No	No	No
Support for the PL/SQL Profiler	No	Yes	No	Yes, with additional install	No	No	Yes
Types of files	SQL & PL/SQL	SQL, PL/SQL, Java, & HTML	SQL, PL/SQL, & Java	SQL, PL/SQL, & HTML	SQL & PL/SQL	SQL & PL/SQL	SQL, PL/SQL, & Java

TABLE 2-2.   Summary of PL/SQL Development Tools

Summary

In this chapter, we have discussed the different environments where a PL/SQL engine can be found, and the application models that are appropriate. We have also examined 6 different PL/SQL development environments that you can use to develop your own PL/SQL programs. In Chapter 3, we will begin our detailed discussion of the PL/SQL language.

PART II

Basic PL/SQL
Features

CHAPTER
3

PL/SQL Basics

he first step in our discussion of PL/SQL is the basic syntax of the language. Syntax rules form the building blocks for any language, PL/SQL included. This chapter discusses the components of a PL/SQL block, variable declarations and datatypes, and the basic procedural constructs, and gives a brief introduction to cursors and subprograms. It also covers PL/SQL style, and shows you techniques that let you write easily understandable code.

All PL/SQL statements are either procedural or SQL statements. *Procedural statements* include variable declarations, procedure calls, and looping constructs. *SQL statements* are used to access the database. This chapter and Chapter 7 focus on the procedural statements of PL/SQL, where as Chapters 4, 5, and 6 cover SQL statements.

The PL/SQL Block

The basic unit in any PL/SQL program is a block. All PL/SQL programs are composed of blocks, which can occur sequentially (one after the other) or nested (one inside the other). There are two different kinds of blocks: anonymous and named. *Anonymous blocks* are generally constructed dynamically and executed only once. This type of block is often issued from a client program to call a subprogram stored in the database. *Named blocks* are blocks that have a name associated with them. Named blocks can be further categorized as follows:

- *Labeled blocks* are anonymous blocks with a label that gives the block a name. These are also generally constructed dynamically and executed only once. Labeled blocks are generally used the same way as anonymous blocks, but the label allows you to refer to variables that otherwise would not be visible.

- *Subprograms* consist of procedures and functions. They can be stored in the database as stand-alone objects, as part of a package, or as methods of an object type. Subprograms generally don't change once they are constructed, and they are executed many times. Subprograms can also be declared within other blocks. Regardless of where they are declared, subprograms are executed explicitly via a call to the procedure or function.

- *Triggers* consist of a PL/SQL block that is associated with an event that occurs in the database. They also generally don't change once they are constructed and are executed many times. Triggers are executed implicitly whenever the triggering event occurs. The triggering event can be a data manipulation language (DML) statement executed against a table in the database. DML statements include INSERT, UPDATE, and DELETE. It can also be a data definition language (DDL) statement such as CREATE or DROP, or a database event such as startup or shutdown.

The following example consists of an anonymous PL/SQL block that inserts two rows into the `temp_table` database table, selects them back, and then echoes them to the screen. The example is in the form of a SQL*Plus session:

```
-- Available online as AnonymousBlock.sql
SQL> DECLARE
  2     /* Declare variables to be used in this block. */
  3     v_Num1      NUMBER := 1;
  4     v_Num2      NUMBER := 2;
  5     v_String1   VARCHAR2(50) := 'Hello World!';
  6     v_String2   VARCHAR2(50) :=
  7       '-- This message brought to you by PL/SQL!';
  8     v_OutputStr VARCHAR2(50);
  9  BEGIN
 10     /* First, insert two rows into temp_table, using the values
 11        of the variables. */
 12     INSERT INTO temp_table (num_col, char_col)
 13       VALUES (v_Num1, v_String1);
 14     INSERT INTO temp_table (num_col, char_col)
 15       VALUES (v_Num2, v_String2);
 16
 17     /* Now query temp_table for the two rows we just inserted, and
 18        output them to the screen using the DBMS_OUTPUT package. */
 19     SELECT char_col
 20       INTO v_OutputStr
 21          FROM temp_table
 22          WHERE num_col = v_Num1;
 23     DBMS_OUTPUT.PUT_LINE(v_OutputStr);
 24
 25     SELECT char_col
 26       INTO v_OutputStr
 27          FROM temp_table
 28          WHERE num_col = v_Num2;
 29     DBMS_OUTPUT.PUT_LINE(v_OutputStr);
 30
 31     /* Rollback our changes */
 32     ROLLBACK;
 33  END;
 34  /
Hello World!
-- This message brought to you by PL/SQL!
PL/SQL procedure successfully completed.
```

NOTE

In order to run the above example, along with most of the other examples in this book, you need to create several database tables, including `temp_table`. *These can all be created using the* `tables.sql` *script, which can be found on the accompanying CD-ROM. Furthermore, many of the examples are online as well. The filenames are indicated at the beginning of each example, and can also be found in the README file on the CD-ROM. For more information on the CD-ROM and its contents, including a description of the sample tables, see Chapter 1. For more information on the DBMS_ OUTPUT package, see Chapter 2.*

In order to name this block, we put a label before the DECLARE keyword, as in the next example. The label can optionally appear after the END keyword as well. Labels and their uses will be discussed in more detail later in this chapter.

```
-- Available online as LabeledBlock.sql
SQL> <<l_InsertIntoTemp>>
  2  DECLARE
  3    /* Declare variables to be used in this block. */
  4    v_Num1      NUMBER := 1;
  5    v_Num2      NUMBER := 2;
  6    v_String1   VARCHAR2(50) := 'Hello World!';
  7    v_String2   VARCHAR2(50) :=
  8      '-- This message brought to you by PL/SQL!';
  9    v_OutputStr VARCHAR2(50);
 10  BEGIN
 11    /* First, insert two rows into temp_table, using the values
 12       of the variables. */
 13    INSERT INTO temp_table (num_col, char_col)
 14      VALUES (v_Num1, v_String1);
 15    INSERT INTO temp_table (num_col, char_col)
 16      VALUES (v_Num2, v_String2);
 17
 18    /* Now query temp_table for the two rows we just inserted, and
 19       output them to the screen using the DBMS_OUTPUT package. */
 20    SELECT char_col
 21      INTO v_OutputStr
 22        FROM temp_table
 23        WHERE num_col = v_Num1;
 24    DBMS_OUTPUT.PUT_LINE(v_OutputStr);
 25
```

```
26    SELECT char_col
27      INTO v_OutputStr
28          FROM temp_table
29          WHERE num_col = v_Num2;
30    DBMS_OUTPUT.PUT_LINE(v_OutputStr);
31
32    /* Rollback our changes */
33    ROLLBACK;
34
35  END l_InsertIntoTemp;
36  /
Hello World!
-- This message brought to you by PL/SQL!
PL/SQL procedure successfully completed.
```

We can make this block into a stored procedure by replacing the DECLARE keyword with the CREATE OR REPLACE PROCEDURE keywords. Procedures are discussed in more detail in Chapters 9 and 10. Again, note that the procedure name is used after the END keyword.

```
-- Available online as part of Procedure.sql
CREATE OR REPLACE PROCEDURE InsertIntoTemp AS
  /* Declare variables to be used in this block. */
  v_Num1      NUMBER := 1;
  v_Num2      NUMBER := 2;
  v_String1   VARCHAR2(50) := 'Hello World!';
  v_String2   VARCHAR2(50) :=
    '-- This message brought to you by PL/SQL!';
  v_OutputStr VARCHAR2(50);
BEGIN
  /* First, insert two rows into temp_table, using the values
     of the variables. */
  INSERT INTO temp_table (num_col, char_col)
    VALUES (v_Num1, v_String1);
  INSERT INTO temp_table (num_col, char_col)
    VALUES (v_Num2, v_String2);

  /* Now query temp_table for the two rows we just inserted, and
     output them to the screen using the DBMS_OUTPUT package. */
  SELECT char_col
    INTO v_OutputStr
      FROM temp_table
      WHERE num_col = v_Num1;
  DBMS_OUTPUT.PUT_LINE(v_OutputStr);

  SELECT char_col
    INTO v_OutputStr
```

```
      FROM temp_table
     WHERE num_col = v_Num2;
  DBMS_OUTPUT.PUT_LINE(v_OutputStr);

  /* Rollback our changes */
  ROLLBACK;

END InsertIntoTemp;
```

Once the procedure is created, we can call it with an anonymous block as follows:

```
-- Available online as part of Procedure.sql
SQL> BEGIN
  2     InsertIntoTemp;
  3  END;
  4  /
Hello World!
-- This message brought to you by PL/SQL!
PL/SQL procedure successfully completed.
```

See Chapters 9 and 10 for more information on creating and calling stored subprograms.

Finally, we can construct a trigger on the `temp_table` table to ensure that only positive values are put into `num_col`. Triggers are discussed in more detail in Chapter 11. This trigger will be called whenever a new row is inserted into `temp_table` or an existing row is updated.

```
-- Available online as part of trigger.sql
CREATE OR REPLACE TRIGGER OnlyPositive
  BEFORE INSERT OR UPDATE OF num_col
  ON temp_table
  FOR EACH ROW
BEGIN
  IF :new.num_col < 0 THEN
    RAISE_APPLICATION_ERROR(-20100, 'Please insert a positive value');
  END IF;
END OnlyPositive;
```

Once the trigger is created, it will be fired whenever an INSERT or UPDATE is issued against `temp_table`. The following SQL*Plus session shows some successful and unsuccessful operations:

```
-- Available online as part of trigger.sql
SQL> -- This INSERT will succeed, since the value is positive.
SQL> INSERT INTO temp_table (num_col, char_col)
```

```
  2     VALUES (1, 'This is row 1');
1 row created.

SQL> -- This one will fail, however, because the value is negative.
SQL> INSERT INTO temp_table (num_col, char_col)
  2     VALUES (-1, 'This is row -1');
INSERT INTO temp_table (num_col, char_col)
                *
ERROR at line 1:
ORA-20100: Please insert a positive value
ORA-06512: at "DEMO.ONLYPOSITIVE", line 3
ORA-04088: error during execution of trigger 'DEMO.ONLYPOSITIVE'
```

Basic Block Structure

All blocks have three distinct sections: the declarative section, the executable section, and the exception section. Only the executable section is required; the other two are optional. For example, here is an anonymous block with all three sections:

```
-- Available online as allthree.sql
DECLARE
  /* Start of declarative section */
  v_StudentID NUMBER(5) := 10000;   -- Numeric variable initialized
                                    -- to 10,000
  v_FirstName VARCHAR2(20);         -- Variable length character string
                                    -- with maximum length of 20
BEGIN
  /* Start of executable section */
  -- Retrieve first name of student with ID 10,000
  SELECT first_name
    INTO v_FirstName
    FROM students
    WHERE id = v_StudentID;
EXCEPTION
  /* Start of exception section */
  WHEN NO_DATA_FOUND THEN
    -- Handle the error condition
    INSERT INTO log_table (info)
      VALUES ('Student 10,000 does not exist!');
END;
```

NOTE
This example references two additional tables that are created by `tables.sql`*:* `students` *and* `log_table`*. Again, see Chapter 1 for the complete description of the sample schema.*

The *declarative section* is where the declarations of all the variables, cursors, and types used by this block are located. Local procedures and functions can also be declared in this section. These subprograms will be visible in this block only. The *executable section* is where the work of the block is done. Both SQL statements and procedural statements can appear in this section. Errors are handled in the *exception section*. Code in this section is not executed unless an error occurs. We will discuss the components of the declarative and executable sections in more detail in the rest of this chapter and Chapters 4–6; Chapter 7 deals with the exception section and how it is used to detect and handle errors.

The keywords DECLARE, BEGIN, EXCEPTION, and END delimit each section. The final semicolon is also required—this is a syntactic part of the block. Based on this, the skeleton of an anonymous block looks like this:

```
DECLARE
   /* Declarative section is here */
BEGIN
   /* Executable section is here */
EXCEPTION
   /* Exception section is here */
END;
```

NOTE
The DECLARE keyword is not necessary when creating a procedure. In fact, it is an error to use it. However, DECLARE is required when creating a trigger. See Chapters 9–11 for more information.

If the declarative section is absent, the block starts with the BEGIN keyword. If the exception section is absent, the EXCEPTION keyword is omitted, and the END keyword followed by a semicolon finishes the block. So, a block with just the executable section would be structured as

```
BEGIN
   /* Executable section is here */
END;
```

while a block with declarative and executable sections, but no exception section, would look like this:

```
DECLARE
   /* Declarative section is here */
BEGIN
   /* Executable section is here */
END;
```

NOTE
The statements in the preceding blocks delimited by
/ and */ are comments. Comments are discussed*
in more detail later in this chapter.

Nested Blocks

A block can be nested within the executable or exception section of an outer block, as the following example illustrates:

```
-- Available online as nested.sql
DECLARE
  /* Start of declarative section */
  v_StudentID NUMBER(5) := 10000;   -- Numeric variable initialized
                                    -- to 10,000
  v_FirstName VARCHAR2(20);         -- Variable length character string
                                    -- with maximum length of 20
BEGIN
  /* Start of executable section */
  -- Retrieve first name of student with ID 10,000
  SELECT first_name
    INTO v_FirstName
    FROM students
    WHERE id = v_StudentID;

  -- Start of a nested block, which contains only an executable
  -- section
  BEGIN
    INSERT INTO log_table (info)
      VALUES ('Hello from a nested block!');
  END;
EXCEPTION
  /* Start of exception section */
  WHEN NO_DATA_FOUND THEN
    -- Start of a nested block, which itself contains an executable
    -- and exception section
    BEGIN
      -- Handle the error condition
      INSERT INTO log_table (info)
        VALUES ('Student 10,000 does not exist!');
    EXCEPTION
      WHEN OTHERS THEN
        -- Something went wrong with the INSERT
        DBMS_OUTPUT.PUT_LINE('Error inserting into log_table!');
    END;
END;
```

Lexical Units

Any PL/SQL program is made up of lexical units—the building blocks of a language. Essentially, a *lexical unit* is a sequence of characters, in the character set allowed for the PL/SQL language. This character set includes

- Upper- and lowercase letters: A–Z and a–z

- Digits: 0–9

- White space: tabs, spaces, and carriage returns

- Mathematical symbols: + – * / < > =

- Punctuation symbols: ( ) { } [ ] ? ! ~ ; : . ' " @ # % $ ^ & _ |

Any symbol in the character set, and only the symbols in the character set, can be used as part of a PL/SQL program. Like SQL, PL/SQL is not case sensitive. Thus, upper- and lowercase letters are equivalent, except inside quoted strings.

Lexical units can be classified as identifiers, delimiters, literals, and comments.

Identifiers

Identifiers are used to name PL/SQL objects, such as variables, cursors, types, and subprograms. Identifiers consist of a letter, optionally followed by any sequence of characters, including letters, numbers, dollar signs, underscores, and pound signs (#). Other characters are illegal. The maximum length for an identifier is 30 characters, and all characters are significant. For example, here are some legal identifiers:

```
x
v_StudentID
TempVar
v1
v2_
social_security_#
```

Here are some illegal identifiers:

```
x+y                             -- Illegal character +
_temp_                          -- Must start with a letter,
                                   not an underscore
First Name                      -- Illegal space
This_is_a_really_long_identifier  -- More than 30 characters
1_variable                      -- Can't start with a digit
```

PL/SQL is not case sensitive, so the following identifiers all mean the same thing to PL/SQL:

```
Room_Description
room_description
ROOM_DESCRIPTION
rOOm_DEscriPTIOn
```

It is good programming practice to have a consistent naming scheme for identifiers and to make them descriptive. See the section "PL/SQL Style Guide" at the end of this chapter for more information.

Reserved Words

Many identifiers, known as *reserved words* (or keywords), have special meaning to PL/SQL. It is illegal to use these words to name your own identifiers. For example, BEGIN and END are used to delimit PL/SQL blocks. Thus, you cannot use them as variable names. For example, the following declarative section is illegal and will generate a compile error because "begin" is a reserved word:

```
DECLARE
  begin NUMBER;
```

These words are only reserved when used as identifiers by themselves. They can appear as part of another identifier. For example, the following declarative section is legal, even though "begin" and "date" are reserved:

```
DECLARE
  v_BeginDate DATE;
```

In this book, reserved words are written in uppercase to improve readability. See the "PL/SQL Style Guide" section at the end of this chapter for more information. Appendix B contains a complete list of reserved words.

Quoted Identifiers

If you want to make an identifier case sensitive, include characters such as spaces, or use a reserved word, you can enclose the identifier in double quotation marks. For example, all of the following are legal and distinct identifiers:

```
"A number"
"Linda's variable"
"x/y"
"X/Y"
```

Like nonquoted identifiers, the maximum length of a quoted identifier is 30 characters (not including the double quotation marks). Any printable character is legal as part of a quoted identifier except a double quotation mark. Quoted identifiers are also useful when you want to use a PL/SQL reserved word in a SQL statement. PL/SQL reserves more words than SQL (this is also indicated by the chart in Appendix B). For example, if you wanted to query a table with a column called "exception" (a reserved word), you could access it with

```
DECLARE
  v_Exception    VARCHAR2(10);
BEGIN
  SELECT "EXCEPTION"
    INTO v_Exception
    FROM exception_table;
END;
```

Note that `"EXCEPTION"` is in uppercase. Oracle objects are stored in uppercase in the data dictionary, unless explicitly created as a quoted lowercase identifier in the CREATE statement. Strings inside double quotation marks are case sensitive, so `"EXCEPTION"` needs to be in uppercase as well.

I don't recommend using reserved words for identifiers, even though it is legal. It is poor programming style and can make the program more difficult to understand. The only case where this may become necessary is when a database table uses a PL/SQL reserved word for a column name. Because PL/SQL has more reserved words than SQL, a table may have a column that is a PL/SQL reserved word, but not a SQL reserved word. The `exception_table` table in the previous example illustrates this case.

TIP
Although the `exception_table` table can still be used in PL/SQL, it is better to rename the offending column. If the table definition cannot be changed, a view can be created with an alternate name for the column. This view can then be used in PL/SQL. Suppose we created `exception_table` with
```
CREATE TABLE exception_table (
  exception    VARCHAR2(20),
  date_occurred DATE);
```
Given this definition, we can create a view with
```
CREATE VIEW exception_view AS
  SELECT exception exception_
         description,
         date_occurred
    FROM exception_table;
```
We can now use `exception_view` instead of `exception_table`, and the column can now be referred to as `exception_description`, which is not reserved.

Delimiters

Delimiters are symbols (either a single character or a sequence of characters) that have special meaning to PL/SQL. They are used to separate identifiers from each other. Table 3-1 lists the delimiters available to PL/SQL.

Symbol	Description	Symbol	Description
+	Addition operator	–	Subtraction operator
*	Multiplication operator	/	Division operator
=	Equality operator	<	Less-than operator
>	Greater-than operator	(	Initial expression delimiter
)	Final expression delimiter	;	Statement terminator
%	Attribute indicator	,	Item separator
.	Component selector	@	Database link indicator
'	Character string delimiter	"	Quoted string delimiter
:	Bind variable indicator	**	Exponentiation operator
<>	Not-equal-to operator	!=	Not-equal-to operator (equivalent to <>)
~=	Not-equal-to operator (equivalent to !=)	^=	Not-equal-to operator (equivalent to ~=)
<=	Less-than-or-equal-to operator	>=	Greater-than-or-equal-to operator
:=	Assignment operator	=>	Association operator
..	Range operator	||	String concatenation operator
<<	Begin label delimiter	>>	End label delimiter
--	Single line comment indicator	/*	Initial multiline comment indicator
*/	Final multiline comment indicator	<space>	Space
<tab>	Tab character	<cr>	Carriage return or new line

TABLE 3-1. *PL/SQL Delimiters*

Literals

A *literal* is a character, numeric, or Boolean value that is not an identifier. As an example, –23.456 and NULL are both literals. The Boolean, character, and numeric types are discussed in the section "PL/SQL Types" later in this chapter.

Character Literals

Character literals, also known as string literals, consist of one or more characters delimited by single quotation marks. (This is the same standard as SQL.) Character literals can be assigned to variables of type CHAR or VARCHAR2 without conversion. For example, all of the following are legal string literals:

```
'12345'
'Four score and seven years ago...'
'100%'
'"'
```

All string literals are considered to have the datatype CHAR. Any printable character in the PL/SQL character set can be part of a literal, including another single quotation mark. A single quotation mark is also used to delimit the literal, so to include a single quotation mark as part of the string, place two single quotation marks next to each other. For example, to put the string "Mike's string" into a literal, we would use

```
'Mike''s string'
```

Thus, in PL/SQL, the string that consists of just a single quotation mark would be identified by

```
''''
```

The first single quotation mark delimits the start of the string, the next two identify the only character in the string (which happens to be a single quotation mark), and the fourth quotation mark delimits the end of the string. Note that this is different from the literal

```
''
```

which denotes a zero-length string. In PL/SQL, the zero-length string literal is considered identical to NULL.

Some character literals represent values in other datatypes, which can be converted either implicitly or explicitly. The literal '12345' can be converted to a number, and the literal '01-JAN-2001' can be converted to a date, for example. See the section "Converting Between Datatypes" later in this chapter for more details.

Numeric Literals

A numeric literal represents either an integer or real value. Numeric literals can be assigned to variables of type NUMBER without conversion. These are the only literals that are valid as part of arithmetic expressions. Integer literals consist of an optional sign (+ or –), followed by digits. No decimal point is used to define an integer literal, because its use will create a real literal. The following are legal integer literals:

```
123
-7
+12
0
```

A real literal consists of an optional sign followed by digits containing one decimal point. The following are all legal real literals:

```
-17.1
23.0
3.
```

Even though 23.0 and 3. actually contain numbers with no fractional part, they are still considered real literals by PL/SQL. Real literals can also be written using scientific notation if desired. The following are also legal real literals:

```
1.345E7
9.87E-3
-7.12e+12
```

After the E or e, there can be only an integer literal. The E stands for *exponent,* and can be interpreted as "times 10 to the power of." So the preceding three values can also be read as

```
1.345E7 = 1.345 times 10 to the power of 7
        = 1.345 x 10,000,000 = 13,450,000
9.87E-3 = 9.87 times 10 to the power of -3 = 9.87 x .001 = 0.00987
-7.12e+12 = -7.12 times 10 to the power of 12
        = -7.12 x 1,000,000,000,000 = -7,120,000,000,000
```

NOTE
Depending on your NLS settings, a different character (such as a comma) may be used instead of a period to separate the integral and fractional parts of a real literal. See the Oracle NLS documentation for more details. NLS is known as globalization in Oracle 9i.

Boolean Literals

There are only three possible Boolean literals: TRUE, FALSE, and NULL. This is different from most languages, where a Boolean can be only TRUE or FALSE. These values can only be assigned to a Boolean variable. Boolean literals represent the truth or falsity of conditions and are used in IF and LOOP statements.

Comments

Comments improve readability and make your programs more understandable. They are ignored by the PL/SQL compiler. Hints to the SQL optimizer, which look like comments within SQL statements, are processed by the SQL engine. There are two kinds of comments: single-line comments and multiline or C-style comments.

Single-Line Comments

A single-line comment can start at any point on a line with two dashes and continues until the end of the line (delimited by a carriage return). Given the PL/SQL block

```
-- Available online as part of comments.sql
DECLARE
  v_Department  CHAR(3);
  v_Course      NUMBER;
BEGIN
  INSERT INTO classes (department, course)
    VALUES (v_Department, v_Course);
END;
```

we can add single-line comments to make this block more understandable, as in the following example:

```
-- Available online as part of comments.sql
DECLARE
  v_Department  CHAR(3);   -- Variable to hold the 3 character
                           -- department code
  v_Course      NUMBER;    -- Variable to hold the course number
BEGIN
  -- Insert the course identified by v_Department and v_Course
  -- into the classes table in the database.
  INSERT INTO classes (department, course)
    VALUES (v_Department, v_Course);
END;
```

NOTE

If the comment extends over more than one line, the double dash (--) is necessary at the start of each line.

Multiline Comments

Multiline comments start with the /* delimiter and end with the */ delimiter. This is the comment style used in the C language, as demonstrated in the following code:

```
-- Available online as part of comments.sql
DECLARE
  v_Department   CHAR(3);   /* Variable to hold the 3 character
                              department name */
  v_Course       NUMBER;    /* Variable to hold the course number */
BEGIN
  /* Insert the course identified by v_Department and v_Course
     into the classes table in the database. */
  INSERT INTO classes (department, course)
    VALUES (v_Department, v_Course);
END;
```

Multiline comments can extend over as many lines as desired. However, they cannot be nested. One comment has to end before another can begin. The following block is illegal because it contains nested comments:

```
-- Available online as part of comments.sql
BEGIN
  /* We are now inside a comment. If we were to begin another
     comment such as /* this */ it would be illegal. */
  NULL;
END;
```

TIP
Strictly speaking, it is possible to have the beginning comment symbols, /*, within a comment—it is the */ of a nested comment that causes the problem by ending the comment as a whole. However, I would recommend against this as it simply adds confusion.

Variable Declarations

Communication with the database takes place through variables in the PL/SQL block. *Variables* are memory locations, which can store data values. As the program runs, the contents of variables can and do change. Information from the database can be assigned to a variable, or the contents of a variable can be inserted into the database. Variables can also be modified directly by PL/SQL commands. These variables are declared in the declarative section of the block. Every variable has a specific type as well, which describes what kind of information can be stored in it. We will discuss types shortly.

Declaration Syntax

Variables are declared in the declarative section of the block. The general syntax for declaring a variable is

> *variable_name type* [CONSTANT] [NOT NULL] [:= *value*];

where *variable_name* is the name of the variable, *type* is the type, and *value* is the initial value of the variable. For example, the following are all legal variable declarations:

```
DECLARE
   v_Description      VARCHAR2(50);
   v_NumberSeats      NUMBER := 45;
   v_Counter          BINARY_INTEGER := 0;
```

Any legal PL/SQL identifier (as defined earlier in the section "Lexical Units") can be used as a variable name. VARCHAR2, NUMBER, and BINARY_INTEGER are valid PL/SQL types. In this example, v_NumberSeats and v_Counter are both initialized, to 45 and 0, respectively. If a variable is not initialized, such as v_Description, it is assigned NULL by default. If NOT NULL is present in the declaration, the variable must be initialized as it is defined. Furthermore, it is illegal to assign NULL to a variable constrained to be NOT NULL, either when it is declared or in the executable or exception section of the block. The following declaration is illegal because v_TempVar is constrained to be NOT NULL, but is not initialized:

```
DECLARE
   v_TempVar NUMBER NOT NULL;
```

We can correct this by assigning a default value to v_TempVar, for example:

```
DECLARE
   v_TempVar NUMBER NOT NULL := 0;
```

If CONSTANT is present in the variable declaration, the variable must be initialized, and its value cannot be changed from this initial value. A constant variable is treated as read-only for the remainder of the block. Constants are often used for values that are known when the block is written, for example:

```
DECLARE
   c_MinimumStudentID CONSTANT NUMBER(5) := 10000;
```

If desired, the keyword DEFAULT can be used instead of := as well:

```
DECLARE
    v_NumberSeats    NUMBER DEFAULT 45;
    v_Counter        BINARY_INTEGER DEFAULT 0;
    v_FirstName      VARCHAR2(20) DEFAULT 'Scott';
```

There can be only one variable declaration per line in the declarative section. The following section is illegal, because two variables are declared on the same line:

```
DECLARE
    v_FirstName, v_LastName   VARCHAR2(20);
```

The correct version of this block would be

```
DECLARE
    v_FirstName VARCHAR2(20);
    v_LastName  VARCHAR2(20);
```

Variable Initialization

Many languages do not define what uninitialized variables contain. As a result, uninitialized variables can contain random or unknown values at runtime. In these languages, leaving uninitialized variables is not good programming style. In general, it is best to initialize a variable if its value can be determined.

PL/SQL, however, does define what an uninitialized variable contains—it is assigned NULL. NULL simply means "missing or unknown value." As a result, it is logical that NULL is assigned by default to any uninitialized variable. This is a unique feature of PL/SQL. Many other programming languages (C and Ada included) do not define the value for uninitialized variables. Other languages (such as Java) require that all variables be initialized.

PL/SQL Types

As of Oracle7, PL/SQL had three categories of types: scalar, composite, and reference. Oracle8 defined two additional type categories: the LOB and object types. Scalar datatypes do not have any components within the type, while composite types do. A reference type is a pointer to another type. Figure 3-1 lists all of the PL/SQL types, and they are described in the following sections.

The predefined PL/SQL types are defined in a package called STANDARD. The contents of this package are available to any PL/SQL block. Besides types, package STANDARD defines the built-in SQL and conversion functions available in PL/SQL.

```
                         SCALAR TYPES
    Numeric Family:      Character Family:   Date/Interval Family:
     BINARY_INTEGER       CHAR                DATE
     DEC                  CHARACTER           INTERVAL DAY TO SECOND³
     DECIMAL              LONG                INTERVAL YEAR TO MONTH³
     DOUBLE PRECISION     NCHAR¹              TIMESTAMP³
     FLOAT                NVARCHAR2¹          TIMESTAMP WITH TIME ZONE³
     INT                  STRING              TIMESTAMP WITH LOCAL TIME ZONE³
     INTEGER              VARCHAR
     NATURAL              VARCHAR2
     NATURALN
     NUMBER              Rowid Family:       Boolean Family:
     NUMERIC              ROWID               BOOLEAN
     PLS_INTEGER          UROWID²
     POSITIVE
     POSITIVEN           Trusted Family:     Raw Family:
     REAL                 MLSLABEL            RAW
     SIGNTYPE                                 LONG RAW
     SMALLINT
```

COMPOSITE TYPES	LOB TYPES	REFERENCE TYPES	OBJECT TYPES
RECORD	BFILE ¹	REF CURSOR	object type³
NESTED TABLE¹	LOB ¹	REF object type¹	SYS.ANYTYPE³
INDEX-BY TABLE	CLOB ¹		SYS.ANYDATA³
VARRAY¹	NLOB ¹		SYS.ANYDATASET³

[1] This type is available in Oracle8 and higher
[2] This type is available in Oracle8i and higher
[3] This type is available in Oracle9i and higher

FIGURE 3-1. *PL/SQL types*

Scalar Types

The legal scalar types consist of the same types valid for a database column, with a number of additions. Scalar types can be divided into seven families—numeric, character, raw, date/interval, rowid, Boolean, and trusted—each of which is described in the following sections.

Numeric Family

Types in the numeric family store integer or real values. There are three basic types—NUMBER, PLS_INTEGER, and BINARY_INTEGER. Variables of type NUMBER can hold either an integer or real quantity, and variables of type BINARY_INTEGER or PLS_INTEGER can hold only integers.

NUMBER   This type can hold a numeric value, either integer or floating point. It is the same as the NUMBER database type. The syntax for declaring a number is

NUMBER (*P,S*)

where *P* is the precision and *S* is the scale. The precision is the number of digits in the value, and the scale is the number of digits to the right of the decimal point. The scale can be negative, which indicates that the value is rounded to the specified number of places to the left of the decimal point. Both precision and scale are optional, but if scale is present, precision must be present as well. Table 3-2 shows different combinations of precision and scale, and their meanings.

The maximum precision is 38, and the scale ranges from –84 to 127.

A *subtype* is an alternate name for a type, which can optionally constrain the legal values for a variable of the subtype. Subtypes are explained in detail in the "User-Defined Subtypes" section later in this chapter. There are a number of subtypes that are equivalent to NUMBER, which essentially rename the NUMBER datatype because

Declaration	Assigned Value	Stored Value
NUMBER	1234.5678	1234.5678
NUMBER(3)	123	123
NUMBER(3)	1234	Error—exceeds precision
NUMBER(4,3)	123.4567	Error—exceeds precision
NUMBER(4,3)	1.234567	1.235[1]
NUMBER(7,2)	12345.67	12345.67
NUMBER(3,–3)	1234	1000[2]
NUMBER(3, –1)	1234	1230[2]

[1] If the assigned value exceeds the scale, the stored value is rounded to the number of digits specified by the scale.

[2] If the scale is negative, the stored value is rounded to the number of digits specified by the scale, to the left of the decimal point.

TABLE 3-2.   *Precision and Scale Values*

none of them are constrained. You may want to use an alternate name for readability, or for compatibility with datatypes from other databases. The equivalent types are

- DEC
- DECIMAL
- DOUBLE PRECISION
- FLOAT
- NUMERIC
- REAL

Among the types that can store floating-point numbers, DEC, DECIMAL, and NUMERIC have the maximum precision of 38 decimal digits. DOUBLE PRECISION and FLOAT have a precision of 126 binary digits, which is approximately 38 decimal digits. REAL has a precision of 63 binary digits, which is approximately 18 decimal digits.

In addition to the above unconstrained subtypes, the INTEGER, INT, and SMALLINT subtypes can store integers with a maximum precision of 38 decimal digits.

BINARY_INTEGER   The NUMBER type is stored in a decimal format, which is optimized for accuracy and storage efficiency. Because of this, arithmetic operations can't be performed directly on NUMBERs. In order to compute using numeric quantities, NUMBERs must be converted into a binary type. The PL/SQL engine will do this automatically if you have an arithmetic expression involving NUMBERs, and will convert the result back to NUMBER if necessary.

However, if you have a whole number value that won't be stored in the database, but will only be used for computations, the BINARY_INTEGER datatype is available. This datatype is used to store signed integer values, which range from –2147483647 to +2147483647. It is stored in a 2's complement binary format (generally the native format for integers), which means that it is available for computations without conversion. Loop counters are often of type BINARY_INTEGER.

Like NUMBER, there are subtypes defined for BINARY_INTEGER. Unlike most of the NUMBER subtypes, however, the BINARY_INTEGER subtypes are *constrained,* which means that they can only hold restricted values. These constrained subtypes of BINARY_INTEGER are listed in Table 3-3.

PLS_INTEGER   PLS_INTEGERs have the same range as BINARY_INTEGERs, from –2147483647 to +2147483647, and are also implemented using the native 2's complement format. However, when a calculation involving a PLS_INTEGER overflows, an error is raised. If a calculation involving a BINARY_INTEGER overflows, the result can be assigned to a NUMBER variable (which has a greater range) with no error. The difference between these two datatypes is illustrated by the following

Subtype	Constraint
NATURAL	0 ... 2147483647
NATURALN	0 ... 2147483647 NOT NULL
POSITIVE	1 ... 2147483647
POSITIVEN	1 ... 2147483647 NOT NULL
SIGNTYPE	–1, 0, 1

TABLE 3-3. *BINARY_INTEGER Subtypes*

SQL*Plus session (see the section "Expressions and Operators" later in this chapter for more information on PL/SQL expressions):

```
-- Available online as integers.sql
SQL> DECLARE
  2    v_BinInt BINARY_INTEGER;
  3  BEGIN
  4    -- Assign the maximum value to v_BinInt.
  5    v_BinInt := 2147483647;
  6
  7    -- Add 1 to v_BinInt (which would cause an overflow), and then
  8    -- subtract it again.  The result of this calculation does fit
  9    -- within the range of a BINARY_INTEGER, and no error is
 10    -- raised.
 11    v_BinInt := v_BinInt + 1 - 1;
 12  END;
 13  /
PL/SQL procedure successfully completed.

SQL> DECLARE
  2    v_PLSInt PLS_INTEGER;
  3  BEGIN
  4    -- Assign the maximum value to v_PLSInt.
  5    v_PLSInt := 2147483647;
  6
  7    -- Add 1 to v_PLSInt (which would cause an overflow), and then
  8    -- subtract it again.  Although the result of the calculation
  9    -- would fit within the range of a PLS_INTEGER, an intermediate
 10    -- value does not, and so ORA-1426 is raised.
 11    v_PLSInt := v_PLSInt + 1 - 1;
 12  END;
 13  /
DECLARE
*
ERROR at line 1:
ORA-01426: numeric overflow
ORA-06512: at line 11
```

Character Family

Variables in the character family are used to hold strings, or character data. The types in the character family are VARCHAR2, CHAR, and LONG, along with NCHAR and NVARCHAR2 (the latter two available with Oracle8 and higher).

VARCHAR2 This type behaves similarly to the VARCHAR2 database type. Variables of type VARCHAR2 can hold variable-length character strings, with a maximum length. The syntax for declaring a VARCHAR2 variable is

VARCHAR2(*L*)

where *L* is the maximum length of the variable. The length is required—there is no default. The maximum length for a VARCHAR2 variable in PL/SQL is 32,767 bytes. Note that a VARCHAR2 database column can only hold 4,000 bytes. If a VARCHAR2 PL/SQL variable is more than 4,000 bytes, it can only be inserted into a database column of type LONG or CLOB, which has a maximum length of 2 gigabytes (4 gigabytes for a CLOB). Likewise, LONG or CLOB data cannot be selected into a VARCHAR2 variable unless it is 32,767 bytes or less in length.

NOTE
In Oracle7, a VARCHAR2 database column could hold 2,000 bytes. Thus, a PL/SQL VARCHAR2 can be inserted into an Oracle7 VARCHAR2 column only if it is less than or equal to 2,000 bytes in length.

The length of a VARCHAR2 is specified in bytes, not in characters. The actual data is stored in the character set for your database, which could be a single-byte character set such as ASCII or EBCDIC Code Page 500, or a variable-length multibyte character set such as Unicode. If the database character set contains multibyte characters, the maximum number of characters that a VARCHAR2 variable can hold may be less than the length specified. This is because a single character may be represented by more than one byte.

The subtypes VARCHAR and STRING are equivalent to VARCHAR2.

TIP
Why are there two types—VARCHAR and VARCHAR2? The VARCHAR type is defined by ANSI, while the VARCHAR2 type is defined by Oracle. Currently, they behave the same. If the ANSI VARCHAR type changes in the future, the Oracle VARCHAR2 type will not.

In Oracle9*i*, the syntax for declaring a VARCHAR2 variable has been expanded to

VARCHAR2(*L* [CHAR | BYTE])

where *L* is again the maximum length of the variable. CHAR or BYTE is used to specify whether *L* is to be measured in characters or bytes, respectively (the default is CHAR). The maximum length, however, is still 32,767 bytes. For example, suppose the database character set is UTF8, which is a variable-width multibyte character set. The maximum width of a character is 3 bytes in UTF8, which means that a variable declared as VARCHAR2(300 BYTE) may be able to hold a maximum of only 100 characters, depending on the actual characters that are stored.

CHAR   Variables of this type are fixed-length character strings. The syntax for declaring a CHAR variable is

CHAR [(*L*)]

where *L* is the maximum length, in bytes. Unlike VARCHAR2, however, specifying the length is optional. If it is not specified, it defaults to 1. If the length isn't specified, the parentheses shouldn't be included either. Because CHAR variables are fixed length, they are blank padded, if necessary, to fill out the maximum length. Because they are blank padded, CHAR variables won't necessarily match in a character comparison. See the section "Character Comparisons" in Chapter 4 for more information on character comparisons.

The maximum length of a CHAR variable is 32,767 bytes. The maximum length of a CHAR database column is 2,000 bytes. Therefore, if a CHAR variable contains more than 2,000 bytes, it can only be inserted into a VARCHAR2 (if the length is <= 4,000 bytes) or LONG database column. Similarly, LONG data can only be selected into a CHAR variable if it is less than 32,767 bytes.

NOTE
In Oracle7, CHAR database columns could hold up to 255 bytes.

Like VARCHAR2, the length of a CHAR variable is specified in bytes, not characters. If the database character set contains multibyte characters, the maximum number of characters a CHAR variable can hold may be less than the length specified.

CHARACTER is a subtype for CHAR, with the same restrictions. VARCHAR2 and CHAR variables have significantly different semantics (see the section "Character Comparisons" in Chapter 4 for more information).

Oracle9i and higher

In Oracle9*i*, the syntax for declaring a CHAR variable has been expanded to

CHAR [(*L* [CHAR | BYTE])]

where *L* is again the maximum length of the variable. CHAR or BYTE is used to specify whether *L* is to be measured in characters or bytes, respectively (the default is CHAR). The maximum length, however, is still 32,767 bytes. As before, suppose the database character set is UTF8, which is a variable-width multibyte character set. The maximum width of a character is 3 bytes in UTF8, which means that a variable declared as CHAR(300 BYTE) may be able to hold a maximum of only 100 characters (blank padded as necessary), depending on the actual characters that are stored.

LONG   Unlike the database LONG type, which can hold up to 2 gigabytes of data, the PL/SQL LONG type is a variable-length string with a maximum length of 32,760 bytes. LONG variables are very similar to VARCHAR2 variables. Similar to the behavior for VARCHAR2 variables, if a LONG database column contains more than 32,760 bytes of data, it cannot be selected into a PL/SQL LONG variable. However, because the maximum length of a PL/SQL LONG is less than a database LONG, a PL/SQL LONG can be inserted into a database column of type LONG with no restrictions.

Oracle8 and higher

NCHAR and NVARCHAR2   Oracle8 provides two additional database types: the NLS character types NCHAR and NVARCHAR2. *NLS character types* are used to store character strings in a different character set from the PL/SQL language itself. This character set is known as the *national character set.*
   NCHARs and NVARCHAR2s are specified and used the same way as CHARs and VARCHAR2s. However, the specification for the length can vary depending on the national character set. If the national character set is fixed width, the length is specified in characters. If the national character set is variable width, the length is specified in bytes.

NOTE
In Oracle9i, the length for NCHAR and NVARCHAR2 is always specified in characters.

For more information on NCHAR, NVARCHAR2, and NLS in general, see the *Server SQL Reference.*

Raw Family

The types in the raw family are used to store binary data. Character variables are automatically converted between character sets by Oracle, if necessary. This can happen if the data is being passed via a database link between two databases, each using different character sets. This will not happen for raw variables.

RAW RAW variables are similar to CHAR variables, except that they are not converted between character sets. The syntax for specifying a RAW variable is

RAW(*L*)

where *L* is the length in bytes of the variable. RAW is used to store fixed-length binary data. Unlike character data, RAW data is not converted between character sets when transmitted between two different databases. The maximum length of a RAW variable is 32,767 bytes. The maximum length of a RAW database column is 2,000 bytes (255 in Oracle7). So if the data is more than 2,000 bytes in length, it cannot be inserted into a RAW database column. It can be inserted, however, into a LONG RAW database column, which has a maximum length of 2 gigabytes. Similarly, if the data in a LONG RAW database column is more than 32,767 bytes in length, it cannot be selected into a PL/SQL RAW variable.

LONG RAW LONG RAW data is similar to LONG data, except that PL/SQL will not convert between character sets. The maximum length of a LONG RAW variable is 32,760 bytes. Again, because the maximum length of a database LONG RAW column is 2 gigabytes, if the actual length of the data is more than 32,760 bytes in length, it cannot be selected into a PL/SQL LONG RAW variable. But because the maximum length of a PL/SQL LONG RAW will fit into a database LONG RAW, there are no restrictions on insertion of PL/SQL LONG RAWs into a database LONG RAW.

Date/Interval Family
There are three kinds of types in the date/interval family: DATE, TIMESTAMP, and INTERVAL. TIMESTAMP and INTERVAL are available with Oracle9*i* and higher.

DATE The DATE PL/SQL type behaves the same way as the DATE database type. The DATE type is used to store both date and time information, including the century, year, month, day, hour, minute, and second. There is no storage for fractional seconds. Internally, a DATE variable is 7 bytes, with one byte for each component (century through second).

Values are assigned to DATE variables either from a character variable or from another DATE variable. Character variables are implicitly converted to dates using the default date format for the current session. For more control, it is best to use the TO_DATE built in function to assign values and the TO_CHAR function to extract them. The built-in conversion functions are described in the "Converting Between Datatypes" section later in this chapter, and also in Chapter 5.

<table>
<tr><td>Oracle9i
and higher</td></tr>
</table>

TIMESTAMP   The TIMESTAMP type is similar to the DATE type in that it holds the year, month, day, hour, minute, and second of a point in time. However, timestamps can store fractional seconds. The syntax for specifying a TIMESTAMP variable is

TIMESTAMP[(P)]

where P is the precision of the fractional part of the seconds field, and defaults to 6.
   The TIMESTAMP WITH TIME ZONE type also includes a specified time zone, in addition to the timestamp data. It is defined with

TIMESTAMP[(P)] WITH TIME ZONE

where P is again the precision of the fractional part of the seconds field.
   The TIMESTAMP WITH LOCAL TIME ZONE type is always stored in the time zone of the database, regardless of the user's time zone. It is defined with

TIMESTAMP[(P)] WITH LOCAL TIME ZONE

where P is again the precision of the fractional part of the seconds field.

<table>
<tr><td>Oracle9i
and higher</td></tr>
</table>

INTERVAL   The INTERVAL type is used to store the amount of time between two timestamps. The INTERVAL YEAR TO MONTH type stores the number of years and months, and is specified with

INTERVAL YEAR[(P)] TO MONTH

where P is the number of digits of the year field, which defaults to 2. The INTERVAL DAY TO SECOND type stores the number of days and seconds, and is specified with

INTERVAL DAY[(DP)] TO SECOND[(SP)]

where DP is the number of digits in the day field (the default is 2), and SP is the number of digits in the fractional part of the second field (the default is 6).

Rowid Family

There are two types in the rowid family: ROWID and UROWID. UROWID is available in Oracle8*i* and higher.

ROWID   The ROWID PL/SQL type is the same as the database ROWID pseudocolumn type. It can hold a *rowid,* which can be thought of as a unique key for every row in the database. Rowids are stored internally as a fixed-length binary quantity whose length varies between operating systems. In order to manipulate rowids, they can be converted to character strings via the built-in function ROWIDTOCHAR. The output of this function is an 18-character string. In Oracle7 databases, this string was in *restricted format*

```
BBBBBBBB.RRRR.FFFF
```

where BBBBBBBB identifies the block within a database file, RRRR the row within the block, and FFFF the file number. Each component of a rowid is represented as a hexadecimal number. For example, the rowid

```
0000001E.00FF.0001
```

identifies the 30th block, the 255th row within this block, in file 1. In Oracle8 and higher databases, the rowid string is in *extended format,* which is also an 18-character string representing a value in base-64 notation. The components of an extended format rowid can be determined using the DBMS_ROWID package, described in Appendix A.

Rowids are not generally constructed by a PL/SQL program; they are selected from the ROWID pseudocolumn of a table. This value can then be used in the WHERE clause of a subsequent UPDATE or DELETE statement.

Oracle **8i**
and higher | **UROWID**   Although every row in a table accessible in an Oracle database has an address, it may not be a physical address. For example, rows in index-organized tables have a *logical rowid* that is based on the primary key of the table. Tables in a non-Oracle database, but accessible through a gateway, also have logical rowids. The UROWID datatype can store both physical rowids (that is, those of the ROWID datatype) and logical rowids. Oracle recommends that UROWID be used for future applications because it is the most versatile.

See *Oracle Concepts* for more information on logical rowids and index-organized tables.

Boolean Family

The only datatype in the Boolean family is BOOLEAN. Boolean variables are used in PL/SQL control structures, such as IF-THEN-ELSE and LOOP statements. A BOOLEAN variable can hold TRUE, FALSE, or NULL only. Thus, the following declarative section is illegal because 0 is not a valid BOOLEAN value:

```
DECLARE
    v_ContinueFlag BOOLEAN := 0;
```

Trusted Family

The only datatype in the trusted family is MLSLABEL. This datatype is used in Trusted Oracle to store variable-length binary labels. With standard Oracle, variables and table columns of type MLSLABEL can only hold the value NULL. Internally, MLSLABEL variables are between 2 and 5 bytes in length. However, they can be converted to and from a character variable automatically. The maximum length of a character representation of an MLSLABEL is 255 bytes.

NOTE
MLSLABEL is not available as of Oracle8i.

Composite Types

The composite types available in PL/SQL are records, tables (both nested and index-by), and varrays. A *composite type* is one that has components within it. A variable of a composite type contains one or more scalar variables (also known as *attributes*). Records are discussed in detail in the section "PL/SQL Records" later in this chapter, and tables and varrays are discussed in Chapter 8.

Reference Types

Once a variable is declared of a scalar or composite type in PL/SQL, the memory storage for this variable is allocated. The variable names this storage and is used to refer to it later in the program. However, there is no way to deallocate the storage and still have the variable remain available—the memory is not freed until the variable is no longer in scope. (See the section "Variable Scope and Visibility" later in this chapter for information on scope.) A reference type does not have this restriction. A *reference type* in PL/SQL is similar to a pointer in C. A variable that is declared of a reference type can point to different storage locations over the life of the program.

The only reference type available with Oracle7 was REF CURSOR. This type, also known as a cursor variable, will be discussed in detail in Chapter 6. Oracle8 introduced the REF object type, which can point to an object.

LOB Types

| Oracle8 and higher | The LOB types are used to store large objects. A *large object* can be either a binary or character value up to 4 gigabytes in size. Large objects can contain unstructured data, which is accessed more efficiently than LONG or LONG RAW data, with fewer restrictions. LOB types are manipulated using the DBMS_LOB package. For more information, see Chapter 12.

Object Types

Oracle8
and higher

An object type is a composite type that has both attributes (variables of other types) and methods (subprogram) within it. Oracle8 allows you to create object types to represent real-world objects. Oracle9*i* extends the object model to include inheritance and subtypes. For more information, see Chapter 12.

Using %TYPE

In many cases, a PL/SQL variable will be used to manipulate data stored in a database table. In this case, the variable should have the same type as the table column. For example, the `first_name` column of the `students` table has type VARCHAR2(20). Based on this, we can declare a variable as follows:

```
DECLARE
  v_FirstName VARCHAR2(20);
```

This is fine, but what happens if the definition of `first_name` is changed? Say the table is altered and `first_name` now has type VARCHAR2(25). Any PL/SQL code that uses this column would have to be changed, as in

```
DECLARE
  v_FirstName VARCHAR2(25);
```

If you have a large amount of PL/SQL code, this can be a time-consuming and error-prone process. Rather than hardcode the type of a variable in this way, you can use the %TYPE attribute. This attribute is appended to a table column reference, or another variable, and returns its type.

```
DECLARE
  v_FirstName students.first_name%TYPE;
```

By using %TYPE, `v_FirstName` will have whatever type the `first_name` column of the `students` table has. The type is determined each time the block is run for anonymous and named blocks, and whenever stored objects (procedures, functions, packages, object types, and triggers) are compiled. %TYPE can also be applied to an earlier PL/SQL variable declaration. The following example shows various applications of the %TYPE attribute:

```
DECLARE
  v_RoomID      classes.room_id%TYPE;   -- NUMBER(5)
  v_RoomID2     v_RoomID%TYPE;          -- NUMBER(5)
  v_TempVar     NUMBER(7,3) NOT NULL := 12.3;
  v_AnotherVar  v_TempVar%TYPE;         -- NUMBER(7,3)
```

If %TYPE is applied to a variable or column that is constrained to be NOT NULL (such as `classes.room_id` or `v_TempVar`), the type it returns does not have this restriction. The preceding block is still legal even though `v_RoomID`, `v_RoomID2`, and `v_AnotherVar` are not initialized because they can hold NULL values.

It is good programming style to use %TYPE, because it makes a PL/SQL program more flexible and able to adapt to changing database definitions.

User-Defined Subtypes

A subtype is a PL/SQL type that is based on an existing type. A subtype can be used to give an alternate name for a type, which describes its intended use. PL/SQL defines several subtypes (for example, DECIMAL and INTEGER are subtypes of NUMBER) in package STANDARD. The syntax for defining a subtype is

SUBTYPE *new_type* IS *original_type*;

where *new_type* is the name of the new subtype, and *original type* refers to the base type. The base type can be a predefined type or subtype, or a %TYPE reference.

```
DECLARE
    SUBTYPE t_LoopCounter IS NUMBER;   -- Define the new subtype
    v_LoopCounter t_LoopCounter;     -- Declare a variable of the subtype
    SUBTYPE t_NameType IS students.first_name%TYPE;
```

The SUBTYPE definition cannot be constrained directly in the definition. The following block is illegal:

```
DECLARE
    SUBTYPE t_LoopCounter IS NUMBER(4);   -- Illegal constraint
```

There is a workaround for this, however. You can declare a dummy variable of the desired type (with the constraint) and use %TYPE in the SUBTYPE definition:

```
DECLARE
    v_DummyVar  NUMBER(4);                -- Dummy variable, won't be used
    SUBTYPE t_LoopCounter is v_DummyVar%TYPE;  -- Returns NUMBER(4)
    v_Counter   t_LoopCounter;
```

| Oracle8*i* and higher | This restriction has been removed in Oracle8*i*. There, the following declare section is legal: |

```
DECLARE
    SUBTYPE t_LoopCounter IS NUMBER(4);   -- Legal in Oracle8i
```

Variable declarations using an unconstrained subtype can also constrain the type:

```
DECLARE
   SUBTYPE  t_Numeric IS NUMBER; -- Define unconstrained subtype,
   v_Counter is t_Numeric(5);    -- but a constrained variable
```

A subtype is considered to be in the same family as its base type.

Converting Between Datatypes

PL/SQL can handle conversions between different families among the scalar datatypes. Within a family, you can convert between datatypes subject to the variable constraints. For example, a CHAR(10) variable cannot be converted into a VARCHAR2(1) variable because there is not enough room. Likewise, precision and scale constraints may prohibit conversion between NUMBER(3,2) and NUMBER(3). In cases of constraint violations, the PL/SQL compiler will not issue an error, but you may get a runtime error, depending on the values in the variables to be converted.

There are two types of conversions, regardless of the type: implicit and explicit.

Explicit Datatype Conversion

The built-in conversion functions available in SQL are also available in PL/SQL. Table 3-4 gives brief descriptions of these functions. When desired, you can use these functions to convert explicitly between variables in different datatype families. For more information and examples on using these conversion functions, see Chapter 5.

Implicit Datatype Conversion

PL/SQL will automatically convert between datatype families when possible. For example, the following block retrieves the current number of credits for student 10002:

```
DECLARE
   v_CurrentCredits  VARCHAR2(5);
BEGIN
   SELECT current_credits
     INTO v_CurrentCredits
     FROM students
     WHERE id = 10002;
END;
```

In the database, `current_credits` is a NUMBER(3) field. However, `v_CurrentCredits` is a VARCHAR2(5) variable. PL/SQL will automatically convert the numeric data into a character string and then assign it to the character variable. PL/SQL can automatically convert between

- Characters and numbers
- Characters and dates

Function	Description	Families Available for Conversion
TO_CHAR	Converts its argument to a VARCHAR2 type, depending on the optional format specifier.	Numeric, date
TO_DATE	Converts its argument to a DATE type, depending on the optional format specifier.	Character
TO_TIMESTAMP*	Converts its argument to a TIMESTAMP type, depending on the optional format specifier.	Character
TO_TIMESTAMP_TZ*	Converts its argument to a TIMESTAMP WITH TIMEZONE type, depending on the optional format specifier.	Character
TO_DSINTERVAL*	Converts its argument to an INTERVAL DAY TO SECOND type, depending on the optional format specifier.	Character
TO_YMINTERVAL*	Converts its argument to an INTERVAL YEAR TO MONTH type, depending on the optional format specifier.	Character
TO_NUMBER	Converts its argument to a NUMBER type, depending on the optional format specifier.	Character
RAWTOHEX	Converts a RAW value to a hexadecimal representation of the binary quantity.	Raw
HEXTORAW	Converts a hexadecimal representation into the equivalent binary quantity.	Character (must be in a hexadecimal representation)
CHARTOROWID	Converts a character representation of a ROWID into the internal binary format.	Character (must be in the 18-character rowid format)
ROWIDTOCHAR	Converts an internal binary ROWID variable into the 18-character external format.	Rowid

*These functions are available in Oracle9*i* and higher.

TABLE 3-4. *PL/SQL and SQL Datatype Conversion Functions*

Even though PL/SQL will implicitly convert between datatypes, it is good programming practice to use an explicit conversion function. In the next example, this is done with the TO_CHAR function:

```
DECLARE
    v_CurrentCredits   VARCHAR2(5);
BEGIN
    SELECT TO_CHAR(current_credits)
      INTO v_CurrentCredits
      FROM students
      WHERE id = 10002;
END;
```

The advantage of this is that an explicit format string can also be used in the TO_CHAR function, if desired. It also makes the intent of the program clearer and emphasizes the type conversion.

Automatic datatype conversion can also take place when PL/SQL is evaluating expressions, which are described fully in the section "Expressions and Operators" later in this chapter. The same guidelines apply there as well; however, use of an explicit conversion function is recommended.

Variable Scope and Visibility

The *scope* of a variable is the portion of the program in which the variable can be accessed. For a PL/SQL variable, this is from the variable declaration until the end of the block. When a variable goes out of scope, the PL/SQL engine will free the memory used to store the variable, because it can no longer be referenced. Figure 3-2 illustrates this. v_Character is in scope only in the inner block; after the END of the inner block, it is out of scope. The scope of v_Number ranges until the END of the outer block. Both variables are in scope in the inner block.

The *visibility* of a variable is the portion of the program where the variable can be accessed without having to qualify the reference. The visibility is always within the scope; if a variable is out of scope, it is not visible. Consider Figure 3-3. At location 1, both v_AvailableFlag and v_SSN are in scope and are visible.

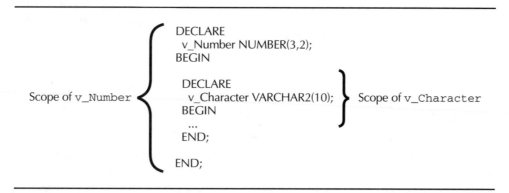

FIGURE 3-2. *Variable scope*

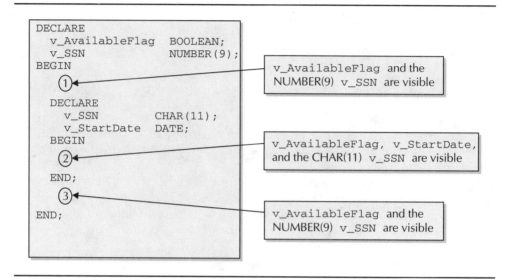

FIGURE 3-3. *Scope and visibility*

At location 2, the same two variables are in scope, but only v_AvailableFlag is still visible. The redeclaration of v_SSN as a CHAR(11) variable has hidden the NUMBER(9) declaration. All four variables are in scope at location 2, but only three are visible: v_AvailableFlag, v_StartDate, and the CHAR(11) v_SSN. By location 3, v_StartDate and the CHAR(11) v_SSN are no longer in scope and hence are no longer visible. The same two variables are in scope and visibility as in location 1: v_AvailableFlag and the NUMBER(9) v_SSN.

If a variable is in scope but is not visible, how does the program reference it? Consider Figure 3-4. This is the same block as Figure 3-3, but a label <<l_Outer>> has been added to the outer block. (Labels are discussed in more detail in the "PL/SQL Control Structures" section later in this chapter.) At location 2, the NUMBER(9) v_SSN is not visible. However, we can refer to it, using the label, as

```
l_Outer.v_SSN
```

Expressions and Operators

Expressions and operators are the glue that holds PL/SQL variables together. These operators define how values are assigned to variables and how these values are manipulated. An *expression* is a sequence of variables and literals, separated by *operators*. The value of an expression is determined by the values of its component variables and literals and the definition of the operators.

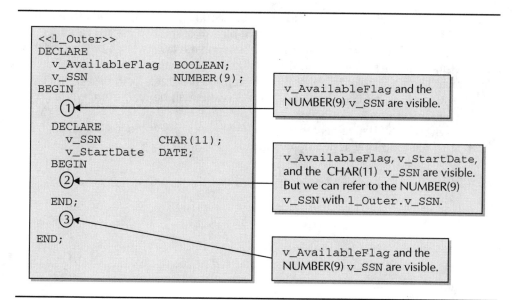

FIGURE 3-4.   *Using a label to reference a variable*

Assignment

The most basic operator is assignment. The syntax is

> *variable* := *expression*;

where *variable* is a PL/SQL variable, and *expression* is a PL/SQL expression. Assignments are legal in the executable and exception handling sections of a block, and when variables are first declared in the declarative section. The following example illustrates some assignments:

```
DECLARE
  v_String1  VARCHAR2(10);
  v_String2  VARCHAR2(15);
  v_Numeric  NUMBER;
BEGIN
  v_String1 := 'Hello';
  v_String2 := v_String1;
  v_Numeric := -12.4;
END;
```

A quantity that can appear on the left-hand side of an assignment operator is known as an *lvalue,* and a quantity that can appear on the right-hand side is known as an *rvalue*. An lvalue must refer to an actual storage location, because the rvalue will be written into it. In the preceding example, all of the lvalues are variables. The PL/SQL engine will allocate storage for variables, and the values `'Hello'` and `-12.4` can be put into this storage. An rvalue can be the contents of a storage location (referenced by a variable) or a literal. The example illustrates both cases: `'Hello'` is a literal, and `v_String1` is a variable. An rvalue will be read from, while an lvalue will be written to. All lvalues are also rvalues.

In a given PL/SQL statement, there can be only one assignment. Unlike languages such as C, the following assignment is *illegal*:

```
DECLARE
  v_Val1 NUMBER;
  v_Val2 NUMBER;
  v_Val3 NUMBER;
BEGIN
  v_Val1 := v_Val2 := v_Val3 := 0;
END;
```

Expressions

PL/SQL expressions are rvalues. As such, an expression is not valid as a statement by itself—it must be part of another statement. For example, an expression can appear on the right-hand side of an assignment operator or as part of a SQL statement. The operators that make up an expression, together with the type of their operands, determine the type of the expression.

An *operand* is the argument to an operator. PL/SQL operators take either one argument (unary) or two arguments (binary). For example, the negation operator (–) is a unary operand, while the multiplication operator (*) is a binary operand. Table 3-5 classifies the PL/SQL operators according to their precedence, or priority. Operators with the highest precedence are listed first.

The *precedence* of the operators in an expression determines the order of evaluation. Consider the following numeric expression:

```
3 + 5 * 7
```

Multiplication has a higher precedence than addition, so this expression evaluates to 38 (3 + 35) rather than 56 (8 * 7). You use parentheses in the expression to override the default order of precedence. For example, in the following form, the expression evaluates to 56:

```
(3 + 5) * 7
```

Operator	Type	Description
**, NOT	Binary	Exponentiation, logical negation
+, −	Unary	Identity, negation
*, /	Binary	Multiplication, division
+, −, ||	Binary	Addition, subtraction, string concatenation
=, !=, <, >, <=, >=, IS NULL, LIKE, BETWEEN, IN	Binary (except for IS NULL, which is unary)	Logical comparison
AND	Binary	Logical conjunction
OR	Binary	Logical inclusion

TABLE 3-5.   *PL/SQL Operators*

Character Expressions

The only character operator is concatenation (||). This operator attaches two or more strings (or arguments which can be converted implicitly to a string) together. For example, the expression

```
'Hello ' || 'World' || '!'
```

evaluates to

```
'Hello World!'
```

If all of the operands in a concatenation expression are of type CHAR, the expression is of type CHAR. If any operand is of type VARCHAR2, the expression is of type VARCHAR2. String literals are considered to be of type CHAR, so the preceding example evaluates to a CHAR value. The expression assigned to v_Result in the following block, however, evaluates to a VARCHAR2 value:

```
DECLARE
  v_TempVar  VARCHAR2(10) := 'PL';
  v_Result   VARCHAR2(20);
BEGIN
  v_Result := v_TempVar || '/SQL';
END;
```

Boolean Expressions

All of the PL/SQL control structures (except GOTO) involve Boolean expressions, also known as conditions. A *Boolean expression* is any expression that evaluates to a Boolean value (TRUE, FALSE, or NULL). For example, all of the following are Boolean expressions:

```
X > Y
NULL
(4 > 5) OR (-1 != Z)
```

Three operators—AND, OR, and NOT—take Boolean arguments and return Boolean values. Their behavior is described by the truth tables in Figure 3-5. These operators implement standard three-valued logic. Essentially, AND returns TRUE only if both of its operands are TRUE, and OR returns FALSE only if both of its operands are FALSE.

NULLs add complexity to Boolean expressions. (Recall that NULL means "missing or unknown value.") The expression

```
TRUE AND NULL
```

evaluates to NULL because we don't know whether the second operand is TRUE or not. For more information, see the section "NULL Conditions" later in this chapter.

NOT	TRUE	FALSE	NULL
	FALSE	TRUE	NULL

AND	TRUE	FALSE	NULL
TRUE	TRUE	FALSE	NULL
FALSE	FALSE	FALSE	FALSE
NULL	NULL	FALSE	NULL

OR	TRUE	FALSE	NULL
TRUE	TRUE	TRUE	TRUE
FALSE	TRUE	FALSE	NULL
NULL	TRUE	NULL	NULL

FIGURE 3-5. *Truth tables*

Comparison, or *relational,* operators take numeric, character, or data operands and return a Boolean value. These operators are defined according to the following table:

Operator	Definition
=	Is equal to (equality)
!=	Is not equal to (inequality)
<	Is less than
>	Is greater than
<=	Is less than or equal to
>=	Is greater than or equal to

The IS NULL operator returns TRUE only if its operand is NULL. NULLs cannot be tested using the relational operators because any relational expression with a NULL operand returns NULL.

The LIKE operator is used for pattern matching in character strings, similar to regular expressions in UNIX. The underscore character (_) matches exactly one character, and the percent character (%) matches zero or more characters. The following expressions all return TRUE:

```
'Scott' LIKE 'Sc%t'
'Scott' LIKE 'Sc_tt'
'Scott' LIKE '%'
```

The BETWEEN operator combines <= and >= in one expression. For example, the following expression returns FALSE

```
100 BETWEEN 110 AND 120
```

whereas this expression returns TRUE:

```
100 BETWEEN 90 and 110
```

The IN operator returns TRUE if its first operand is contained in the set identified by the second operand. For example, the following expression returns FALSE:

```
'Scott' IN ('Mike', 'Pamela', 'Fred')
```

If the set contains NULLs, they are ignored, because a comparison with NULL will always return NULL.

PL/SQL Control Structures

PL/SQL, like other third-generation languages, has a variety of control structures that allow you to control the behavior of the block as it runs. These structures include conditional statements and loops. It is these structures, combined with variables, that give PL/SQL its power and flexibility.

IF-THEN-ELSE

The syntax for an IF-THEN-ELSE statement is

> **IF** *boolean_expression1* **THEN**
>   *sequence_of_statements*;
> [**ELSIF** *boolean_expression2* **THEN**
>   *sequence_of_statements*;]
>   ...
> [**ELSE**
>   *sequence_of_statements*;]
> **END IF**;

where *boolean_expression* is any expression that evaluates to a Boolean value, defined in the previous section, "Boolean Expressions." The ELSIF and ELSE clauses are optional, and there can be as many ELSIF clauses as desired. For example, the following block shows an IF-THEN-ELSE statement with one ELSIF clause and one ELSE clause:

```
-- Available online as if1.sql
DECLARE
  v_NumberSeats rooms.number_seats%TYPE;
  v_Comment VARCHAR2(35);
BEGIN
  /* Retrieve the number of seats in the room identified by ID 20008.
     Store the result in v_NumberSeats. */
  SELECT number_seats
    INTO v_NumberSeats
    FROM rooms
    WHERE room_id = 20008;
  IF v_NumberSeats < 50 THEN
    v_Comment := 'Fairly small';
  ELSIF v_NumberSeats < 100 THEN
    v_Comment := 'A little bigger';
  ELSE
```

```
     v_Comment := 'Lots of room';
  END IF;
END;
```

The behavior of the preceding block is the same as the keywords imply. If the first condition evaluates to TRUE, the first sequence of statements is executed. In this case, the first condition is

```
v_NumberSeats < 50
```

and the first sequence of statements is

```
v_Comment := 'Fairly small';
```

If the number of seats is not less than 50, the second condition

```
v_NumberSeats < 100
```

is evaluated. If this evaluates to TRUE, the second sequence of statements

```
v_Comment := 'A little bigger';
```

is executed. Finally, if the number of seats is not less than 100, the final sequence of statements

```
v_Comment := 'Lots of room';
```

is executed. Each sequence of statements is executed only if its associated Boolean condition evaluates to TRUE.

In the example, each sequence of statements has only one procedural statement. However, in general, you can have as many statements (procedural or SQL) as desired. The following block illustrates this:

```
-- Available online as if2.sql
DECLARE
  v_NumberSeats rooms.number_seats%TYPE;
  v_Comment VARCHAR2(35);
BEGIN
  /* Retrieve the number of seats in the room identified by ID 20008.
     Store the result in v_NumberSeats. */
  SELECT number_seats
    INTO v_NumberSeats
    FROM rooms
    WHERE room_id = 20008;
  IF v_NumberSeats < 50 THEN
    v_Comment := 'Fairly small';
```

```
      INSERT INTO temp_table (char_col)
        VALUES ('Nice and cozy');
   ELSIF v_NumberSeats < 100 THEN
     v_Comment := 'A little bigger';
      INSERT INTO temp_table (char_col)
        VALUES ('Some breathing room');
   ELSE
     v_Comment := 'Lots of room';
   END IF;
END;
```

NOTE

Be aware of the spelling of ELSIF—there is only one E and no space. This syntax comes from the Ada language.

NULL Conditions

A sequence of statements in an IF-THEN-ELSE statement is executed only if its associated condition evaluates to TRUE. If the condition evaluates to FALSE or NULL, the sequence of statements is not executed. Consider the following two blocks as an example:

```
/* Block 1 */
DECLARE
  v_Number1 NUMBER;
  v_Number2 NUMBER;
  v_Result  VARCHAR2(7);
BEGIN
  ...
  IF v_Number1 < v_Number2 THEN
    v_Result := 'Yes';
  ELSE
    v_Result := 'No';
  END IF;
END;

/* Block 2 */
 DECLARE
v_Number1 NUMBER;
v_Number2 NUMBER;
v_Result VARCHAR2(7);
BEGIN
  ...
  IF v_Number1 >= v_Number2 THEN
    v_Result := 'No';
```

```
    ELSE
      v_Result := 'Yes';
    END IF;
END;
```

Do these blocks behave the same? Suppose that `v_Number1` is 3 and `v_Number2` is 7. The condition in block 1 (3 < 7) will thus evaluate to TRUE, and `v_Result` will be set to 'Yes'. Similarly, the condition in block 2 (3 >= 7) will evaluate to FALSE, and `v_Result` will also be set to 'Yes'. For any non-NULL values of `v_Number1` and `v_Number2`, the blocks have the same behavior.

Now suppose that `v_Number1` is 3 but `v_Number2` is NULL. What happens now? The condition in block 1 (3 < NULL) will evaluate to NULL, so the ELSE clause will be executed, assigning 'No' to `v_Result`. The condition in block 2 (3 >= NULL) will also evaluate to NULL, so the ELSE clause will be executed, assigning 'Yes' to `v_Result`. If either `v_Number1` or `v_Number2` is NULL, the blocks behave differently.

If we add a check for NULL to the preceding blocks, we can make them behave the same:

```
/* Block 1 */
DECLARE
  v_Number1 NUMBER;
  v_Number2 NUMBER;
  v_Result  VARCHAR2(7);
BEGIN
  ...
  IF v_Number1 IS NULL OR
      v_Number2 IS NULL THEN
    v_Result := 'Unknown';
  ELSIF v_Number1 < v_Number2 THEN
    v_Result := 'Yes';
  ELSE
    v_Result := 'No';
  END IF;
END;

/* Block 2 */
DECLARE
  v_Number1 NUMBER;
  v_Number2 NUMBER;
  v_Result VARCHAR2(7);
BEGIN
  ...
  IF v_Number1 IS NULL OR
      v_Number2 IS NULL THEN
    v_Result := 'Unknown';
```

```
    ELSIF v_Number1 >= v_Number2 THEN
      v_Result := 'No';
    ELSE
      v_Result := 'Yes';
    END IF;
  END;
```

The IS NULL condition will evaluate to TRUE only if the variable it is checking is NULL. If the variable is not NULL, the condition will evaluate to FALSE. By adding this check to the preceding blocks, we assign 'Unknown' to v_Result if either variable is NULL. The block will only check whether v_Number1 is greater than v_Number2 if it is assured that both are non-NULL, in which case the remainder of the blocks behave the same.

CASE

| Oracle9i
and higher |

In many cases, an IF-THEN-ELSE block is used to execute different statements, depending on the value of an input variable. For example, consider the following block, which selects a course for a student based on their major:

```
-- Available online as part of case.sql
DECLARE
  v_Major students.major%TYPE;
  v_CourseName VARCHAR2(10);
BEGIN
  -- Retrieve the major for a given student
  SELECT major
    INTO v_Major
    FROM students
    WHERE ID = 10011;

  -- Based on the major, choose a course
  IF v_Major = 'Computer Science' THEN
    v_CourseName := 'CS  101';
  ELSIF v_Major = 'Economics' THEN
    v_CourseName := 'ECN 203';
  ELSIF v_Major = 'History' THEN
    v_CourseName := 'HIS 101';
  ELSIF v_Major = 'Music' THEN
    v_CourseName := 'MUS 100';
  ELSIF v_Major = 'Nutrition' THEN
    v_CourseName := 'NUT 307';
  ELSE
    v_CourseName := 'Unknown';
  END IF;
  DBMS_OUTPUT.PUT_LINE(v_CourseName);
END;
```

The preceding code continually tests the value of a single variable, v_Major, in each of the different ELSIF statements. Oracle9*i* provides a simplified construction that accomplishes the same thing, known as the CASE statement. Similar to a switch statement in C, CASE has the following structure:

```
CASE test_var
  WHEN value1 THEN sequence_of_statements1;
  WHEN value2 THEN sequence_of_statements2;
  ...
  WHEN valuen THEN sequence_of_statementsn;
  [ELSE else_sequence;]
END CASE;
```

where *test_var* is the variable or expression to be tested, *value1* through *valuen* are the comparison values, and *sequence_of_statements1* through *sequence_of_statementsn* are the corresponding code to be executed. If *test_var* equals *value2*, for example, *sequence_of_statements2* will be executed. If none of the values are equal, then *else_sequence* will be executed.

We can rewrite our example using CASE, as follows:

```
-- Available online as part of case.sql
DECLARE
  v_Major students.major%TYPE;
  v_CourseName VARCHAR2(10);
BEGIN
  -- Retrieve the major for a given student
  SELECT major
    INTO v_Major
    FROM students
    WHERE ID = 10011;

  -- Based on the major, choose a course
  CASE v_Major
    WHEN 'Computer Science' THEN
      v_CourseName := 'CS  101';
    WHEN 'Economics' THEN
      v_CourseName :='ECN 203';
    WHEN 'History' THEN
      v_CourseName := 'HIS 101';
    WHEN 'Music' THEN
      v_CourseName := 'MUS 100';
    WHEN 'Nutrition' THEN
      v_CourseName := 'NUT 307';
    ELSE
      v_CourseName := 'Unknown';
```

```
    END CASE;

    DBMS_OUTPUT.PUT_LINE(v_CourseName);
END;
```

NOTE
*The test variable used in a CASE statement is not
limited to a single variable as in the above example.
It can be an arbitrarily complex expression, possibly
containing function calls. Either way, however, it is
evaluated exactly once, at the beginning of execution
of the CASE statement. Furthermore, the types of
value1 through valuen must be compatible with
the type of the test expression.*

Once a given *sequence_of_statements* is executed, control passes immediately
to the statement following the CASE. There is no need for a break statement, like a
C switch.

CASE Statements with no ELSE Clause

The ELSE clause of a CASE statement is optional. In this situation, if the test
expression does not match any of the test values, PL/SQL will raise the predefined
error CASE_NOT_FOUND, which is equivalent to ORA-6592, as the following
SQL*Plus session shows:

```
-- Available online as part of case.sql
SQL> DECLARE
  2    v_TestVar NUMBER := 1;
  3  BEGIN
  4    -- Since none of the WHEN clauses tests for the value 1,
  5    -- this will raise ORA-6592.
  6    CASE v_TestVar
  7      WHEN 2 THEN DBMS_OUTPUT.PUT_LINE('Two!');
  8      WHEN 3 THEN DBMS_OUTPUT.PUT_LINE('Three!');
  9      WHEN 4 THEN DBMS_OUTPUT.PUT_LINE('Four!');
 10    END CASE;
 11  END;
 12  /
DECLARE
*
ERROR at line 1:
ORA-06592: CASE not found while executing CASE statement
ORA-06512: at line 6
```

This is equivalent to an ELSE clause, which looks like

```
ELSE RAISE CASE_NOT_FOUND;
```

For more information on exceptions and how to handle them, see Chapter 7.

Labeled CASE Statements

A CASE statement can optionally be labeled, like a PL/SQL block. We will see later in this chapter that loops can be labeled in a similar manner. If a CASE statement is labeled, then the label can also appear after the END CASE clause, as the following example illustrates:

```
-- Available online as part of case.sql
DECLARE
  v_TestVar NUMBER := 1;
BEGIN
  -- This CASE statement is labeled.
  <<MyCase>>
  CASE v_TestVar
    WHEN 1 THEN DBMS_OUTPUT.PUT_LINE('One!');
    WHEN 2 THEN DBMS_OUTPUT.PUT_LINE('Two!');
    WHEN 3 THEN DBMS_OUTPUT.PUT_LINE('Three!');
    WHEN 4 THEN DBMS_OUTPUT.PUT_LINE('Four!');
  END CASE MyCase;
END;
```

A label after END CASE is legal only if the CASE statement itself is labeled, and the two labels must match.

Searched CASE Statements

The examples that we have seen have all been *test* CASE statements—each WHEN clause compared a value against a single test expression. CASE statements can also be *searched*, using the following structure:

```
CASE
  WHEN test1 THEN sequence_of_statements1;
  WHEN test2 THEN sequence_of_statements2;
  ...
  WHEN testn THEN sequence_of_statementsn;
  [ELSE else_sequence;]
END CASE;
```

There is no test expression; rather, each WHEN clause contains a Boolean expression. Like an IF-THEN statement, if a given test expression evaluates to TRUE, then the corresponding *sequence_of_statements* is executed. The following example illustrates a searched CASE statement. Note that the test expressions do not have to test the same thing.

```
-- Available online as part of case.sql
SQL> DECLARE
  2     v_Test1 NUMBER := 2;
  3     v_Test2 VARCHAR2(20) := 'Goodbye';
  4   BEGIN
  5     CASE
  6       WHEN v_Test1 = 1 THEN
  7         DBMS_OUTPUT.PUT_LINE('One!');
  8         DBMS_OUTPUT.PUT_LINE('Another one!');
  9       WHEN v_Test1 > 1 THEN
 10         DBMS_OUTPUT.PUT_LINE('> 1!');
 11         DBMS_OUTPUT.PUT_LINE('Still > 1!');
 12       WHEN v_Test2 = 'Goodbye' THEN
 13         DBMS_OUTPUT.PUT_LINE('Goodbye!');
 14         DBMS_OUTPUT.PUT_LINE('Adios!');
 15       ELSE
 16         DBMS_OUTPUT.PUT_LINE('No match');
 17     END CASE;
 18   END;
 19   /
> 1!
Still > 1!
PL/SQL procedure successfully completed.
```

The preceding example also illustrates some WHEN clauses that have more than one statement within them. Note as well that, even though `v_Test2` does equal Goodbye, and thus the third WHEN condition would evaluate to TRUE, it is not executed because a previous condition has already evaluated to TRUE.

Loops

PL/SQL provides a facility for executing statements repeatedly, via *loops.* Loops are divided into four categories. Simple loops, WHILE loops, and numeric FOR loops are loops that are discussed in the following sections. Cursor FOR loops are discussed in Chapter 6.

Simple Loops

The most basic kind of loops, simple loops, have the syntax

```
LOOP
  sequence_of_statements;
END LOOP;
```

The *sequence_of_statements* will be executed infinitely, because this loop has no stopping condition. However, we can add one with the EXIT statement, which has the following syntax:

```
EXIT [WHEN condition];
```

For example, the following block inserts 50 rows into `temp_table` (see Chapter 4 for information on INSERT and other SQL statements):

```
-- Available online as simple.sql
DECLARE
  v_Counter BINARY_INTEGER := 1;
BEGIN
  LOOP
    -- Insert a row into temp_table with the current value of the
    -- loop counter.
    INSERT INTO temp_table
      VALUES (v_Counter, 'Loop index');
    v_Counter := v_Counter + 1;
    -- Exit condition - when the loop counter > 50 we will
    -- break out of the loop.
    IF v_Counter > 50 THEN
      EXIT;
    END IF;
  END LOOP;
END;
```

The statement

```
EXIT WHEN condition;
```

is equivalent to

```
IF condition THEN
  EXIT;
END IF;
```

So, we can rewrite the example with the following block, which behaves exactly the same way:

```
-- Available online as exitwhen.sql
DECLARE
  v_Counter BINARY_INTEGER := 1;
BEGIN
  LOOP
    -- Insert a row into temp_table with the current value of the
    -- loop counter.
    INSERT INTO temp_table
      VALUES (v_Counter, 'Loop index');
    v_Counter := v_Counter + 1;
    -- Exit condition - when the loop counter > 50 we will
    -- break out of the loop.
    EXIT WHEN v_Counter > 50;
  END LOOP;
END;
```

WHILE Loops

The syntax for a WHILE loop is

```
WHILE condition LOOP
  sequence_of_statements;
END LOOP;
```

The *condition* is evaluated before each iteration of the loop. If it evaluates to TRUE, *sequence_of_statements* is executed. If *condition* evaluates to FALSE or NULL, the loop is finished and control resumes after the END LOOP statement. Now we can rewrite the example using a WHILE loop, as follows:

```
-- Available online as while1.sql
DECLARE
  v_Counter BINARY_INTEGER := 1;
BEGIN
  -- Test the loop counter before each loop iteration to
  -- insure that it is still less than 50.
  WHILE v_Counter <= 50 LOOP
    INSERT INTO temp_table
      VALUES (v_Counter, 'Loop index');
    v_Counter := v_Counter + 1;
  END LOOP;
END;
```

The EXIT or EXIT WHEN statement can still be used inside a WHILE loop to exit the loop prematurely, if desired.

Keep in mind that if the loop condition does not evaluate to TRUE the first time it is checked, the loop is not executed at all. If we remove the initialization of v_Counter in our example, the condition v_Counter < 50 will evaluate to NULL, and no rows will be inserted into temp_table:

```
-- Available online as while2.sql
DECLARE
  v_Counter BINARY_INTEGER;
BEGIN
  -- This condition will evaluate to NULL, since v_Counter
  -- is initialized to NULL by default.
  WHILE v_Counter <= 50 LOOP
    INSERT INTO temp_table
      VALUES (v_Counter, 'Loop index');
    v_Counter := v_Counter + 1;
  END LOOP;
END;
```

Numeric FOR Loops

The number of iterations for simple loops and WHILE loops is not known in advance—it depends on the loop condition. Numeric FOR loops, on the other hand, have a defined number of iterations. The syntax is

```
FOR loop_counter IN [REVERSE] low_bound .. high_bound LOOP
  sequence_of_statements;
END LOOP;
```

where *loop_counter* is an implicitly declared index variable, *low_bound* and *high_bound* specify the number of iterations, and *sequence_of_statements* is the content of the loop.

The bounds of the loop are evaluated once. This determines the total number of iterations that *loop_counter* will take on the values ranging from *low_bound* to *high_bound*, incrementing by 1 each time until the loop is complete. We can rewrite our looping example using a FOR loop as follows:

```
-- Available online as forloop.sql
BEGIN
  FOR v_Counter IN 1..50 LOOP
    INSERT INTO temp_table
      VALUES (v_Counter, 'Loop Index');
  END LOOP;
END;
```

Scoping Rules   The loop index for a FOR loop is implicitly declared as a BINARY_INTEGER. It is not necessary to declare it prior to the loop. If it is declared, the loop index will hide the outer declaration in the same way that a variable declaration in an inner block can hide a declaration in an outer block. See the following example:

```
-- Available online as forscope.sql
DECLARE
  v_Counter  NUMBER := 7;
BEGIN
  -- Inserts the value 7 into temp_table.
  INSERT INTO temp_table (num_col)
    VALUES (v_Counter);
  -- This loop redeclares v_Counter as a BINARY_INTEGER, which hides
  -- the NUMBER declaration of v_Counter.
  FOR v_Counter IN 20..30 LOOP
    -- Inside the loop, v_Counter ranges from 20 to 30.
    INSERT INTO temp_table (num_col)
      VALUES (v_Counter);
  END LOOP;
  -- Inserts another 7 into temp_table.
  INSERT INTO temp_table (num_col)
    VALUES (v_Counter);
END;
```

Using REVERSE   If the REVERSE keyword is present in the FOR loop, the loop index will iterate from the high value to the low value. Note in the following example that the syntax is the same—the low value is still referenced first:

```
BEGIN
  FOR v_Counter in REVERSE 10..50 LOOP
    -- v_Counter will start with 50, and will be decremented by
    -- 1 each time through the loop.
    NULL;
  END LOOP;
END;
```

Loop Ranges   The high and low values don't have to be numeric literals. They can be any expression that can be converted to a numeric value. Here is an example:

```
DECLARE
  v_LowValue  NUMBER := 10;
  v_HighValue NUMBER := 40;
BEGIN
  FOR v_Counter IN REVERSE v_LowValue .. v_HighValue LOOP
    INSERT INTO temp_table
      VALUES (v_Counter, 'Dynamically specified loop ranges');
  END LOOP;
END;
```

This allows the low bound and high bound to be determined dynamically.

GOTOs and Labels

PL/SQL also includes a GOTO statement. The syntax is

GOTO *label*;

where *label* is a label defined in the PL/SQL block. Labels are enclosed in double angle brackets. When a GOTO statement is evaluated, control immediately passes to the statement identified by the label. For example, we can implement our looping example with the following:

```
-- Available online as goto.sql
DECLARE
  v_Counter  BINARY_INTEGER := 1;
BEGIN
  LOOP
    INSERT INTO temp_table
      VALUES (v_Counter, 'Loop count');
    v_Counter := v_Counter + 1;
    IF v_Counter >= 50 THEN
      GOTO l_EndOfLoop;
    END IF;
  END LOOP;

  <<l_EndOfLoop>>
  INSERT INTO temp_table (char_col)
    VALUES ('Done!');
END;
```

Restrictions on GOTO

PL/SQL enforces restrictions on the use of GOTO. It is illegal to branch into an inner block, loop, or IF statement. The following illegal example illustrates this:

```
BEGIN
  GOTO l_InnerBlock;   -- Illegal, cannot branch to an inner block.
  BEGIN
    ...
    <<l_InnerBlock>>
    ...
  END;

  GOTO l_InsideIf;   -- Illegal, cannot branch into an IF statement.
  IF x > 3 THEN
    ...
    <<l_InsideIf>>
    INSERT INTO ...
  END IF;
END;
```

If these were legal, statements inside the IF statement could be executed even if the IF condition did not evaluate to TRUE. In the preceding example, the INSERT statement could be executed if x = 2.

It is also illegal for a GOTO to branch from one IF clause to another:

```
BEGIN
  IF x > 3 THEN
    ...
    GOTO l_NextCondition;
  ELSE
    <<l_NextCondition>>
    ...
  END IF;
END;
```

Finally, it is illegal to branch from an exception handler back into the current block. We will discuss exceptions and their handlers in Chapter 7.

```
DECLARE
  v_Room   rooms%ROWTYPE;
BEGIN
  -- Retrieve a single row from the rooms table.
  SELECT *
    INTO v_Room
    FROM rooms
    WHERE rowid = 1;
  <<l_Insert>>
  INSERT INTO temp_table (char_col)
    VALUES ('Found a row!');
EXCEPTION
  WHEN NO_DATA_FOUND THEN
    GOTO l_Insert;  -- Illegal, cannot branch into current block
END;
```

Labeling Loops

Loops themselves can be labeled. If so, the label can be used on the EXIT statement to indicate which loop is to be exited, as in the following example:

```
BEGIN
  <<l_Outer>>
  FOR v_OuterIndex IN 1..50 LOOP
    ...
    <<l_Inner>>
    FOR v_InnerIndex IN 2..10 LOOP
      ...
      IF v_OuterIndex > 40 THEN
```

```
        EXIT l_Outer;   -- Exits both loops
      END IF;
    END LOOP l_Inner;
END LOOP l_Outer;
```

If a loop is labeled, the label name can optionally be included after the END LOOP statement, as the preceding example indicates.

GOTO Guidelines

Be careful when using GOTO. Unnecessary GOTO statements can create *spaghetti code*—code that jumps around from place to place with no apparent reason and is very difficult to understand and maintain.

Just about all cases where a GOTO could be used can be rewritten using other PL/SQL control structures, such as loops or conditionals. Exceptions can also be used to exit out of a deeply nested loop, rather than branching to the end.

NULL as a Statement

In some cases, you may want to explicitly indicate that no action is to take place. This can be done via the NULL statement. The NULL statement does not do anything; it just serves as a placeholder. See the following example:

```
-- Available online as null.sql
DECLARE
  v_TempVar  NUMBER := 7;
BEGIN
  IF v_TempVar < 5 THEN
    INSERT INTO temp_table (char_col)
      VALUES ('Too small');
  ELSIF v_TempVar < 20 THEN
    NULL; -- Do nothing
  ELSE
    INSERT INTO temp_table (char_col)
      VALUES ('Too big');
  END IF;
END;
```

Pragmas

Pragmas are compiler directives, similar to #pragma or #define directives in C. They serve as instructions to the PL/SQL compiler. The compiler will act on the pragma during the compilation of the block. For example, the RESTRICT_REFERENCES pragma places restrictions on what kinds of SQL statements and package variables can be in a function. In addition to compiling the function as normal, the compiler needs to verify that the restrictions are met. The RESTRICT_REFERENCES pragma is described in Chapter 10. PL/SQL has a number of pragmas, which we will see throughout this book.

Pragmas are another concept that PL/SQL and Ada have in common.

PL/SQL Records

The scalar types (NUMBER, VARCHAR2, DATE, and so on) are already predefined in package STANDARD. Therefore, in order to use one of these types in your program, you need only declare a variable of the required type. Composite types, on the other hand, are user defined. In order to use a composite type, you must first define the type, and then declare variables of that type—similar to the syntax for declaring a subtype that we saw earlier in this chapter, in the section "User-Defined SubTypes." We will see this in the following sections.

PL/SQL records are similar to C structures. A record provides a way to deal with separate but related variables as a unit. Consider the following declarative section:

```
DECLARE
  v_StudentID  NUMBER(5);
  v_FirstName  VARCHAR2(20);
  v_LastName   VARCHAR2(20);
```

All three of these variables are logically related, because they refer to common fields in the `students` table. By declaring a record type for these variables, the relationship between them is apparent, and they can be manipulated as a unit. See the following example:

```
DECLARE
  /* Define a record type to hold common student information */
  TYPE t_StudentRecord IS RECORD (
    StudentID  NUMBER(5),
    FirstName  VARCHAR2(20),
    LastName   VARCHAR2(20));

  /* Declare a variable of this type. */
  v_StudentInfo  t_StudentRecord;
```

The general syntax for defining a record type is

```
TYPE record_type IS RECORD (
  field1 type1 [NOT NULL] [:= expr1],
  field2 type2 [NOT NULL] [:= expr2],
  ...
  fieldn typen [NOT NULL] [:= exprn]);
```

where *record_type* is the name of the new type, *field1* through *fieldn* are the names of the fields within the record, and *type1* through *typen* are the types of the associated fields. A record can have as many fields as desired. Each field declaration looks essentially the same as a variable declaration outside a record, including NOT NULL constraints and initial values. *expr1* through *exprn* represent the initial value of each field. Like a variable declaration outside a record, the initial value and NOT NULL constraint are optional. The following declare section first defines the record type t_SampleRecord and then declares two records of that type:

```
DECLARE
  TYPE t_SampleRecord IS RECORD (
    Count          NUMBER(4),
    Name           VARCHAR2(10) := 'Scott',
    EffectiveDate  DATE,
    Description    VARCHAR2(45) NOT NULL := 'Unknown');
  v_Sample1  t_SampleRecord;
  v_Sample2  t_SampleRecord;
```

Similar to declarations that are not inside record definitions, if a field is constrained to be NOT NULL, it must have an initial value. Any field without an initial value is initialized to NULL. You can use either the DEFAULT keyword or := to specify the default value.

In order to refer to a field within a record, dot notation is used. The syntax is

record name.field name

The following example shows how fields in v_Sample1 and v_Sample2 are referenced:

```
BEGIN
  /* SYSDATE is a built-in function which returns the current
     date and time. */
  v_Sample1.EffectiveDate := SYSDATE;
  v_Sample2.Description := 'Pesto Pizza';
END;
```

A reference like this is an rvalue, so it can be used on either side of an assignment operator.

Record Assignment

In order for one record to be assigned to another, both records must be of the same type. For example, given the previous declarations of v_Sample1 and v_Sample2, the following assignment is legal:

```
v_Sample1 := v_Sample2;
```

A record assignment like this one will use *copy semantics*—the values of the fields in v_Sample1 will be assigned the values of the corresponding fields in v_Sample2. Even if you have two different types that happen to have the same field definitions, the records cannot be assigned to each other. The following example is illegal, and raises the error "PLS-382: expression is of wrong type":

```
-- Available online as RecordAssignment.sql
DECLARE
  TYPE t_Rec1Type IS RECORD (
    Field1 NUMBER,
    Field2 VARCHAR2(5));
  TYPE t_Rec2Type IS RECORD (
    Field1 NUMBER,
    Field2 VARCHAR2(5));
  v_Rec1 t_Rec1Type;
  v_Rec2 t_Rec2Type;
BEGIN
  /* Even though v_Rec1 and v_Rec2 have the same field names
     and field types, the record types themselves are different.
     This is an illegal assignment which raises PLS-382. */
  v_Rec1 := v_Rec2;

  /* However, the fields are the same type, so the following
     are legal assignments. */
  v_Rec1.Field1 := v_Rec2.Field1;
  v_Rec2.Field2 := v_Rec2.Field2;
END;
```

A record can also be assigned to a SELECT statement. This will retrieve data from the database and store it in the record. The fields in the record should match the fields in the select list of the query. Chapter 4 describes the SELECT statement in more detail. The following example illustrates this:

```
-- Available online as RecordSelect.sql
DECLARE
  -- Define a record to match some fields in the students table.
  -- Note the use of %TYPE for the fields.
  TYPE t_StudentRecord IS RECORD (
    FirstName   students.first_name%TYPE,
    LastName    students.last_name%TYPE,
    Major       students.major%TYPE);

  -- Declare a variable to receive the data.
  v_Student   t_StudentRecord;
BEGIN
```

```
  -- Retrieve information about student with ID 10,000.
  -- Note how the query is returning columns which match the
  -- fields in v_Student.
  SELECT first_name, last_name, major
    INTO v_Student
    FROM students
    WHERE ID = 10000;
END;
```

Oracle9i
and higher   Oracle9*i* also allows records to be used in INSERT and UPDATE statements, to modify data in the database as opposed to querying it. See Chapter 4 for more information.

Using %ROWTYPE

It is common in PL/SQL to declare a record with the same types as a database row. PL/SQL provides the %ROWTYPE operator to facilitate this. Similar to %TYPE, %ROWTYPE will return a type based on the table definition. For example, a declaration such as

```
DECLARE
    v_RoomRecord  rooms%ROWTYPE;
```

will define a record whose fields correspond to the columns in the rooms table. Specifically, v_RoomRecord will look like this:

```
(room_id       NUMBER(5),
 building      VARCHAR2(15),
 room_number   NUMBER(4),
 number_seats  NUMBER(4),
 description   VARCHAR2(50))
```

As with %TYPE, any NOT NULL constraint defined on the column is not included. However, the length of VARCHAR2 and CHAR columns and the precision and scale for NUMBER columns are included.

If the table definition changes, %ROWTYPE changes along with it. Like %TYPE, %ROWTYPE is evaluated each time an anonymous block is submitted to the PL/SQL engine and each time a stored object is compiled.

PL/SQL Style Guide

There are no absolute rules for the style of a program. Program style includes things such as variable names, use of capitalization and white space, and the use of comments. These are not things that will necessarily affect how a program runs—two different styles for the same program will still do the same thing.

However, a program that is written with good style will be much easier to understand and maintain than a poorly written program.

Good style means that it will take less time to understand what the program is doing when seeing it for the first time. Also, it will help you understand what the program is doing, both as you write it and when you see it a month later.

As an example, consider the following two blocks. Which one is easier to understand?

```
declare
x number;
y number;
begin if x < 10 then y := 7; else y := 3; end if; end;

DECLARE
  v_Test   NUMBER;   -- Variable which will be examined
  v_Result NUMBER;   -- Variable to store the result
BEGIN
  -- Examine v_Test, and assign 7 to v_Result if v_Test < 10.
  IF v_Test < 10 THEN
    v_Result := 7;
  ELSE
    v_Result := 3;
  END IF;
END;
```

Both blocks accomplish the same thing. However, the program flow in the second block is significantly easier to understand.

This section covers several points of style. I feel that if you follow these recommendations, you will produce better code. All of the examples in this book follow these guidelines and serve as illustrations of this style of PL/SQL programming.

Style of Comments

Comments are the main mechanism for informing the reader what the purpose of a program is and how it works. I recommend putting comments

- *At the start of each block and/or procedure.* These comments should explain what the block or procedure is supposed to do. Especially for procedures, it is important to list which variables or parameters will be read by the procedure (input) and which variables or parameters will be written to by the procedure (output). Also, it is a good idea to list the database objects accessed. This way the dependencies of the procedure are explicitly available.

■ *By each variable declaration.* Describe what the variable will be used for. Often, these can simply be one-line comments, such as

```
v_SSN CHAR(11);   -- Social Security Number
```

■ *Before each major section of the block.* You don't necessarily need comments around every statement, but a comment explaining the purpose of the next group of statements is useful. The algorithm used may be apparent from the code itself, so it is better to describe the purpose of the algorithm and what the results will be used for, rather than the details of the method.

It's possible to have too many comments, which just get in the way of the code. When deciding on whether or not a comment is appropriate, ask yourself, "What would a programmer seeing this for the first time want to know?" Remember that the programmer may be yourself a month or two after you write the code!

Comments should be meaningful and not restate what the PL/SQL code itself says. For example, the following comment doesn't tell us anything more than the PL/SQL does and thus isn't really useful:

```
DECLARE
   v_Temp NUMBER := 0;   -- Assign 0 to v_Temp
```

However, this comment is better, because it tells us the purpose of the v_Temp variable:

```
DECLARE
   v_Temp NUMBER := 0;   -- Temporary variable used in main loop
```

Style of Variable Names

The key to variable names is to make them descriptive. The declaration

```
x number;
```

doesn't tell us anything about what x will be used for. However,

```
v_StudentID  NUMBER(5);
```

tells us that this variable will probably be used for a student ID number, even without an explanatory comment by the declaration. Remember, the maximum length of a PL/SQL identifier is 30 characters, and all of them are significant. Thirty characters is generally enough for a descriptive name.

The variable name can also tell us the use of the variable. I use a one-letter code separated by an underscore from the rest of the variable to indicate this, as in the following example:

```
v_VariableName     Program variable
e_ExceptionName    User-defined exception
t_TypeName         User-defined type
p_ParameterName    Parameter to a procedure or function
c_ConstantValue    Variable constrained with the CONSTANT clause
```

Style of Capitalization

PL/SQL is not case sensitive. However, I feel that proper use of upper- and lowercase significantly increases program readability. I generally follow these rules:

- Reserved words are in uppercase: BEGIN, DECLARE, and ELSIF, for example.

- Built-in functions are in uppercase: SUBSTR, COUNT, and TO_CHAR.

- Predefined types are in uppercase: NUMBER(7,2), BOOLEAN, and DATE.

- SQL keywords are in uppercase: SELECT, INTO, UPDATE, and WHERE.

- Database objects are in lowercase: log_table, classes, and students.

- Variable names are in mixed case, with a capital letter for each word in the name: v_HireDate, e_TooManyStudents, and t_StudentRecordType.

Style of Indentation

Use of *white space* (carriage returns, spaces, and tabs) is one of the simplest things you can do, and it can have the largest effect on program readability. Compare the two identical nested IF-THEN-ELSE constructs shown here:

```
IF x < y THEN IF z IS NULL THEN x := 3; ELSE x := 2; END IF; ELSE
   x := 4; END IF;

IF x < y THEN
   IF z IS NULL THEN
     x := 3;
   ELSE
     x := 2;
   END IF;
ELSE
   x := 4;
END IF;
```

I generally indent each line within a block by two spaces. I indent the contents of a block from the DECLARE..END keywords, and I indent loops and IF-THEN-ELSE statements. SQL statements that are continued over multiple lines are also indented, as in

```
SELECT id, first_name, last_name
  INTO v_StudentID, v_FirstName, v_LastName
  FROM STUDENTS
  WHERE id = 10002;
```

Style in General

As you write more PL/SQL code, you will probably develop your own programming style. These guidelines are by no means required, but I have found them useful in my own PL/SQL development, and I use them in the examples in this book. It is a good idea to show your code to another programmer and ask him or her what it does. If another programmer can describe what the program does and the outline of how it works, then you have documented it well and written in a good style.

In addition, many development organizations have guidelines for good code documentation and style, which can apply to other languages besides PL/SQL. The converse is also true: if you have an established C coding style, you can probably adapt it for use in PL/SQL.

Summary

In this chapter, we have covered the basic building blocks of PL/SQL: the structure of a PL/SQL block, variables and datatypes (scalar, composite, and reference), expressions and operators, datatype conversion rules, and the basic control structures. We also discussed PL/SQL style, which can help you write more understandable and manageable code. Now that we understand these fundamental concepts, we can continue in Chapter 4 by adding SQL to the procedural constructs we have discussed. We will defer the discussion of collections, which are the remaining composite types, and which are covered in Chapter 8.

CHAPTER
4

SQL within PL/SQL

tructured Query Language (SQL) defines how data in Oracle is manipulated. The procedural constructs we examined in the last chapter become more useful when combined with the processing power of SQL because they allow PL/SQL programs to manipulate data in Oracle. This chapter discusses the SQL statements that are permitted in PL/SQL and the transaction control statements that guarantee consistency of the data. Chapter 5 discusses the built-in SQL functions.

SQL Statements

SQL statements can be divided into five categories, as described here. Table 4-1 gives some example statements. The *Server SQL Reference* manual describes all of the SQL statements in detail.

- Data manipulation language (DML) statements change the data in tables, or query data in a database table, but do not change the structure of a table or other object.

- Data definition language (DDL) statements create, drop, or alter the structure of a schema object. Commands that change permissions on schema objects are also DDL.

- Transaction control statements guarantee the consistency of the data by organizing SQL statements into logical transactions, which either succeed or fail as a unit.

- Session control statements change the settings for a single database session—for example, to enable SQL tracing or turn on an event.

- System control statements change the settings for the entire database—for example, to enable or disable archiving.

NOTE
Certain client-side tools that allow PL/SQL have their own commands. These commands are valid in that environment only. For example, SQL*Plus allows commands such as spool *(echo to a file) or* set serveroutput *(echo the contents of the DBMS_ OUTPUT buffer to the screen). Likewise, Pro*C allows embedded SQL commands such as* allocate *(create memory for a cursor variable) or* connect *(establish a connection to the database). For more information on client-side tools such as these, see Chapter 2.*

Category	Sample SQL Statements
Data manipulation language (DML)	SELECT, INSERT, UPDATE, DELETE, EXPLAIN PLAN
Data definition language (DDL)	DROP, CREATE, ALTER, GRANT, REVOKE
Transaction control	COMMIT, ROLLBACK, SAVEPOINT, SET TRANSACTION
Session control	ALTER SESSION, SET ROLE
System control	ALTER SYSTEM

TABLE 4-1. *Categories of SQL Statements*

Using SQL in PL/SQL

The only SQL statements allowed directly in a PL/SQL program are DML and transaction control statements. Specifically, DDL statements are illegal. EXPLAIN PLAN, although classified as DML, is also illegal. In order to explain why this is the case, we need to look at the way PL/SQL is designed.

In general, a programming language can bind variables in two ways: early or late. *Binding* a variable is the process of identifying the storage location associated with an identifier in the program. In PL/SQL, binding also involves checking the database for permission to access the object referenced. A language that uses *early binding* does the bind during the compile phase, while a language that uses *late binding* postpones the bind until runtime. Early binding means that the compile phase will take longer (because the work of binding has to be done), but execution will be faster because the bind has already been completed. Late binding shortens the compile time but lengthens the execution time.

PL/SQL was intentionally designed to use early binding. This decision was made so that execution of a block would be as fast as possible, because all of the database objects have been verified by the compiler. This makes sense because PL/SQL blocks can be stored in the database via procedures, functions, packages, and triggers. These objects are stored in compiled form, so that when needed they can be loaded from the database into memory and run. For more information on stored objects, see Chapters 9–11. As a result of this design decision, DDL statements are prohibited. A DDL statement will modify a database object, so the permissions must be validated again. Validating the permissions would require that the identifiers be bound, and this has already been done during the compile.

To further illustrate this, consider the following hypothetical PL/SQL block:

```
BEGIN
  CREATE TABLE temp_table (
    num_value    NUMBER,
    char_value   CHAR(10));
  INSERT INTO temp_table (num_value, char_value)
    VALUES (10, 'Hello');
END;
```

In order to compile this, the `temp_table` identifier needs to be bound. This process will check to see whether this table exists. However, the table won't exist until the block is run. But because the block can't even compile, there is no way that it can run.

DML and transaction control statements are the only SQL statements that don't have the potential to modify schema objects or permissions on schema objects, thus they are the only legal SQL statements in PL/SQL.

Using Dynamic SQL

There is, however, a technique that allows all valid SQL statements, including DDL, to be issued from PL/SQL: dynamic SQL. Dynamic SQL allows you to create a SQL statement dynamically at runtime, and then parse and execute it. The statement doesn't actually get created until runtime, so the PL/SQL compiler doesn't have to bind the identifiers in the statement, which allows the block to compile. There are two techniques for dynamic SQL in PL/SQL: native dynamic SQL (Oracle8*i* and higher) and the DBMS_SQL package. We could use dynamic SQL to execute the CREATE TABLE statement in the preceding block, for example. However, the INSERT statement would fail to compile because the table wouldn't exist until the block is run. The solution to this problem is to use dynamic SQL to execute the INSERT statement as well. The following block uses native dynamic SQL to both create `temp_table`, and then insert into it:

```
BEGIN
  EXECUTE IMMEDIATE 'CREATE TABLE temp_table (
    num_value    NUMBER,
    char_value   CHAR(10))';
  EXECUTE IMMEDIATE 'INSERT INTO temp_table (num_value, char_value)
    VALUES (10, ''Hello'')';
END;
```

See Chapter 12 for more information on dynamic SQL.

DML in PL/SQL

The allowable DML statements are SELECT, INSERT, UPDATE, and DELETE. Each of these commands operates as its name implies: SELECT returns rows from a database table that match the criteria given by its WHERE clause, INSERT adds rows to a database table, UPDATE modifies the rows in a database table that match the WHERE clause, and DELETE removes rows identified by the WHERE clause. Besides the WHERE clause, these statements can have other clauses, which are described later in this section.

When SQL statements are executed from SQL*Plus, the results are returned to the screen, as shown in Figure 4-1. For an UPDATE, INSERT, or DELETE statement, SQL*Plus returns the number of rows processed. For a SELECT statement, the rows that match the query are echoed to the screen.

```
 Oracle SQL*Plus                                                _ □ ×
File  Edit  Search  Options  Help
SQL> SELECT first_name, last_name, major
  2      FROM students
  3      ORDER BY major;

FIRST_NAME             LAST_NAME              MAJOR
--------------------   --------------------   -------------------------
Scott                  Smith                  Computer Science
Joanne                 Junebug                Computer Science
Manish                 Murgratroid            Economics
Barbara                Blues                  Economics
Margaret               Mason                  History
Patrick                Poll                   History
Timothy                Taller                 History
David                  Dinsmore               Music
Rose                   Riznit                 Music
Ester                  Elegant                Nutrition
Rita                   Razmataz               Nutrition

11 rows selected.

SQL> UPDATE CLASSES
  2      SET num_credits = 3
  3      WHERE department = 'HIS'
  4      AND course = 101;

1 row updated.

SQL> commit;

Commit complete.

SQL>
```

FIGURE 4-1.   *Results of executing SQL statements in SQL*Plus*

Notice the UPDATE statement in Figure 4-1:

```
UPDATE CLASSES
   SET num_credits = 3
   WHERE department = 'HIS'
   AND course = 101;
```

All of the values that are used to change the contents of the `classes` table are hardcoded—they are known at the time this statement is written. PL/SQL removes this restriction with variables. Variables are allowed wherever an expression is allowed in the SQL statement. When used in this manner, they are known as *bind variables*. For example, in the preceding UPDATE statement, we could replace the hardcoded value for the number of credits with a bind variable:

```
-- Available online as BindVariable.sql
DECLARE
  v_NumCredits  classes.num_credits%TYPE;
BEGIN
  /* Assign to v_NumCredits */
  v_NumCredits := 3;
  UPDATE CLASSES
    SET num_credits = v_NumCredits
    WHERE department = 'HIS'
    AND course = 101;
END;
```

Instead of being echoed to the screen like in SQL*Plus, the output of queries is stored in variables as well. Not everything in a SQL statement can be replaced by a variable—only expressions. Notably, the table and column names have to be known. This is required because of early binding—names of Oracle objects have to be known at compile time. By definition, the value of a variable is not known until runtime. Dynamic SQL can be used to overcome this restriction as well.

SELECT

A SELECT statement retrieves data from the database into PL/SQL variables. The general form of a SELECT statement is shown here:

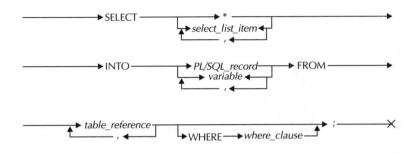

Each component is described in the following table:

SELECT Clause	Description
select_list_item	Column (or expression) to be selected. Each *select_list_item* is separated by a comma and can optionally be identified by an alias. The complete set of select list items is known as the *select list*. The * syntax is shorthand for the entire row. This will bring back every field in the table or tables, in the order in which the fields were defined.
variable	PL/SQL variable into which a select list item will go. Each variable must be type compatible with its associated select list item, and there must be the same number of select list items and output variables.
PL/SQL_record	Can be used instead of a list of variables. The record should contain fields that correspond to the select list and allow easier manipulation of the returned data. Records combine related fields in one syntactic unit, so they can be manipulated as a group as well as individually. Records are described in more detail in Chapter 3. If the select list is just *, and the select is from a single table, this record could be defined as *table_reference*%ROWTYPE.

SELECT Clause	Description
table_reference	Identifies the table from which to get the data. A single query can select from more than one *table_reference*, in which case they are separated by commas. A query of this type is known as a *join*. A *table_reference* does not need to be the name of a database table. For example, it could be a synonym, a table at a remote database specified with a database link, a view, a nested table column (Oracle9*i* and higher), or an inline view. See the section "Table References" later in this chapter for more information.
where_clause	Criteria for the query. This clause identifies the rows that will be returned by the query. It is made up of Boolean conditions joined by the Boolean operators, and is also described in more detail later in this chapter in the section "The WHERE Clause."

NOTE
There are significantly more clauses that are available for a SELECT statement. These include the ORDER BY and GROUP BY clauses, for example. SELECT statements can also be combined with set operators such as UNION and MINUS. For more information, see the Server SQL Reference.

The form of the SELECT statement described here should return no more than one row. The WHERE clause will be compared against each row in the table. If it matches more than one row, PL/SQL will return this error message:

```
ORA-1427: Single-row query returns more than one row
```

In this case, you should use a cursor to retrieve each row individually. See Chapter 6 for information about cursors. The following example illustrates two different SELECT statements:

```
-- Available online as select.sql
DECLARE
  v_StudentRecord   students%ROWTYPE;
  v_Department      classes.department%TYPE;
  v_Course          classes.course%TYPE;
BEGIN
  -- Retrieve one record from the students table, and store it
```

```
-- in v_StudentRecord. Note that the WHERE clause will only
-- match one row in the table.
-- Note also that the query is returning all of the fields in
-- the students table (since we are selecting *). Thus the
-- record into which we fetch is defined as students%ROWTYPE.
SELECT *
  INTO v_StudentRecord
  FROM students
  WHERE id = 10000;

-- Retrieve two fields from the classes table, and store them
-- in v_Department and v_Course. Again, the WHERE clause will
-- only match one row in the table.
SELECT department, course
  INTO v_Department, v_Course
  FROM classes
  WHERE room_id = 20003;
END;
```

INSERT

The syntax for the INSERT statement is shown here. Note that there is no WHERE clause directly in the statement.

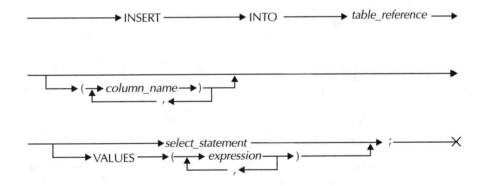

The *table_reference* clause refers to an Oracle table (or certain views), *column_ name* refers to a column in this table, and *expression* is a SQL or PL/SQL expression, as defined in the previous chapter. Table references are discussed in more detail later in this chapter in the section "Table References." If the INSERT statement contains a *select_statement*, the select list should match the columns to be inserted. A query of this type is known as a *subquery*, since it is within another SQL statement.

NOTE
Like SELECT, INSERT can take some other forms as well. For example, you can have a subquery as part of the VALUES clause. See the Server SQL Reference *for more information.*

The following example includes several valid INSERT statements:

```
-- Available online as insert.sql
DECLARE
  v_StudentID   students.id%TYPE;
BEGIN
  -- Retrieve a new student ID number
  SELECT student_sequence.NEXTVAL
    INTO v_StudentID
    FROM dual;

  -- Add a row to the students table
  INSERT INTO students (id, first_name, last_name)
    VALUES (v_StudentID, 'Timothy', 'Taller');

  -- Add a second row, but use the sequence number directly
  -- in the INSERT statement.
  INSERT INTO students (id, first_name, last_name)
    VALUES (student_sequence.NEXTVAL, 'Patrick', 'Poll');
END;
```

The following example is invalid, since the select list of the subquery does not match the columns to be inserted. This statement returns the Oracle error "ORA-913: Too many values."

```
INSERT INTO rooms
  SELECT * FROM classes;
```

This next example, however, is legal. It doubles the size of the `temp_table` table by inserting a second copy of each row.

```
INSERT INTO temp_table
  SELECT * FROM temp_table;
```

Oracle8 with the objects option provides an additional clause for INSERT statements: the REF INTO clause. When used with object tables, this will return a reference to the object inserted. See Chapter 12 for more information.

UPDATE

The syntax for the UPDATE statement is shown here:

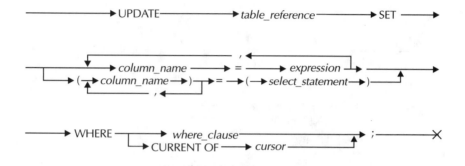

The *table_reference* clause refers to the table (or certain views) being updated, *column_name* is a column whose value will be changed, and *expression* is a SQL expression as defined in Chapter 3. If the statement contains a *select_statement*, the select list should match the columns in the SET clause. The special syntax CURRENT OF *cursor* is used with a cursor definition, and will be discussed in Chapter 6.

The following block illustrates two UPDATE statements:

```
-- Available online as update.sql
DECLARE
  v_Major            students.major%TYPE;
  v_CreditIncrease   NUMBER := 3;
BEGIN
  -- This UPDATE statement will add 3 to the current_credits
  -- field of all students who are majoring in History.
  v_Major := 'History';
  UPDATE students
    SET current_credits = current_credits + v_CreditIncrease
    WHERE major = v_Major;

  -- This UPDATE statement will update both columns of
  -- temp_table, for all rows.
  UPDATE temp_table
    SET num_col = 1, char_col = 'abcd';
END;
```

DELETE

The DELETE statement removes rows from a database table. The WHERE clause of the statement indicates which rows are to be removed. Here is the syntax for the DELETE statement:

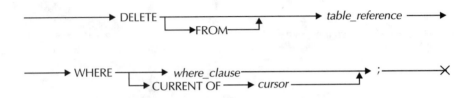

The *table_reference* clause refers to an Oracle table (or certain views), and the *where_clause* defines the set of rows to be deleted. The special syntax CURRENT OF *cursor* is used with a cursor definition, and will be discussed in Chapter 6. Table references and the WHERE clause are discussed in detail in the sections that follow.

The following block illustrates some different DELETE statements:

```
-- Available online as delete.sql
DECLARE
  v_StudentCutoff   NUMBER;
BEGIN
  v_StudentCutoff := 10;
  -- Delete any classes which don't have enough students registered.
  DELETE FROM classes
    WHERE current_students < v_StudentCutoff;

  -- Delete any Economics students who don't have any credits yet.
  DELETE FROM students
    WHERE current_credits = 0
    AND   major = 'Economics';
END;
```

> **NOTE**
> The first DELETE statement in the above block, as well as some of the examples in the following section, will raise constraint errors if the tables were created using the `tables.sql` creation script. This is because of the referential integrity constraints on the `classes` table. For more information on referential integrity constraints, see the Server SQL Reference.

The WHERE Clause

The SELECT, UPDATE, and DELETE statements all include the WHERE clause as an integral part of their operations. This clause defines which statements make up the *active set*—the set of rows returned by a query (SELECT) or acted upon by an UPDATE or DELETE statement.

A WHERE clause consists of conditions, joined together by the Boolean operators AND and OR. Conditions usually take the form of comparisons—for example, in the following DELETE statement:

```
-- Available online as part of WhereClause.sql
DECLARE
  v_Department  CHAR(3);
BEGIN
  v_Department := 'CS';
  -- Remove all Computer Science classes
  DELETE FROM classes
    WHERE department = v_Department;
END;
```

The preceding block will remove all rows in the `classes` table for which the condition evaluates to TRUE (those in which the `department` column = 'CS'). There are several things to note about comparisons such as these, including the importance of variable names and how characters are compared.

Variable Names

Suppose we change the name of the variable in the preceding block from `v_Department` to `department`:

```
-- Available online as part of WhereClause.sql
DECLARE
  Department  CHAR(3);
BEGIN
  Department := 'CS';
  -- Remove all Computer Science classes
  DELETE FROM classes
    WHERE department = Department;
END;
```

This simple change has a dramatic effect on the results of the statement—the modified block will remove *all* rows in the classes table, not just the ones in which `department` = 'CS'! This happens because of the way the identifiers in a SQL statement are parsed. When the PL/SQL engine sees a condition such as

```
expr1 = expr2
```

expr1 and *expr2* are first checked to see if they match columns in the table being operated upon, then checked to see if they are variables in the PL/SQL block. PL/SQL is not case sensitive, so in the preceding block both department and Department are associated with the column in the classes table, rather than the variable. This condition will evaluate to TRUE for every row in the table; thus, all rows will be deleted.

If the block has a label, we can still use the same name for a variable as a table column by prepending the label to the variable reference. This block has the desired effect—namely, to delete only those rows where department = 'CS':

```
-- Available online as part of WhereClause.sql
<<l_DeleteBlock>>
DECLARE
  Department   CHAR(3);
BEGIN
  Department := 'CS';
  -- Remove all Computer Science classes
  DELETE FROM classes
    WHERE department = l_DeleteBlock.Department;
END;
```

Although this method can be used to get the desired behavior, it is still not good programming style to use the same name for a PL/SQL variable as for a table column. This and other PL/SQL style guidelines are discussed at the end of Chapter 3.

Character Comparisons

When two character values are being compared, as in the previous example, Oracle can use two different kinds of comparison semantics: blank-padded or non-blank-padded. These comparison semantics differ in how character strings of different lengths are compared. Suppose we are comparing two character strings, string1 and string2. For *blank-padded* semantics, the following algorithm is used:

1. If string1 and string2 are of different lengths, pad the shorter value with blanks first so that they are both the same length.

2. Compare each string, character by character, starting from the left. Suppose the character in string1 is char1, and the character in string2 is char2.

3. If ASCII(char1) < ASCII(char2), string1 < string2. If ASCII(char1) > ASCII(char2), string1 > string2. If ASCII(char1) = ASCII(char2), continue to the next character in string1 and string2.

4. If the ends of string1 and string2 are reached, then the strings are equal.

Using blank-padded semantics, the following conditions will all return TRUE:

```
'abc' = 'abc'
'abc   ' = 'abc'   -- Note the trailing blanks in the first string
'ab' < 'abc'
'abcd' > 'abcc'
```

The *non-blank-padded* comparison algorithm is a little different:

1. Compare each string, character by character, starting from the left. Suppose the character in string1 is char1, and the character in string2 is char2.

2. If ASCII(char1) < ASCII(char2), string1 < string2. If ASCII(char1) > ASCII(char2), string1 > string2. If ASCII(char1) = ASCII(char2), continue to the next character in string1 and string2.

3. If string1 ends before string2, then string1 < string2. If string2 ends before string1, then string1 > string2.

Using non-blank-padded character comparison semantics, the following comparisons will return TRUE:

```
'abc' = 'abc'
'ab' < 'abc'
'abcd' > 'abcc'
```

However, the following comparison will return FALSE since the strings are of different lengths. This is the basic difference between the two comparison methods.

```
'abc   ' = 'abc'   -- Note the trailing blanks in the first string
```

Having defined these two different methods, when is each one used? PL/SQL will use blank-padded semantics only when both values being compared are *fixed-length* values. If either value is variable length, non-blank-padded semantics are used. The CHAR datatype is fixed length, and the VARCHAR2 datatype is variable length. Character literals (enclosed in single quotes) are always considered to be fixed length.

If a statement isn't acting upon the correct rows, check the datatypes used in the WHERE clause. The following block will *not* delete any rows because the v_Department variable is VARCHAR2 rather than CHAR:

```
-- Available online as part of WhereClause.sql
DECLARE
 v_Department   VARCHAR2(3);
BEGIN
```

```
   v_Department := 'CS';
   -- Remove all Computer Science classes
   DELETE FROM classes
     WHERE department = v_Department;
END;
```

The `department` column of the `classes` table is CHAR. Any computer science classes will thus have a value of 'CS ' for `department` (note the trailing blank). Since `v_Department` = 'CS' (no trailing blank) and is of a variable-length datatype, the DELETE statement does not affect any rows.

To ensure that your WHERE clauses have the desired effect, make sure that the variables in the PL/SQL block have the same datatype as the database columns to which they are compared. Using %TYPE can guarantee this.

Bulk Binds

Oracle **8*i***
and higher SQL statements in PL/SQL blocks are sent to the SQL engine to be executed. The SQL engine can in turn send data back to the PL/SQL engine. For example, consider the following block:

```
-- Available online as part of bulkDemo.sql
DECLARE
  TYPE t_Numbers IS TABLE OF temp_table.num_col%TYPE
    INDEX BY BINARY_INTEGER;
  TYPE t_Chars IS TABLE OF temp_table.char_col%TYPE
    INDEX BY BINARY_INTEGER;
  v_Numbers t_Numbers;
  v_Chars t_Chars;
BEGIN
  -- Fill up the arrays with 500 rows.
  FOR v_Count IN 1..500 LOOP
    v_Numbers(v_Count) := v_Count;
    v_Chars(v_Count) := 'Row number ' || v_Count;
  END LOOP;

  -- And insert them into the database.
  FOR v_Count IN 1..500 LOOP
    INSERT INTO temp_table VALUES
      (v_Numbers(v_Count), v_Chars(v_Count));
  END LOOP;
END;
```

NOTE
This block uses a PL/SQL index-by table, which is similar to a C or Java array. For more information on index-by tables and the other collection types, see Chapter 8.

When we run this block, 500 rows are inserted into `temp_table`. However, each INSERT is done individually. This results in 500 context switches between PL/SQL and SQL.

Oracle8*i* eliminates all but one of these context switches by passing the entire PL/SQL table to the SQL engine in one step, which is known as a *bulk bind*. Bulk binds are done using the FORALL statement, as in the following block:

```
-- Available online as part of bulkDemo.sql
DECLARE
  TYPE t_Numbers IS TABLE OF temp_table.num_col%TYPE
    INDEX BY BINARY_INTEGER;
  TYPE t_Chars IS TABLE OF temp_table.char_col%TYPE
    INDEX BY BINARY_INTEGER;
  v_Numbers t_Numbers;
  v_Chars t_Chars;
BEGIN
  -- Fill up the arrays with 500 rows.
  FOR v_Count IN 1..500 LOOP
    v_Numbers(v_Count) := v_Count;
    v_Chars(v_Count) := 'Row number ' || v_Count;
  END LOOP;

  -- And insert them into the database using bulk binds.

  FORALL v_Count IN 1..500
    INSERT INTO temp_table VALUES
      (v_Numbers(v_Count), v_Chars(v_Count));
END;
```

Bulk binds can also be used with queries, to retrieve more than one row of the active set at a time. For more information on bulk binds, see Chapter 12.

The RETURNING Clause

It is often desirable to know information about rows modified by a DML statement once the statement has been issued—for example, the rowid of a newly inserted row. One way of accomplishing this is to issue a SELECT after the statement. However, this involves a second SQL statement and call to the RDBMS kernel. Oracle8 provides a shortcut: the RETURNING clause. This clause is valid at the end of any DML statement, and is used to get information about the row or rows just processed. The syntax is described below.

expr is a valid PL/SQL or SQL expression, which can include columns or pseudocolumns of the current table, and *variable* is the PL/SQL variable into which the results will be stored. Corresponding *expr*s and *variable*s must be type compatible. (Pseudocolumns, including ROWID, are discussed later in this chapter in the section "Pseudocolumns.") The following SQL*Plus session illustrates several uses of the RETURNING clause:

```
-- Available online as part of ReturningInto.sql
SQL> DECLARE
  2    v_NewRowid ROWID;
  3    v_FirstName students.first_name%TYPE;
  4    v_LastName students.last_name%TYPE;
  5    v_ID students.ID%TYPE;
  6  BEGIN
  7    -- Insert a new row into the students table, and get the
  8    -- rowid of the new row at the same time.
  9    INSERT INTO students
 10      (ID, first_name, last_name, major, current_credits)
 11    VALUES
 12      (student_sequence.NEXTVAL, 'Xavier', 'Xemes', 'Nutrition', 0)
 13    RETURNING rowid INTO v_NewRowid;
 14
 15    DBMS_OUTPUT.PUT_LINE('Newly inserted rowid is ' || v_NewRowid);
 16
 17    -- Update this new row to increase the credits, and get
 18    -- the first and last name back.
 19    UPDATE students
 20      SET current_credits = current_credits + 3
 21      WHERE rowid = v_NewRowid
 22      RETURNING first_name, last_name INTO v_FirstName, v_LastName;
 23
 24    DBMS_OUTPUT.PUT_LINE('Name: ' || v_FirstName || ' ' || v_LastName);
 25
```

```
26     -- Delete the row,and get the ID of the deleted row back.
27     DELETE FROM students
28       WHERE rowid = v_NewRowid
29       RETURNING ID INTO v_ID;
30
31     DBMS_OUTPUT.PUT_LINE('ID of new row was ' || v_ID);
32  END;
33  /
Newly inserted rowid is AAAF3MAAFAAAAATAAM
Name: Xavier Xemes
ID of new row was 10012
PL/SQL procedure successfully completed.
```

Table References

All of the DML operations reference a table. This reference can in general look like

[*schema.*]*table*[*@dblink*]

where *schema* identifies the owner of the table, and *dblink* is a database link to a remote database where the table resides in the given *schema*.

When a user connects to the database using their username and password, all table references that do not explicitly specify a schema will refer to tables in that user's schema. Subsequent SQL statements issued during the session will reference this schema by default. If a table reference is unqualified, as in

```
UPDATE students
   SET major = 'Music'
   WHERE id = 10005;
```

the table name (students in this example) must name a table in the default schema. If it does not, an error such as

```
ORA-942: table or view does not exist
```

or

```
PLS-201: identifier must be declared
```

will be reported. The default schema is the one to which you connect before executing any SQL or PL/SQL commands. If the table is in another schema, it can be qualified by the schema name, as in

```
UPDATE example.students
   SET major = 'Music'
   WHERE id = 10005;
```

The preceding UPDATE will work if the connection is made to the `example` schema, or to another schema that has been granted the UPDATE privilege on the `students` table.

> **NOTE**
> *Oracle 8i and higher provide the TABLE() function, which can be used to create table references dynamically from stored nested tables or other expressions. Oracle 9i allows the use of a table function to generate the data dynamically as well. For more information on TABLE() with stored nested tables, see Chapter 8. For more information on table functions, see Chapter 12.*

Database Links

If you have SQL*Net installed on your system, you can take advantage of database links. A *database link* is a reference to a remote database, which can be located on a completely different system from the local database. The following DDL statement creates a database link:

```
CREATE DATABASE LINK link_name
  CONNECT TO username IDENTIFIED BY password
  USING sqlnet_string;
```

The name of the database link, *link_name*, follows the usual rules for a database identifier. *username* and *password* identify a schema on the remote database, and *sqlnetstring* is a valid connect string for the remote database. Assuming that the appropriate schemas have been created and SQL*Net is installed, the following is an example of a database link creation:

```
CREATE DATABASE LINK example_backup
  CONNECT TO example IDENTIFIED BY example
  USING 'backup_database';
```

For more information on how to install and configure SQL*Net, consult the *SQL*Net User's Guide and Reference*. Given the preceding link, we can now update the `students` table remotely with

```
UPDATE students@example_backup
  SET major = 'Music'
  WHERE id = 10005;
```

When a database link is used as part of a transaction, the transaction is said to be a *distributed transaction*, because it modifies more than one database. These are handled automatically by the two-phase commit mechanism. For more information on distributed transactions and their administration and implications, consult the *Server SQL Reference.*

Synonyms

Table references can be complicated, especially if a schema and/or database link is included. In order to make maintenance easier, Oracle allows you to create a synonym for a complicated reference. The *synonym* essentially renames the table reference, similar to an alias for a select list item. However, a synonym is a data dictionary object and is created by the CREATE SYNONYM DDL statement:

    CREATE SYNONYM *synonym_name* FOR *reference*;

Replace *synonym_name* with the name of your synonym and *reference* with the schema object that is referenced. Note that this schema object can be a table, as in the following example, or it could be a procedure, sequence, or other database object:

```
CREATE SYNONYM backup_students
    FOR students@example_backup;
```

Given this synonym, we can rewrite our distributed UPDATE statement with

```
UPDATE backup_students
    SET major = 'Music'
    WHERE id = 10005;
```

NOTE
Creating a synonym does not grant any privileges on the referenced object—it just provides an alternate name for the object.

Pseudocolumns

Pseudocolumns are additional functions that can be called only from SQL statements. Syntactically, they are treated like columns in a table. However, they don't actually exist in the same way that table columns do. Rather, they are evaluated as part of the SQL statement execution.

CURRVAL and NEXTVAL

These two pseudocolumns, CURRVAL and NEXTVAL, are used with sequences. A *sequence* is an Oracle object that is used to generate unique numbers. A sequence is created with the CREATE SEQUENCE DDL command. Once a sequence is created, you can access it with

> *sequence*.CURRVAL

and

> *sequence*.NEXTVAL

where *sequence* is the name of the sequence. CURRVAL returns the current value of the sequence, and NEXTVAL increments the sequence and returns the new value. Both CURRVAL and NEXTVAL return NUMBER values. CURRVAL can only be accessed in a given session after at least one NEXTVAL has been issued.

Sequence values can be used in the select list of a query, in the VALUES clause of an INSERT statement, and in the SET clause of an UPDATE statement. They cannot be used in the WHERE clause or in a PL/SQL procedural statement, however. The following are legal examples of using CURRVAL and NEXTVAL:

```
-- Available online as part of tables.sql
CREATE SEQUENCE student_sequence
  START WITH 10000
  INCREMENT BY 1;

-- This statement will use 10,000 as the id value
INSERT INTO students (id, first_name, last_name, major,
                      current_credits)
  VALUES (student_sequence.NEXTVAL, 'Scott', 'Smith',
          'Computer Science', 11);
-- This statement will use 10,001 as the id value
INSERT INTO students (id, first_name, last_name, major,
                      current_credits)
  VALUES (student_sequence.NEXTVAL, 'Margaret', 'Mason',
          'History', 4);
```

Assuming that `tables.sql` has been used to create 12 rows in the `students` table, the following SQL*Plus session illustrates the use of CURRVAL:

```
SQL> SELECT student_sequence.CURRVAL
  2    FROM dual;
CURRVAL
---------
   10011
```

LEVEL

LEVEL is used only inside a SELECT statement that implements a hierarchical tree walk over a table, using the START WITH and CONNECT BY clauses. The LEVEL pseudocolumn will return the current level of the tree as a NUMBER value. For more information, see the *Server SQL Reference*.

ROWID

The ROWID pseudocolumn is used in the select list of a query. It returns the row identifier of that particular row. The external format of a ROWID is a character string, as described in Chapter 3. The ROWID pseudocolumn returns a value of type ROWID. For example, the following query returns all of the rowids in the `rooms` table:

```
SQL> SELECT ROWID
  2     FROM rooms;
ROWID
------------------
AAAF3PAAFAAAABDAAA
AAAF3PAAFAAAABDAAB
AAAF3PAAFAAAABDAAC
AAAF3PAAFAAAABDAAD
AAAF3PAAFAAAABDAAE
AAAF3PAAFAAAABDAAF
AAAF3PAAFAAAABDAAG
AAAF3PAAFAAAABDAAH
AAAF3PAAFAAAABDAAI
9 rows selected.
```

NOTE
The format of a ROWID is different in Oracle7 and Oracle8. Index-organized tables (new in Oracle8i) have a different ROWID format as well. Furthermore, a non-Oracle database accessed through a gateway may have still another ROWID format. However, the external format for all ROWIDs is a character string. See Chapter 3 for more information.

ROWNUM

ROWNUM will return the current row number in a query. It is useful for limiting the total number of rows, and it is used primarily in the WHERE clause of queries and the SET clause of UPDATE statements. ROWNUM returns a NUMBER value. For example, the following query returns only the first two rows from `students`:

```
SELECT *
  FROM students
  WHERE ROWNUM < 3;
```

The first row has ROWNUM 1, the second has ROWNUM 2, and so on. The ROWNUM value is assigned to a row *before* a sort is done (via the ORDER BY clause). As a result, you cannot use ROWNUM to retrieve the *n* highest rows in the search order. Consider this statement:

```
SELECT first_name, last_name
  FROM students
  WHERE ROWNUM < 3
  ORDER BY first_name;
```

While this statement will return two rows from the students table, sorted by `first_name`, they won't necessarily be the first two rows in the entire sort order. To guarantee this, it is best to declare a cursor for this query and only fetch the first two rows. Chapter 6 discusses cursors and how to use them. An inline view with the ORDER BY can also be used. See the *Server SQL Reference* for information on inline views.

GRANT, REVOKE, and Privileges

While DDL statements such as GRANT and REVOKE can't be used directly in PL/SQL, they do have an effect on which SQL statements are legal. In order to perform an operation such as INSERT or DELETE on an Oracle table, you need permission to perform the operation. These permissions are manipulated via the GRANT and REVOKE SQL commands.

Object versus System Privileges

There are two different kinds of privileges: object and system. An *object privilege* allows an operation on a particular object (such as a table). A *system privilege* allows operations on an entire class of objects.

Table 4-2 describes the available object privileges. The DDL object privileges (ALTER, INDEX, REFERENCES) can't be utilized directly in PL/SQL (except in dynamic SQL), because they allow DDL operations on the object in question.

There are many system privileges, for just about any DDL operation possible. For example, the CREATE TABLE system privilege allows the grantee to create tables. The CREATE ANY TABLE system privilege allows the grantee to create tables in other schemas. The *Server SQL Reference* documents all of the available system privileges.

Object Privilege	Kinds of Objects	Description
ALTER	Tables, sequences	Allows grantee to issue an ALTER statement (such as ALTER TABLE) on the object.
DELETE	Tables, views, and updatable materialized views	Allows grantee to issue a DELETE statement against the object.
EXECUTE	Procedures, functions, packages, and object types	Allows grantee to execute the stored PL/SQL object. (Stored objects are discussed in Chapters 9–11.)
INDEX	Tables	Allows grantee to create an index on the table via the CREATE INDEX command.
INSERT	Tables, views, and updatable materialized views	Allows grantee to issue an INSERT statement against the object.
ON COMMIT REFRESH[2]	Materialized views	Allows grantee to create a refresh-on-commit materialized view on the specified table.
QUERY REWRITE[2]	Materialized views	Allows grantee to create a query-rewrite materialized view on the specified table.

TABLE 4-2. *SQL Object Privileges*

Object Privilege	Kinds of Objects	Description
READ[1]	Directories	Allows grantee to read from the specified directory.
REFERENCES[1]	Tables	Allows grantee to create a constraint that refers to the table.
SELECT	Tables, views, sequences, and materialized views	Allows grantee to issue a SELECT statement against the object.
UNDER[3]	Object types	Allows grantee to create a subtype under the specified type, if the supertype has invoker's rights.
UPDATE	Tables, views, and updatable materialized views	Allows grantee to issue an UPDATE statement against the object.

[1]Available in Oracle8 and higher
[2]Available in Oracle8i and higher
[3]Available in Oracle9i and higher

TABLE 4-2. *SQL Object Privileges* (continued)

GRANT and REVOKE

The GRANT statement is used to allow another schema access to a privilege, and the REVOKE statement is used to remove the access allowed by GRANT. Both statements can be used for object and system privileges.

GRANT

The basic syntax of GRANT for object privileges is

    GRANT privilege ON object TO grantee [WITH GRANT OPTION];

where *privilege* is the desired privilege, *object* is the object to which access is granted, and *grantee* is the user who will receive the privilege. For example, assuming that `userA` is a valid database schema, the following GRANT statement is legal:

```
GRANT SELECT ON classes TO userA;
```

If the WITH GRANT OPTION is specified, then `userA` can in turn grant the privilege to another user. More than one privilege can be specified in one GRANT statement, for example:

```
GRANT UPDATE, DELETE ON students TO userA;
```

For system privileges, the syntax is

GRANT *privilege* TO *grantee* [WITH ADMIN OPTION];

where *privilege* is the system privilege to be granted, and *grantee* is the user receiving the privilege. If WITH ADMIN OPTION is included, then *grantee* can grant the privilege to other users as well. For example:

```
GRANT CREATE TABLE, ALTER ANY PROCEDURE to userA;
```

Similar to the GRANT statement for object privileges, more than one system privilege can be specified in the same statement.

Since GRANT is a DDL statement, it takes effect immediately and issues an implicit COMMIT after execution.

REVOKE

The syntax for REVOKE for object privileges is

REVOKE *privilege* ON *object* FROM *grantee* [CASCADE CONSTRAINTS] [FORCE];

where *privilege* is the privilege to be revoked, *object* is the object on which the privilege is granted, and *grantee* is the recipient of the privilege. For example, the following is a legal REVOKE command:

```
REVOKE SELECT ON classes FROM userA;
```

If the CASCADE CONSTRAINTS clause is included and the REFERENCES privilege is being revoked, all referential integrity constraints created by *grantee* with this privilege are dropped as well. The FORCE keyword is used when revoking the EXECUTE privilege on an object type with table dependencies.

Multiple privileges can also be revoked with one statement, as in

```
REVOKE UPDATE, DELETE, INSERT ON students FROM userA;
```

To revoke a system privilege, the syntax is

REVOKE *privilege* FROM *grantee*;

where *privilege* is the system privilege to be revoked, and *grantee* is the user who will no longer have this privilege. For example:

```
REVOKE ALTER TABLE, EXECUTE ANY PROCEDURE FROM userA;
```

Roles

In a large Oracle system, with many different user accounts, administrating privileges can be a challenge. To ease this, Oracle provides a facility known as roles. A *role* is essentially a collection of privileges, both object and system. Consider the following series of statements:

```
CREATE ROLE table_query;
GRANT SELECT ON students TO table_query;
GRANT SELECT ON classes TO table_query;
GRANT SELECT ON rooms TO table_query;
```

The `table_query` role has SELECT privileges on three different tables. We can now grant this role to additional users, with

```
GRANT table_query TO userA;
GRANT table_query TO userB;
```

Now, `userA` and `userB` have SELECT privileges on the three tables. This is easier to administer than the six separate GRANTs that would otherwise have been required.

The role PUBLIC is predefined by Oracle. Every user has been automatically granted this role. Thus, you can issue a statement such as

```
GRANT privilege TO PUBLIC;
```

which grants the privilege to every Oracle user at once.

Oracle predefines several other roles, which include common system privileges. The privileges as of Oracle9i for some of the roles are listed in Table 4-3. The predefined Oracle user SYSTEM is automatically granted all of these roles.

Role Name	Privileges Granted
CONNECT	ALTER SESSION, CREATE CLUSTER, CREATE DATABASE LINK, CREATE SEQUENCE, CREATE SESSION, CREATE SYNONYM, CREATE TABLE, CREATE VIEW
RESOURCE	CREATE CLUSTER, CREATE INDEXTYPE, CREATE OPERATOR, CREATE PROCEDURE, CREATE SEQUENCE, CREATE TABLE, CREATE TRIGGER, CREATE TYPE
DBA	All system privileges (with the ADMIN OPTION, so they can be granted again), plus EXP_FULL_DATABASE and IMP_FULL_DATABASE
EXP_FULL_DATABASE	ADMINISTER RESOURCE, BACKUP ANY TABLE, EXECUTE ANY PROCEDURE, EXECUTE ANY TYPE, SELECT ANY TABLE, plus INSERT, UPDATE, DELETE on the system tables `sys.incexp`, `sys.incvid`, and `sys.incfil`

TABLE 4-3.   *Predefined System Roles*

NOTE
Oracle does not guarantee that these roles will be predefined in future versions.

Typically, the CONNECT and RESOURCE roles are granted to the database users who will be creating objects, and just the CONNECT role is granted to users who query objects. Users with just CONNECT would need additional object privileges on the objects that they will need to access.

Transaction Control

A *transaction* is a series of SQL statements that either succeeds or fails as a unit. Transactions are a standard part of relational databases and prevent inconsistent data. The classic example of this is a bank transaction: Consider the following two

SQL statements, which implement a transfer of `transaction_amount` dollars between two bank accounts identified as `from_acct` and `to_acct`:

```
UPDATE accounts
  SET balance = balance - transaction_amount
  WHERE account_no = from_acct;
UPDATE accounts
  SET balance = balance + transaction_amount
  WHERE account_no = to_acct;
```

Suppose the first UPDATE statement succeeds, but the second statement fails due to an error (perhaps the database or network went down). The data is now inconsistent—`from_acct` has been debited, but `to_acct` has not been credited. Needless to say, this is not a good situation—especially if you are the owner of `from_acct`. We prevent this by combining the two statements into a transaction, whereby either both statements will succeed or both statements will fail. This prevents inconsistent data.

A transaction begins with the first SQL statement issued after the previous transaction, or the first SQL statement after connecting to the database. The transaction ends with the COMMIT or ROLLBACK statement.

COMMIT versus ROLLBACK

When a COMMIT statement is issued to the database, the transaction is ended, and

- All work done by the transaction is made permanent.
- Other sessions can see the changes made by this transaction.
- Any locks acquired by the transaction are released.

The syntax for the COMMIT statement is

COMMIT [WORK];

The optional WORK keyword is available for increased readability. Until a transaction is committed, only the session executing that transaction can see the changes made by that session. This is illustrated in Figure 4-2. Session A issues the INSERT statement first. Session B issues a query against the `rooms` table, but does not see the INSERT done by session A, since it hasn't been committed. Session A then commits, and the second SELECT by session B will see the new inserted row.

```
              Session A                          Session B

    INSERT INTO rooms
      (room_id, building, room_number,
       number_seats, description)
    VALUES
      (99991, 'Building 7', 310,
       50, 'Discussion Room E');
                                        SELECT *
                                          FROM rooms
       COMMIT                             WHERE building = 'Building 7';

Time

                                        SELECT *
                                          FROM rooms
                                          WHERE building = 'Building 7';
```

FIGURE 4-2. *Two sessions*

When a ROLLBACK statement is issued to the database, the transaction is ended, and

- All work done by the transaction is undone, as if it hadn't been issued.

- Any locks acquired by the transaction are released.

The syntax for the ROLLBACK statement is

ROLLBACK [WORK];

Just like COMMIT, the WORK keyword is optional and is available for increased readability. An explicit ROLLBACK statement is often used when an error that prevents further work is detected by the program. If a session disconnects from the database without ending the current transaction with COMMIT or ROLLBACK, the transaction is automatically rolled back by the database.

NOTE
SQL*Plus will automatically issue a COMMIT when you exit. The `autocommit` option will issue a COMMIT after every SQL statement, as well. This does not affect the SQL statements inside a PL/SQL block, since SQL*Plus doesn't have control until the block finishes. If SQL*plus is exited without ending a transaction, it is implicitly committed. If a statement ends with an error, SQL*Plus may roll it back.

Savepoints

The ROLLBACK statement undoes the entire transaction, as we have seen. With the SAVEPOINT command, however, only part of the transaction need be undone. The syntax for SAVEPOINT is

SAVEPOINT *name*;

where *name* is the savepoint's name. Savepoint names follow the usual rules for SQL identifiers (see Chapter 3). Note that savepoints are not declared in the declarative section, since they are global to a transaction, and the transaction can continue past the end of the block. Once a savepoint is defined, the program can roll back to the savepoint via the following syntax:

ROLLBACK [WORK] TO SAVEPOINT *name*;

When a ROLLBACK TO SAVEPOINT is issued, the following things occur:

- Any work done since the savepoint is undone. The savepoint remains active, however. It can be rolled back to again, if desired.

- Any locks and resources acquired by the SQL statements since the savepoint will be released.

- The transaction is *not* finished, because SQL statements are still pending.

Consider the following fragment of a PL/SQL block:

```
BEGIN
    INSERT INTO temp_table (char_col) VALUES ('Insert One');
    SAVEPOINT A;
```

```
    INSERT INTO temp_table (char_col) VALUES ('Insert Two');
    SAVEPOINT B;
    INSERT INTO temp_table (char_col) VALUES ('Insert Three');
    SAVEPOINT C;
    /* Missing statements here */
    COMMIT;
END;
```

If we put

```
ROLLBACK TO B;
```

in for the missing statements, the third INSERT and savepoint C will be undone. But the first two INSERTs will be processed. If, on the other hand, we put

```
ROLLBACK TO A;
```

in for the missing statements, the second and third INSERTs will be undone, leaving only the first INSERT.

SAVEPOINT is often used before a complicated section of a transaction. If this part of the transaction fails, it can be rolled back, allowing the earlier part to continue.

Transactions versus Blocks

It is important to note the distinction between transactions and PL/SQL blocks. When a block starts, it does not mean that a transaction starts. Likewise, the start of a transaction need not coincide with the start of a block. For example, suppose we issue the following statements from the SQL*Plus prompt:

```
INSERT INTO classes
    (department, course, description, max_students,
     current_students, num_credits, room_id)
  VALUES ('CS', 101, 'Computer Science 101', 50, 10, 4, 99998);
BEGIN
  UPDATE rooms
    SET room_id = room_id + 1;
  ROLLBACK WORK;
END;
```

Note that we have issued an INSERT statement and then an anonymous PL/SQL block. The block issues an UPDATE and then a ROLLBACK. This ROLLBACK undoes not only the UPDATE statement, but the prior INSERT as well. Both the INSERT statement and the block are part of the same database session, thus the same transaction.

Similarly, a single PL/SQL block can contain multiple transactions. Consider the following:

```
DECLARE
   v_NumIterations    NUMBER;
BEGIN
   -- Loop from 1 to 500, inserting these values into temp_table.
   -- Commit every 50 rows.
   FOR v_LoopCounter IN 1..500 LOOP
     INSERT INTO temp_table (num_col) VALUES (v_LoopCounter);
     v_NumIterations := v_NumIterations + 1;
     IF v_NumIterations = 50 THEN
       COMMIT;
       v_NumIterations := 0;
     END IF;
   END LOOP;
END;
```

This block will insert the numbers 1 through 500 into `temp_table` and will commit after every 50 rows. So, there will be a total of ten transactions during the execution of one block.

Autonomous Transactions

Oracle**8i** and higher
Prior to Oracle8i, there was no way in which some SQL operations within a transaction could be committed independent of the rest of the operations. Oracle8i allows this, however, through autonomous transactions. An *autonomous transaction* is a transaction that is started within the context of another transaction, known as the *parent transaction*, but is independent of it. The autonomous transaction can be committed or rolled back regardless of the state of the parent transaction.

PRAGMA AUTONOMOUS_TRANSACTION

The only way to execute an autonomous transaction is from within a PL/SQL block. The block is marked as autonomous by using a pragma in the declarative section, as the following example illustrates:

```
-- Available online as part of autoTrans.sql
CREATE OR REPLACE PROCEDURE Autonomous AS
   PRAGMA AUTONOMOUS_TRANSACTION;
BEGIN
   INSERT INTO temp_table VALUES (-10, 'Hello from Autonomous!');
   COMMIT;
END Autonomous;
```

NOTE
Procedure creation is discussed in Chapter 9.

The pragma indicates to the PL/SQL compiler that this block is to be treated as autonomous. If we call `Autonomous` from the following PL/SQL block,

```
-- Available online as part of autoTrans.sql
BEGIN
   -- Insert into temp_table from the parent transaction.
   INSERT INTO temp_table VALUES (-10, 'Hello from the parent!');

   -- Call Autonomous, which will be independent of this
   -- transaction.
   Autonomous;

   -- Even though we rollback the parent transaction, the insert
   -- done from Autonomous is still committed.
   ROLLBACK;
END;
```

only one row will be in `temp_table`. The INSERT from the parent block has been rolled back along with the rollback of the parent transaction, but the INSERT from the procedure is still committed:

```
-- Available online as part of autoTrans.sql
SQL> SELECT * FROM temp_table WHERE num_col = -10;
   NUM_COL CHAR_COL
--------- -----------------------------------------------
       -10 Hello from Autonomous!
```

Location of the Pragma   PRAGMA AUTONOMOUS_TRANSACTION must appear in the declarative section of the block, and only one pragma is allowed in the block. It can go anywhere in the declarative section, but it is good style to put it at the beginning.

Types of Autonomous Blocks   Not all blocks can be marked as autonomous. Only the following are legal:

- Top-level anonymous blocks

- Local, stand-alone, and packaged subprograms

- Methods of an object type

- Database triggers

In particular, nested PL/SQL blocks cannot be autonomous. Also, only individual subprograms within a package can be marked as autonomous—the package itself cannot be. The following SQL*Plus session illustrates some valid and invalid locations for the pragma. Note that if the pragma is located in an invalid place, the PLS-710 compile error is raised.

```
-- Available online as autoPragma.sql
SQL> -- The pragma is legal in top-level anonymous blocks:
SQL> DECLARE
  2     PRAGMA AUTONOMOUS_TRANSACTION;
  3  BEGIN
  4     COMMIT;
  5  END;
  6  /
PL/SQL procedure successfully completed.

SQL> -- But it is not legal in nested blocks:
SQL> BEGIN
  2     DECLARE
  3       PRAGMA AUTONOMOUS_TRANSACTION;
  4     BEGIN
  5       COMMIT;
  6     END;
  7  END;
  8  /
     PRAGMA AUTONOMOUS_TRANSACTION;
            *
ERROR at line 3:
ORA-06550: line 3, column 12:
PLS-00710: PRAGMA AUTONOMOUS_TRANSACTION cannot be declared here

SQL> -- It is valid in both stand-alone and local subprograms.
SQL> CREATE OR REPLACE PROCEDURE Auto1 AS
  2     PRAGMA AUTONOMOUS_TRANSACTION;
  3
  4     PROCEDURE Local IS
  5       PRAGMA AUTONOMOUS_TRANSACTION;
  6     BEGIN
  7       ROLLBACK;
  8     END Local;
  9  BEGIN
 10     Local;
 11     COMMIT;
 12  END Auto1;
 13  /
Procedure created.
SQL> show errors
```

```
No errors.

SQL> -- It is valid in a packaged procedure.
SQL> CREATE OR REPLACE PACKAGE Auto2 AS
  2    PROCEDURE P;
  3  END Auto2;
  4  /
Package created.
SQL> show errors
No errors.

SQL> CREATE OR REPLACE PACKAGE BODY Auto2 AS
  2    PROCEDURE P IS
  3      PRAGMA AUTONOMOUS_TRANSACTION;
  4    BEGIN
  5      COMMIT;
  6    END P;
  7  END Auto2;
  8  /
Package body created.
SQL> show errors
No errors.

SQL> -- But not valid at the package level.
SQL> CREATE OR REPLACE PACKAGE Auto3 AS
  2    PRAGMA AUTONOMOUS_TRANSACTION;
  3    PROCEDURE P;
  4    PROCEDURE Q;
  5  END Auto3;
  6  /
Warning: Package created with compilation errors.
SQL> show errors
Errors for PACKAGE AUTO3:

LINE/COL ERROR
-------- -------------------------------------------------------------
2/10     PLS-00710: PRAGMA AUTONOMOUS_TRANSACTION cannot be declared
         here
```

NOTE
Packages are also discussed in Chapter 9.

Properties of Autonomous Transactions

An autonomous transaction begins with the first SQL statement in an autonomous
block, and ends with a COMMIT or ROLLBACK statement. Any transaction control

statement can be used in an autonomous transaction, including COMMIT, ROLLBACK, SAVEPOINT, ROLLBACK TO SAVEPOINT, and SET TRANSACTION.

Savepoints are local to the current transaction. Thus, you can't rollback to a savepoint in the parent transaction, as illustrated by the following:

```
-- Available online as autoSavepoints.sql
SQL> CREATE OR REPLACE PROCEDURE AutoProc AS
  2    PRAGMA AUTONOMOUS_TRANSACTION;
  3  BEGIN
  4    ROLLBACK TO SAVEPOINT A;
  5  END AutoProc;
  6  /
Procedure created.

SQL> BEGIN
  2    SAVEPOINT A;
  3    INSERT INTO temp_table (char_col)
  4      VALUES ('Savepoint A!');
  5    -- Even though A is a valid savepoint in the parent
  6    -- transaction, it is not in the autonomous transaction.
  7    -- So this will raise an error.
  8    AutoProc;
  9  END;
 10  /
BEGIN
*
ERROR at line 1:
ORA-01086: savepoint 'A' never established
ORA-06512: at "EXAMPLE.AUTOPROC", line 4
ORA-06512: at line 8
```

Ending Autonomous Transactions

An autonomous transaction ends with a COMMIT or ROLLBACK statement. It does not end when the block containing it ends. If an autonomous block ends without ending the transaction, an ORA-6519 error is raised and the autonomous transaction is rolled back:

```
-- Available online as part of autoTrans.sql
SQL> DECLARE
  2    PRAGMA AUTONOMOUS_TRANSACTION;
  3  BEGIN
  4    INSERT INTO temp_table (num_col) VALUES (1);
  5  END;
  6  /
DECLARE
*
```

```
ERROR at line 1:
ORA-06519: active autonomous transaction detected and rolled back
ORA-06512: at line 4
```

Summary

In this chapter, we have discussed the SQL language in general, and the DML and transaction control statements allowed in PL/SQL in particular. We've also explored privileges and roles, and we've seen how transactions prevent inconsistent data. In the next chapter, we will discuss the built-in SQL functions. Chapter 6 discusses cursors, which are used for multirow queries. Cursors will build on the concepts in this and the next chapter.

CHAPTER
5

Built-in SQL
Functions

he basic SQL commands we saw in Chapter 4 are enhanced by many predefined functions. In this chapter, we will examine the different kinds of functions and discuss some of their uses.

Introduction

SQL provides a number of predefined functions that can be called from a SQL statement. For example, the following SELECT statement uses the UPPER function to return the first names of students, in all uppercase rather than the case in which they were stored:

```
SELECT UPPER(first_name)
   FROM students;
```

Many SQL functions can be called from PL/SQL procedural statements as well. For example, the following block also uses the UPPER function, but in an assignment statement:

```
DECLARE
   v_FirstName   students.first_name%TYPE;
BEGIN
   v_FirstName := UPPER('Charlie');
END;
```

SQL functions can be divided into categories based on the type of arguments each function expects. The UPPER function, for example, expects a character argument. If you supply an argument that is not in the correct family, it is converted automatically by PL/SQL before the function is called, in accordance with the datatype conversion rules we saw in Chapter 3. SQL functions can also be classified as group or single-row functions. A *group function* operates on many rows of data and returns a single result. Group functions are valid only in the select list or HAVING clause of a query. They are not allowed in PL/SQL procedural statements. COUNT is an example of a group function. *Single-row functions*, such as UPPER, operate on one value and return another value. They are allowed anywhere an expression is allowed in SQL statements, and also in PL/SQL procedural statements.

The following sections describe the built-in functions available. Within each section, the functions are described in alphabetical order. For brevity, the functions are described in a table that contains the function parameters, the version in which the function was introduced, where it is allowed, and a description. Examples are provided where necessary. Some of the functions take optional arguments. These are indicated by square brackets ([]) in the function's syntax.

NOTE
The versions listed in the following sections are Oracle7, Oracle8, Oracle8i, and Oracle9i. In all cases, the function is available in the latest maintenance release for each of the major versions (that is, 7.3 for Oracle7 and 8.1.7 for Oracle8i). The function may also be available in earlier maintenance releases.

Character Functions Returning Character Values

These functions all take arguments in the character family (except CHR and NCHR) and return character values. The majority of the functions return a VARCHAR2 value, except where noted. The return type of character functions is subject to the same restrictions as the base database type, namely that VARCHAR2 values are limited to 4,000 characters (2,000 in Oracle7), and CHAR values are limited to 2,000 characters (255 in Oracle7). When used in procedural statements, they can be assigned to either VARCHAR2 or CHAR PL/SQL variables.

These functions are described in the following table:

Function	Version Available	Where Allowed
CHR(x [USING NCHAR_CS])	Oracle7 (USING NCHAR_CS from Oracle8)	Procedural and SQL statements. USING NCHAR_CS is valid in procedural statements in Oracle9i only, and in SQL statements in earlier releases.

Returns the character that has the value equivalent to *x* in the database character set. CHR and ASCII are opposite functions. CHR returns the character given the character number, and ASCII returns the character number given the character. If USING NCHAR_CS (Oracle8 and higher) is specified, the national database character set is used instead of the character set. The NCHR (Oracle9i and higher) function is the same as CHR with USING_NCHAR_CS.

Function	Version Available	Where Allowed
CONCAT(*string1, string2*)	Oracle7	Procedural and SQL statements

Returns *string1* concatenated with *string2*. This function is identical to the || operator. The returned value is always VARCHAR2, in the character set of *string1*.

INITCAP(*string*)	Oracle7	Procedural and SQL statements

Returns *string* with the first character of each word capitalized and the remaining characters of each word in lowercase. Words are separated by spaces or nonalphanumeric characters. Characters that are not letters are unaffected. The return type is the same as *string*.

LOWER(*string*)	Oracle7	Procedural and SQL statements

Returns *string* with all characters in lowercase. Any characters that are not letters are left intact. If *string* has the CHAR datatype, the result is also CHAR. If *string* is VARCHAR2, the result is VARCHAR2.

LPAD(*string1, x [,string2]*)	Oracle7	Procedural and SQL statements

Returns *string1* padded on the left to length *x* with the characters in *string2*. If *string2* is less than *x* characters, it is duplicated as necessary. If *string2* is more than *x* characters, only the first *x* characters of *string2* are used. If *string2* is not specified, it defaults to a single blank. Note that *x* is specified in terms of display length, rather than actual length. If the database character set is multibyte, the display length can be longer than the actual length of the string in bytes. LPAD behaves similarly to RPAD, except that it pads on the left rather than the right.

LTRIM(*string1, string2*)	Oracle7	Procedural and SQL statements

Returns *string1* with the leftmost characters appearing in *string2* removed. *string2* defaults to a single blank. The database will scan *string1*, starting from the leftmost position. When the first character not in *string2* is encountered, the result is returned. LTRIM behaves similarly to RTRIM, except that it trims from the left rather than the right.

REPLACE (*string, search_str [,replace_str]*)	Oracle7	Procedural and SQL statements

Returns *string* with every occurrence of *search_str* replaced with *replace_str*. If *replace_str* is not specified, all occurrences of *search_str* are removed. REPLACE is a subset of the functionality provided by TRANSLATE.

Function	Version Available	Where Allowed
RPAD(*string1, x, [,string2]*)	Oracle7	Procedural and SQL statements

Returns *string1* padded on the right to length *x* with the characters in *string2*. If *string2* is less than *x* characters, it is duplicated as necessary. If *string2* is more than *x* characters, only the first *x* is used. If *string2* is not specified, it defaults to a single blank. Note that *x* is specified in terms of display length rather than actual length. If the database character set is multibyte, the display length can be longer than the actual length of the string in bytes. RPAD behaves similarly to LPAD, except that it pads on the right rather than the left.

Function	Version Available	Where Allowed
RTRIM(*string1 [,string2]*)	Oracle7	Procedural and SQL statements

Returns *string1* with the rightmost characters appearing in *string2* removed. *string2* defaults to a single blank. The database will scan *string1*, starting from the rightmost position. When the first character not in *string2* is encountered, the result is returned. RTRIM behaves similarly to LTRIM.

Function	Version Available	Where Allowed
SOUNDEX(*string*)	Oracle7	Procedural and SQL statements

Returns the phonetic representation of *string*. See the following section for details.

Function	Version Available	Where Allowed
SUBSTR(*string, a [,b]*)	Oracle7	Procedural and SQL statements

Returns a portion of *string*, with *a* and *b* measured in characters. See the following section for details.

Function	Version Available	Where Allowed
SUBSTRB(*string, a [,b]*)	Oracle7	Procedural and SQL statements

Returns a portion of *string*, with *a* and *b* measured in bytes. See the following section for details.

Function	Version Available	Where Allowed
SUBSTRC(*string, a [,b]*)	Oracle9*i*	Procedural and SQL statements

Returns a portion of *string*, with *a* and *b* measured in Unicode complete characters. See the following section for details.

Function	Version Available	Where Allowed
SUBSTR2(*string, a [,b]*)	Oracle9*i*	Procedural and SQL statements

Returns a portion of *string*, with *a* and *b* measured in UCS2 codepoints. See the following section for details.

Function	Version Available	Where Allowed
SUBSTR4(*string, a* [,*b*])	Oracle9i	Procedural and SQL statements

Returns a portion of *string*, with *a* and *b* measured in UCS4 codepoints. See the following section for details.

TRANSLATE(*string*, *from_str, to_str*)	Oracle7	Procedural and SQL statements

Returns *string* with all occurrences of each character in *from_str* replaced by the corresponding character in *to_str*. TRANSLATE is a superset of the functionality provided by REPLACE. If *from_str* is longer than *to_str*, any extra characters in *from_str* not in *to_str* are removed from *string*, since they have no corresponding characters. *to_str* cannot be empty. Oracle interprets the empty string to be the same as NULL, and if any argument to TRANSLATE is NULL, the result is NULL as well.

TRIM ([{ { LEADING | TRAILING | BOTH } [*trim_char*])	*trim_char*} FROM] *string*)	Oracle8i	Procedural and SQL statements

Returns *string* with leading, trailing, or both occurrences of *trim_char* removed. *trim_char* must be a single character, and defaults to a blank. If none of LEADING, TRAILING, or BOTH is specified, occurrences of *trim_char* are removed from both ends of *string*.

UPPER(*string*)	Oracle7	Procedural and SQL statements

Returns *string* with all letters in uppercase. If string has datatype CHAR, the return value is also CHAR. If string has datatype VARCHAR2, the return value is VARCHAR2. Characters that are not letters are left intact in the returned value.

SUBSTR, SUBSTRB, SUBSTRC, SUBSTR2, and SUBSTR4

Syntax
```
SUBSTR(string, a [,b])
SUBSTRB(string, a [,b])
SUBSTRC(string, a [,b])
SUBSTR2(string, a [,b])
SUBSTR4(string, a [,b])
```

Purpose   Returns a portion of *string* starting at character *a*, *b* characters long. If *a* is 0, it is treated as 1 (the beginning of the string). If *a* is positive, characters are returned counting from the left. If *a* is negative, characters are returning starting from the end of *string*, and counting from the right. If *b* is not present, it defaults to the entire string. If *b* is less than 1, NULL is returned. If a floating-point value is passed for either *a* or *b*, the value is truncated to an integer first. The return type is always the same type as *string*.

The different versions of SUBSTR use different meanings for *a* and *b*, as the following table illustrates:

Function	Units for *a* and *b*
SUBSTR	Characters in the input database character set
SUBSTRB	Bytes
SBUSTRC	Unicode complete characters
SUBSTR2	USC2 codepoints
SUBSTR4	UCS4 codepoints

Example

```
SELECT SUBSTR('abc123def', 4, 4) "First"
   FROM dual;
First
-----
123d

SELECT SUBSTR('abc123def', -4, 4) "Second"
   FROM dual;
Second
------
3def

SELECT SUBSTR('abc123def', 5) "Third"
   FROM dual;

Third
-----
23def
```

SOUNDEX

Syntax
SOUNDEX(*string*)

Purpose   Returns the phonetic representation of *string*. This is useful for comparing words that are spelled differently but sound alike. The phonetic representation is defined in *The Art of Computer Programming, Volume 3: Sorting and Searching*, by Donald E. Knuth. The algorithm for developing the phonetic spelling is as follows:

- Keep the first letter of the string, but remove occurrences of *a, e, h, i, o, w,* and *y.*

- Assign numbers to the remaining letters as follows:

    1. *b, f, p, v*

    2. *c, g, j, k, q, s, x, z*

    3. *d, t*

    4. *l*

    5. *m, n*

    6. *r*

- If two or more letters with the same number (such as *c* and *j*) were next to each other in the original word, or have only *h* or *w* between them, remove all but the first.

- Return the first 4 bytes padded with 0.

Example

```
SQL> SELECT first_name, SOUNDEX(first_name)
  2    FROM students;

FIRST_NAME           SOUN
-------------------- ----
Scott                S300
Margaret             M626
Joanne               J500
Manish               M520
Patrick              P362
Timothy              T530
Barbara              B616
David                D130
Ester                E236
Rose                 R200
Rita                 R300
Shay                 S000
```

```
SELECT first_name
  FROM students
  WHERE SOUNDEX(first_name) = SOUNDEX('skit');
FIRST_NAME
--------------------
Scott
```

Character Functions Returning Numeric Values

These functions take character arguments and return numeric results. The arguments can be either CHAR or VARCHAR2. Although many results are in fact integer values, the return value is simply NUMBER, with no precision or scale defined. These functions are described in the following table:

Function	Version Available	Where Allowed
ASCII(*string*)	Oracle7	Procedural and SQL statements

Returns the decimal representation of the first byte of *string* in the database character set. Note that the function is still called ASCII even if the character set is not 7-bit ASCII. CHR and ASCII are opposite functions. CHR returns the character given the character number, and ASCII returns the character number given the character.

INSTR(*string1, string2* [,*a*] [,*b*])	Oracle7	Procedural and SQL statements

Returns the position within *string1* where *string2* is contained, with *a* and *b* measured in characters. See the following sections for details.

INSTRB(*string1, string2* [,*a*] [,*b*])	Oracle7	Procedural and SQL statements

Returns the position within *string1* where *string2* is contained, with *a* and *b* measured in bytes. See the following sections for details.

INSTRC(*string1, string2* [,*a*] [,*b*])	Oracle9*i*	Procedural and SQL statements

Returns the position within *string1* where *string2* is contained, with *a* and *b* measured in Unicode complete characters. See the following sections for details.

INSTR2(*string1, string2* [,*a*] [,*b*])	Oracle9*i*	Procedural and SQL statements

Returns the position within *string1* where *string2* is contained, with *a* and *b* measured UCS2 codepoints. See the following sections for details.

Function	Version Available	Where Allowed
INSTR4(*string1*, *string2* [,*a*] [,*b*])	Oracle9*i*	Procedural and SQL statements

Returns the position within *string1* where *string2* is contained, with *a* and *b* measured in UCS4 codepoints. See the following sections for details.

LENGTH(*string*)	Oracle7	Procedural and SQL statements

Returns the length of *string*, measured in characters. See the following sections for details.

LENGTHB(*string*)	Oracle7	Procedural and SQL statements

Returns the length of *string*, measured in bytes. See the following sections for details.

LENGTHC(*string*)	Oracle9*i*	Procedural and SQL statements

Returns the length of *string*, measured in Unicode complete characters. See the following sections for details.

LENGTH2(*string*)	Oracle9*i*	Procedural and SQL statements

Returns the length of *string*, measured in UCS2 codepoints. See the following sections for details.

LENGTH4(*string*)	Oracle9*i*	Procedural and SQL statements

Returns the length of *string*, measured in UCS4 codepoints. See the following sections for details.

INSTR, INSTRB, INSTRC, INSTR2, and INSTR4

Syntax
```
INSTR(string1, string2 [,a] [,b])
INSTRB(string1, string2 [,a] [,b])
INSTRC(string1, string2 [,a] [,b])
INSTR2(string1, string2 [,a] [,b])
INSTR4(string1, string2 [,a] [,b])
```

Purpose   Returns the position within *string1* where *string2* is contained. *string1* is scanned from the left, starting at position *a*. If *a* is negative, then *string1* is scanned from the right. The position of the *b*th occurrence is returned. Both *a* and *b* default to 1, which would return the first occurrence of *string2* within *string1*. If *string2* isn't found subject to *a* and *b*, 0 is returned. Positions are relative to the beginning of *string1* regardless of the values of *a* and *b*.

The different versions of INSTR use different meanings for *a* and *b*, as the following table illustrates:

Function	Units for *a* and *b*
INSTR	Characters in the input database character set
INSTRB	Bytes
INSTRC	Unicode complete characters
INSTR2	USC2 codepoints
INSTR4	UCS4 codepoints

Example

```
SELECT INSTR('Scott''s spot', 'ot', 1, 2) "First"
  FROM dual;
    First
---------
       11

SELECT INSTR('Scott''s spot', 'ot', -1, 2) "Second"
  FROM dual;
    Second
---------
        3

SELECT INSTR('Scott''s spot', 'ot', 5) "Third"
  FROM dual;
    Third
---------
       11

SELECT INSTR('Scott''s spot', 'ot', 12) "Fourth"
  FROM dual;
    Fourth
---------
        0
```

LENGTH, LENGTHB, LENGTHC, LENGTH2, and LENGTH4

Syntax

LENGTH(*string*)
LENGTHB(*string*)
LENGTHC(*string*)
LENGTH2(*string*)
LENGTH4(*string*)

Purpose   Returns the length of *string*. Since CHAR values are blank-padded, if *string* has datatype CHAR, the trailing blanks are included in the length. If *string* is NULL, the function returns NULL. The different versions of LENGTH use different meanings for the returned value, as the following table illustrates:

Function	Units for Returned Value
LENGTH	Characters in the input database character set
LENGTHB	Bytes
LENGTHC	Unicode complete characters
LENGTH2	USC2 codepoints
LENGTH4	UCS4 codepoints

Example

```
SELECT LENGTH('Mary had a little lamb') "Length"
  FROM dual;
  Length
---------
      22
```

NLS Functions

Except for NCHR, these functions take character arguments and return character values. All of the functions in this section are designed to work with data in different character sets, or with different NLS parameters than the default. For more information on NLS (which is known as Globalization in Oracle9*i*), see the Oracle documentation.

These functions are described in the following table:

Function	**Version Available**	**Where Allowed**
CONVERT(*string, dest_ charset* [,*source_charset*])	Oracle7	Procedural and SQL statements

Converts the input *string* into the specified character set *dest_charset. source_ charset* is the character set of the input value—if it is not specified then it defaults to the database character set. The input can be a CHAR, VARCHAR2, NCHAR, NVARCHAR2, CLOB, or NCLOB. The return value is VARCHAR2.

If a character in the input string does not appear in *dest_charset*, a replacement character (as defined by *dest_charset*) will be used.

NCHR(*x*)	Oracle9*i*	Procedural and SQL statements

Returns the character that has the value equivalent to *x* in the database national character set. NCHR(*x*) is equivalent to CHR(*x* USING NCHAR_CS).

NLS_CHARSET_DECL_ LEN(*byte_width, charset*)	Oracle8	Procedural and SQL statements

Returns the declaration width (in characters) of an NCHAR value. *byte_width* is the length of the value in bytes, and *charset* is the character set ID of the value.

NLS_CHARSET_ ID(*charset_name*)	Oracle8	Procedural and SQL statements

Returns the numeric ID of the specified character set name *charset_name*. Specifying 'CHAR_CS' for *charset*_name will return the ID of the database character set, and 'NCHAR_CS' for *charset*_name will return the ID of the database national character set. If *charset_name* is not a valid character set name, NULL is returned. NLS_CHARSET_ID and NLS_CHARSET_NAME are inverse functions.

NLS_CHARSET_ NAME(*charset_ID*)	Oracle8	Procedural and SQL statements

Returns the name of the specified character set ID *charset_ID*. If *charset_ID* is not a valid character set ID, NULL is returned. NLS_CHARSET_NAME and NLS_CHARSET_ID are inverse functions.

NLS_INITCAP(*string* [,*nlsparams*])	Oracle7	Procedural and SQL statements

Returns *string* with the first character of each word capitalized and the remaining characters of each word in lowercase. *nlsparams* specifies a different sorting sequence than the default for the session. If it is not specified, NLS_INITCAP behaves the same as INITCAP. *nlsparams* should be of the form 'NLS_SORT = *sort*' where *sort* specifies a linguistic sort sequence. For more information on NLS parameters and how they are used, see the *Server SQL Reference*.

Function	Version Available	Where Allowed
NLS_LOWER(*string* [,*nlsparams*])	Oracle7	Procedural and SQL statements

Returns *string* with all letters in lowercase. Characters that are not letters are left intact. *nlsparams* has the same form and serves the same purpose as in NLS_INITCAP. If *nlsparams* is not included, NLS_LOWER behaves the same as LOWER.

Function	Version Available	Where Allowed
NLS_UPPER(*string* [,*nlsparams*])	Oracle7	Procedural and SQL statements

Returns *string* with all letters in uppercase. Characters that are not letters are left intact. *nlsparams* has the same form and behaves the same as in NLS_INITCAP. If *nlsparams* isn't specified, NLS_UPPER behaves the same as UPPER.

Function	Version Available	Where Allowed
NLSSORT(*string* [,*nlsparams*])	Oracle7	Procedural and SQL statements

Returns the string of bytes used to sort *string*. All character values are converted into byte strings such as this for consistency among different database character sets. *nlsparams* behaves the same as it does for NLS_INITCAP. If *nlsparams* is omitted, the default sort sequence for your session is used. For more information on sort sequences, see the "National Language Support" section of the *Server SQL Reference*.

Function	Version Available	Where Allowed
TRANSLATE(*string* USING {CHAR_CS | NCHAR_CS })	Oracle8	Procedural and SQL statements

TRANSLATE...USING converts the input *string* argument into either the database character set (if CHAR_CS is specified) or the database national character set (if NCHAR_CS is specified). *string* can be CHAR, VARCHAR2, NCHAR, or NVARCHAR2. If CHAR_CS is specified, the return type is VARCHAR2, and if NCHAR_CS is specified, the return type is NVARCHAR2. TRANSLATE...USING provides a subset of the CONVERT functionality. Note that if the input contains UCS2 characters or backslash characters, you should use the UNISTR function (available with Oracle9i and higher).

Function	Version Available	Where Allowed
UNISTR(*s*)	Oracle9i	Procedural and SQL statements

Returns the string *s* translated into the database Unicode character set. *s* can contain escaped UCS2 codepoint characters, which consist of a backslash followed by the hexadecimal codepoint number. Thus, to include a backslash in the string you must use a double backslash (\\). UNISTR is similar to TRANSLATE...USING, except that it translates only into Unicode and accepts escaped characters.

Numeric Functions

These functions take NUMBER arguments and return NUMBER values. The return values of the transcendental and trigonometric functions are accurate to 36 decimal digits. ACOS, ASIN, ATAN, and ATAN2 are accurate to 30 decimal digits. The functions are described in the following table:

Function	Version Available	Where Allowed
ABS(x)	Oracle7	Procedural and SQL statements

Returns the absolute value of x.

Function	Version Available	Where Allowed
ACOS(x)	Oracle7	Procedural and SQL statements

Returns the arc cosine of x. x should range from -1 to 1, and the output ranges from 0 to Π, expressed in radians.

Function	Version Available	Where Allowed
ASIN(x)	Oracle7	Procedural and SQL statements

Returns the arc sine of x. x should range from -1 to 1, and the output ranges from $-\Pi/2$ to $-\Pi/2$, expressed in radians.

Function	Version Available	Where Allowed
ATAN(x)	Oracle7	Procedural and SQL statements

Returns the arc tangent of x. The output ranges from $-\Pi/2$ to $-\Pi/2$, expressed in radians.

Function	Version Available	Where Allowed
ATAN2(x, y)	Oracle7	Procedural and SQL statements

Returns the arc tangent of x and y. The output ranges from $-\Pi$ to Π, depending on the signs of x and y, and is expressed in radians. ATAN2(x, y) is the same as ATAN(x/y).

Function	Version Available	Where Allowed
BITAND(x, y)	Oracle7	Procedural and SQL statements

Returns the bitwise AND of x and y, each of which must be non-negative integer values. This function is equivalent to the && operator in C. Note that there is no BITOR function, but the UTL_RAW package does provide additional bit operators that work on RAW values.

Function	Version Available	Where Allowed
CEIL(x)	Oracle7	Procedural and SQL statements

Returns the smallest integer greater than or equal to x.

Function	Version Available	Where Allowed
COS(x)	Oracle7	Procedural and SQL statements

Returns the cosine of x. x is an angle expressed in radians.

Function	Version Available	Where Allowed
COSH(x)	Oracle7	Procedural and SQL statements

Returns the hyperbolic cosine of x.

Function	Version Available	Where Allowed
EXP(x)	Oracle7	Procedural and SQL statements

Returns e raised to the xth power. $e = 2.71828183...$

Function	Version Available	Where Allowed
FLOOR(x)	Oracle7	Procedural and SQL statements

Returns the largest integer equal to or less than x.

Function	Version Available	Where Allowed
LN(x)	Oracle7	Procedural and SQL statements

Returns the natural logarithm of x. x must be greater than 0.

Function	Version Available	Where Allowed
LOG(x, y)	Oracle7	Procedural and SQL statements

Returns the logarithm base x of y. The base must be a positive number other than 0 or 1, and y can be any positive number.

Function	Version Available	Where Allowed
MOD(x, y)	Oracle7	Procedural and SQL statements

Returns the remainder of x divided by y. If y is 0, x is returned.

Function	Version Available	Where Allowed
POWER(x, y)	Oracle7	Procedural and SQL statements

Returns x raised to the yth power. The base x and the exponent y need not be positive integers, but if x is negative, y must be an integer.

Function	Version Available	Where Allowed
ROUND(x [,y])	Oracle7	Procedural and SQL statements

Returns x rounded to y places to the right of the decimal point. y defaults to 0, which rounds x to the nearest integer. If y is negative, digits left of the decimal point are rounded. y must be an integer.

Function	Version Available	Where Allowed
SIGN(x)	Oracle7	Procedural and SQL statements

If $x < 0$, returns -1. If $x = 0$, returns 0. If $x > 0$, returns 1.

SIN(x)	Oracle7	Procedural and SQL statements

Returns the sine of x, which is an angle expressed in radians.

SINH(x)	Oracle7	Procedural and SQL statements

Returns the hyperbolic sine of x.

SQRT(x)	Oracle7	Procedural and SQL statements

Returns the square root of x. x cannot be negative.

TAN(x)	Oracle7	Procedural and SQL statements

Returns the tangent of x, which is an angle expressed in radians.

TANH(x)	Oracle7	Procedural and SQL statements

Returns the hyperbolic tangent of x.

TRUNC(x [,y])	Oracle7	Procedural and SQL statements

Returns x truncated (as opposed to rounded) to y decimal places. y defaults to 0, which truncates x to an integer value. If y is negative, digits left of the decimal point are truncated.

WIDTH_BUCKET(x, min, max, num_buckets)	Oracle 9i	SQL statements only

See the following section for details.

WIDTH_BUCKET

Syntax
WIDTH_BUCKET(x, min, max, num_buckets)

Purpose   WIDTH_BUCKET allows you to create equal-length histograms based on the input parameters. The range min...max is divided into num_buckets sections, with each section of equal size. The section into which *x* falls is then returned. If *x* is less than *min*, 0 is returned. If *x* is greater than or equal to *max*, *num_buckets*+1 is returned. Neither *min* nor *max* can be NULL, and *num_buckets* must evaluate to a positive integer. If *x* is NULL, then NULL is returned.

Example

The following example sets up 20 buckets, each of size 50 (1,000/20):

```
SELECT number_seats, WIDTH_BUCKET(number_seats, 1, 1000, 20) Bucket
  FROM rooms;

NUMBER_SEATS    BUCKET
------------  ----------
        1000        21
         500        10
          50         1
          50         1
          50         1
          10         1
        1000        21
          75         2
          50         1
```

Date and Datetime Functions

The date functions take arguments of type DATE. Except for the MONTHS_BETWEEN function, which returns a NUMBER, all of the functions return DATE or datetime values. Date arithmetic is also discussed in this section. The functions are described in the following table.

Function	Version Available	Where Allowed
ADD_MONTHS(*d*, *x*)	Oracle7	Procedural and SQL statements

Returns the date *d* plus *x* months. *x* can be any integer. If the resultant month has fewer days than the month of *d*, the last day of the resultant month is returned. If not, the result has the same day component as *d*. The time component of *d* and the result are the same.

CURRENT_DATE	Oracle9*i*	Procedural and SQL statements

Returns the current date in the session time zone as a DATE value. This function is similar to SYSDATE, except that SYSDATE is not sensitive to the current session time zone.

Function	Version Available	Where Allowed
CURRENT_TIMESTAMP [(*precision*)]	Oracle9*i*	Procedural and SQL statements

Returns the current date in the session time zone, as a TIMESTAMP WITH TIMEZONE value. If *precision* is specified, it represents the decimal precision on the number of seconds returned. It defaults to 6.

DBTIMEZONE	Oracle9*i*	Procedural and SQL statements

Returns the time zone of the database. The format is the same as used in the CREATE DATABASE statement, or most recent ALTER DATABASE.

EXTRACT({YEAR, MONTH, DAY, HOUR, MINUTE, SECOND, TIMEZONE_HOUR, TIMEZONE_MINUTE, TIMEZONE_REGION, TIMEZONE_ABBR} FROM *datetime_or_ interval*)	DATE fields only in Oracle8*i*, all datetime fields in Oracle9*i*	Procedural and SQL statements

Returns the selected data from *datetime_or_interval*, which must be either a DATE, DATETIME, or INTERVAL expression. The requested field must be valid for the expression—for example, you cannot extract TIMEZONE from a DATE value. If the field is not valid, Oracle9*i* will raise "ORA-30076: invalid extract field for extract source".

LAST_DAY(*d*)	Oracle7	Procedural and SQL statements

Returns the date of the last day of the month that contains *d*. This function can be used to determine how many days are left in the current month.

LOCALTIMESTAMP [(*precision*)]	Oracle9*i*	Procedural and SQL statements

Returns the current date in the session time zone as a TIMESTAMP value. If *precision* is specified, it represents the decimal precision on the number of seconds returned. It defaults to 6. LOCALTIMESTAMP returns a TIMESTAMP value, while CURRENT_TIMESTAMP returns a TIMESTAMP WITH TIMEZONE value.

Function	Version Available	Where Allowed
MONTHS_BETWEEN(*date1*, *date2*)	Oracle7	Procedural and SQL statements

Returns the number of months between *date1* and *date2*. If both *date1* and *date2* have the same day component, or if both are the last days of their respective months, the result is an integer. Otherwise, the result will contain the fractional portion of a 31-day month.

Function	Version Available	Where Allowed
NEW_TIME(*d*, *zone1*, *zone2*)	Oracle7	Procedural and SQL statements

Returns the date and time in time zone *zone2* when the date and time in time zone *zone1* are *d*. The return type is DATE. *zone1* and *zone2* are character strings with meanings described in Table 5-1. Additional time zone names can be determined in Oracle9*i* by querying the v$timezone_names view.

Function	Version Available	Where Allowed
NEXT_DAY(*d*, *string*)	Oracle7	Procedural and SQL statements

Returns the date of the first day named by *string* that is later than the date *d*. *string* specifies a day of the week in the language of the current session. The time component of the returned value is the same as the time component of *d*. The case of *string* is not significant.

Function	Version Available	Where Allowed
ROUND(*d* [,*format*])	Oracle7	Procedural and SQL statements

Rounds the date *d* to the unit specified by *format*. The available values for *format* for ROUND and TRUNC are described in Table 5-2. If *format* is not specified, it defaults to 'DD', which rounds *d* to the nearest day.

Function	Version Available	Where Allowed
SESSIONTIMEZONE	Oracle9*i*	Procedural and SQL statements

Returns the time zone of the current session. The return type is a character string in either a time zone offset or a time zone region name. The format is the same as used in the most recent ALTER SESSION statement, if specified.

Function	Version Available	Where Allowed
SYS_EXTRACT_UTC(*datetime*)	Oracle9*i*	Procedural and SQL statements

Returns the time in UTC (Coordinated Universal Time, formerly Greenwich Mean Time) from the supplied *datetime*, which must include a time zone.

Function	Version Available	Where Allowed
SYSDATE	Oracle7	Procedural and SQL statements

Returns the current date and time, of type DATE. When used in distributed SQL statements, SYSDATE returns the date and time of the local database.

SYSTIMESTAMP	Oracle9*i*	Procedural and SQL statements

Returns the current date and time, of type TIMESTAMP WITH TIMEZONE. When used in distributed SQL statements, SYSTIMESTAMP returns the date and time of the local database.

TRUNC(*d* [,*format*])	Oracle7	Procedural and SQL statements

Returns the date *d* truncated to the unit specified by *format*. The available format models and their effects are the same as ROUND, described in Table 5-2. If *format* is omitted, it defaults to 'DD', which truncates *d* to the nearest day.

TZ_OFFSET(*timezone*)	Oracle9*i*	Procedural and SQL statements

Returns the offset as a character string between the supplied *timezone* and UTC. *timezone* can be specified as either a time zone name (as in Table 5-1 or the v$timezone_names view), or an offset in the format '+/- HH:MI'. The functions SESSIONTIMEZONE and DBTIMEZONE can be used as well. The offset is returned in the '+/- HH:MI' format.

String	Time Zone
AST	Atlantic standard time
ADT	Atlantic daylight time
BST	Bering standard time
BDT	Bering daylight time
CST	Central standard time
CDT	Central daylight time
EST	Eastern standard time

TABLE 5-1. *Time Zone Format Strings*

String	Time Zone
EDT	Eastern daylight time
GMT	Greenwich mean time
HST	Alaska-Hawaii standard time
HDT	Alaska-Hawaii daylight time
MST	Mountain standard time
MDT	Mountain daylight time
NST	Newfoundland standard time
PST	Pacific standard time
PDT	Pacific daylight time
YST	Yukon standard time
YDT	Yukon daylight time

TABLE 5-1. *Time Zone Format Strings* (continued)

Format Model	Rounding or Truncating Unit
CC, SCC	Century
SYYYY, YYYY, YEAR, SYEAR, YYY, YY, Y	Year (rounds up on July 1)
IYYY, IY, IY, I	ISO year
Q	Quarter (rounds up on the 16th day of the second month of the quarter)
MONTH, MON, MM, RM	Month (rounds up on the sixteenth day)
WW	Same day of the week as the first day of the year
IW	Same day of the week as the first day of the ISO year
W	Same day of the week as the first day of the month

TABLE 5-2. *ROUND and TRUNC Date Formats*

Format Model	Rounding or Truncating Unit
DDD, DD, J	Day
Day, DY, D	Starting day of the week
HH, HH12, HH24	Hour
MI	Minute

TABLE 5-2. *ROUND and TRUNC Date Formats* (continued)

Date and Datetime Arithmetic

Applying the arithmetic operators to dates, datetimes, intervals, and numbers is described according to Table 5-3. Note that when subtracting two date values, the result is a number.

Operation	Type of Returned Value	Result
$d1 - d2$	NUMBER	Returns the difference in days between $d1$ and $d2$. This value is expressed as a number, with the real part representing a fraction of a day.
$dt1 - dt2$	INTERVAL	Returns the interval between $dt1$ and $dt2$.
$i1 - i2$	INTERVAL	Returns the difference between $i1$ and $i2$.
$d1 + d2$	N/A	Illegal—can only subtract two dates.
$dt1 + dt2$	N/A	Illegal—can only subtract two datetimes.
$i1 + i2$	INTERVAL	Returns the sum of $i1$ and $i2$.
$d1 + n$	DATE	Adds n days to $d1$ and returns the result as a DATE. n can be a real number, including a fraction of a day.
$d1 - n$	DATE	Subtracts n days from $d1$ and returns the result as a DATE. n can be a real number, including a fraction of a day.

TABLE 5-3. *Semantics of Date Arithmetic*

Operation	Type of Returned Value	Result
dt1 + i1	DATETIME	Returns the sum of *dt1* and *i1*.
dt1 – i1	DATETIME	Returns the difference of *dt1* and *i1*.
*i1 * n*	INTERVAL	Returns the value of *i1* times *n*.
i1 / n	INTERVAL	Returns the value of *i1* divided by *n*.

d1, d2 represent date values.

dt1, dt2 represent datetime values

i1, i2 represent interval values

n represents a number value

TABLE 5-3. *Semantics of Date Arithmetic* (continued)

See the Oracle documentation for examples on date arithmetic.

Conversion Functions

The conversion functions are used to convert between PL/SQL datatypes. PL/SQL will do many of these conversions automatically, via an implicit call to a conversion function. However, you have no control over the format specifiers used in implicit calls, and it can make your code more difficult to understand. Consequently, it is good programming style to use an explicit conversion function rather than relying on PL/SQL's implicit conversions. The conversion functions are described in the following table and sections:

Function	Version Available	Where Allowed
ASCIISTR(*string*)	Oracle9*i*	Procedural and SQL statements

Returns a string containing only valid SQL characters plus a slash. Any characters in *string* (which can be in any character set) that are not valid are converted into a numeric equivalent, with a slash in front of them.

Function	Version Available	Where Allowed
BIN_TO_NUM (*num* [,*num*]...)	Oracle9*i*	SQL statements only

Converts a bit vector into its equivalent number. The argument to BIN_TO_ NUM is a list of comma-separated *num*s, each of which must be 0 or 1 only. For example, BIN_TO_NUM(1,0,1,1) returns 11 because the binary representation of 11 is 1011. BIN_TO_NUM is useful when using grouping sets and the GROUP BY clause.

CHARTOROWID(*string*)	Oracle7	Procedural and SQL statements

Converts a CHAR or VARCHAR2 value containing the external format of a ROWID into the internal binary format. The argument *string* must be a character string containing the external format of a ROWID, as described in Chapter 2. CHARTOROWID is the inverse of ROWIDTOCHAR.

COMPOSE(*string*)	Oracle9*i*	SQL statements only

Returns *string* (which can be in any character set) in its fully normalized Unicode form in the same character set. See the Oracle documentation for more details on Unicode and normalized form. *string* can be CHAR, VARCHAR2, NCHAR, NVARCHAR2, CLOB, or NCLOB.

DECOMPOSE(*string*)	Oracle9*i*	SQL statements only

Returns a Unicode string which is the canonical decomposition of *string* (which can be in any character set). See the Oracle documentation for more details on Unicode and canonical decomposition. *string* can be CHAR, VARCHAR2, NCHAR, NVARCHAR2, CLOB, or NCLOB.

FROM_TZ(*timestamp, timezone*)	Oracle9*i*	Procedural and SQL statements

Returns a TIMESTAMP WITH TIMEZONE value, which is the combination of *timestamp*, which does not have time zone information, and the supplied *timezone*.

HEXTORAW(*string*)	Oracle7	Procedural and SQL statements

Converts the binary value represented by *string* to a RAW value. *string* should contain hexadecimal values. Every two characters in *string* represent 1 byte of the resultant RAW. HEXTORAW and RAWTOHEX are inverse functions.

Function	Version Available	Where Allowed
NUMTODSINTERVAL(*x*, *unit*)	Oracle9*i*	Procedural and SQL statements

Converts *x*, which should be a number, into an INTERVAL DAY TO SECOND value. *unit* is a character string (of CHAR, VARCHAR2, NCHAR, or NVARCHAR2 type), and must be one of 'DAY', 'HOUR', 'MINUTE', or 'SECOND'. *unit* is not case sensitive, and the default precision of the return value is 9.

Function	Version Available	Where Allowed
NUMTOYMINTERVAL (*x*, *unit*)	Oracle9*i*	Procedural and SQL statements

Converts *x*, which should be a number, into an INTERVAL YEAR TO MONTH value. *unit* is a character string (of CHAR, VARCHAR2, NCHAR, or NVARCHAR2 type), and must be one of 'YEAR' or 'MONTH'. *unit* is not case sensitive, and the default precision of the return value is 9.

Function	Version Available	Where Allowed
REFTOHEX(*refvalue*)	Oracle9*i*	Procedural and SQL statements

Returns a hexadecimal representation of the REF *refvalue*.

Function	Version Available	Where Allowed
RAWTOHEX(*rawvalue*)	Oracle7	Procedural and SQL statements

Converts the RAW *rawvalue* to a character string containing the hexadecimal representation. Each byte of *rawvalue* is converted into a two-character string. RAWTOHEX and HEXTORAW are inverse functions.

Function	Version Available	Where Allowed
RAWTONHEX(*rawvalue*)	Oracle9*i*	Procedural and SQL statements

Converts the RAW *rawvalue* to a character string containing the hexadecimal representation. Each byte of *rawvalue* is converted into a two-character string. RAWTONHEX behaves similar to RAWTOHEX, except that the return type is NVARCHAR2 rather than VARCHAR2.

Function	Version Available	Where Allowed
ROWIDTOCHAR(*rowid*)	Oracle7	Procedural and SQL statements

Converts the ROWID value *rowid* to its external character string representation (which can be different forms, depending on the original *rowid* value). ROWIDTOCHAR and CHARTOROWID are inverse functions.

Function	Version Available	Where Allowed
ROWIDTONCHAR(*rowid*)	Oracle9*i*	Procedural and SQL statements

Converts the ROWID value *rowid* to its external character string representation (which can be different forms, depending on the original *rowid* value). The return type is NCHAR, rather than CHAR.

Function	Version Available	Where Allowed
TO_CHAR	Oracle7	Procedural and SQL statements

Converts its arguments to a character type. See the following sections for details.

Function	Version Available	Where Allowed
TO_CLOB(*string*)	Oracle9*i*	Procedural and SQL statement

Converts *string* to a CLOB. *string* can be a literal, or can be another LOB column. If the argument contains NCHAR data, it is converted into the database character set.

Function	Version Available	Where Allowed
TO_DATE	Oracle7	Procedural and SQL statements

Converts its arguments to a date type. See the following sections for details.

Function	Version Available	Where Allowed
TO_DSINTERVAL(*string* [,*nlsparams*])	Oracle9*i*	Procedural and SQL statements

Converts *string* (which can be CHAR, VARCHAR2, NCHAR, or NVARCHAR2) to an INTERVAL DAY TO SECOND type. If present, *nlsparams* can contain only the NLS_NUMERIC_CHARARCTERS specification of the decimal and group characters.

Function	Version Available	Where Allowed
TO_LOB(*long_column*)	Oracle8*i*	SELECT statements only

Converts *long_column* into a LOB. This function is used to convert LONG or LONG RAW data to CLOB or BLOB, respectively.

Function	Version Available	Where Allowed
TO_MULTI_BYTE(*string*)	Oracle7	Procedural and SQL statements

Returns *string* with all single-byte characters replaced by their equivalent multibyte characters. This function is only relevant if the database character set contains both single-byte and multibyte characters. If not, *string* is returned without change. TO_MULTI_BYTE and TO_SINGLE_BYTE are inverse functions.

Function	Version Available	Where Allowed
TO_NCHAR	Oracle9*i*	Procedural and SQL statements

TO_NCHAR behaves the same as TO_CHAR, except that the result is in the national character set rather than the database character set. See the following sections for more information on TO_CHAR.

Function	Version Available	Where Allowed
TO_NCLOB(*string*)	Oracle9*i*	Procedural and SQL statements

Converts *string* to a NCLOB. *string* can be a literal, or can be another LOB column. Data in *string* is converted into the database national character set if necessary.

TO_NUMBER	Oracle7	Procedural and SQL statements

Converts its argument to a number type. See the following sections for details.

TO_SINGLE_BYTE(*string*)	Oracle7	Procedural and SQL statements

Converts all multibyte characters found in *string* to their equivalent single-byte characters. This function is only relevant if the database character set contains both single-byte and multibyte characters. If not, *string* is returned unchanged. TO_SINGLE_BYTE and TO_MULTI_BYTE are inverse functions.

TO_TIMESTAMP	Oracle9*i*	Procedural and SQL statements

Converts its argument to a TIMESTAMP type. See the following sections for details.

TO_TIMESTAMP_TZ	Oracle9*i*	Procedural and SQL statements

Converts its argument to a TIMESTAMP with TIMEZONE type. See the following sections for details.

TO_YMINTERVAL(*string*)	Oracle9*i*	Procedural and SQL statements

Converts *string* (which can be CHAR, VARCHAR2, NCHAR, or NVARCHAR2) to an INTERVAL YEAR TO MONTH type. TO_YMINTERVAL is similar to TO_DSINTERVAL, except that it does not take NLS parameters as an argument and converts to a YEAR TO MONTH interval instead of a DAY TO SECOND interval.

TO_CHAR (Dates and Datetimes)

Syntax
TO_CHAR(*d* [,*format* [,*nlsparams*]])

Purpose   Converts the date or timestamp *d* to a VARCHAR2 character string. If *format* is specified, it is used to control how the result is structured. A format string is made up of *format elements*. Each element returns a portion of the date or timestamp value, such as the month. The date format elements that are valid in TO_CHAR are described in Table 5-4. If *format* is not specified, the default date, timestamp, or timestamp with time zone format for your session is used. If *nlsparams* is specified, it controls the language for the month and day components of the returned string. The format of *nlsparams* is

'NLS_DATE_LANGUAGE = *language*'

where *language* represents the desired language. For more information on TO_ CHAR and date format elements, see the *Server SQL Reference*.

Example

```
SELECT TO_CHAR(SYSDATE, 'DD-MON-YY HH24:MI:SS') "Right Now"
  FROM dual;
Right Now
-----------------
10-AUG-01 15:44:54
```

Date Format Element	Description
Punctuation	All punctuation symbols are reproduced in the result string.
"text"	Text contained in double quotes is likewise reproduced.
AD, A.D.	AD indicator, with or without periods.
AM, A.M.	Ante meridiem indicator, with or without periods.
BC, B.C.	BC indicator, with or without periods.
CC, SCC	Century. SCC returns BC dates as negative values.
D	Day of week (1–7).
DAY[1]	Name of day, padded with blanks to length of nine characters.
DD	Day of month (1–31).
DDD	Day of year (1–366).
DY[1]	Abbreviated name of day.

TABLE 5-4. *Valid Date and Datetime Format Elements*

Date Format Element	Description
E[2]	Abbreviated era name (Japanese Imperial, ROC Official, and Thai Buddha calendars only).
EE[2]	Full era name (Japanese Imperial, ROC Official, and Thai Buddha calendars only).
FF[2]	Fractional seconds, with no radix.
HH, HH12	Hour of day (1–12).
HH24	Hour of day (0–23).
IW	Week of year (1–52, 1–53) based on the ISO standard.
IYY, IY, I	Last three, two, or one digits of the ISO year.
IYYY	Four-digit year based on the ISO standard.
J	Julian day. The number of days since January 1, 4712 BC. The corresponding output will be an integer value.
MI	Minute (0–59).
MM	Month (1–12). JAN = 1, DEC = 12.
MON[1]	Abbreviated name of month.
MONTH[1]	Name of month, padded with blanks to nine characters.
PM, P.M.	Post meridiem indicator, with and without periods.
Q	Quarter of year (1–4). JAN-MAR = 1.
RM	Roman numeral month (I–XII). JAN = I, DEC = XII.
RR	Last two digits of year for years in other centuries.
RRRR	Round year, similar to RR except takes four digits as well as two.
SS	Second (0–59).
SSSSS	Seconds past midnight (0–86399). The format model 'J.SSSSS' will always yield a numeric value.
TZD[2]	Daylight savings information
TZH[2]	Time zone hour

TABLE 5-4.   *Valid Date and Datetime Format Elements* (continued)

Date Format Element	Description
TZM[2]	Time zone minute
TZR[2]	Time zone region (such as 'US/Pacific')
WW	Week of year (1–53). Week 1 starts on the first day of the year and continues to the seventh day. Thus, the weeks do not necessarily start on Sunday.
W	Week of month (1–5). Weeks are defined as they are for the WW element.
X[2]	Local radix character
Y, YYY	Year with comma in this position.
YEAR, SYEAR[1]	Year spelled out. SYEAR returns BC dates as negative.
YYYY, SYYYY	Four-digit year. SYYYY returns BC dates as negative.
YYY, YY, Y	Last three, two, or one digit(s) of year.

[1]These elements are case sensitive. For example, 'MON' will return 'JAN', and 'Mon' will return 'Jan.'

[2]These elements are new in Oracle9*i*.

TABLE 5-4.   *Valid Date and Datetime Format Elements* (continued)

TO_CHAR (numbers)

Syntax
TO_CHAR(*num* [,*format* [,*nlsparams*]])

Purpose   Converts the NUMBER argument *num* to a VARCHAR2. If specified, *format* governs the conversion. Available number formats are described in Table 5-5. If *format* is not specified, the resultant string will have exactly as many characters as necessary to hold the significant digits of *num*. *nlsparams* is used to specify the decimal and group separator, along with the currency symbol. It can have the format

'NLS_NUMERIC_CHARS = ''*dg*'' NLS_CURRENCY = ''*string*''

where *d* and *g* represent the decimal and group separators, respectively. *string* represents the currency symbol. For example, in the United States the decimal separator is typically a period (.), the group separator is a comma (,), and the currency symbol is a dollar ($). See *Oracle Globalization* for complete details on National Language Support (which is known as Globalization in Oracle9*i*).

Example

```
SELECT TO_CHAR(123456, '99G99G99') "Result"
  FROM dual;
Result
---------
 12,34,56

SELECT TO_CHAR(123456, 'L99G99D99',
             'NLS_NUMERIC_CHARACTERS = '',.''
              NLS_CURRENCY = ''Money'' ') "Result 2"
  FROM dual;
Result 2
-------------
Money12,34.56
```

Format Element	Sample Format String	Description
$	$999	Returns value with a leading dollar sign, regardless of the currency symbol. This can be used in addition to leading or trailing zeros.
B	B999	Returns blanks for the integer part of a decimal number when the integer part is zero.
MI	999MI	Returns a negative value with a trailing minus sign rather than a leading minus. A positive value will have a trailing blank.
S	S9999	Returns a leading sign: + for positive numbers, – for negative numbers.
S	9999S	Returns a trailing sign: + for positive numbers, – for negative numbers.
PR	99PR	Returns a negative value in <angle brackets>. A positive value will have a leading and trailing blank.

TABLE 5-5. *Number Format Elements*

Format Element	Sample Format String	Description
D	99D9	Returns a decimal point separator in the specified position. The number of 9s on either side specifies the maximum number of digits.
G	9G999	Returns a group separator in the position specified. G can appear more than once in the format string.
C	C99	Returns the ISO currency symbol in the specified position. C can also appear more than once in the format string.
L	L999	Returns the local currency symbol in the specified position.
,	999,999	Returns a comma in the specified position, regardless of the group separator.
.	99.99	Returns a decimal point in the specified position, regardless of the decimal separator.
V	99V999	Returns a value multiplied by 10^n, where n is the number of 9s after the V. The value is rounded if necessary.
EEEE	9.99EEEE	Returns the value using scientific notation.
RM	RM	Returns the value using uppercase Roman numerals.
rm	rm	Returns the value using lowercase Roman numerals.
FM	FM90.99	Returns a value with no leading or trailing blanks.
0	0999	Returns leading zeros rather than blanks.
0	9990	Returns trailing zeros rather than blanks.
9	99	Each 9 represents a significant digit in the result. The return value has the number of significant digits equal to the number of 9s, with a leading minus if negative. Any leading zeros are left blank.

TABLE 5-5. *Number Format Elements* (continued)

TO_DATE

Syntax

TO_DATE(*string* [,*format* [,*nlsparams*]])

Purpose   Converts the CHAR or VARCHAR2 *string* into a DATE. *format* is a date format string, as described in Table 5-4. If *format* is not specified, the default date format for the session is used. *nlsparams* is used the same way for TO_DATE as it is for TO_CHAR. TO_DATE and TO_CHAR are inverse functions.

Example

```
DECLARE
  v_CurrentDate  DATE;
BEGIN
  v_CurrentDate := TO_DATE('January 7, 1973', 'Month DD, YYYY');
END;
```

TO_NUMBER

Syntax

TO_NUMBER(*string* [,*format* [,*nlsparams*]])

Purpose   Converts the CHAR or VARCHAR2 *string* to a NUMBER value. If *format* is specified, *string* should correspond to the number format. *nlsparams* behaves the same as it does for TO_CHAR. TO_NUMBER and TO_CHAR are inverse functions.

Example

```
DECLARE
  v_Num  NUMBER;
BEGIN
  v_Num := TO_NUMBER('$12345.67', '$99999.99');
END;
```

Oracle**9i** and higher # TO_TIMESTAMP and TO_TIMESTAMP_TZ

Syntax

TO_TIMESTAMP(*string* [,*format* [,*nlsparams*]])
TO_TIMESTAMP_TZ(*string* [,*format* [,*nlsparams*]])

Purpose   Converts the CHAR or VARCHAR2 *string* into a TIMESTAMP or TIMESTAMP WITH TIMEZONE. *format* is a date format string, as described in Table 5-4. If *format* is not specified, the default date format for the session is used. *nlsparams* is used the same way for TO_TIMESTAMP and TO_TIMESTAMP_TZ as it is for TO_CHAR.

Where Allowed   Procedural and SQL statements

Example

```
DECLARE
  v_CurrentDate   TIMESTAMP;
BEGIN
  v_CurrentDate := TO_TIMESTAMP('January 7, 1973', 'Month DD, YYYY');
END;
```

Aggregate and Analytic Functions

Aggregate functions return a single result based on many rows—as opposed to single-row functions, which return one result for each row. For example, the COUNT function returns the number of rows meeting the criteria specified by the WHERE clause of a SELECT statement. These functions are valid in the select list of a query and the GROUP BY or HAVING clause only.

Most of these functions can accept qualifiers on their arguments. These qualifiers are DISTINCT and ALL. If the DISTINCT qualifier is passed, only distinct values returned by the query are considered. The ALL qualifier causes the function to consider all of the values returned by the query. If none is specified, ALL is the default.

Oracle**9i** and higher

Oracle9*i* introduces the OVER clause, which is valid after any of the functions listed in this section. When the OVER clause is used, the function is known as an analytic function instead of an aggregate. Analytic functions can return multiple rows for each group, rather than the single value of aggregate functions. The OVER clause specifies a sliding window within the group. For more information, see the *SQL Reference*.

These functions are described in the following table:

Function	Version Available
AVG([DISTINCT | ALL] *col*)	Oracle7
Returns the average of the column values.	

Function	Version Available
CORR(*x1, x2*)	Oracle9*i*

Returns the coefficient of correlation of the set of pairs made up of the numeric expressions *x1* and *x2*. After elimination of any rows with a NULL *x1* or *x2*, the result is determined by COVAR_POP(*x1, x2*) / (STDDEV_POP(*x1*) * STDDEV_POP(*x2*)).

COUNT(* | [DISTINCT | ALL] *col*)	Oracle7

Returns the number of rows in the query. If * is passed, the total number of rows is returned. If a select list item is passed instead, the non-NULL values are counted.

COVAR_POP(*x1, x2*)	Oracle9*i*

Returns the population covariance of the set of pairs made up of the numeric expressions *x1* and *x2*. The result is determined by (SUM(*x1* * *x2*) – SUM(*x2*) * SUM(*x1*) / *n*) / *n*, where *n* is the number of pairs with non-NULL entries.

COVAR_SAMP(*x1, x2*)	Oracle9*i*

Returns the same covariance of the set of pairs made up of the numeric expressions *x1* and *x2*. After elimination of any rows with a NULL *x1* or *x2*, the result is determined by (SUM(*x1* * *x2*) – SUM(*x1*) * SUM(*x2*) / *n*) / (*n* – 1) where *n* is the number of pairs with non-NULL entries.

CUME_DIST	Oracle9*i*

Returns the cumulative distribution of a value within a group of values. See the *SQL Reference* for more details.

DENSE_RANK	Oracle9*i*

Returns the rank of a row within an ordered group of rows, where the ranks are consecutive integers beginning with 1. See the *SQL Reference* for more details.

GROUP_ID()	Oracle9*i*

Returns a unique number value used to distinguish groups in a GROUP BY clause.

GROUPING	Oracle9*i*

Distinguishes superaggregrate rows from regular grouped rows. See the *SQL Reference* for more details.

GROUPING_ID	Oracle9*i*

Returns a number corresponding to the GROUPING bit vector for a row. See the *SQL Reference* for more details.

Function	Version Available
MAX([DISTINCT | ALL] *col*)	Oracle7

Returns the maximum value of the select list item. Note that DISTINCT and ALL have no effect, since the maximum value would be the same in either case.

MIN([DISTINCT | ALL] *col*)	Oracle7

Returns the minimum value of the select list item. Note that DISTINCT and ALL have no effect, since the minimum value would be the same in either case.

PERCENTILE_CONT	Oracle9*i*

This function is an inverse distribution function that assumes a continuous distribution model. See the *SQL Reference* for more details.

PERCENTILE_DISC	Oracle9*i*

This function is an inverse distribution function that assumes a discrete distribution model. See the *SQL Reference* for more details.

PERCENT_RANK	Oracle9*i*

Returns the rank of a given row as a value between 0 and 1. See the *SQL Reference* for more details.

RANK	Oracle9*i*

Returns the rank of a given row. Ranks need not be consecutive, as equal rows receive the same rank. See the *SQL Reference* for more details.

REGR functions	Oracle9*i*

These functions (REGR_SLOPE, REGR_INTERCEPT, REGR_COUNT, REGR_R2, REGR_AVGX, REGR_AVGY, REGR_SXX, REGR_SYY, and REGR_SXY) fit an ordinary least-squares regression line to the set of pairs. See the *SQL Reference* for more details.

STDDEV([DISTINCT | ALL] *col*)	Oracle7

Returns the standard deviation of the select list item. This is defined as the square root of the variance.

STDDEV_POP(*col*)	Oracle9*i*

Computes the population standard deviation and returns the square root of the population variance.

STDDEV_SAMP(*col*)	Oracle9*i*

Computes the cumulative standard deviation and returns the square root of the sample variance.

Function	Version Available
SUM([DISTINCT | ALL] *col*)	Oracle7

Returns the sum of the values for the select list item.

VAR_POP(*x*)	Oracle9*i*

Returns the population variance of a set of numbers after discarding the NULL values. The result is determined by $(SUM(x^2) - SUM(x)^2 / COUNT(x)) / COUNT(x)$

VAR_SAMP(*x*)	Oracle9*i*

Returns the sample variance of a set of numbers after discarding the NULL values. The result is determined by $(SUM(x^2) - SUM(x)^2 / COUNT(x)) / (COUNT(x) - 1)$

VARIANCE([DISTINCT | ALL] *col*)	Oracle7

Returns the variance of *col*.

Other Functions

This section lists the remaining functions that do not fit in the previous categories.

Function	Version Available	Where Allowed
BFILENAME(*directory, file_name*)	Oracle8	Procedural and SQL statements

Returns the BFILE locator associated with the physical file *file_name* on the operating system. *directory* must be a DIRECTORY object in the data dictionary.

COALESCE(*expr1, ..., [exprn]*)	Oracle9*i*	Procedural and SQL statements

Returns the first non-NULL *expr* in the argument list. If all expressions are NULL, COALESCE returns NULL. This is a generalization of the NVL function.

Function	Version Available	Where Allowed
DECODE(*base_expr*, *compare1, value1, compare2, value2, ... default*)	Oracle7	SQL statements only

The DECODE function is similar to a series of nested IF-THEN-ELSE statements. The *base_expr* is compared to each of *compare1, compare2*, and so forth in sequence. If *base_expr* matches the *i*th *compare* item, the *i*th *value* is returned. If *base_expr* doesn't match any of the *compare* values, *default* is returned.

Each *compare* value is evaluated in turn. If a match is found, the remaining *compare* values, if any, are not evaluated. A NULL *base_expr* is considered equivalent to a NULL *compare* value. Each *compare* value is converted to the datatype of the first *compare* value, if necessary. This datatype is also the type of the returned value.

DUMP	Oracle7	SQL statements only

See the following sections for details.

EMPTY_BLOB/EMPTY_CLOB	Oracle8	Procedural and SQL statements

Returns an empty LOB locator. EMPTY_CLOB returns a character locator, and EMPTY_BLOB returns a binary locator.

EXISTSNODE(*XMLType_instance*, *Xpath_string*)	Oracle9*i*	SQL statements only

Determines whether traversal of the XML document identified by *XMLType_instance* using the path in *Xpath_string* returns any nodes. Returns a NUMBER value, which is 0 if there are no nodes, and > 0 if there are. See the Oracle documentation for more information on using XML types.

Function	Version Available	Where Allowed
EXTRACT(*XMLType_instance, Xpath_string*)	Oracle9*i*	SQL statements only

Returns the portion of the XML document identified by *XMLType_instance* after applying *Xpath_string*. See the Oracle documentation for more information on using XML types.

Function	Version Available	Where Allowed
GREATEST(*expr1* [,*expr2*] ...)	Oracle7	Procedural and SQL statements

Returns the greatest expression of its arguments. Each expression is implicitly converted to the type of *expr1* before the comparisons are made. If *expr1* is a character type, non-blank-padded character comparisons are used, and the result has datatype VARCHAR2.

Function	Version Available	Where Allowed
LEAST(*expr1* [,*expr2*] ...)	Oracle7	Procedural and SQL statements

Returns the least value in the list of expressions. LEAST behaves similarly to GREATEST, in that all expressions are implicitly converted to the datatype of the first. All character comparisons are done with non-blank-padded character comparison semantics.

Function	Version Available	Where Allowed
NULLIF (*a*, *b*)	Oracle9*i*	SQL statements only

Returns NULL if *a* is equal to *b*, and *a* if they are not equal.

Function	Version Available	Where Allowed
NVL(*expr1, expr2*)	Oracle7	Procedural and SQL statements

If *expr1* is NULL, returns *expr2*; otherwise, returns *expr1*. The return value has the same datatype as *expr1* unless *expr1* is a character string, in which case the return value has datatype VARCHAR2. This function is useful to ensure that the active set of a query contains no NULL values.

Function	Version Available	Where Allowed
NVL2(*expr1, expr2, expr3*)	Oracle9*i*	Procedural and SQL statements

If *expr1* is NULL, then returns *expr2*; otherwise, *expr3* is returned. The return value has the type of *expr2*, unless *expr2* is character data, in which case the return type is VARCHAR2.

Function	Version Available	Where Allowed
SYS_CONNECT_BY_PATH	Oracle9*i*	SELECT statements only

SYS_CONNECT_BY_PATH returns the path of a column value from root to node. It is valid only in hierarchical queries. See the *SQL Reference* for more details.

Function	Version Available	Where Allowed
SYS_CONTEXT(*namespace, parameter* [,*length*])	Oracle8*i*	Procedural and SQL statements

Returns the value of *parameter* associated with the context *namespace*. Parameters and namespaces are set with the DBMS_SESSION.SET_CONTEXT procedure. The return value is VARCHAR2 with a maximum length of 256 bytes, unless the *length* parameter is specified, which is the maximum length if so.

SYS_DBURIGEN	Oracle9*i*	SQL statements only

Generates a URL for retrieving an XML document from the database. See the Oracle documentation for more information on using XML types.

SYS_GUID	Oracle8*i*	Procedural and SQL statements

Returns a globally unique identifier as a 16-byte RAW value.

SYS_TYPEID(*object_type*)	Oracle9*i*	Procedural and SQL statements

Returns the type ID of the most specific type of *object_type*.

SYS_XMLAGG	Oracle9*i*	Procedural and SQL statements

Aggregates several XML documents or document fragments together into one document. See the Oracle documentation for more information on using XML types.

SYS_XMLGEN	Oracle9*i*	Procedural and SQL statements

Returns an XML document fragment based on data in the database. See the Oracle documentation for more information on using XML types.

TREAT(*expr* AS [REF] [*schema.*]*type*)	Oracle9*i*	SQL statements only

TREAT is used to change the declared type of an expression. You can only change the declared type to a subtype or supertype of the given expression. Returns *expr* as if it were of the type *schema.type*, or a REF to it, if specified.

UID	Oracle7	Procedural and SQL statements

Returns an integer that uniquely identifies the current database user. UID takes no arguments.

Function	Version Available	Where Allowed
USER	Oracle7	Procedural and SQL statements

Returns a VARCHAR2 value containing the name of the current Oracle user. USER takes no arguments.

USERENV	Oracle7	Procedural and SQL statements

See the following sections for details.

VSIZE(*x*)	Oracle9*i*	Procedural and SQL statements

Returns the number of bytes in the internal representation of *x*.

DUMP

Syntax
DUMP(*expr* [,*number_format* [,*start_position*] [,*length*]]])

Purpose   Returns a VARCHAR2 value that contains information about the internal representation of *expr*. *number_format* specifies the base of the values returned according to the following table:

number_format	Result Returned In
8	Octal notation
10	Decimal notation
16	Hexadecimal notation
17	Single characters

If *number_format* is not specified, the result is returned in decimal notation. If *start_position* and *length* are specified, *length* bytes starting at *start_position* are returned. The default is to return the entire representation. The datatype is returned as a number corresponding to internal datatypes according to the following table:

Code	Datatype	Available In
1	VARCHAR2	Oracle7
2	NUMBER	Oracle7

Code	Datatype	Available In
8	LONG	Oracle7
12	DATE	Oracle7
23	RAW	Oracle7
24	LONG RAW	Oracle7
69	ROWID	Oracle7
96	CHAR	Oracle7
112	CLOB	Oracle8
113	BLOB	Oracle8
114	BFILE	Oracle8
180	TIMESTAMP	Oracle9*i*
181	TIMESTAMP WITH TIMEZONE	Oracle9*i*
182	INTERVAL YEAR TO MONTH	Oracle9*i*
183	INTERVAL DAY TO SECOND	Oracle9*i*
208	UROWID	Oracle8*i*
231	TIMESTAMP WITH LOCAL TIMEZONE	Oracle9*i*

Example

```
SELECT first_name, DUMP(first_name) "Dump"
   FROM students
FIRST_NAME          Dump
------------------- -------------------------------------------
Scott               Typ=1 Len=5: 83,99,111,116,116
Margaret            Typ=1 Len=8: 77,97,114,103,97,114,101,116
Joanne              Typ=1 Len=6: 74,111,97,110,110,101
Manish              Typ=1 Len=6: 77,97,110,105,115,104
Patrick             Typ=1 Len=7: 80,97,116,114,105,99,107
Timothy             Typ=1 Len=7: 84,105,109,111,116,104,121

SELECT first_name, DUMP(first_name, 17) "Dump"
   FROM students
FIRST_NAME          Dump
------------------- -------------------------------------------
Scott               Typ=1 Len=5: S,c,o,t,t
Margaret            Typ=1 Len=8: M,a,r,g,a,r,e,t
Joanne              Typ=1 Len=6: J,o,a,n,n,e
```

```
Manish                  Typ=1 Len=6: M,a,n,i,s,h
Patrick                 Typ=1 Len=7: P,a,t,r,i,c,k
Timothy                 Typ=1 Len=7: T,i,m,o,t,h,y

SELECT first_name, DUMP(first_name, 17, 2, 4) "Dump"
  FROM students;
FIRST_NAME              Dump
------------------- -----------------------------------
Scott                   Typ=1 Len=5: c,o,t,t
Margaret                Typ=1 Len=8: a,r,g,a
Joanne                  Typ=1 Len=6: o,a,n,n
Manish                  Typ=1 Len=6: a,n,i,s
Patrick                 Typ=1 Len=7: a,t,r,i
```

USERENV

Syntax

USERENV(*option*)

Purpose   Returns a VARCHAR2 value containing information about the current session, based on *option*. The behavior is described according to the following table:

Value of option	Behavior of USERENV(Option)
'OSDBA'	If the current session has the OSDBA role enabled, returns 'TRUE'; otherwise, returns 'FALSE'. Note that the return value is VARCHAR2, not BOOLEAN.
'LABEL'	Valid in Trusted Oracle only. Returns the current session label. For more information, see the *Trusted Oracle7 Server Administrator's Guide*.
'LANGUAGE'	Returns the language and territory currently used by your session, along with the database character set. These are NLS parameters. The returned value has the form *language_territory.characterset*.
'TERMINAL'	Returns an operating system-dependent identifier for the current session's terminal. For distributed SQL statements, the identifier for the local session is returned.
'SESSIONID'	Returns the auditing session identifier, if the initialization parameter AUDIT_TRAIL is set to TRUE. USERENV ('SESSIONID') is not valid in distributed SQL statements.

Value of option	Behavior of USERENV(Option)
'ENTRYID'	Returns the available auditing entry identifier, if the initialization parameter AUDIT_TRAIL is set to TRUE. USERENV('ENTRYID') is not valid in distributed SQL statements.
'LANG'*	Returns the ISO abbreviation for the language name. This is a shorter format than USERENV('LANGUAGE').

*USERENV('LANG') is valid in Oracle8 and higher.

Example

```
SELECT USERENV('TERMINAL'), USERENV('LANGUAGE')
  FROM dual;
USERENV( USERENV('LANGUAGE')
-------- --------------------------------------------
Windows  AMERICAN_AMERICA.WE8ISO8859P1
```

Summary

In this chapter, we have discussed the different types of built-in functions in detail, including where each type is appropriate. In the next chapter, we will discuss cursors, which are used for multirow queries. Cursors will build on the concepts that we have examined so far.

CHAPTER

6

Cursors

n Chapters 4 and 5, we discussed how SQL statements can be used in PL/SQL. This functionality is enhanced through the use of cursors, which allow a program to take explicit control of SQL statement processing. In this chapter, we will see how cursors are used for multirow queries and other SQL statements. We will also discuss cursor variables, which allow more dynamic use of cursors.

What Is a Cursor?

In order to process a SQL statement, Oracle will allocate an area of memory known as the *context area*. The context area contains information necessary to complete the processing, including the number of rows processed by the statement, a pointer to the parsed representation of the statement, and in the case of a query, the *active set*, which is the set of rows returned by the query.

A *cursor* is a handle, or pointer, to the context area. Through the cursor, a PL/SQL program can control the context area and what happens to it as the statement is processed. The following PL/SQL block illustrates a cursor fetch loop, in which multiple rows of data are returned from a query:

```
-- Available online as CursorLoop.sql
DECLARE
  /* Output variables to hold the results of the query */
  v_StudentID    students.id%TYPE;
  v_FirstName    students.first_name%TYPE;
  v_LastName     students.last_name%TYPE;

  /* Bind variable used in the query */
  v_Major        students.major%TYPE := 'Computer Science';

  /* Cursor declaration */
  CURSOR c_Students IS
    SELECT id, first_name, last_name
      FROM students
      WHERE major = v_Major;
BEGIN
  /* Identify the rows in the active set, and prepare for further
     processing of the data */
  OPEN c_Students;
  LOOP
    /* Retrieve each row of the active set into PL/SQL variables */
    FETCH c_Students INTO v_StudentID, v_FirstName, v_LastName;

    /* If there are no more rows to fetch, exit the loop */
    EXIT WHEN c_Students%NOTFOUND;
```

```
  END LOOP;

  /* Free resources used by the query */
  CLOSE c_Students;
END;
```

This example illustrates an *explicit* cursor, in which the cursor name is explicitly assigned to a SELECT statement via the CURSOR...IS statement. An *implicit* cursor is used for all other SQL statements. Processing an explicit cursor involves four steps, which are described in the next section. Processing an implicit cursor, on the other hand, is taken care of automatically by PL/SQL.

Processing Explicit Cursors

The four PL/SQL steps necessary for explicit cursor processing are as follows:

1. Declare the cursor.

2. Open the cursor for a query.

3. Fetch the results into PL/SQL variables.

4. Close the cursor.

The cursor declaration is the only step that can go in the declarative section of a block—the other three steps are found in the executable or exception sections.

Declaring a Cursor

Declaring a cursor defines the name of the cursor and associates it with a SELECT statement. The syntax is

CURSOR *cursor_name* IS *select_statement*;

where *cursor_name* is the name of the cursor, and *select_statement* is the query to be processed by this cursor. Cursor names follow the usual scope and visibility rules for PL/SQL identifiers, as described in Chapter 3. Because a cursor name is a PL/SQL identifier, it must be declared before it is referenced. Any SELECT statements are legal, including joins and statements with the UNION or MINUS clause.

NOTE
select_statement *contains no INTO clause. When using explicit cursors, the INTO clause is part of the FETCH statement.*

A cursor declaration can reference PL/SQL variables as well. These variables are considered bind variables. The usual scoping rules apply, so these variables must be visible at the point of the cursor declaration. For example, the following declarative section is legal:

```
DECLARE
  v_Department    classes.department%TYPE;
  v_Course        classes.course%TYPE;
  CURSOR c_Classes IS
    SELECT * from classes
      WHERE department = v_Department
      AND course = v_Course;
```

The next declarative section is illegal, because v_Department and v_Course are not declared before they are referenced:

```
DECLARE
  CURSOR c_Classes IS
    SELECT * from classes
      WHERE department = v_Department
      AND course = v_Course;
  v_Department    classes.department%TYPE;
  v_Course        classes.course%TYPE;
```

To ensure that all variables referenced in a cursor declaration are declared before the reference, you can declare all cursors at the end of a declarative section. This is the convention used in this book. The only exception to this is when the cursor name itself is used in a reference, such as the %ROWTYPE attribute (which creates a record with fields corresponding to the select list of the cursor). In this case, the cursor must be declared before a reference to it.

Opening a Cursor

The syntax for opening a cursor is

OPEN *cursor_name*;

where *cursor_name* identifies a cursor that has previously been declared. When a cursor is opened, the following things happen:

- The values of the bind variables are examined.

- Based on the values of the bind variables and the contents of the table(s) referenced in the query, the active set is determined.

- The active set pointer is set to the first row.

Bind variables are examined at cursor open time, and only at cursor open time. For example, consider the following PL/SQL block:

```
DECLARE
    v_RoomID        classes.room_id%TYPE;
    v_Building      rooms.building%TYPE;
    v_Department    classes.department%TYPE;
    v_Course        classes.course%TYPE;
    CURSOR c_Buildings IS
      SELECT building
        from rooms, classes
        where rooms.room_id = classes.room_id
        and department = v_Department
        and course = v_Course;
BEGIN
    -- Assign to bind variables before the cursor OPEN.
    v_Department := 'HIS';
    v_Course := 101;

    -- Open the cursor.
    OPEN c_Buildings;

    -- Reassign the bind variables - this has no effect,
    -- since the cursor is already open.
    v_Department := 'XXX';
    v_Course := -1;
END;
```

When c_Buildings is opened, v_Department and v_Course contain 'HIS' and 101, respectively. These are the values used in the query. Even though v_Department and v_Course are changed after the OPEN, the active set of the query does not change. In order for the new values to be examined, the cursor would have to be closed and reopened. In accordance with the transaction model (which we discussed in Chapter 4), the query will see changes made to the database that have been committed prior to the OPEN statement, and changes made to the database by the current transaction. If another session has made data changes, but has not yet committed them, those changes will not be visible.

The active set, or the set of rows that match the query, is determined at cursor open time. The previous query, for example, returns one row ('Building Seven'). The WHERE clause is evaluated against the table or tables referenced in the FROM clause of the query, and any rows for which the condition evaluates to TRUE are added to the active set. A pointer into the set is also established at cursor open time. This pointer indicates which row is to be fetched next by the cursor.

Once a cursor has been opened, it cannot be reopened unless it is first closed. If OPEN is issued against an already open cursor, Oracle will raise ORA-6511, as the following example illustrates:

```
-- Available online as AlreadyOpen.sql
SQL> DECLARE
  2     v_StudentID students.ID%TYPE;
  3
  4     CURSOR c_AllStudentIDs IS
  5       SELECT ID FROM students;
  6  BEGIN
  7    OPEN c_AllStudentIDs;
  8
  9    -- Open it again.  This will raise ORA-6511.
 10    OPEN c_AllStudentIDs;
 11  END;
 12  /
DECLARE
*
ERROR at line 1:
ORA-06511: PL/SQL: cursor already open
ORA-06512: at line 5
ORA-06512: at line 10
```

Fetching from a Cursor

The INTO clause for the query is part of the FETCH statement. The FETCH statement has two forms:

FETCH *cursor_name* INTO *list_of_variables*;

and

FETCH *cursor_name* INTO *PL/SQL_record*;

where *cursor_name* identifies a previously declared and opened cursor, *list_of_variables* is a comma-separated list of previously declared PL/SQL variables, and *PL/SQL_record* is a previously declared PL/SQL record. In either case, the variable or variables in the INTO clause must be type compatible with the select list of the query. Given the preceding c_Buildings cursor declaration, the following FETCH statement is legal:

```
FETCH c_Buildings INTO v_Building;
```

The following example illustrates legal and illegal FETCH statements:

 `-- Available online as BadFetch.sql`

```
DECLARE
  v_Department   classes.department%TYPE;
  v_Course       classes.course%TYPE;
  CURSOR c_AllClasses IS
    SELECT *
      FROM classes;
  v_ClassesRecord  c_AllClasses%ROWTYPE;
BEGIN
  OPEN c_AllClasses;

  -- This is a legal FETCH statement, returning the first
  -- row into a PL/SQL record which matches the select list
  -- of the query.
  FETCH c_AllClasses INTO v_ClassesRecord;

  -- This FETCH statement is illegal, since the select list
  -- of the query returns all 7 columns in the classes table
  -- but we are only fetching into 2 variables.
  -- This will raise the error "PLS-394: wrong number of values
  -- in the INTO list of a FETCH statement".
  FETCH c_AllClasses INTO v_Department, v_Course;
END;
```

After each FETCH, the active set pointer is increased to the next row. Thus, each FETCH will return successive rows in the active set, until the entire set is returned.

The %NOTFOUND attribute, described in the "Cursor Attributes" section, is used to determine when the entire active set has been retrieved. The last FETCH will not assign values to the output variables—they will still contain their prior values.

NOTE
FETCH statements such as these will retrieve a single row at a time. In Oracle8i and higher, you can fetch more than one row at a time into a collection, using the BULK COLLECT clause. For more information, see Chapter 12.

Closing a Cursor

When all of the active set has been retrieved, the cursor should be closed. This tells PL/SQL that the program is finished with the cursor, and the resources associated with it can be freed. These resources include the storage used to hold the active set, as well as any temporary space used for determining the active set. The syntax for closing a cursor is

> CLOSE cursor_name;

where cursor_name identifies a previously opened cursor. Once a cursor is closed, it is illegal to fetch from it. Doing so will yield the Oracle error

ORA-1001: Invalid Cursor

or

ORA-1002: Fetch out of Sequence

Similarly, it is illegal to close an already closed cursor, which will also raise the ORA-1001 error.

Cursor Attributes

There are four attributes available in PL/SQL that can be applied to cursors. Cursor attributes are appended to a cursor name in a PL/SQL block, similar to %TYPE and %ROWTYPE. However, instead of returning a type, cursor attributes return a value that can be used in expressions. The attributes are %FOUND, %NOTFOUND, %ISOPEN, and %ROWCOUNT. (Oracle8i introduces a new attribute, %BULK_ ROWCOUNT, used for array fetches. See Chapter 12 for more information about array fetches, also known as bulk binds.) They are described in the following sections, each of which refers to the listing in Figure 6-1. For this example, assume that temp_table has two rows. The data for these rows is listed in the following table:

num_col	char_col
10	'Hello'
20	'There'

%FOUND　　%FOUND is a Boolean attribute. It returns TRUE if the previous FETCH returned a row and FALSE if it didn't. If %FOUND is checked while the cursor isn't open, ORA-1001 (invalid cursor) is returned. The following table uses the numbered locations in Figure 6-1 to illustrate the behavior of %FOUND:

Location	Value of c_TempData%FOUND	Explanation
1	Error: ORA-1001	c_TempData hasn't been opened yet. There is no active set associated with it.

Location	Value of c_TempData%FOUND	Explanation
2	NULL	Although c_TempData has been opened, no fetch has been done. The value of the attribute can't be determined.
3	TRUE	The prior fetch returned the first row in temp_table.
4	TRUE	The prior fetch returned the second row in temp_table.
5	FALSE	The prior fetch didn't return any data because all rows in the active set have been retrieved.
6	Error: ORA-1001	c_TempData has been closed, clearing all stored information about the active set.

```
DECLARE
  -- Cursor declaration
  CURSOR c_TempData IS
    SELECT * from temp_table;
  -- Record to store the fetched data
  v_TempRecord c_TempData%ROWTYPE;
BEGIN
  <-- location 1 >
  OPEN c_TempData;              -- Open cursor
  <-- location 2 >
  FETCH c_TempData INTO v_TempRecord;  -- Fetch first row
  <-- location 3 >
  FETCH c_TempData INTO v_TempRecord;  -- Fetch second row
  <-- location 4 >
  FETCH c_TempData INTO v_TempRecord;  -- Third fetch
  <-- location 5 >
  CLOSE c_TempData;
  <-- location 6 >
END;
```

FIGURE 6-1. *Cursor Attribute Example*

%NOTFOUND %NOTFOUND behaves opposite to %FOUND—if the prior fetch returns a row, then %NOTFOUND is FALSE. %NOTFOUND returns TRUE only if the prior fetch does not return a row. It is often used as the exit condition for a fetch loop. The following table describes the behavior of %NOTFOUND for the example in Figure 6-1.

Location	Value of `c_TempData%NOTFOUND`	Explanation
1	Error: ORA-1001	`c_TempData` hasn't been opened yet. There is no active set associated with it.
2	NULL	Although `c_TempData` has been opened, no fetch has been done. The value of the attribute can't be determined.
3	FALSE	The prior fetch returned the first row in `temp_table`.
4	FALSE	The prior fetch returned the second row in `temp_table`.
5	TRUE	The prior fetch didn't return any data because all rows in the active set have been retrieved.
6	Error: ORA-1001	`c_TempData` has been closed, clearing all stored information about the active set.

%ISOPEN This Boolean attribute is used to determine whether or not the associated cursor is open. If so, %ISOPEN returns TRUE; otherwise, it returns FALSE. This is illustrated in the following table:

Location	Value of `c_TempData%ISOPEN`	Explanation
1	FALSE	`c_TempData` hasn't been opened yet.
2	TRUE	`c_TempData` has been opened.
3	TRUE	`c_TempData` is still open.
4	TRUE	`c_TempData` is still open.
5	TRUE	`c_TempData` is still open.
6	FALSE	`c_TempData` has been closed.

%ROWCOUNT   This numeric attribute returns the number of rows fetched by the cursor so far. If referenced when its associated cursor is not open, ORA-1001 is returned. The behavior of %ROWCOUNT is described in the following table:

Location	Value of c_TempData%ROWCOUNT	Explanation
1	Error: ORA-1001	c_TempData hasn't been opened yet. There is no active set associated with it.
2	0	c_TempData has been opened, but no fetch has been done.
3	1	The first row from temp_table has been fetched.
4	2	The second row from temp_table has been fetched.
5	2	Two rows have been fetched from temp_table so far.
6	Error: ORA-1001	c_TempData has been closed, removing all information about the active set.

Cursor Attribute Comparison   Table 6-1 shows the value of all four cursor attributes as the block progresses, for comparison.

Location	c_TempData% FOUND	c_TempData% NOTFOUND	c_TempData% ISOPEN	c_TempData% ROWCOUNT
1	ORA-1001	ORA-1001	FALSE	ORA-1001
2	NULL	NULL	TRUE	0
3	TRUE	FALSE	TRUE	1
4	TRUE	FALSE	TRUE	2
5	FALSE	TRUE	TRUE	2
6	ORA-1001	ORA-1001	FALSE	ORA-1001

TABLE 6-1.   *Behavior of All Cursor Attributes*

Parameterized Cursors

There is an additional way of using bind variables in a cursor. A *parameterized* cursor takes arguments, similar to a procedure. (Procedures are discussed in more detail in Chapters 9 and 10.) Consider the c_Classes cursor, which we examined earlier in this chapter:

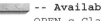

```
-- Available online as part of Parameterized.sql
DECLARE
  v_Department    classes.department%TYPE;
  v_Course        classes.course%TYPE;
  CURSOR c_Classes IS
    SELECT *
      FROM classes
       WHERE department = v_Department
       AND course = v_Course;
```

c_Classes contains two bind variables, v_Department and v_Course. We can modify c_Classes into a parameterized cursor that is equivalent, as follows:

```
-- Available online as part of Parameterized.sql
DECLARE
  CURSOR c_Classes(p_Department classes.department%TYPE,
                   p_Course classes.course%TYPE) IS
  SELECT *
    FROM classes
    WHERE department = p_Department
    AND course = p_Course;
```

With a parameterized cursor, the OPEN statement is used to pass the actual values into the cursor. We could open c_Classes with

```
-- Available online as part of Parameterized.sql
OPEN c_Classes('HIS', 101);
```

In this case, 'HIS' would be passed in for p_Department, and 101 for p_Course. Parameters can be passed using positional or named notation, as well. For more information on parameter passing in general, see Chapter 9.

Processing Implicit Cursors

Explicit cursors are used to process SELECT statements that return more than one row, as we have seen in the previous sections. However, all SQL statements are executed inside a context area and thus have a cursor that points to this context area. This cursor is known as the *SQL cursor*. Unlike explicit cursors, the SQL cursor is not opened or closed by the program. PL/SQL implicitly opens the SQL cursor, processes the SQL statement in it, and closes the cursor afterwards.

The implicit cursor is used to process INSERT, UPDATE, DELETE, and SELECT... INTO statements. Because the SQL cursor is opened and closed by the PL/SQL engine, the OPEN, FETCH, and CLOSE commands are not relevant. However, the cursor attributes can be applied to the SQL cursor. For example, the following block will perform an INSERT statement if the UPDATE statement does not match any rows:

```
-- Available online as part of NoMatch.sql
BEGIN
  UPDATE rooms
    SET number_seats = 100
    WHERE room_id = 99980;
  -- If the previous UPDATE statement didn't match any rows,
  -- insert a new row into the rooms table.
  IF SQL%NOTFOUND THEN
    INSERT INTO rooms (room_id, number_seats)
      VALUES (99980, 100);
  END IF;
END;
```

We can also accomplish the same thing by using SQL%ROWCOUNT:

```
-- Available online as part of NoMatch.sql
BEGIN
  UPDATE rooms
    SET number_seats = 100
    WHERE room_id = 99980;
  -- If the previous UPDATE statement didn't match any rows,
  -- insert a new row into the rooms table.
  IF SQL%ROWCOUNT = 0 THEN
    INSERT INTO rooms (room_id, number_seats)
      VALUES (99980, 100);
  END IF;
END;
```

Although SQL%NOTFOUND can be used with SELECT...INTO statements, it is not really useful to do so. This is because a SELECT...INTO statement will raise the Oracle error

```
ORA-1403: no data found
```

when it does not match any rows. This error causes control to pass immediately to the exception-handling section of the block, preventing the check for SQL%NOTFOUND. This is illustrated by the following SQL*Plus session:

```
-- Available online as NoDataFound.sql
SQL> DECLARE
```

```
 2     -- Record to hold room information.
 3     v_RoomData    rooms%ROWTYPE;
 4   BEGIN
 5     -- Retrieve information about room ID -1.
 6     SELECT *
 7       INTO v_RoomData
 8       FROM rooms
 9       WHERE room_id = -1;
10
11     -- The following statement will never be executed, since
12     -- control passes immediately to the exception handler.
13     IF SQL%NOTFOUND THEN
14       DBMS_OUTPUT.PUT_LINE('SQL%NOTFOUND is true!');
15     END IF;
16   EXCEPTION
17     WHEN NO_DATA_FOUND THEN
18       DBMS_OUTPUT.PUT_LINE('NO_DATA_FOUND raised!');
19   END;
20   /
NO_DATA_FOUND raised!
PL/SQL procedure successfully completed.
```

Exception handling is discussed in detail in Chapter 7. Note that it is possible to check SQL%NOT FOUND inside a NO_DATA_FOUND exception handler, but SQL%NOT FOUND will always evaluate to TRUE at this point.

SQL%ISOPEN is also valid; however, it will always evaluate to FALSE because the implicit cursor is automatically closed after the statement within it has been processed.

Cursor Fetch Loops

The most common operation with cursors is to fetch all of the rows in the active set. This is done via a *fetch loop,* which is simply a loop that processes each of the rows in the active set, one by one. The following sections examine several different kinds of cursor fetch loops and their uses.

Simple Loops

In this first style of fetch loop, the simple loop syntax (LOOP…END LOOP) is used for the cursor processing. Explicit cursor attributes are used to control how many times the loop executes. An example of this type of fetch loop is given here:

```
-- Available online as SimpleLoop.sql
DECLARE
   -- Declare variables to hold information about the students
   -- majoring in History.
```

```
    v_StudentID    students.id%TYPE;
    v_FirstName    students.first_name%TYPE;
    v_LastName     students.last_name%TYPE;

    -- Cursor to retrieve the information about History students
    CURSOR c_HistoryStudents IS
      SELECT id, first_name, last_name
        FROM students
        WHERE major = 'History';
BEGIN
  -- Open the cursor and initialize the active set
  OPEN c_HistoryStudents;
  LOOP
      -- Retrieve information for the next student
      FETCH c_HistoryStudents INTO v_StudentID, v_FirstName, v_LastName;

      -- Exit loop when there are no more rows to fetch
      EXIT WHEN c_HistoryStudents%NOTFOUND;

      -- Process the fetched rows.  In this case sign up each
      -- student for History 301 by inserting them into the
      -- registered_students table. Record the first and last
      -- names in temp_table as well.
      INSERT INTO registered_students (student_id, department, course)
        VALUES (v_StudentID, 'HIS', 301);

      INSERT INTO temp_table (num_col, char_col)
        VALUES (v_StudentID, v_FirstName || ' ' || v_LastName);

  END LOOP;

  -- Free resources used by the cursor
  CLOSE c_HistoryStudents;

END;
```

Note the placement of the EXIT WHEN statement immediately after the FETCH statement. After the last row has been retrieved, c_HistoryStudents%NOTFOUND becomes TRUE, and the loop is exited. The EXIT WHEN statement is also before the processing of the data. This is done to ensure that the processing will not handle any NULL rows.

Consider the following loop, which is very similar to the previous one, except that the EXIT WHEN statement has been moved to the end of the loop:

```
-- Available online as ExitWhen.sql
DECLARE
  -- Declare variables to hold information about the students
```

```
   -- majoring in History.
   v_StudentID    students.id%TYPE;
   v_FirstName    students.first_name%TYPE;
   v_LastName     students.last_name%TYPE;

   -- Cursor to retrieve the information about History students
   CURSOR c_HistoryStudents IS
     SELECT id, first_name, last_name
       FROM students
       WHERE major = 'History';
BEGIN
  -- Open the cursor and initialize the active set
  OPEN c_HistoryStudents;
  LOOP
     -- Retrieve information for the next student
     FETCH c_HistoryStudents INTO v_StudentID, v_FirstName, v_LastName;

     -- Process the fetched rows, in this case sign up each
     -- student for History 301 by inserting them into the
     -- registered_students table. Record the first and last
     -- names in temp_table as well.
     INSERT INTO registered_students (student_id, department, course)
       VALUES (v_StudentID, 'HIS', 301);

     INSERT INTO temp_table (num_col, char_col)
       VALUES (v_StudentID, v_FirstName || ' ' || v_LastName);

     -- Exit loop when there are no more rows to fetch
     EXIT WHEN c_HistoryStudents%NOTFOUND;

  END LOOP;

  -- Free resources used by the cursor
  CLOSE c_HistoryStudents;
END;
```

The last FETCH will not modify v_StudentID, v_FirstName, and
v_LastName because there are no more rows in the active set. The output
variables will thus still have the values for the prior FETCHed rows. Because the
check is after the processing, however, these duplicate values are inserted into the
registered_students and temp_table tables, which is not the desired effect.

WHILE Loops

A cursor fetch loop can also be constructed using the WHILE…LOOP syntax, as
illustrated by the following example:

```
-- Available online as WhileLoop.sql
DECLARE
  -- Cursor to retrieve the information about History students
  CURSOR c_HistoryStudents IS
    SELECT id, first_name, last_name
      FROM students
      WHERE major = 'History';

  -- Declare a record to hold the fetched information.
  v_StudentData  c_HistoryStudents%ROWTYPE;
BEGIN
  -- Open the cursor and initialize the active set
  OPEN c_HistoryStudents;

  -- Retrieve the first row, to set up for the WHILE loop
  FETCH c_HistoryStudents INTO v_StudentData;

  -- Continue looping while there are more rows to fetch
  WHILE c_HistoryStudents%FOUND LOOP
    -- Process the fetched rows, in this case sign up each
    -- student for History 301 by inserting them into the
    -- registered_students table. Record the first and last
    -- names in temp_table as well.
    INSERT INTO registered_students (student_id, department, course)
      VALUES (v_StudentData.ID, 'HIS', 301);

    INSERT INTO temp_table (num_col, char_col)
      VALUES (v_StudentData.ID,
              v_StudentData.first_name || ' ' || v_StudentData.last_name);

    -- Retrieve the next row. The %FOUND condition will be checked
    -- before the loop continues again.
    FETCH c_HistoryStudents INTO v_StudentData;
  END LOOP;

  -- Free resources used by the cursor
  CLOSE c_HistoryStudents;
END;
```

This fetch loop behaves the same as the first LOOP…END LOOP example in the previous section. Note that the FETCH statement appears twice: once before the loop and once after the loop processing. This is necessary so that the loop condition (c_HistoryStudents%FOUND) will be evaluated for each loop iteration.

Cursor FOR Loops

Both of the FETCH loops just described require explicit processing of the cursor, with OPEN, FETCH, and CLOSE statements. PL/SQL provides a simpler type of loop, which implicitly handles the cursor processing. This is known as a cursor FOR loop. An example, which again is equivalent to the previous two examples, is illustrated here:

```
-- Available online as ForLoop.sql
DECLARE
   -- Cursor to retrieve the information about History students
   CURSOR c_HistoryStudents IS
     SELECT id, first_name, last_name
       FROM students
       WHERE major = 'History';
BEGIN
   -- Begin the loop. An implicit OPEN of c_HistoryStudents
   -- is done here.
   FOR v_StudentData IN c_HistoryStudents LOOP
     -- An implicit FETCH is done here.
     -- c_HistoryStudents%NOTFOUND is also implicitly checked, to
     -- see if we are done fetching.

     -- Process the fetched rows, in this case sign up each
     -- student for History 301 by inserting them into the
     -- registered_students table. Record the first and last
     -- names in temp_table as well.
     INSERT INTO registered_students (student_id, department, course)
       VALUES (v_StudentData.ID, 'HIS', 301);

     INSERT INTO temp_table (num_col, char_col)
       VALUES (v_StudentData.ID,
               v_StudentData.first_name || ' ' || v_StudentData.last_name);

   END LOOP;
   -- Now that the loop is finished, an implicit CLOSE of
   -- c_HistoryStudents is done.
END;
```

There are two important things to note about this example. First, the record v_StudentData is *not* declared in the declarative section of the block. This variable is *implicitly* declared by the PL/SQL compiler, similar to the loop index for a numeric FOR loop. The type of this variable is c_HistoryStudents%ROWTYPE, and the scope of v_StudentData is only the FOR loop itself. The implicit declaration of the loop index, and the scope of this declaration, is the same behavior as a numeric FOR loop, as described in Chapter 3. Because of this, you cannot assign to a loop variable inside a cursor FOR loop.

Second, c_HistoryStudents is implicitly opened, fetched from, and closed by the loop at the places indicated by the comments. Before the loop starts, the cursor is opened. Before each loop iteration, the %FOUND attribute is checked to make sure there are remaining rows in the active set. When the active set is completely fetched, the cursor is closed as the loop ends.

Cursor FOR loops have the advantage of providing the functionality of a cursor fetch loop simply and cleanly, with a minimum of syntax.

Implicit FOR Loops

The syntax for a FOR loop can be shortened even more. In addition to the record, the cursor itself can be implicitly declared, as the following example illustrates.

```
-- Available online as ImplicitFOR.sql
BEGIN
  -- Begin the loop. An implicit OPEN is done here.
  FOR v_StudentData IN (SELECT id, first_name, last_name
                          FROM students
                          WHERE major = 'History') LOOP
    -- An implicit FETCH is done here, and %NOTFOUND is checked

    -- Process the fetched rows, in this case sign up each
    -- student for History 301 by inserting them into the
    -- registered_students table. Record the first and last
    -- names in temp_table as well.
    INSERT INTO registered_students (student_id, department, course)
      VALUES (v_StudentData.ID, 'HIS', 301);

    INSERT INTO temp_table (num_col, char_col)
      VALUES (v_StudentData.ID,
              v_StudentData.first_name || ' ' || v_StudentData.last_name);
  END LOOP;
  -- Now that the loop is finished, an implicit CLOSE is done.
END;
```

The query is contained within parenthesis within the FOR statement itself. In this case, both the record v_StudentData and the cursor are implicitly declared. The cursor has no name, however.

NO_DATA_FOUND versus %NOTFOUND

The NO_DATA_FOUND exception is raised only for SELECT...INTO statements, when the WHERE clause of the query does not match any rows. When the WHERE clause of an explicit cursor does not match any rows, the %NOTFOUND attribute is set to TRUE instead. If the WHERE clause of an UPDATE or DELETE statement does not match any rows, SQL%NOTFOUND is set to TRUE, rather than raising NO_DATA_FOUND. Because of this, all of the fetch loops shown so far use %NOTFOUND or %FOUND to determine the exit condition for the loop, rather than the NO_DATA_FOUND exception.

SELECT FOR UPDATE Cursors

Very often, the processing done in a fetch loop modifies the rows that have been retrieved by the cursor. PL/SQL provides a convenient syntax for doing this. This method consists of two parts: the FOR UPDATE clause in the cursor declaration and the WHERE CURRENT OF clause in an UPDATE or DELETE statement.

FOR UPDATE

The FOR UPDATE clause is part of a SELECT statement. It is legal as the last clause of the statement, after the ORDER BY clause (if it is present). The syntax is

SELECT...FROM...FOR UPDATE [OF *column_reference*] [NOWAIT]

where *column_reference* is a column in the table against which the query is performed. A list of columns can also be used. For example, the following declarative section defines two cursors that are both legal forms of the SELECT...FOR UPDATE syntax:

```
DECLARE
  -- This cursor lists two columns for the UPDATE clause.
  CURSOR c_AllStudents IS
    SELECT *
      FROM students
      FOR UPDATE OF first_name, last_name;

  -- This cursor does not list any columns.
  CURSOR c_LargeClasses IS
    SELECT department, course
      FROM classes
      WHERE max_students > 50
      FOR UPDATE;
```

Normally, a SELECT operation will not take any locks on the rows being accessed. This allows other sessions connected to the database to change the data being selected. The result set is still consistent, however. At OPEN time, when the active set is determined, Oracle takes a snapshot of the table. Any changes that have been committed prior to this point are reflected in the active set. Any changes made after this point, even if they are committed, are not reflected unless the cursor is reopened, which will evaluate the active set again. However, if the FOR UPDATE clause is present, exclusive row locks are taken on the rows in the active set before the OPEN returns. These locks prevent other sessions from changing the rows in the active set until the transaction is committed or rolled back.

If another session already has locks on the rows in the active set, then the SELECT...FOR UPDATE operation will wait for these locks to be released by the other session. There is no time-out for this waiting period; the SELECT...FOR

UPDATE will hang until the other session releases the lock. To handle this situation, the NOWAIT clause is available. If the rows are locked by another session, the OPEN will return immediately with the Oracle error

```
ORA-54: resource busy and acquire with NOWAIT specified
```

In this case, you may want to retry the OPEN later or change the active set to fetch unlocked rows.

| Oracle**9i** |
| and higher |

In Oracle9i, you can use the syntax

SELECT...FROM...FOR UPDATE [OF *column_reference*] [WAIT *n*]

where *n* is the number of seconds to wait. If the rows are not unlocked within *n* seconds, then the ORA-54 error will be returned.

WHERE CURRENT OF

If the cursor is declared with the FOR UPDATE clause, the WHERE CURRENT OF clause can be used in an UPDATE or DELETE statement. The syntax for this clause is

WHERE CURRENT OF *cursor*

where *cursor* is the name of a cursor that has been declared with a FOR UPDATE clause. The WHERE CURRENT OF clause evaluates to the row that was just retrieved by the cursor. For example, the following block will update the current credits for all registered students in HIS 101:

```
-- Available online as ForUpdate.sql
DECLARE
  -- Number of credits to add to each student's total
  v_NumCredits   classes.num_credits%TYPE;

  -- This cursor will select only those students who are currently
  -- registered for HIS 101.
  CURSOR c_RegisteredStudents IS
    SELECT *
      FROM students
      WHERE id IN (SELECT student_id
                     FROM registered_students
                     WHERE department= 'HIS'
                     AND course = 101)
    FOR UPDATE OF current_credits;

BEGIN
  -- Set up the cursor fetch loop.
```

```
FOR v_StudentInfo IN c_RegisteredStudents LOOP
-- Determine the number of credits for HIS 101.
SELECT num_credits
  INTO v_NumCredits
  FROM classes
  WHERE department = 'HIS'
  AND course = 101;

-- Update the row we just retrieved from the cursor.
UPDATE students
  SET current_credits = current_credits + v_NumCredits
  WHERE CURRENT OF c_RegisteredStudents;
END LOOP;

-- Commit our work, and release the lock.
COMMIT;
END;
```

Note that the UPDATE statement updates only the column listed in the FOR UPDATE clause of the cursor declaration. If no columns are listed, any column can be updated. (PL/SQL will let you update any column, even those not mentioned specifically in the FOR UPDATE clause, but this is not good style.)

It is legal to execute a query with a FOR UPDATE clause, but not reference the rows fetched via WHERE CURRENT OF. In this case, the rows are still locked and thus can only be modified by the current session (which holds the lock). UPDATE and DELETE statements that modify these rows will not block if they are executed by the session holding the lock. However, it is illegal to use WHERE CURRENT on a cursor that has not been declared FOR UPDATE.

Fetching Across Commits

Note that the COMMIT in the example in the previous section is done after the fetch loop is complete. This is done because a COMMIT will release any locks held by the session. Because the FOR UPDATE clause acquires locks, these will be released by the COMMIT. When this happens, the cursor is invalidated. Any subsequent fetches will return the Oracle error

```
ORA-1002: fetch out of sequence
```

Consider the following example, which raises this error:

```
-- Available online as part of commit.sql
DECLARE
  -- Cursor to retrieve all students, and lock the rows as well.
  CURSOR c_AllStudents IS
    SELECT *
```

```
        FROM students
        FOR UPDATE;

  -- Variable for retrieved data.
  v_StudentInfo   c_AllStudents%ROWTYPE;
BEGIN
  -- Open the cursor. This will acquire the locks.
  OPEN c_AllStudents;

  -- Retrieve the first record.
  FETCH c_AllStudents INTO v_StudentInfo;

  -- Issue a COMMIT. This will release the locks, invalidating the
  -- cursor.
  COMMIT;

  -- This FETCH will raise the ORA-1002 error.
  FETCH c_AllStudents INTO v_StudentInfo;
END;
```

Thus, if there is a COMMIT inside a SELECT...FOR UPDATE fetch loop, any fetches done after the COMMIT will fail. So, it is not advisable to use a COMMIT inside the loop. If the cursor is not defined as a SELECT...FOR UPDATE, there is no problem.

TIP

Even if you are not doing a SELECT...FOR UPDATE, committing inside a fetch loop is not necessarily advisable. If the query affects a large number of rows, for example, you may receive "ORA-1555: snapshot too old" errors.

What do you do if you want to update the row just fetched from the cursor and use a COMMIT inside the fetch loop? The WHERE CURRENT OF clause isn't available, because the cursor can't be defined with a FOR UPDATE clause. However, you can use the primary key of the table in the WHERE clause of the UPDATE, as illustrated by the following example:

```
-- Available online as part of commit.sql
DECLARE
  -- Number of credits to add to each student's total
  v_NumCredits  classes.num_credits%TYPE;

  -- This cursor will select only those students who are currently
  -- registered for HIS 101.
```

```
    CURSOR c_RegisteredStudents IS
      SELECT *
        FROM students
        WHERE id IN (SELECT student_id
                       FROM registered_students
                       WHERE department= 'HIS'
                       AND course = 101);

BEGIN
  -- Set up the cursor fetch loop.
  FOR v_StudentInfo IN c_RegisteredStudents LOOP
  -- Determine the number of credits for HIS 101.
  SELECT num_credits
    INTO v_NumCredits
    FROM classes
    WHERE department = 'HIS'
    AND course = 101;

  -- Update the row we just retrieved from the cursor.
  UPDATE students
    SET current_credits = current_credits + v_NumCredits
    WHERE id = v_Studentinfo.id;

  -- We can commit inside the loop, since the cursor is
  -- not declared FOR UPDATE.
  COMMIT;
  END LOOP;
END;
```

This example essentially simulates the WHERE CURRENT OF clause, but does not create locks on the rows in the active set. As a result, it may not perform as expected if other sessions are accessing the data concurrently.

TIP
If the table used in the query does not have a primary key, you may be able to use the ROWID pseudocolumn instead. You can fetch the rowid of each row into a PL/SQL variable (declared with the ROWID or UROWID type), and use this in a WHERE clause like WHERE rowid = v_RowID.

Cursor Variables

All of the explicit cursor examples we have seen so far are examples of *static cursors*— the cursor is associated with one SQL statement, and this statement is known when the block is compiled. A *cursor variable,* on the other hand, can be associated with different queries at runtime. Cursor variables are analogous to PL/SQL variables, which can hold different values at runtime. Static cursors are analogous to PL/SQL constants because they can only be associated with one runtime query.

NOTE
Dynamic SQL also allows you to associate different statements with a variable. See Chapter 12 for more information on dynamic SQL.

In order to use a cursor variable, it must first be declared. Storage for it must then be allocated at runtime because a cursor variable is a REF type. It is then opened, fetched, and closed similar to a static cursor. Cursor variables are used most often inside a stored procedure that returns the variable to a client-side program. This technique allows a stored procedure to open a query, and return the result set to the client for processing there. See Chapters 9 and 10 for more information on stored procedures.

Declaring a Cursor Variable

A cursor variable is a reference type. Before Oracle8, it was the only reference type available. (Oracle8 and higher allow REFs to object types. For more information on object types, see Chapter 12.) As we discussed in Chapter 3, a reference type is similar to a pointer in C. It can refer to different storage locations as the program runs. In order to use a reference type, first the variable has to be declared, and then the storage has to be allocated. Reference types in PL/SQL are declared using the syntax

    REF *type*

where *type* is a previously defined type. The REF keyword indicates that the new type will be a pointer to the defined type. The type of a cursor variable is therefore REF CURSOR. The complete syntax for defining a cursor variable type is

    TYPE *type_name* IS REF CURSOR [RETURN *return_type*];

where *type_name* is the name of the new reference type, and *return_type* is a record type indicating the types of the select list that will eventually be returned by the cursor variable.

The return type for a cursor variable must be a record type. It can be declared explicitly as a user-defined record or implicitly using %ROWTYPE. Once the reference type is defined, the variable can be declared. The following declarative section shows different declarations for cursor variables:

```
-- Available online as part of RefCursors.sql
DECLARE
   -- Definition using %ROWTYPE.
   TYPE t_StudentsRef IS REF CURSOR
     RETURN students%ROWTYPE;

   -- Define a new record type,
   TYPE t_NameRecord IS RECORD (
     first_name   students.first_name%TYPE,
     last_name    students.last_name%TYPE);

   -- a variable of this type,
   v_NameRecord  t_NameRecord;

   -- And a cursor variable using the record type.
   TYPE t_NamesRef IS REF CURSOR
     RETURN t_NameRecord;

   -- We can declare another type, using %TYPE for the previously
   -- defined record.
   TYPE t_NamesRef2 IS REF CURSOR
     RETURN v_NameRecord%TYPE;

   -- Declare cursor variables using the above types.
   v_StudentCV t_StudentsRef;
   v_NameCV    t_NamesRef;
```

Constrained and Unconstrained Cursor Variables

The cursor variables in the previous section are *constrained*—they are declared for a specific return type only. When the variable is later opened, it must be opened for a query whose select list matches the return type of the cursor. If not, the predefined exception ROWTYPE_MISMATCH is raised.

PL/SQL also allows the declaration of *unconstrained* cursor variables. An unconstrained cursor variable does not have a RETURN clause. When an unconstrained cursor variable is later opened, it can be opened for any query. The following declarative section declares an unconstrained cursor variable:

```
-- Available online as part of RefCursors.sql
DECLARE
   -- Define an unconstrained reference type,
   TYPE t_FlexibleRef IS REF CURSOR;
```

```
-- and a variable of that type.
v_CursorVar t_FlexibleRef;
```

Allocating Storage for Cursor Variables

A cursor variable is a reference type, so no storage is allocated for it when it is declared. Before it can be used, it needs to point to a valid area of memory. This memory can be created in two ways: by allocating it in a client-side program, or by allocating it on the server by the PL/SQL engine.

Client-Side Allocation

In a typical case, a cursor variable is opened on the server and then passed to a client program through a bind variable. It is the responsibility of the client program to allocate the storage for the variable. Depending on the language in which the client-side program is written, the cursor variable is allocated in different ways. We will see examples of Pro*C client allocations in this section. Cursor variables can also be used from client-side OCI or JDBC programs as well. For more information on using cursor variables from these environments, see the Oracle documentation.

Pro*C Allocation   In order to allocate storage when using the Pro*C precompiler, you need to declare a variable of type SQL_CURSOR. It is then allocated with the EXEC SQL ALLOCATE command. For example, the following Pro*C fragment declares and allocates a cursor variable:

```
SQL_CURSOR v_CursorVar;
EXEC SQL ALLOCATE :v_CursorVar;
```

A host cursor variable is unconstrained, because it has no return type associated with it.

Server-Side Allocation

Cursor variables can also be used entirely on the server, within PL/SQL. In this case, the variable is automatically allocated when necessary, just like other types. When the variable goes out of scope and thus no longer references the storage, it is deallocated. Cursor variables can not be declared in a package, however.

Opening a Cursor Variable for a Query

In order to associate a cursor variable with a particular SELECT statement, the OPEN syntax is extended to allow the query to be specified. This is done with the OPEN FOR syntax,

OPEN *cursor variable* FOR *select_statement*;

where *cursor_variable* is a previously declared cursor variable, and *select_statement* is the desired query. If the cursor variable is constrained, the select list must match the return type of the cursor. If it is constrained, the error

```
ORA-6504: PL/SQL: return types of result set variables or query
          do not match
```

is returned. For more information on PL/SQL errors and how to handle them, see Chapter 7. For example, given a cursor variable declaration like this

```
DECLARE
    TYPE t_ClassesRef IS REF CURSOR RETURN classes%ROWTYPE;
    v_ClassesCV t_ClassesRef;
```

we can open v_ClassesCV with

```
OPEN v_ClassesCV FOR
   SELECT * FROM classes;
```

If, on the other hand, we attempt to open v_ClassesCV this way

```
OPEN v_ClassesCV FOR
    SELECT department, course FROM classes
```

we would receive ORA-6504 because the select list of the query does not match the return type of the cursor variable.

OPEN...FOR behaves the same way as OPEN—any bind variables in the query are examined and the active set is determined. Following the OPEN...FOR, the cursor variable is open, and can be fetched from. This fetch can either be done on the server with the FETCH statement (just like a regular cursor) or on the client.

NOTE
The query used in OPEN FOR must be hardcoded in the program—it cannot be contained in a variable. This restriction is lifted in Oracle8i with native dynamic SQL, however. See Chapter 12 for details.

Closing Cursor Variables

On the server, cursor variables are closed just like static cursors—with the CLOSE statement. This frees the resources used for the query. It does not necessarily free the storage for the cursor variable itself, however. The storage for the variable is freed when the variable goes out of scope. It is illegal to close a cursor or cursor variable that is already closed.

On the client, cursor variables are closed just like other cursors, using whatever mechanism is appropriate.

Cursor Variable Example I

The following is a complete Pro*C program that demonstrates the use of cursor variables. It uses an embedded PL/SQL block to select from either the classes or the rooms table, depending on user input. For the benefit of those who may not be familiar with C, the code is more heavily commented than usual.

```
-- Available online as cursor1.pc
/* Include C and SQL header files. */
#include <stdio.h>
EXEC SQL INCLUDE SQLCA;


/* Character string to hold the username and password. */
char *v_Username = "example/example";

/* SQL Cursor variable */
SQL_CURSOR v_CursorVar;

/* Integer variable used to control table selection. */
int v_Table;

/* Output variables for rooms. */
int v_RoomID;
VARCHAR v_Description[2001];

/* Output variables for classes. */
VARCHAR v_Department[4];
int v_Course;



/* Error handling routine. Print out the error, and exit. */
void handle_error() {
  printf("SQL Error occurred!\n");
  printf("%.*s\n", sqlca.sqlerrm.sqlerrml, sqlca.sqlerrm.sqlerrmc);
  EXEC SQL ROLLBACK WORK RELEASE;
  exit(1);
}

int main() {
  /* Character string to hold user input. */
  char v_Choice[20];
```

```
/* Set up the error handling. Whenever a SQL error occurs, we
   will call the handle_error() routine. */
EXEC SQL WHENEVER SQLERROR DO handle_error();

/* Connect to the database. */
EXEC SQL CONNECT :v_Username;
printf("Connected to Oracle.\n");

/* Allocate the cursor variable. */
EXEC SQL ALLOCATE :v_CursorVar;

/* Print a message asking the user for input, and retrieve their
   selection into v_Choice. */
printf("Choose from (C)lasses or (R)ooms. Enter c or r: ");
gets(v_Choice);

/* Determine the correct table. */
if (v_Choice[0] == 'c')
  v_Table = 1;
else
  v_Table = 2;

/* Open the cursor variable using an embedded PL/SQL block. */
EXEC SQL EXECUTE
  BEGIN
    IF :v_Table = 1 THEN
      /* Open variable for the classes table. */
      OPEN :v_CursorVar FOR
        SELECT department, course
          FROM classes;
    ELSE
      /* Open variable for the rooms table. */
      OPEN :v_CursorVar FOR
        SELECT room_id, description
          FROM rooms;
    END IF;
  END;
END-EXEC;

/* Exit the loop when we are done fetching. */
EXEC SQL WHENEVER NOT FOUND DO BREAK;

/* Begin the fetch loop. */
for (;;) {
  if (v_Table == 1) {
    /* Fetch class info. */
    EXEC SQL FETCH :v_CursorVar
      INTO :v_Department, :v_Course;
```

```
      /* Display it to the screen. Since v_Department is a
         VARCHAR, use the .len field for the actual length
         and the .arr field for the data. */
      printf("%.*s %d\n", v_Department.len, v_Department.arr,
                          v_Course);
    }
    else {
      /* Fetch room info. */
      EXEC SQL FETCH :v_CursorVar
        INTO :v_RoomID, v_Description;

      /* Display it to the screen. Since v_Description is a
         VARCHAR, use the .len field for the actual length
         and the .arr field for the data. */
      printf("%d %.*s\n", v_RoomID, v_Description.len,
                          v_Description.arr);
    }
  }

  /* Close the cursor. */
  EXEC SQL CLOSE :v_CursorVar;

  /* Disconnect from the database. */
  EXEC SQL COMMIT WORK RELEASE;
}
```

In the preceding program, the cursor is opened on the server (via the embedded anonymous block) and fetched from and closed back on the client. Because the cursor variable is declared as a host variable, it is unconstrained. Thus, we were able to use the same variable for selecting both from classes and from rooms. The cursor is also closed on the client.

Cursor Variable Example 2

The following example is similar to the Pro*C example in the previous section, but is written entirely in PL/SQL. It is a stored procedure that selects from classes or rooms, depending on its input. For more information on stored procedures, see Chapters 9 and 10.

```
-- Available online as cursor2.sql
CREATE OR REPLACE PROCEDURE ShowCursorVariable
  /* Demonstrates the use of a cursor variable on the server.
     If p_Table is 'classes', then information from the classes
     table is inserted into temp_table.  If p_Table is 'rooms'
     then information from rooms is inserted. */
  (p_Table IN VARCHAR2) AS
```

```
/* Define the cursor variable type */
TYPE t_ClassesRooms IS REF CURSOR;

/* and the variable itself. */
v_CursorVar t_ClassesRooms;

/* Variables to hold the output. */
v_Department  classes.department%TYPE;
v_Course      classes.course%TYPE;
v_RoomID      rooms.room_id%TYPE;
v_Description rooms.description%TYPE;
BEGIN
-- Based on the input parameter, open the cursor variable.
IF p_Table = 'classes' THEN
  OPEN v_CursorVar FOR
    SELECT department, course
      FROM classes;
ELSIF p_table = 'rooms' THEN
  OPEN v_CursorVar FOR
    SELECT room_id, description
      FROM rooms;
ELSE
  /* Wrong value passed as input - raise an error */
  RAISE_APPLICATION_ERROR(-20000,
    'Input must be ''classes'' or ''rooms''');
END IF;

/* Fetch loop.  Note the EXIT WHEN clause after the. */
LOOP
  IF p_Table = 'classes' THEN
    FETCH v_CursorVar INTO
      v_Department, v_Course;
    EXIT WHEN v_CursorVar%NOTFOUND;

    INSERT INTO temp_table (num_col, char_col)
      VALUES (v_Course, v_Department);
  ELSE
    FETCH v_CursorVar INTO
      v_RoomID, v_Description;
    EXIT WHEN v_CursorVAR%NOTFOUND;

    INSERT INTO temp_table (num_col, char_col)
      VALUES (v_RoomID, SUBSTR(v_Description, 1, 60));
  END IF;
END LOOP;

/* Close the cursor. */
```

```
    CLOSE v_CursorVar;

    COMMIT;
END ShowCursorVariable;
```

Restrictions on Using Cursor Variables

Cursor variables are a powerful feature, and they can greatly simplify processing because they allow different kinds of data to be returned in the same variable. However, there are a number of restrictions associated with their use, which are described below:

- Cursor variables cannot be defined in a package. The type itself can, but the variable cannot.

- Remote subprograms cannot return the value of a cursor variable. Cursor variables can be passed between client- and server-side PL/SQL (such as from an Oracle Forms client), but not between two servers.

- PL/SQL collections (index-by tables, nested tables, and varrays) cannot store cursor variables. Similarly, database tables and views cannot store REF CURSOR columns. You can, however, have an array of client-side cursor variables (such as JDBC ResultSets).

- You cannot use cursor variables with dynamic SQL in Pro*C.

- The query associated with a cursor variable in the OPEN...FOR statement cannot be FOR UPDATE. This restriction has been lifted in Oracle8i and higher.

Summary

In this chapter, we discussed the steps necessary for processing cursors, which allow explicit control of SQL statement processing. For explicit cursors, the steps include declaring, opening, fetching, and closing the cursor. Cursor attributes are used to determine the current state of a cursor, and thus how to manipulate it. In addition, we discussed different kinds of fetch loops. The chapter concluded with a discussion of cursor variables and their uses. The next chapter discusses error handling in PL/SQL.

CHAPTER
7

Error Handling

ny well-written program must have the ability to handle errors intelligently and recover from them if possible. PL/SQL implements error handling with *exceptions* and *exception handlers.* Exceptions can be associated with Oracle errors or with your own user-defined errors. In this chapter, we will discuss the syntax of exceptions and exception handlers, how exceptions are raised and handled, and the rules of exception propagation. The chapter closes with guidelines on using exceptions.

What Is an Exception?

In Chapter 1, we discussed how PL/SQL is based on the Ada language. One of the features of Ada that is also incorporated into PL/SQL is the exception mechanism. By using exceptions and exception handlers, you can make your PL/SQL programs robust and able to deal with both unexpected and expected errors during execution. PL/SQL exceptions are similar to Java exceptions as well. For example, Java exceptions are thrown and caught in a manner like PL/SQL. Unlike Java, however, PL/SQL exceptions are not objects and have no methods defined on them.

What kinds of errors can occur in a PL/SQL program? Errors can be classified as described in Table 7-1.

Exceptions are designed for run-time error handling, rather than compile-time error handling. Errors that occur during the compilation phase are detected by the PL/SQL engine and reported back to the user. The program cannot handle these, because the program has not yet run. For example, the following block will raise the compilation error:

```
PLS-201: identifier 'SSTUDENTS' must be declared
```

Error Type	Reported By	How Handled
Compile-time	PL/SQL compiler	Interactively—compiler reports errors, and you have to correct them.
Runtime	PL/SQL runtime engine	Programmatically—exceptions are raised and caught by exception handlers.

TABLE 7-1. *Types of PL/SQL Errors*

because 'students' is misspelled in the SELECT statement:

```
DECLARE
   v_NumStudents NUMBER;
BEGIN
   SELECT COUNT(*)
     INTO v_NumStudents
     FROM sstudents;
END;
```

Exceptions and exception handlers are the method by which the program reacts and deals with runtime errors. Runtime errors include SQL errors such as

```
ORA-1: unique constraint violated
```

and procedural errors such as

```
ORA-06502: PL/SQL: numeric or value error
```

NOTE
PL/SQL has a facility known as dynamic SQL that allows you to create and run arbitrary SQL statements and PL/SQL blocks at runtime. If you dynamically run a PL/SQL block, which itself contains a compilation error, this error will be raised at runtime and can be caught by an exception handler. For more information on dynamic SQL, see Chapter 12.

When an error occurs, an exception is *raised.* When this happens, control is passed to the exception handler, which is a separate section of the program. This separates the error handling from the rest of the program, which makes the logic of the program easier to understand. This also ensures that all errors will be trapped.

In a language that doesn't use the exception model for error handling (such as C), in order to ensure that your program can handle errors in all cases, you must explicitly insert error-handling code. See the following code for an example:

```
int x = 1, y = 2, z = 3;
f(x);   /* Function call, passing x as an argument. */
if <an error occurred>
  handle_error(...);
y = 1 / z;
if <an error occurred>
  handle_error(...);
```

```
z = x + y;
if <an error occurred>
  handle_error(...);
```

Note that a check for errors must occur after each statement in the program. If you forget to insert the check, the program will not properly handle an error situation. In addition, the error handling can clutter up the program, making it difficult to understand the program's logic. Compare the preceding example to this similar example in PL/SQL:

```
DECLARE
  x NUMBER := 1;
  y NUMBER := 2;
  z NUMBER := 3;
BEGIN
  f(x);
  y := 1 / z;
  z := x + y;
EXCEPTION
  WHEN OTHERS THEN
    /* Handler to execute for all errors */
    handle_error(...);
END;
```

Note that the error handling is separated from the program logic. This solves both problems with the C example, namely

- Program logic is easier to understand because it is clearly visible.

- No matter which statement fails, the program will detect and handle the error. Note that program execution will not continue from the statement that raised the error, however. Instead, execution will continue to the exception handler, and then to any outer block.

Declaring Exceptions

Exceptions are declared in the declarative section of the block, raised in the executable section, and handled in the exception section. There are two types of exceptions: *user-defined* and *predefined*.

User-Defined Exceptions

A user-defined exception is an error that is defined by the programmer. The error that it signifies is not necessarily an Oracle error—it could be an error with the data, for example. Predefined exceptions, on the other hand, correspond to common SQL and PL/SQL errors.

User-defined exceptions are declared in the declarative section of a PL/SQL block. Just like variables, exceptions have a type (EXCEPTION) and scope. For example:

```
DECLARE
  e_TooManyStudents EXCEPTION;
```

e_TooManyStudents is an identifier that will be visible until the end of this block. Note that the scope of an exception is the same as the scope of any other variable or cursor in the same declarative section. See Chapter 3 for information on the scope and visibility rules for PL/SQL identifiers.

Predefined Exceptions

Oracle has predefined several exceptions that correspond to the most common Oracle errors. Like the predefined types (NUMBER, VARCHAR2, and so on), the identifiers for these exceptions are defined in the STANDARD package (see Chapter 3 for more information on predefined types and the STANDARD package). Because of this, they are already available to the program—it is not necessary to declare them in the declarative section like a user-defined exception. These predefined exceptions are described in Table 7-2.

NOTE
It is possible to associate user-defined exceptions with Oracle errors, as well. See the "The EXCEPTION_INIT Pragma" section later in this chapter for more information.

Oracle Error	Equivalent Exception	Description
ORA-0001	DUP_VAL_ON_INDEX	Unique constraint violated.
ORA-0051	TIMEOUT_ON_RESOURCE	Time-out occurred while waiting for resource.
ORA-0061	TRANSACTION_BACKED_OUT[1]	The transaction was rolled back due to deadlock.
ORA-1001	INVALID_CURSOR	Illegal cursor operation.
ORA-1012	NOT_LOGGED_ON	Not connected to Oracle.

TABLE 7-2.   *Predefined Oracle Exceptions*

Oracle Error	Equivalent Exception	Description
ORA-1017	LOGIN_DENIED	Invalid username/password.
ORA-1403	NO_DATA_FOUND	No data found.
ORA-1410	SYS_INVALID_ROWID[2]	Conversion to a universal rowid failed.
ORA-1422	TOO_MANY_ROWS	A SELECT...INTO statement matches more than one row.
ORA-1476	ZERO_DIVIDE	Division by zero.
ORA-1722	INVALID_NUMBER	Conversion to a number failed—for example, "1A" is not valid.
ORA-6500	STORAGE_ERROR	Internal PL/SQL error raised if PL/SQL runs out of memory.
ORA-6501	PROGRAM_ERROR	Internal PL/SQL error.
ORA-6502	VALUE_ERROR	Truncation, arithmetic, or conversion error.
ORA-6504	ROWTYPE_MISMATCH	Host cursor variable and PL/SQL cursor variable have incompatible row types.
ORA-6511	CURSOR_ALREADY_OPEN	Attempt to open a cursor that is already open.
ORA-6530	ACCESS_INTO_NULL[1]	Attempt to assign values to the attributes of a NULL object.
ORA-6531	COLLECTION_IS_NULL[1]	Attempt to apply collection methods other than EXISTS to a NULL PL/SQL table or varray.
ORA-6532	SUBSCRIPT_OUTSIDE_LIMIT[1]	Reference to a nested table or varray index outside the declared range (such as −1).

TABLE 7-2. *Predefined Oracle Exceptions* (continued)

Oracle Error	Equivalent Exception	Description
ORA-6533	SUBSCRIPT_BEYOND_COUNT[1]	Reference to a nested table or varray index higher than the number of elements in the collection.
ORA-6592	CASE_NOT_FOUND[3]	No matching WHEN clause in a CASE statement is found.
ORA-30625	SELF_IS_NULL[2]	Attempt to call a method on a NULL object instance.

[1]This exception is predefined in Oracle8 and higher.

[2]This exception is predefined in Oracle8*i* and higher.

[3]This exception is predefined in Oracle9*i* and higher.

TABLE 7-2. *Predefined Oracle Exceptions* (continued)

Short descriptions of some of the predefined exceptions follow. For more information on these errors, see the *PL/SQL User's Guide*.

INVALID_CURSOR   This error is raised when an illegal cursor operation is performed, such as attempting to close a cursor that is already closed. The analogous situation of attempting to open a cursor that is already open causes CURSOR_ALREADY_OPEN to be raised.

NO_DATA_FOUND   This exception can be raised in two different situations. The first is when a SELECT...INTO statement does not return any rows. If the statement returns more than one row, TOO_MANY_ROWS is raised. The second situation is an attempt to reference a PL/SQL index-by table element that has not been assigned a value. For example, the following anonymous block will raise NO_DATA_FOUND:

```
-- Available online as NoDataFound.sql
SQL> DECLARE
  2     TYPE t_NumberTableType IS TABLE OF NUMBER
  3       INDEX BY BINARY_INTEGER;
  4     v_NumberTable t_NumberTableType;
  5     v_TempVar NUMBER;
  6  BEGIN
```

```
7    v_TempVar := v_NumberTable(1);
8  END;
9  /
DECLARE
*
ERROR at line 1:
ORA-01403: no data found
ORA-06512: at line 7
```

See Chapter 8 for more information on PL/SQL index-by tables.

INVALID_NUMBER   This exception is raised in a SQL statement when an attempted conversion from a character string to a number fails. In a procedural statement, VALUE_ERROR is raised instead. For example, the following statement raises INVALID_NUMBER because 'X' is not a valid number:

```
INSERT INTO students (id, first_name, last_name)
   VALUES, ('X', 'SCOTT', 'Smith');
```

STORAGE_ERROR and PROGRAM_ERROR   These are internal exceptions, which are not normally raised. If they occur, either your machine has run out of memory (STORAGE_ERROR) or a PL/SQL internal error occurred (PROGRAM_ERROR). Internal errors are often caused by bugs in the PL/SQL engine and should be reported to Oracle Technical Support.

VALUE_ERROR   This exception is raised when an arithmetic, conversion, truncation, or constraint error occurs in a procedural statement. If the error occurs in an SQL statement, an error such as INVALID_NUMBER is raised instead. The error can occur as a result of an assignment statement, a SELECT...INTO statement, RETURNING INTO parameters of a SQL statement, or subprogram parameters. All of these situations result in a value being assigned to a PL/SQL variable. If there is a problem with this assignment, VALUE_ERROR is raised.

| Oracle**8i** and higher | Prior to Oracle8*i*, the error message text for VALUE_ERROR was simply "Numeric or Value Error." In Oracle8*i*, however, the error message text will contain the specific cause of the error. This is reflected in the following examples, both of which raise VALUE_ERROR:

```
-- Available online as ValueError.sql
SQL> DECLARE
  2    v_TempVar VARCHAR2(3);
  3  BEGIN
  4    v_TempVar := 'ABCD';
  5  END;
  6  /
```

```
DECLARE
*
ERROR at line 1:
ORA-06502: PL/SQL: numeric or value error: character string buffer too
   small
ORA-06512: at line 4

SQL> DECLARE
  2     v_TempVar NUMBER(2);
  3   BEGIN
  4     SELECT id
  5       INTO v_TempVar
  6       FROM students
  7       WHERE last_name = 'Smith';
  8   END;
  9   /
DECLARE
*
ERROR at line 1:
ORA-06502: PL/SQL: numeric or value error: number precision too large
ORA-06512: at line 4
```

ROWTYPE_MISMATCH   This exception is raised when the types of a host cursor variable and a PL/SQL cursor variable do not match. For example, if the actual and formal return types don't match for a procedure that takes a cursor variable as an argument, ROWTYPE_MISMATCH is raised. See Chapter 6 for more information on cursor variables and an example that raises this exception.

Raising Exceptions

When the error associated with an exception occurs, the exception is raised (just like Java exceptions are thrown). User-defined exceptions are raised explicitly via the RAISE statement, while predefined exceptions (or user-defined exceptions associated with an Oracle error through the EXCEPTION_INIT pragma) are raised implicitly when their associated Oracle error occurs. If an Oracle error that is not associated with an exception occurs, an exception is also raised. This exception can be caught with an OTHERS handler (see the "The OTHERS Exception Handler" section later in this chapter for details). Predefined exceptions can be raised explicitly via the RAISE statement as well, if desired. Continuing the example started earlier in the "User-Defined Exceptions" section, we have

```
-- Available online as part of UserDefined.sql
DECLARE
   -- Exception to indicate an error condition
   e_TooManyStudents EXCEPTION;
```

```
  -- Current number of students registered for HIS-101
  v_CurrentStudents NUMBER(3);

  -- Maximum number of students allowed in HIS-101
  v_MaxStudents NUMBER(3);
BEGIN
  /* Find the current number of registered students, and the maximum
     number of students allowed. */
  SELECT current_students, max_students
    INTO v_CurrentStudents, v_MaxStudents
    FROM classes
    WHERE department = 'HIS' AND course = 101;

  /* Check the number of students in this class. */
  IF v_CurrentStudents > v_MaxStudents THEN
    /* Too many students registered -- raise exception. */
    RAISE e_TooManyStudents;
  END IF;
END;
```

When an exception is raised, control immediately passes to the exception section of the block. If there is no exception section, the exception is propagated to the enclosing block (see the "Exception Propagation" section later in the chapter for more information). Once control passes to the exception handler, there is *no* way to return to the executable section of the block. This is illustrated in Figure 7-1.

Predefined exceptions are automatically raised when the associated Oracle error occurs. For example, the following PL/SQL block will raise the DUP_VAL_ON_INDEX exception:

```
-- Available online as DupValOnIndex.sql
BEGIN
  INSERT INTO students (id, first_name, last_name)
    VALUES (20000, 'John', 'Smith');
  INSERT INTO students (id, first_name, last_name)
    VALUES (20000, 'Susan', 'Ryan');
END;
```

The exception is raised because the `id` column of the `students` table is a primary key and therefore has a unique constraint defined on it. When the second INSERT statement attempts to insert 20000 into this column, the error

```
ORA-0001: unique constraint (<constraint name>)violated
```

is raised. This corresponds to the DUP_VAL_ON_INDEX exception.

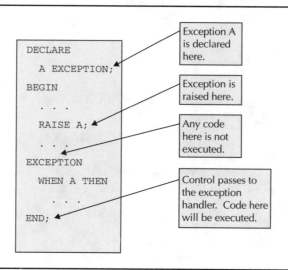

FIGURE 7-1. *Control passing to exception handler*

Handling Exceptions

When an exception is raised, control passes to the exception section of the block, as we saw in Figure 7-1. The exception section consists of *handlers* for some or all of the exceptions. An exception handler contains the code that is executed when the error associated with the exception occurs, and the exception is raised. The syntax for the exception section is as follows:

> **EXCEPTION**
>   **WHEN** *exception_name* **THEN**
>   *sequence_of_statements1;*
>   **WHEN** *exception_name* **THEN**
>   *sequence_of_statements2;*
>   [**WHEN** OTHERS **THEN**
>   *sequence_of_statements3;*]
> **END**;

Each exception handler consists of the WHEN clause and statements to execute when the exception is raised. The WHEN clause identifies which exception this handler is for. Continuing the example started earlier, we have

```
-- Available online as part of UserDefined.sql
DECLARE
```

```
   -- Exception to indicate an error condition
   e_TooManyStudents EXCEPTION;

   -- Current number of students registered for HIS-101
   v_CurrentStudents NUMBER(3);

   -- Maximum number of students allowed in HIS-101
   v_MaxStudents NUMBER(3);
BEGIN
   /* Find the current number of registered students, and the maximum
      number of students allowed. */
   SELECT current_students, max_students
     INTO v_CurrentStudents, v_MaxStudents
     FROM classes
     WHERE department = 'HIS' AND course = 101;

   /* Check the number of students in this class. */
   IF v_CurrentStudents > v_MaxStudents THEN
     /* Too many students registered -- raise exception. */
     RAISE e_TooManyStudents;
   END IF;
EXCEPTION
 WHEN e_TooManyStudents THEN
   /* Handler which executes when there are too many students
      registered for HIS-101. We will insert a log message
      explaining what has happened. */
    INSERT INTO log_table (info)
      VALUES ('History 101 has ' || v_CurrentStudents ||
              'students: max allowed is ' || v_MaxStudents);
 END;
```

A single handler can also be executed for more than one exception. Simply list the exception names in the WHEN clause separated by the keyword OR:

```
EXCEPTION
   WHEN NO_DATA_FOUND OR TOO_MANY_ROWS THEN
     INSERT INTO log_table (info)
       VALUES ('A select error occurred.');
 END;
```

NOTE
Unlike Java, an exception section of a block can have handlers for exceptions that are not actually raised by the executable section, and it can also not handle exceptions that could be raised by the executable section. The PL/SQL compiler does not currently validate the exception section in this manner.

A given exception can be handled by at most one handler in an exception section. If there is more than one handler for an exception, the PL/SQL compiler will raise PLS-483, as shown by the following SQL*Plus session:

```
-- Available online as DuplicateHandlers.sql
SQL> DECLARE
  2      -- Declare 2 user defined exceptions
  3      e_Exception1 EXCEPTION;
  4      e_Exception2 EXCEPTION;
  5  BEGIN
  6      -- Raise just exception 1.
  7      RAISE e_Exception1;
  8  EXCEPTION
  9    WHEN e_Exception2 THEN
 10      INSERT INTO log_table (info)
 11        VALUES ('Handler 1 executed!');
 12    WHEN e_Exception1 THEN
 13      INSERT INTO log_table (info)
 14        VALUES ('Handler 3 executed!');
 15    WHEN e_Exception1 OR e_Exception2 THEN
 16      INSERT INTO log_table (info)
 17        VALUES ('Handler 4 executed!');
 18  END;
 19  /
   WHEN e_Exception1 OR e_Exception2 THEN
   *
ERROR at line 15:
ORA-06550: line 15, column 3:
PLS-00483: exception 'E_EXCEPTION2' may appear in at most one exception
           handler in this block
ORA-06550: line 0, column 0:
PL/SQL: Compilation unit analysis terminated
```

The OTHERS Exception Handler

PL/SQL defines a special exception handler, known as WHEN OTHERS. This handler will execute for all raised exceptions that are not handled by any other WHEN clauses defined in the current exception section (similar to the generic Exception class in Java). It should always be the last handler in the block, so that all previous (and more specific) handlers will be scanned first. WHEN OTHERS will trap all exceptions, be they user-defined or predefined. It is good programming practice to have an OTHERS handler at the top level of your program (the outermost block) to ensure that no errors go undetected. If not, the error will propagate out to the calling environment (see the "Exception Propagation" section for more details). This can cause undesirable effects, such as the current transaction being rolled back.

The next listing continues the previous example by adding an OTHERS handler:

```
-- Available online as part of UserDefined.sql
DECLARE
  -- Exception to indicate an error condition
  e_TooManyStudents EXCEPTION;

  -- Current number of students registered for HIS-101
  v_CurrentStudents NUMBER(3);

  -- Maximum number of students allowed in HIS-101
  v_MaxStudents NUMBER(3);
BEGIN
  /* Find the current number of registered students, and the maximum
     number of students allowed. */
  SELECT current_students, max_students
    INTO v_CurrentStudents, v_MaxStudents
    FROM classes
    WHERE department = 'HIS' AND course = 101;

  /* Check the number of students in this class. */
  IF v_CurrentStudents > v_MaxStudents THEN
    /* Too many students registered -- raise exception. */
    RAISE e_TooManyStudents;
  END IF;
EXCEPTION
  WHEN e_TooManyStudents THEN
    /* Handler which executes when there are too many students
       registered for HIS-101. We will insert a log message
       explaining what has happened. */
    INSERT INTO log_table (info)
      VALUES ('History 101 has ' || v_CurrentStudents ||
              'students: max allowed is ' || v_MaxStudents);
  WHEN OTHERS THEN
    /* Handler which executes for all other errors. */
    INSERT INTO log_table (info) VALUES ('Another error occurred');
END;
```

The OTHERS exception handler in this example simply records the fact that an error occurred. However, it doesn't record which error. We can determine which error raised the exception that is being handled by an OTHERS handler through the predefined functions SQLCODE and SQLERRM, described next.

TIP
Do not code an exception handler like
WHEN OTHERS THEN NULL;
because it will silently trap any unexpected errors,
and not record the fact that they occurred. A good
OTHERS handler will log the error, and possibly
additional information, for later analysis.

SQLCODE and SQLERRM   Inside an OTHERS handler, it is often useful to know
which Oracle error raised the exception, whether or not the error has a predefined
exception for it. One reason would be to log which error occurred, rather than the
fact that an error happened. Or, you may want to do different things depending on
which error was raised. PL/SQL provides this information via two built-in functions:
SQLCODE and SQLERRM. SQLCODE returns the current error code, and SQLERRM
returns the current error message text. For a user-defined exception, SQLCODE
returns 1 and SQLERRM returns "User-defined Exception."

NOTE
The DBMS_UTILITY.FORMAT_ERROR_STACK
function also returns the current error message and
can be used in addition to SQLERRM. See Appendix
A for more information.

Here is the complete PL/SQL block that we have developed so far, with a complete
OTHERS exception handler:

```
-- Available online as part of UserDefined.sql
DECLARE
  -- Exception to indicate an error condition
  e_TooManyStudents EXCEPTION;

  -- Current number of students registered for HIS-101
  v_CurrentStudents NUMBER(3);

  -- Maximum number of students allowed in HIS-101
  v_MaxStudents NUMBER(3);

  -- Code and text of other runtime errors
  v_ErrorCode log_table.code%TYPE;
  v_ErrorText log_table.message%TYPE;
BEGIN
  /* Find the current number of registered students, and the maximum
     number of students allowed. */
```

```
    SELECT current_students, max_students
      INTO v_CurrentStudents, v_MaxStudents
      FROM classes
      WHERE department = 'HIS' AND course = 101;

  /* Check the number of students in this class. */
  IF v_CurrentStudents > v_MaxStudents THEN
    /* Too many students registered -- raise exception. */
    RAISE e_TooManyStudents;
  END IF;
EXCEPTION
  WHEN e_TooManyStudents THEN
    /* Handler which executes when there are too many students
       registered for HIS-101. We will insert a log message
       explaining what has happened. */
    INSERT INTO log_table (info)
      VALUES ('History 101 has ' || v_CurrentStudents ||
              'students: max allowed is ' || v_MaxStudents);
  WHEN OTHERS THEN
    /* Handler which executes for all other errors. */
    v_ErrorCode := SQLCODE;
    -- Note the use of SUBSTR here.
    v_ErrorText := SUBSTR(SQLERRM, 1, 200);
    INSERT INTO log_table (code, message, info) VALUES
      (v_ErrorCode, v_ErrorText, 'Oracle error occurred');
END;
```

The maximum length of an Oracle error message is 512 characters. In the preceding listing, v_ErrorText is only 200 characters (to match the code field of the log_table table). If the error message text is longer than 200 characters, the assignment

```
v_ErrorText := SQLERRM;
```

will itself raise the predefined exception VALUE_ERROR. To prevent this, we use the SUBSTR built-in function to ensure that at most 200 characters of the error message text are assigned to v_ErrorText. For more information on SUBSTR and other predefined PL/SQL functions, see Chapter 5.

Note that the values of SQLCODE and SQLERRM are assigned to local variables first; then these variables are used in a SQL statement. Because these functions are procedural, they cannot be used directly inside a SQL statement.

SQLERRM can also be called with a single number argument. In this case, it returns the text associated with the number. This argument should always be negative. If SQLERRM is called with zero, the message

```
ORA-0000: normal, successful completion
```

is returned. If SQLERRM is called with any positive value other than +100, messages such as

non-ORACLE Exception

are returned. SQLERRM(100) returns

ORA-1403: no data found

When called from an exception handler, SQLCODE will return a negative value indicating the Oracle error. The only exception to this is the error "ORA-1403: no data found," in which case SQLCODE returns +100. (100 corresponds to the ANSI specification for the NO DATA FOUND error.)

If SQLERRM (with no arguments) is called from the executable section of a block, it always returns

ORA-0000: normal, successful completion

and SQLCODE returns 0. All of these situations are shown in the following SQL*Plus session:

```
-- Available online as SQLERRM.sql
SQL> BEGIN
  2      DBMS_OUTPUT.PUT_LINE('SQLERRM(0): ' || SQLERRM(0));
  3      DBMS_OUTPUT.PUT_LINE('SQLERRM(100): ' || SQLERRM(100));
  4      DBMS_OUTPUT.PUT_LINE('SQLERRM(10): ' || SQLERRM(10));
  5      DBMS_OUTPUT.PUT_LINE('SQLERRM: ' || SQLERRM);
  6      DBMS_OUTPUT.PUT_LINE('SQLERRM(-1): ' || SQLERRM(-1));
  7      DBMS_OUTPUT.PUT_LINE('SQLERRM(-54): ' || SQLERRM(-54));
  8  END;
  9  /
SQLERRM(0): ORA-0000: normal, successful completion
SQLERRM(100): ORA-01403: no data found
SQLERRM(10):  -10: non-ORACLE exception
SQLERRM: ORA-0000: normal, successful completion
SQLERRM(-1): ORA-00001: unique constraint (.) violated
SQLERRM(-54): ORA-00054: resource busy and acquire with NOWAIT
  specified
PL/SQL procedure successfully completed.
```

TIP

It is generally more useful to use SQLERRM with no parameters, rather than passing a parameter (such as SQLCODE). The version with no parameters will return the complete error message, with any substituted strings, such as the constraint name in the case of the ORA-1 error in the previous example.

The EXCEPTION_INIT Pragma

You can associate a named exception with a particular Oracle error. This gives you the ability to trap this error specifically, rather than via an OTHERS handler. This is done via the EXCEPTION_INIT pragma. For more information on pragmas and how they are used, see Chapter 3. The EXCEPTION_INIT pragma is used as follows,

> PRAGMA EXCEPTION_INIT (*exception_name, oracle_error_number*);

where *exception_name* is the name of an exception declared prior to the pragma, and *oracle_error_number* is the desired error code to be associated with this named exception. This pragma must be in the declarative section. The following example will raise the `e_MissingNull` user-defined exception if the "ORA-1400: mandatory NOT NULL column missing or NULL during insert" error is encountered at runtime:

```
-- Available online as ExceptionInit.sql
DECLARE
  e_MissingNull EXCEPTION;
  PRAGMA EXCEPTION_INIT(e_MissingNull, -1400);
BEGIN
  INSERT INTO students (id) VALUES (NULL);
EXCEPTION
  WHEN e_MissingNull then
    INSERT INTO log_table (info) VALUES ('ORA-1400 occurred');
END;
```

Only one user-defined exception can be associated with an Oracle error with each occurrence of PRAGMA EXCEPTION_INIT. Inside the exception handler, SQLCODE and SQLERRM will return the code and message for the Oracle error that occurred, rather than "User-Defined Exception."

Using RAISE_APPLICATION_ERROR

You can use the built-in function RAISE_APPLICATION_ERROR to create your own error messages, which can be more descriptive than named exceptions. User-defined errors are passed out of the block the same way as Oracle errors to the calling environment. The syntax of RAISE_APPLICATION_ERROR is

> RAISE_APPLICATION_ERROR(*error_number, error_message,* [*keep_errors*]);

where *error_number* is a value between -20,000 and -20,999, *error_message* is the text associated with this error, and *keep_errors* is a Boolean value. The *error_message* parameter must be less than 512 characters. The Boolean parameter, *keep_errors*, is optional. If *keep_errors* is TRUE, the new error is added to the list of errors already

raised (if one exists). If it is FALSE, which is the default, the new error will replace
the current list of errors.

For example, the following procedure checks various conditions before
registering a student for a class. Procedures are discussed in more detail starting
in Chapter 9.

```
-- Available online as part of Register.sql
/* Registers the student identified by the p_StudentID parameter in
   the class identified by the p_Department and p_Course
   parameters. */
CREATE OR REPLACE PROCEDURE Register (
  p_StudentID IN students.id%TYPE,
  p_Department IN classes.department%TYPE,
  p_Course IN classes.course%TYPE) AS

  v_CurrentStudents classes.current_students%TYPE;
  v_MaxStudents classes.max_students%TYPE;
  v_NumCredits classes.num_credits%TYPE;
  v_Count NUMBER;
BEGIN
  /* Determine the current number of students registered, and the
     maximum number of students allowed to register. */
  BEGIN
    SELECT current_students, max_students, num_credits
      INTO v_CurrentStudents, v_MaxStudents, v_NumCredits
      FROM classes
      WHERE course = p_Course
      AND department = p_Department;

    /* Make sure there is enough room for this additional student. */
    IF v_CurrentStudents + 1 > v_MaxStudents THEN
      RAISE_APPLICATION_ERROR(-20000,
        'Can''t add more students to ' || p_Department || ' ' ||
        p_Course);
    END IF;
  EXCEPTION
    WHEN NO_DATA_FOUND THEN
      /* Class information passed to this procedure doesn't exist. */
      RAISE_APPLICATION_ERROR(-20001,
        p_Department || ' ' || p_Course || ' doesn''t exist');
  END;

  /* Ensure that the student is not currently registered */
  SELECT COUNT(*)
    INTO v_Count
    FROM registered_students
    WHERE student_id = p_StudentID
```

```
   AND department = p_Department
   AND course = p_Course;
 IF v_Count = 1 THEN
   RAISE_APPLICATION_ERROR(-20002,
     'Student ' || p_StudentID || ' is already registered for ' ||
     p_Department || ' ' || p_Course);
 END IF;

 /* There is enough room, and the student is not already in the
    class.  Update the necessary tables. */
 INSERT INTO registered_students (student_id, department, course)
   VALUES (p_StudentID, p_Department, p_Course);
 UPDATE students
   SET current_credits = current_credits + v_NumCredits
   WHERE ID = p_StudentID;
 UPDATE classes
   SET current_students = current_students + 1
   WHERE course = p_Course
   AND department = p_Department;
END Register;
```

The Register procedure uses RAISE_APPLICATION_ERROR in three different places. First, the procedure determines the current number of students registered for the class. This is done with the first SELECT...INTO statement. If this statement returns NO_DATA_FOUND, control passes to the exception handler, and RAISE_ APPLICATION_ERROR is used to notify the user that the class doesn't exist. If the class does exist, the procedure then verifies that there is room for the new student. If there isn't, RAISE_APPLICATION_ERROR is again used to notify the user that there isn't enough room. The third check is to ensure that the student is not already registered for the class, which is done with the second SELECT...INTO statement. If all of these tests pass, the student is actually added to the class by updating the registered_students, students, and classes tables.

Assuming that the tables are in their initial state (as created by tables.sql), the following SQL*Plus session illustrates the behavior of the Register procedure and the errors it raises:

```
-- Available online as part of Register.sql
SQL> -- Illustrate the ORA-2001 and ORA-2002 errors
SQL> exec Register(10000, 'CS', 999);
BEGIN Register(10000, 'CS', 999); END;
*
ERROR at line 1:
ORA-20001: CS 999 doesn't exist
ORA-06512: at "DEMO.REGISTER", line 28
ORA-06512: at line 1
```

```
SQL> exec Register(10000, 'CS', 102);
BEGIN Register(10000, 'CS', 102); END;
*
ERROR at line 1:
ORA-20002: Student 10000 is already registered for CS 102
ORA-06512: at "DEMO.REGISTER", line 40
ORA-06512: at line 1

SQL> -- Register 2 students for MUS 410, which will raise ORA-2003
SQL> exec Register(10002, 'MUS', 410);
PL/SQL procedure successfully completed.

SQL> exec Register(10005, 'MUS', 410);
BEGIN Register(10005, 'MUS', 410); END;
*
ERROR at line 1:
ORA-20000: Can't add more students to MUS 410
ORA-06512: at "DEMO.REGISTER", line 23
ORA-06512: at line 1
```

Compare the above output to the anonymous block below, which illustrates an anonymous block that simply raises the NO_DATA_FOUND exception:

```
-- Available online as part of Register.sql
SQL> BEGIN
  2     RAISE NO_DATA_FOUND;
  3  END;
  4  /
BEGIN
*
ERROR at line 1:
ORA-01403: no data found
ORA-06512: at line 2
```

The format of both outputs is the same—an Oracle error number and text associated with it. Note that both also include an ORA-6512 statement indicating the line that caused the error. So, RAISE_APPLICATION_ERROR can be used to return error conditions to the user in a manner consistent with other Oracle errors. This is very useful, because no special error handling is necessary for user-defined errors vs. predefined ones.

Exception Propagation

Exceptions can occur in the declarative, the executable, or the exception section of a PL/SQL block. We have seen in the previous section what happens when exceptions are raised in the executable portion of the block, and there is a handler for the exception. But what if there isn't a handler, or the exception is raised from a different section of the block? The process that governs this is known as *exception propagation*.

Exceptions Raised in the Executable Section

When an exception is raised in the executable section of a block, PL/SQL uses the following algorithm to determine which exception handler to invoke:

1. If the current block has a handler for the exception, execute it and complete the block successfully. Control then passes to the enclosing block.

2. If there is no handler for the current exception, propagate the exception by raising it in the enclosing block. Step 1 will then be executed for the enclosing block. If there is no enclosing block, the exception will be propagated out to the calling environment, such as SQL*Plus.

Before we can examine this algorithm in detail, we need to define an *enclosing block*. A block can be embedded inside another block. In this case, the outer block encloses the inner block. See the following example:

```
DECLARE
   -- Begin outer block.
   ...
BEGIN
   ...
   DECLARE
      -- Begin inner block 1. This is embedded in the outer block.
   ...
   BEGIN
      ...
   END;
   ...
   BEGIN
      -- Begin inner block 2. This is also embedded in the outer block.
      -- Note that this block doesn't have a declarative part.
      ...
   END;
   ...
   -- End outer block.
END;
```

In the preceding listing, inner blocks 1 and 2 are both enclosed by the outer block. Any unhandled exceptions in blocks 1 and 2 will be propagated to the outer block.

A procedure call will also create an enclosing block, and is illustrated in the following example:

```
BEGIN
  -- Begin outer block.
  -- Call a procedure. The procedure will be enclosed by this
  -- outer block.
  F(...);
EXCEPTION
  WHEN OTHERS THEN
    -- Any exceptions raised by F will be caught here
END;
```

If procedure F raises an unhandled exception, it will be propagated to the outer block, because it encloses the procedure.

Different cases for the exception propagation algorithm are illustrated in examples 1, 2, and 3, in the following sections.

Propagation Example I

The example shown here illustrates application of rule 1. Exception A is raised and handled in the sub-block. Control then returns to the outer block.

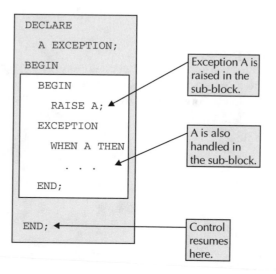

Propagation Example 2

In this example, rule 2 is applied for the sub-block. The exception is propagated to the enclosing block, where rule 1 is applied. The enclosing block then completes successfully.

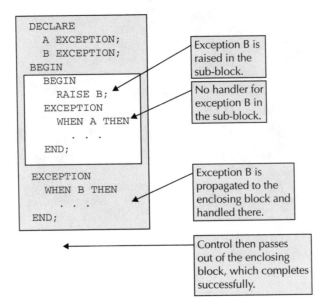

Propagation Example 3

Here, rule 2 is applied for the sub-block. The exception is propagated to the enclosing block, where there is still no handler for it. Rule 2 is applied again, and the enclosing block completes unsuccessfully with an unhandled exception.

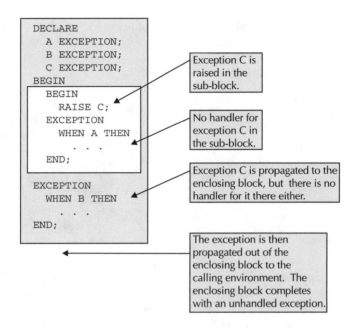

Exceptions Raised in the Declarative Section

If an assignment in the declarative section raises an exception, the exception is immediately propagated to the enclosing block. Once there, the rules given in the previous section are applied to propagate the exception further. Even if there is a handler in the current block, it is *not* executed. Examples 4 and 5 illustrate this.

Propagation Example 4

In this example, the VALUE_ERROR exception is raised by the following declaration:

```
v_Number NUMBER(3) := 'ABC';
```

This exception is immediately propagated to the enclosing block. Even though there is an OTHERS exception handler in this block, it is not executed. If this block had been enclosed in an outer block, the outer block would have been able to catch this exception. (Example 5 illustrates this scenario.)

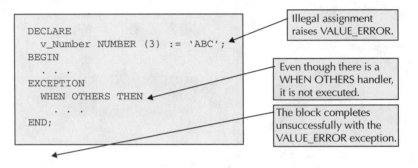

```
DECLARE
   v_Number NUMBER (3) := 'ABC';
BEGIN
   . . .
EXCEPTION
   WHEN OTHERS THEN
      . . .
END;
```

Illegal assignment raises VALUE_ERROR.

Even though there is a WHEN OTHERS handler, it is not executed.

The block completes unsuccessfully with the VALUE_ERROR exception.

Propagation Example 5

Similar to example 4, the VALUE_ERROR exception is raised in the declarative section of the inner block. The exception is immediately propagated to the outer block. Because the outer block has an OTHERS exception handler, the exception is handled and the outer block completes successfully.

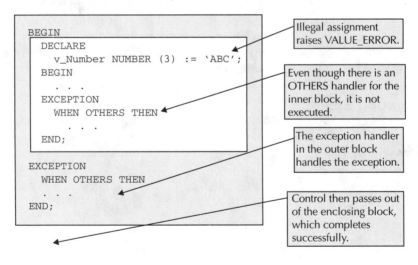

```
BEGIN
   DECLARE
   v_Number NUMBER (3) := 'ABC';
   BEGIN
      . . .
   EXCEPTION
      WHEN OTHERS THEN
         . . .
   END;

EXCEPTION
   WHEN OTHERS THEN
      . . .
END;
```

Illegal assignment raises VALUE_ERROR.

Even though there is an OTHERS handler for the inner block, it is not executed.

The exception handler in the outer block handles the exception.

Control then passes out of the enclosing block, which completes successfully.

Exceptions Raised in the Exception Section

Exceptions can also be raised while in an exception handler, either explicitly via the RAISE statement or implicitly via a runtime error. In either case, the exception is propagated immediately to the enclosing block, like exceptions raised in the declarative section. This is done because only one exception at a time can be "active" in the exception section. As soon as one is handled, another can be raised. But there cannot be more than one exception raised simultaneously. Examples 6, 7, and 8 illustrate this scenario.

Propagation Example 6

In this example, exception A is raised and then handled. But in the exception handler for A, exception B is raised. This exception is immediately propagated to the outer block, bypassing the handler for B. Similar to example 5, if this block had been enclosed in an outer block, this outer block could have caught exception B. (Example 7 illustrates the latter case.)

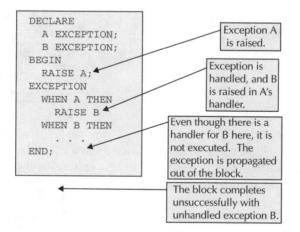

```
DECLARE
    A EXCEPTION;
    B EXCEPTION;
BEGIN
    RAISE A;
EXCEPTION
    WHEN A THEN
        RAISE B
    WHEN B THEN
        . . .
END;
```

Exception A is raised.

Exception is handled, and B is raised in A's handler.

Even though there is a handler for B here, it is not executed. The exception is propagated out of the block.

The block completes unsuccessfully with unhandled exception B.

Propagation Example 7

Similar to example 6, exception B is raised in the handler for exception A. This exception is immediately propagated to the enclosing block, bypassing the inner handler for B. However, in example 7 we have an outer block that handles exception B and completes successfully.

Propagation Example 8

As examples 6 and 7 illustrate, RAISE can be used to raise another exception inside a handler. In an exception handler, RAISE can also be used without an argument. If RAISE doesn't have an argument, the current exception is propagated to the enclosing block. This technique is useful for logging the error and/or doing any necessary cleanup because of it, and then notifying the enclosing block that it occurred. Example 8 illustrates this final scenario.

Note that there is a COMMIT after the INSERT statement in example 8. This ensures that the INSERT will be committed to the database, in case the transaction is rolled back. See Chapter 4 for more information about transactions.

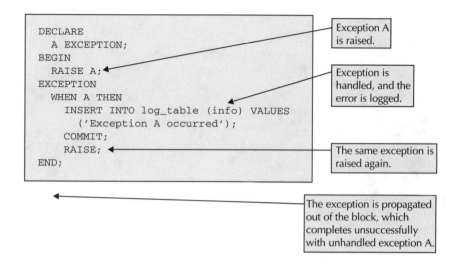

Exception Guidelines

This section contains guidelines and tips on how best to use exceptions in your programs. These guidelines include the scope of exceptions, how to avoid unhandled exceptions, and how to identify which statement raised a given exception. They should help you use exceptions more effectively in your own programs, and avoid some common pitfalls.

Scope of Exceptions

Exceptions are scoped just like variables. If a user-defined exception is propagated out of its scope, it can no longer be referenced by name. The next example illustrates this:

```
-- Available online as part of OutOfScope.sql
SQL> BEGIN
  2     DECLARE
  3        e_UserDefinedException EXCEPTION;
  4     BEGIN
  5        RAISE e_UserDefinedException;
```

```
 6    END;
 7  EXCEPTION
 8    /* e_UserDefinedException is out of scope here - can only be
 9       handled by an OTHERS handler */
10    WHEN OTHERS THEN
11      /* Just re-raise the exception, which will be propagated to
12         the calling environment */
13      RAISE;
14  END;
15  /
BEGIN
*
ERROR at line 1:
ORA-06510: PL/SQL: unhandled user-defined exception
ORA-06512: at line 13
```

In general, if a user-defined error is to be propagated out of a block, it is best to define the exception in a package so that it will still be visible outside the block, or to use RAISE_APPLICATION_ERROR instead. See the section "Using RAISE_APPLICATION_ERROR" earlier in this chapter for more information. If we create a package called Globals and define e_UserDefinedException in this package, the exception will still be visible in the outer block. See the following example:

-- **Available online as part of OutOfScope.sql**
```
CREATE OR REPLACE PACKAGE Globals AS
/* This package contains global declarations. Objects declared here
   will be visible via qualified references for any other blocks or
   procedures. Note that this package does not have a package body. */

  /* A user-defined exception. */
  e_UserDefinedException EXCEPTION;
END Globals;
```

Given package Globals, we can rewrite the preceding listing as

-- **Available online as part of OutOfScope.sql**
```
BEGIN
  BEGIN
    RAISE Globals.e_UserDefinedException;
  END;
EXCEPTION
  /* Since e_UserDefinedException is still visible, we can handle it
     explicitly */
  WHEN Globals.e_UserDefinedException THEN
    /* Just re-raise the exception, which will be propagated to the
       calling environment */
    RAISE;
END;
```

Package `Globals` can also be used for common PL/SQL tables, variables, and types, in addition to exceptions. See Chapters 9 and 10 for more information on packages.

Avoiding Unhandled Exceptions

It is good programming practice to avoid unhandled exceptions. This can be done via an OTHERS handler at the topmost level of your program. This handler may simply log the error and where it occurred. This way, you ensure that no error will go undetected. Here's an example:

```
DECLARE
    v_ErrorNumber NUMBER;        -- Variable to hold the error number
    v_ErrorText VARCHAR2(200);   -- Variable to hold error message text
BEGIN
    /* Normal PL/SQL processing */
    ...
EXCEPTION
    WHEN OTHERS THEN
        /* Log all exceptions so we complete successfully */
        v_ErrorNumber := SQLCODE;
        v_ErrorText := SUBSTR(SQLERRM, 1, 200);
        INSERT INTO log_table (code, message, info) VALUES
            (v_ErrorNumber, v_ErrorText, 'Oracle error occurred at ' ||
            TO_CHAR(SYSDATE, 'DD-MON-YY HH24:MI:SS'));
END;
```

Masking Location of the Error

Because the same exception section is examined for the entire block, it can be difficult to determine which SQL statement caused the error. Consider the following example:

```
BEGIN
    SELECT ...
    SELECT ...
    SELECT ...
EXCEPTION
    WHEN NO_DATA_FOUND THEN
        -- Which select statement raised the exception?
END;
```

There are two methods to solve this. The first is to increment a counter identifying the SQL statement:

```
DECLARE
    -- Variable to hold the select statement number
    v_SelectCounter NUMBER := 1;
```

```
BEGIN
  SELECT ...
  v_SelectCounter := 2;
  SELECT ...
  v_SelectCounter := 3;
  SELECT ...
EXCEPTION
  WHEN NO_DATA_FOUND THEN
    INSERT INTO log_table (info) VALUES ('No data found in select ' ||
      v_SelectCounter);
END;
```

The second method is to put each statement into its own sub-block:

```
BEGIN
  BEGIN
    SELECT ...
  EXCEPTION
    WHEN NO_DATA_FOUND THEN
      INSERT INTO log_table (info) VALUES ('No data found in
        select 1;);
  END;
  BEGIN
    SELECT ...
  EXCEPTION
    WHEN NO_DATA_FOUND THEN
      INSERT INTO log_table (info) VALUES ('No data found in
        select 2');
  END;
  BEGIN
    SELECT ...
  EXCEPTION
    WHEN NO_DATA_FOUND THEN
      INSERT INTO log_table (info) VALUES ('No data found in
        select 3');
  END;
END;
```

A General Error Handler

One problem with exceptions is that when an exception occurs, there is no easy
way to tell what part of the code was executing at the time. PL/SQL does provide a
solution to this, with the DBMS_UTILITY.FORMAT_CALL_STACK function. This
built-in function will return the current call stack, as a VARCHAR2 value. Consider
the following example, with procedures A, B, and C:

```
-- Available online as part of ErrorPkg.sql
CREATE OR REPLACE PROCEDURE C AS
  v_CallStack VARCHAR2(2000);
BEGIN
  v_CallStack := DBMS_UTILITY.FORMAT_CALL_STACK;
  INSERT INTO temp_table (char_col) VALUES (v_CallStack);
  INSERT INTO temp_table (num_col)
    VALUES (-1);
END C;
CREATE OR REPLACE PROCEDURE B AS
BEGIN
  C;
END B;
CREATE OR REPLACE PROCEDURE A AS
BEGIN
  B;
END A;
```

Note that A calls B, which calls C. If we call procedure A, we get output similar to the following:

```
----- PL/SQL Call Stack -----
  object      line   object
  handle    number   name
  16998f0        4   procedure DEMO.C
  1699ca0        3   procedure EXAMPLE.B
  169f918        3   procedure EXAMPLE.A
  1667ef0        1   anonymous block
```

Similar to FORMAT_CALL_STACK, DBMS_UTILITY_FORMAT_ERROR_STACK will return the current sequence of errors. Given these two functions, we can write a general error handler that will record both the location of an error and what the error is.

Here are the table definitions necessary for this package:

```
-- Available online as part of ErrorPkg.sql
CREATE TABLE errors (
  module        VARCHAR2(50),
  seq_number    NUMBER,
  error_number  NUMBER,
  error_mesg    VARCHAR2(100),
  error_stack   VARCHAR2(2000),
  call_stack    VARCHAR2(2000),
  timestamp     DATE,
  PRIMARY KEY (module, seq_number));

CREATE TABLE call_stacks (
```

```
module          VARCHAR2(50),
seq_number      NUMBER,
call_order      NUMBER,
object_handle   VARCHAR2(10),
line_num        NUMBER,
object_name     VARCHAR2(80),
PRIMARY KEY (module, seq_number, call_order),
FOREIGN KEY (module, seq_number) REFERENCES errors ON DELETE
  CASCADE);

CREATE TABLE error_stacks (
module          VARCHAR2(50),
seq_number      NUMBER,
error_order     NUMBER,
facility        CHAR(3),
error_number    NUMBER(5),
error_mesg      VARCHAR2(100),
PRIMARY KEY (module, seq_number, error_order),
FOREIGN KEY (module, seq_number) REFERENCES errors ON DELETE
  CASCADE);

CREATE SEQUENCE error_seq
  START WITH 1
  INCREMENT BY 1;
```

Given the above definitions, here is the `ErrorPkg` package:

```
-- Available online as part of ErrorPkg.sql
/* Generic error-handling package, using
   DBMS_UTILITY.FORMAT_ERROR_STACK and DBMS_UTILITY.FORMAT_CALL_STACK.
   This package will store general error information in the errors
   table, with detailed call stack and error stack information in the
   call_stacks and error_stacks tables, respectively. */
CREATE OR REPLACE PACKAGE ErrorPkg AS

  -- Entry point for handling errors.  HandleAll should be called
  -- from all exception handlers where you want the error to be
  -- logged.  p_Top should be TRUE only at the topmost level of
  -- procedure nesting.  It should be FALSE at other levels.
  PROCEDURE HandleAll(p_Top BOOLEAN);

  -- Prints the error and call stacks (using DBMS_OUTPUT) for the
  -- given module and sequence number.
  PROCEDURE PrintStacks(p_Module IN errors.module%TYPE,
                        p_SeqNum IN errors.seq_number%TYPE);

  -- Unwinds the call and error stacks, and stores them in the errors
```

```
    -- and call_stacks tables.  Returns the sequence number under which
    -- the error is stored.
    -- If p_CommitFlag is TRUE, then the inserts are committed.
    -- In order to use StoreStacks, an error must have been handled.
    -- Thus HandleAll should have been called with p_Top = TRUE.
  PROCEDURE StoreStacks(p_Module IN errors.module%TYPE,
                        p_SeqNum OUT errors.seq_number%TYPE,
                        p_CommitFlag BOOLEAN DEFAULT FALSE);
END ErrorPkg;

CREATE OR REPLACE PACKAGE BODY ErrorPkg AS

  v_NewLine     CONSTANT CHAR(1) := CHR(10);

  v_Handled      BOOLEAN := FALSE;
  v_ErrorStack   VARCHAR2(2000);
  v_CallStack    VARCHAR2(2000);

  PROCEDURE HandleAll(p_Top BOOLEAN) IS
  BEGIN
    IF p_Top THEN
      v_Handled := FALSE;
    ELSIF NOT v_Handled THEN
      v_Handled := TRUE;
      v_ErrorStack := DBMS_UTILITY.FORMAT_ERROR_STACK;
      v_CallStack := DBMS_UTILITY.FORMAT_CALL_STACK;
    END IF;
  END HandleAll;

  PROCEDURE PrintStacks(p_Module IN errors.module%TYPE,
                        p_SeqNum IN errors.seq_number%TYPE) IS
    v_TimeStamp errors.timestamp%TYPE;
    v_ErrorMsg  errors.error_mesg%TYPE;

    CURSOR c_CallCur IS
      SELECT object_handle, line_num, object_name
        FROM call_stacks
        WHERE module = p_Module
        AND seq_number = p_SeqNum
        ORDER BY call_order;

    CURSOR c_ErrorCur IS
      SELECT facility, error_number, error_mesg
        FROM error_stacks
        WHERE module = p_Module
        AND seq_number = p_SeqNum
        ORDER BY error_order;
  BEGIN
```

```
SELECT timestamp, error_mesg
  INTO v_TimeStamp, v_ErrorMsg
  FROM errors
  WHERE module = p_Module
  AND seq_number = p_SeqNum;

-- Output general error information.
DBMS_OUTPUT.PUT(TO_CHAR(v_TimeStamp, 'DD-MON-YY HH24:MI:SS'));
DBMS_OUTPUT.PUT(' Module: ' || p_Module);
DBMS_OUTPUT.PUT(' Error #' || p_SeqNum || ': ');
DBMS_OUTPUT.PUT_LINE(v_ErrorMsg);

-- Output the call stack.
DBMS_OUTPUT.PUT_LINE('Complete Call Stack:');
DBMS_OUTPUT.PUT_LINE(' Object Handle  Line Number  Object Name');
DBMS_OUTPUT.PUT_LINE(' -------------  -----------  -----------');
FOR v_CallRec in c_CallCur LOOP
  DBMS_OUTPUT.PUT(RPAD(' ' || v_CallRec.object_handle, 15));
  DBMS_OUTPUT.PUT(RPAD(' ' || TO_CHAR(v_CallRec.line_num), 13));
  DBMS_OUTPUT.PUT_LINE(' ' || v_CallRec.object_name);
END LOOP;

-- Output the error stack.
DBMS_OUTPUT.PUT_LINE('Complete Error Stack:');
FOR v_ErrorRec in c_ErrorCur LOOP
  DBMS_OUTPUT.PUT(' ' || v_ErrorRec.facility || '-');
  DBMS_OUTPUT.PUT(TO_CHAR(v_ErrorRec.error_number) || ': ');
  DBMS_OUTPUT.PUT_LINE(v_ErrorRec.error_mesg);
END LOOP;

END PrintStacks;

PROCEDURE StoreStacks(p_Module IN errors.module%TYPE,
                      p_SeqNum OUT errors.seq_number%TYPE,
                      p_CommitFlag BOOLEAN DEFAULT FALSE) IS
  v_SeqNum      NUMBER;

  v_Index       NUMBER;
  v_Length      NUMBER;
  v_End         NUMBER;

  v_Call        VARCHAR2(100);
  v_CallOrder   NUMBER := 1;
  v_Handle      call_stacks.object_handle%TYPE;
  v_LineNum     call_stacks.line_num%TYPE;
  v_ObjectName  call_stacks.object_name%TYPE;

  v_Error       VARCHAR2(120);
```

```
   v_ErrorOrder NUMBER := 1;
   v_Facility    error_stacks.facility%TYPE;
   v_ErrNum      error_stacks.error_number%TYPE;
   v_ErrMsg      error_stacks.error_mesg%TYPE;

   v_FirstErrNum errors.error_number%TYPE;
   v_FirstErrMsg errors.error_mesg%TYPE;
BEGIN
  -- First get the error sequence number.
  SELECT error_seq.nextval
    INTO v_SeqNum
    FROM dual;

  p_SeqNum := v_SeqNum;

  -- Insert the first part of the header information into the
  -- errors table.
  INSERT INTO errors
    (module, seq_number, error_stack, call_stack, timestamp)
  VALUES
    (p_Module, v_SeqNum, v_ErrorStack, v_CallStack, SYSDATE);

  -- Unwind the error stack to get each error out.  We do this by
  -- scanning the error stack string.  Start with the index at the
  -- beginning of the string.
  v_Index := 1;

  -- Loop through the string, finding each newline.  A newline ends
  -- each error on the stack.
  WHILE v_Index <  LENGTH(v_ErrorStack) LOOP
    -- v_End is the position of the newline.
    v_End := INSTR(v_ErrorStack, v_NewLine, v_Index);

    -- Thus, the error is between the current index and the
    -- newline.
    v_Error := SUBSTR(v_ErrorStack, v_Index, v_End - v_Index);

    -- Skip over the current error, for the next iteration.
    v_Index := v_Index + LENGTH(v_Error) + 1;

    -- An error looks like 'facility-number: mesg'.  We need to get
    -- each piece out for insertion.

    -- First, the facility is the first 3 characters of the error.
    v_Facility := SUBSTR(v_Error, 1, 3);

    -- Remove the facility and the dash (always 4 characters).
    v_Error := SUBSTR(v_Error, 5);
```

```
-- Now we can get the error number.
v_ErrNum :=
  TO_NUMBER(SUBSTR(v_Error, 1, INSTR(v_Error, ':') - 1));

-- Remove the error number, colon and space (always 7
-- characters).
v_Error := SUBSTR(v_Error, 8);

-- What's left is the error message.
v_ErrMsg := v_Error;

-- Insert the errors, and grab the first error number and
-- message while we're at it.
INSERT INTO error_stacks
  (module, seq_number, error_order, facility, error_number,
   error_mesg)
VALUES
  (p_Module, p_SeqNum, v_ErrorOrder, v_Facility, v_ErrNum,
   v_ErrMsg);

IF v_ErrorOrder = 1 THEN
  v_FirstErrNum := v_ErrNum;
  v_FirstErrMsg := v_Facility || '-' || TO_NUMBER(v_ErrNum) ||
                  ': ' || v_ErrMsg;
END IF;

v_ErrorOrder := v_ErrorOrder + 1;
END LOOP;

-- Update the errors table with the message and code.
UPDATE errors
  SET error_number = v_FirstErrNum,
      error_mesg = v_FirstErrMsg
  WHERE module = p_Module
  AND seq_number = v_SeqNum;

-- Now we need to unwind the call stack, to get each call out.
-- We do this by scanning the call stack string.  Start with the
-- index after the first call on the stack.  This will be after
-- the first occurrence of 'name' and the newline.
v_Index := INSTR(v_CallStack, 'name') + 5;

-- Loop through the string, finding each newline.  A newline ends
-- each call on the stack.
WHILE v_Index <  LENGTH(v_CallStack) LOOP
  -- v_End is the position of the newline.
  v_End := INSTR(v_CallStack, v_NewLine, v_Index);
```

```
  -- Thus, the call is between the current index and the newline.
  v_Call := SUBSTR(v_CallStack, v_Index, v_End - v_Index);

  -- Skip over the current call, for the next iteration.
  v_Index := v_Index + LENGTH(v_Call) + 1;

  -- Within a call, we have the object handle, then the line
  -- number, then the object name, separated by spaces.  We need
  -- to separate them out for insertion.

  -- Trim white space from the call first.
  v_Call := LTRIM(v_Call);

  -- First get the object handle.
  v_Handle := SUBSTR(v_Call, 1, INSTR(v_Call, ' '));

  -- Now, remove the object handle, then the white space from
  -- the call.
  v_Call := SUBSTR(v_Call, LENGTH(v_Handle) + 1);
  v_Call := LTRIM(v_Call);

  -- Now we can get the line number.
  v_LineNum := TO_NUMBER(SUBSTR(v_Call, 1, INSTR(v_Call, ' ')));

  -- Remove the line number, and white space.
  v_Call := SUBSTR(v_Call, LENGTH(v_LineNum) + 1);
  v_Call := LTRIM(v_Call);

  -- What is left is the object name.
  v_ObjectName := v_Call;

  -- Insert all calls except the call for ErrorPkg.
  IF v_CallOrder > 1 THEN
    INSERT INTO call_stacks
      (module, seq_number, call_order, object_handle, line_num,
       object_name)
    VALUES
      (p_Module, v_SeqNum, v_CallOrder, v_Handle, v_LineNum,
       v_ObjectName);
  END IF;

  v_Callorder := v_CallOrder + 1;

END LOOP;

IF p_CommitFlag THEN
  COMMIT;
END IF;
```

```
   END StoreStacks;

END ErrorPkg;
```

Now, suppose we put a trigger on `temp_table` (this requires the CREATE TRIGGER privilege) to raise the ZERO_DIVIDE exception, and modify A, B, and C as follows:

```
-- Available online as part of ErrorPkg.sql
CREATE OR REPLACE TRIGGER temp_insert
  BEFORE INSERT ON temp_table
BEGIN
  RAISE ZERO_DIVIDE;
END ttt_insert;

CREATE OR REPLACE PROCEDURE C AS
BEGIN
  INSERT INTO temp_table (num_col) VALUES (7);
EXCEPTION
  WHEN OTHERS THEN
    ErrorPkg.HandleAll(FALSE);
    RAISE;
END C;

CREATE OR REPLACE PROCEDURE B AS
BEGIN
  C;
EXCEPTION
  WHEN OTHERS THEN
    ErrorPkg.HandleAll(FALSE);
    RAISE;
END B;

CREATE OR REPLACE PROCEDURE A AS
  v_ErrorSeq NUMBER;
BEGIN
  B;
EXCEPTION
  WHEN OTHERS THEN
    ErrorPkg.HandleAll(TRUE);
    ErrorPkg.StoreStacks('Error Test', v_ErrorSeq, TRUE);
    ErrorPkg.PrintStacks('Error Test', v_ErrorSeq);
END A;
```

The important thing to note is that, except for the top level (procedure A), all of the exception handlers look like

```
WHEN OTHERS THEN
    ErrorPkg.HandleAll(FALSE);
RAISE;
```

This tells `ErrorPkg` to record the call and error stack if necessary, then propagate the error out to the calling procedure. At the top level, `HandleAll` should be called with TRUE. This tells `ErrorPkg` that it is at the top level, and that no more propagating will occur. `StoreStacks` then stores the call and error stacks in the `errors`, `error_stacks`, and `call_stacks` tables, indexed by a module name. The module should be the name of the package, or other determining identifier. All errors are stored using both the module name, and the error number, which is returned by `StoreStacks`. A call to `PrintStacks` will query the error tables and print the results using DBMS_OUTPUT. For example, if we call A from SQL*Plus, we see the following:

```
-- Available online as part of ErrorPkg.sql
SQL> SET SERVEROUTPUT ON SIZE 1000000 FORMAT TRUNCATED
SQL> exec A;
31-MAY-01 01:42:47  Module: Error Test  Error #1:  ORA-1476: divisor
  is equal to zero
Complete Call Stack:
  Object Handle  Line Number  Object Name
  -------------  -----------  -----------
  85463480       6            procedure DEMO.C
  85457294       3            procedure DEMO.B
  85459b84       4            procedure DEMO.A
  85402580       1            anonymous block
Complete Error Stack:
  ORA-1476: divisor is equal to zero
  ORA-6512: at "DEMO.TEMP_INSERT", line 2
  ORA-4088: error during execution of trigger 'DEMO.TEMP_INSERT'

PL/SQL procedure successfully completed.
```

Summary

This chapter explained how PL/SQL programs can detect and react intelligently to runtime errors. The mechanism provided by PL/SQL to do this includes exceptions and exception handlers. We have seen how exceptions are defined and how they correspond to either user-defined errors or predefined Oracle errors. We have also discussed the rules for exception propagation, including exceptions raised in all parts of a PL/SQL block. The chapter concluded with guidelines on using exceptions.

CHAPTER
8

Collections

t is often convenient to manipulate many variables at once, as one unit. Datatypes like this are known as *collections*. Oracle7 provided one collection type: an index-by table. Oracle8 added two more collection types: nested tables and varrays. Oracle9*i* adds the ability to create multilevel collections—that is, collections of collections. All of the collection types are similar to arrays in other languages. In this chapter, we will discuss each of these collection types and their features.

Declaring and Using Collection Types

As we saw in Chapter 3, PL/SQL has two composite types: records and collections. A record allows you to treat several variables as a unit—all the fields of the students table, for example. Records are similar to structs in C. Collections are also composite types, in that they allow you to treat several variables as a unit. Instead of combining several different variables of different types, however, a collection combines variables of the same type, similar to a C or Java array. There are three collection types: index-by tables, nested tables, and varrays.

Index-by tables were first introduced in PL/SQL 2.0 (with Oracle7 Release 7.0), and were significantly enhanced in PL/SQL 2.3 (with Oracle7 Release 7.3). *Nested tables,* introduced with Oracle8, extend the functionality of index-by tables by adding extra collection methods (known as *table attributes* for index-by tables). Nested tables can also be stored in database tables (which is why they are called nested) and can be manipulated directly using SQL. Index-by tables, on the other hand, exist entirely within PL/SQL and cannot be stored directly in a database table. Collectively, index-by tables and nested tables are known as *PL/SQL tables.*

NOTE
In Oracle7, index-by tables were known as PL/SQL tables. Oracle8 PL/SQL tables include both index-by and nested tables.

The third collection type is the *varray.* Varrays were introduced in Oracle8 and are similar to PL/SQL tables in how they are accessed. However, varrays are declared with a fixed number of elements, whereas PL/SQL tables have no declared upper limit.

In this section, we will examine how to declare and use all three collection types. The differences and similarities between them are summarized at the end of the section.

Index-By Tables

Index-by tables are syntactically similar to C or Java arrays. In order to declare an index-by table, you first define the table type within a PL/SQL block, and then declare a variable of this type (just like for a record). The general syntax for defining an index-by table type is

TYPE *tabletype* IS TABLE OF *type* INDEX BY BINARY_INTEGER;

where *tabletype* is the name of the new type being defined, and *type* is a predefined type or a reference to a type via %TYPE or %ROWTYPE. The following declarative section illustrates several different PL/SQL table types and variable declarations:

```
-- Available online as part of indexBy.sql
DECLARE
  TYPE NameTab IS TABLE OF students.first_name%TYPE
    INDEX BY BINARY_INTEGER;
  TYPE DateTab IS TABLE OF DATE
    INDEX BY BINARY_INTEGER;
  v_Names NameTab;
  v_Dates DateTab;
```

NOTE
The INDEX BY BINARY_INTEGER clause is required as part of the table definition. This clause is not present for nested tables.

Once the type and the variable are declared, we can refer to an individual element in the PL/SQL table by using the syntax

tablename(*index*)

where *tablename* is the name of a table and *index* is either a variable of type BINARY_INTEGER or a variable or expression that can be converted to a BINARY_INTEGER. Given the declarations for the different table types, we could continue the above PL/SQL block with

```
-- Available online as part of indexBy.sql
BEGIN
  v_Names(1) := 'Scott';
  v_Dates(-4) := SYSDATE - 1;
END;
```

A table reference, like a record or variable reference, is an lvalue because it points to storage that has been allocated by the PL/SQL engine.

Index-By Tables versus C or Java Arrays

Consider the following PL/SQL block, which creates an index-by table and assigns values to some of its elements:

```
-- Available online as part of indexBy.sql
DECLARE
  TYPE CharacterTab IS TABLE OF VARCHAR2(10)
    INDEX BY BINARY_INTEGER;
  v_Characters CharacterTab;
BEGIN
  -- Assign to three elements of the table.  Note that the key
  -- values are not sequential.
  v_Characters(0)  := 'Harold';
  v_Characters(-7) := 'Susan';
  v_Characters(3)  := 'Steve';
END;
```

Although assignment to table elements is syntactically similar to assignment to a C or Java array, index-by tables are implemented differently. An index-by table is similar to a database table, with two columns—key and value. The type of key is BINARY_INTEGER, and the type of value is whatever datatype is specified in the definition—VARCHAR2(10) in the previous example.

After executing the assignments in the above block, the data structure of v_Characters will look like Table 8-1. There are several things to note about index-by tables that are illustrated by this example:

■ Index-by tables are unconstrained. The only limit (other than available memory) on the number of rows is that the key is a BINARY_INTEGER, and is therefore constrained to the values that can be represented by the BINARY_INTEGER type (–2147483647 … +2147483647).

■ The elements in an index-by table are not necessarily in any particular order. Because they are not stored contiguously in memory like an array, elements can be inserted under arbitrary keys. (If you pass an index-by table from PL/SQL to a host array in C or Java, the elements should be numbered sequentially starting from 1.)

■ The keys used for an index-by table don't have to be sequential. Any BINARY_INTEGER value or expression can be used for a table index.

■ The only type allowed for the key is BINARY_INTEGER.

Nonexistent Elements

An assignment to element *i* in an index-by table actually creates element *i* if it does not already exist, similar to an INSERT operation on a database table. References to element *i* are likewise similar to a SELECT operation. In fact, if element *i* is referenced

Key	Value
0	Harold
−7	Susan
3	Steve

TABLE 8-1. *Contents of v_Characters*

before it has been created, the PL/SQL engine will return "ORA-1403: No data found," just like a database table. This is illustrated by the following SQL*Plus session:

```
-- Available online as part of indexBy.sql
SQL> DECLARE
  2    TYPE NumberTab IS TABLE OF NUMBER
  3      INDEX BY BINARY_INTEGER;
  4    v_Numbers NumberTab;
  5  BEGIN
  6    -- Assign to several of the elements.
  7    FOR v_Count IN 1..10 LOOP
  8      v_Numbers(v_Count) := v_Count * 10;
  9    END LOOP;
 10
 11    -- And print them out
 12    DBMS_OUTPUT.PUT_LINE('Table elements: ');
 13    FOR v_Count IN 1..10 LOOP
 14      DBMS_OUTPUT.PUT_LINE('  v_Numbers(' || v_Count || '): ' ||
 15                    v_Numbers(v_Count));
 16    END LOOP;
 17
 18    -- Read from v_Numbers(11).  Since it hasn't been assigned a
 19    -- value, this will raise NO_DATA_FOUND.
 20    BEGIN
 21      DBMS_OUTPUT.PUT_LINE('v_Numbers(11): ' || v_Numbers(11));
 22    EXCEPTION
 23      WHEN NO_DATA_FOUND THEN
 24        DBMS_OUTPUT.PUT_LINE(
 25          'No data found reading v_Numbers(11)!');
 26    END;
 27  END;
 28  /
Table elements:
v_Numbers(1): 10
v_Numbers(2): 20
v_Numbers(3): 30
v_Numbers(4): 40
```

```
v_Numbers(5): 50
v_Numbers(6): 60
v_Numbers(7): 70
v_Numbers(8): 80
v_Numbers(9): 90
v_Numbers(10): 100
No data found reading v_Numbers(11)!
PL/SQL procedure successfully completed.
```

NOTE
See Chapter 2 for information on the DBMS_ OUTPUT package, and Chapter 7 for information on the exception-handling features of PL/SQL.

Elements can be deleted from an index-by table using the DELETE method described later in this chapter in the "Collection Methods" section.

Index-By Tables of Nonscalar Types

In Oracle7 Release 7.3, the only nonscalar type supported by index-by tables was a record. Oracle8 allowed index-by tables of object types, and Oracle9i allows index-by tables of any collection type. For information on index-by tables of collections, see the section "Multilevel Collections" later in this chapter.

Index-By Tables of Records   The following example illustrates an index-by table of records:

```
-- Available online as tabRecord.sql
DECLARE
  TYPE StudentTab IS TABLE OF students%ROWTYPE
    INDEX BY BINARY_INTEGER;
  /* Each element of v_Students is a record */
  v_Students StudentTab;
BEGIN
  /* Retrieve the record with id = 10,001 and store it into
     v_Students(10001). */
  SELECT *
    INTO v_Students(10001)
    FROM students
    WHERE id = 10001;

  /* Directly assign to v_Students(1). */
  v_Students(1).first_name := 'Larry';
  v_Students(1).last_name := 'Lemon';
END;
```

Because each element of this table is a record, we can refer to fields within this record with the syntax

table(index).field

as the above example illustrates.

 Index-By Tables of Object Types Oracle8 allows index-by tables of object types, as the following example illustrates:

```
-- Available online as tabObject.sql
CREATE OR REPLACE TYPE MyObject AS OBJECT (
  field1 NUMBER,
  field2 VARCHAR2(20),
  field3 DATE);
/

DECLARE
  TYPE ObjectTab IS TABLE OF MyObject
    INDEX BY BINARY_INTEGER;
  /* Each element of v_Objects is an instance of the MyObject object
   * type. */
  v_Objects ObjectTab;
BEGIN
  /* Directly assign to v_Objects(1).  First we have to initialize
   * the object type. */
  v_Objects(1) := MyObject(1, NULL, NULL);
  v_Objects(1).field2 := 'Hello World!';
  v_Objects(1).field3 := SYSDATE;
END;
```

NOTE
Object types are first created with the SQL CREATE TYPE command. Object instances of a created type can then be created. For more information on object types, see Chapter 12.

Nested Tables

The basic functionality of a nested table is the same as an index-by table. A nested table can be thought of as a database table with two columns—key and value—as we saw in the previous section. Elements can be deleted from the middle of a nested table, leaving a sparse table with nonsequential keys, like index-by tables. However, nested tables must be created with sequential keys, and the keys cannot be negative. Furthermore, nested tables can be stored in the database while index-by tables cannot. The maximum number of rows in a nested table is 2 gigabytes, which is also the maximum key value.

The syntax for creating a nested table type is

TYPE *table_name* is TABLE OF *table_type* [NOT NULL];

where *table_name* is the name of the new type, and *table_type* is the type of each element in the nested table. *table_type* can be a user-defined object type or it can be an expression using %TYPE, but it cannot be BOOLEAN, NCHAR, NCLOB, NVARCHAR2, or REF CURSOR. Prior to Oracle9*i*, *table_type* cannot be TABLE or VARRAY either. This restriction is lifted in Oracle9*i* (see the section "Multilevel Collections" later in this chapter for details). If NOT NULL is present, elements of the nested table cannot be NULL.

NOTE
The only syntactic difference between index-by tables and nested tables is the presence of the INDEX BY BINARY_INTEGER clause. If this clause is not present, the type is a nested table type. If this clause is present, the type is an index-by table type.

The following declarative section shows some valid nested table declarations:

```
-- Available online as part of nested.sql
DECLARE
  -- Define a nested table type based on an object type
  TYPE ObjectTab IS TABLE OF MyObject;

  -- A nested table type based on %ROWTYPE
  TYPE StudentsTab IS TABLE OF students%ROWTYPE;

  -- Variables of the above types
  v_ClassList StudentsTab;
  v_ObjectList ObjectTab;
```

NOTE
The MyObject *object type was defined in the previous section.*

Nested Table Initialization

When an index-by table is created but does not yet have any elements, it is simply empty. However, when a nested table is declared but does not yet have any elements (as in the preceding block), it is initialized to be atomically NULL, like other PL/SQL types. If you try to add an element to a NULL nested table, the error "ORA-6531: Reference to uninitialized collection," which corresponds to the predefined exception COLLECTION_IS_NULL, is raised. Continuing the previous example, the following execution section will raise this error:

```
-- Available online as part of nested.sql
BEGIN
  -- This assignment will raise COLLECTION_IS_NULL because
  -- v_ObjectList is atomically NULL.
  v_ObjectList(1) :=
    MyObject(-17, 'Goodbye', TO_DATE('01-01-2001', 'DD-MM-YYYY'));
END;
```

So, how do you initialize a nested table? This can be done by using the constructor. The constructor for a nested table has the same name as the table type itself. However, it has a varying number of arguments, each of which should be compatible with the table element type. The arguments become elements of the table, starting sequentially with index 1. The following SQL*Plus session illustrates the use of nested table constructors:

```
-- Available online as tConstruct.sql
SQL> DECLARE
  2     TYPE NumbersTab IS TABLE OF NUMBER;
  3
  4     -- Create a table with one element.
  5     v_Tab1 NumbersTab := NumbersTab(-1);
  6
  7     -- Create a table with five elements.
  8     v_Primes NumbersTab := NumbersTab(1, 2, 3, 5, 7);
  9
 10     -- Create a table with no elements.
 11     v_Tab2 NumbersTab := NumbersTab();
 12  BEGIN
 13     -- Assign to v_Tab1(1). This will replace the value already
 14     -- in v_Tab(1), which was initialized to -1.
 15     v_Tab1(1) := 12345;
 16
 17     -- Print out the contents of v_Primes.
```

```
18    FOR v_Count IN 1..5 LOOP
19      DBMS_OUTPUT.PUT(v_Primes(v_Count) || ' ');
20    END LOOP;
21    DBMS_OUTPUT.NEW_LINE;
22  END;
23  /
1 2 3 5 7
PL/SQL procedure successfully completed.
```

Empty Tables Note the declaration of v_Tab2 in the preceding block:

```
-- Create a table with no elements.
v_Tab2 t_NumbersTab := t_NumbersTab();
```

v_Tab2 is initialized by calling the constructor with no arguments. This creates a table that has no elements, but is not atomically NULL. The following SQL*Plus session illustrates this:

```
-- Available online as nullTable.sql
SQL> DECLARE
  2    TYPE WordsTab IS TABLE OF VARCHAR2(50);
  3
  3    -- Create a NULL table.
  4    v_Tab1 WordsTab;
  5
  5    -- Create a table with one element, which itself is NULL.
  6    v_Tab2 WordsTab := WordsTab();
  7  BEGIN
  8    IF v_Tab1 IS NULL THEN
  9      DBMS_OUTPUT.PUT_LINE('v_Tab1 is NULL');
 10    ELSE
 11      DBMS_OUTPUT.PUT_LINE('v_Tab1 is not NULL');
 12    END IF;
 13
 13    IF v_Tab2 IS NULL THEN
 14      DBMS_OUTPUT.PUT_LINE('v_Tab2 is NULL');
 15    ELSE
 16      DBMS_OUTPUT.PUT_LINE('v_Tab2 is not NULL');
 17    END IF;
 18  END;
 19  /
v_Tab1 is NULL
v_Tab2 is not NULL
PL/SQL procedure successfully completed.
```

Adding Elements to an Existing Table

Although a table is unconstrained, you cannot assign to an element that does not yet exist, and would thus cause the table to increase in size. If you attempt to do this, PL/SQL will raise the error "ORA-6533: Subscript beyond count," which is equivalent to the SUBSCRIPT_BEYOND_COUNT predefined exception. This is illustrated by the following SQL*Plus session:

```
-- Available online as tabAssign.sql
SQL> DECLARE
  2    TYPE NumbersTab IS TABLE OF NUMBER;
  3    v_Numbers NumbersTab := NumbersTab(1, 2, 3);
  4  BEGIN
  5    -- v_Numbers was initialized to have 3 elements. So the
  6    -- following assignments are all legal.
  7    v_Numbers(1) := 7;
  8    v_Numbers(2) := -1;
  9
 10    -- However, this assignment will raise ORA-6533.
 11    v_Numbers(4) := 4;
 12  END;
 13  /
DECLARE
*
ERROR at line 1:
ORA-06533: Subscript beyond count
ORA-06512: at line 11
```

TIP
You can increase the size of a nested table by using the EXTEND method, described later in this chapter in the "Collection Methods" section.

Varrays

Oracle **8**
and higher

A *varray* (variable length array) is a datatype very similar to an array in C or Java. Syntactically, a varray is accessed similar to a nested or index-by table. However, a varray has a fixed upper bound on its size, specified as part of the type declaration. Rather than being a sparse data structure with no upper bound, elements are inserted into a varray starting at index 1, up to the maximum length declared in the varray type. The maximum size of a varray is 2 gigabytes, like a nested table.

The storage for a varray is the same as a C or Java array; namely, the elements are stored contiguously in memory. This is different from the storage for a nested table, which is more like a database table.

Declaring a Varray

A varray type is declared using the syntax:

> TYPE *type_name* IS {VARRAY | VARYING ARRAY} (*maximum_size*)
>   OF *element_type* [NOT NULL];

where *type_name* is the name of the new varray type, *maximum_size* is an integer specifying the maximum number of elements in the varray, and *element_type* is a PL/SQL scalar, record, or object type. The *element_type* can be specified using %TYPE, but cannot be BOOLEAN, NCHAR, NCLOB, NVARCHAR2, or REF CURSOR. Prior to Oracle9i, *element_type* cannot be TABLE or VARRAY either. This restriction is lifted in Oracle9i (see the section "Multilevel Collections" later in this chapter for details). The following declarative section shows some legal varray types:

```
-- Available online as part of varray.sql
DECLARE
  -- Some valid varray types.
  -- This is a list of numbers, each of which is constrained to
  -- be not null.
  TYPE NumberList IS VARRAY(10) OF NUMBER(3) NOT NULL;

  -- A list of PL/SQL records.
  TYPE StudentList IS VARRAY(100) OF students%ROWTYPE;

  -- A list of objects.
  TYPE ObjectList is VARRAY(25) OF MyObject;
```

Varray Initialization

Similar to tables, varrays are initialized using a constructor. The number of arguments passed to the constructor becomes the initial length of the varray, and must be less than or equal to the maximum length specified in the varray type. The following SQL*Plus session illustrates this:

```
-- Available online as vConstruct.sql
SQL> DECLARE
  2      -- Define a VARRAY type.
  3      TYPE Numbers IS VARRAY(20) OF NUMBER(3);
  4
  4      -- Declare a NULL varray.
  5      v_NullList Numbers;
  6
  6      -- This varray has 2 elements.
```

```
 7    v_List1 Numbers := Numbers(1, 2);
 8
 8    -- This varray has one element, which itself is NULL.
 9    v_List2 Numbers := Numbers(NULL);
10  BEGIN
11    IF v_NullList IS NULL THEN
12      DBMS_OUTPUT.PUT_LINE('v_NullList is NULL');
13    END IF;
14
14    IF v_List2(1) IS NULL THEN
15      DBMS_OUTPUT.PUT_LINE('v_List2(1) is NULL');
16    END IF;
17  END;
18  /
v_NullList is NULL
v_List2(1) is NULL
PL/SQL procedure successfully completed.
```

Manipulating Varray Elements

Like nested tables, the initial size of a varray is set by the number of elements used in the constructor when it is declared. Assignments to elements outside this range will raise the error "ORA-6533: Subscript beyond count," just like a nested table. The following SQL*Plus session illustrates this:

```
-- Available online as part of vAssign.sql
SQL> DECLARE
 2    TYPE Strings IS VARRAY(5) OF VARCHAR2(10);
 3
 4    -- Declare a varray with three elements
 5    v_List Strings :=
 6      Strings('One', 'Two', 'Three');
 7  BEGIN
 8    -- Subscript between 1 and 3, so this is legal.
 9    v_List(2) := 'TWO';
10
11    -- Subscript beyond count, raises ORA-6533.
12    v_List(4) := '!!!';
13  END;
14  /
DECLARE
*
ERROR at line 1:
ORA-06533: Subscript beyond count
ORA-06512: at line 12
```

TIP
*Like nested tables, the size of a varray can be
increased using the EXTEND method, described later
in this chapter in the "Collection Methods" section.
Unlike a nested table, however, a varray cannot be
extended past the maximum size declared for the
varray type.*

Assignments to elements outside the maximum size of the varray, or attempts to extend the varray past the maximum size, will raise the error "ORA-6532: Subscript outside of limit," which is equivalent to the predefined exception SUBSCRIPT_OUTSIDE_LIMIT. This is illustrated by the following:

```
-- Available online as part of vAssign.sql
SQL> DECLARE
  2      TYPE Strings IS VARRAY(5) OF VARCHAR2(10);
  3      -- Declare a varray with four elements,
  4      v_List Strings :=
  5        Strings('One', 'Two', 'Three', 'Four');
  6  BEGIN
  7      -- Subscript between 1 and 4, so this is legal.
  8      v_List(2) := 'TWO';
  9
 10      -- Extend the table to 5 elements and set the value.
 11      v_List.EXTEND;
 12      v_List(5) := 'Five';
 13
 14      -- Attempt to extend the table to 6 elements.  This will raise
 15      -- ORA-6532.
 16      v_list.EXTEND;
 17  END;
 18  /
DECLARE
*
ERROR at line 1:
ORA-06532: Subscript outside of limit
ORA-06512: at line 16
```

Multilevel Collections

Oracle9*i*
and higher All of the examples we have seen so far involve one-dimensional collections. Oracle9*i* allows collections of more than one dimension—that is, a collection of collections. This construct is known as a *multilevel collection*. The type declaration for a multilevel collection is the same as for a one-dimensional collection, except that

the collection type is itself a collection. The following declaration section illustrates some multilevel collection types:

```
-- Available online as part of multilevel.sql
DECLARE
  -- First declare an index-by table of numbers
  TYPE t_Numbers IS TABLE OF NUMBER
    INDEX BY BINARY_INTEGER;

  -- Now declare a type which is an index-by table of t_Numbers.
  -- This is a multilevel collection.
  TYPE t_MultiNumbers IS TABLE OF t_Numbers
    INDEX BY BINARY_INTEGER;

  -- We can also have a varray of the index-by table
  TYPE t_MultiVarray IS VARRAY(10) OF t_Numbers;

  -- Or a nested table
  TYPE t_MultiNested IS TABLE OF t_Numbers;

  v_MultiNumbers t_MultiNumbers;
```

An element of a multilevel collection is itself a collection, so we use two sets of parentheses to access an element of the contained collection, as the following illustrates:

```
-- Available online as part of multilevel.sql
BEGIN
  v_MultiNumbers(1)(1) := 12345;
END;
```

Comparison Between Collection Types

This section describes some of the similarities and differences between the three collection types we have examined. Table 8-2 summarizes the behavior of the types, which are discussed in the following sections.

Varrays versus Nested Tables

Varrays and nested tables have similarities, including

- Both types (plus index-by tables) allow access to individual elements using subscript notation within PL/SQL.

- Both types can be stored in database tables (when declared outside a PL/SQL block).

- Collection methods can be applied to both.

Index-By Tables	Nested Tables	Varrays
First available in Oracle7.0, enhanced in 7.3	First available in Oracle8	First available in Oracle8
Elements are accessed syntactically through parentheses	Elements are accessed syntactically through parentheses	Elements are accessed syntactically through parentheses
Oracle 7.3 introduced table attributes for manipulation	Can use additional collection methods in addition to the 7.3 attributes	Can use additional collection methods in addition to the 7.3 attributes
Cannot be stored in database tables	Can be stored in database tables	Can be stored in database tables
Keys can be positive or negative	Keys must be positive	Keys must be positive
Have no explicit maximum size	Have no explicit maximum size	Are constrained to a maximum size in the type definition
Can map to host arrays	Cannot map to host arrays	Cannot map to host arrays
Can be sparse with nonsequential key values	Can be sparse with nonsequential key values	Always have space allocated for each of the elements and have sequential key values
Cannot be atomically NULL	Can be atomically NULL	Can be atomically NULL
Referencing nonexistent elements raises NO_DATA_FOUND	Referencing nonexistent elements raises SUBSCRIPT_BEYOND_COUNT	Referencing nonexistent elements raises SUBSCRIPT_BEYOND_COUNT
Can be declared inside PL/SQL blocks only	Can be declared inside PL/SQL blocks, or outside with CREATE TYPE*	Can be declared inside PL/SQL blocks, or outside with CREATE TYPE*
Elements are assigned directly, without initialization	The table must be initialized and extended before elements can be assigned	The varray must be initialized before elements can be assigned

*See the section "Schema-Level Types" later in this chapter for details of the CREATE TYPE statement and how it is used.

TABLE 8-2. *Collection Types*

However, there are also some differences:

- Varrays have a maximum size, whereas nested tables do not have an explicit maximum size.

- When stored in the database, varrays retain the ordering and subscript values for the elements, whereas nested tables do not.

Nested Tables versus Index-By Tables

Nested tables are similar to index-by tables in many ways. For example:

- Both table datatypes have the same structure.

- Individual elements in both are accessed using subscript notation.

- The methods available for nested tables include all of the table attributes for index-by tables.

However, there are also several significant differences:

- Nested tables can be manipulated using SQL and can be stored in the database, whereas index-by tables cannot.

- Nested tables have a legal subscript range of 1 … 2147483647, whereas index-by tables have a range of -2147483647 … 2147483647. Thus, index-by tables can have negative subscripts whereas nested tables cannot.

- Nested tables can be atomically NULL (testable with the IS NULL operator).

- Nested tables must be initialized and/or extended in order to add elements.

- Nested tables have additional methods available, such as EXTEND and TRIM (described in the "Collection Methods" section later in this chapter).

- PL/SQL will automatically convert between a host array and an index-by table, but cannot convert between a host array and a nested table.

Collections in the Database

All of the examples we have examined so far involve the manipulation of collections in PL/SQL blocks. However, nested tables and varrays can be stored in database tables as well. In the following sections, we will discuss how to access and manipulate stored collections, as well as some of the implications.

Implications of Stored Collections

Storing collections in the database has implications with regard to the way that the table types need to be declared, and the syntax of creating tables with collection columns. We will examine these implications in this section.

Schema-Level Types

In order to store and retrieve a collection from a database table, the collection type must be known to both PL/SQL and SQL. This means that it cannot be local to a PL/SQL block, and instead should be declared using a CREATE TYPE statement, similar to an object type. The following example illustrates this:

```
-- Available online as typeLocation.sql
SQL> -- Create a stored type which is visible to SQL and PL/SQL.
SQL> CREATE OR REPLACE TYPE NameList AS
  2     VARRAY(20) OF VARCHAR2(30);
  3  /
Type created.
SQL> DECLARE
  2     -- This type is local to this block.
  3     TYPE DateList IS VARRAY(10) OF DATE;
  4
  4     -- We can create variables of both DateList and NameList here.
  5     v_Dates DateList;
  6     v_Names NameList;
  7  BEGIN
  8     NULL;
  9  END;
 10  /
PL/SQL procedure successfully completed.

SQL> DECLARE
  2     -- Since NameList is global to PL/SQL, we can reference it in
  3     -- another block as well.
  4     v_Names2 NameList;
  5  BEGIN
  6     NULL;
  7  END;
  8  /
PL/SQL procedure successfully completed.
```

TIP
When issuing the CREATE OR REPLACE TYPE statement from SQL*Plus, the final / is needed, similar to after a PL/SQL block. See Chapter 2 for more information on SQL*Plus.

A type created at the schema level (with CREATE OR REPLACE TYPE) is considered global to PL/SQL, with scope and visibility rules similar to any other database object. A schema-level type can also be used as a database column, as we will see in the sections that follow.

A type declared local to a PL/SQL block, however, is visible only in that block and is not available for a database column. A type declared in a package header is visible throughout PL/SQL (in accordance with the PL/SQL scoping rules), but is still not available for a database column. Only schema-level types can be used for database columns.

The books Table   In the following sections, we will create tables and types that will model the library used by the students. To facilitate this, we need the following table:

```
-- Available online as part of tables.sql
CREATE TABLE books (
   catalog_number NUMBER(4)      PRIMARY KEY,
   title          VARCHAR2(40),
   author1        VARCHAR2(40),
   author2        VARCHAR2(40),
   author3        VARCHAR2(40),
   author4        VARCHAR2(40)
);
```

where the catalog_number uniquely identifies a given book, and author1 through author4 contain the book's authors, in "last_name, first_name" format. The following rows are inserted into books by tables.sql:

```
INSERT INTO books (catalog_number, title, author1)
   VALUES (1000, 'Oracle8i Advanced PL/SQL Programming',
                 'Urman, Scott');

INSERT INTO books (catalog_number, title, author1, author2, author3)
   VALUES (1001, 'Oracle8i: A Beginner''s Guide',
                 'Abbey, Michael', 'Corey, Michael J.',
                 'Abramson, Ian');

INSERT INTO books (catalog_number, title, author1, author2, author3,
                 author4)
   VALUES (1002, 'Oracle8 Tuning',
                 'Corey, Michael J.', 'Abbey, Michael',
                 'Dechichio, Daniel J.', 'Abramson, Ian');

INSERT INTO books (catalog_number, title, author1, author2)
   VALUES (2001, 'A History of the World',
                 'Arlington, Arlene', 'Verity, Victor');
```

```
INSERT INTO books (catalog_number, title, author1)
   VALUES (3001, 'Bach and the Modern World', 'Foo, Fred');

INSERT INTO books (catalog_number, title, author1)
   VALUES (3002, 'Introduction to the Piano',
                 'Morenson, Mary');
```

Structure of Stored Varrays

A varray can be used as the type for a database column. In this case, the entire varray is stored within one database row, alongside the other columns. Different rows contain different varrays. For example, consider the following declarations:

```
-- Available online as part of tables.sql
CREATE OR REPLACE TYPE BookList AS VARRAY(10) OF NUMBER(4);

CREATE TABLE class_material (
   department        CHAR(3),
   course            NUMBER(3),
   required_reading  BookList
);
```

> **NOTE**
> *Varray data that is larger than 4K will actually be stored separately from the rest of the table columns, in a LOB. In Oracle8i and higher, you can specify the storage parameters for the LOB separately in the CREATE TABLE statement. See the SQL Reference Guide for more information on CREATE TABLE, and Chapter 12 for more information about LOBs.*

The `class_material` table contains a list of the catalog numbers of the required books for a given class. This list is stored as a varray column. The type for any varray column must be known to the database and stored in the data dictionary, so the CREATE TYPE statement is necessary. The storage for `class_material` (with some sample data) is illustrated by Figure 8-1. Note that the entire varray (which can consist of up to ten elements) is stored in a single database column, `required_reading`.

class_material

Department	Course	Required_Reading		
MUS	100	3001	3002	
CS	102	1000	1001	1002
HIS	101	2001		

FIGURE 8-1. *Varrays in the database*

Structure of Stored Nested Tables

Like a varray, a nested table can be stored as a database column. Each row of the database table can contain a different nested table. For example, suppose we want to model the library catalog. We can do this with the following definitions:

```
-- Available online as part of tables.sql
CREATE OR REPLACE TYPE StudentList AS TABLE OF NUMBER(5);

CREATE TABLE library_catalog (
  catalog_number NUMBER(4),
    FOREIGN KEY (catalog_number) REFERENCES books(catalog_number),
  num_copies     NUMBER,
  num_out        NUMBER,
  checked_out    StudentList)
NESTED TABLE checked_out STORE AS co_tab;
```

The `library_catalog` table contains four columns, including the catalog number of the books in the collection, and a nested table containing the IDs of the students who have checked out copies. There are a couple of things to note about storing nested tables:

- The table type is used in the table definition, just like a column object or built-in type. It must be a schema-level type created with the CREATE TYPE statement.

- For each nested table in a given database table, the NESTED TABLE clause is required. This clause indicates the name of the store table.

A *store table* is a system-generated table that is used to store the actual data in the nested table. Unlike a stored varray, the data for a nested table is not stored inline with the rest of the table columns; it is stored separately. The checked_out column will actually store a REF (similar to a pointer) into the co_tab table, where the list of student IDs will be stored. The storage for library_catalog is illustrated by Figure 8-2. For each row of library_catalog, checked_out contains a REF to the corresponding rows in co_tab.

NOTE
The store table (co_tab in the above example) can exist in another schema, and can have different storage parameters from the main table. The store table can be described, and exists in user_tables, but cannot be accessed directly. If you attempt to query or modify the store table directly, you will get the Oracle error "ORA-22812: Cannot reference nested table column's storage table." The contents of the store table are manipulated through SQL on the main table. For more information on the NESTED TABLE clause of CREATE TABLE, see the Oracle SQL Reference.

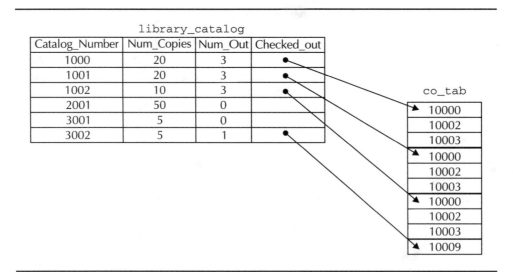

FIGURE 8-2. *Nested tables in the database*

Manipulating Entire Collections

You can manipulate a stored collection in its entirety using SQL DML statements, as we will see in the following sections. These types of operations affect the collection as a whole, rather than the individual elements. Elements within a collection can be manipulated using PL/SQL, or through the SQL operators that we will discuss in "SQL Table Operators" later in this chapter.

INSERT

The INSERT statement is used to insert a collection into a database row. The collection must first be created and initialized, and can also be a PL/SQL variable. The following example will insert rows into `class_material` corresponding to Figure 8-1:

```
-- Available online as part of collectionDML.sql
DECLARE
    v_CSBooks BookList := BookList(1000, 1001, 1002);
    v_HistoryBooks BookList := BookList(2001);
BEGIN
    -- INSERT using a newly constructed varray of 2 elements.
    INSERT INTO class_material
        VALUES ('MUS', 100, BookList(3001, 3002));

    -- INSERT using a previously initialized varray of 3 elements.
    INSERT INTO class_material VALUES ('CS', 102, v_CSBooks);

    -- INSERT using a previously initialized varray of 1 element.
    INSERT INTO class_material VALUES ('HIS', 101, v_HistoryBooks);
END;
```

UPDATE

Similarly, UPDATE is used to modify a stored collection. After completion of the following example, `library_catalog` will look like Figure 8-2.

```
-- Available online as part of collectionDML.sql
DECLARE
    v_StudentList1 StudentList := StudentList(10000, 10002, 10003);
    v_StudentList2 StudentList := StudentList(10000, 10002, 10003);
    v_StudentList3 StudentList := StudentList(10000, 10002, 10003);
BEGIN
    -- First insert rows with NULL nested tables.
    INSERT INTO library_catalog (catalog_number, num_copies, num_out)
        VALUES (1000, 20, 3);
    INSERT INTO library_catalog (catalog_number, num_copies, num_out)
        VALUES (1001, 20, 3);
```

```
INSERT INTO library_catalog (catalog_number, num_copies, num_out)
  VALUES (1002, 10, 3);
INSERT INTO library_catalog (catalog_number, num_copies, num_out)
  VALUES (2001, 50, 0);
INSERT INTO library_catalog (catalog_number, num_copies, num_out)
  VALUES (3001, 5, 0);
INSERT INTO library_catalog (catalog_number, num_copies, num_out)
  VALUES (3002, 5, 1);

-- Now update using the PL/SQL variables.
UPDATE library_catalog
  SET checked_out = v_StudentList1
  WHERE catalog_number = 1000;
UPDATE library_catalog
  SET checked_out = v_StudentList2
  WHERE catalog_number = 1001;
UPDATE library_catalog
  SET checked_out = v_StudentList3
  WHERE catalog_number = 1002;

-- And update the last row using a new variable.
UPDATE library_catalog
  SET checked_out = StudentList(10009)
  WHERE catalog_number = 3002;
END;
```

DELETE

DELETE can remove a row containing a collection, as the following example illustrates:

```
-- Available online as part of collectionDML.sql
DELETE FROM library_catalog
  WHERE catalog_number = 3001;
```

SELECT

Collections are retrieved from the database into PL/SQL variables using the SELECT statement, just like any other database type. Once the collection is in PL/SQL, it can be manipulated using procedural statements.

Querying Varrays   The PrintRequired procedure, which will print the required books for a given class, demonstrates how to SELECT a stored varray into a PL/SQL variable, where it can be manipulated.

```
-- Available online as part of PrintRequired.sql
CREATE OR REPLACE PROCEDURE PrintRequired(
  p_Department IN class_material.department%TYPE,
  p_Course IN class_material.course%TYPE) IS
```

```
      v_Books class_material.required_reading%TYPE;
      v_Title books.title%TYPE;
   BEGIN
      -- Fetch the entire varray.
      SELECT required_reading
        INTO v_Books
        FROM class_material
        WHERE department = p_Department
        AND course = p_Course;

      DBMS_OUTPUT.PUT('Required reading for ' || RTRIM(p_Department));
      DBMS_OUTPUT.PUT_LINE(' ' || p_Course || ':');

      -- Loop over the table, printing out each row.
      FOR v_Index IN 1..v_Books.COUNT LOOP
        SELECT title
          INTO v_Title
          FROM books
          WHERE catalog_number = v_Books(v_Index);
        DBMS_OUTPUT.PUT_LINE(
          '  ' || v_Books(v_Index) || ': ' || v_Title);
      END LOOP;
   END PrintRequired;
```

Assuming that class_material looks like Figure 8-1, we can call
PrintRequired and receive the following output:

-- **Available online as part of PrintRequired.sql**
```
SQL> DECLARE
  2     CURSOR c_Courses IS
  3       SELECT department, course
  4         FROM class_material
  5         ORDER BY department;
  6  BEGIN
  7    FOR v_Rec IN c_Courses LOOP
  8      PrintRequired(v_Rec.department, v_Rec.course);
  9    END LOOP;
 10  END;
 11  /
Required reading for CS 102:
  1000: Oracle8i Advanced PL/SQL Programming
  1001: Oracle8i: A Beginner's Guide
  1002: Oracle8 Tuning
Required reading for HIS 101:
  2001: A History of the World
Required reading for MUS 100:
  3001: Bach and the Modern World
  3002: Introduction to the Piano
PL/SQL procedure successfully completed.
```

Querying Nested Tables   When a nested table is retrieved into a PL/SQL variable, it is assigned keys starting at 1, and ranging to the number of elements in the table. The latter can be determined with the COUNT method. The Library.PrintCheckedOut procedure, which will print the names of the students who have a particular book checked out, demonstrates this.

```
-- Available online as part of Library.sql
CREATE OR REPLACE PACKAGE Library AS
  -- Prints out the students who have a particular book checked out.
  PROCEDURE PrintCheckedOut(
    p_CatalogNumber IN library_catalog.catalog_number%TYPE);
  ...
END Library;

CREATE OR REPLACE PACKAGE BODY Library AS
  PROCEDURE PrintCheckedOut(
    p_CatalogNumber IN library_catalog.catalog_number%TYPE) IS

    v_StudentList StudentList;
    v_Student students%ROWTYPE;
    v_Book      books%ROWTYPE;
    v_FoundOne BOOLEAN := FALSE;
  BEGIN
    -- Select the entire nested table into a PL/SQL variable.
    SELECT checked_out
      INTO v_StudentList
      FROM library_catalog
      WHERE catalog_number = p_CatalogNumber;

    SELECT *
      INTO v_Book
      FROM books
      WHERE catalog_number = p_CatalogNumber;

    DBMS_OUTPUT.PUT_LINE(
      'Students who have ' || v_Book.catalog_number || ': ' ||
      v_Book.title || ' checked out: ');

    -- Loop over the nested table, and print out the student names.
    IF v_StudentList IS NOT NULL THEN
      FOR v_Index IN 1..v_StudentList.COUNT LOOP
        v_FoundOne := TRUE;

        SELECT *
          INTO v_Student
          FROM students
```

```
          WHERE ID = v_StudentList(v_Index);

        DBMS_OUTPUT.PUT_LINE('   ' || v_Student.first_name || ' ' ||
                                  v_Student.last_name);
      END LOOP;
    END IF;

    IF NOT v_FoundOne THEN
      DBMS_OUTPUT.PUT_LINE('  None');
    END IF;
  END PrintCheckedOut;
  ...
END Library;
```

The following example shows the output from `Library.PrintCheckedOut`, assuming that `library_catalog` looks like Figure 8-2:

```
-- Available online as part of callLibrary.sql
SQL> BEGIN
  2    Library.PrintCheckedOut(1000);
  3  END;
  4  /
Students who have 1000: Oracle8i Advanced PL/SQL Programming checked
  out:
Scott Smith
Joanne Junebug
Manish Murgatroid
PL/SQL procedure successfully completed.
```

Stored Tables with Nonsequential Keys   Nested tables stored in the database cannot be manipulated directly with PL/SQL, only with SQL. As a result of this, the key values are not recorded. As we saw in the last example, when a nested table is SELECTed from the database, the keys are renumbered sequentially from 1. Consequently, if you INSERT a nested table with nonsequential keys into the database, the keys will change. This is illustrated by the following. First, we declare a nested table type and database table that uses it:

```
-- Available online as part of nonSequential.sql
CREATE OR REPLACE TYPE DateTab AS
  TABLE OF DATE;
/

CREATE TABLE famous_dates (
  key        VARCHAR2(100) PRIMARY KEY,
  date_list  DateTab)
  NESTED TABLE date_list STORE AS dates_tab;
```

Once we have the table and type created, we can run the following PL/SQL block:

```
-- Available online as part of nonSequential.sql
DECLARE
    -- Create a nested table with 5 dates.
    v_Dates DateTab := DateTab(TO_DATE('04-JUL-1776', 'DD-MON-YYYY'),
                               TO_DATE('12-APR-1861', 'DD-MON-YYYY'),
                               TO_DATE('05-JUN-1968', 'DD-MON-YYYY'),
                               TO_DATE('26-JAN-1986', 'DD-MON-YYYY'),
                               TO_DATE('01-JAN-2001', 'DD-MON-YYYY'));

    -- Local procedure to print out a DateTab.
    PROCEDURE Print(p_Dates IN DateTab) IS
      v_Index BINARY_INTEGER := p_Dates.FIRST;
    BEGIN
       WHILE v_Index <= p_Dates.LAST LOOP
          DBMS_OUTPUT.PUT('  ' || v_Index || ': ');
          DBMS_OUTPUT.PUT_LINE(TO_CHAR(p_Dates(v_Index),
                                        'DD-MON-YYYY'));
          v_Index := p_Dates.NEXT(v_Index);
       END LOOP;
    END Print;

BEGIN
    -- Delete element 2 of the table.  This will result in a table of
    -- 4 elements.
    v_Dates.DELETE(2);

    DBMS_OUTPUT.PUT_LINE('Initial value of the table:');
    Print(v_Dates);

    -- INSERT the nested table into the database, and then SELECT it
    -- back out.
    INSERT INTO famous_dates (key, date_list)
      VALUES ('Dates in American History', v_Dates);

    SELECT date_list
      INTO v_Dates
      FROM famous_dates
      WHERE key = 'Dates in American History';

    DBMS_OUTPUT.PUT_LINE('Table after INSERT and SELECT:');
    Print(v_Dates);
END;
```

This block first creates a nested table of five elements, and then deletes the second element. The shortened table is then inserted into the database, and selected back out. The output is as follows:

```
Initial value of the table:
1: 04-JUL-1776
3: 05-JUN-1968
4: 26-JAN-1986
5: 01-JAN-2001
Table after INSERT and SELECT:
1: 04-JUL-1776
2: 05-JUN-1968
3: 26-JAN-1986
4: 01-JAN-2001
```

The keys have been renumbered, although the data has remained the same.

Manipulating Individual Collection Elements

The examples we have seen so far have modified the entire stored collection. It is also possible, however, to manipulate individual collection elements using both PL/SQL and SQL.

PL/SQL Manipulations

The Library package also contains the CheckOut and CheckIn procedures, each of which selects the nested table into a PL/SQL variable, manipulates it, and then updates library_catalog again. We've already seen the PrintCheckedOut procedure, and the following listing completes the package:

```
-- Available online as part of Library.sql
CREATE OR REPLACE PACKAGE Library AS
  ...
  -- Checks out the book with p_CatalogNumber to the student with
  -- p_StudentID.
  PROCEDURE CheckOut(
    p_CatalogNumber IN library_catalog.catalog_number%TYPE,
    p_StudentID IN NUMBER);

  -- Checks in the book with p_CatalogNumber from the student with
  -- p_StudentID.
  PROCEDURE CheckIn(
    p_CatalogNumber IN library_catalog.catalog_number%TYPE,
    p_StudentID IN NUMBER);
END Library;
```

```
CREATE OR REPLACE PACKAGE BODY Library AS
  ...
  -- Checks out the book with p_CatalogNumber to the student with
  -- p_StudentID.
  PROCEDURE CheckOut(
    p_CatalogNumber IN library_catalog.catalog_number%TYPE,
    p_StudentID IN NUMBER) IS

    v_NumCopies library_catalog.num_copies%TYPE;
    v_NumOut library_catalog.num_out%TYPE;
    v_CheckedOut library_catalog.checked_out%TYPE;
  BEGIN
    -- First verify that the book exists, and that there is a copy
    -- available to be checked out.
    BEGIN
      SELECT num_copies, num_out, checked_out
        INTO v_NumCopies, v_NumOut, v_CheckedOut
        FROM library_catalog
        WHERE catalog_number = p_CatalogNumber
        FOR UPDATE;
    EXCEPTION
      WHEN NO_DATA_FOUND THEN
        RAISE_APPLICATION_ERROR(-20000,
          'There is no book with catalog number ' ||
          p_CatalogNumber || ' in the library');
    END;

    IF v_NumCopies = v_NumOut THEN
      RAISE_APPLICATION_ERROR(-20001,
        'All of the copies of book ' || p_CatalogNumber ||
        ' are checked out');
    END IF;

    -- Search the list to see if this student already has this book.
    IF v_CheckedOut IS NOT NULL THEN
      FOR v_Counter IN 1..v_CheckedOut.COUNT LOOP
        IF v_CheckedOut(v_Counter) = p_StudentID THEN
          RAISE_APPLICATION_ERROR(-20002,
            'Student ' || p_StudentID || ' already has book ' ||
            p_CatalogNumber || ' checked out');
        END IF;
      END LOOP;
    END IF;

    -- Make room in the list
    IF v_CheckedOut IS NULL THEN
      v_CheckedOut := StudentList(NULL);
    ELSE
      v_CheckedOut.EXTEND;
```

```
      END IF;

      -- Check out the book by adding it to the list.
      v_CheckedOut(v_CheckedOut.COUNT) := p_StudentID;

      -- And put it back in the database, adding 1 to num_out.
      UPDATE library_catalog
        SET checked_out = v_CheckedOut,
            num_out = num_out + 1
        WHERE catalog_number = p_CatalogNumber;
    END CheckOut;

  -- Checks in the book with p_CatalogNumber from the student with
  -- p_StudentID.
  PROCEDURE CheckIn(
    p_CatalogNumber IN library_catalog.catalog_number%TYPE,
    p_StudentID IN NUMBER) IS

    v_NumCopies library_catalog.num_copies%TYPE;
    v_NumOut library_catalog.num_out%TYPE;
    v_CheckedOut library_catalog.checked_out%TYPE;
    v_AlreadyCheckedOut BOOLEAN := FALSE;
  BEGIN
    -- First verify that the book exists
    BEGIN
      SELECT num_copies, num_out, checked_out
        INTO v_NumCopies, v_NumOut, v_CheckedOut
        FROM library_catalog
        WHERE catalog_number = p_CatalogNumber
        FOR UPDATE;
    EXCEPTION
      WHEN NO_DATA_FOUND THEN
        RAISE_APPLICATION_ERROR(-20000,
          'There is no book with catalog number ' ||
          p_CatalogNumber || ' in the library');
    END;

    -- Search the list to verify that this student has checked it
    -- out.
    IF v_CheckedOut IS NOT NULL THEN
      FOR v_Counter IN 1..v_CheckedOut.COUNT LOOP
        IF v_CheckedOut(v_Counter) = p_StudentID THEN
          v_AlreadyCheckedOut := TRUE;
          -- Delete it from the list.
          v_CheckedOut.DELETE(v_Counter);
        END IF;
      END LOOP;
    END IF;
```

```
IF NOT v_AlreadyCheckedOut THEN
  RAISE_APPLICATION_ERROR(-20003,
    'Student ' || p_StudentID || ' does not have book ' ||
    p_CatalogNumber || ' checked out');
END IF;

-- And put it back in the database, subtracting from num_out.
UPDATE library_catalog
  SET checked_out = v_CheckedOut,
      num_out = num_out - 1
  WHERE catalog_number = p_CatalogNumber;
  END CheckIn;
END Library;
```

Again assuming that class_material and library_catalog look
like Figures 8-1 and 8-2, we can call CheckOut and CheckIn and receive
the following output:

```
-- Available online as part of callLibrary.sql
SQL> DECLARE
  2    CURSOR c_History101Students IS
  3      SELECT student_ID
  4        FROM registered_students
  5        WHERE department = 'HIS'
  6        AND course = 101;
  7    v_RequiredReading class_material.required_reading%TYPE;
  8  BEGIN
  9    -- Check out the required books for all students in HIS 101:
 10
 11    -- Get the books required for HIS 101
 12    SELECT required_reading
 13      INTO v_RequiredReading
 14      FROM class_material
 15      WHERE department = 'HIS'
 16      AND course = 101;
 17
 18    -- Loop over the History 101 students
 19    FOR v_Rec IN c_History101Students LOOP
 20      -- Loop over the required reading list
 21      FOR v_Index IN 1..v_RequiredReading.COUNT LOOP
 22        -- And check out the book!
 23        Library.CheckOut(v_RequiredReading(v_Index),
 24                          v_Rec.student_ID);
 25      END LOOP;
 26    END LOOP;
 27
 28    -- Print out the students who have the book checked out now
```

```
29      Library.PrintCheckedOut(2001);
30
31      -- Check in the book for some of the students
32      Library.CheckIn(2001, 10001);
33      Library.CheckIn(2001, 10002);
34      Library.CheckIn(2001, 10003);
35
36      -- And print again.
37      Library.PrintCheckedOut(2001);
38   END;
39   /
Students who have 2001: A History of the World checked out:
  Scott Smith
  Margaret Mason
  Joanne Junebug
  Manish Murgatroid
  Patrick Poll
  Timothy Taller
  Barbara Blues
  David Dinsmore
  Ester Elegant
  Rose Riznit
  Rita Razmataz
Students who have 2001: A History of the World checked out:
  Scott Smith
  Patrick Poll
  Timothy Taller
  Barbara Blues
  David Dinsmore
  Ester Elegant
  Rose Riznit
  Rita Razmataz
PL/SQL procedure successfully completed.
```

SQL Table Operators

Oracle **8i** and higher   You can also manipulate the elements of a stored nested table directly using SQL with the TABLE operator. With this operator, you do not have to select the nested table into PL/SQL, manipulate it, and then update it back in the database. Elements of stored varrays cannot be manipulated directly with DML, however—they must be manipulated in PL/SQL.

TABLE is defined as follows:

TABLE(*subquery*)

where *subquery* is a query that returns a nested table column.

NOTE
TABLE was introduced with Oracle8i. In Oracle8, the THE operator was available, which operates the same as TABLE. THE is deprecated in Oracle8i, however, and TABLE should be used instead.

For example, we can change the `Library.PrintCheckedOut` procedure to use TABLE as follows:

```
-- Available online as part of LibraryOperator.sql
PROCEDURE PrintCheckedOut(
    p_CatalogNumber IN library_catalog.catalog_number%TYPE) IS

    v_StudentList StudentList;
    v_Student students%ROWTYPE;
    v_Book    books%ROWTYPE;
    v_FoundOne BOOLEAN := FALSE;

  CURSOR c_CheckedOut IS
    SELECT column_value ID
      FROM TABLE(SELECT checked_out
                   FROM library_catalog
                  WHERE catalog_number = p_CatalogNumber);
BEGIN
    SELECT *
      INTO v_Book
      FROM books
     WHERE catalog_number = p_CatalogNumber;

    DBMS_OUTPUT.PUT_LINE(
      'Students who have ' || v_Book.catalog_number || ': ' ||
      v_Book.title || ' checked out: ');

    -- Loop over the nested table, and print out the student names.
    FOR v_Rec IN c_CheckedOut LOOP
      v_FoundOne := TRUE;

        SELECT *
          INTO v_Student
          FROM students
         WHERE ID = v_Rec.ID;

        DBMS_OUTPUT.PUT_LINE('  ' || v_Student.first_name || ' ' ||
                             v_Student.last_name);
    END LOOP;

    IF NOT v_FoundOne THEN
```

```
       DBMS_OUTPUT.PUT_LINE('  None');
    END IF;
  END PrintCheckedOut;
```

For more information on using TABLE, see the *Oracle SQL Reference*.

Querying Stored Varrays   Although elements of a stored varray cannot be manipulated with DML statements (unlike a nested table), a varray can be queried using the TABLE operator. In this case, TABLE takes a varray column and returns the elements within it as if the varray were a separate one-column table itself. The name of the column is `column_value`. For example, we can query `class_material` as follows:

```
SQL> SELECT department, course, column_value
  2    FROM class_material, TABLE(required_reading);

DEP    COURSE COLUMN_VALUE
---    ------- ------------
MUS       100         3001
MUS       100         3002
CS        102         1000
CS        102         1001
CS        102         1002
HIS       101         2001
6 rows selected.
```

Collection Methods

Nested tables and varrays are object types, and as such they have methods defined on them. Likewise, index-by tables have attributes. An attribute or collection method is invoked using the syntax:

collection_instance.method_or_attribute

where *collection_instance* is a collection variable (not the type name), and *method_ or_attribute* is one of the methods or attributes described in this section. These methods can be called only from procedural statements, and not from SQL statements.

All of the following examples assume the following declarations:

```
-- Available online as part of tables.sql
CREATE OR REPLACE TYPE NumTab AS TABLE OF NUMBER;
CREATE OR REPLACE TYPE NumVar AS VARRAY(25) OF NUMBER;
CREATE OR REPLACE PACKAGE IndexBy AS
  TYPE NumTab IS TABLE OF NUMBER INDEX BY BINARY_INTEGER;
END IndexBy;
```

NOTE
*The IndexBy package allows NumTab to
be referenced from PL/SQL blocks using the
IndexBy.NumTab syntax. For more information
on packages, see Chapters 9 and 10.*

The methods are listed in Table 8-3, and are described in the sections that follow.

EXISTS

EXISTS is used to determine whether the referenced element is present in the collection. The syntax is

EXISTS(*n*)

where *n* is an integer expression. It returns TRUE if the element specified by *n* exists, even if it is NULL. If *n* is out of range, EXISTS returns FALSE, rather than raising the SUBSCRIPT_OUTSIDE_LIMIT exception (for nested tables or varrays) or ORA-1403 (for index-by tables). EXISTS and DELETE can be used to maintain sparse nested tables. The following example illustrates the usage of EXISTS:

```
-- Available online as exists.sql
SQL> DECLARE
  2    v_NestedTable NumTab := NumTab(-7, 14.3, 3.14159, NULL, 0);
  3    v_Count BINARY_INTEGER := 1;
  4    v_IndexByTable IndexBy.NumTab;
  5  BEGIN
  6    -- Loop over v_NestedTable, and print out the elements, using
  7    -- EXISTS to indicate the end of the loop.
  8    LOOP
  9      IF v_NestedTable.EXISTS(v_Count) THEN
 10        DBMS_OUTPUT.PUT_LINE(
 11          'v_NestedTable(' || v_Count || '): ' ||
 12          v_NestedTable(v_Count));
 13        v_Count := v_Count + 1;
 14      ELSE
 15        EXIT;
 16      END IF;
 17    END LOOP;
 18
 18    -- Assign the same elements to the index-by table.
 19    v_IndexByTable(1) := -7;
 20    v_IndexByTable(2) := 14.3;
 21    v_IndexByTable(3) := 3.14159;
 22    v_IndexByTable(4) := NULL;
 23    v_IndexByTable(5) := 0;
 24
 24    -- And do a similar loop.
 25    v_Count := 1;
 26    LOOP
 27      IF v_IndexByTable.EXISTS(v_Count) THEN
```

```
28          DBMS_OUTPUT.PUT_LINE(
29            'v_IndexByTable(' || v_Count || '): ' ||
30            v_IndexByTable(v_Count));
31          v_Count := v_Count + 1;
32        ELSE
33          EXIT;
34        END IF;
35      END LOOP;
36    END;
37    /
v_NestedTable(1): -7
v_NestedTable(2): 14.3
v_NestedTable(3): 3.14159
v_NestedTable(4):
v_NestedTable(5): 0
v_IndexByTable(1): -7
v_IndexByTable(2): 14.3
v_IndexByTable(3): 3.14159
v_IndexByTable(4):
v_IndexByTable(5): 0
PL/SQL procedure successfully completed.
```

Method or Attribute	Return Type	Description	Valid for
EXISTS	BOOLEAN	Returns TRUE if the specified element exists in the collection	Index-by tables, nested tables, varrays
COUNT	NUMBER	Returns the number of elements in a collection	Index-by tables, nested tables, varrays
LIMIT	NUMBER	Returns the maximum number of elements for a collection	Nested tables (always returns NULL), varrays
FIRST & LAST	BINARY_ INTEGER	Returns the index of the first (or last) element in a collection	Index-by tables, nested tables, varrays
NEXT & PRIOR	BINARY_ INTEGER	Returns the index of the next (or prior) element, relative to a given element, in a collection	Index-by tables, nested tables, varrays
EXTEND	N/A	Adds elements to a collection	Nested tables, varrays (up to the maximum size for the type)
TRIM	N/A	Removes elements from the end of a collection	Nested tables, varrays
DELETE	N/A	Removes specified elements from a collection	Index-by tables, nested tables

TABLE 8-3. *Collection Methods*

As the above example shows, if element *n* of a collection contains NULL, EXISTS(*n*) will return TRUE. EXISTS can also be applied to an atomically NULL nested table or varray, in which case it will always return FALSE.

COUNT

COUNT returns the number of elements currently in a collection, as an integer. It takes no arguments and is valid wherever an integer expression is valid. The following SQL*Plus session illustrates the use of COUNT:

```
-- Available online as count.sql
SQL> DECLARE
  2    v_NestedTable NumTab := NumTab(1, 2, 3);
  3    v_Varray NumVar := NumVar(-1, -2, -3, -4);
  4    v_IndexByTable IndexBy.NumTab;
  5  BEGIN
  6    -- First add some elements to the index-by table.  Note that
  7    -- the index values are not sequential.
  8    v_IndexByTable(1) := 1;
  9    v_IndexByTable(8) := 8;
 10    v_IndexByTable(-1) := -1;
 11    v_IndexByTable(100) := 100;
 12
 13    -- And print out the counts.
 14    DBMS_OUTPUT.PUT_LINE(
 15      'Nested Table Count: ' || v_NestedTable.COUNT);
 16    DBMS_OUTPUT.PUT_LINE(
 17      'Varray Count: ' || v_Varray.COUNT);
 18    DBMS_OUTPUT.PUT_LINE(
 19      'Index-By Table Count: ' || v_IndexByTable.COUNT);
 20  END;
 21  /
Nested Table Count: 3
Varray Count: 4
Index-By Table Count: 4
PL/SQL procedure successfully completed.
```

For varrays, COUNT always equals LAST (described later in this section) because elements can't be deleted from a varray. However, elements can be deleted from the middle of a nested table, so COUNT could be different from LAST for a table. COUNT is useful when selecting a nested table from the database, because the number of elements is unknown at that point. COUNT ignores deleted elements when computing the total.

LIMIT

LIMIT returns the current maximum number of elements for a collection. Because nested tables have no maximum size, LIMIT always returns NULL when applied to a nested table. LIMIT is not valid for index-by tables. The following SQL*Plus session illustrates the use of LIMIT:

```
-- Available online as limit.sql
SQL> DECLARE
  2    v_Table NumTab := NumTab(1, 2, 3);
  3    v_Varray NumVar := NumVar(1234, 4321);
  4  BEGIN
  5    -- Output the limit and count for the collections.
  6    DBMS_OUTPUT.PUT_LINE('Varray limit: ' || v_Varray.LIMIT);
  7    DBMS_OUTPUT.PUT_LINE('Varray count: ' || v_Varray.COUNT);
  8    IF v_Table.LIMIT IS NULL THEN
  9      DBMS_OUTPUT.PUT_LINE('Table limit is NULL');
 10    ELSE
 11      DBMS_OUTPUT.PUT_LINE('Table limit: ' || v_Table.LIMIT);
 12    END IF;
 13    DBMS_OUTPUT.PUT_LINE('Table count: ' || v_Table.COUNT);
 14  END;
 15  /
Varray limit: 25
Varray count: 2
Table limit is NULL
Table count: 3
PL/SQL procedure successfully completed.
```

Note that the varray limit is 25, as defined in the CREATE TYPE statement, even though v_Varray currently contains only two elements. COUNT returns the current number of elements, as described in the previous section.

FIRST and LAST

FIRST returns the index of the first element of a collection, and LAST returns the index of the last element. For a varray, FIRST always returns 1 and LAST always returns the value of COUNT, because a varray is dense and elements cannot be deleted. FIRST and LAST can be used along with NEXT and PRIOR to loop through a collection, as illustrated by the example in the next section.

NEXT and PRIOR

NEXT and PRIOR are used to increment and decrement the key for a collection. The syntax is

NEXT(*n*)
PRIOR(*n*)

where *n* is an integer expression. NEXT(*n*) returns the key of the element immediately after the element at position *n*, and PRIOR(*n*) returns the key of the element immediately prior to the element at position *n*. If there is no next or prior element, NEXT and PRIOR will return NULL. The following SQL*Plus session illustrates how to use NEXT and PRIOR, along with FIRST and LAST, to loop through a nested table:

```
-- Available online as collectionLoops.sql
SQL> DECLARE
  2     TYPE CharTab IS TABLE OF CHAR(1);
  3     v_Characters CharTab :=
  4        CharTab('M', 'a', 'd', 'a', 'm', ',', ' ',
  5                'I', '''', 'm', ' ', 'A', 'd', 'a', 'm');
  6
  7     v_Index INTEGER;
  8  BEGIN
  9     -- Loop forward over the table.
 10     v_Index := v_Characters.FIRST;
 11     WHILE v_Index <= v_Characters.LAST LOOP
 12       DBMS_OUTPUT.PUT(v_Characters(v_Index));
 13       v_Index := v_Characters.NEXT(v_Index);
 14     END LOOP;
 15     DBMS_OUTPUT.NEW_LINE;
 16
 17     -- Loop backward over the table.
 18     v_Index := v_Characters.LAST;
 19     WHILE v_Index >= v_Characters.FIRST LOOP
 20       DBMS_OUTPUT.PUT(v_Characters(v_Index));
 21       v_Index := v_Characters.PRIOR(v_Index);
 22     END LOOP;
 23     DBMS_OUTPUT.NEW_LINE;
 24  END;
 25  /
Madam, I'm Adam
madA m'I ,madaM
PL/SQL procedure successfully completed.
```

FIRST, LAST, NEXT, and PRIOR work the same way for varrays and index-by tables as well.

EXTEND

EXTEND is used to add elements to the end of a nested table or varray. It is not valid for index-by tables. EXTEND has three forms:

EXTEND
EXTEND(*n*)
EXTEND(*n*, *i*)

EXTEND with no arguments simply adds a NULL element to the end of the collection, with index LAST+1. EXTEND(*n*) adds *n* NULL elements to the end of the table, and EXTEND(*n*, *i*) adds *n* copies of element *i* to the end of the table. If the collection has been created with a NOT NULL constraint, then only the last form can be used, because it does not add a NULL element.

Because a nested table does not have an explicit maximum size, you can call EXTEND with *n* as large as needed (the maximum size is 2G, subject to memory constraints). A varray, however, can be extended only up to the maximum size, so *n* can be (LIMIT − COUNT) at most. The following SQL*Plus session illustrates the use of EXTEND:

```
-- Available online as extend.sql
SQL> DECLARE
  2    v_NumbersTab NumTab := NumTab(1, 2, 3, 4, 5);
  3    v_NumbersList NumVar := NumVar(1, 2, 3, 4, 5);
  4  BEGIN
  5    BEGIN
  6      -- This assignment will raise SUBSCRIPT_BEYOND_COUNT, since
  7      -- v_NumbersTab has only 5 elements.
  8      v_NumbersTab(26) := -7;
  9    EXCEPTION
 10      WHEN SUBSCRIPT_BEYOND_COUNT THEN
 11        DBMS_OUTPUT.PUT_LINE(
 12          'ORA-6533 raised for assignment to v_NumbersTab(26)');
 13    END;
 14
 15    -- We can fix this by adding 30 additional elements to
 16    -- v_NumbersTab.
 17    v_NumbersTab.EXTEND(30);
 18
 19    -- And now do the assignment.
 20    v_NumbersTab(26) := -7;
 21
 22    -- For a varray, we can extend it only up to the maximum size
 23    -- (also given by LIMIT).  For example, the following will
 24    -- raise SUBSCRIPT_OUTSIDE_LIMIT:
 25    BEGIN
 26      v_NumbersList.EXTEND(30);
 27    EXCEPTION
 28      WHEN SUBSCRIPT_OUTSIDE_LIMIT THEN
 29        DBMS_OUTPUT.PUT_LINE(
 30          'ORA-6532 raised for v_NumbersList.EXTEND(30)');
 31    END;
 32
 33    -- But this is legal.
```

```
34    v_NumbersList.EXTEND(20);
35
36    -- And we can now assign to the highest element in the varray.
37    v_NumbersList(25) := 25;
38  END;
39  /
ORA-6533 raised for assignment to v_NumbersTab(26)
ORA-6532 raised for v_NumbersList.EXTEND(30)
PL/SQL procedure successfully completed.
```

EXTEND operates on the internal size of a collection, which includes any deleted elements for a nested table. When an element is deleted (using the DELETE method described later in this section), the data for that element is removed, but the key remains. The following example illustrates the interaction between EXTEND and DELETE:

```
-- Available online as extendDelete.sql
DECLARE
  -- Initialize a nested table to 5 elements.
  v_Numbers NumTab := NumTab(-2, -1, 0, 1, 2);

  -- Local procedure to print out a table.
  -- Note the use of FIRST, LAST, and NEXT.
  PROCEDURE Print(p_Table IN NumTab) IS
    v_Index INTEGER;
  BEGIN
    v_Index := p_Table.FIRST;
    WHILE v_Index <= p_Table.LAST LOOP
      DBMS_OUTPUT.PUT('Element ' || v_Index || ': ');
      DBMS_OUTPUT.PUT_LINE(p_Table(v_Index));
      v_Index := p_Table.NEXT(v_Index);
    END LOOP;
  END Print;

BEGIN
  DBMS_OUTPUT.PUT_LINE('At initialization, v_Numbers contains');
  Print(v_Numbers);

  -- Delete element 3.  This removes the '0', but keeps a placeholder
  -- where it was.
  v_Numbers.DELETE(3);

  DBMS_OUTPUT.PUT_LINE('After delete, v_Numbers contains');
  Print(v_Numbers);

  -- Add 2 copies of element 1 onto the table.  This will add elements
  -- 6 and 7.
```

```
    v_Numbers.EXTEND(2, 1);

    DBMS_OUTPUT.PUT_LINE('After extend, v_Numbers contains');
    Print(v_Numbers);

    DBMS_OUTPUT.PUT_LINE('v_Numbers.COUNT = ' || v_Numbers.COUNT);
    DBMS_OUTPUT.PUT_LINE('v_Numbers.LAST = ' || v_Numbers.LAST);
END;
```

This example produces the following output. Note the values of COUNT and LAST after the DELETE and EXTEND operation.

```
At initialization, v_Numbers contains
Element 1: -2
Element 2: -1
Element 3: 0
Element 4: 1
Element 5: 2
After delete, v_Numbers contains
Element 1: -2
Element 2: -1
Element 4: 1
Element 5: 2
After extend, v_Numbers contains
Element 1: -2
Element 2: -1
Element 4: 1
Element 5: 2
Element 6: -2
Element 7: -2
v_Numbers.COUNT = 6
v_Numbers.LAST = 7
```

TRIM

TRIM is used to remove elements from the end of a nested table or varray. It has two forms, defined with

TRIM
TRIM(n)

With no arguments, TRIM removes one element from the end of the collection. Otherwise, n elements are removed. If n is greater than COUNT, the SUBSCRIPT_ BEYOND_COUNT exception is raised. After the TRIM, COUNT will be smaller because the elements have been removed.

Similar to EXTEND, TRIM operates on the internal size of a collection, including any elements removed with DELETE. This is illustrated by the following example:

```
-- Available online as trim.sql
DECLARE
  -- Initialize a table to 7 elements.
  v_Numbers NumTab := NumTab(-3, -2, -1, 0, 1, 2, 3);

  -- Local procedure to print out a table.
  PROCEDURE Print(p_Table IN NumTab) IS
    v_Index INTEGER;
  BEGIN
    v_Index := p_Table.FIRST;
    WHILE v_Index <= p_Table.LAST LOOP
      DBMS_OUTPUT.PUT('Element ' || v_Index || ': ');
      DBMS_OUTPUT.PUT_LINE(p_Table(v_Index));
      v_Index := p_Table.NEXT(v_Index);
    END LOOP;
    DBMS_OUTPUT.PUT_LINE('COUNT = ' || p_Table.COUNT);
    DBMS_OUTPUT.PUT_LINE('LAST = ' || p_Table.LAST);
  END Print;

BEGIN
  DBMS_OUTPUT.PUT_LINE('At initialization, v_Numbers contains');
  Print(v_Numbers);

  -- Delete element 6.
  v_Numbers.DELETE(6);
  DBMS_OUTPUT.PUT_LINE('After delete , v_Numbers contains');
  Print(v_Numbers);

  -- Trim the last 3 elements.  This will remove the 2 and 3, but
  -- also remove the (now empty) spot where 1 was.
  v_Numbers.TRIM(3);
  DBMS_OUTPUT.PUT_LINE('After trim, v_Numbers contains');
  Print(v_Numbers);
END;
```

See Chapter 9 for information on how to create procedures. This example produces the following output:

```
At initialization, v_Numbers contains
Element 1: -3
Element 2: -2
Element 3: -1
Element 4: 0
Element 5: 1
```

```
Element 6: 2
Element 7: 3
COUNT = 7
LAST = 7
After delete , v_Numbers contains
Element 1: -3
Element 2: -2
Element 3: -1
Element 4: 0
Element 5: 1
Element 7: 3
COUNT = 6
LAST = 7
After trim, v_Numbers contains
Element 1: -3
Element 2: -2
Element 3: -1
Element 4: 0
COUNT = 4
LAST = 4
```

DELETE

DELETE will remove one or more elements from an index-by table or nested table. DELETE has no effect on a varray because of its fixed size (and in fact, it is illegal to call DELETE on a varray). DELETE has three forms:

DELETE
DELETE(*n*)
DELETE(*m,n*)

With no arguments, DELETE will remove the entire table. DELETE(*n*) will remove the element at index *n*, and DELETE(*m,n*) will remove all the elements between indexes *m* and *n*. After the DELETE, COUNT will be smaller, reflecting the new size of the nested table. If the element of the table to be deleted does not exist, DELETE will not raise an error, but will simply skip that element. The following example illustrates the use of DELETE:

```
-- Available online as delete.sql
DECLARE
  -- Initialize a table to 10 elements.
  v_Numbers NumTab := NumTab(10, 20, 30, 40, 50, 60, 70, 80, 90, 100);

  -- Local procedure to print out a table.
  PROCEDURE Print(p_Table IN NumTab) IS
```

```
    v_Index INTEGER;
  BEGIN
    v_Index := p_Table.FIRST;
    WHILE v_Index <= p_Table.LAST LOOP
      DBMS_OUTPUT.PUT('Element ' || v_Index || ': ');
      DBMS_OUTPUT.PUT_LINE(p_Table(v_Index));
      v_Index := p_Table.NEXT(v_Index);
    END LOOP;
    DBMS_OUTPUT.PUT_LINE('COUNT = ' || p_Table.COUNT);
    DBMS_OUTPUT.PUT_LINE('LAST = ' || p_Table.LAST);
  END Print;

BEGIN
  DBMS_OUTPUT.PUT_LINE('At initialization, v_Numbers contains');
  Print(v_Numbers);

  -- Delete element 6.
  DBMS_OUTPUT.PUT_LINE('After delete(6), v_Numbers contains');
  v_Numbers.DELETE(6);
  Print(v_Numbers);

  -- Delete elements 7 through 9.
  DBMS_OUTPUT.PUT_LINE('After delete(7,9), v_Numbers contains');
  v_Numbers.DELETE(7,9);
  Print(v_Numbers);
END;
```

This example produces the following output:

```
At initialization, v_Numbers contains
Element 1: 10
Element 2: 20
Element 3: 30
Element 4: 40
Element 5: 50
Element 6: 60
Element 7: 70
Element 8: 80
Element 9: 90
Element 10: 100
COUNT = 10
LAST = 10
After delete(6), v_Numbers contains
Element 1: 10
Element 2: 20
Element 3: 30
Element 4: 40
```

```
Element 5: 50
Element 7: 70
Element 8: 80
Element 9: 90
Element 10: 100
COUNT = 9
LAST = 10
After delete(7,9), v_Numbers contains
Element 1: 10
Element 2: 20
Element 3: 30
Element 4: 40
Element 5: 50
Element 10: 100
COUNT = 6
LAST = 10
```

Summary

Collections are useful constructs for any programming language. In this chapter, we have examined the three types of collections: index-by tables, nested tables, and varrays. We have discussed the differences between the collection types, including how to use collection methods and how to store and manipulate collections in the database. Depending on your needs, you can use whichever collection is most appropriate.

PART
III

More PL/SQL
Features

CHAPTER
9

Creating Procedures, Functions, and Packages

s we saw in Chapter 3, there are two main kinds of PL/SQL blocks: anonymous and named. An anonymous block (beginning with either DECLARE or BEGIN) is compiled each time it is issued. It also is not stored in the database, and cannot be called directly from other PL/ SQL blocks. The constructs that we will look at in this and the next two chapters—procedures, functions, packages, and triggers—are all named blocks and thus do not have these restrictions. They can be stored in the database and run when appropriate. In this chapter, we will explore the syntax of creating procedures, functions, and packages. In Chapter 10, we will examine how to use them and some of their implications. Chapter 11 focuses on database triggers.

Procedures and Functions

PL/SQL procedures and functions behave very much like procedures and functions in other 3GLs (third-generation languages). They share many of the same properties. Collectively, procedures and functions are also known as *subprograms*. As an example, the following code creates a procedure in the database:

```
-- Available online as part of AddNewStudent.sql
CREATE OR REPLACE PROCEDURE AddNewStudent (
  p_FirstName   students.first_name%TYPE,
  p_LastName    students.last_name%TYPE,
  p_Major       students.major%TYPE) AS
BEGIN
  -- Insert a new row in the students table. Use
  -- student_sequence to generate the new student ID, and
  -- 0 for current_credits.
  INSERT INTO students (ID, first_name, last_name,
                        major, current_credits)
    VALUES (student_sequence.nextval, p_FirstName, p_LastName,
            p_Major, 0);
END AddNewStudent;
```

Once this procedure is created, we can call it from another PL/SQL block:

```
-- Available online as part of AddNewStudent.sql
BEGIN
  AddNewStudent('Zelda', 'Zudnik', 'Computer Science');
END;
```

This example illustrates several notable points:

■ The `AddNewStudent` procedure is created first with the CREATE OR REPLACE PROCEDURE statement. When a procedure is created, it is first compiled, and then stored in the database in compiled form. This compiled code can then be run later from another PL/SQL block. (The source code for the procedure is also stored. (See the section "Stored Subprograms and the Data Dictionary" in Chapter 10 for more information.)

■ When the procedure is called, parameters can be passed. In the preceding example, the new student's first name, last name, and major are passed to the procedure at runtime. Inside the procedure, the parameter p_FirstName will have the value `Zelda`, p_LastName will have the value `Zudnik`, and p_Major will have the value `Computer Science` because these literals are passed to the procedure when it is called.

■ A procedure call is a PL/SQL statement by itself. It is not called as part of an expression. When a procedure is called, control passes to the first executable statement inside the procedure. When the procedure finishes, control resumes at the statement following the procedure call. In this regard, PL/SQL procedures behave the same as procedures in other 3GLs. Functions are called as part of an expression, as we will see later in this section.

■ A procedure is a PL/SQL block, with a declarative section, an executable section, and an exception-handling section. As in an anonymous block, only the executable section is required. AddNewStudent has only an executable section.

Subprogram Creation

Similar to other data dictionary objects, subprograms are created using the CREATE statement. Procedures are created with CREATE PROCEDURE, and functions are created with CREATE FUNCTION. We will examine the details of these statements in the following sections.

Creating a Procedure

The basic syntax for the CREATE [OR REPLACE] PROCEDURE statement is

```
CREATE [OR REPLACE] PROCEDURE procedure_name
  [ (argument [{IN | OUT | IN OUT}] type,
   ...
   argument [{IN | OUT | IN OUT}] type) ] {IS | AS}
procedure_body
```

where *procedure_name* is the name of the procedure to be created, *argument* is the name of a procedure parameter, *type* is the type of the associated parameter, and *procedure_body* is a PL/SQL block that makes up the code of the procedure. See the section "Subprogram Parameters" later in this chapter for information on procedure and function parameters, and the meaning of the IN, OUT, and IN OUT keywords. The argument list is optional. In this case, there are no parentheses either in the procedure declaration or in the procedure call.

NOTE
Oracle8i added two additions to the CREATE [OR REPLACE] PROCEDURE statement: the NOCOPY keyword, discussed later in this chapter in the section "Passing Parameters by Reference and by Value," and the AUTHID clause, discussed in Chapter 10.

In order to change the code of a procedure, the procedure must be dropped and then re-created. Because this is a common operation while the procedure is under development, the OR REPLACE keywords allow this to be done in one operation. If the procedure exists, it is dropped first, without a warning message. (To drop a procedure, use the DROP PROCEDURE command, described in the "Dropping Procedures and Functions" section later in this chapter.) If the procedure does not already exist, it is simply created. If the procedure exists and the OR REPLACE keywords are not present, the CREATE statement will return the Oracle error "ORA-955: Name is already used by an existing object."

As with other CREATE statements, creating a procedure is a DDL operation, so an implicit COMMIT is done both before and after the procedure is created. Either the IS or the AS keyword can be used—they are equivalent.

The Procedure Body   The body of a procedure is a PL/SQL block with declarative, executable, and exception sections. The declarative section is located between the IS or AS keyword and the BEGIN keyword. The executable section (the only one that is required) is located between the BEGIN and EXCEPTION keywords, or between the BEGIN and END keywords if there is no exception-handling section. The exception section, if present, is located between the EXCEPTION and END keywords.

TIP
There is no DECLARE keyword in a procedure or function declaration. The IS or AS keyword is used instead. This syntax originally comes from Ada, on which PL/SQL is based.

The structure of a procedure creation statement therefore looks like this:

CREATE OR REPLACE PROCEDURE *procedure_name* [*parameter_list*] **AS**
 /* Declarative section is here */
BEGIN
 /* Executable section is here */
EXCEPTION
 /* Exception section is here */
END [*procedure_name*];

The procedure name can optionally be included after the final END statement in the procedure declaration. If there is an identifier after the END, it must match the name of the procedure.

TIP
It is good style to include the procedure name in the final END statement because it makes the procedure easier to read, emphasizes the END that matches the CREATE statement, and enables the PL/SQL compiler to flag mismatched BEGIN-END pairs as early as possible.

Creating a Function
A function is very similar to a procedure. Both take parameters, which can be of any mode (parameters and modes are described later in this chapter in the section "Subprogram Parameters"). Both are different forms of PL/SQL blocks, with a declarative, executable, and exception section. Both can be stored in the database or declared within a block. (Procedures and functions not stored in the database are discussed in Chapter 10, in the section "Subprogram Locations.") However, a procedure call is a PL/SQL statement by itself, while a function call is called as part of an expression. For example, the following function returns TRUE if the specified class is 80 percent full or more, and FALSE otherwise:

```
-- Available online as AlmostFull.sql
CREATE OR REPLACE FUNCTION AlmostFull (
  p_Department classes.department%TYPE,
  p_Course     classes.course%TYPE)
  RETURN BOOLEAN IS

  v_CurrentStudents NUMBER;
  v_MaxStudents     NUMBER;
```

```
    v_ReturnValue        BOOLEAN;
    v_FullPercent        CONSTANT NUMBER := 80;
BEGIN
  -- Get the current and maximum students for the requested
  -- course.
  SELECT current_students, max_students
    INTO v_CurrentStudents, v_MaxStudents
    FROM classes
    WHERE department = p_Department
    AND course = p_Course;

  -- If the class is more full than the percentage given by
  -- v_FullPercent, return TRUE. Otherwise, return FALSE.
  IF (v_CurrentStudents / v_MaxStudents * 100) >= v_FullPercent THEN
    v_ReturnValue := TRUE;
  ELSE
    v_ReturnValue := FALSE;
  END IF;

  RETURN v_ReturnValue;
END AlmostFull;
```

The AlmostFull function returns a Boolean value. It can be called from the following PL/SQL block. Note that the function call is not a statement by itself—it is used as part of the IF statement inside the loop.

-- **Available online as callFunction.sql**
```
SQL> DECLARE
  2     CURSOR c_Classes IS
  3       SELECT department, course
  4         FROM classes;
  5   BEGIN
  6     FOR v_ClassRecord IN c_Classes LOOP
  7       -- Output all the classes which don't have very much room
  8       IF AlmostFull(v_ClassRecord.department,
  9                       v_ClassRecord.course) THEN
 10         DBMS_OUTPUT.PUT_LINE(
 11           v_ClassRecord.department || ' ' ||
 12           v_ClassRecord.course || ' is almost full!');
 13       END IF;
 14     END LOOP;
 15   END;
 16   /
MUS 410 is almost full!
PL/SQL procedure successfully completed.
```

NOTE
The DBMS_OUTPUT.PUT_LINE procedure will output its argument to the screen in SQL*Plus, provided that you have used the "set serveroutput on" option. For more information, see Chapter 2.

Function Syntax   The syntax for creating a stored function is very similar to the syntax for a procedure. It is

CREATE [OR REPLACE] FUNCTION *function_name*
[(*argument* [{IN | OUT | IN OUT}] *type*,

  ...
  argument [{IN | OUT | IN OUT}] *type*)]
RETURN *return_type* {IS | AS}
function_body

where *function_name* is the name of the function, *argument* and *type* are the same as for procedures, *return_type* is the type of the value that the function returns, and *function_body* is a PL/SQL block containing the code for the function. The same rules apply for a function body as for a procedure body—for example, the function name can optionally appear after the final END.

Similar to procedures, the argument list is optional. In this case, there are no parentheses either in the function declaration or in the function call. However, the function return type is required, because the function call is part of an expression. The type of the function is used to determine the type of the expression containing the function call.

NOTE
Like procedures, the NOCOPY keyword and AUTHID clause are available with Oracle8i.

The RETURN Statement   Inside the body of the function, the RETURN statement is used to return control to the calling environment with a value. The general syntax of the RETURN statement is

RETURN *expression*;

where *expression* is the value to be returned. When RETURN is executed, *expression* will be converted to the type specified in the RETURN clause of the function definition, if it is not already of that type. At this point, control immediately returns to the calling environment.

There can be more than one RETURN statement in a function, although only one of them will be executed. It is an error for a function to end without executing a RETURN. The following example illustrates multiple RETURN statements in one function. Even though there are five different RETURN statements in the function, only one of them is executed. Which one is executed depends on how full the class specified by p_Department and p_Course is.

```
-- Available online as ClassInfo.sql
CREATE OR REPLACE FUNCTION ClassInfo(
  /* Returns 'Full' if the class is completely full,
     'Some Room' if the class is over 80% full,
     'More Room' if the class is over 60% full,
     'Lots of Room' if the class is less than 60% full, and
     'Empty' if there are no students registered. */
  p_Department classes.department%TYPE,
  p_Course     classes.course%TYPE)
  RETURN VARCHAR2 IS

  v_CurrentStudents NUMBER;
  v_MaxStudents     NUMBER;
  v_PercentFull     NUMBER;
BEGIN
  -- Get the current and maximum students for the requested
  -- course.
  SELECT current_students, max_students
    INTO v_CurrentStudents, v_MaxStudents
    FROM classes
    WHERE department = p_Department
    AND course = p_Course;

  -- Calculate the current percentage.
  v_PercentFull := v_CurrentStudents / v_MaxStudents * 100;

  IF v_PercentFull = 100 THEN
    RETURN 'Full';
  ELSIF v_PercentFull > 80 THEN
    RETURN 'Some Room';
  ELSIF v_PercentFull > 60 THEN
    RETURN 'More Room';
  ELSIF v_PercentFull > 0 THEN
    RETURN 'Lots of Room';
  ELSE
    RETURN 'Empty';
  END IF;
END ClassInfo;
```

When used in a function, the RETURN statement must have an expression associated with it. RETURN can also be used in a procedure, however. In this case, it has no arguments, which causes control to pass back to the calling environment immediately. The current values of the formal parameters declared as OUT or IN OUT are passed back to the actual parameters, and execution continues from the statement following the procedure call. (See the section "Subprogram Parameters" later in this chapter for more information on parameters.)

Dropping Procedures and Functions

Similar to dropping a table, procedures and functions can also be dropped. This removes the procedure or function from the data dictionary. The syntax for dropping a procedure is

    DROP PROCEDURE *procedure_name*;

and the syntax for dropping a function is

    DROP FUNCTION *function_name*;

where *procedure_name* is the name of an existing procedure, and *function_name* is the name of an existing function. For example, the following statement drops the AddNewStudent procedure:

```
DROP PROCEDURE AddNewStudent;
```

If the object to be dropped is a function, you must use DROP FUNCTION, and if the object is a procedure, you must use DROP PROCEDURE. Like CREATE, DROP is a DDL command, so an implicit COMMIT is done both before and after the statement. If the subprogram does not exist, the DROP statement will raise the error "ORA-4043: Object does not exist."

Subprogram Parameters

As in other 3GLs, you can create procedures and functions that take parameters. These parameters can have different modes, and may be passed by value or by reference. We will examine how to do this in the next few sections.

Parameter Modes

Given the AddNewStudent procedure shown earlier, we can call this procedure from the following anonymous PL/SQL block:

```
-- Available online as callANS.sql
DECLARE
  -- Variables describing the new student
  v_NewFirstName  students.first_name%TYPE := 'Cynthia';
  v_NewLastName   students.last_name%TYPE := 'Camino';
```

```
    v_NewMajor        students.major%TYPE := 'History';
BEGIN
    -- Add Cynthia Camino to the database.
    AddNewStudent(v_NewFirstName, v_NewLastName, v_NewMajor);
END;
```

The variables declared in the preceding block (v_NewFirstName, v_NewLastName, v_NewMajor) are passed as arguments to AddNewStudent. In this context, they are known as *actual parameters*, whereas the parameters in the procedure declaration (p_FirstName, p_LastName, p_Major) are known as *formal parameters*. Actual parameters contain the values passed to the procedure when it is called, and they receive results from the procedure when it returns (depending on the mode). The values of the actual parameters are the ones that will be used in the procedure. The formal parameters are the placeholders for the values of the actual parameters. When the procedure is called, the formal parameters are assigned the values of the actual parameters. Inside the procedure, they are referred to by the formal parameters. When the procedure returns, the actual parameters are assigned the values of the formal parameters. These assignments follow the normal rules for PL/SQL assignment, including type conversion, if necessary.

Formal parameters can have three modes—IN, OUT, or IN OUT. (Oracle 8i adds the NOCOPY modifier, described in the next section.) If the mode is not specified for a formal parameter, it defaults to IN. The differences between each mode are described in Table 9-1 and are illustrated in the following example:

NOTE
The ModeTest example shows legal and illegal PL/SQL assignments. If you remove the comment from the illegal statement, you will receive compilation errors.

```
-- Available online as ModeTest.sql
CREATE OR REPLACE PROCEDURE ModeTest (
    p_InParameter     IN NUMBER,
    p_OutParameter    OUT NUMBER,
    p_InOutParameter  IN OUT NUMBER) IS

    v_LocalVariable   NUMBER := 0;
BEGIN
    DBMS_OUTPUT.PUT_LINE('Inside ModeTest:');
    IF (p_InParameter IS NULL) THEN
        DBMS_OUTPUT.PUT('p_InParameter is NULL');
    ELSE
        DBMS_OUTPUT.PUT('p_InParameter = ' || p_InParameter);
    END IF;
```

```
IF (p_OutParameter IS NULL) THEN
  DBMS_OUTPUT.PUT('  p_OutParameter is NULL');
ELSE
  DBMS_OUTPUT.PUT('  p_OutParameter = ' || p_OutParameter);
END IF;

IF (p_InOutParameter IS NULL) THEN
  DBMS_OUTPUT.PUT_LINE('  p_InOutParameter is NULL');
ELSE
  DBMS_OUTPUT.PUT_LINE('  p_InOutParameter = ' ||
                       p_InOutParameter);
END IF;

/* Assign p_InParameter to v_LocalVariable. This is legal,
   since we are reading from an IN parameter and not writing
   to it. */
v_LocalVariable := p_InParameter;  -- Legal

/* Assign 7 to p_InParameter. This is ILLEGAL, since we
   are writing to an IN parameter. */
-- p_InParameter := 7;  -- Illegal

/* Assign 7 to p_OutParameter. This is legal, since we
   are writing to an OUT parameter. */
p_OutParameter := 7;  -- Legal

/* Assign p_OutParameter to v_LocalVariable. In Oracle7 version
   7.3.4, and Oracle8 version 8.0.4 or higher (including 8i),
   this is legal.  Prior to 7.3.4, it is illegal to read from an
   OUT parameter. */
v_LocalVariable := p_OutParameter;  -- Possibly illegal

/* Assign p_InOutParameter to v_LocalVariable. This is legal,
   since we are reading from an IN OUT parameter. */
v_LocalVariable := p_InOutParameter;  -- Legal

/* Assign 8 to p_InOutParameter. This is legal, since we
   are writing to an IN OUT parameter. */
p_InOutParameter := 8;  -- Legal

DBMS_OUTPUT.PUT_LINE('At end of ModeTest:');
IF (p_InParameter IS NULL) THEN
  DBMS_OUTPUT.PUT('p_InParameter is NULL');
ELSE
  DBMS_OUTPUT.PUT('p_InParameter = ' || p_InParameter);
END IF;
```

```
    IF (p_OutParameter IS NULL) THEN
      DBMS_OUTPUT.PUT('  p_OutParameter is NULL');
    ELSE
      DBMS_OUTPUT.PUT('  p_OutParameter = ' || p_OutParameter);
    END IF;

    IF (p_InOutParameter IS NULL) THEN
      DBMS_OUTPUT.PUT_LINE('  p_InOutParameter is NULL');
    ELSE
      DBMS_OUTPUT.PUT_LINE('  p_InOutParameter = ' ||
                          p_InOutParameter);
    END IF;

END ModeTest;
```

NOTE
It is illegal to read from OUT parameters in Oracle versions prior to 7.3.4 and in 8.0.3, but legal in Oracle8 version 8.0.4 and higher. See the section "Reading from OUT Parameters" later in this chapter for more details.

Passing Values Between Formal and Actual Parameters   We can call ModeTest with the following block:

```
-- Available online as part of callMT.sql
DECLARE
  v_In NUMBER := 1;
  v_Out NUMBER := 2;
  v_InOut NUMBER := 3;
BEGIN
  DBMS_OUTPUT.PUT_LINE('Before calling ModeTest:');
  DBMS_OUTPUT.PUT_LINE('v_In = ' || v_In ||
                      ' v_Out = ' || v_Out ||
                      ' v_InOut = ' || v_InOut);

  ModeTest(v_In, v_Out, v_InOut);

  DBMS_OUTPUT.PUT_LINE('After calling ModeTest:');
  DBMS_OUTPUT.PUT_LINE('  v_In = ' || v_In ||
                      ' v_Out = ' || v_Out ||
                      ' v_InOut = ' || v_InOut);
END;
```

Mode	Description
IN	The value of the actual parameter is passed into the procedure when the procedure is invoked. Inside the procedure, the formal parameter acts like a PL/SQL constant—it is considered *read-only* and cannot be changed. When the procedure finishes and control returns to the calling environment, the actual parameter is not changed.
OUT	Any value the actual parameter has when the procedure is called is ignored. Inside the procedure, the formal parameter acts like an uninitialized PL/SQL variable, and thus has a value of NULL. It can be read from and written to. When the procedure finishes and control returns to the calling environment, the contents of the formal parameter are assigned to the actual parameter. (In Oracle8*i*, this behavior can be altered by using the NOCOPY modifier—see the section "Passing Parameters by Value and by Reference" later in this chapter.)
IN OUT	This mode is a combination of IN and OUT. The value of the actual parameter is passed into the procedure when the procedure is invoked. Inside the procedure, the formal parameter acts like an initialized variable, and can be read from and written to. When the procedure finishes and control returns to the calling environment, the contents of the formal parameter are assigned to the actual parameter (subject to NOCOPY in Oracle8*i*, as for OUT).

TABLE 9-1. *Parameter Modes*

This produces output as shown here:

```
Before calling ModeTest:
v_In = 1  v_Out = 2  v_InOut = 3
Inside ModeTest:
p_InParameter = 1  p_OutParameter is NULL  p_InOutParameter = 3
At end of ModeTest:
p_InParameter = 1  p_OutParameter = 7  p_InOutParameter = 8
After calling ModeTest:
v_In = 1  v_Out = 7  v_InOut = 8
```

This output shows that the OUT parameter has been initialized to NULL inside the procedure. Also, the values of the IN and IN OUT formal parameters at the end of the procedure have been copied back to the actual parameters when the procedure ends.

NOTE
If the procedure raises an exception, the values of IN OUT and OUT formal parameters are not copied to their corresponding actual parameters (subject to NOCOPY in Oracle8i). See the section "Exceptions Raised Inside Subprograms" later in this chapter.

Literals or Constants as Actual Parameters   Because of this copying, the actual parameter that corresponds to an IN OUT or OUT parameter must be a variable, and cannot be a constant or expression. There must be a location where the returned value can be stored. For example, we can replace v_In with a literal when we call ModeTest:

```
-- Available online as part of callMT.sql
DECLARE
  v_Out NUMBER := 2;
  v_InOut NUMBER := 3;
BEGIN
  ModeTest(1, v_Out, v_InOut);
END;
```

But if we replace v_Out with a literal, we get the following illegal example:

```
-- Available online as part of callMT.sql
SQL> DECLARE
  2    v_InOut NUMBER := 3;
  3  BEGIN
  4    ModeTest(1, 2, v_InOut);
  5  END;
  6  /
DECLARE
*
ERROR at line 1:
ORA-06550: line 4, column 15:
PLS-00363: expression '2' cannot be used as an assignment target
ORA-06550: line 4, column 3:
PL/SQL: Statement ignored
```

Compilation Checks   The PL/SQL compiler will check for legal assignments when the procedure is created. For example, if we remove the comments on the assignment to `p_InParameter`, `ModeTest` generates the following error if we attempt to compile it:

```
PLS-363: expression 'P_INPARAMETER' cannot be used as an
          assignment target
```

Reading From OUT Parameters   Prior to version 7.3.4 and in 8.0.3, it is illegal to read from an OUT parameter in a procedure. If we attempt to compile `ModeTest` against an 8.0.3 database, for example, we receive the following error:

```
PLS-00365: 'P_OUTPARAMETER' is an OUT parameter and cannot be read
```

One workaround for this issue is to declare OUT parameters as IN OUT. Table 9-2 shows which Oracle versions allow reading from OUT parameters and which do not.

Constraints on Formal Parameters

When a procedure is called, the values of the actual parameters are passed in, and they are referred to using the formal parameters inside the procedure. The constraints on the variables are passed as well, as part of the parameter passing mechanism. In a procedure declaration, it is illegal to constrain CHAR and VARCHAR2 parameters with a length, and NUMBER parameters with a precision and/or scale, as the constraints will be taken from the actual parameters. For example, the following procedure declaration is illegal and will generate a compile error (we will see more information about how to detect compile errors in Chapter 10):

```
-- Available online as part of ParameterLength.sql
CREATE OR REPLACE PROCEDURE ParameterLength (
  p_Parameter1 IN OUT VARCHAR2(10),
  p_Parameter2 IN OUT NUMBER(3,1)) AS
BEGIN
  p_Parameter1 := 'abcdefghijklm';
  p_Parameter2 := 12.3;
END ParameterLength;
```

Oracle Version	Legal to Read OUT Parameters?
Prior to 7.3.4	No
7.3.4	Yes
8.0.3	No
8.0.4 and higher	Yes

TABLE 9-2.   *The Legality of Reading OUTs*

The correct declaration for this procedure would be

```
-- Available online as part of ParameterLength.sql
CREATE OR REPLACE PROCEDURE ParameterLength (
  p_Parameter1 IN OUT VARCHAR2,
  p_Parameter2 IN OUT NUMBER) AS
BEGIN
  p_Parameter1 := 'abcdefghijklmno';
  p_Parameter2 := 12.3;
END ParameterLength;
```

So, what are the constraints on `p_Parameter1` and `p_Parameter2`? They come from the actual parameters. If we call `ParameterLength` with

```
-- Available online as part of ParameterLength.sql
DECLARE
  v_Variable1 VARCHAR2(40);
  v_Variable2 NUMBER(7,3);
BEGIN
  ParameterLength(v_Variable1, v_Variable2);
END;
```

then `p_Parameter1` will have a maximum length of 40 (coming from the actual parameter `v_Variable1`) and `p_Parameter2` will have precision 7 and scale 3 (coming from the actual parameter `v_Variable2`). It is important to be aware of this. Consider the following block, which also calls `ParameterLength`:

```
-- Available online as part of ParameterLength.sql
DECLARE
  v_Variable1 VARCHAR2(10);
  v_Variable2 NUMBER(7,3);
BEGIN
  ParameterLength(v_Variable1, v_Variable2);
END;
```

The only difference between this block and the prior one is that `v_Variable1`, and hence `p_Parameter1`, has a length of 10 rather than 40. Because `ParameterLength` assigns a character string of length 15 to `p_Parameter1` (and hence `v_Variable1`), there is not enough room in the string. This will result in the following Oracle errors when the procedure is called:

```
DECLARE
*
ERROR at line 1:
ORA-06502: PL/SQL: numeric or value error: character string buffer too
  small
ORA-06512: at "DEMO.PARAMETERLENGTH", line 5
ORA-06512: at line 5
```

The source of the error is not in the procedure—it is in the code that calls the procedure. In addition, the ORA-6502 is a runtime error, not a compile error. Thus, the block compiled successfully, and the error was actually raised when the procedure returned and the PL/SQL engine attempted to copy the actual value `'abcdefghijklmno'` into the formal parameter.

TIP

In order to avoid errors such as ORA-6502, document any constraint requirements of the actual parameters when the procedure is created. This documentation could consist of comments stored with the procedure, and should include a description of what the procedure does in addition to any parameter definitions. Alternatively, you can use %TYPE to declare the formal parameters, as described in the next section.

%TYPE and Procedure Parameters   Although formal parameters cannot be declared with constraints, they can be constrained by using %TYPE. If a formal parameter is declared using %TYPE, and the underlying type is constrained, the constraint will be on the formal parameter rather than the actual parameter. If we declare `ParameterLength` with

```
-- Available online as part of ParameterLength.sql
CREATE OR REPLACE PROCEDURE ParameterLength (
  .p_Parameter1 IN OUT VARCHAR2,
  p_Parameter2 IN OUT students.current_credits%TYPE) AS
BEGIN
  p_Parameter2 := 12345;
END ParameterLength;
```

then `p_Parameter2` will be constrained with precision of 3, because that is the precision of the `current_credits` column. Even if we call `ParameterLength` with an actual parameter of enough precision, the formal precision is taken. Thus, the following example will generate the ORA-6502 error:

```
-- Available online as part of ParameterLength.sql
SQL> DECLARE
  2    v_Variable1 VARCHAR2(1);
  3    -- Declare v_Variable2 with no constraints
  4    v_Variable2 NUMBER;
  5  BEGIN
  6    -- Even though the actual parameter has room for 12345, the
  7    -- constraint on the formal parameter is taken and we get
  8    -- ORA-6502 on this procedure call.
```

```
 9     ParameterLength(v_Variable1, v_Variable2);
10   END;
11   /
DECLARE
*
ERROR at line 1:
ORA-06502: PL/SQL: numeric or value error: number precision too large
ORA-06512: at "EXAMPLE.PARAMETERLENGTH", line 5
ORA-06512: at line 9
```

NOTE
The ORA-6502 error message was enhanced for Oracle8i. Prior to Oracle8i, the error is reported simply as "ORA-6502: PL/SQL numeric or value error," regardless of the actual cause of the error. For example, the error message text is different in the previous two examples, which show the Oracle8i behavior.

Exceptions Raised Inside Subprograms

If an error occurs inside a subprogram, an exception is raised. This exception may be user-defined or predefined. If the procedure has no exception handler for this error (or if an exception is raised from within an exception handler), control immediately passes out of the procedure to the calling environment, in accordance with the exception propagation rules (see Chapter 7 for more details). However, in this case, the values of OUT and IN OUT formal parameters are *not* returned to the actual parameters. The actual parameters will have the same values as they would have had if the procedure had not been called. For example, suppose we create the following procedure:

```
-- Available online as part of RaiseError.sql
/* Illustrates the behavior of unhandled exceptions and
 * OUT variables. If p_Raise is TRUE, then an unhandled
 * error is raised. If p_Raise is FALSE, the procedure
 * completes successfully.
 */
CREATE OR REPLACE PROCEDURE RaiseError (
  p_Raise IN BOOLEAN,
  p_ParameterA OUT NUMBER) AS
BEGIN
  p_ParameterA := 7;

  IF p_Raise THEN
    /* Even though we have assigned 7 to p_ParameterA, this
```

```
        * unhandled exception causes control to return immediately
        * without returning 7 to the actual parameter associated
        * with p_ParameterA.
        */
      RAISE DUP_VAL_ON_INDEX;
    ELSE
      -- Simply return with no error. This will return 7 to the
      -- actual parameter.
      RETURN;
    END IF;
END RaiseError;
```

If we call `RaiseError` with the following block,

```
-- Available online as part of RaiseError.sql
DECLARE
  v_TempVar NUMBER := 1;
BEGIN
  DBMS_OUTPUT.PUT_LINE('Initial value: ' || v_TempVar);
  RaiseError(FALSE, v_TempVar);
  DBMS_OUTPUT.PUT_LINE('Value after successful call: ' ||
                       v_TempVar);

  v_TempVar := 2;
  DBMS_OUTPUT.PUT_LINE('Value before 2nd call: ' || v_TempVar);
  RaiseError(TRUE, v_TempVar);
EXCEPTION
  WHEN OTHERS THEN
    DBMS_OUTPUT.PUT_LINE('Value after unsuccessful call: ' ||
                         v_TempVar);
END;
```

we get the following output:

```
Initial value: 1
Value after successful call: 7
Value before 2nd call: 2
Value after unsuccessful call: 2
```

Before the first call to `RaiseError`, `v_TempVar` contained 1. The first call was successful, and `v_TempVar` was assigned the value 7. The block then changed `v_TempVar` to 2 before the second call to `RaiseError`. This second call did not complete successfully, and `v_TempVar` was unchanged at 2 (rather than being changed to 7 again).

NOTE
The semantics of exception handling change when an OUT or IN OUT parameter is declared with the NOCOPY hint. See the section "Exception Semantics with NOCOPY," later in this chapter, for details.

Passing Parameters by Reference and by Value

A subprogram parameter can be passed in one of two ways—by reference or by value. When a parameter is passed *by reference,* a pointer to the actual parameter is passed to the corresponding formal parameter. When a parameter is passed *by value,* on the other hand, it is copied from the actual parameter into the formal parameter. Passing by reference is generally faster, because it avoids the copy. This is especially true for collection parameters (tables and varrays, which are discussed in Chapter 8), due to their larger size. By default, PL/SQL will pass IN parameters by reference, and IN OUT and OUT parameters by value. This is done to preserve the exception semantics that we discussed in the previous section, and so that constraints on actual parameters can be verified. Prior to Oracle8*i*, there is no way to modify this behavior.

Using NOCOPY   Oracle8*i* includes a compiler hint known as NOCOPY. The syntax for declaring a parameter with this hint is

parameter_name [mode] NOCOPY *datatype*

where *parameter_name* is the name of the parameter, *mode* is the parameter mode (IN, OUT, or IN OUT), and *datatype* is the parameter datatype. If NOCOPY is present, the PL/SQL compiler will try to pass the parameter by reference, rather than by value. NOCOPY is a compiler hint, rather than a directive, so it will not always be taken (see the section "NOCOPY Restrictions" for details on when NOCOPY will be heeded). The following example illustrates the syntax of NOCOPY:

```
-- Available online as part of NoCopyTest.sql
CREATE OR REPLACE PROCEDURE NoCopyTest (
  p_InParameter    IN NUMBER,
  p_OutParameter   OUT NOCOPY VARCHAR2,
  p_InOutParameter IN OUT NOCOPY CHAR) IS
BEGIN
  NULL;
END NoCopyTest;
```

Using NOCOPY on an IN parameter will generate a compilation error, because IN parameters are always passed by reference and NOCOPY thus doesn't apply.

Exception Semantics with NOCOPY   When a parameter is passed by reference, any modifications to the formal parameter also modify the actual parameter, because both point to the same location. This means that if a procedure exits with an unhandled exception after the formal parameter has been changed, the original value of the actual parameter will be lost. Suppose we modify RaiseError to use NOCOPY, as follows:

```
-- Available online as part of NoCopyTest.sql
CREATE OR REPLACE PROCEDURE RaiseError (
  p_Raise IN BOOLEAN,
  p_ParameterA OUT NOCOPY NUMBER) AS
BEGIN
  p_ParameterA := 7;
  IF p_Raise THEN
    RAISE DUP_VAL_ON_INDEX;
  ELSE
    RETURN;
  END IF;
END RaiseError;
```

The only change is that p_ParameterA will now be passed by reference, rather than by value. Suppose we call RaiseError with the following:

```
-- Available online as part of NoCopyTest.sql
DECLARE
  v_TempVar NUMBER := 1;
BEGIN
  DBMS_OUTPUT.PUT_LINE('Initial value: ' || v_TempVar);
  RaiseError(FALSE, v_TempVar);
  DBMS_OUTPUT.PUT_LINE('Value after successful call: ' ||
                        v_TempVar);

  v_TempVar := 2;
  DBMS_OUTPUT.PUT_LINE('Value before 2nd call: ' || v_TempVar);
  RaiseError(TRUE, v_TempVar);
EXCEPTION
  WHEN OTHERS THEN
    DBMS_OUTPUT.PUT_LINE('Value after unsuccessful call: ' ||
                          v_TempVar);
END;
```

This is the same block we saw earlier in the section "Exceptions Raised Inside Subprograms." The output of this block, however, is different now:

```
Initial value: 1
Value after successful call: 7
Value before 2nd call: 2
Value after unsuccessful call: 7
```

The actual parameter has been modified both times, even when the exception was raised.

NOCOPY Restrictions   In some cases, NOCOPY will be ignored, and the parameter will be passed by value. No error is generated in these cases. Remember that NOCOPY is a hint, and the compiler is not obligated to follow it. NOCOPY will be ignored in the following situations:

■   The actual parameter is a member of an index-by table. If the actual parameter is an entire table, however, this restriction does not apply.

■   The actual parameter is constrained by a precision, scale, or NOT NULL constraint. This restriction does not apply to a character parameter constrained by a maximum length, though. The reason for this is that the PL/SQL compiler checks for constraint violations only when returning from a subprogram, when copying the value back from the formal parameter to the actual parameter. If there is a constraint violation, the original value of the actual parameter needs to be unchanged, which is impossible with NOCOPY.

■   The actual and formal parameters are both records, and they were declared either implicitly as a loop control variable or using %ROWTYPE, and the constraints on the corresponding fields differ.

■   Passing the actual parameter requires an implicit datatype conversion.

■   The subprogram is involved in a remote procedure call (RPC). An RPC is a procedure call made over a database link to a remote server. Because the parameters must be transferred over the network, it is not possible to pass them by reference.

TIP
As the last point above illustrates, if the subprogram is part of an RPC, NOCOPY will be ignored. If you modify an existing application to make some of the calls RPCs, rather than local calls, the exception semantics can change.

Benefits of NOCOPY   The primary advantage of NOCOPY is that it may increase performance. This is especially valuable when passing large PL/SQL tables, as the following example illustrates:

```
-- Available online as CopyFast.sql
CREATE OR REPLACE PACKAGE CopyFast AS
  -- PL/SQL table of students.
  TYPE StudentArray IS
    TABLE OF students%ROWTYPE;

  -- Three procedures which take a parameter of StudentArray, in
  -- different ways.  They each do nothing.
  PROCEDURE PassStudents1(p_Parameter IN StudentArray);
  PROCEDURE PassStudents2(p_Parameter IN OUT StudentArray);
  PROCEDURE PassStudents3(p_Parameter IN OUT NOCOPY StudentArray);

  -- Test procedure.
  PROCEDURE Go;
END CopyFast;

CREATE OR REPLACE PACKAGE BODY CopyFast AS
  PROCEDURE PassStudents1(p_Parameter IN StudentArray) IS
  BEGIN
    NULL;
  END PassStudents1;

  PROCEDURE PassStudents2(p_Parameter IN OUT StudentArray) IS
  BEGIN
    NULL;
  END PassStudents2;

  PROCEDURE PassStudents3(p_Parameter IN OUT NOCOPY StudentArray) IS
  BEGIN
    NULL;
  END PassStudents3;

  PROCEDURE Go IS
    v_StudentArray StudentArray := StudentArray(NULL);
    v_StudentRec students%ROWTYPE;
    v_Time1 NUMBER;
    v_Time2 NUMBER;
    v_Time3 NUMBER;
    v_Time4 NUMBER;
  BEGIN
    -- Fill up the array with 50,001 copies of David Dinsmore's
    -- record.
    SELECT *
      INTO v_StudentArray(1)
      FROM students
```

```
        WHERE ID = 10007;
   v_StudentArray.EXTEND(50000, 1);

   -- Call each version of PassStudents, and time them.
   -- DBMS_UTILITY.GET_TIME will return the current time, in
   -- hundredths of a second.
   v_Time1 := DBMS_UTILITY.GET_TIME;
   PassStudents1(v_StudentArray);
   v_Time2 := DBMS_UTILITY.GET_TIME;
   PassStudents2(v_StudentArray);
   v_Time3 := DBMS_UTILITY.GET_TIME;
   PassStudents3(v_StudentArray);
   v_Time4 := DBMS_UTILITY.GET_TIME;

   -- Output the results.
   DBMS_OUTPUT.PUT_LINE('Time to pass IN: ' ||
                        TO_CHAR((v_Time2 - v_Time1) / 100));
   DBMS_OUTPUT.PUT_LINE('Time to pass IN OUT: ' ||
                        TO_CHAR((v_Time3 -   v_Time2) / 100));
   DBMS_OUTPUT.PUT_LINE('Time to pass IN OUT NOCOPY: ' ||
                        TO_CHAR((v_Time4 - v_Time3) / 100));
   END Go;
END CopyFast;
```

NOTE
This example uses a package to group together related procedures. Packages are described in the section "Packages" later in this chapter. See also Chapter 8 for information on collections and how the EXTEND method is used, and Appendix A for information about DBMS_UTILITY.

Each of the PassStudents procedures does nothing—the procedures simply take a parameter that is a PL/SQL table of students. The parameter is 50,001 records, so it is reasonably large. The difference between the procedures is that PassStudents1 takes the parameter as an IN, PassStudents2 as an IN OUT, and PassStudents3 as IN OUT NOCOPY. Thus, PassStudents2 should pass the parameter by value and the other two by reference. We can see this by looking at the results of calling CopyFast.Go:

```
SQL> BEGIN
  2    CopyFast.Go;
  3  END;
  4  /
Time to pass IN: 0
Time to pass IN OUT: 4.28
Time to pass IN OUT NOCOPY: 0
PL/SQL procedure successfully completed.
```

Although the actual results may differ on your system, the time for passing the IN OUT parameter by value should be significantly more than passing the IN and IN OUT NOCOPY parameters by reference.

Subprograms with No Parameters

If there are no parameters for a procedure, there are no parentheses in either the procedure declaration or the procedure call. This is also true for functions. The following example illustrates this:

```
-- Available online as noparams.sql
CREATE OR REPLACE PROCEDURE NoParamsP AS
BEGIN
  DBMS_OUTPUT.PUT_LINE('No Parameters!');
END NoParamsP;

CREATE OR REPLACE FUNCTION NoParamsF
  RETURN DATE AS
BEGIN
  RETURN SYSDATE;
END NoParamsF;

BEGIN
  NoParamsP;
  DBMS_OUTPUT.PUT_LINE('Calling NoParamsF on ' ||
    TO_CHAR(NoParamsF, 'DD-MON-YYYY'));
END;
```

NOTE
With the CALL syntax available with Oracle8i, the parentheses are optional. See the section "The CALL Statement" later in this chapter for details.

Positional and Named Notation

In all of the examples shown so far in this chapter, the actual arguments are associated with the formal arguments by position. Given a procedure declaration such as

```
-- Available online as part of CallMe.sql
CREATE OR REPLACE PROCEDURE CallMe(
  p_ParameterA VARCHAR2,
  p_ParameterB NUMBER,
  p_ParameterC BOOLEAN,
  p_ParameterD DATE) AS
BEGIN
  NULL;
END CallMe;
```

and a calling block such as

```
-- Available online as part of CallMe.sql
DECLARE
  v_Variable1 VARCHAR2(10);
  v_Variable2 NUMBER(7,6);
  v_Variable3 BOOLEAN;
  v_Variable4 DATE;
BEGIN
  CallMe(v_Variable1, v_Variable2, v_Variable3, v_Variable4);
END;
```

the actual parameters are associated with the formal parameters by position:
v_Variable1 is associated with p_ParameterA, v_Variable2 is associated with
p_ParameterB, and so on. This is known as *positional notation*. Positional notation
is more commonly used, and it is also the notation used in other 3GLs such as C.
      Alternatively, we can call the procedure using *named notation*:

```
-- Available online as part of CallMe.sql
DECLARE
  v_Variable1 VARCHAR2(10);
  v_Variable2 NUMBER(7,6);
  v_Variable3 BOOLEAN;
  v_Variable4 DATE;
BEGIN
  CallMe(p_ParameterA => v_Variable1,
         p_ParameterB => v_Variable2,
         p_ParameterC => v_Variable3,
         p_ParameterD => v_Variable4);
END;
```

In named notation, the formal parameter and the actual parameter are both
included for each argument. This allows us to rearrange the order of the arguments, if
desired. For example, the following block also calls CallMe, with the same arguments:

```
-- Available online as part of CallMe.sql
DECLARE
  v_Variable1 VARCHAR2(10);
  v_Variable2 NUMBER(7,6);
  v_Variable3 BOOLEAN;
  v_Variable4 DATE;
BEGIN
  CallMe(p_ParameterB => v_Variable2,
         p_ParameterC => v_Variable3,
         p_ParameterD => v_Variable4,
         p_ParameterA => v_Variable1);
END;
```

Positional and named notation can be mixed in the same call as well, if desired. The first arguments must be specified by position, and the remaining arguments can be specified by name. The following block illustrates this method:

```
-- Available online as part of CallMe.sql
DECLARE
  v_Variable1 VARCHAR2(10);
  v_Variable2 NUMBER(7,6);
  v_Variable3 BOOLEAN;
  v_Variable4 DATE;
BEGIN
  -- First 2 parameters passed by position, the second 2 are
  -- passed by name.
  CallMe(v_Variable1, v_Variable2,
        p_ParameterC => v_Variable3,
        p_ParameterD => v_Variable4);
END;
```

Named notation is another feature of PL/SQL that comes from Ada. When should you use positional notation, and when should you use named notation? Neither is more efficient than the other, so the only preference is one of style. Some of the style differences are illustrated in Table 9-3.

I generally use positional notation, as I prefer to write succinct code. It is important to use good names for the actual parameters, however. On the other hand, if the procedure takes a large number of arguments (more than ten is a good measure), named notation is desirable, because it is easier to match the formal and actual parameters. Procedures with this many arguments are fairly rare, however. Named notation is also useful for procedures with default arguments (see the next section for details).

TIP
The more parameters a procedure has, the more difficult it is to call and make sure that all of the required parameters are present. If you have a significant number of parameters that you would like to pass to or from a procedure, consider defining a record type with the parameters as fields within the record. Then you can use a single parameter of the record type. (Note that if the calling environment is not PL/SQL, you may not be able to bind a record type, however.) PL/SQL has no explicit limit on the number of parameters.

Positional Notation	Named Notation
Relies more on good names for the actual parameters to illustrate what each is used for.	Clearly illustrates the association between the actual and formal parameters.
Names used for the formal and actual parameters are independent; one can be changed without modifying the other.	Can be more difficult to maintain because all calls to the procedure using named notation must be changed if the *names* of the formal parameters are changed.
Can be more difficult to maintain because all calls to the procedure using positional notation must be changed if the *order* of the formal parameters is changed.	The *order* used for the formal and actual parameters is independent; one can be changed without modifying the other.
More succinct than named notation.	Requires more coding, because both the formal and actual parameters are included in the procedure call.
Parameters with default values must be at the end of the argument list.	Allows default values for formal parameters to be used, regardless of which parameter has the default.

TABLE 9-3. *Positional versus Named Notation*

Parameter Default Values

Similar to variable declarations, the formal parameters to a procedure or function can have default values. If a parameter has a default value, it does not have to be passed from the calling environment. If it is passed, the value of the actual parameter will be used instead of the default. A default value for a parameter is included using the syntax

```
parameter_name [mode] parameter_type
  {:= | DEFAULT} initial_value
```

where *parameter_name* is the name of the formal parameter, *mode* is the parameter mode (IN, OUT, or IN OUT), *parameter_type* is the parameter type (either predefined or user-defined), and *initial_value* is the value to be assigned to the formal parameter by default. Either := or the DEFAULT keyword can be used. For example, we can rewrite the `AddNewStudent` procedure to assign the economics major by default to all new students, unless overridden by an explicit argument:

```
-- Available online as part of default.sql
CREATE OR REPLACE PROCEDURE AddNewStudent (
  p_FirstName   students.first_name%TYPE,
  p_LastName    students.last_name%TYPE,
  p_Major       students.major%TYPE DEFAULT 'Economics') AS
BEGIN
  -- Insert a new row in the students table. Use
  -- student_sequence to generate the new student ID, and
  -- 0 for current_credits.
  INSERT INTO students VALUES (student_sequence.nextval,
    p_FirstName, p_LastName, p_Major, 0);
END AddNewStudent;
```

The default value will be used if the `p_Major` formal parameter does not have an actual parameter associated with it in the procedure call. We can do this with positional notation

```
-- Available online as part of default.sql
BEGIN
  AddNewStudent('Simon', 'Salovitz');
END;
```

or with named notation:

```
-- Available online as part of default.sql
BEGIN
  AddNewStudent(p_FirstName => 'Veronica',
                p_LastName => 'Vassily');
END;
```

If positional notation is used, all parameters with default values that don't have an associated actual parameter must be at the end of the parameter list. Consider the following example:

```
-- Available online as part of DefaultTest.sql
CREATE OR REPLACE PROCEDURE DefaultTest (
  p_ParameterA NUMBER DEFAULT 10,
  p_ParameterB VARCHAR2 DEFAULT 'abcdef',
  p_ParameterC DATE DEFAULT SYSDATE) AS
BEGIN
  DBMS_OUTPUT.PUT_LINE(
    'A: ' || p_ParameterA ||
    ' B: ' || p_ParameterB ||
    ' C: ' || TO_CHAR(p_ParameterC, 'DD-MON-YYYY'));
END DefaultTest;
```

All three parameters to `DefaultTest` take default arguments. If we wanted to take the default value for `p_ParameterB` only, but specify values for `p_ParameterA` and `p_ParameterC`, we would have to use named notation, as follows:

```
-- Available online as part of DefaultTest.sql
SQL> BEGIN
  2     DefaultTest(p_ParameterA => 7, p_ParameterC => '30-DEC-95');
  3  END;
  4  /
A: 7  B: abcdef  C: 30-DEC-1995
PL/SQL procedure successfully completed.
```

If we wanted to use the default value for `p_ParameterB`, we would also have to use the default value for `p_ParameterC` when using positional notation. When using positional notation, all default parameters for which there are no associated actual parameters must be at the end of the parameter list, as in the following example:

```
-- Available online as part of DefaultTest.sql
SQL> BEGIN
  2     -- Uses the default value for both p_ParameterB and
  3     -- p_ParameterC.
  4     DefaultTest(7);
  5  END;
  6  /
A: 7  B: abcdef  C: 17-OCT-1999
PL/SQL procedure successfully completed.
```

TIP
When using default values, make them the last parameters in the argument list if possible. This way, either positional or named notation can be used.

The CALL Statement

| Oracle8*i* |
| and higher |

Oracle8*i* adds a new SQL statement to call stored subprograms: the CALL statement. It can be used to call both PL/SQL and Java subprograms with a PL/SQL wrapper, and has the syntax

CALL *subprogram_name* ([*argument_list*]) [INTO *host_variable*];

where *subprogram_name* is a stand-alone or packaged subprogram. It can also be an object type method, and can be at a remote database. The *argument_list* is a comma-delimited list of arguments, and *host_variable* is a host variable used to retrieve the return value of functions. The following SQL*Plus session illustrates some legal and illegal uses of the CALL statement:

```
-- Available online as calls.sql
SQL> CREATE OR REPLACE PROCEDURE CallProc1(p1 IN VARCHAR2 := NULL) AS
  2  BEGIN
  3    DBMS_OUTPUT.PUT_LINE('CallProc1 called with ' || p1);
  4  END CallProc1;
  5  /
Procedure created.

SQL> CREATE OR REPLACE PROCEDURE CallProc2(p1 IN OUT VARCHAR2) AS
  2  BEGIN
  3    DBMS_OUTPUT.PUT_LINE('CallProc2 called with ' || p1);
  4    p1 := p1 || ' returned!';
  5  END CallProc2;
  6  /
Procedure created.

SQL> CREATE OR REPLACE FUNCTION CallFunc(p1 IN VARCHAR2)
  2    RETURN VARCHAR2 AS
  3  BEGIN
  4    DBMS_OUTPUT.PUT_LINE('CallFunc called with ' || p1);
  5    RETURN p1;
  6  END CallFunc;
  7  /
Function created.

SQL> -- Some valid calls direct from SQL.
SQL> CALL CallProc1('Hello!');
CallProc1 called with Hello!
Call completed.

SQL> CALL CallProc1();
CallProc1 called with
Call completed.

SQL> VARIABLE v_Output VARCHAR2(50);
SQL> CALL CallFunc('Hello!') INTO :v_Output;
CallFunc called with Hello!
Call completed.

SQL> PRINT v_Output
V_OUTPUT
-----------------------------------------------------------------
Hello!
```

```
SQL> CALL CallProc2(:v_Output);
CallProc2 called with Hello!
Call completed.

SQL> PRINT v_Output
V_OUTPUT
-------------------------------------------------------------------
Hello! returned!

SQL> -- This is illegal
SQL> BEGIN
  2    CALL CallProc1();
  3  END;
  4  /
  CALL CallProc1();
       *
ERROR at line 2:
ORA-06550: line 2, column 8:
PLS-00103: Encountered the symbol "CALLPROC1" when expecting one of the
following:
:= . ( @ % ;
The symbol ":=" was substituted for "CALLPROC1" to continue.

SQL> -- But these are legal
SQL> DECLARE
  2    v_Result VARCHAR2(50);
  3  BEGIN
  4    EXECUTE IMMEDIATE 'CALL CallProc1(''Hello from PL/SQL'')';
  5    EXECUTE IMMEDIATE
  6      'CALL CallFunc(''Hello from PL/SQL'') INTO :v_Result'
  7      USING OUT v_Result;
  8  END;
  9  /
CallProc1 called with Hello from PL/SQL
CallFunc called with Hello from PL/SQL
PL/SQL procedure successfully completed.
```

The example illustrates the following points:

■ CALL is a SQL statement. It is not valid inside a PL/SQL block, but is valid when executed using dynamic SQL. (Inside a PL/SQL block, you can call the subprogram using the PL/SQL syntax.) See Chapter 12 for more information about dynamic SQL.

■ The parentheses are always required, even if the subprogram takes no arguments (or has default values for all the arguments).

■ The INTO clause is used for the output variables of functions only. IN OUT or OUT parameters are specified as part of the *argument_list*.

TIP
SQL*Plus versions earlier than 8.1 do not accept the CALL statement as valid SQL. You can use the EXECUTE SQL*Plus command instead. For more information, see Chapter 2.

Procedures versus Functions

Procedures and functions share many of the same features:

■ Both can return more than one value via OUT parameters.

■ Both can have declarative, executable, and exception-handling sections.

■ Both can accept default values.

■ Both can be called using positional or named notation.

■ Both can accept NOCOPY parameters (Oracle8*i* and higher).

So when is a function appropriate, and when is a procedure appropriate? It generally depends on how many values the subprogram is expected to return and how those values will be used. The rule of thumb is that if there is more than one return value, use a procedure. If there is only one return value, a function can be used. Although it is legal for a function to have OUT parameters (and thus return more than one value), it is generally considered poor programming style. Functions can also be called from within a SQL statement. (See Chapter 10 for more information.)

Packages

Another Ada feature incorporated in the design of PL/SQL is the *package*. A package is a PL/SQL construct that allows related objects to be stored together. A package has two separate parts: the specification and the body. Each of them is stored separately in the data dictionary. Unlike procedures and functions, which can be contained locally in a block or stored in the database, a package can only be stored; it cannot be local. Besides allowing related objects to be grouped together, packages are useful because they are less restrictive than stored subprograms with respect to dependencies. They also have performance advantages, which we will discuss in the next chapter.

A package is essentially a named declarative section. Anything that can go in the declarative part of a block can go in a package. This includes procedures, functions, cursors, types, and variables. One advantage of putting these objects into a package is the ability to reference them from other PL/SQL blocks, so packages also provide global variables (within a single database session) for PL/SQL.

Package Specification

The *package specification* (also known as the *package header*) contains information about the contents of the package. However, it does not contain the code for any subprograms. Consider the following example:

```
-- Available online as part of ClassPackage.sql
CREATE OR REPLACE PACKAGE ClassPackage AS
  -- Add a new student into the specified class.
  PROCEDURE AddStudent(p_StudentID  IN students.id%TYPE,
                       p_Department IN classes.department%TYPE,
                       p_Course     IN classes.course%TYPE);

  -- Removes the specified student from the specified class.
  PROCEDURE RemoveStudent(p_StudentID  IN students.id%TYPE,
                          p_Department IN classes.department%TYPE,
                          p_Course     IN classes.course%TYPE);

  -- Exception raised by RemoveStudent.
  e_StudentNotRegistered EXCEPTION;

  -- Table type used to hold student info.
  TYPE t_StudentIDTable IS TABLE OF students.id%TYPE
    INDEX BY BINARY_INTEGER;

  -- Returns a PL/SQL table containing the students currently
  -- in the specified class.
  PROCEDURE ClassList(p_Department  IN  classes.department%TYPE,
                      p_Course      IN  classes.course%TYPE,
                      p_IDs         OUT t_StudentIDTable,
                      p_NumStudents IN OUT BINARY_INTEGER);
END ClassPackage;
```

ClassPackage contains three procedures, a type, and an exception. The general syntax for creating a package header is

```
CREATE [OR REPLACE] PACKAGE package_name {IS | AS}
  type_definition |
  procedure_specification |
  function_specification |
  variable_declaration |
  exception_declaration |
  cursor_declaration |
  pragma_declaration
END [package_name];
```

where *package_name* is the name of the package. The *elements* within the package (procedure and function specifications, variables, and so on) are the same as they would be in the declarative section of an anonymous block. The same syntax rules apply for a package header as for a declarative section, except for procedure and function declarations. These rules are as follows:

- Package elements can appear in any order. However, as in a declarative section, an object must be declared before it is referenced. If a cursor contains a variable as part of the WHERE clause, for example, the variable must be declared before the cursor declaration.

- All types of elements do not have to be present. A package can contain only procedure and function specifications, for example, without declaring any exceptions or types.

- Any declarations for procedures and functions must be forward declarations. A *forward declaration* simply describes the subprogram and its arguments (if any), but does not include the code. See the section "Forward Declarations" in Chapter 10 for more information. This rule is different from the declarative section of a block, where both forward declarations and the actual code for procedures or functions may be found. The code that implements the package's procedures and functions is found in the package body.

Package Body

The *package body* is a separate data dictionary object from the package header. It cannot be successfully compiled unless the package header has already been successfully compiled. The body contains the code for the forward subprogram declarations in the package header. It can also contain additional declarations that

are global to the package body, but are not visible in the specification. The
following example shows the package body for `ClassPackage`:

```
-- Available online as part of ClassPackage.sql
CREATE OR REPLACE PACKAGE BODY ClassPackage AS
  -- Add a new student for the specified class.
  PROCEDURE AddStudent(p_StudentID  IN students.id%TYPE,
                       p_Department IN classes.department%TYPE,
                       p_Course     IN classes.course%TYPE) IS
  BEGIN
    INSERT INTO registered_students (student_id, department, course)
      VALUES (p_StudentID, p_Department, p_Course);
  END AddStudent;

  -- Removes the specified student from the specified class.
  PROCEDURE RemoveStudent(p_StudentID  IN students.id%TYPE,
                          p_Department IN classes.department%TYPE,
                          p_Course     IN classes.course%TYPE) IS
  BEGIN
    DELETE FROM registered_students
      WHERE student_id = p_StudentID
      AND department = p_Department
      AND course = p_Course;

    -- Check to see if the DELETE operation was successful. If
    -- it didn't match any rows, raise an error.
    IF SQL%NOTFOUND THEN
      RAISE e_StudentNotRegistered;
    END IF;
  END RemoveStudent;

  -- Returns a PL/SQL table containing the students currently
  -- in the specified class.
  PROCEDURE ClassList(p_Department  IN  classes.department%TYPE,
                      p_Course      IN  classes.course%TYPE,
                      p_IDs         OUT t_StudentIDTable,
                      p_NumStudents IN OUT BINARY_INTEGER) IS

    v_StudentID  registered_students.student_id%TYPE;

    -- Local cursor to fetch the registered students.
    CURSOR c_RegisteredStudents IS
      SELECT student_id
        FROM registered_students
        WHERE department = p_Department
        AND course = p_Course;
  BEGIN
    /* p_NumStudents will be the table index. It will start at
```

```
    *  0, and be incremented each time through the fetch loop.
    *  At the end of the loop, it will have the number of rows
    *  fetched, and therefore the number of rows returned in
    *  p_IDs.
    */
   p_NumStudents := 0;

   OPEN c_RegisteredStudents;
   LOOP
     FETCH c_RegisteredStudents INTO v_StudentID;
     EXIT WHEN c_RegisteredStudents%NOTFOUND;

     p_NumStudents := p_NumStudents + 1;
     p_IDs(p_NumStudents) := v_StudentID;
   END LOOP;
  END ClassList;
END ClassPackage;
```

The package body contains the code for the forward declarations in the package header, and can also contain additional variables, cursors, types, or subprograms. Objects in the header that are not forward declarations (such as the e_StudentNotRegistered exception) can be referenced directly in the package body.

The package body is optional. If the package header does not contain any procedures or functions (only variable declarations, cursors, types, and so on), the body does not have to be present. This technique is valuable for declaring global variables and types, because all objects in a package are visible outside the package. (Scope and visibility of packaged elements are discussed in the next section.)

Any forward declaration in the package header must be fleshed out in the package body. The specification for the procedure or function must be the same in both. This includes the name of the subprogram, the names of its parameters, and the modes of the parameters. For example, the following package header does not match the package body, because the body uses a different parameter list for FunctionA:

-- Available online as packageError.sql
```
CREATE OR REPLACE PACKAGE PackageA AS
   FUNCTION FunctionA(p_Parameter1 IN NUMBER,
                      p_Parameter2 IN DATE)
     RETURN VARCHAR2;
END PackageA;

CREATE OR REPLACE PACKAGE BODY PackageA AS
   FUNCTION FunctionA(p_Parameter1 IN CHAR)
     RETURN VARCHAR2;
END PackageA;
```

If we try to create `PackageA` as above, we get the following errors for the package body:

```
PLS-00328: A subprogram body must be defined for the forward
           declaration of FUNCTIONA.

PLS-00323: subprogram or cursor 'FUNCTIONA' is declared in a
           package specification and must be defined in the package
           body.
```

Packages and Scope

Any object declared in a package header is in scope and is visible outside the package, by qualifying the object with the package name. For example, we can call `ClassPackage.RemoveStudent` from the following PL/SQL block:

```
BEGIN
  ClassPackage.RemoveStudent(10006, 'HIS', 101);
END;
```

The procedure call is the same as it would be for a stand-alone procedure. The only difference is that it is prefixed by the package name. Packaged procedures can have default parameters, and they can be called using either positional or named notation, just like stand-alone stored procedures.

This also applies to user-defined types defined in the package. In order to call `ClassList`, for example, we need to declare a variable of type `ClassPackage.t_StudentIDTable` (see Chapter 8 for more information on declaring and using PL/SQL collection types):

```
-- Available online as callCL.sql
DECLARE
  v_HistoryStudents ClassPackage.t_StudentIDTable;
  v_NumStudents     BINARY_INTEGER := 20;
BEGIN
  -- Fill the PL/SQL table with the first 20 History 101
  -- students.
  ClassPackage.ClassList('HIS', 101, v_HistoryStudents,
                         v_NumStudents);

  -- Insert these students into temp_table.
  FOR v_LoopCounter IN 1..v_NumStudents LOOP
    INSERT INTO temp_table (num_col, char_col)
      VALUES (v_HistoryStudents(v_LoopCounter),
              'In History 101');
  END LOOP;
END;
```

Inside the package body, objects in the header can be referenced without the package name. For example, the RemoveStudent procedure can reference the exception with simply e_StudentNotRegistered instead of the full ClassPackage.e_StudentNotRegistered. The fully qualified name can be used if desired, however.

Scope of Objects in the Package Body

As currently written, ClassPackage.AddStudent and ClassPackage.RemoveStudent simply update the registered_students table. This is not really enough, however. They also should update students and classes to reflect the newly added (or removed) student. We can do this by adding a procedure to the package body, as shown here:

```
-- Available online as part of ClassPackage2.sql
CREATE OR REPLACE PACKAGE BODY ClassPackage AS
  -- Utility procedure that updates students and classes to reflect
  -- the change.  If p_Add is TRUE, then the tables are updated for
  -- the addition of the student to the class.  If it is FALSE,
  -- then they are updated for the removal of the student.
  PROCEDURE UpdateStudentsAndClasses(
    p_Add       IN BOOLEAN,
    p_StudentID IN students.id%TYPE,
    p_Department IN classes.department%TYPE,
    p_Course    IN classes.course%TYPE) IS

    -- Number of credits for the requested class
    v_NumCredits  classes.num_credits%TYPE;
  BEGIN
    -- First determine NumCredits.
    SELECT num_credits
      INTO v_NumCredits
      FROM classes
      WHERE department = p_Department
      AND course = p_Course;

    IF (p_Add) THEN
      -- Add NumCredits to the student's course load
      UPDATE STUDENTS
        SET current_credits = current_credits + v_NumCredits
        WHERE ID = p_StudentID;

      -- And increase current_students
      UPDATE classes
        SET current_students = current_students + 1
        WHERE department = p_Department
        AND course = p_Course;
```

```
    ELSE
      -- Remove NumCredits from the students course load
      UPDATE STUDENTS
        SET current_credits = current_credits - v_NumCredits
        WHERE ID = p_StudentID;

      -- And decrease current_students
      UPDATE classes
        SET current_students = current_students - 1
        WHERE department = p_Department
        AND course = p_Course;
    END IF;
  END UpdateStudentsAndClasses;

  -- Add a new student for the specified class.
  PROCEDURE AddStudent(p_StudentID  IN students.id%TYPE,
                       p_Department IN classes.department%TYPE,
                       p_Course     IN classes.course%TYPE) IS
  BEGIN
    INSERT INTO registered_students (student_id, department, course)
      VALUES (p_StudentID, p_Department, p_Course);

    UpdateStudentsAndClasses(TRUE, p_StudentID, p_Department,
                                   p_Course);
END AddStudent;

  -- Removes the specified student from the specified class.
  PROCEDURE RemoveStudent(p_StudentID  IN students.id%TYPE,
                          p_Department IN classes.department%TYPE,
                          p_Course     IN classes.course%TYPE) IS
  BEGIN
    DELETE FROM registered_students
      WHERE student_id = p_StudentID
      AND department = p_Department
      AND course = p_Course;

    -- Check to see if the DELETE operation was successful. If
    -- it didn't match any rows, raise an error.
    IF SQL%NOTFOUND THEN
      RAISE e_StudentNotRegistered;
    END IF;

    UpdateStudentsAndClasses(FALSE, p_StudentID, p_Department,
                                    p_Course);
  END RemoveStudent;

  ...
END ClassPackage;
```

`UpdateStudentsAndClasses` is declared local to the package body. Its scope is therefore the package body itself. Consequently, it can be called from other procedures in the body (namely `AddStudent` and `RemoveStudent`), but it is not visible from outside the body.

Overloading Packaged Subprograms

Inside a package, procedures and functions can be *overloaded*. This means that there is more than one procedure or function with the same name, but with different parameters. This is a very useful feature because it allows the same operation to be applied to objects of different types. For example, suppose we want to add a student to a class either by specifying the student ID or by specifying the first and last names. We could do this by modifying `ClassPackage` as follows:

```
-- Available online as overload.sql
CREATE OR REPLACE PACKAGE ClassPackage AS
  -- Add a new student into the specified class.
  PROCEDURE AddStudent(p_StudentID  IN students.id%TYPE,
                       p_Department IN classes.department%TYPE,
                       p_Course     IN classes.course%TYPE);

  -- Also adds a new student, by specifying the first and last
  -- names, rather than ID number.
  PROCEDURE AddStudent(p_FirstName IN students.first_name%TYPE,
                       p_LastName  IN students.last_name%TYPE,
                       p_Department IN classes.department%TYPE,
                       p_Course     IN classes.course%TYPE);
  ...
END ClassPackage;

CREATE OR REPLACE PACKAGE BODY ClassPackage AS
  -- Add a new student for the specified class.
  PROCEDURE AddStudent(p_StudentID  IN students.id%TYPE,
                       p_Department IN classes.department%TYPE,
                       p_Course     IN classes.course%TYPE) IS
  BEGIN
    INSERT INTO registered_students (student_id, department, course)
      VALUES (p_StudentID, p_Department, p_Course);
  END AddStudent;

  -- Add a new student by name, rather than ID.
  PROCEDURE AddStudent(p_FirstName IN students.first_name%TYPE,
                       p_LastName  IN students.last_name%TYPE,
                       p_Department IN classes.department%TYPE,
                       p_Course     IN classes.course%TYPE) IS
    v_StudentID students.ID%TYPE;
```

```
BEGIN
  /* First we need to get the ID from the students table. */
  SELECT ID
    INTO v_StudentID
    FROM students
    WHERE first_name = p_FirstName
    AND last_name = p_LastName;

  -- Now we can add the student by ID.
  INSERT INTO registered_students (student_id, department, course)
    VALUES (v_StudentID, p_Department, p_Course);
  END AddStudent;
  ...
END ClassPackage;
```

We can now add a student to Music 410 with either

```
BEGIN
  ClassPackage.AddStudent(10000, 'MUS', 410);
END;
```

or

```
BEGIN
  ClassPackage.AddStudent('Rita', 'Razmataz', 'MUS', 410);
END;
```

Overloading can be a very useful technique when the same operation can be done on arguments of different types. Overloading is subject to several restrictions, however.

- You cannot overload two subprograms if their parameters differ only in name or mode. The following two procedures cannot be overloaded, for example:

  ```
  PROCEDURE OverloadMe(p_TheParameter IN NUMBER);
  PROCEDURE OverloadMe(p_TheParameter OUT NUMBER);
  ```

- You cannot overload two functions based only on their return type. For example, the following functions cannot be overloaded:

  ```
  FUNCTION OverloadMeToo RETURN DATE;
  FUNCTION OverloadMeToo RETURN NUMBER;
  ```

- Finally, the parameters of overloaded functions must differ by type family—you cannot overload on the same family. For example, because both CHAR and VARCHAR2 are in the same family, you can't overload the following procedures:

```
PROCEDURE OverloadChar(p_TheParameter IN CHAR);
PROCEDURE OverloadChar(p_TheParameter IN VARCHAR2);
```

NOTE
The PL/SQL compiler will actually allow you to create a package that has subprograms that violate the preceding restrictions. However, the runtime engine will not be able to resolve the references and will always generate a "PLS-307: Too many declarations of 'subprogram' match this call" error.

Object Types and Overloading

Oracle8i and higher | Packaged subprograms can also be overloaded based on user-defined object types. For example, suppose we create the following two object types:

```
-- Available online as part of objectOverload.sql
CREATE OR REPLACE TYPE t1 AS OBJECT (
  f NUMBER
);

CREATE OR REPLACE TYPE t2 AS OBJECT (
  f NUMBER
);
```

We can now create a package and package body that contains procedures that are overloaded based on the object type of their parameter:

```
-- Available online as part of objectOverload.sql
CREATE OR REPLACE PACKAGE Overload AS
  PROCEDURE Proc(p_Parameter1 IN t1);
  PROCEDURE Proc(p_Parameter1 IN t2);
END Overload;

CREATE OR REPLACE PACKAGE BODY Overload AS
  PROCEDURE Proc(p_Parameter1 IN t1) IS
  BEGIN
    DBMS_OUTPUT.PUT_LINE('Proc(t1): ' || p_Parameter1.f);
  END Proc;

  PROCEDURE Proc(p_Parameter1 IN t2) IS
  BEGIN
    DBMS_OUTPUT.PUT_LINE('Proc(t2): ' || p_Parameter1.f);
  END Proc;
END Overload;
```

As the following example shows, the correct procedure is called based on the type of the argument:

```
-- Available online as part of objectOverload.sql
SQL> DECLARE
  2    v_Obj1 t1 := t1(1);
  3    v_OBj2 t2 := t2(2);
  4  BEGIN
  5    Overload.Proc(v_Obj1);
  6    Overload.proc(v_Obj2);
  7  END;
  8  /
Proc(t1): 1
Proc(t2): 2
PL/SQL procedure successfully completed.
```

See Chapter 12 for more information on object types.

Package Initialization

The first time a packaged subprogram is called, or any reference to a packaged variable or type is made, the package is *instantiated*. This means that the package is read from disk into memory, and the compiled code of the called subprogram is run. At this point, memory is allocated for all variables defined in the package. Each session will have its own copy of packaged variables, ensuring that two sessions executing subprograms in the same package use different memory locations.

In many cases, initialization code needs to be run the first time the package is instantiated within a session. This can be done by adding an initialization section to the package body, after all other objects, with the syntax

CREATE OR REPLACE PACKAGE BODY *package_name* {IS | AS}

...

BEGIN

  initialization_code;

END [*package_name*];

where *package_name* is the name of the package, and *initialization_code* is the code to be run. For example, the following package implements a random number function:

```
-- Available online as Random.sql
CREATE OR REPLACE PACKAGE Random AS
  -- Random number generator.  Uses the same algorithm as the
  -- rand() function in C.
```

```
-- Used to change the seed.  From a given seed, the same
-- sequence of random numbers will be generated.
PROCEDURE ChangeSeed(p_NewSeed IN NUMBER);

-- Returns a random integer between 1 and 32767.
FUNCTION Rand RETURN NUMBER;

-- Same as Rand, but with a procedural interface.
PROCEDURE GetRand(p_RandomNumber OUT NUMBER);

-- Returns a random integer between 1 and p_MaxVal.
FUNCTION RandMax(p_MaxVal IN NUMBER) RETURN NUMBER;

-- Same as RandMax, but with a procedural interface.
PROCEDURE GetRandMax(p_RandomNumber OUT NUMBER,
                     p_MaxVal IN NUMBER);
END Random;

CREATE OR REPLACE PACKAGE BODY Random AS

  /* Used for calculating the next number. */
  v_Multiplier  CONSTANT NUMBER := 22695477;
  v_Increment   CONSTANT NUMBER := 1;

  /* Seed used to generate random sequence. */
  v_Seed        number := 1;

  PROCEDURE ChangeSeed(p_NewSeed IN NUMBER) IS
  BEGIN
    v_Seed := p_NewSeed;
  END ChangeSeed;

  FUNCTION Rand RETURN NUMBER IS
  BEGIN
    v_Seed := MOD(v_Multiplier * v_Seed + v_Increment,
              (2 ** 32));
    RETURN BITAND(v_Seed/(2 ** 16), 32767);
  END Rand;

  PROCEDURE GetRand(p_RandomNumber OUT NUMBER) IS
  BEGIN
    -- Simply call Rand and return the value.
    p_RandomNumber := Rand;
  END GetRand;

  FUNCTION RandMax(p_MaxVal IN NUMBER) RETURN NUMBER IS
  BEGIN
```

```
    RETURN MOD(Rand, p_MaxVal) + 1;
END RandMax;

PROCEDURE GetRandMax(p_RandomNumber OUT NUMBER,
                     p_MaxVal IN NUMBER) IS
BEGIN
  -- Simply call RandMax and return the value.
  p_RandomNumber := RandMax(p_MaxVal);
END GetRandMax;

BEGIN
  /* Package initialization.  Initialize the seed to the current
     time in seconds. */
  ChangeSeed(TO_NUMBER(TO_CHAR(SYSDATE, 'SSSSS')));
END Random;
```

In order to retrieve a random number, you can simply call `Random.Rand`. The sequence of random numbers is controlled by the initial seed—the same sequence is generated for a given seed. Thus, in order to provide more random values, we need to initialize the seed to a different value each time the package is instantiated. To accomplish this, the `ChangeSeed` procedure is called from the package initialization section.

NOTE
*Oracle8 includes a built-in package DBMS_
RANDOM, which can also be used to provide
random numbers. See Appendix A for more
information on the built-in packages.*

Summary

We have examined three types of named PL/SQL blocks in this chapter: procedures, functions, and packages. We discussed the syntax for creating each of these, paying particular attention to various types of parameter passing. In the next chapter, we see more uses of procedures, functions, and packages. Chapter 10 focuses on types of subprograms, how they are stored in the data dictionary, and calling stored subprograms from SQL statements. In Chapter 11, we cover a fourth type of named block: database triggers.

CHAPTER
10

Using Procedures, Functions, and Packages

n the last chapter, we discussed the details of creating procedures, packages, and functions. In this chapter, we will look at some of their features, including the difference between stored and local subprograms, how stored subprograms interact with the data dictionary, and how to call stored subprograms from SQL statements. We will also examine some new Oracle8*i* and Oracle9*i* features of stored subprograms. We will examine triggers in Chapter 11.

Subprogram Locations

Subprograms and packages can be stored in the data dictionary, as all of the examples in the previous chapter have shown. The subprogram is created first with the CREATE OR REPLACE command, and then it is called from another PL/SQL block. In addition to this, however, a subprogram can be defined within the declarative section of a block. In this case, it is known as a *local subprogram*. Packages must be stored in the data dictionary and cannot be local.

Stored Subprograms and the Data Dictionary

When a subprogram is created with CREATE OR REPLACE, it is stored in the data dictionary. In addition to the source text, the subprogram is stored in compiled form, which is known as *p-code*. The p-code has all of the references in the subprogram evaluated, and the source code is translated into a form that is easily readable by the PL/SQL engine. When the subprogram is called, the p-code is read from disk, if necessary, and executed. Once it is read from disk, the p-code is stored in the shared pool portion of the system global area (SGA), where it can be accessed by multiple users as needed. Like all of the contents of the shared pool, p-code is aged out of the shared pool according to a least recently used (LRU) algorithm.

P-code is analogous to the object code generated by other 3GL compilers, or to Java bytecodes that can be read by a Java runtime system. Since the p-code has the object references in the subprogram evaluated (this is a property of early binding, which we saw in Chapter 4), executing the p-code is a comparatively inexpensive operation.

NOTE
*Oracle9*i *allows you to compile a subprogram into native operating system code rather than p-code. See the section "Native Compilation" later in this chapter for more details.*

Information about the subprogram is accessible through various data dictionary views. The `user_objects` view contains information about all objects owned by the current user, including stored subprograms. This information includes when the object was created and last modified, the type of the object (table, sequence, function, and so on), and the validity of the object. The user_source view contains the original source code for the object. The user_errors view contains information about compile errors.

Consider the following simple procedure:

```
CREATE OR REPLACE PROCEDURE Simple AS
  v_Counter NUMBER;
BEGIN
  v_Counter := 7;
END Simple;
```

After this procedure is created, user_objects shows it as valid, and user_source contains the source code for it. User_errors has no rows, because the procedure was compiled successfully. This is illustrated in Figure 10-1.

```
Oracle SQL*Plus
File  Edit  Search  Options  Help
SQL> SELECT object_name, object_type, status
  2     FROM user_objects WHERE object_name = 'SIMPLE';

OBJECT_NAME                          OBJECT_TYPE      STATUS
------------------------------------ ---------------- -------
SIMPLE                               PROCEDURE        VALID

SQL> SELECT text FROM user_source
  2     WHERE name = 'SIMPLE' ORDER BY line;

TEXT
----------------------------------------------------
PROCEDURE Simple AS
  v_Counter NUMBER;
BEGIN
  v_Counter := 7;
END Simple;

SQL> SELECT line, position, text
  2     FROM user_errors
  3     WHERE name = 'SIMPLE'
  4     ORDER BY sequence;

no rows selected

SQL>
```

FIGURE 10-1. *Data dictionary views after successful compilation*

If, however, we change the code of `Simple` so that it has a compile error (note the missing semicolon), such as

```
CREATE OR REPLACE PROCEDURE Simple AS
  v_Counter NUMBER;
BEGIN
  v_Counter := 7
END Simple;
```

and examine the same three data dictionary views (as shown in Figure 10-2), we see several differences. `User_source` still shows the source code for the procedure. However, in `user_objects` the status is listed as 'INVALID' rather than 'VALID'. And `user_errors` contains the PLS-103 compilation error.

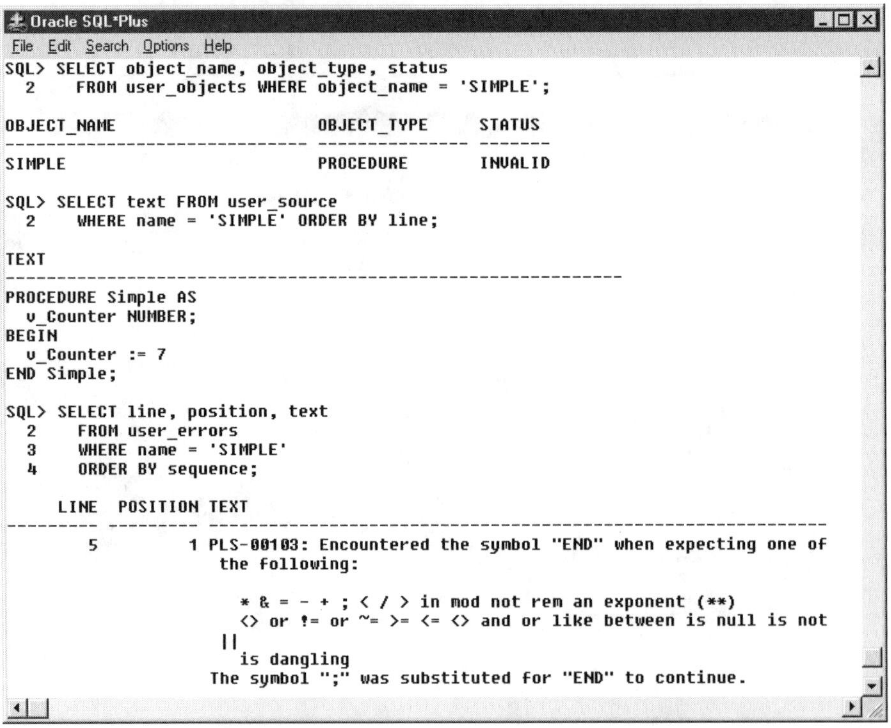

FIGURE 10-2. *Data dictionary views after unsuccessful compilation*

TIP
In SQL*Plus, the `show errors` *command will query* `user_errors` *for you and format the output for readability. It will return information about errors for the last object that you created. You can use* `show errors` *after receiving the message "Warning: Procedure created with compilation errors." See Chapter 2 for more information on PL/SQL development environments.*

A stored subprogram that is invalid is still stored in the database. However, it cannot be called successful until the error is fixed. If an invalid procedure is called, the PLS-905 error is returned, as the following example illustrates:

```
SQL> BEGIN Simple; END;
  2  /
BEGIN Simple; END;
      *
ERROR at line 1:
ORA-06550: line 1, column 7:
PLS-00905: object EXAMPLE.SIMPLE is invalid
ORA-06550: line 1, column 7:
PL/SQL: Statement ignored
```

The data dictionary is discussed in more detail in Appendix C.

Native Compilation

Similar to Java bytecode, p-code is then run by the PL/SQL engine, which interprets the p-code and runs it. This is a very portable design, in that the same PL/SQL code can be run in different databases, possibly on different platforms. However, because it is interpreted, it is not as fast as code, which is compiled to native operating system code.

In Oracle9*i*, you can choose to have PL/SQL compiled to native code. This will create a shared library, which is then run by the Oracle shadow process. In order to use this feature, you must have a C compiler installed on your system, as the PL/SQL compiler will generate C code that is then compiled into the native library.

For details on how to do this, see the Oracle documentation.

Local Subprograms

A local subprogram, declared in the declarative section of a PL/SQL block, is illustrated in the following example:

```
-- Available online as localSub.sql
SQL> DECLARE
```

```
 2   CURSOR c_AllStudents IS
 3     SELECT first_name, last_name
 4       FROM students;
 5
 6   v_FormattedName VARCHAR2(50);
 7
 8   /* Function which will return the first and last name
 9      concatenated together, separated by a space. */
10   FUNCTION FormatName(p_FirstName IN VARCHAR2,
11                       p_LastName IN VARCHAR2)
12     RETURN VARCHAR2 IS
13   BEGIN
14     RETURN p_FirstName || ' ' || p_LastName;
15   END FormatName;
16
17  -- Begin main block.
18  BEGIN
19    FOR v_StudentRecord IN c_AllStudents LOOP
20      v_FormattedName :=
21        FormatName(v_StudentRecord.first_name,
22                   v_StudentRecord.last_name);
23      DBMS_OUTPUT.PUT_LINE(v_FormattedName);
24    END LOOP;
25  END;
26  /
Scott Smith
Margaret Mason
Joanne Junebug
Manish Murgatroid
Patrick Poll
Timothy Taller
Barbara Blues
David Dinsmore
Ester Elegant
Rose Riznit
Rita Razmataz
Shay Shariatpanahy
PL/SQL procedure successfully completed.
```

The FormatName function is declared in the declarative section of the block. The function name is a PL/SQL identifier and thus follows the same scope and visibility rules as any other PL/SQL identifier. Specifically, it is only visible in the block in which it is declared. Its scope extends from the point of declaration until the end of the block. No other block can call FormatName, since it would not be visible from another block.

Local Subprograms as Part of Stored Subprograms

Local subprograms can also be declared as part of the declarative section of a stored subprogram, as the following example illustrates. In this case, FormatName can be called only from within StoredProc, since that is the limit of its scope.

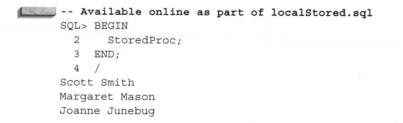

```
-- Available online as part of localStored.sql
CREATE OR REPLACE PROCEDURE StoredProc AS
/* Local declarations, which include a cursor, variable, and a
      function. */
  CURSOR c_AllStudents IS
    SELECT first_name, last_name
      FROM students;

  v_FormattedName VARCHAR2(50);

  /* Function which will return the first and last name
     concatenated together, separated by a space. */
  FUNCTION FormatName(p_FirstName IN VARCHAR2,
                      p_LastName IN VARCHAR2)
    RETURN VARCHAR2 IS
  BEGIN
    RETURN p_FirstName || ' ' || p_LastName;
  END FormatName;

-- Begin main block.
BEGIN
  FOR v_StudentRecord IN c_AllStudents LOOP
    v_FormattedName :=
      FormatName(v_StudentRecord.first_name,
                 v_StudentRecord.last_name);
    DBMS_OUTPUT.PUT_LINE(v_FormattedName);
  END LOOP;
END StoredProc;
```

Given the preceding stored procedure, we can call it and receive the same output as for the previous anonymous block example, as follows:

```
-- Available online as part of localStored.sql
SQL> BEGIN
  2    StoredProc;
  3   END;
  4   /
Scott Smith
Margaret Mason
Joanne Junebug
```

```
Manish Murgatroid
Patrick Poll
Timothy Taller
Barbara Blues
David Dinsmore
Ester Elegant
Rose Riznit
Rita Razmataz
Shay Shariatpanahy
PL/SQL procedure successfully completed.
```

Location of Local Subprograms

Any local subprogram must be declared at the end of the declarative section. If we were to move FormatName above the declaration for c_AllStudents, as the following SQL*Plus session illustrates, we would get a compile error:

```
-- Available online as localError.sql
SQL> DECLARE
  2     /* Declare FormatName first. This will generate a compile
  3        error, since all other declarations have to be before
  4        any local subprograms. */
  5     FUNCTION FormatName(p_FirstName IN VARCHAR2,
  6                         p_LastName IN VARCHAR2)
  7       RETURN VARCHAR2 IS
  8     BEGIN
  9       RETURN p_FirstName || ' ' || p_LastName;
 10     END FormatName;
 11
 12     CURSOR c_AllStudents IS
 13       SELECT first_name, last_name
 14         FROM students;
 15
 16     v_FormattedName VARCHAR2(50);
 17  -- Begin main block
 18  BEGIN
 19     NULL;
 20  END;
 21  /
   CURSOR c_AllStudents IS
   *
ERROR at line 12:
ORA-06550: line 12, column 3:
PLS-00103: Encountered the symbol "CURSOR" when expecting one of the
           following:
begin function package pragma procedure form
```

Forward Declarations

Since the names of local PL/SQL subprograms are identifiers, they must be declared before they are referenced. This is normally not a problem. However, in the case of mutually referential subprograms, this does present a difficulty. Consider the following example:

```
-- Available online as mutual.sql
SQL> DECLARE
  2    v_TempVal BINARY_INTEGER := 5;
  3
  4    -- Local procedure A. Note that the code of A calls procedure B.
  5    PROCEDURE A(p_Counter IN OUT BINARY_INTEGER) IS
  6    BEGIN
  7      DBMS_OUTPUT.PUT_LINE('A(' || p_Counter || ')');
  8      IF p_Counter > 0 THEN
  9        B(p_Counter);
 10        p_Counter := p_Counter - 1;
 11      END IF;
 12    END A;
 13
 14    -- Local procedure B. Note that the code of B calls procedure A.
 15    PROCEDURE B(p_Counter IN OUT BINARY_INTEGER) IS
 16    BEGIN
 17      DBMS_OUTPUT.PUT_LINE('B(' || p_Counter || ')');
 18      p_Counter := p_Counter - 1;
 19      A(p_Counter);
 20    END B;
 21  BEGIN
 22    B(v_TempVal);
 23  END;
 24  /
DECLARE
*
ERROR at line 1:
ORA-06550: line 9, column 7:
PLS-00201: identifier 'B' must be declared
ORA-06550: line 9, column 7:
PL/SQL: Statement ignored
```

As the above SQL*Plus session shows, this example is impossible to compile. Since procedure A calls procedure B, B must be declared prior to A so that the reference to B can be resolved. Since procedure B calls procedure A, A must be declared prior to B so that the reference to A can be resolved. Both of these can't be true at the same time. In order to rectify this, we can use a forward declaration. This is simply a procedure name and its formal parameters, which allows mutually referential procedures to exist. Forward declarations are also used in package headers. The following example illustrates this technique:

```
-- Available online as forwardDeclaration.sql
DECLARE
  v_TempVal BINARY_INTEGER := 5;

  -- Forward declaration of procedure B.
  PROCEDURE B(p_Counter IN OUT BINARY_INTEGER);

  PROCEDURE A(p_Counter IN OUT BINARY_INTEGER) IS
  BEGIN
    DBMS_OUTPUT.PUT_LINE('A(' || p_Counter || ')');
    IF p_Counter > 0 THEN
      B(p_Counter);
      p_Counter := p_Counter - 1;
    END IF;
  END A;

  PROCEDURE B(p_Counter IN OUT BINARY_INTEGER) IS
  BEGIN
    DBMS_OUTPUT.PUT_LINE('B(' || p_Counter || ')');
    p_Counter := p_Counter - 1;
    A(p_Counter);
  END B;
BEGIN
  B(v_TempVal);
END;
```

The output from the above block is shown here:

```
B(5)
A(4)
B(4)
A(3)
B(3)
A(2)
B(2)
A(1)
B(1)
A(0)
```

Overloading Local Subprograms

As we saw in Chapter 9, subprograms declared in packages can be overloaded. This is also true for local subprograms, as the following example illustrates:

```
-- Available online as overloadedLocal.sql
DECLARE
  -- Two overloaded local procedures
  PROCEDURE LocalProc(p_Parameter1 IN NUMBER) IS
  BEGIN
    DBMS_OUTPUT.PUT_LINE('In version 1, p_Parameter1 = ' ||
                          p_Parameter1);
  END LocalProc;

  PROCEDURE LocalProc(p_Parameter1 IN VARCHAR2) IS
  BEGIN
    DBMS_OUTPUT.PUT_LINE('In version 2, p_Parameter1 = ' ||
                          p_Parameter1);
  END LocalProc;
BEGIN
  -- Call version 1
  LocalProc(12345);

  -- And version 2
  LocalProc('abcdef');
END;
```

The output from the preceding example is

```
In version 1, p_Parameter1 = 12345
In version 2, p_Parameter1 = abcdef
```

Stored versus Local Subprograms

Stored subprograms and local subprograms behave differently and they have different properties. When should each be used? I generally prefer to use stored subprograms, and will usually put them in a package. If you develop a useful subprogram, it is likely that you will want to call it from more than one block. In order to do this, the subprogram must be stored in the database. The size and complexity benefits are also usually a factor. The only procedures and functions that I would declare local to a block would tend to be short ones, which are only called from one specific section of the program (their containing block). Local subprograms of this sort are generally used to avoid code duplication within a single block. This usage is similar to C macros. Table 10-1 summarizes the differences between stored and local subprograms.

Stored Subprograms	Local Subprograms
The stored subprogram is stored in compiled p-code in the database; when the procedure is called, it does not have to be compiled.	The local subprogram is compiled as part of its containing block. If the containing block is anonymous and is run multiple times, the subprogram has to be compiled each time.
Stored subprograms can be called from any block submitted by a user who has EXECUTE privileges on the subprogram.	Local subprograms can be called only from the block containing the subprogram.
By keeping the subprogram code separate from the calling block, the calling block is shorter and easier to understand. The subprogram and calling block can also be maintained separately, if desired.	The subprogram and the calling block are one and the same, which can lead to confusion. If a change to the calling block is made, the subprogram will be recompiled as part of the recompilation of the containing block.
The compiled p-code can be pinned in the shared pool using the DBMS_SHARED_POOL.KEEP packaged procedure.* This can improve performance.	Local subprograms cannot be pinned in the shared pool by themselves.
Stand-alone stored subprograms cannot be overloaded, but packaged subprograms can be overloaded within the same package.	Local subprograms can be overloaded within the same block.

*The DBMS_SHARED_POOL package is discussed later in this chapter in the section "Pinning and the Shared Pool."

TABLE 10-1.   *Stored versus Local Subprograms*

Considerations of Stored Subprograms and Packages

Storing subprograms and packages as data dictionary objects has advantages. For example, it allows them to be shared among database users as needed. There are several implications of this, however. These include dependencies among stored objects, how package state is handled, and the privileges necessary to run stored subprograms and packages.

Subprogram Dependencies

When a stored procedure or function is compiled, all of the Oracle objects that it references are recorded in the data dictionary. The procedure is *dependent* on these objects. We have seen that a subprogram that has compile errors is marked as invalid in the data dictionary. A stored subprogram can also become invalid if a DDL operation is performed on one of its dependent objects. The best way to illustrate this is by example. The AlmostFull function (defined in Chapter 9) queries the classes table. The dependencies of AlmostFull are illustrated in Figure 10-3. AlmostFull depends on only one object: classes. This is indicated by the arrow in the figure.

Now suppose we create a procedure that calls AlmostFull and inserts the results into temp_table. This procedure is RecordFullClasses:

```
-- Available online as RecordFullClasses.sql
CREATE OR REPLACE PROCEDURE RecordFullClasses AS
  CURSOR c_Classes IS
    SELECT department, course
      FROM classes;
BEGIN
  FOR v_ClassRecord IN c_Classes LOOP
    -- Record all classes which don't have very much room left
    -- in temp_table.
    IF AlmostFull(v_ClassRecord.department, v_ClassRecord.course)
    THEN
      INSERT INTO temp_table (char_col) VALUES
        (v_ClassRecord.department || ' ' || v_ClassRecord.course ||
        ' is almost full!');
    END IF;
  END LOOP;
END RecordFullClasses;
```

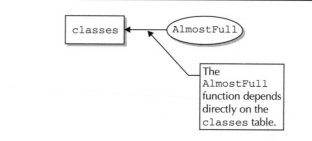

FIGURE 10-3. *AlmostFull dependencies*

The dependency information is illustrated by the arrows in Figure 10-4. `RecordFullClasses` depends both on `AlmostFull` and on `temp_table`. These are *direct* dependencies, because `RecordFullClasses` refers directly to both `AlmostFull` and `temp_table`. `AlmostFull` depends on `classes`, so `RecordFullClasses` has an *indirect* dependency on `classes`.

If a DDL operation is performed on `classes`, all objects that depend on `classes` (directly or indirectly) are invalidated. Suppose we alter the `classes` table in our example by adding an extra column:

```
ALTER TABLE classes ADD (
    student_rating  NUMBER(2)  -- Difficulty rating from 1 to 10
);
```

This will cause both `AlmostFull` and `RecordFullClasses` to become invalid, since they depend on `classes`. This is illustrated by the SQL*Plus session in Figure 10-5.

Automatic Recompilation

If a dependent object is invalidated, the PL/SQL engine will automatically attempt to recompile it the next time it is called. Since neither `RecordFullClasses` nor `AlmostFull` references the new column in `classes`, this recompilation will be successful. The SQL*Plus session in Figure 10-6, which continues the session in Figure 10-5, illustrates this.

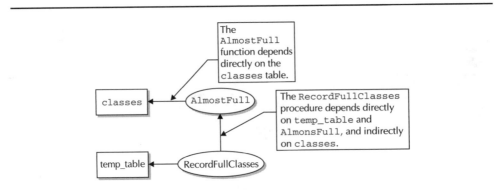

FIGURE 10-4. *RecordFullClasses dependencies*

```
Oracle SQL*Plus                                                    _ □ ×
File  Edit  Search  Options  Help
SQL> SELECT object_name, object_type, status
  2    FROM user_objects
  3    WHERE object_name IN ('ALMOSTFULL', 'RECORDFULLCLASSES');

OBJECT_NAME                      OBJECT_TYPE     STATUS
-------------------------------- --------------- -------
RECORDFULLCLASSES                PROCEDURE       VALID
ALMOSTFULL                       FUNCTION        VALID

SQL> ALTER TABLE classes ADD (
  2    student_rating  NUMBER(2)  -- Difficulty rating from 1 to 10
  3  );

Table altered.

SQL> SELECT object_name, object_type, status
  2    FROM user_objects
  3    WHERE object_name IN ('ALMOSTFULL', 'RECORDFULLCLASSES');

OBJECT_NAME                      OBJECT_TYPE     STATUS
-------------------------------- --------------- -------
RECORDFULLCLASSES                PROCEDURE       INVALID
ALMOSTFULL                       FUNCTION        INVALID

SQL>
```

FIGURE 10-5.   *Invalidation as a result of a DDL operation*

CAUTION
*The automatic recompilation can fail (especially
if a table description is modified). In this case,
the calling block will receive a compilation error.
However, this error will occur at runtime, not
compile time.*

Packages and Dependencies

As the previous example showed, stored subprograms can be invalidated if their
dependent objects are modified. The situation is different for packages, however.
Consider the dependency picture for ClassPackage (which we saw in Chapter 9)
in Figure 10-7. The package body depends on registered_students and the
package header. But, the package header does not depend on the package body, or
on registered_students. This is one advantage of packages—we can change
the package body without having to change the header. Therefore, other objects

```
Oracle SQL*Plus                                                    _ □ ×
File  Edit  Search  Options  Help
Table altered.                                                        ▲

SQL> SELECT object_name, object_type, status
  2    FROM user_objects
  3      WHERE object_name IN ('ALMOSTFULL', 'RECORDFULLCLASSES');

OBJECT_NAME                   OBJECT_TYPE      STATUS
----------------------------- ---------------- -------
RECORDFULLCLASSES             PROCEDURE        INVALID
ALMOSTFULL                    FUNCTION         INVALID

SQL> exec RecordFullClasses;

PL/SQL procedure successfully completed.

SQL> SELECT object_name, object_type, status
  2    FROM user_objects
  3      WHERE object_name IN ('ALMOSTFULL', 'RECORDFULLCLASSES');

OBJECT_NAME                   OBJECT_TYPE      STATUS
----------------------------- ---------------- -------
RECORDFULLCLASSES             PROCEDURE        VALID
ALMOSTFULL                    FUNCTION         VALID

SQL>                                                                 ▼
◄                                                                   ►
```

FIGURE 10-6. *Automatic recompilation after invalidation*

that depend on the header won't have to be recompiled at all, since they never get invalidated. If the header is changed, this automatically invalidates the body, since the body depends on the header.

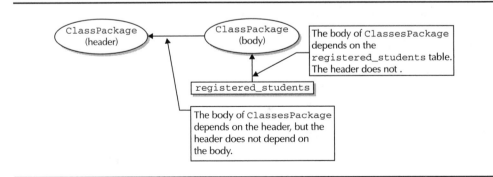

FIGURE 10-7. *ClassPackage dependencies*

NOTE
There are certain cases where a change in the package body necessitates a change in the header. For example, if the arguments to a procedure need to be changed, the header and body would have to be modified to match. The header would not have to be modified if the implementation of a body procedure were changed without affecting its declaration, however. Similarly, if you are using the signature dependency model (described in the section "How Invalidations Are Determined"), only changes to the signatures of objects in the package specification will invalidate the body. In addition, if you add an object to a package header (such as a cursor or variable), the body will be invalidated.

We can also see this behavior from the following SQL*Plus session:

```
-- Available online as dependencies.sql
SQL> -- First create a simple table.
SQL> CREATE TABLE simple_table (f1 NUMBER);
Table created.

SQL> -- Now create a packaged procedure which references the table.
SQL> CREATE OR REPLACE PACKAGE Dependee AS
  2    PROCEDURE Example(p_Val IN NUMBER);
  3  END Dependee;
  4  /
Package created.

SQL> CREATE OR REPLACE PACKAGE BODY Dependee AS
  2    PROCEDURE Example(p_Val IN NUMBER) IS
  3    BEGIN
  4      INSERT INTO simple_table VALUES (p_Val);
  5    END Example;
  6  END Dependee;
  7  /
Package body created.

SQL> -- Now create a procedure which references Dependee.
SQL> CREATE OR REPLACE PROCEDURE Depender(p_Val IN NUMBER) AS
  2  BEGIN
  3    Dependee.Example(p_Val + 1);
```

```
  4   END Depender;
  5   /
Procedure created.

SQL> -- Query user_objects to see that all objects are valid.
SQL> SELECT object_name, object_type, status
  2     FROM user_objects
  3     WHERE object_name IN ('DEPENDER', 'DEPENDEE',
  4                           'SIMPLE_TABLE');
OBJECT_NAME                         OBJECT_TYPE    STATUS
------------------------------ ------------- -------
SIMPLE_TABLE                        TABLE          VALID
DEPENDEE                            PACKAGE        VALID
DEPENDEE                            PACKAGE BODY   VALID
DEPENDER                            PROCEDURE      VALID

SQL> -- Change the package body only.  Note that the header is
SQL> -- unchanged.
SQL> CREATE OR REPLACE PACKAGE BODY Dependee AS
  2     PROCEDURE Example(p_Val IN NUMBER) IS
  3     BEGIN
  4        INSERT INTO simple_table VALUES (p_Val - 1);
  5     END Example;
  6   END Dependee;
  7   /
Package body created.

SQL> -- Now user_objects shows that Depender is still valid.
SQL> SELECT object_name, object_type, status
  2     FROM user_objects
  3     WHERE object_name IN ('DEPENDER', 'DEPENDEE',
  4                           'SIMPLE_TABLE');
OBJECT_NAME                         OBJECT_TYPE    STATUS
------------------------------ ------------- -------
SIMPLE_TABLE                        TABLE          VALID
DEPENDEE                            PACKAGE        VALID
DEPENDEE                            PACKAGE BODY   VALID
DEPENDER                            PROCEDURE      VALID

SQL> -- Even if we drop the table, it only invalidates the
SQL> -- package body.
SQL> DROP TABLE simple_table;
Table dropped.
```

```
SQL> SELECT object_name, object_type, status
  2      FROM user_objects
  3      WHERE object_name IN ('DEPENDER', 'DEPENDEE',
  4                            'SIMPLE_TABLE');
OBJECT_NAME                          OBJECT_TYPE     STATUS
------------------------------------ --------------- -------
DEPENDEE                             PACKAGE         VALID
DEPENDEE                             PACKAGE BODY    INVALID
DEPENDER                             PROCEDURE       VALID
```

NOTE
The data dictionary views user_dependencies, all_dependencies, *and* dba_dependencies *directly list the relationships between schema objects. For more information on these views, see Appendix C.*

Figure 10-8 shows the dependencies of the objects created by this script.

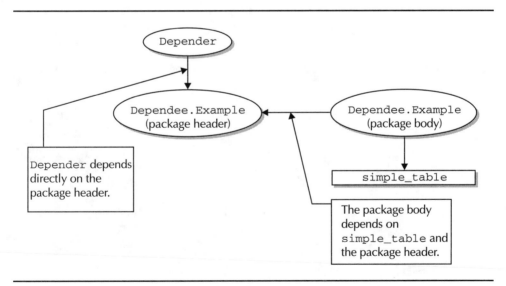

FIGURE 10-8.   *More package dependencies*

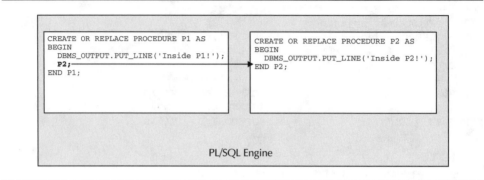

FIGURE 10-9. *P1 and P2 in the same database*

How Invalidations Are Determined

When an object is altered, its dependent objects are invalidated, as we have seen. If all of the objects are in the same database, the dependent objects are invalidated as soon as the base object is altered. This can be done quickly, because the data dictionary tracks the dependencies. Suppose we create two procedures P1 and P2, as illustrated in Figure 10-9. P1 depends on P2, which means that recompiling P2 will invalidate P1. The following SQL*Plus session illustrates this:

```
-- Available online as part of remoteDependencies.sql
SQL> -- Create two procedures.  P1 depends on P2.
SQL> CREATE OR REPLACE PROCEDURE P2 AS
  2  BEGIN
  3    DBMS_OUTPUT.PUT_LINE('Inside P2!');
  4  END P2;
  5  /
Procedure created.

SQL> CREATE OR REPLACE PROCEDURE P1 AS
  2  BEGIN
  3    DBMS_OUTPUT.PUT_LINE('Inside P1!');
  4    P2;
  5  END P1;
  6  /
Procedure created.
```

```
SQL> -- Verify that both procedures are valid.
SQL> SELECT object_name, object_type, status
  2     FROM user_objects
  3     WHERE object_name IN ('P1', 'P2');
OBJECT_NAME                      OBJECT_TYPE      STATUS
------------------------------   ---------------  -------
P2                               PROCEDURE        VALID
P1                               PROCEDURE        VALID

SQL> -- Recompile P2, which invalidates P1 immediately.
SQL> ALTER PROCEDURE P2 COMPILE;
Procedure altered.

SQL> -- Query again to see this.
SQL> SELECT object_name, object_type, status
  2     FROM user_objects
  3     WHERE object_name IN ('P1', 'P2');
OBJECT_NAME                      OBJECT_TYPE      STATUS
------------------------------   ---------------  -------
P2                               PROCEDURE        VALID
P1                               PROCEDURE        INVALID
```

Suppose, however, that `P1` and `P2` are in different databases, and `P1` calls `P2` over a database link. This situation is illustrated by Figure 10-10. In this case,

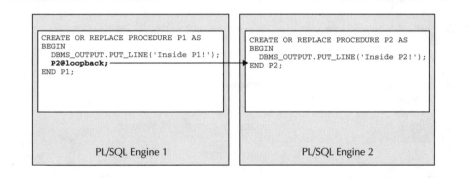

FIGURE 10-10.   *P1 and P2 in different databases*

recompiling `P2` does not immediately invalidate `P1`, as the following SQL*Plus session shows:

```
-- Available online as part of remoteDependencies.sql
SQL> -- Create a database link which points back to the current
SQL> -- instance.  You will have to modify connect_string and set
SQL> -- up SQL*Net appropriately for your system..
SQL> CREATE DATABASE LINK loopback
  2    USING 'connect_string';
Database link created.

SQL> -- Change P1 to call P2 over the link.
SQL> CREATE OR REPLACE PROCEDURE P1 AS
  2    BEGIN
  3      DBMS_OUTPUT.PUT_LINE('Inside P1!');
  4      P2@loopback;
  5    END P1;
  6  /
Procedure created.

SQL> -- Verify that both are valid.
SQL> SELECT object_name, object_type, status
  2    FROM user_objects
  3    WHERE object_name IN ('P1', 'P2');
OBJECT_NAME                    OBJECT_TYPE      STATUS
------------------------------ ---------------- -------
P2                             PROCEDURE        VALID
P1                             PROCEDURE        VALID

SQL> -- Now when we recompile P2, P1 is not invalidated immediately.
SQL> ALTER PROCEDURE P2 COMPILE;
Procedure altered.

SQL> SELECT object_name, object_type, status
  2    FROM user_objects
  3    WHERE object_name IN ('P1', 'P2');
OBJECT_NAME                    OBJECT_TYPE      STATUS
------------------------------ ---------------- -------
P2                             PROCEDURE        VALID
P1                             PROCEDURE        VALID
```

NOTE
In the above example, the database link is actually a loopback, which points to the same database. The observed behavior, however, is the same as if `P1` and `P2` were actually in separate databases. Using a loopback enables us to query the status of `P1` and `P2` in one SELECT statement.

Why is the behavior different in the remote case? The answer lies in the fact that the data dictionary does not track remote dependencies. It would thus be too expensive to invalidate all the dependent objects, because they could be in different databases (that may or may not even be accessible at the time of the invalidation).

Instead, the validity of remote objects is checked at runtime. When P1 is called, the remote data dictionary is queried to determine the status of P2 (if the remote database is inaccessible, an error is raised). P1 and P2 are compared to see if P1 needs to be recompiled. There are two different methods of comparison—the timestamp and signature methods.

NOTE

It is not necessary to have a database link to utilize runtime validity checking. If P1 were in a client-side PL/SQL engine (such as Oracle Forms), and P2 was in the server, the situation is similar, and either the timestamp or signature method will be used. See Chapter 2 for more information about different PL/SQL execution environments.

Timestamp Model   With this model, the timestamps of the last modifications of the two objects are compared. The last_ddl_time field of user_objects contains this timestamp. If the base object has a newer timestamp than the dependent object, the dependent object will be recompiled. There are several issues with this model, however:

- The date comparison does not take the locations of the two PL/SQL engines into account. If they are in different time zones, the comparison will not be valid.

- Even if the two engines are in the same time zone, the timestamp model can result in unnecessary recompilations. In the above example, P2 was simply recompiled but was not actually changed. P1 does not really have to be recompiled, but because it has an older timestamp it would be.

- Slightly more serious is when P1 is contained in a client-side PL/SQL engine, such as Oracle Forms. In this case, it may not be possible to recompile P1, because the source for it may not be included with the runtime version of Forms.

Signature Model   PL/SQL provides a different method for determining when remote dependent objects need to be recompiled that resolves the issues with the timestamp model. This method is called the "signature model." When a procedure is created, a *signature* is stored in the data dictionary in addition to the p-code. The signature encodes the types and order of the parameters. With this model, the signature of P2 will change only when the parameters change. When P1 is compiled the first time, the signature of P2 is included (rather than the timestamp). Thus, P1 only needs to be recompiled when the signature of P2 changes.

In order to use the signature model, the parameter REMOTE_DEPENDENCIES_ MODE must be set to SIGNATURE. This is a parameter in the database initialization file. (The name and location of the initialization file, commonly called init.ora, varies depending on your system.) It can also be set interactively. There are three ways of setting this mode:

- Add the line REMOTE_DEPENDENCIES_MODE=SIGNATURE to the database initialization file. The next time the database is started, the mode will be set to SIGNATURE for all sessions.

- Issue the command

  ```
  ALTER SYSTEM SET REMOTE_DEPENDENCIES_MODE = SIGNATURE;
  ```

  This will affect the entire database (all sessions) from the time the statement is issued. You must have the ALTER SYSTEM system privilege to issue this command.

- Issue the command

  ```
  ALTER SESSION SET REMOTE_DEPENDENCIES_MODE = SIGNATURE;
  ```

  This will only affect your session. Objects created after this point in the current session will use the signature method.

In all of these options, TIMESTAMP can be used instead of SIGNATURE to use the timestamp model. TIMESTAMP is the default. There are several things to be aware of when using the signature method:

- Signatures don't get modified if the default values of formal parameters are changed. Suppose P2 has a default value for one of its parameters, and P1 is using this default value. If the default value in the specification for P2 is changed, P1 will not be recompiled by default. The old value for the default parameter will still be used until P1 is manually recompiled. This applies for IN parameters only.

- If P1 is calling a packaged procedure P2, and a new overloaded version of P2 is added to the remote package, the signature is not changed. P1 will still use the old version (not the new overloaded one) until P1 is recompiled manually.

- To manually recompile a procedure, use the command

ALTER PROCEDURE *procedure_name* COMPILE;

where *procedure_name* is the name of the procedure to be compiled. For functions, use

ALTER FUNCTION *function_name* COMPILE;

where *function_name* is the name of the function to be compiled. And for packages, use any of the following:

ALTER PACKAGE *package_name* COMPILE;
ALTER PACKAGE *package_name* COMPILE SPECIFICATION;
ALTER PACKAGE *package_name* COMPILE BODY;

where *package_name* is the name of the package. If SPECIFICATION is present, only the package header is compiled. If BODY is present, only the package body is compiled. If neither is present, both are compiled.

For more information on the signature model, see the *Oracle Server Application Developer's Guide.*

Package Runtime State

When a package is first instantiated, the package code is read from disk into the shared pool. However, the runtime state of a package—namely, the packaged variables and cursors—are kept in session memory. This means that each session has its own copy of the runtime state. It is initialized when the package is instantiated and remains until the session is closed, even if the package state is aged out of the shared pool. As we saw in Chapter 9, variables declared in a package header have global scope. They are visible for any PL/SQL block that has EXECUTE privilege for the package. Since the package state persists until the end of the session, variables in a package header can be used as global variables. The following example illustrates this:

```
-- Available online as PersistPkg.sql
CREATE OR REPLACE PACKAGE PersistPkg AS
  -- Type which holds an array of student ID's.
  TYPE t_StudentTable IS TABLE OF students.ID%TYPE
    INDEX BY BINARY_INTEGER;

  -- Maximum number of rows to return each time.
  v_MaxRows NUMBER := 5;
```

```
    -- Returns up to v_MaxRows student ID's.
    PROCEDURE ReadStudents(p_StudTable OUT t_StudentTable,
                           p_NumRows   OUT NUMBER);

END PersistPkg;

CREATE OR REPLACE PACKAGE BODY PersistPkg AS
  -- Query against students.  Since this is global to the package
  -- body, it will remain past a database call.
  CURSOR StudentCursor IS
    SELECT ID
      FROM students
      ORDER BY last_name;

  PROCEDURE ReadStudents(p_StudTable OUT t_StudentTable,
                         p_NumRows   OUT NUMBER) IS
    v_Done BOOLEAN := FALSE;
    v_NumRows NUMBER := 1;
  BEGIN
    IF NOT StudentCursor%ISOPEN THEN
      -- First open the cursor
      OPEN StudentCursor;
    END IF;

    -- Cursor is open, so we can fetch up to v_MaxRows
    WHILE NOT v_Done LOOP
      FETCH StudentCursor INTO p_StudTable(v_NumRows);
      IF StudentCursor%NOTFOUND THEN
        -- No more data, so we're finished.
        CLOSE StudentCursor;
        v_Done := TRUE;
      ELSE
        v_NumRows := v_NumRows + 1;
        IF v_NumRows > v_MaxRows THEN
          v_Done := TRUE;
        END IF;
      END IF;
    END LOOP;

    -- Return the actual number of rows fetched.
    p_NumRows := v_NumRows - 1;
```

```
    END ReadStudents;
END PersistPkg;
```

PersistPkg.ReadStudents will select from the StudentsCursor cursor. Since this cursor is declared at the package level (not inside ReadStudents), it will remain past a call to ReadStudents. We can call PersistPkg.ReadStudents with the following block:

```
-- Available online as callRS.sql
DECLARE
  v_StudentTable PersistPkg.t_StudentTable;
  v_NumRows NUMBER := PersistPkg.v_MaxRows;
  v_FirstName students.first_name%TYPE;
  v_LastName students.last_name%TYPE;
BEGIN
  PersistPkg.ReadStudents(v_StudentTable, v_NumRows);
  DBMS_OUTPUT.PUT_LINE(' Fetched ' || v_NumRows || ' rows:');
  FOR v_Count IN 1..v_NumRows LOOP
    SELECT first_name, last_name
      INTO v_FirstName, v_LastName
      FROM students
      WHERE ID = v_StudentTable(v_Count);
    DBMS_OUTPUT.PUT_LINE(v_FirstName || ' ' || v_LastName);
  END LOOP;
END;
```

The output from executing the above block three times is shown in Figure 10-11. On each call, different data is returned because the cursor has remained open in between each call.

Serially Reusable Packages

PL/SQL lets you mark a package as serially reusable. The runtime state of a *serially reusable* package will last only for each database call, rather than for the entire session. A serially reusable package has the syntax

    PRAGMA SERIALLY_REUSABLE;

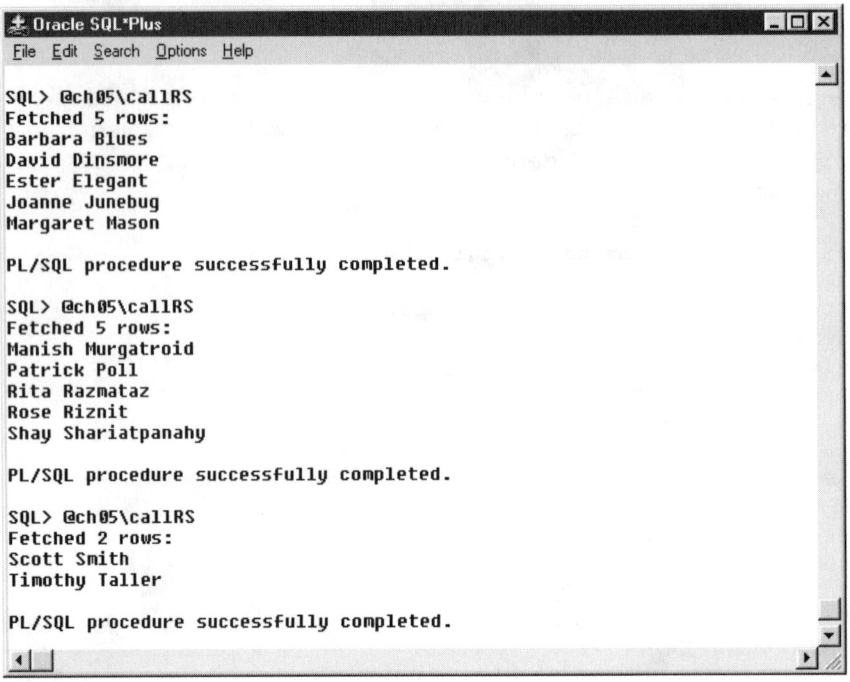

```
Oracle SQL*Plus                                    _ □ ×
File  Edit  Search  Options  Help

SQL> @ch05\callRS
Fetched 5 rows:
Barbara Blues
David Dinsmore
Ester Elegant
Joanne Junebug
Margaret Mason

PL/SQL procedure successfully completed.

SQL> @ch05\callRS
Fetched 5 rows:
Manish Murgatroid
Patrick Poll
Rita Razmataz
Rose Riznit
Shay Shariatpanahy

PL/SQL procedure successfully completed.

SQL> @ch05\callRS
Fetched 2 rows:
Scott Smith
Timothy Taller

PL/SQL procedure successfully completed.
```

FIGURE 10-11.   *Calling ReadStudents*

in the package header (and also the package body, if present). If we modify PersistPkg to include this pragma, the output changes. The modified package is below, and the output is shown in Figure 10-12.

```
-- Available online as PersistPkg2.sql
CREATE OR REPLACE PACKAGE PersistPkg AS
  PRAGMA SERIALLY_REUSABLE;

  -- Type which holds an array of student ID's.
  TYPE t_StudentTable IS TABLE OF students.ID%TYPE
    INDEX BY BINARY_INTEGER;

  -- Maximum number of rows to return each time.
  v_MaxRows NUMBER := 5;

  -- Returns up to v_MaxRows student ID's.
  PROCEDURE ReadStudents(p_StudTable OUT t_StudentTable,
```

```
                    p_NumRows    OUT NUMBER);

END PersistPkg;

CREATE OR REPLACE PACKAGE BODY PersistPkg AS
  PRAGMA SERIALLY_REUSABLE;

  -- Query against students.  Even though this is global to the
  -- package body, it will be reset after each database call,
  -- because the package is now serially reusable.
  CURSOR StudentCursor IS
    SELECT ID
      FROM students
      ORDER BY last_name;
  ...
END PersistPkg;
```

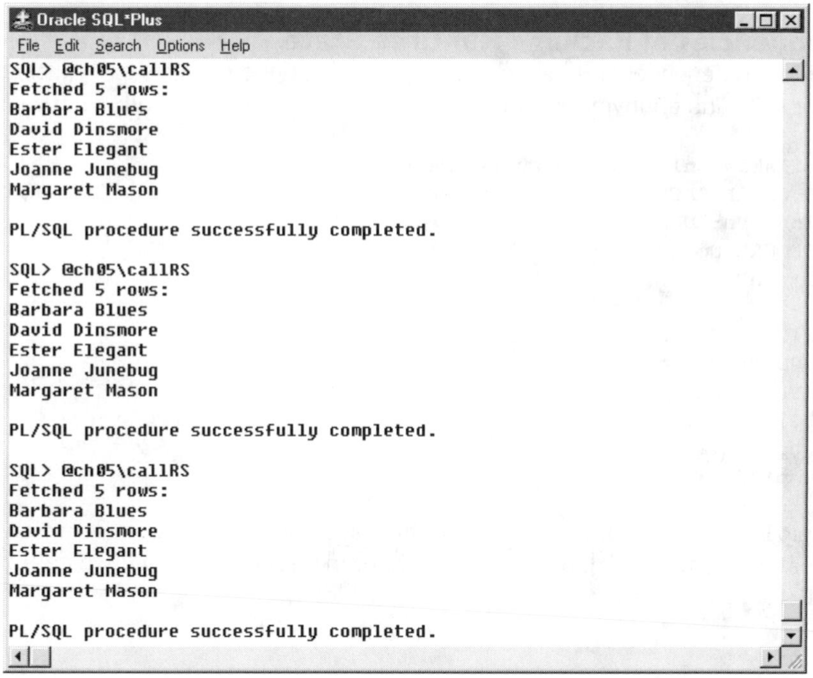

```
Oracle SQL*Plus                                          _ □ ×
 File  Edit  Search  Options  Help
SQL> @ch05\callRS
Fetched 5 rows:
Barbara Blues
David Dinsmore
Ester Elegant
Joanne Junebug
Margaret Mason

PL/SQL procedure successfully completed.

SQL> @ch05\callRS
Fetched 5 rows:
Barbara Blues
David Dinsmore
Ester Elegant
Joanne Junebug
Margaret Mason

PL/SQL procedure successfully completed.

SQL> @ch05\callRS
Fetched 5 rows:
Barbara Blues
David Dinsmore
Ester Elegant
Joanne Junebug
Margaret Mason

PL/SQL procedure successfully completed.
```

FIGURE 10-12.   *Calling a serially reusable ReadStudents*

Note the difference between the two versions—the nonserially reusable version will maintain the state of the cursor over database calls, while the serially reusable version resets the state (and thus the output) each time. The differences between serially reusable and nonserially reusable packages are summarized in the following table. Serially reusable packages can save memory, at the expense of package state being reset after each call.

Serially Reusable Packages	**Nonserially Reusable Packages**
Runtime state is kept in shared memory, and is freed after every database call.	Runtime state is kept in process memory, and lasts for the life of the database session.
The maximum memory used is proportional to the number of concurrent users of the package.	The maximum memory used is proportional to the number of concurrently logged-on users, which is typically much higher.

Dependencies of Package Runtime State

In addition to dependencies between stored objects, dependencies can exist between package state and anonymous blocks. For example, consider the following package:

```
-- Available online as anonymousDependencies.sql
CREATE OR REPLACE PACKAGE SimplePkg AS
  v_GlobalVar NUMBER := 1;
  PROCEDURE UpdateVar;
END SimplePkg;

CREATE OR REPLACE PACKAGE BODY SimplePkg AS
  PROCEDURE UpdateVar IS
  BEGIN
    v_GlobalVar := 7;
  END UpdateVar;
END SimplePkg;
```

SimplePkg contains a package global—v_GlobalVar. Suppose we create SimplePkg from one database session. Then, in a second session, we call SimplePkg.UpdateVar with the following block:

```
BEGIN
  SimplePkg.UpdateVar;
END;
```

Now, back in the first session, we re-create `SimplePkg` by running the creation script again. Finally, we issue the same anonymous block in session 2. We get the following:

```
BEGIN
*
ERROR at line 1:
ORA-04068: existing state of packages has been discarded
ORA-04061: existing state of package "EXAMPLE.SIMPLEPKG" has been
           invalidated
ORA-04065: not executed, altered or dropped package
           "EXAMPLE.SIMPLEPKG"
ORA-06508: PL/SQL: could not find program unit being called
ORA-06512: at line 2
```

What has happened here? The dependency picture for this situation is shown in Figure 10-13. The anonymous block depends on `SimplePkg`, in the same sense that we have seen earlier. This is a compile-time dependency, in that it is determined when the anonymous block is first compiled. However, there is also a runtime dependency—on the packaged variable, since each session has its own copy of packaged variables. Thus, when `SimplePkg` is recompiled the runtime dependency is followed, which invalidates the block and raises the ORA-4068 error.

Runtime dependencies exist only on package state. This includes variables and cursors declared in a package. If the package had no global variables, the second execution of the anonymous block would have succeeded.

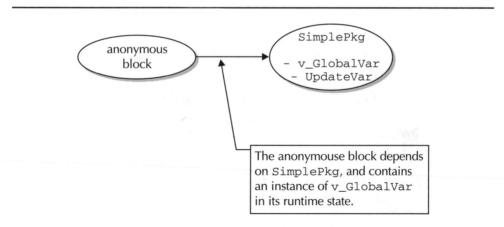

FIGURE 10-13.   *Package global dependencies*

Privileges and Stored Subprograms

Stored subprograms and packages are objects in the data dictionary, and as such they are owned by a particular database user, or schema. Other users can access these objects if they are granted the correct privileges on them. Privileges and roles also come into play when creating a stored object, with regard to the access available inside the subprogram.

EXECUTE Privilege

In order to allow access to a table, the SELECT, INSERT, UPDATE, and DELETE object privileges are used. The GRANT statement gives these privileges to a database user or a role. For stored subprograms and packages, the relevant privilege is EXECUTE. Consider the `RecordFullClasses` procedure, which we examined earlier in this chapter:

```
-- Available online as part of execute.sql
CREATE OR REPLACE PROCEDURE RecordFullClasses AS
  CURSOR c_Classes IS
    SELECT department, course
      FROM classes;
BEGIN
  FOR v_ClassRecord IN c_Classes LOOP
    -- Record all classes which don't have very much room left
    -- in temp_table.
    IF AlmostFull(v_ClassRecord.department, v_ClassRecord.course) THEN
      INSERT INTO temp_table (char_col) VALUES
        (v_ClassRecord.department || ' ' || v_ClassRecord.course ||
          ' is almost full!');
    END IF;
  END LOOP;
END RecordFullClasses;
```

NOTE
The online example execute.sql will first create the users UserA and UserB, and then create the necessary objects for the examples in this section. You may have to modify the password used for the DBA account in order to get the example to work on your system. You can see the output from running execute.sql in execute.out, also available online.

Suppose that the objects on which `RecordFullClasses` depends (the function `AlmostFull` and tables `classes` and `temp_table`) are all owned by the database user `UserA`. `RecordFullClasses` is owned by `UserA` as well. If we grant the EXECUTE privilege on `RecordFullClasses` to another database user, say `UserB`, with

-- **Available online as part of execute.sql**
```
GRANT EXECUTE ON RecordFullClasses TO UserB;
```

then `UserB` can execute `RecordFullClasses` with the following block. Note that dot notation is used to indicate the schema:

-- **Available online as part of execute.sql**
```
BEGIN
  UserA.RecordFullClasses;
END;
```

In this scenario, all of the database objects are owned by `UserA`. This situation is illustrated in Figure 10-14. The dotted line signifies the GRANT statement from

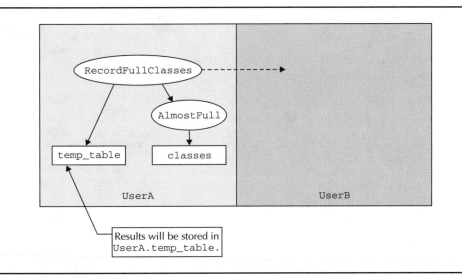

FIGURE 10-14. *Database objects owned by UserA*

UserA to UserB, while the solid lines signify object dependencies. After executing the above block, the results will be inserted into UserA.temp_table.

Now suppose that UserB has another table, also called temp_table, as illustrated in Figure 10-15. If UserB calls UserA.RecordFullClasses (by executing the anonymous block above), which table gets modified? The table in UserA does. This concept can be expressed as follows:

By default, a subprogram executes under the privilege set of its owner.

Even though UserB is calling RecordFullClasses, RecordFullClasses is owned by UserA. Thus, the identifier temp_table will evaluate to the table belonging to UserA, *not* UserB.

Oracle8*i* includes a new feature known as "Invoker's rights," which enables you to specify if a procedure executes under the privilege set of its owner, or of its caller. See the section "Invoker's versus Definer's Rights" later in this chapter for details.

Stored Subprograms and Roles

Let's modify the situation in Figure 10-15 slightly. Suppose UserA does not own temp_table or RecordFullClasses, and these are owned by UserB. Furthermore, suppose we have modified RecordFullClasses to explicitly refer to the objects in UserA. This is illustrated by the following listing and Figure 10-16:

```
-- Available online as part of execute.sql
CREATE OR REPLACE PROCEDURE RecordFullClasses AS
  CURSOR c_Classes IS
    SELECT department, course
      FROM UserA.classes;
BEGIN
  FOR v_ClassRecord IN c_Classes LOOP
    -- Record all classes which don't have very much room left
    -- in temp_table.
    IF UserA.AlmostFull(v_ClassRecord.department,
                        v_ClassRecord.course) THEN
      INSERT INTO temp_table (char_col) VALUES
        (v_ClassRecord.department || ' ' || v_ClassRecord.course ||
         ' is almost full!');
    END IF;
  END LOOP;
END RecordFullClasses;
```

In order for RecordFullClasses to compile correctly, UserA must have granted the SELECT privilege on classes and the EXECUTE privilege on AlmostFull to UserB. The dotted lines in Figure 10-16 represent this. Furthermore, this grant must be

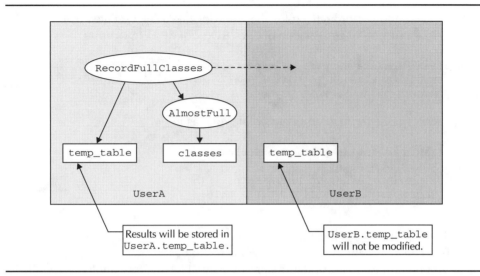

FIGURE 10-15. *temp_table owned by UserB and UserA*

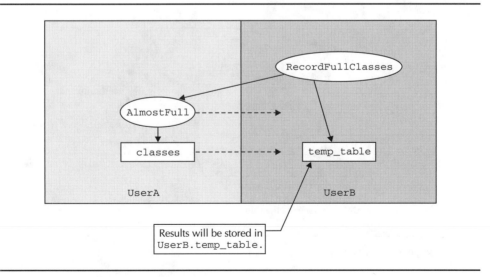

FIGURE 10-16. *RecordFullClasses owned by UserB*

done explicitly and *not* through a role. The following GRANTs, executed by UserA, would allow a successful compilation of UserB.RecordFullClasses:

```
-- Available online as part of execute.sql
GRANT SELECT ON classes TO UserB;
GRANT EXECUTE ON AlmostFull TO UserB;
```

A GRANT done through an intermediate role, as in

```
-- Available online as part of execute.sql
CREATE ROLE UserA_Role;
GRANT SELECT ON classes TO UserA_Role;
GRANT EXECUTE ON AlmostFull TO UserA_Role;
GRANT UserA_Role to UserB;
```

will not work. The role is illustrated in Figure 10-17.

So we can clarify the rule in the previous section as:

A subprogram executes under the privileges that have been granted explicitly to its owner, not via a role.

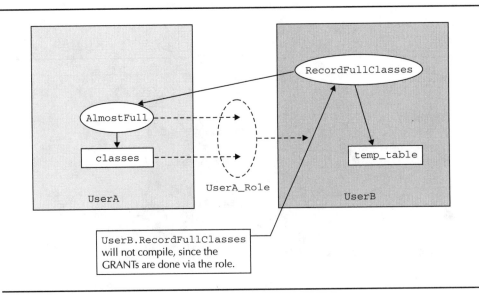

FIGURE 10-17. *GRANTs done via a role*

If the grants had been done via a role, we would have received PLS-201 errors when we tried to compile `RecordFullClasses`:

```
PLS-201: identifier 'CLASSES' must be declared
PLS-201: identifier 'ALMOSTFULL' must be declared
```

This rule also applies for triggers and packages, which are stored in the database as well. Essentially, *the only objects available inside a stored procedure, function, package, or trigger are the ones owned by the owner of the subprogram, or explicitly granted to the owner.*

Why is this? To explain this restriction, we need to examine binding. PL/SQL uses early binding—references are evaluated when a subprogram is compiled, not when it is run. GRANT and REVOKE are both DDL statements. They take effect immediately, and the new privileges are recorded in the data dictionary. All database sessions will see the new privilege set. However, this is not necessarily true for roles. A role can be granted to a user, and that user can then choose to disable the role with the SET ROLE command. The distinction is that SET ROLE applies to one database session only, while GRANT and REVOKE apply to all sessions. A role can be disabled in one session but enabled in other sessions.

In order to allow privileges granted via a role to be used inside stored subprograms and triggers, the privileges would have to be checked every time the procedure is run. The privileges are checked as part of the binding process. But early binding means that the privileges are checked at compile time, not runtime. In order to maintain early binding, *all roles are disabled inside stored procedures, functions, packages, and triggers.*

Invoker's versus Definer's Rights

Oracle**8i** and higher | Consider the situation that we examined earlier in this chapter, in the section "EXECUTE Privilege," and illustrated by Figure 10-15. In this situation, both `UserA` and `UserB` own a copy of `temp_table`, and `RecordFullClasses`, since it is owned by `UserA`, inserts into `UserA.temp_table`. `RecordFullClasses` is known as a *definer's rights* procedure, because unqualified external references within it are resolved under the privilege set of its owner, or definer.

Oracle8i introduces a different kind of external reference resolution. In an *invoker's rights* subprogram, external references are resolved under the privilege set of the caller, not the owner. An invoker's rights routine is created by using the AUTHID clause. It is valid for stand-alone subprograms, package specifications, and object type specifications (see Chapter 12 for information about object types) only.

Individual subprograms within a package must be all invoker's or definer's, not a mix. The syntax of AUTHID is given here:

CREATE [OR REPLACE] FUNCTION *function_name*
[*parameter_list*] RETURN *return_type*
[AUTHID {CURRENT_USER | DEFINER}] {IS | AS}
function_body;

CREATE [OR REPLACE] PROCEDURE *procedure_name*
[*parameter_list*]
[AUTHID {CURRENT_USER | DEFINER}] {IS | AS}
function_body;

CREATE [OR REPLACE] PACKAGE *package_spec_name*
[AUTHID {CURRENT_USER | DEFINER}] {IS | AS}
package_spec;

If CURRENT_USER is specified in the AUTHID clause, the object will have invoker's rights. If DEFINER is specified, then the object will have definer's rights. The default if the AUTHID clause is not present is definer's rights.

For example, the following version of `RecordFullClasses` is an invoker's rights procedure:

```
-- Available online as part of invokers.sql
CREATE OR REPLACE PROCEDURE RecordFullClasses
  AUTHID CURRENT_USER AS

  -- Note that we have to preface classes and AlmostFull with
  -- UserA, since both of these are owned by UserA only.
  CURSOR c_Classes IS
    SELECT department, course
      FROM UserA.classes;
BEGIN
  FOR v_ClassRecord IN c_Classes LOOP
    -- Record all classes which don't have very much room left
    -- in temp_table.
    IF UserA.AlmostFull(v_ClassRecord.department,
                        v_ClassRecord.course) THEN
      INSERT INTO temp_table (char_col) VALUES
        (v_ClassRecord.department || ' ' || v_ClassRecord.course ||
         ' is almost full!');
    END IF;
  END LOOP;
END RecordFullClasses;
```

NOTE
The online example invokers.sql *will first create the users* UserA *and* UserB, *and then create the necessary objects for the examples in this section. You may have to modify the password used for the DBA account in order to get the example to work on your system. You can see the output from running* invokers.sql *in* invokers.out, *also available online.*

If UserB executes RecordFullClasses, the insert will be done in UserB.temp_table. If UserA executes it, the insert will be done in UserA.temp_table. This is illustrated by the following SQL*Plus session and Figure 10-18:

```
-- Available online as part of invokers.sql
SQL> connect UserA/UserA
Connected.
SQL> -- Call as UserA.  This will insert into UserA.temp_table.
SQL> BEGIN
  2    RecordFullClasses;
  3    COMMIT;
  4  END;
  5  /
PL/SQL procedure successfully completed.

SQL> -- Query temp_table.  There should be 1 row.
SQL> SELECT * FROM temp_table;
   NUM_COL CHAR_COL
---------- -----------------------------------------------------------
           MUS 410 is almost full!

SQL> -- Connect as UserB.
SQL> -- Now the call to RecordFullClasses will insert into
SQL> -- UserB.temp_table.
SQL> BEGIN
  2    UserA.RecordFullClasses;
  3    COMMIT;
  4  END;
  5  /
PL/SQL procedure successfully completed.

SQL> -- So we should have one row here as well.
SQL> SELECT * FROM temp_table;
   NUM_COL CHAR_COL
---------- -----------------------------------------------------------
           MUS 410 is almost full!
```

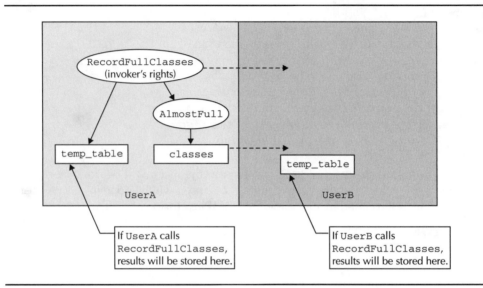

FIGURE 10-18.   *Invoker's rights* `RecordFullClasses`

Resolution with Invoker's Rights   In an invoker's rights routine, external references in SQL statements will be resolved using the caller's privilege set. However, references in PL/SQL statements (such as assignments or procedure calls) are still resolved under the owner's privilege set. This is why, in Figure 10-18, GRANTs need be done only on `RecordFullClasses` and the `classes` table. Since the call to `AlmostFull` is a PL/SQL reference, it will always be done under `UserA`'s privilege set, and thus it does not need to be GRANTed to `UserB`.

However, suppose that the GRANT on `classes` was not done. In this case, `UserA` can successfully compile and run the procedure, because all of the SQL objects are accessible from `UserA`'s privilege set. But `UserB` will receive an ORA-942 error upon calling `RecordFullClasses`. This is illustrated by Figure 10-19 and the following SQL*Plus session:

```
-- Available online as part of invokers.sql
SQL> connect UserB/UserB
Connected.
SQL> BEGIN
  2    UserA.RecordFullClasses;
  3  END;
  4  /
```

```
BEGIN
*
ERROR at line 1:
ORA-00942: table or view does not exist
ORA-06512: at "USERA.RECORDFULLCLASSES", line 7
ORA-06512: at "USERA.RECORDFULLCLASSES", line 10
ORA-06512: at line 2
```

NOTE
The error received here is ORA-942, and not PLS-201. It is a database compilation error, but we receive it at runtime.

Roles and Invoker's Rights   Suppose the GRANT on classes was done via a role, and not directly. Recall from the situation in Figure 10-17 that definer's rights procedures must have all privileges GRANTed explicitly. For invoker's rights routines, however, this is not the case. Because the external references for invoker's rights

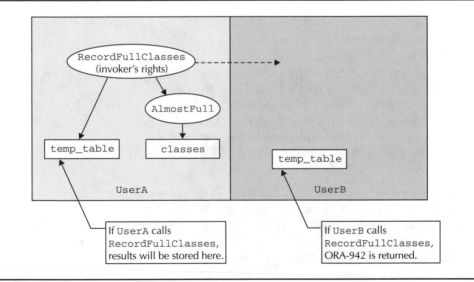

FIGURE 10-19. *Revoked SELECT on* `classes`

routines is done at runtime, the current privilege set is available. This implies that privileges GRANTed via a role to the *caller* will be accessible. This is illustrated by the following SQL*Plus session and Figure 10-20:

```
-- Available online as part of invokers.sql
SQL> connect UserA/UserA
Connected.
CREATE ROLE UserA_Role;
Role created.
SQL> GRANT SELECT ON classes TO UserA_Role;
Grant succeeded.
SQL> GRANT UserA_Role TO UserB;
Grant succeeded.
SQL> -- Connect as UserB and call.
SQL> connect UserB/UserB
Connected.
SQL> -- Now the call to RecordFullClasses will succeed.
SQL> BEGIN
  2     UserA.RecordFullClasses;
  3     COMMIT;
  4  END;
  5  /
PL/SQL procedure successfully completed.
```

NOTE
References that are resolved at the time of procedure compilation must still be GRANTed directly. Only those references that are resolved at runtime can be GRANTed via a role. This also implies that the SET ROLE command (if executed through dynamic SQL) can be used with runtime references.

Triggers, Views, and Invoker's Rights   A database trigger will always be executed with definer's rights, and will execute under the privilege set of the schema that owns the triggering table. This is also true for a PL/SQL function that is called from a view. In this case, the function will execute under the privilege set of the view's owner.

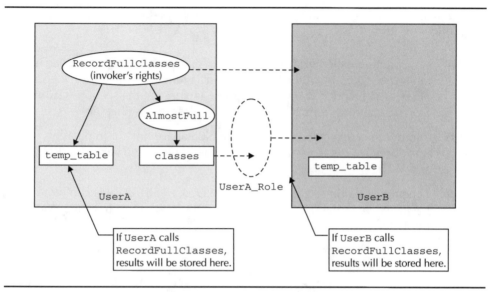

FIGURE 10-20. *Roles and invoker's rights*

Using Stored Functions in SQL Statements

In general, because calls to subprograms are procedural, they cannot be called from SQL statements. However, if a stand-alone or packaged function meets certain restrictions, it can be called during execution of a SQL statement. This feature was first introduced in PL/SQL 2.1 (Oracle7 Release 7.1), and has been enhanced for Oracle8*i*.

User-defined functions are called the same way as built-in functions such as TO_CHAR, UPPER, or ADD_MONTHS. Depending on where a user-defined function is used, and what version of Oracle you are running, it must meet different restrictions. These restrictions are defined in terms of purity levels.

Purity Levels

There are four different purity levels for functions. A *purity level* defines what kinds of data structures the function reads or modifies. The available levels are listed in Table 10-2. Depending on the purity level of a function, it is subject to the following restrictions:

- Any function called from a SQL statement cannot modify any database tables (WNDS). (In Oracle8i and higher, a function called from a non-SELECT statement can modify database tables. See the section "Calling Stored Functions from SQL in Oracle8i" later in this chapter.)

- In order to be executed remotely (via a database link) or in parallel, a function must not read or write the value of packaged variables (RNPS and WNPS).

- Functions called from the SELECT, VALUES, or SET clauses can write packaged variables. Functions in all other clauses must have the WNPS purity level.

- A function is only as pure as the subprograms it calls. If a function calls a stored procedure that does an UPDATE, for example, the function does not have the WNDS purity level and thus cannot be used inside a SELECT statement.

Purity Level	Meaning	Description
WNDS	Writes no database state	The function does not modify any database tables (using DML statements).
RNDS	Reads no database state	The function does not read any database tables (using the SELECT statement).
WNPS	Writes no package state	The function does not modify any packaged variables (no packaged variables are used on the left side of an assignment or in a FETCH statement).
RNPS	Reads no package state	The function does not examine any packaged variables (no packaged variables appear on the right side of an assignment or as part of a procedural or SQL expression).

TABLE 10-2. *Function Purity Levels*

■ Regardless of their purity level, stored PL/SQL functions cannot be called from a CHECK constraint clause of a CREATE TABLE or ALTER TABLE command, or be used to specify a default value for a column, because these situations require an unchanging definition.

In addition to the preceding restrictions, a user-defined function must also meet the following requirements to be callable from a SQL statement. Note that all the built-in functions must meet these requirements as well.

■ The function has to be stored in the database, either stand-alone or as part of a package. It must not be local to another block.

■ The function can take only IN parameters, no IN OUT or OUT.

■ The formal parameters must use only database types, not PL/SQL types such as BOOLEAN or RECORD. Database types include NUMBER, CHAR, VARCHAR2, ROWID, LONG, RAW, LONG RAW, DATE, as well as the new types introduced for Oracle8*i* and Oracle9*i*.

■ The return type of the function must also be a database type.

■ The function must not end the current transaction with COMMIT or ROLLBACK, or rollback to a savepoint prior to the function execution.

■ It also must not issue any ALTER SESSION or ALTER SYSTEM commands.

As an example, the `FullName` function takes a student ID number as input and returns the concatenated first and last names:

-- **Available online as part of FullName.sql**
```
CREATE OR REPLACE FUNCTION FullName (
  p_StudentID  students.ID%TYPE)
  RETURN VARCHAR2 IS

  v_Result  VARCHAR2(100);
BEGIN
  SELECT first_name || ' ' || last_name
    INTO v_Result
    FROM students
    WHERE ID = p_StudentID;

  RETURN v_Result;
END FullName;
```

FullName meets all of the restrictions, so we can call it from SQL statements, as the following SQL*Plus session illustrates:

```
-- Available online as part of FullName.sql
SQL> SELECT ID, FullName(ID) "Full Name"
  2    FROM students;
      ID Full Name
--------- -------------------------------
   10000 Scott Smith
   10001 Margaret Mason
   10002 Joanne Junebug
   10003 Manish Murgratroid
   10004 Patrick Poll
   10005 Timothy Taller
   10006 Barbara Blues
   10007 David Dinsmore
   10008 Ester Elegant
   10009 Rose Riznit
   10010 Rita Razmataz
   10011 Shay Shariatpanahy
12 rows selected.
SQL> INSERT INTO temp_table (char_col)
  2    VALUES (FullName(10010));
1 row created.
```

RESTRICT_REFERENCES

The PL/SQL engine can determine the purity level of stand-alone functions. When the function is called from a SQL statement, the purity level is checked. If it does not meet the restrictions, an error is returned. For packaged functions, however, the RESTRICT_REFERENCES pragma is required (prior to Oracle8i). This pragma specifies the purity level of a given function, with the syntax

PRAGMA RESTRICT_REFERENCES(*subprogram_or_package_name*,
  WNDS [, WNPS] [, RNDS] [, RNPS]);

where *subprogram_or_package_name* is the name of a package, or a packaged subprogram. (With Oracle8 and higher, you can also use the DEFAULT or TRUST keywords. See the sections "DEFAULT Keyword" and "TRUST Keyword" later in this chapter for details.) Because WNDS is required for all functions used in SQL statements, it is also required for the pragma. (This restriction is relaxed in Oracle8i.) The purity levels can be specified in any order. The pragma goes in the package header, with the specification for the function. For example, the StudentOps package uses RESTRICT_REFERENCES twice:

```
-- Available online as StudentOps.sql
CREATE OR REPLACE PACKAGE StudentOps AS
  FUNCTION FullName(p_StudentID IN students.ID%TYPE)
    RETURN VARCHAR2;
  PRAGMA RESTRICT_REFERENCES(FullName, WNDS, WNPS, RNPS);

  /* Returns the number of History majors. */
  FUNCTION NumHistoryMajors
    RETURN NUMBER;
  PRAGMA RESTRICT_REFERENCES(NumHistoryMajors, WNDS);
END StudentOps;

CREATE OR REPLACE PACKAGE BODY StudentOps AS
  -- Packaged variable to hold the number of history majors.
  v_NumHist NUMBER;

  FUNCTION FullName(p_StudentID IN students.ID%TYPE)
    RETURN VARCHAR2 IS
    v_Result  VARCHAR2(100);
  BEGIN
    SELECT first_name || ' ' || last_name
      INTO v_Result
      FROM students
      WHERE ID = p_StudentID;

    RETURN v_Result;
  END FullName;

  FUNCTION NumHistoryMajors RETURN NUMBER IS
    v_Result NUMBER;
  BEGIN
    IF v_NumHist IS NULL THEN
      /* Determine the answer. */
      SELECT COUNT(*)
        INTO v_Result
        FROM students
        WHERE major = 'History';
      /* And save it for future use. */
      v_NumHist := v_Result;
    ELSE
      v_Result := v_NumHist;
    END IF;

    RETURN v_Result;
  END NumHistoryMajors;
END StudentOps;
```

NOTE
In Oracle8i and higher, the pragma is no longer required. The PL/SQL engine can verify the purity level of all functions at runtime as needed. For more information, see the section "Calling Stored Functions from SQL in Oracle8i" later in this chapter.

Rationale for RESTRICT_REFERENCES   Why is the pragma required for packaged functions, but not for stand-alone functions? The answer lies in the relationship between the package header and package body. Remember that PL/SQL blocks calling a packaged function will depend only on the package header, and not the body. Furthermore, the body may not even exist when the calling block is created. Consequently, the PL/SQL compiler needs the pragma to determine the purity levels of the packaged function, to verify that it is being used correctly in the calling block. Whenever the package body is subsequently modified (or created for the first time) the function code is also checked against the pragma. The pragma is checked at compile time, not runtime.

TIP
Strictly speaking, the PL/SQL engine can verify the purity level at runtime, as it does for stand-alone functions prior to Oracle8i. However, using the pragma means that the engine does not need to verify the level at runtime, which is a performance benefit. Thus, in Oracle8i it is advantageous to use RESTRICT_REFERENCES, even though it is no longer required.

Initialization Section   The code in the initialization section of a package can have a purity level as well. The first time any function in the package is called, the initialization section is run. Consequently, a packaged function is only as pure as the initialization section of the containing package. The purity level for a package is also done with RESTRICT_REFERENCES, but with the package name rather than a function name:

```
CREATE OR REPLACE PACKAGE StudentOps AS
   PRAGMA RESTRICT_REFERENCES (StudentOps, WNDS);
...
END StudentOps;
```

Oracle**8** and higher | **DEFAULT Keyword**   If there is no RESTRICT_REFERENCES pragma associated with a given packaged function, it will not have any purity level asserted. However, with Oracle8 and higher you can change the default purity level for a package. The DEFAULT keyword is used instead of the subprogram name in the pragma:

> PRAGMA RESTRICT_REFERENCES(**DEFAULT**,
> WNDS [, WNPS] [, RNDS] [, RNPS]);

Any subsequent subprograms in the package must comply with the purity levels specified. For example, consider the `DefaultPragma` package:

```
-- Available online as DefaultPragma.sql
CREATE OR REPLACE PACKAGE DefaultPragma AS
  FUNCTION F1 RETURN NUMBER;
  PRAGMA RESTRICT_REFERENCES(F1, RNDS, RNPS);

  PRAGMA RESTRICT_REFERENCES(DEFAULT, WNDS, WNPS, RNDS, RNPS);
  FUNCTION F2 RETURN NUMBER;

  FUNCTION F3 RETURN NUMBER;
END DefaultPragma;

CREATE OR REPLACE PACKAGE BODY DefaultPragma AS
  FUNCTION F1 RETURN NUMBER IS
  BEGIN
    INSERT INTO temp_table (num_col, char_col)
      VALUES (1, 'F1!');
    RETURN 1;
  END F1;

  FUNCTION F2 RETURN NUMBER IS
  BEGIN
    RETURN 2;
  END F2;

  -- This function violates the default pragma.
  FUNCTION F3 RETURN NUMBER IS
  BEGIN
    INSERT INTO temp_table (num_col, char_col)
      VALUES (1, 'F3!');
    RETURN 3;
  END F3;
END DefaultPragma;
```

The default pragma (which asserts all four purity levels) will be applied to both F2 and F3. Since F3 INSERTs into `temp_table`, it violates the pragma. Compiling the above package will return the following errors:

```
PL/SQL: Compilation unit analysis terminated
PLS-00452: Subprogram 'F3' violates its associated pragma
```

Overloaded Functions   RESTRICT_REFERENCES can appear anywhere in the package specification, after the function declaration. It can apply to only one function definition, however. For overloaded functions, the pragma applies to the nearest definition prior to the pragma. In the following example, each pragma applies to the version of TestFunc just prior to it:

```
-- Available online as part of Overload.sql
CREATE OR REPLACE PACKAGE Overload AS
  FUNCTION TestFunc(p_Parameter1 IN NUMBER)
    RETURN VARCHAR2;
  PRAGMA RESTRICT_REFERENCES(TestFunc, WNDS, RNDS, WNPS, RNPS);

  FUNCTION TestFunc(p_ParameterA IN VARCHAR2,
                    p_ParameterB IN DATE)
    RETURN VARCHAR2;
  PRAGMA RESTRICT_REFERENCES(TestFunc, WNDS, RNDS, WNPS, RNPS);
END Overload;

CREATE OR REPLACE PACKAGE BODY Overload AS
  FUNCTION TestFunc(p_Parameter1 IN NUMBER)
    RETURN VARCHAR2 IS
  BEGIN
    RETURN 'Version 1';
  END TestFunc;

  FUNCTION TestFunc(p_ParameterA IN VARCHAR2,
                    p_ParameterB IN DATE)
    RETURN VARCHAR2 IS
  BEGIN
    RETURN 'Version 2';
  END TestFunc;
END Overload;
```

The following SQL*Plus session illustrates that both overloaded versions are callable from SQL:

```
-- Available online as part of Overload.sql
SQL> SELECT Overload.TestFunc(1) FROM dual;
OVERLOAD.TESTFUNC(1)
---------------------------------------------------------
Version 1

SQL> SELECT Overload.TestFunc('abc', SYSDATE) FROM dual;
OVERLOAD.TESTFUNC('ABC',SYSDATE)
---------------------------------------------------------
Version 2
```

TIP

*I generally prefer to code the RESTRICT_
REFERENCES pragma immediately after each
function, so that it is clear to which version it
applies.*

Built-In Packages   The procedures in the built-in packages supplied with PL/SQL were, in general, not considered pure as of Oracle7.3 and PL/SQL 2.3. This included DBMS_OUTPUT, DBMS_PIPE, DBMS_ALERT, DBMS_SQL, and UTL_FILE. However, the necessary pragmas were added to these packages in later versions where possible. Table 10-3 shows when the pragmas were added for the more commonly used packages. Since the pragma is not necessary starting with Oracle8*i*, all built-in packaged functions that meet the restrictions can be used in SQL statements as of Oracle8*i*. If you call a built-in packaged function in Oracle8*i* and it does not meet the restrictions, an error will be raised at runtime.

NOTE

*The pragmas have been added to some of these
packages for the RDBMS patch sets, so they may
be available in versions prior to the ones listed in
Table 10-3. You can check the source for the
package header (usually found in the* rdbms/
admin *directory under $ORACLE_HOME) to verify
the purity level for a particular PL/SQL version.*

Package	Pragma Added as of Version
DBMS_ALERT	N/A—REGISTER contains a COMMIT
DBMS_JOB	N/A—Jobs run in a separate process and thus can't be called from SQL
DBMS_OUTPUT	7.3.3
DBMS_PIPE	7.3.3
DBMS_SQL	N/A—EXECUTE and PARSE can be used to execute DDL statements, which would cause an implicit COMMIT
STANDARD	7.3.3 (This includes the RAISE_APPLICATION_ERROR procedure.)
UTL_FILE	8.0.6
UTL_HTTP	7.3.3

TABLE 10-3. *RESTRICT_REFERENCES for Built-In Packages*

Default Parameters

When calling a function from a procedural statement, you can use the default values for formal parameters, if they are present. When calling a function from a SQL statement, however, all parameters must be specified. Furthermore, you have to use positional notation and not named notation. The following call to FullName is illegal:

```
SELECT FullName(p_StudentID => 10000) FROM dual;
```

Calling Stored Functions from SQL in Oracle8*i*

Oracle **8*i*** and higher
As we have seen in the past sections, the RESTRICT_REFERENCES pragma enforces compile-time purity levels. Prior to Oracle8*i*, packaged functions need the pragma in order to be callable from SQL. Oracle8*i*, however, relaxes this restriction. If the pragma is not present, the database will verify the purity level of a function at runtime.

This is especially useful for external routines (those written in Java or C, for example). In this case, the PL/SQL compiler can't check the purity level, since the PL/SQL compiler doesn't actually compile the function. (See Chapter 12 for more information on external routines.) Thus, the check has to be performed at runtime.

The check is only performed if the function is called from within an executing SQL statement. If the pragma is present, the check is not performed. Consequently, using the pragma will save some execution time, and will also serve to document the behavior of the function.

For example, suppose we remove the pragmas from `StudentOps`:

```
-- Available online as part of StudentOps2.sql
CREATE OR REPLACE PACKAGE StudentOps AS
  FUNCTION FullName(p_StudentID IN students.ID%TYPE)
    RETURN VARCHAR2;

  /* Returns the number of History majors. */
  FUNCTION NumHistoryMajors
    RETURN NUMBER;
END StudentOps;
```

We can still call these functions from SQL, as the following SQL*Plus session shows:

```
SQL> SELECT StudentOps.FullName(ID)
  2    FROM students
  3    WHERE major = 'History';
STUDENTOPS.FULLNAME(ID)
-----------------------
Margaret Mason
Patrick Poll
Timothy Taller
SQL> INSERT INTO temp_table (num_col)
  2    VALUES (StudentOps.NumHistoryMajors);
1 row created.
SQL> SELECT * FROM temp_table;
  NUM_COL CHAR_COL
--------- --------
        3
```

If you attempt to call an illegal function from a SQL statement, Oracle8*i* will issue an error such as "ORA-14551: Cannot perform a DML operation inside a query," as the following example shows. Consider the `InsertTemp` function:

```
-- Available online as part of InsertTemp.sql
CREATE OR REPLACE FUNCTION InsertTemp(
  p_Num IN temp_table.num_col%TYPE,
  p_Char IN temp_table.char_col%type)
  RETURN NUMBER AS
BEGIN
  INSERT INTO temp_table (num_col, char_col)
    VALUES (p_Num, p_Char);
  RETURN 0;
END InsertTemp;
```

Calling it from within a SELECT statement yields the following results:

```
-- Available online as part of InsertTemp.sql
SQL> SELECT InsertTemp(1, 'Hello')
  2    FROM dual;
SELECT InsertTemp(1, 'Hello')
       *
ERROR at line 1:
ORA-14551: cannot perform a DML operation inside a query
ORA-06512: at "EXAMPLE.INSERTTEMP", line 6
ORA-06512: at line 1
```

TRUST Keyword

Although RESTRICT_REFERENCES is no longer required (and, in fact, cannot be used for external routines), code written prior to Oracle8*i* may use it. The pragma can also be used to speed processing, as we discussed in the previous section. Thus, you may want to call a function that does not have the pragma from one that is declared pure. To aid this, Oracle8*i* provides an additional keyword that can be used in the pragma, in addition to or instead of the purity levels—TRUST.

If the TRUST keyword is present, the restrictions listed in the pragma are not enforced. Rather, they are trusted to be true. This allows you to write new code that does not use RESTRICT_REFERENCES, and call the new code from functions that are declared pure. For example, consider the following package:

```
-- Available online as TrustPkg.sql
CREATE OR REPLACE PACKAGE TrustPkg AS
  FUNCTION ToUpper (p_a VARCHAR2) RETURN VARCHAR2 IS
    LANGUAGE JAVA
    NAME 'Test.Uppercase(char[]) return char[]';
  PRAGMA RESTRICT_REFERENCES(ToUpper, WNDS, TRUST);

  PROCEDURE Demo(p_in IN VARCHAR2, p_out OUT VARCHAR2);
  PRAGMA RESTRICT_REFERENCES(Demo, WNDS);
END TrustPkg;

CREATE OR REPLACE PACKAGE BODY TrustPkg AS
  PROCEDURE Demo(p_in IN VARCHAR2, p_out OUT VARCHAR2) IS
  BEGIN
    p_out := ToUpper(p_in);
  END Demo;
END TrustPkg;
```

`TrustPkg.ToUpper` is an external routine—the body of the function is actually written in Java, and will return its input parameter in all uppercase. Since the body is not in PL/SQL, the TRUST keyword is necessary for the pragma. Then, because ToUpper is trusted to have the WNDS purity, we can call ToUpper from Demo.

NOTE
Although TrustPkg can be compiled without having the Java stored procedure present, it cannot be run without first creating Test.Uppercase.

Calling Functions from DML Statements

Prior to Oracle8*i*, a function called from a DML statement could not update the database (that is, it must assert the WNDS purity level). With Oracle8*i*, however, this restriction has been relaxed. Now, a function called from a DML statement must not read from or modify the table(s) being modified by that DML statement, but it can update other tables. For example, consider the UpdateTemp function:

```
-- Available online as part of DMLUpdate.sql
CREATE OR REPLACE FUNCTION UpdateTemp(p_ID IN students.ID%TYPE)
  RETURN students.ID%TYPE AS
BEGIN
  INSERT INTO temp_table (num_col, char_col)
    VALUES(p_ID, 'Updated!');
  RETURN p_ID;
END UpdateTemp;
```

Prior to Oracle8*i*, executing the following UPDATE statement would raise an error:

```
-- Available online as part of DMLUpdate.sql
SQL> UPDATE students
  2     SET major = 'Nutrition'
  3     WHERE UpdateTemp(ID) = ID;
   WHERE UpdateTemp(ID) = ID
         *
ERROR at line 3:
ORA-06571: Function UPDATETEMP does not guarantee not to update
database
```

With Oracle8*i*, however, it succeeds because UpdateTemp does not modify students, only temp_table.

NOTE
A function called from a parallelized DML statement must not modify the database, even tables not currently being modified.

Pinning in the Shared Pool

The *shared pool* is the portion of the SGA that contains, among other things, the p-code of compiled subprograms as they are run. The first time a stored subprogram is called, the p-code is loaded from disk into the shared pool. Once the object is no longer referenced, it is free to be aged out. Objects are aged out of the shared pool using an LRU (least recently used) algorithm. See *Oracle Concepts* for more information on the shared pool and how it works.

The DBMS_SHARED_POOL package allows you to pin objects in the shared pool. When an object is *pinned*, it will never be aged out until you request it, no matter how full the pool gets or how often the object is accessed. This can improve performance, as it takes time to reload a package from disk. Pinning an object also helps minimize fragmentation of the shared pool. DBMS_SHARED_POOL has four procedures: DBMS_SHARED_POOL.KEEP, DBMS_SHARED_POOL.UNKEEP, DBMS_SHARED_POOL.SIZES, and DBMS_SHARED_POOL.ABORTED_REQUEST_THRESHOLD.

KEEP

The DBMS_SHARED_POOL.KEEP procedure is used to pin objects in the pool. Packages, triggers, sequences, object types, and Java objects (Oracle8*i* and higher), and SQL statements can be pinned.

KEEP is defined with

```
PROCEDURE KEEP(name VARCHAR2,
               flag CHAR DEFAULT 'P');
```

The parameters are described in the following table. Once an object has been kept, it will not be removed until the database is shut down or the DBMS_SHARED_POOL.UNKEEP procedure is used. Note that DBMS_SHARED_POOL.KEEP does not load the package into the shared pool immediately; rather, it will be pinned the first time it is subsequently loaded.

Parameter	Type	Description
name	VARCHAR2	Name of the object. This can be an object name or the identifier associated with a SQL statement. The SQL identifier is the concatenation of the `address` and `hash_value` fields in the `v$sqlarea` view (by default, selectable only by SYS) and is returned by the SIZES procedure.

Parameter	Type	Description
flag	CHAR	Determines the type of the object. The values for *flag* have the following meanings: P—Package, function, or procedure Q—Sequence R—Trigger T—Object type (Oracle8 and higher) JS—Java source (Oracle8*i* and higher) JC—Java class (Oracle8*i* and higher) JR—Java resource (Oracle8*i* and higher) JD—Java shared data (Oracle8*i* and higher) C—SQL cursor

UNKEEP

UNKEEP is the only way to remove a kept object from the shared pool, without restarting the database. Kept objects are never aged out automatically. UNKEEP is defined with

        PROCEDURE UNKEEP(*name* VARCHAR2,
                        flag CHAR DEFAULT 'P');

The arguments are the same as for KEEP. If the specified object does not already exist in the shared pool, an error is raised.

SIZES

SIZES will echo the contents of the shared pool to the screen. It is defined with

        PROCEDURE SIZES(*minsize* NUMBER);

Objects with a size greater than *minsize* will be returned. SIZES uses DBMS_ OUTPUT to return the data, so be sure to use "set serveroutput on" in SQL*Plus or Server Manager before calling the procedure.

ABORTED_REQUEST_THRESHOLD

When the database determines that there is not enough memory in the shared pool to satisfy a given request, it will begin aging objects out until there is enough memory. If enough objects are aged out, this can have a performance impact on other database sessions. The ABORTED_REQUEST_THRESHOLD can be used to remedy this. It is defined with

PROCEDURE ABORTED_REQUEST_THRESHOLD(*threshold_size* NUMBER);

Once this procedure is called, Oracle will not start aging objects from the pool unless at least *threshold_size* bytes is needed.

Summary

We have continued our discussion of three types of named PL/SQL blocks in this chapter—procedures, functions, and packages. This included the differences between local and stored subprograms, and how dependencies among stored subprograms work. We also discussed how to call stored subprograms from SQL statements. We closed the chapter with a discussion of the DBMS_SHARED_POOL package. In the next chapter, we will cover a fourth type of named PL/SQL block—database triggers.

CHAPTER
11

Database Triggers

he fourth type of named PL/SQL block is the trigger. Triggers share many of the same characteristics as subprograms (which we have examined in the previous two chapters), but they have some significant differences. In this chapter, we will examine how to create different types of triggers and discuss some possible applications.

Types of Triggers

Triggers are similar to procedures or functions, in that they are named PL/SQL blocks with declarative, executable, and exception handling sections. Like packages, triggers must be stored as stand-alone objects in the database and cannot be local to a block or package. As we have seen in the past two chapters, a procedure is executed explicitly from another block via a procedure call, which can also pass arguments. On the other hand, a trigger is executed implicitly whenever the triggering event happens, and a trigger doesn't accept arguments. The act of executing a trigger is known as *firing* the trigger. The triggering event can be a DML (INSERT, UPDATE, or DELETE) operation on a database table or certain kinds of views. Oracle8*i* extended this functionality by allowing triggers to fire on a system event, such as database startup or shutdown, and certain kinds of DDL operations. We will discuss the triggering events in detail later in this chapter.

Triggers can be used for many things, including the following:

- Maintaining complex integrity constraints not possible through declarative constraints enabled at table creation

- Auditing information in a table by recording the changes made and who made them

- Automatically signaling other programs that action needs to take place when changes are made to a table

- Publishing information about various events in a publish-subscribe environment

There are three main kinds of triggers: DML, instead-of, and system triggers. In the following sections, we will introduce each kind. We will see more details later in the section "Creating Triggers."

NOTE
*Oracle8i and higher allow triggers to be written in
either PL/SQL or other languages that can be called
as external routines. See the section "Trigger Bodies"
later in this chapter for more information (as well as
Chapter 12).*

DML Triggers

A *DML trigger* is fired by a DML statement, and the type of statement determines
the type of the DML trigger. DML triggers can be defined for INSERT, UPDATE, or
DELETE operations. They can be fired before or after the operation, and they can
also fire on row or statement operations.

As an example, suppose we want to track statistics about different majors,
including the number of students registered and the total credits taken. We are going
to store these results in the major_stats table:

```
-- Available online as part of tables.sql
CREATE TABLE major_stats (
  major           VARCHAR2(30),
  total_credits   NUMBER,
  total_students NUMBER);
```

In order to keep major_stats up-to-date, we can create a trigger on
students that will update major_stats every time students is modified. The
UpdateMajorStats trigger, shown next, does this. After any DML operation on
students, the trigger will execute. The body of the trigger queries students and
updates major_stats with the current statistics.

```
-- Available online as UpdateMajorStats.sql
CREATE OR REPLACE TRIGGER UpdateMajorStats
  /* Keeps the major_stats table up-to-date with changes made
     to the students table. */
  AFTER INSERT OR DELETE OR UPDATE ON students
DECLARE
  CURSOR c_Statistics IS
    SELECT major, COUNT(*) total_students,
           SUM(current_credits) total_credits
      FROM students
      GROUP BY major;
BEGIN
  /* First delete from major_stats.  This will clear the
     statistics, and is necessary to account for the deletion
     of all students in a given major. */
  DELETE FROM major_stats;
```

```
/* Now loop through each major, and insert the appropriate row into
   major_stats. */
FOR v_StatsRecord in c_Statistics LOOP
  INSERT INTO major_stats (major, total_credits, total_students)
    VALUES (v_StatsRecord.major, v_StatsRecord.total_credits,
            v_StatsRecord.total_students);
END LOOP;
END UpdateMajorStats;
```

A statement trigger can be fired for more than one type of triggering statement. For example, `UpdateMajorStats` is fired on INSERT, UPDATE, and DELETE statements. The triggering event specifies one or more of the DML operations that should fire the trigger.

Instead-Of Triggers

Oracle **8** and higher | Oracle8 provided an additional kind of trigger. *Instead-of* triggers can be defined on views (either relational or object) only. Unlike a DML trigger, which executes in addition to the DML operation, an instead-of trigger will execute instead of the DML statement that fired it. Instead-of triggers must be row level. For example, consider the `classes_rooms` view:

```
-- Available online as part of insteadOf.sql
CREATE OR REPLACE VIEW classes_rooms AS
  SELECT department, course, building, room_number
  FROM rooms, classes
  WHERE rooms.room_id = classes.room_id;
```

It is illegal to INSERT into this view directly, because it is a join of two tables and the INSERT requires that both underlying tables be modified, as the following SQL*Plus session shows:

```
-- Available online as part of insteadOf.sql
SQL> INSERT INTO classes_rooms (department, course, building,
                                room_number)
  2    VALUES ('MUS', 100, 'Music Building', 200);
INSERT INTO classes_rooms (department, course, building, room_number)
                                                 *
ERROR at line 1:
ORA-01776: cannot modify more than one base table through a join view
```

However, we can create an instead-of trigger which does the correct thing for an INSERT, namely to update the underlying tables:

```
-- Available online as part of insteadOf.sql
CREATE TRIGGER ClassesRoomsInsert
  INSTEAD OF INSERT ON classes_rooms
```

```
DECLARE
  v_roomID rooms.room_id%TYPE;
BEGIN
  -- First determine the room ID
  SELECT room_id
    INTO v_roomID
    FROM rooms
    WHERE building = :new.building
    AND room_number = :new.room_number;

  -- And now update the class
  UPDATE CLASSES
    SET room_id = v_roomID
    WHERE department = :new.department
    AND course = :new.course;
END ClassesRoomsInsert;
```

With the `ClassesRoomsInsert` trigger in place, the INSERT statement succeeds and does the correct thing.

NOTE

As currently written, `ClassesRoomsInsert` does not have any error checking. We will rectify this later in this chapter in the section "Creating Instead-Of Triggers."

System Triggers

Oracle8*i* and higher provide a third kind of trigger. A *system trigger* fires when a system event, such as database startup or shutdown, occurs, rather than on a DML operation on a table. A system trigger can also be fired on DDL operations, such as table creation. For example, suppose we want to record whenever a data dictionary object is created. We can do this by creating a table as follows:

```
-- Available online as part of LogCreations.sql
CREATE TABLE ddl_creations (
  user_id        VARCHAR2(30),
  object_type    VARCHAR2(20),
  object_name    VARCHAR2(30),
  object_owner   VARCHAR2(30),
  creation_date DATE);
```

Once this table is available, we can create a system trigger to record the relevant information. The `LogCreations` trigger does just that—after every CREATE operation on the current schema, it records information about the object just created in `ddl_creations`.

```
-- Available online as part of LogCreations.sql
CREATE OR REPLACE TRIGGER LogCreations
  AFTER CREATE ON SCHEMA
BEGIN
  INSERT INTO ddl_creations (user_id, object_type, object_name,
                             object_owner, creation_date)
    VALUES (USER, SYS.DICTIONARY_OBJ_TYPE, SYS.DICTIONARY_OBJ_NAME,
            SYS.DICTIONARY_OBJ_OWNER, SYSDATE);
END LogCreations;
```

Creating Triggers

Regardless of the type, all triggers are created using the same syntax. The general syntax for creating a trigger is

```
CREATE [OR REPLACE] TRIGGER trigger_name
  {BEFORE | AFTER | INSTEAD OF} triggering_event
[referencing_clause]
  [WHEN trigger_condition]
  [FOR EACH ROW]
  trigger_body;
```

where *trigger_name* is the name of the trigger, *triggering_event* specifies the event that fires the trigger (possibly including a specific table or view), and *trigger_body* is the main code for the trigger. The *referencing_clause* is used to refer to the data in the row currently being modified by a different name. The *trigger_condition* in the WHEN clause, if present, is evaluated first, and the body of the trigger is executed only when this condition evaluates to TRUE. We will see more examples of different kinds of triggers in the following sections.

NOTE
The trigger body cannot exceed 32K. If you have a trigger that exceeds this size, you can reduce it by moving some of the code to separately compiled packages or stored procedures, and calling these from the trigger body. It is generally a good idea to keep trigger bodies small, because of the frequency with which they execute.

Creating DML Triggers

A DML trigger is fired on an INSERT, UPDATE, or DELETE operation on a database table. It can be fired either before or after the statement executes, and can be fired once per affected row, or once per statement. The combination of these factors determines the type of the trigger. There are a total of 12 possible types: 3 statements × 2 timing × 2 levels. For example, all of the following are valid DML trigger types:

- Before UPDATE statement level

- After INSERT row level

- Before DELETE row level

Table 11-1 summarizes the various options. A trigger can also be fired for more than one kind of DML statement on a given table—INSERT and UPDATE, for example. Any code in the trigger will be executed along with the triggering statement itself, as part of the same transaction.

Category	Values	Comments
Statement	INSERT, DELETE, or UPDATE	Defines which kind of DML statement causes the trigger to fire.
Timing	BEFORE or AFTER	Defines whether the trigger fires before or after the statement is executed.
Level	Row or statement	If the trigger is a row-level trigger, it fires once for each row affected by the triggering statement. If the trigger is a statement-level trigger, it fires once, either before or after the statement. A row-level trigger is identified by the FOR EACH ROW clause in the trigger definition.

TABLE 11-1. *Types of DML Triggers*

A table can have any number of triggers defined on it, including more than one of a given DML type. For example, you can define two after DELETE statement-level triggers. All triggers of the same type will fire sequentially. (For more information on the order of trigger firing, see the following section.)

TIP
Prior to PL/SQL 2.1 (Oracle7 Release 7.1), a table could have only one trigger of each type defined on it, for a maximum of 12. Thus, the COMPATIBLE initialization parameter must be 7.1 or higher (which it almost certainly will be) to have duplicate triggers of the same type on one table.

The triggering event for a DML trigger specifies the name of the table (and column) on which the trigger will fire. In Oracle8i and higher, a trigger can also fire on a column of a nested table. See Chapter 8 for more information on nested tables.

Order of DML Trigger Firing

Triggers are fired as the DML statement is executed. The algorithm for executing a DML statement is given here:

1. Execute the before statement-level triggers, if present.

2. For each row affected by the statement:

   A. Execute the before row-level triggers, if present.

   B. Execute the statement itself.

   C. Execute the after row-level triggers, if present.

3. Execute the after statement-level triggers, if present.

To illustrate this, suppose we create all four kinds of UPDATE triggers on the `classes` table—before and after, statement and row level. We will create three before row triggers and two after statement triggers as well, as follows:

```
-- Available online as firingOrder.sql
CREATE SEQUENCE trig_seq
  START WITH 1
  INCREMENT BY 1;

CREATE OR REPLACE PACKAGE TrigPackage AS
  -- Global counter for use in the triggers
  v_Counter NUMBER;
END TrigPackage;
```

```
CREATE OR REPLACE TRIGGER ClassesBStatement
  BEFORE UPDATE ON classes
BEGIN
  -- Reset the counter first.
  TrigPackage.v_Counter := 0;

  INSERT INTO temp_table (num_col, char_col)
    VALUES (trig_seq.NEXTVAL,
      'Before Statement: counter = ' || TrigPackage.v_Counter);

  -- And now increment it for the next trigger.
  TrigPackage.v_Counter := TrigPackage.v_Counter + 1;
END ClassesBStatement;

CREATE OR REPLACE TRIGGER ClassesAStatement1
  AFTER UPDATE ON classes
BEGIN
  INSERT INTO temp_table (num_col, char_col)
    VALUES (trig_seq.NEXTVAL,
      'After Statement 1: counter = ' || TrigPackage.v_Counter);

  -- Increment for the next trigger.
  TrigPackage.v_Counter := TrigPackage.v_Counter + 1;
END ClassesAStatement1;

CREATE OR REPLACE TRIGGER ClassesAStatement2
  AFTER UPDATE ON classes
BEGIN
  INSERT INTO temp_table (num_col, char_col)
    VALUES (trig_seq.NEXTVAL,
      'After Statement 2: counter = ' || TrigPackage.v_Counter);

  -- Increment for the next trigger.
  TrigPackage.v_Counter := TrigPackage.v_Counter + 1;
END ClassesAStatement2;

CREATE OR REPLACE TRIGGER ClassesBRow1
  BEFORE UPDATE ON classes
  FOR EACH ROW
BEGIN
  INSERT INTO temp_table (num_col, char_col)
    VALUES (trig_seq.NEXTVAL,
      'Before Row 1: counter = ' || TrigPackage.v_Counter);

  -- Increment for the next trigger.
  TrigPackage.v_Counter := TrigPackage.v_Counter + 1;
END ClassesBRow1;
```

```
CREATE OR REPLACE TRIGGER ClassesBRow2
  BEFORE UPDATE ON classes
  FOR EACH ROW
BEGIN
  INSERT INTO temp_table (num_col, char_col)
    VALUES (trig_seq.NEXTVAL,
      'Before Row 2: counter = ' || TrigPackage.v_Counter);

  -- Increment for the next trigger.
  TrigPackage.v_Counter := TrigPackage.v_Counter + 1;
END ClassesBRow2;

CREATE OR REPLACE TRIGGER ClassesBRow3
  BEFORE UPDATE ON classes
  FOR EACH ROW
BEGIN
  INSERT INTO temp_table (num_col, char_col)
    VALUES (trig_seq.NEXTVAL,
      'Before Row 3: counter = ' || TrigPackage.v_Counter);

  -- Increment for the next trigger.
  TrigPackage.v_Counter := TrigPackage.v_Counter + 1;
END ClassesBRow3;

CREATE OR REPLACE TRIGGER ClassesARow
  AFTER UPDATE ON classes
  FOR EACH ROW
BEGIN
  INSERT INTO temp_table (num_col, char_col)
    VALUES (trig_seq.NEXTVAL,
      'After Row: counter = ' || TrigPackage.v_Counter);

  -- Increment for the next trigger.
  TrigPackage.v_Counter := TrigPackage.v_Counter + 1;
END ClassesARow;
```

Suppose we now issue the following UPDATE statement:

```
-- Available online as part of firingOrder.sql
UPDATE classes
  SET num_credits = 4
  WHERE department IN ('HIS', 'CS');
```

This statement affects four rows. The before and after statement-level triggers are each executed once, and the before and after row-level triggers are each executed four times. If we then select from `temp_table`, we get

`-- Available online as part of firingOrder.sql`
```
SQL> SELECT * FROM temp_table
  2    ORDER BY num_col;
  NUM_COL CHAR_COL
--------- ------------------------------------
        1 Before Statement: counter = 0
        2 Before Row 3: counter = 1
        3 Before Row 2: counter = 2
        4 Before Row 1: counter = 3
        5 After Row: counter = 4
        6 Before Row 3: counter = 5
        7 Before Row 2: counter = 6
        8 Before Row 1: counter = 7
        9 After Row: counter = 8
       10 Before Row 3: counter = 9
       11 Before Row 2: counter = 10
       12 Before Row 1: counter = 11
       13 After Row: counter = 12
       14 Before Row 3: counter = 13
       15 Before Row 2: counter = 14
       16 Before Row 1: counter = 15
       17 After Row: counter = 16
       18 After Statement 2: counter = 17
       19 After Statement 1: counter = 18
```

As each trigger is fired, it will see the changes made by the earlier triggers, as well as any database changes made by the statement so far. This can be seen by the counter value printed by each trigger. (See Chapter 10 for more information about using packaged variables.)

The order in which triggers of the same type are fired is not defined. As in the above example, each trigger will see changes made by earlier triggers. If the order is important, combine all of the operations into one trigger.

NOTE
When you create a snapshot log for a table, Oracle will automatically create an after row trigger for the table, that will update the log after every DML statement. You should be aware of this if you need to create an additional after row trigger on that table. There are also additional restrictions on triggers and snapshots (known as materialized views in Oracle9i). For more information, see Oracle Server Replication.

Correlation Identifiers in Row-Level Triggers

A row-level trigger fires once per row processed by the triggering statement. Inside the trigger, you can access the data in the row that is currently being processed. This is accomplished through two correlation identifiers—`:old` and `:new`. A *correlation identifier* is a special kind of PL/SQL bind variable. The colon in front of each indicates that they are bind variables, in the sense of host variables used in embedded PL/SQL, and indicates that they are not regular PL/SQL variables. The PL/SQL compiler will treat them as records of type

triggering_table%ROWTYPE

where *triggering_table* is the table for which the trigger is defined. Thus, a reference such as

:new.*field*

will be valid only if *field* is a field in the triggering table. The meanings of `:old` and `:new` are described in Table 11-2. Although syntactically they are treated as records, in reality they are not (this is discussed in the section "Pseudorecords"). `:old` and `:new` are also known as *pseudorecords*, for this reason.

NOTE
`:old` is undefined for INSERT statements, and `:new` is undefined for DELETE statements. The PL/SQL compiler will not generate an error if you use `:old` in an INSERT or `:new` in a DELETE, but the field values of both will be NULL.

| Oracle8*i* and higher | Oracle8*i* defined an additional correlation identifier—`:parent`. If the trigger is defined on a nested table, `:old` and `:new` refer to the rows in the nested table, whereas `:parent` refers to the current row of the parent table. For more information on using `parent:`, see the Oracle documentation.

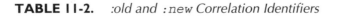

Triggering Statement	:old	:new
INSERT	Undefined—all fields are NULL.	Values that will be inserted when the statement is complete.

TABLE 11-2. *:old and :new Correlation Identifiers*

Triggering Statement	:old	:new
UPDATE	Original values for the row before the update.	New values that will be updated when the statement is complete.
DELETE	Original values before the row is deleted.	Undefined—all fields are NULL.

TABLE 11-2. `:old` and `:new` *Correlation Identifiers* (continued)

Using :old and :new   The GenerateStudentID trigger, shown next, uses
:new. It is a before INSERT trigger, and its purpose is to fill in the ID field of
students with a value generated from the student_sequence sequence.

```
-- Available online as part of GenerateStudentID.sql
CREATE OR REPLACE TRIGGER GenerateStudentID
  BEFORE INSERT OR UPDATE ON students
  FOR EACH ROW
BEGIN
  /* Fill in the ID field of students with the next value from
     student_sequence. Since ID is a column in students, :new.ID
     is a valid reference. */
  SELECT student_sequence.NEXTVAL
    INTO :new.ID
    FROM dual;
END GenerateStudentID;
```

GenerateStudentID actually modifies the value of :new.ID. This is one of
the useful features of :new—when the statement is actually executed, whatever
values are in :new will be used. With GenerateStudentID, we can issue an
INSERT statement such as

```
-- Available online as part of GenerateStudentID.sql
INSERT INTO students (first_name, last_name)
  VALUES ('Lolita', 'Lazarus');
```

without generating an error. Even though we haven't specified a value for the primary-
key column ID (which is required), the trigger will supply it. In fact, if we do specify a
value for ID, it will be ignored because the trigger changes it. If we issue

```
-- Available online as part of GenerateStudentID.sql
INSERT INTO students (ID, first_name, last_name)
  VALUES (-7, 'Zelda', 'Zoom');
```

the ID column will be populated from `student_sequence.NEXTVAL`, rather than containing -7.

As a result of this, you cannot change `:new` in an after row-level trigger, because the statement has already been processed. In general, `:new` is modified only in a before row-level trigger, and `:old` is never modified, only read from.

The `:new` and `:old` records are only valid inside row-level triggers. If you try to reference either inside a statement-level trigger, you will get a compile error. Because a statement-level trigger executes once—even if there are many rows processed by the statement— `:old` and `:new` have no meaning. Which row would they refer to?

Pseudorecords   Although `:new` and `:old` are syntactically treated as records of *triggering_table*%ROWTYPE, in reality they are not. As a result, operations that would normally be valid on records are not valid for `:new` and `:old`. For example, they cannot be assigned as entire records. Only the individual fields within them may be assigned. The following example illustrates this:

```
-- Available online as pseudoRecords.sql
CREATE OR REPLACE TRIGGER TempDelete
  BEFORE DELETE ON temp_table
  FOR EACH ROW
DECLARE
  v_TempRec temp_table%ROWTYPE;
BEGIN
  /* This is not a legal assignment, since :old is not truly
     a record. */
  v_TempRec := :old;

  /* We can accomplish the same thing, however, by assigning
     the fields individually. */
  v_TempRec.char_col := :old.char_col;
  v_TempRec.num_col := :old.num_col;
END TempDelete;
```

In addition, `:old` and `:new` cannot be passed to procedures or functions that take arguments of *triggering_table*%ROWTYPE.

REFERENCING Clause   If desired, you can use the REFERENCING clause to specify a different name for `:old` and `:new`. This clause is found after the triggering event, before the WHEN clause, with syntax

REFERENCING [OLD AS *old_name*] [NEW AS *new_name*]

In the trigger body, you can use :*old_name* and :*new_name* instead of :old and :new. Note that the correlation identifiers do *not* have colons within the REFERENCING clause. Below is an alternate version of the GenerateStudentID trigger, which uses REFERENCING to refer to :new as :new_student:

-- **Available online as part of GenerateStudentID.sql**
```
CREATE OR REPLACE TRIGGER GenerateStudentID
  BEFORE INSERT OR UPDATE ON students
  REFERENCING new AS new_student
  FOR EACH ROW
BEGIN
  /* Fill in the ID field of students with the next value from
     student_sequence. Since ID is a column in students,
      :new_student.ID is a valid reference. */
  SELECT student_sequence.nextval
    INTO :new_student.ID
    FROM dual;
END GenerateStudentID;
```

The WHEN Clause

The WHEN clause is valid for row-level triggers only. If present, the trigger body will be executed only for those rows that meet the condition specified by the WHEN clause. The WHEN clause looks like

> WHEN *trigger_condition*

where *trigger_condition* is a Boolean expression. It will be evaluated for each row. The :new and :old records can be referenced inside *trigger_condition* as well, but like REFERENCING, the colon is *not* used there. The colon is only valid in the trigger body. For example, the body of the CheckCredits trigger is only executed if the current credits being taken by a student are more than 20:

```
CREATE OR REPLACE TRIGGER CheckCredits
  BEFORE INSERT OR UPDATE OF current_credits ON students
  FOR EACH ROW
  WHEN (new.current_credits > 20)
BEGIN
  /* Trigger body goes here. */
END;
```

CheckCredits could also be written as follows:

```
CREATE OR REPLACE TRIGGER CheckCredits
    BEFORE INSERT OR UPDATE OF current_credits ON students
    FOR EACH ROW
BEGIN
    IF :new.current_credits > 20 THEN
      /* Trigger body goes here. */
    END IF;
END;
```

Trigger Predicates: INSERTING, UPDATING, and DELETING

The UpdateMajorStats trigger earlier in this chapter is an INSERT, UPDATE, and DELETE trigger. Inside a trigger of this type (which will fire for different kinds of DML statements) there are three Boolean functions that you can use to determine what the operation is. These predicates are INSERTING, UPDATING, and DELETING. Their behavior is described in the following table.

Predicate	Behavior
INSERTING	TRUE if the triggering statement is an INSERT; FALSE otherwise.
UPDATING	TRUE if the triggering statement is an UPDATE; FALSE otherwise.
DELETING	TRUE if the triggering statement is a DELETE; FALSE otherwise.

NOTE
Oracle8i defined additional functions that can be called from within a trigger body, similar to trigger predicates. See the section "Event Attribute Functions" later in this chapter for more details.

The LogRSChanges trigger uses these predicates to record all changes made to the registered_students table. In addition to the change, it records the user who makes the change. The records are kept in the RS_audit table, which looks like this:

```
-- Available online as part of tables.sql
CREATE TABLE RS_audit (
    change_type     CHAR(1)     NOT NULL,
    changed_by      VARCHAR2(8) NOT NULL,
```

```
timestamp       DATE        NOT NULL,
old_student_id  NUMBER(5),
old_department  CHAR(3),
old_course      NUMBER(3),
old_grade       CHAR(1),
new_student_id  NUMBER(5),
new_department  CHAR(3),
new_course      NUMBER(3),
new_grade       CHAR(1)
);
```

LogRSChanges is created with:

-- **Available online as LogRSChanges.sql**

```
CREATE OR REPLACE TRIGGER LogRSChanges
  BEFORE INSERT OR DELETE OR UPDATE ON registered_students
  FOR EACH ROW
DECLARE
  v_ChangeType CHAR(1);
BEGIN
  /* Use 'I' for an INSERT, 'D' for DELETE, and 'U' for UPDATE. */
  IF INSERTING THEN
    v_ChangeType := 'I';
  ELSIF UPDATING THEN
    v_ChangeType := 'U';
  ELSE
    v_ChangeType := 'D';
  END IF;

  /* Record all the changes made to registered_students in
     RS_audit. Use SYSDATE to generate the timestamp, and
     USER to return the userid of the current user. */
  INSERT INTO RS_audit
    (change_type, changed_by, timestamp,
     old_student_id, old_department, old_course, old_grade,
     new_student_id, new_department, new_course, new_grade)
  VALUES
    (v_ChangeType, USER, SYSDATE,
     :old.student_id, :old.department, :old.course, :old.grade,
     :new.student_id, :new.department, :new.course, :new.grade);
END LogRSChanges;
```

Triggers are commonly used for auditing, as in LogRSChanges. Although this is available as part of the database, triggers allow for more customized and flexible recording. LogRSChanges could be modified, for example, to record changes only made by certain people. It could also check to see if users have permission to make changes and raise an error (with RAISE_APPLICATION_ERROR) if they don't.

Creating Instead-Of Triggers

Unlike DML triggers, which fire in addition to the INSERT, UPDATE, or DELETE operation (either before or after them), instead-of triggers fire instead of a DML operation. Also, instead-of triggers can be defined only on views, whereas DML triggers are defined on tables. Instead-of triggers are used in two cases:

- To allow a view that would otherwise not be modifiable to be modified

- To modify the columns of a nested table column in a view

We will discuss the first case in this section. For more information on nested tables, see Chapter 8.

Modifiable versus Nonmodifiable Views

A *modifiable view* is one against which you can issue a DML statement. In general, a view is modifiable if it does not contain any of the following:

- Set operators (UNION, UNION ALL, MINUS)

- Aggregate functions (SUM, AVG, etc.)

- GROUP BY, CONNECT BY, or START WITH clauses

- The DISTINCT operator

- Joins

There are, however, some views that contain joins that are modifiable. In general, a join view is modifiable if the DML operation on it modifies only one base table at a time, and if the DML statement meets the conditions in Table 11-3. (For more information on modifiable vs. nonmodifiable join views, see *Oracle Concepts.*) If a view is nonmodifiable, you can write an instead-of trigger on it that does the correct thing, thus allowing it to be modified. An instead-of trigger can also be written on a modifiable view, if additional processing is required.

Table 11-3 refers to key-preserved tables. A table is *key-preserved* if, after a join with another table, the keys in the original table are also keys in the resultant join. For more details on key-preserved tables, see the *Application Developer's Guide— Fundamentals.*

DML Operation	Permitted if
INSERT	The statement does not refer, implicitly or explicitly, to the columns of a nonkey-preserved table.
UPDATE	The updated columns map to columns of a key-preserved table.
DELETE	There is exactly one key-preserved table in the join.

TABLE 11-3. *Modifiable Join Views*

Instead-Of Example

Consider the `classes_rooms` view that we saw earlier in this chapter:

```
-- Available online as part of insteadOf.sql
CREATE OR REPLACE VIEW classes_rooms AS
  SELECT department, course, building, room_number
  FROM rooms, classes
  WHERE rooms.room_id = classes.room_id;
```

As we saw earlier, it is illegal to INSERT into this view. Although it is legal to issue an UPDATE or DELETE against this view, they do not necessarily do the correct thing. For example, a DELETE from `classes_rooms` will delete the corresponding rows from `classes`. What is the correct DML behavior for `classes_rooms`? This could vary, depending on your business rules. Suppose, however, that they have the following meanings:

Operation	Meaning
INSERT	Assign the newly inserted class to the newly inserted room. This results in an update of `classes`.
UPDATE	Change the room assigned to a class. This can result in an update of either `classes` or `rooms`, depending on which columns of `classes_rooms` are updated.
DELETE	Clear the room ID from the deleted class. This results in an update of `classes`, to set the ID to NULL.

The `ClassesRoomsInstead` trigger enforces the above rules and allows DML operations to be performed correctly against `classes_rooms`. This is a more complete version of the `ClassesRoomsInsert` trigger that we saw in the introductory sections of this chapter:

```
-- Available online as ClassesRoomInstead.sql
CREATE OR REPLACE TRIGGER ClassesRoomsInstead
  INSTEAD OF INSERT OR UPDATE OR DELETE ON classes_rooms
  FOR EACH ROW
DECLARE
  v_roomID rooms.room_id%TYPE;
  v_UpdatingClasses BOOLEAN := FALSE;
  v_UpdatingRooms BOOLEAN := FALSE;

  -- Local function that returns the room ID, given a building
  -- and room number.  This function will raise ORA-20000 if the
  -- building and room number are not found.
  FUNCTION getRoomID(p_Building IN rooms.building%TYPE,
                     p_Room IN rooms.room_number%TYPE)
    RETURN rooms.room_id%TYPE IS

    v_RoomID rooms.room_id%TYPE;
  BEGIN
    SELECT room_id
      INTO v_RoomID
      FROM rooms
      WHERE building = p_Building
      AND room_number = p_Room;
    RETURN v_RoomID;
  EXCEPTION
    WHEN NO_DATA_FOUND THEN
      RAISE_APPLICATION_ERROR(-20000, 'No matching room');
  END getRoomID;

  -- Local procedure which checks if the class identified by
  -- p_Department and p_Course exists.  If not, it raises
  -- ORA-20001.
  PROCEDURE verifyClass(p_Department IN classes.department%TYPE,
                        p_Course IN classes.course%TYPE) IS
    v_Dummy NUMBER;
  BEGIN
    SELECT 0
      INTO v_Dummy
      FROM classes
      WHERE department = p_Department
      AND course = p_Course;
  EXCEPTION
    WHEN NO_DATA_FOUND THEN
      RAISE_APPLICATION_ERROR(-20001,
        p_Department || ' ' || p_Course || ' doesn''t exist');
```

```
    END verifyClass;

BEGIN
    IF INSERTING THEN
      -- This essentially assigns a class to a given room.  The logic
      -- here is the same as the "updating rooms" case below:  First,
      -- determine the room ID:
        v_RoomID := getRoomID(:new.building, :new.room_number);

        -- And then update classes with the new ID.
        UPDATE CLASSES
          SET room_id = v_RoomID
          WHERE department = :new.department
          AND course = :new.course;


    ELSIF UPDATING THEN
      -- Determine if we are updating classes, or updating rooms.
      v_UpdatingClasses := (:new.department != :old.department) OR
                           (:new.course != :old.course);
      v_UpdatingRooms := (:new.building != :old.building) OR
                         (:new.room_number != :old.room_number);

      IF (v_UpdatingClasses) THEN
        -- In this case, we are changing the class assigned for a
        -- given room.  First make sure the new class exists.
        verifyClass(:new.department, :new.course);

        -- Get the room ID,
        v_RoomID := getRoomID(:old.building, :old.room_number);

        -- Then clear the room for the old class,
        UPDATE classes
          SET room_ID = NULL
          WHERE department = :old.department
          AND course = :old.course;

        -- And finally assign the old room to the new class.
        UPDATE classes
          SET room_ID = v_RoomID
          WHERE department = :new.department
          AND course = :new.course;
      END IF;

      IF v_UpdatingRooms THEN
        -- Here, we are changing the room for a given class.  This
        -- logic is the same as the "inserting" case above, except
        -- that classes is updated with :old instead of :new.
        -- First, determine the new room ID.
        v_RoomID := getRoomID(:new.building, :new.room_number);
```

```
      -- And then update classes with the new ID.
      UPDATE CLASSES
         SET room_id = v_RoomID
         WHERE department = :old.department
         AND course = :old.course;
      END IF;

   ELSE
      -- Here, we want to clear the class assigned to the room,
      -- without actually removing rows from the underlying tables.
      UPDATE classes
         SET room_ID = NULL
         WHERE department = :old.department
         AND course = :old.course;
      END IF;
END ClassesRoomsInstead;
```

NOTE
The FOR EACH ROW clause is optional for an instead-of trigger. All instead-of triggers are row level, whether or not the clause is present.

`ClassesRoomsInstead` uses trigger predicates to determine the DML operation being performed, and to take the appropriate action. Figure 11-1 contains the original contents for `classes`, `rooms`, and `classes_rooms`. Suppose we then issue the following INSERT statement:

classes			rooms			classes_rooms			
Dept.	Course	Room ID	Room ID	Building	Room Number	Department	Course	Building	Room Number
HIS	101	20000	20000	Building 7	201	HIS	101	Building 7	201
CS	101	20001	20001	Building 6	101	CS	101	Building 6	101
ECN	203	20002	20002	Building 6	150	ECN	203	Building 6	150
CS	102	20003	20003	Building 6	160	CS	102	Building 6	160
HIS	301	20004	20004	Building 6	170	HIS	301	Building 6	170
MUS	410	20005	20005	Music Building	100	MUS	410	Music Building	100
MUS	100								
ECN	101	20007	20006	Music Building	200	ECN	101	Building 7	300
NUT	307	20008				NUT	307	Building 7	310
			20007	Building 7	300				
			20008	Building 7	310				

FIGURE 11-1. *Original Contents of* `classes`, `rooms`, *and* `classes_rooms`

```
-- Available online as part of ClassesRoomsInstead.sql
INSERT INTO classes_rooms
   VALUES ('MUS', 100, 'Music Building', 200);
```

The trigger causes `classes` to be updated to reflect the new room assignment. This is illustrated by Figure 11-2. Now, suppose we issue the following UPDATE statement:

```
-- Available online as part of ClassesRoomsInstead.sql
UPDATE classes_rooms
   SET department = 'NUT', course = 307
   WHERE building = 'Building 7' AND room_number = 201;
```

`classes` has been updated again, to reflect the new changes. History 101 now doesn't have a room assigned, and Nutrition 307 has the room originally assigned to History 101. This is illustrated by Figure 11-3. Finally, suppose we issue the following DELETE statement:

```
-- Available online as part of ClassesRoomsInstead.sql
DELETE FROM classes_rooms
   WHERE building = 'Building 6';
```

The updates to `classes` now set `room_ID` to NULL for those classes originally in Building 6, as illustrated by Figure 11-4. Note that throughout all the above DML statements, `rooms` remained unchanged, and only `classes` was updated.

classes			rooms			classes_rooms			
Dept.	Course	Room ID	Room ID	Building	Room Number	Department	Course	Building	Room Number
HIS	101	20000	20000	Building 7	201	HIS	101	Building 7	201
CS	101	20001	20001	Building 6	101	CS	101	Building 6	101
ECN	203	20002	20002	Building 6	150	ECN	203	Building 6	150
CS	102	20003	20003	Building 6	160	CS	102	Building 6	160
HIS	301	20004	20004	Building 6	170	HIS	301	Building 6	170
MUS	410	20005	20005	Music Building	100	MUS	410	Music Building	100
MUS	**100**	**20006**	20006	Music Building	200	ECN	101	Building 7	300
ECN	101	20007	20007	Building 7	300	NUT	307	Building 7	310
NUT	307	20008	20008	Building 7	310	**MUS**	**100**	**Music Building**	**200**

FIGURE 11-2. *Contents after INSERT*

classes			rooms			classes_rooms			
Dept.	Course	Room ID	Room ID	Building	Room Number	Department	Course	Building	Room Number
HIS	101	20000	20000	Building 7	201	HIS	301	Building 6	170
CS	101	20001	20001	Building 6	101	CS	101	Building 6	101
ECN	203	20002	20002	Building 6	150	ECN	203	Building 6	150
CS	102	20003	20003	Building 6	160	CS	102	Building 6	160
HIS	301	20004	20004	Building 6	170	MUS	410	Music Building	100
MUS	410	20005	20005	Music Building	100				
MUS	100	20006				ECN	101	Building 7	300
ECN	101	20007	20006	Music Building	200	**NUT**	**307**	**Building 7**	**210**
HIS	**307**					MUS	100	Music Building	200
			20007	Building 7	300				
			20008	Building 7	310				

FIGURE 11-3. *Contents after UPDATE*

Creating System Triggers

As we have seen in the previous sections, both DML and instead-of triggers fire on (or instead of) DML events, namely INSERT, UPDATE, or DELETE statements. System

classes			rooms			classes_rooms			
Dept.	Course	Room ID	Room ID	Building	Room Number	Department	Course	Building	Room Number
NUT	307	20000	20000	Building 7	201	MUS	410	Music Building	100
CS	**101**		20001	Building 6	101				
ECN	**203**		20002	Building 6	150	ECN	101	Building 7	300
CS	**102**		20003	Building 6	160	NUT	307	Building 7	310
HIS	**301**		20004	Building 6	170	MUS	100	Music Building	200
MUS	410	20005	20005	Music Building	100				
MUS	100	20006							
ECN	101	20007	20006	Music Building	200				
HIS	101								
			20007	Building 7	300				
			20008	Building 7	310				

FIGURE 11-4. *Contents after DELETE*

triggers, on the other hand, fire on two different kinds of events: DDL or database. *DDL events* include CREATE, ALTER, or DROP statements, whereas *database events* include startup/shutdown of the server, logon/logoff of a user, and a server error. The syntax for creating a system trigger is as follows:

```
CREATE [OR REPLACE] TRIGGER [schema.]trigger_name
   {BEFORE | AFTER}
   {ddl_event_list | database_event_list}
   ON {DATABASE | [schema.]SCHEMA}
   [when_clause]
   trigger_body;
```

where *ddl_event_list* is one or more DDL events (separated by the OR keyword), and *database_event_list* is one or more database events (separated by the OR keyword).

Table 11-4 describes the DDL and database events, along with their allowed timings (BEFORE or AFTER). You cannot create an instead-of system trigger. There is no database event for TRUNCATE.

NOTE
You must have the ADMINISTER DATABASE TRIGGER system privilege in order to create a system trigger. See the section "Trigger Privileges" later in this chapter for more information.

Event	Timings Allowed	Description
STARTUP	AFTER	Fired when an instance is started up.
SHUTDOWN	BEFORE	Fired when an instance is shut down. This event may not fire if the database is shutdown abnormally (as in a shutdown abort).
SERVERERROR	AFTER	Fired whenever an error occurs.

TABLE 11-4. *System DDL and Database Events*

Event	Timings Allowed	Description
LOGON	AFTER	Fired after a user has successfully connected to the database.
LOGOFF	BEFORE	Fired at the start of a user logoff.
CREATE	BEFORE, AFTER	Fired before or after a schema object is created.
DROP	BEFORE, AFTER	Fired before or after a schema object is dropped.
ALTER	BEFORE, AFTER	Fired before or after a schema object is altered.

TABLE 11-4. *System DDL and Database Events* (continued)

Database versus Schema Triggers

A system trigger can be defined at the database level or a schema level. A database-level trigger will fire whenever the triggering event occurs, whereas a schema-level trigger will fire only when the triggering event occurs for the specified schema. The DATABASE and SCHEMA keywords determine the level for a given system trigger. If the schema is not specified with the SCHEMA keyword, it defaults to the schema that owns the trigger. For example, suppose we create the following trigger while connected as `UserA`:

```
-- Available online as part of DatabaseSchema.sql
CREATE OR REPLACE TRIGGER LogUserAConnects
  AFTER LOGON ON SCHEMA
BEGIN
  INSERT INTO example.temp_table
    VALUES (1, 'LogUserAConnects fired!');
END LogUserAConnects;
```

`LogUserAConnects` will record in `temp_table` whenever `UserA` connects to the database. We can do likewise for `UserB` by creating the following while connected as `UserB`:

```
-- Available online as part of DatabaseSchema.sql
CREATE OR REPLACE TRIGGER LogUserBConnects
  AFTER LOGON ON SCHEMA
BEGIN
```

```
INSERT INTO example.temp_table
  VALUES (2, 'LogUserBConnects fired!');
END LogUserBConnects;
```

Finally, we can create the following trigger while connected as `example`. `LogAllConnects` will record all connects to the database, because it is a database-level trigger.

-- Available online as part of DatabaseSchema.sql
```
CREATE OR REPLACE TRIGGER LogAllConnects
  AFTER LOGON ON DATABASE
BEGIN
  INSERT INTO example.temp_table
    VALUES (3, 'LogAllConnects fired!');
END LogAllConnects;
```

NOTE
You must first create UserA and UserB, and grant the appropriate permissions, before running the above examples. See DatabaseSchema.sql for more details.

We can now see the effects of the different triggers in the following SQL*Plus session:

-- Available online as part of DatabaseSchema.sql
```
SQL> connect UserA/UserA
Connected.
SQL> connect UserB/UserB
Connected.
SQL> connect example/example
Connected.
SQL>
SQL> SELECT * FROM temp_table;
   NUM_COL CHAR_COL
---------- -----------------------------------------------------------
         3 LogAllConnects fired!
         2 LogUserBConnects fired!
         3 LogAllConnects fired!
         3 LogAllConnects fired!
         1 LogUserAConnects fired!
```

`LogAllConnects` has fired three times (once for all three connections), while `LogUserAConnects` and `LogUserBConnects` have only fired once, as expected.

NOTE
STARTUP and SHUTDOWN triggers are relevant only at the database level. It is not illegal to create them at the schema level, but they will not fire.

Event Attribute Functions

Within a system trigger, there are several event attribute functions that are available. Similar to the trigger predicates (INSERTING, UPDATING, and DELETING), they allow a trigger body to get information about the triggering event. Although it is legal to call these functions from other PL/SQL blocks (not necessarily in a system trigger body), they will not always return a valid result. The event attribute functions are described in Table 11-5.

The `LogCreations` trigger, which we saw at the beginning of this chapter, uses some of the attribute functions. Unlike trigger predicates, event attribute functions are stand-alone PL/SQL functions that are owned by SYS. There are no synonyms defined for them by default, so they must be prefixed by SYS in order to resolve them.

```
-- Available online as part of LogCreations.sql
CREATE OR REPLACE TRIGGER LogCreations
  AFTER CREATE ON SCHEMA
BEGIN
  INSERT INTO ddl_creations (user_id, object_type, object_name,
                             object_owner, creation_date)
    VALUES (USER, SYS.DICTIONARY_OBJ_TYPE, SYS.DICTIONARY_OBJ_NAME,
            SYS.DICTIONARY_OBJ_OWNER, SYSDATE);
END LogCreations;
```

Attribute Function	Datatype	System Event Applicable for	Description
SYSEVENT	VARCHAR2(20)	All events	Returns the system event that fired the trigger.
INSTANCE_ NUM	NUMBER	All events	Returns the current instance number. This will always be 1 unless you are running with Oracle Real Application Clusters.

TABLE 11-5. *Event Attribute Functions*

Attribute Function	Datatype	System Event Applicable for	Description
DATABASE_ NAME	VARCHAR2(50)	All events	Returns the current database name.
SERVER_ERROR	NUMBER	SERVERERROR	Takes a single NUMBER argument. Returns the error at the position on the error stack indicated by the argument. The position 1 is the top of the stack.
IS_ SERVERERROR	BOOLEAN	SERVERERROR	Takes an error number as an argument, and returns TRUE if the Oracle error indicated is on the error stack.
LOGIN_USER	VARCHAR2(30)	All events	Returns the userid of the user that fired the trigger.
DICTIONARY_ OBJ_TYPE	VARCHAR2(20)	CREATE, DROP, ALTER	Returns the type of dictionary object on which the DDL operation that fired the trigger occurred.
DICTIONARY_ OBJ_NAME	VARCHAR2(30)	CREATE, DROP, ALTER	Returns the name of the dictionary object on which the DDL operation that fired the trigger occurred.
DICTIONARY_ OBJ_OWNER	VARCHAR2(30)	CREATE, DROP, ALTER	Returns the owner of the dictionary object on which the DDL operation that fired the trigger occurred.

TABLE 11-5. *Event Attribute Functions* (continued)

Attribute Function	Datatype	System Event Applicable for	Description
DES_ ENCRYPTED_ PASSWORD	VARCHAR2(30)	CREATE or ALTER USER	Returns the DES encrypted password of the user being created or altered.

TABLE 11-5. *Event Attribute Functions* (continued)

Using the SERVERERROR Event

The SERVERERROR event can be used to track errors that occur in the database. The error code is available inside the trigger through the SERVER_ERROR attribute function. This function allows you to determine the error codes that are on the stack. However, it does not tell you the messages associated with those codes.

This can be remedied with the DBMS_UTILTITY.FORMAT_ERROR_STACK procedure. Although the trigger itself did not cause the error, the error stack is available to PL/SQL through this procedure. This is illustrated by the following example, which will record errors in the following table:

```
-- Available online as part of LogErrors.sql
CREATE TABLE error_log (
  timestamp     DATE,
  username      VARCHAR2(30),
  instance      NUMBER,
  database_name VARCHAR2(50),
  error_stack   VARCHAR2(2000)
  );
```

We can create a trigger that inserts into `error_log` as follows:

```
-- Available online as part of LogErrors.sql
CREATE OR REPLACE TRIGGER LogErrors
  AFTER SERVERERROR ON DATABASE
BEGIN
  INSERT INTO error_log
    VALUES (SYSDATE, SYS.LOGIN_USER, SYS.INSTANCE_NUM, SYS.
            DATABASE_NAME, DBMS_UTILITY.FORMAT_ERROR_STACK);
END LogErrors;
```

Finally, we can generate some errors and see that LogErrors correctly records them. Note that the trigger captures errors in SQL, runtime PL/SQL errors, and compile-time PL/SQL errors.

```
-- Available online as part of LogErrors.sql
SQL> SELECT * FROM non_existent_table;
SELECT * FROM non_existent_table
              *
ERROR at line 1:
ORA-00942: table or view does not exist
SQL> BEGIN
  2     INSERT INTO non_existent_table VALUES ('Hello!');
  3  END;
  4  /
   INSERT INTO non_existent_table VALUES ('Hello!');
               *
ERROR at line 2:
ORA-06550: line 2, column 15:
PLS-00201: identifier 'NON_EXISTENT_TABLE' must be declared
ORA-06550: line 2, column 3:
PL/SQL: SQL Statement ignored
SQL> BEGIN
  2     -- This is a syntax error!
  3     DELETE FROM students
  4  END;
  5  /
END;
*
ERROR at line 4:
ORA-06550: line 4, column 1:
PLS-00103: Encountered the symbol "END" when expecting one of the
following:
. @ ; return RETURNING_ <an identifier>
<a double-quoted delimited-identifier> partition where
The symbol ";" was substituted for "END" to continue.
SQL> DECLARE
  2     v_StringVar VARCHAR2(2);
  3  BEGIN
  4     -- This is a runtime error!
  5     v_StringVar := 'abcdef';
  6  END;
  7  /
DECLARE
*
ERROR at line 1:
ORA-06502: PL/SQL: numeric or value error: character string buffer too small
ORA-06512: at line 5
```

```
SQL> SELECT *
  2    FROM error_log;

TIMESTAMP USERNAME   INSTANCE DATABASE
--------- -------- --------- --------
ERROR_STACK
-----------------------------------------------------------------
12-OCT-01 EXAMPLE          1 V901
ORA-00942: table or view does not exist

12-OCT-01 EXAMPLE          1 V901
ORA-06550: line 2, column 15:
PLS-00201: identifier 'NON_EXISTENT_TABLE' must be declared
ORA-06550: line 2, column 3:
PL/SQL: SQL Statement ignored

12-OCT-01 EXAMPLE          1 V901
ORA-06550: line 4, column 1:
PLS-00103: Encountered the symbol "END" when expecting one of
 the following:

   . @ ; return RETURNING_ <an identifier>
   <a double-quoted delimited-identifier> partition where
The symbol ";" was substituted for "END" to continue.

12-OCT-01 EXAMPLE          1 V901
ORA-06502: PL/SQL: numeric or value error: character string
buffer too small
ORA-06512: at line 5
```

System Triggers and Transactions

Depending on the triggering event, the transactional behavior of a system trigger varies. A system trigger will either fire as a separate transaction that is committed upon successful completion of the trigger, or it will fire as part of the current user transaction. STARTUP, SHUTDOWN, SERVERERROR, and LOGON triggers all fire as separate transactions, while LOGOFF and DDL triggers fire as part of the current transaction.

It is important to note, however, that the work done by the trigger will generally be committed regardless. In the case of a DDL trigger, the current transaction (namely the CREATE, ALTER, or DROP statement) is automatically committed, which commits the work in the trigger. The work in a LOGOFF trigger will also be committed as part of the final transaction in the session.

NOTE
Because system triggers are generally committed anyway, declaring them as autonomous will not have any effect.

System Triggers and the WHEN Clause

Just like DML triggers, system triggers can use the WHEN clause to specify a condition on the trigger firing. However, there are restrictions on the types of conditions that can be specified for each type of system trigger, namely

- STARTUP and SHUTDOWN triggers cannot have any conditions.

- SERVERERROR triggers can use the ERRNO test to check for a specific error only.

- LOGON and LOGOFF triggers can check the userid or username with the USERID or USERNAME tests.

- DDL triggers can check the type and name of the object being modified, and can check the userid or username.

Other Trigger Issues

In this section, we will discuss some remaining issues about triggers. These include the namespace for trigger names, various restrictions on using triggers, and different kinds of trigger bodies. The section closes with a discussion of the privileges related to triggers.

Trigger Names

The namespace for trigger names is different from that of other subprograms. A *namespace* is the set of legal identifiers available for use as the names of an object. Procedures, packages, and tables all share the same namespace. This means that, within one database schema, all objects in the same namespace must have unique names. For example, it is illegal to give the same name to a procedure and a package.

Triggers, however, exist in a separate namespace. This means that a trigger can have the same name as a table or procedure. Within one schema, however, a given name can be used for only one trigger. For example, we can create a trigger called `major_stats` on the `major_stats` table, but it is illegal to create a procedure also called `major_stats`, as the following SQL*Plus session shows:

```
-- Available online as samename.sql
SQL> -- Legal, since triggers and tables are in different namespaces.
```

```
SQL> CREATE OR REPLACE TRIGGER major_stats
  2    BEFORE INSERT ON major_stats
  3  BEGIN
  4    INSERT INTO temp_table (char_col)
  5      VALUES ('Trigger fired!');
  6  END major_stats;
  7  /
Trigger created.

SQL> -- Illegal, since procedures and tables are in the same namespace.
SQL> CREATE OR REPLACE PROCEDURE major_stats AS
  2  BEGIN
  3    INSERT INTO temp_table (char_col)
  4      VALUES ('Procedure called!');
  5  END major_stats;
  6  /
CREATE OR REPLACE PROCEDURE major_stats AS
*
ERROR at line 1:
ORA-00955: name is already used by an existing object
```

TIP

Although it is possible to use the same name for a trigger and a table, I don't recommend it. It is better to give each trigger a unique name that identifies its function as well as the table on which it is defined, or prefix triggers with a common sequence of characters (such as TRG_).

Restrictions on Triggers

The body of a trigger is a PL/SQL block. (Oracle8*i* allowed other types of trigger bodies—see the next section for details.) Any statement that is legal in a PL/SQL block is legal in a trigger body, subject to the following restrictions:

■ A trigger may not issue any transaction control statements—COMMIT, ROLLBACK, SAVEPOINT, or SET TRANSACTION. The PL/SQL compiler will allow a trigger to be created that contains one of these statements, but you will receive an error when the trigger is fired. This is because it is fired as part of the execution of the triggering statement and is in the same transaction as the triggering statement. When the triggering statement is committed or rolled back, the work in the trigger is committed or rolled back as well. (In Oracle8*i* and higher, you can create a trigger that executes as an autonomous transaction, in which case the work in the trigger can be committed or rolled back independent of the state of the triggering statement. See Chapter 4 for more information about autonomous transactions.)

- Likewise, any procedures or functions that are called by the trigger body cannot issue any transaction control statements (unless they are also declared as autonomous in Oracle8*i* and higher).

- The trigger body cannot declare any LONG or LONG RAW variables. Also, :new and :old cannot refer to a LONG or LONG RAW column in the table for which the trigger is defined.

- In Oracle8 and higher, code in a trigger body may reference and use LOB (Large OBject) columns, but it may not modify the values of the columns. This is also true for object columns.

There are also restrictions on which tables a trigger body may access. Depending on the type of trigger and the constraints on the tables, tables may be mutating. This situation is discussed in detail in the section "Mutating Tables" later in this chapter.

Trigger Bodies

Oracle**8i** and higher | Prior to Oracle8*i*, trigger bodies must be PL/SQL blocks. In Oracle8*i* and higher, however, a trigger body can consist of a CALL statement instead. The procedure that is called can be a PL/SQL stored subprogram, or it can be a wrapper for a C or Java routine. This allows you to create triggers where the functional code is written in Java. For example, suppose we want to record connects and disconnects to the database in the following table:

```
-- Available online as part of tables.sql
CREATE TABLE connect_audit (
  user_name   VARCHAR2(30),
  operation   VARCHAR2(30),
  timestamp   DATE);
```

We can use the following package to record connects and disconnects:

```
-- Available online as LogPkg1.sql
CREATE OR REPLACE PACKAGE LogPkg AS
  PROCEDURE LogConnect(p_UserID IN VARCHAR2);
  PROCEDURE LogDisconnect(p_UserID IN VARCHAR2);
END LogPkg;

CREATE OR REPLACE PACKAGE BODY LogPkg AS
  PROCEDURE LogConnect(p_UserID IN VARCHAR2) IS
  BEGIN
```

```
      INSERT INTO connect_audit (user_name, operation, timestamp)
         VALUES (p_USerID, 'CONNECT', SYSDATE);
    END LogConnect;

    PROCEDURE LogDisconnect(p_UserID IN VARCHAR2) IS
    BEGIN
      INSERT INTO connect_audit (user_name, operation, timestamp)
         VALUES (p_USerID, 'DISCONNECT', SYSDATE);
    END LogDisconnect;
END LogPkg;
```

Both `LogPkg.LogConnect` and `LogPkg.LogDisconnect` take a username as an argument, and insert a row into `connect_audit`. Finally, we can call them from a LOGON and LOGOFF trigger as follows:

```
-- Available online as LogConnects.sql
CREATE OR REPLACE TRIGGER LogConnects
  AFTER LOGON ON DATABASE
  CALL LogPkg.LogConnect(SYS.LOGIN_USER)
/

CREATE OR REPLACE TRIGGER LogDisconnects
  BEFORE LOGOFF ON DATABASE
  CALL LogPkg.LogDisconnect(SYS.LOGIN_USER)
/
```

NOTE

Because `LogConnects` *and* `LogDisconnects` *are system triggers on the database (as opposed to a schema), you must have the ADMINISTER DATABASE TRIGGER system privilege to create them.*

The trigger body for both `LogConnects` and `LogDisconnects` is simply a CALL statement, which indicates the procedure to be executed. The current user is passed as the only argument. In the above example, the target of the CALL is a standard PL/SQL packaged procedure. However, it could just as easily be a wrapper for a C or Java external routine. For example, suppose we load the following Java class into the database:

```
// Available online as Logger.java
import java.sql.*;
import oracle.jdbc.driver.*;

public class Logger {
  public static void LogConnect(String userID)
    throws SQLException {
```

```
    // Get default JDBC connection
    Connection conn = new OracleDriver().defaultConnection();

    String insertString =
      "INSERT INTO connect_audit (user_name, operation, timestamp)" +
      " VALUES (?, 'CONNECT', SYSDATE)";

    // Prepare and execute a statement that does the insert
    PreparedStatement insertStatement =
      conn.prepareStatement(insertString);
    insertStatement.setString(1, userID);
    insertStatement.execute();
  }

  public static void LogDisconnect(String userID)
    throws SQLException {
    // Get default JDBC connection
    Connection conn = new OracleDriver().defaultConnection();

    String insertString =
      "INSERT INTO connect_audit (user_name, operation, timestamp)" +
      " VALUES (?, 'DISCONNECT', SYSDATE)";

    // Prepare and execute a statement that does the insert
    PreparedStatement insertStatement =
      conn.prepareStatement(insertString);
    insertStatement.setString(1, userID);
    insertStatement.execute();
  }
}
```

If we then create LogPkg as a wrapper for this class,

```
-- Available online as LogPkg2.sql
CREATE OR REPLACE PACKAGE LogPkg AS
  PROCEDURE LogConnect(p_UserID IN VARCHAR2);
  PROCEDURE LogDisconnect(p_UserID IN VARCHAR2);
END LogPkg;

CREATE OR REPLACE PACKAGE BODY LogPkg AS
  PROCEDURE LogConnect(p_UserID IN VARCHAR2) IS
    LANGUAGE JAVA
    NAME 'Logger.LogConnect(java.lang.String)';

  PROCEDURE LogDisconnect(p_UserID IN VARCHAR2) IS
    LANGUAGE JAVA
    NAME 'Logger.LogDisconnect(java.lang.String)';
END LogPkg;
```

we can use the same triggers to achieve the desired effect. See Chapter 12 for more information about external routines.

NOTE
Trigger predicates such as INSERTING, UPDATING, and DELETING, and the :old and :new correlation identifiers (and :parent), can be used only if the trigger body is a complete PL/SQL block and not a CALL statement.

Trigger Privileges

There are five system privileges that apply to triggers, which are described in Table 11-6. In addition to these, the owner of a trigger must have the necessary object privileges on the objects referenced by the trigger. A trigger is a compiled object, so these privileges must be granted directly and not through a role.

System Privilege	Description
CREATE TRIGGER	Allows the grantee to create a trigger in his or her own schema.
CREATE ANY TRIGGER	Allows the grantee to create triggers in any schema except SYS. It is not recommended to create triggers on data dictionary tables.
ALTER ANY TRIGGER	Allows the grantee to enable, disable, or compile database triggers in any schema except SYS. Note that if the grantee does not have CREATE ANY TRIGGER, he or she cannot change trigger code.
DROP ANY TRIGGER	Allows the grantee to drop database triggers in any schema except SYS.
ADMINISTER DATABASE TRIGGER	Allows the grantee to create or alter a system trigger on the database (as opposed to the current schema). The grantee must also have either CREATE TRIGGER or CREATE ANY TRIGGER.

TABLE 11-6. *System Privileges Related to Triggers*

Triggers and the Data Dictionary

Similar to stored subprograms, certain data dictionary views contain information about triggers and their status. These views are updated whenever a trigger is created or dropped.

Data Dictionary Views

When a trigger is created, its source code is stored in the data dictionary view `user_triggers`. This view includes the trigger body, WHEN clause, triggering table, and the trigger type. For example, the following query returns information about `UpdateMajorStats`:

```
SQL> SELECT trigger_type, table_name, triggering_event
  2    FROM user_triggers
  3    WHERE trigger_name = 'UPDATEMAJORSTATS';
TRIGGER_TYPE      TABLE_NAME       TRIGGERING_EVENT
---------------   --------------   --------------------------
AFTER STATEMENT   STUDENTS         INSERT OR UPDATE OR DELETE
```

`user_triggers` contains information about the triggers owned by the current user. There are also two additional views: `all_triggers` contains information about the triggers which are accessible to the current user (but might be owned by a different user), and `dba_triggers` contains information about all triggers in the database. For more information on data dictionary views, see Appendix C.

Dropping and Disabling Triggers

Similar to procedures and packages, triggers can be dropped. The command to do this has the syntax

    DROP TRIGGER triggername;

where *triggername* is the name of the trigger to be dropped. This permanently removes the trigger from the data dictionary. Similar to subprograms, the OR REPLACE clause can be specified in the trigger CREATE statement. In this case, the trigger is dropped first, if it already exists.

Unlike procedures and packages, however, a trigger can be disabled without dropping it. When a trigger is disabled, it still exists in the data dictionary but is never fired. To disable a trigger, use the ALTER TRIGGER statement:

    ALTER TRIGGER triggername {DISABLE | ENABLE};

where *triggername* is the name of the trigger. All triggers are enabled by default when they are created. ALTER TRIGGER can disable and then reenable any trigger. For example, the following code disables and then reenables `UpdateMajorStats`:

```
SQL> ALTER TRIGGER UpdateMajorStats DISABLE;
Trigger altered.

SQL> ALTER TRIGGER UpdateMajorStats ENABLE;
Trigger altered.
```

All triggers for a particular table can be enabled or disabled using the ALTER TABLE command as well, by adding the ENABLE ALL TRIGGERS or the DISABLE ALL TRIGGERS clause. For example:

```
SQL> ALTER TABLE students
  2      ENABLE ALL TRIGGERS;
Table altered.

SQL> ALTER TABLE students
  2      DISABLE ALL TRIGGERS;
Table altered.
```

The `status` column of `user_triggers` contains either ENABLED or DISABLED, indicating the current status of a trigger. Disabling a trigger does not remove it from the data dictionary, like dropping it would.

Trigger P-Code

When a package or subprogram is stored in the data dictionary, the compiled p-code is stored in addition to the source code for the object. This is also true for triggers. This means that triggers can be called without recompilation, and that dependency information is stored. Thus, they can be automatically invalidated in the same manner as packages and subprograms. When a trigger is invalidated, it will be recompiled the next time it is fired.

Mutating Tables

There are restrictions on the tables and columns that a trigger body may access. In order to define these restrictions, it is necessary to understand mutating and constraining tables. A *mutating table* is a table that is currently being modified by a DML statement. For a trigger, this is the table on which the trigger is defined. Tables that may need to be updated as a result of DELETE CASCADE referential integrity constraints are also mutating. (For more information on referential integrity constraints, see the *Oracle Server Reference*.) A *constraining table* is a table that might need to be read from for a referential integrity constraint. To illustrate these definitions, consider the `registered_students` table, which is created with

```
-- Available online as part of tables.sql
CREATE TABLE registered_students (
  student_id NUMBER(5) NOT NULL,
  department CHAR(3)    NOT NULL,
  course     NUMBER(3) NOT NULL,
  grade      CHAR(1),
  CONSTRAINT rs_grade
    CHECK (grade IN ('A', 'B', 'C', 'D', 'E')),
  CONSTRAINT rs_student_id
    FOREIGN KEY (student_id) REFERENCES students (id),
  CONSTRAINT rs_department_course
    FOREIGN KEY (department, course)
    REFERENCES classes (department, course)
);
```

Registered_students has two declarative referential integrity constraints. As such, both students and classes are constraining tables for registered_ students. Because of the constraints, classes and students may need to be modified and/or queried by the DML statement. Also, registered_students itself is mutating during execution of a DML statement against it.

SQL statements in a trigger body may not

- Read from or modify any mutating table of the triggering statement. This includes the triggering table itself.

- Read from or modify the primary-, unique-, or foreign-key columns of a constraining table of the triggering table. They may, however, modify the other columns if desired.

These restrictions apply to all row-level triggers. They apply for statement triggers only when the statement trigger would be fired as a result of a DELETE CASCADE operation.

NOTE
If an INSERT statement affects only one row, the before and after row triggers for that row do not treat the triggering table as mutating. This is the only case where a row-level trigger may read from or modify the triggering table. Statements such as INSERT INTO table SELECT . . . always treat the triggering table as mutating, even if the subquery returns only one row.

As an example, consider the `CascadeRSInserts` trigger, shown next. Even though it modifies both `students` and `classes`, it is legal because the columns in `students` and `classes` that are modified are not key columns. In the next section, we will examine an illegal trigger.

```
-- Available online as CascadeRSInserts.sql
CREATE OR REPLACE TRIGGER CascadeRSInserts
  /* Keep the registered_students, students, and classes
     tables in synch when an INSERT is done to registered_students. */
  BEFORE INSERT ON registered_students
  FOR EACH ROW
DECLARE
  v_Credits classes.num_credits%TYPE;
BEGIN
  -- Determine the number of credits for this class.
  SELECT num_credits
    INTO v_Credits
    FROM classes
    WHERE department = :new.department
    AND course = :new.course;

  -- Modify the current credits for this student.
  UPDATE students
    SET current_credits = current_credits + v_Credits
    WHERE ID = :new.student_id;

  -- Add one to the number of students in the class.
  UPDATE classes
    SET current_students = current_students + 1
    WHERE department = :new.department
    AND course = :new.course;
END CascadeRSInserts;
```

Mutating Table Example

Suppose we want to limit the number of students in each major to five. We could accomplish this with a before INSERT or UPDATE row-level trigger on `students`, given here:

```
-- Available online as part of LimitMajors.sql
CREATE OR REPLACE TRIGGER LimitMajors
  /* Limits the number of students in each major to 5.
     If this limit is exceeded, an error is raised through
     raise_application_error. */
  BEFORE INSERT OR UPDATE OF major ON students
  FOR EACH ROW
```

```
DECLARE
  v_MaxStudents CONSTANT NUMBER := 5;
  v_CurrentStudents NUMBER;
BEGIN
  -- Determine the current number of students in this
  -- major.
  SELECT COUNT(*)
    INTO v_CurrentStudents
    FROM students
    WHERE major = :new.major;

  -- If there isn't room, raise an error.
  IF v_CurrentStudents + 1 > v_MaxStudents THEN
    RAISE_APPLICATION_ERROR(-20000,
      'Too many students in major ' || :new.major);
  END IF;
END LimitMajors;
```

At first glance, this trigger seems to accomplish the desired result. However, if we update `students` and fire the trigger, we get

`-- Available online as part of LimitMajors.sql`

```
SQL> UPDATE students
  2     SET major = 'History'
  3     WHERE ID = 10003;
UPDATE students
  *
ERROR at line 1:
ORA-04091: table EXAMPLE.STUDENTS is mutating, trigger/function
           may not see it
ORA-06512: at "EXAMPLE.LIMITMAJORS", line 7
ORA-04088: error during execution of trigger 'EXAMPLE.LIMITMAJORS'
```

The ORA-4091 error results because `LimitMajors` queries its own triggering table, which is mutating. ORA-4091 is raised when the trigger is fired, not when it is created.

Workaround for the Mutating Table Error

`Students` is mutating only for a row-level trigger. This means that we cannot query it in a row-level trigger, but we can in a statement-level trigger. However, we cannot simply make `LimitMajors` into a statement trigger because we need to use the value of `:new.major` in the trigger body. The solution for this is to create two triggers—a row and a statement level. In the row-level trigger, we record the value of `:new.major`, but we don't query `students`. The query is done in the statement-level trigger and uses the value recorded in the row trigger.

How do we record this value? One way is to use a PL/SQL table inside a package. This way, we can save multiple values per update. Also, each session gets its own instantiation of packaged variables, so we don't have to worry about simultaneous updates by different sessions. This solution is implemented with the `student_data` package and the `RLimitMajors` and `SLimitMajors` triggers:

```
-- Available online as part of mutating.sql
CREATE OR REPLACE PACKAGE StudentData AS
  TYPE t_Majors IS TABLE OF students.major%TYPE
    INDEX BY BINARY_INTEGER;
  TYPE t_IDs IS TABLE OF students.ID%TYPE
    INDEX BY BINARY_INTEGER;

  v_StudentMajors t_Majors;
  v_StudentIDs    t_IDs;
  v_NumEntries    BINARY_INTEGER := 0;
END StudentData;

CREATE OR REPLACE TRIGGER RLimitMajors
  BEFORE INSERT OR UPDATE OF major ON students
  FOR EACH ROW
BEGIN
  /* Record the new data in StudentData. We don't make any
     changes to students, to avoid the ORA-4091 error. */
  StudentData.v_NumEntries := StudentData.v_NumEntries + 1;
  StudentData.v_StudentMajors(StudentData.v_NumEntries) :=
    :new.major;
  StudentData.v_StudentIDs(StudentData.v_NumEntries) := :new.id;
END RLimitMajors;

CREATE OR REPLACE TRIGGER SLimitMajors
  AFTER INSERT OR UPDATE OF major ON students
DECLARE
  v_MaxStudents      CONSTANT NUMBER := 5;
  v_CurrentStudents  NUMBER;
  v_StudentID        students.ID%TYPE;
  v_Major            students.major%TYPE;
BEGIN
  /* Loop through each student inserted or updated, and verify
     that we are still within the limit. */
  FOR v_LoopIndex IN 1..StudentData.v_NumEntries LOOP
    v_StudentID := StudentData.v_StudentIDs(v_LoopIndex);
    v_Major := StudentData.v_StudentMajors(v_LoopIndex);

    -- Determine the current number of students in this major.
    SELECT COUNT(*)
      INTO v_CurrentStudents
```

```
      FROM students
      WHERE major = v_Major;

    -- If there isn't room, raise an error.
    IF v_CurrentStudents > v_MaxStudents THEN
      RAISE_APPLICATION_ERROR(-20000,
        'Too many students for major ' || v_Major ||
        ' because of student ' || v_StudentID);
    END IF;
  END LOOP;

  -- Reset the counter so the next execution will use new data.
  StudentData.v_NumEntries := 0;
END SLimitMajors;
```

NOTE
*Be sure to drop the incorrect LimitMajors trigger
before running the above script.*

We can now test this series of triggers by updating students until we have too
many history majors:

```
-- Available online as part of mutating.sql
SQL> UPDATE students
  2     SET major = 'History'
  3     WHERE ID = 10003;
1 row updated.

SQL> UPDATE students
  2     SET major = 'History'
  3     WHERE ID = 10002;
1 row updated.

SQL> UPDATE students
  2     SET major = 'History'
  3     WHERE ID = 10009;
UPDATE students
       *
ERROR at line 1:
ORA-20000: Too many students for major History because of student 10009
ORA-06512: at "EXAMPLE.SLIMITMAJORS", line 19
ORA-04088: error during execution of trigger 'EXAMPLE.SLIMITMAJORS'
```

This is the desired behavior. This technique can be applied to occurrences of
ORA-4091 when a row-level trigger reads from or modifies a mutating table. Instead

of doing the illegal processing in the row-level trigger, we defer the processing to an after statement-level trigger, where it is legal. The packaged PL/SQL tables are used to store the rows that were changed.

There are several things to note about this technique:

- The PL/SQL tables are contained in a package so that they will be visible to both the row- and the statement-level trigger. The only way to ensure that variables are global is to put them in a package.

- A counter variable, `StudentData.v_NumEntries`, is used. This is initialized to zero when the package is created. It is incremented by the row-level trigger. The statement-level trigger references it and then resets it to zero after processing. This is necessary so that the next UPDATE statement issued by this session will have the correct value.

- The check in `SLimitMajors` for the maximum number of students had to be changed slightly. Because this is now an after statement trigger, `v_CurrentStudents` will hold the number of students in the major after the insert or update, not before. Thus, the check for `v_CurrentStudents + 1`, which we did in `LimitMajors`, is replaced by `v_CurrentStudents`.

- A database table could have been used instead of PL/SQL tables. I don't recommend this technique, because simultaneous sessions issuing an UPDATE would interfere with each other (in Oracle8i and higher you could use a temporary table, however). Packaged PL/SQL tables are unique among sessions, which avoids the problem.

Summary

As we have seen, triggers are a valuable addition to PL/SQL and Oracle. They can be used to enforce data constraints that are much more complex than normal referential integrity constraints. Oracle8i extended triggers to events beyond DML operations on a table or view, as well. Triggers complete our discussion of named PL/SQL blocks in the past three chapters. In the final chapter, we will see some of the advanced features of PL/SQL.

CHAPTER
12

Advanced Features

n Chapters 3 through 11, we covered the introductory features of PL/SQL. In this chapter, we will briefly discuss, with small examples, some of the more advanced features. For more information on these features, please consult either *Oracle8*i *Advanced PL/SQL Programming* (the follow-up to this book) or the Oracle documentation.

Language Features

In this section, we will briefly examine some of the advanced features of PL/SQL that are built into the language. These include external routines, native dynamic SQL, bulk binds, object types, large objects, and pipelined and table functions.

External Routines

PL/SQL is especially suited for working with Oracle, due to its integration with SQL. In fact, this is why the language was designed. However, there are other tasks for which other languages are more appropriate. For example, C excels at computation-intensive tasks and integration with the file system and other system devices. Java is an excellent portable language with a well-defined security model that works well for Internet applications. If your application needs to perform tasks that are not well suited for PL/SQL, another language may be appropriate. In this case, it is necessary to communicate between modules of the application that are written in different languages.

Prior to Oracle8, the only way to communicate between PL/SQL and another language (such as C) was to use the DBMS_PIPE and/or DBMS_ALERT packages. This typically required setting up a daemon process written using the Oracle Call Interface (OCI) or the precompilers.

| Oracle **8**
and higher | Oracle8, however, simplified this communication through external routines. An *external routine* is a procedure or function written in a language other than PL/SQL but callable from a PL/SQL program. This is done by publishing the external routine to PL/SQL through a PL/SQL-callable entry point (also know as the *wrapper*) that maps to the actual external code. A PL/SQL program then calls the wrapper, which in turn invokes the external code. External routines were first introduced in Oracle8 (where they were known as *external procedures*). In Oracle8, the only supported language for external routines was C. There, the AS EXTERNAL clause was available to create the PL/SQL wrapper. |

| Oracle **8***i*
and higher | Oracle8*i* extended external routines to support Java. PL/SQL wrappers are also extended to include call specifications. A *call specification* is a means of publishing an external routine (regardless of its native language) to PL/SQL. Call specifications use the AS LANGUAGE clause. |

C External Routines

For a C external routine, you must first compile your C function into a shared library located on the operating system. Then, you must set up the listener to support the connection to the external routine driver extproc. Third, you create a data dictionary library object to represent the shared library on the operating system. Finally, you create the wrapper to call the routine.

For example, assume that you have written a C function sendMail with a prototype like the following:

```
int sendMail(
   char *subject,
   char *message,
   char *from,
   char *recipient);
```

If this function is compiled into a shared library on the file system, say /libs/libmail.so, you then create a library object to represent the location of the shared object as follows:

```
CREATE OR REPLACE LIBRARY SendMailLibrary
   AS '/libs/libmail.so';
```

Once the library has been created, you can create a wrapper as follows:

```
CREATE OR REPLACE PROCEDURE SendMailC (
   p_Subject IN VARCHAR2,
   p_Message IN VARCHAR2,
   p_From IN VARCHAR2,
   p_Recipient IN VARCHAR2)
AS EXTERNAL
LIBRARY SendMailLibrary
NAME "sendMail"
PARAMETERS (p_Subject STRING,
            p_Message STRING,
            p_From STRING,
            p_Recipient STRING);
```

The AS EXTERNAL clause specifies the library and C function names, along with the PARAMETERS clause, which defines the mappings between PL/SQL and C datatypes. Once these steps have been completed, you can call the SendMailC routine from PL/SQL. This will in turn call the C sendMail function to actually send the message.

C external routines are run by a separate process. When you invoke an external routine, a process known as extproc is started automatically by the server (using information in the Net8 configuration files). In turn, extproc then loads the shared library identified by the LIBRARY clause and calls the function.

Java External Routines

For a Java external routine, you load the Java class into the database (it will run within the Oracle JVM within the database). Like a C external routine, you then create a wrapper to enable PL/SQL to call it. Unlike C routines, there is no library on the operating system, and setup of the listener is not required.

Similar to the C example, suppose you create a Java class and method as follows:

```
public class sendMail
{
  public static void send(
    String subject,
    String message,
    String from,
    String recipient)
  {
    ...
  }
}
```

Only static methods can be called from PL/SQL, although those methods can call other nonstatic methods also loaded into the database. Once this class is loaded into the database, the PL/SQL wrapper can be created as follows:

```
CREATE OR REPLACE PROCEDURE SendMailJava(
  p_Subject IN VARCHAR2,
  p_Message IN VARCHAR2,
  p_From IN VARCHAR2,
  p_Recipient IN VARCHAR2)
AS LANGAUGE JAVA
NAME 'sendMail.send(java.lang.String, java.lang.String,
                    java.lang.String, java.lang.String)';
```

The NAME clause specifies the signature of the Java method that is to be called. Note that the full names of the types used in the method are required. Similar to the wrapper for the C routine, once SendMailJava has been created, you can call it from other PL/SQL routines. This will in turn invoke the Java sendMail.send() method to actually send the message.

Unlike C external routines, Java external routines are run directly within the database. The JVM contained within the server will run the Java method directly. There is no need to call extproc.

Native Dynamic SQL

Oracle **8i**
and higher

As we have seen, PL/SQL uses early binding to execute SQL statements. This has the consequence that only DML statements can be included directly in PL/SQL blocks. This can be rectified, however, through *dynamic SQL*. Rather than being parsed along with the PL/SQL block, dynamic SQL is parsed and subsequently executed at runtime.

There are two techniques for executing dynamic SQL in PL/SQL. The first is the DBMS_SQL package, which is described later in this chapter in the "Advanced Packages" section. The second technique, introduced in Oracle8i, is native dynamic SQL. Native dynamic SQL, as its name implies, is an integral part of the language itself. As a consequence, it is significantly simpler to use and faster than DBMS_SQL.

Executing Nonquery Statements and PL/SQL Blocks

The basic statement used in nonquery statements (DML and DDL) and PL/SQL blocks is the EXECUTE IMMEDATE statement, as the following SQL*Plus session illustrates:

```
-- Available online as execImmediate.sql
SQL> DECLARE
  2    v_SQLString  VARCHAR2(200);
  3    v_PLSQLBlock VARCHAR2(200);
  4  BEGIN
  5    -- First create a temporary table, using a literal.  Note that
  6    -- there is no trailing semicolon in the string.
  7    EXECUTE IMMEDIATE
  8      'CREATE TABLE execute_table (col1 VARCHAR(10))';
  9
 10    -- Insert some rows using a string.  Again, there is no
 11    -- trailing semicolon inside the string.
 12    FOR v_Counter IN 1..10 LOOP
 13      v_SQLString :=
 14        'INSERT INTO execute_table
 15            VALUES (''Row ' || v_Counter || ''')';
 16      EXECUTE IMMEDIATE v_SQLString;
 17    END LOOP;
 18
 19    -- Print out the contents of the table using an anonymous
 20    -- PL/SQL block.  Here we put the entire block into a single
 21    -- string (including the semicolon).
 22    v_PLSQLBlock :=
 23      'BEGIN
 24        FOR v_Rec IN (SELECT * FROM execute_table) LOOP
 25          DBMS_OUTPUT.PUT_LINE(v_Rec.col1);
 26        END LOOP;
 27      END;';
```

```
28
29      -- And now we execute the anonymous block.
30      EXECUTE IMMEDIATE v_PLSQLBlock;
31
32      -- Finally, drop the table.
33      EXECUTE IMMEDIATE 'DROP TABLE execute_table';
34   END;
35   /
Row 1
Row 2
Row 3
Row 4
Row 5
Row 6
Row 7
Row 8
Row 9
Row 10
PL/SQL procedure successfully completed.
```

The preceding example illustrates various uses of EXECUTE IMMEDIATE: to execute DDL, DML, and anonymous PL/SQL blocks. The string to be executed can be a literal enclosed in single quotes, as the CREATE TABLE and DROP TABLE statements are, or it can be a PL/SQL character string variable, as the INSERT and anonymous blocks are. Note that the trailing semicolon is *not* included for DML and DDL statements, but is for anonymous blocks.

EXECUTE IMMEDIATE is also used to execute statements with bind variables. In this case, the string to be executed contains *placeholders*, which are identified by a colon. The placeholders are matched by position with PL/SQL variables that are found in the USING clause of EXECUTE IMMEDIATE, as the following example illustrates:

```
-- Available online as execBind.sql
DECLARE
  v_SQLString  VARCHAR2(1000);
  v_PLSQLBlock VARCHAR2(1000);

  CURSOR c_EconMajor IS
    SELECT *
      FROM students
      WHERE major = 'Economics';
BEGIN
  -- Insert ECN 103 into classes, using a string for the SQL
  -- statement.
  v_SQLString :=
    'INSERT INTO CLASSES (department, course, description,
                          max_students, current_students,
```

```
                              num_credits)
            VALUES (:dep, :course, :descr, :max_s, :cur_s, :num_c)';

    -- Execute the INSERT, using literal values.
    EXECUTE IMMEDIATE v_SQLString USING
      'ECN', 103, 'Economics 103', 10, 0, 3;

    -- Register all of the Economics majors for the new class.
    FOR v_StudentRec IN c_EconMajor LOOP
      -- Here we have a literal SQL statement, but PL/SQL variables
      -- in the USING clause.
      EXECUTE IMMEDIATE
          'INSERT INTO registered_students
              (student_ID, department, course, grade)
            VALUES (:id, :dep, :course, NULL)'
        USING v_StudentRec.ID, 'ECN', 103;

      -- Update the number of students for the class, using an
      -- anonymous PL/SQL block.
      v_PLSQLBlock :=
        'BEGIN
           UPDATE classes SET current_students = current_students + 1
           WHERE department = :d and course = :c;
         END;';

      EXECUTE IMMEDIATE v_PLSQLBlock USING 'ECN', 103;
    END LOOP;
END;
```

Executing Queries

Queries are executed using the OPEN FOR statement, similar to cursor variables.
The difference is that the string containing the query can be a PL/SQL variable,
rather than a literal. The resulting cursor variable can be fetched from, just like
any other variable. For binds, the USING clause is available, just like EXECUTE
IMMEDIATE. This is illustrated by the following package:

```
-- Available online as part of NativeDynamic.sql
CREATE OR REPLACE PACKAGE NativeDynamic AS
  TYPE t_RefCur IS REF CURSOR;

  -- Selects from students using the supplied WHERE clause,
  -- and returns the opened cursor variable.
  FUNCTION StudentsQuery(p_WhereClause IN VARCHAR2)
    RETURN t_RefCur;

  -- Selects from students based on the supplied major,
  -- and returns the opened cursor variable.
```

```
     FUNCTION StudentsQuery2(p_Major IN VARCHAR2)
        RETURN t_RefCur;
  END NativeDynamic;


  CREATE OR REPLACE PACKAGE BODY NativeDynamic AS
     -- Selects from students using the supplied WHERE clause,
     -- and returns the opened cursor variable.
     FUNCTION StudentsQuery(p_WhereClause IN VARCHAR2)
       RETURN t_RefCur IS
       v_ReturnCursor t_RefCur;
       v_SQLStatement VARCHAR2(500);
     BEGIN
       -- Build the query using the supplied WHERE clause
       v_SQLStatement := 'SELECT * FROM students ' || p_WhereClause;

       -- Open the cursor variable, and return it.
       OPEN v_ReturnCursor FOR v_SQLStatement;
       RETURN v_ReturnCursor;
     END StudentsQuery;

     -- Selects from students based on the supplied major,
     -- and returns the opened cursor variable.
     FUNCTION StudentsQuery2(p_Major IN VARCHAR2)
       RETURN t_RefCur IS
       v_ReturnCursor t_RefCur;
       v_SQLStatement VARCHAR2(500);
     BEGIN
       v_SQLStatement := 'SELECT * FROM students WHERE major = :m';

       -- Open the cursor variable, and return it.
       OPEN v_ReturnCursor FOR v_SQLStatement USING p_Major;
       RETURN v_ReturnCursor;
     END StudentsQuery2;
  END NativeDynamic;
```

We can call NativeDynamic as follows:

```
-- Available online as part of NativeDynamic.sql
SQL> DECLARE
  2     v_Student students%ROWTYPE;
  3     v_StudentCur NativeDynamic.t_RefCur;
  4  BEGIN
  5     -- Call StudentsQuery to open the cursor for students with
  6     -- even IDs.
  7     v_StudentCur :=
  8       NativeDynamic.StudentsQuery('WHERE MOD(id, 2) = 0');
  9
 10     -- Loop through the opened cursor, and print out the results.
```

```
11    DBMS_OUTPUT.PUT_LINE('The following students have even IDs:');
12    LOOP
13      FETCH v_StudentCur INTO v_Student;
14      EXIT WHEN v_StudentCur%NOTFOUND;
15      DBMS_OUTPUT.PUT_LINE('  ' || v_Student.id || ': ' ||
16                           v_Student.first_name || ' ' ||
17                           v_Student.last_name);
18    END LOOP;
19    CLOSE v_StudentCur;
20
21    -- Call StudentsQuery2 to open the cursor for music majors.
22    v_StudentCur :=
23      NativeDynamic.StudentsQuery2('Music');
24
25    -- Loop through the opened cursor, and print out the results.
26    DBMS_OUTPUT.PUT_LINE(
27      'The following students are music majors:');
28    LOOP
29      FETCH v_StudentCur INTO v_Student;
30      EXIT WHEN v_StudentCur%NOTFOUND;
31      DBMS_OUTPUT.PUT_LINE('  ' || v_Student.id || ': ' ||
32                           v_Student.first_name || ' ' ||
33                           v_Student.last_name);
34    END LOOP;
35    CLOSE v_StudentCur;
36  END;
37  /
The following students have even IDs:
  10000: Scott Smith
  10002: Joanne Junebug
  10004: Patrick Poll
  10006: Barbara Blues
  10008: Ester Elegant
  10010: Rita Razmataz
The following students are music majors:
  10007: David Dinsmore
  10009: Rose Riznit
PL/SQL procedure successfully completed.
```

Queries with EXECUTE IMMEDIATE   EXECUTE IMMEDIATE can also be used for single-row queries, either with or without bind variables. With bulk binds (described in the next section), it can be used for multirow queries as well. The requirement is that all of the rows be retrieved in a single operation. The following SQL*Plus session illustrates this use of EXECUTE IMMEDIATE:

```
-- Available online as part of NativeDynamic.sql
SQL> DECLARE
  2    v_SQLQuery VARCHAR2(200);
```

```
 3    v_Class classes%ROWTYPE;
 4    v_Description classes.description%TYPE;
 5  BEGIN
 6    -- First select into a single variable.
 7    v_SQLQuery :=
 8      'SELECT description ' ||
 9      '  FROM classes ' ||
10      '  WHERE department = ''ECN''' ||
11      '  AND course = 203';
12
13    EXECUTE IMMEDIATE v_SQLQuery
14      INTO v_Description;
15
16    DBMS_OUTPUT.PUT_LINE('Fetched ' || v_Description);
17
18    -- Now select into a record, using a bind variable.
19    v_SQLQuery :=
20      'SELECT * ' ||
21      '  FROM classes ' ||
22      '  WHERE description = :description';
23    EXECUTE IMMEDIATE v_SQLQuery
24      INTO v_Class
25      USING v_Description;
26
27    DBMS_OUTPUT.PUT_LINE(
28      'Fetched ' || v_Class.department || ' ' || v_Class.course);
29
30    -- Fetch more than one row, which will raise ORA-1422.
31    v_SQLQuery := 'SELECT * FROM classes';
32    EXECUTE IMMEDIATE v_SQLQuery
33      INTO v_Class;
34  END;
35  /
Fetched Economics 203
Fetched ECN 203
DECLARE
*
ERROR at line 1:
ORA-01422: exact fetch returns more than requested number of rows
ORA-06512: at line 32
```

Note the ORA-1422 error in the above example—this occurs because the query returned more than one row.

Bulk Binds

Oracle**8*i***
and higher SQL statements in PL/SQL blocks are sent to the SQL engine to be executed. The SQL engine can in turn send data back to the PL/SQL engine (as the result of a query). In many cases, data to be inserted or updated in the database is first put into a PL/SQL collection, and then this collection is iterated over with a FOR loop to send the information to the SQL engine. This results in a context switch between PL/SQL and SQL for each row in the collection.

Oracle8*i* and higher allow you to pass all rows in a collection to the SQL engine in one operation, eliminating all but one context switch. This is known as a *bulk bind*, and is done with the FORALL statement, and is illustrated by the following example:

```
-- Available online as part of FORALL.sql
DECLARE
  TYPE t_Numbers IS TABLE OF temp_table.num_col%TYPE;
  TYPE t_Strings IS TABLE OF temp_table.char_col%TYPE;
  v_Numbers t_Numbers := t_Numbers(1);
  v_Strings t_Strings := t_Strings(1);

  -- Prints the total number of rows in temp_table.
  PROCEDURE PrintTotalRows(p_Message IN VARCHAR2) IS
    v_Count NUMBER;
  BEGIN
    SELECT COUNT(*)
      INTO v_Count
      FROM temp_table;
    DBMS_OUTPUT.PUT_LINE(p_Message || ': Count is ' || v_Count);
  END PrintTotalRows;

BEGIN
  -- First delete from temp_table.
  DELETE FROM temp_table;

  -- Fill up the PL/SQL nested tables with 1000 values.
  v_Numbers.EXTEND(1000);
  v_Strings.EXTEND(1000);
  FOR v_Count IN 1..1000 LOOP
    v_Numbers(v_Count) := v_Count;
    v_Strings(v_Count) := 'Element #' || v_Count;
  END LOOP;

  -- Insert all 1000 elements using a single FORALL statement.
  FORALL v_Count IN 1..1000
    INSERT INTO temp_table VALUES
      (v_Numbers(v_Count), v_Strings(v_Count));

  -- There should be 1000 rows now.
  PrintTotalRows('After first insert');

  -- Insert elements 501 through 1000 again.
  FORALL v_Count IN 501..1000
```

```
          INSERT INTO temp_table VALUES
            (v_Numbers(v_Count), v_Strings(v_Count));

      -- We should now have 1500 rows
      PrintTotalRows('After second insert');

      -- Update all of the rows.
      FORALL v_Count IN 1..1000
        UPDATE temp_table
          SET char_col = 'Changed!'
          WHERE num_col = v_Numbers(v_Count);

      -- Even though there are only 1000 elements, the previous
      -- statement updated 1500 rows, since the WHERE clause matched
      -- 2 rows for each of the last 500.
      DBMS_OUTPUT.PUT_LINE(
        'Update processed ' || SQL%ROWCOUNT || ' rows.');

      -- Likewise, this DELETE will remove 300 rows
      FORALL v_Count IN 401..600
        DELETE FROM temp_table
          WHERE num_col = v_Numbers(v_Count);

      -- So there should be 1200 left.
      PrintTotalRows('After delete');
END;
```

The output from the above block is as follows:

```
After first insert: Count is 1000
After second insert: Count is 1500
Update processed 1500 rows.
After delete: Count is 1200
```

As this example illustrates, FORALL is syntactically similar to a FOR loop. It can be used with any collection type, and for INSERT, DELETE, and UPDATE statements. The range specified by FORALL must be contiguous, and all the elements in that range must exist.

Transactional Issues

If there is an error processing one of the rows in a bulk DML operation, only that row is rolled back. The prior rows are still processed. This is the same behavior as bulk operations with OCI or the precompilers, and is illustrated by the following example:

```
-- Available online as part of FORALL.sql
SQL> DECLARE
  2    TYPE t_Strings IS TABLE OF temp_table.char_col%TYPE
```

```
 3       INDEX BY BINARY_INTEGER;
 4     TYPE t_Numbers IS TABLE OF temp_table.num_col%TYPE
 5       INDEX BY BINARY_INTEGER;
 6     v_Strings t_Strings;
 7     v_Numbers t_Numbers;
 8   BEGIN
 9     -- Delete from the table, and set up the index-by table.
10     DELETE FROM temp_table;
11     FOR v_Count IN 1..10 LOOP
12       v_Strings(v_Count) := '123456789012345678901234567890';
13       v_Numbers(v_Count) := v_Count;
14     END LOOP;
15
16     FORALL v_Count IN 1..10
17       INSERT INTO temp_table (num_col, char_col)
18         VALUES (v_Numbers(v_Count), v_Strings(v_Count));
19
20     -- Add an extra character to v_Strings(6).
21     v_Strings(6) := v_Strings(6) || 'a';
22
23     -- This bulk update will fail on the sixth row, but the
24     -- first 5 rows will still be updated.
25     FORALL v_Count IN 1..10
26       UPDATE temp_table
27         SET char_col = char_col || v_Strings(v_Count)
28         WHERE num_col = v_Numbers(v_Count);
29   EXCEPTION
30     WHEN OTHERS THEN
31       DBMS_OUTPUT.PUT_LINE('Got exception: ' || SQLERRM);
32       COMMIT;
33   END;
34   /
Got exception: ORA-01401: inserted value too large for column
PL/SQL procedure successfully completed.

SQL> -- This query should show that the first 5 rows have been
SQL> -- modified.
SQL> SELECT char_col
  2    FROM temp_table
  3    ORDER BY num_col;

CHAR_COL
--------------------------------------------------------------
123456789012345678901234567890123456789012345678901234567890
123456789012345678901234567890123456789012345678901234567890
123456789012345678901234567890123456789012345678901234567890
123456789012345678901234567890123456789012345678901234567890
123456789012345678901234567890123456789012345678901234567890
123456789012345678901234567890
```

```
123456789012345678901234567890
123456789012345678901234567890
123456789012345678901234567890
123456789012345678901234567890
10 rows selected.
```

Oracle**9i**
and higher With Oracle9*i*, a new SAVE EXCEPTIONS clause is available with the FORALL statement. With this clause, any errors that occur during the batch processing will be saved, and processing will continue. You can use the new SQL%BULK_ EXCEPTIONS attribute, which acts as a PL/SQL table, to see the exceptions, as the following SQL*Plus session illustrates:

```
-- Available online as part of FORALL.sql
SQL> DECLARE
  2    TYPE t_Strings IS TABLE OF temp_table.char_col%TYPE
  3      INDEX BY BINARY_INTEGER;
  4    TYPE t_Numbers IS TABLE OF temp_table.num_col%TYPE
  5      INDEX BY BINARY_INTEGER;
  6    v_Strings t_Strings;
  7    v_Numbers t_Numbers;
  8    v_NumErrors NUMBER;
  9  BEGIN
 10    -- Delete from the table, and set up the index-by table.
 11    DELETE FROM temp_table;
 12    FOR v_Counst IN 1..10 LOOP
 13      v_Strings(v_Count) := '123456789012345678901234567890';
 14      v_Numbers(v_Count) := v_Count;
 15    END LOOP;
 16
 17    FORALL v_Count IN 1..10
 18      INSERT INTO temp_table (num_col, char_col)
 19        VALUES (v_Numbers(v_Count), v_Strings(v_Count));
 20
 21    -- Add an extra character to v_Strings(6).
 22    v_Strings(6) := v_Strings(6) || 'a';
 23
 24    -- This bulk update will fail on the sixth row, and continue
 25    -- processing.
 26    FORALL v_Count IN 1..10 SAVE EXCEPTIONS
 27      UPDATE temp_table
 28        SET char_col = char_col || v_Strings(v_Count)
 29        WHERE num_col = v_Numbers(v_Count);
 30  EXCEPTION
 31    WHEN OTHERS THEN
 32      DBMS_OUTPUT.PUT_LINE('Got exception: ' || SQLERRM);
 33      -- Print out any errors.
 34      v_NumErrors := SQL%BULK_EXCEPTIONS.COUNT;
 35      DBMS_OUTPUT.PUT_LINE(
```

```
36               'Number of errors during processing: ' || v_NumErrors);
37          FOR v_Count IN 1..v_NumErrors LOOP
38            DBMS_OUTPUT.PUT_LINE('Error ' || v_Count || ', iteration ' ||
39               SQL%BULK_EXCEPTIONS(v_Count).error_index || ' is: ' ||
40               SQLERRM(0 - SQL%BULK_EXCEPTIONS(v_Count).error_code));
41          END LOOP;
42
43          COMMIT;
44   END;
45   /
Got exception: ORA-24381: error(s) in array DML
Number of errors during processing: 1
Error 1, iteration 6 is: ORA-01401: inserted value too large for column
PL/SQL procedure successfully completed.

SQL> -- This query should show that rows 1-5, and 7-10 have been
SQL> -- modified, even though row 6 had an error.
SQL> SELECT char_col
  2    FROM temp_table
  3    ORDER BY num_col;


CHAR_COL
------------------------------------------------------------
12345678901234567890123456789012345678901234567890
12345678901234567890123456789012345678901234567890
12345678901234567890123456789012345678901234567890
12345678901234567890123456789012345678901234567890
12345678901234567890123456789012345678901234567890
12345678901234567890
12345678901234567890123456789012345678901234567890
12345678901234567890123456789012345678901234567890
12345678901234567890123456789012345678901234567890
12345678901234567890123456789012345678901234567890
10 rows selected.
```

BULK COLLECT Clause

The FORALL statement is used for DML operations, as we saw in the last section. The equivalent clause for a bulk fetch is the BULK COLLECT clause. BULK COLLECT is used as part of the SELECT INTO, FETCH INTO, or RETURNING INTO clause, and will retrieve rows from the query into the indicated collections, as illustrated by the following example:

```
-- Available online as part of BULK_COLLECT.sql
DECLARE
  TYPE t_Numbers IS TABLE OF temp_table.num_col%TYPE;
  TYPE t_Strings IS TABLE OF temp_table.char_col%TYPE;
  v_Numbers t_Numbers := t_Numbers(1);
```

```
  v_Strings t_Strings := t_Strings(1);
  v_Numbers2 t_Numbers;
  v_Strings2 t_Strings;

  CURSOR c_char IS
    SELECT char_col
    FROM temp_table
    WHERE num_col > 800
    ORDER BY num_col;
BEGIN
  -- First load temp_table with 1500 rows, 500 of which are
  -- duplicates.
  v_Numbers.EXTEND(1500);
  v_Strings.EXTEND(1500);
  FOR v_Count IN 1..1000 LOOP
    v_Numbers(v_Count) := v_Count;
    v_Strings(v_Count) := 'Element #' || v_Count;
    IF v_Count > 500 THEN
      v_Numbers(v_Count + 500) := v_Count;
      v_Strings(v_Count + 500) := 'Element #' || v_Count;
    END IF;
  END LOOP;

  DELETE FROM temp_table;
  FORALL v_Count IN 1..1500
    INSERT INTO temp_table (num_col, char_col)
      VALUES (v_Numbers(v_Count), v_Strings(v_Count));

  -- Grab all of the rows back into the nested tables in one
  -- operation.
  SELECT num_col, char_col
    BULK COLLECT INTO v_Numbers, v_Strings
    FROM temp_table
    ORDER BY num_col;

  DBMS_OUTPUT.PUT_LINE(
    'First query fetched ' || v_Numbers.COUNT || ' rows');

  -- The table does not have to be initialized, the BULK COLLECT
  -- will add elements as needed:
  SELECT num_col
    BULK COLLECT INTO v_Numbers2
    FROM temp_table;

  DBMS_OUTPUT.PUT_LINE(
    'Second query fetched ' || v_Numbers2.COUNT || ' rows');

  -- We can bulk fetch from a cursor as well.
  OPEN c_char;
```

```
    FETCH c_char BULK COLLECT INTO v_Strings2;
    CLOSE c_char;

    DBMS_OUTPUT.PUT_LINE(
      'Cursor fetch retrieved ' || v_Strings2.COUNT || ' rows');
END;
```

The output from the above block is as follows:

```
First query fetched 1500 rows
Second query fetched 1500 rows
Cursor fetch retrieved 400 rows
PL/SQL procedure successfully completed.
```

BULK COLLECT can be used for both implicit cursors (SELECT INTO) and explicit cursors (FETCH INTO). It will fetch the data starting at index 1, and successively overwrite elements in the output collection until it retrieves all the requested rows.

BULK COLLECT and RETURNING INTO   BULK COLLECT can be used as part of the RETURNING INTO clause as well, to return information from a DML statement, as the following example illustrates:

```
-- Available online as part of BULK_COLLECT.sql
SQL> DECLARE
  2    TYPE t_Numbers IS TABLE OF temp_table.num_col%TYPE
  3      INDEX BY BINARY_INTEGER;
  4    TYPE t_Strings IS TABLE OF temp_table.char_col%TYPE
  5      INDEX BY BINARY_INTEGER;
  6    v_Numbers t_Numbers;
  7    v_Strings t_Strings;
  8  BEGIN
  9    -- Delete from the table, and then insert 55 rows.  Also set
 10    -- up t_Numbers here.
 11    DELETE FROM temp_table;
 12    FOR v_Outer IN 1..10 LOOP
 13      FOR v_Inner IN 1..v_Outer LOOP
 14        INSERT INTO temp_table (num_col, char_col)
 15          VALUES (v_Outer, 'Element #' || v_Inner);
 16      END LOOP;
 17      v_Numbers(v_Outer) := v_Outer;
 18    END LOOP;
 20
 21    -- Delete some of the rows, but save the character data.
 21    FORALL v_Count IN 1..5
 22      DELETE FROM temp_table
 23        WHERE num_col = v_Numbers(v_Count)
 24        RETURNING char_col BULK COLLECT INTO v_Strings;
```

```
25
26    -- v_Strings now contains 15 rows, which is 1+2+3+4+5.
27    DBMS_OUTPUT.PUT_LINE('After delete:');
28    FOR v_Count IN 1..v_Strings.COUNT LOOP
29      DBMS_OUTPUT.PUT_LINE(
30        '  v_Strings(' || v_Count || ') = ' || v_Strings(v_Count));
31    END LOOP;
32  END;
33  /
After delete:
v_Strings(1) = Element #1
v_Strings(2) = Element #1
v_Strings(3) = Element #2
v_Strings(4) = Element #1
v_Strings(5) = Element #2
v_Strings(6) = Element #3
v_Strings(7) = Element #1
v_Strings(8) = Element #2
v_Strings(9) = Element #3
v_Strings(10) = Element #4
v_Strings(11) = Element #1
v_Strings(12) = Element #2
v_Strings(13) = Element #3
v_Strings(14) = Element #4
v_Strings(15) = Element #5
PL/SQL procedure successfully completed.
```

Object Types

| Oracle 8 and higher |

One of the major PL/SQL enhancements in Oracle8 was object types. Oracle8 extended the relational model of Oracle7 and earlier releases to include objects. An object type contains both attributes and methods. For example, consider the Point type, created with the following:

```
-- Available online as part of Point.sql
CREATE OR REPLACE TYPE Point AS OBJECT (
  -- A point is represented by its location on an X-Y Cartesian
  -- grid.
  x NUMBER,
  y NUMBER,

  -- Returns a string '(x, y)'
  MEMBER FUNCTION ToString RETURN VARCHAR2,
  PRAGMA RESTRICT_REFERENCES(ToString, RNDS, WNDS, RNPS, WNPS),

  -- Returns the distance between p and the current Point (SELF).
  -- If p is not specified then it defaults to (0, 0).
  MEMBER FUNCTION Distance(p IN Point DEFAULT Point(0,0))
```

```
    RETURN NUMBER,
  PRAGMA RESTRICT_REFERENCES(Distance, RNDS, WNDS, RNPS, WNPS),

  -- Returns the sum of p and and the current Point.
  MEMBER FUNCTION Plus(p IN Point) RETURN Point,
  PRAGMA RESTRICT_REFERENCES(Plus, RNDS, WNDS, RNPS, WNPS),

  -- Returns the current Point * n.
  MEMBER FUNCTION Times(n IN NUMBER) RETURN Point,
  PRAGMA RESTRICT_REFERENCES(Times, RNDS, WNDS, RNPS, WNPS)
);

CREATE OR REPLACE TYPE BODY Point AS
  -- Returns a string '(x, y)'
  MEMBER FUNCTION ToString RETURN VARCHAR2 IS
    v_Result VARCHAR2(20);
    v_xString VARCHAR2(8) := SUBSTR(TO_CHAR(x), 1, 8);
    v_yString VARCHAR2(8) := SUBSTR(TO_CHAR(y), 1, 8);
  BEGIN
    v_Result := '(' || v_xString || ', ';
    v_Result := v_Result || v_yString || ')';
    RETURN v_Result;
  END ToString;

  -- Returns the distance between p and the current Point (SELF).
  -- If p is not specified then it defaults to (0, 0).
  MEMBER FUNCTION Distance(p IN Point DEFAULT Point(0,0))
    RETURN NUMBER IS
  BEGIN
    RETURN SQRT(POWER(x - p.x, 2) + POWER(y - p.y, 2));
  END Distance;

  -- Returns the sum of p and the current Point.
  MEMBER FUNCTION Plus(p IN Point) RETURN Point IS
    v_Result Point;
  BEGIN
    v_Result := Point(x + p.x, y + p.y);
    RETURN v_Result;
  END Plus;

  -- Returns the current Point * n.
  MEMBER FUNCTION Times(n IN NUMBER) RETURN Point IS
    v_Result Point;
  BEGIN
    v_Result := Point(x * n, y * n);
    RETURN v_Result;
  END Times;
END;
```

The Point type models a single point on an X-Y Cartesian grid. We can observe the following about object types:

■ Object types are similar in syntax to packages, in that they have both a header and a body. Like packages, the body depends on the header.

■ Attributes, like x and y in the preceding example, are declared similar to PL/SQL variables. Methods, like ToString, Distance, Plus, and Times, are declared similar to PL/SQL subprograms, except that they have the keyword MEMBER.

■ Like a PL/SQL record, you can refer to object attributes using dot notation.

Once we have the type defined, we can declare objects of that type, and call methods on them, as the following SQL*Plus session illustrates:

```
-- Available online as part of Point.sql
SQL> DECLARE
  2     v_Point1 Point := Point(1, 2);
  3     v_Point2 Point;
  4     v_Point3 Point;
  5  BEGIN
  6     v_Point2 := v_Point1.Times(4);
  7     v_Point3 := v_Point1.Plus(v_Point2);
  8     DBMS_OUTPUT.PUT_LINE('Point 2: ' || v_Point2.ToString);
  9     DBMS_OUTPUT.PUT_LINE('Point 3: ' || v_Point3.ToString);
 10     DBMS_OUTPUT.PUT_LINE('Distance between origin and point 1: ' ||
 11       v_Point1.Distance);
 12     DBMS_OUTPUT.PUT_LINE('Distance between point 1 and point 2: ' ||
 13       v_Point1.Distance(v_Point2));
 14  END;
 15  /
Point 2: (4, 8)
Point 3: (5, 10)
Distance between origin and point 1:
 2.2360679774997896964091736687312762354
Distance between point 1 and point 2:
 6.7082039324993690892275210061938287063
PL/SQL procedure successfully completed.
```

This block shows that objects are initialized by a constructor, which takes all of the attributes as arguments. The constructor is implicitly created as part of the object type.

Storing Objects in the Database
Objects can be stored in database tables, and manipulated using SQL. A table can store objects as columns, or the table can be an object table, in which case each

row represents an object instance. The two types of tables, as well as some sample SQL statements, are illustrated by the following example:

```
-- Available online as part of PointSQL.sql
SQL> CREATE TABLE point_object_tab OF Point;
Table created.

SQL> CREATE TABLE point_column_tab (
  2    key VARCHAR2(20),
  3    value Point);
Table created.

SQL> DECLARE
  2    v_Point Point := Point(1, 1);
  3    v_NewPoint Point;
  4    v_Key point_column_tab.key%TYPE;
  5    v_XCoord NUMBER;
  6    v_YCoord NUMBER;
  7  BEGIN
  8    -- Insert into both tables.
  9    INSERT INTO point_object_tab VALUES (v_Point);
 10    INSERT INTO point_column_tab VALUES ('My Point', v_Point);
 11
 12    -- If we just query the object table, we get back each row as a
 13    -- set of select list items, as if it were a relational table.
 14    SELECT *
 15      INTO v_XCoord, v_YCoord
 16      FROM point_object_tab;
 17    DBMS_OUTPUT.PUT_LINE('Relational query of object table: ' ||
 18      v_XCoord || ', ' || v_YCoord);
 19
 20    -- But if we use the VALUE operator, we get each row as an
 21    -- object.
 22    SELECT VALUE(ot)
 23      INTO v_NewPoint
 24      FROM point_object_tab ot;
 25    DBMS_OUTPUT.PUT_LINE('object table: ' || v_NewPoint.ToString);
 26
 27    -- Selecting from an object column always returns an object
 28    -- instance.
 29    SELECT key, value
 30      INTO v_Key, v_NewPoint
 31      FROM point_column_tab;
 32    DBMS_OUTPUT.PUT_LINE('column table: ' || v_NewPoint.ToString);
 33
 34  END;
 35  /
Relational query of object table: 1, 1
object table: (1, 1)
PL/SQL procedure successfully completed.
```

In order to query a row in an object table and get the result back as an object (as opposed to individual columns), you must use the VALUE operator, as the preceding example shows.

Object References

Objects that are stored in the database are said to be *persistent*. A persistent object can have a reference to it. An object reference is a pointer to the object, rather than the object itself. Object references can be retrieved by using the REF operator in a query, or by using the REF INTO clause of an INSERT statement, as the following illustrates:

```
-- Available online as part of PointSQL.sql
SQL> DECLARE
  2    v_PointRef REF Point;
  3    v_Point Point;
  4  BEGIN
  5    DELETE FROM point_object_tab;
  6
  7    -- Insert some points into the object table.
  8    INSERT INTO point_object_tab (x, y)
  9      VALUES (0, 0);
 10    INSERT INTO point_object_tab (x, y)
 11      VALUES (1, 1);
 12
 13    -- Retrieve a reference to the second row
 14    SELECT REF(ot)
 15      INTO v_PointRef
 16      FROM point_object_tab ot
 17      WHERE x = 1 AND y = 1;
 18
 19    -- Dereference it to get an actual point
 20    SELECT DEREF(v_PointRef)
 21      INTO v_Point
 22      FROM dual;
 23    DBMS_OUTPUT.PUT_LINE('Selected reference ' ||
 24      v_Point.ToString);
 25
 26    -- We can also get a reference to a newly inserted row
 27    -- with REF INTO
 28    INSERT INTO point_object_tab ot (x, y)
 29      VALUES (10, 10)
 30      RETURNING REF(ot) INTO v_PointRef;
 31  END;
 32  /
Selected reference (1, 1)
PL/SQL procedure successfully completed.
```

Large Objects

A *large object* (LOB) is simply a database field that holds a large amount of data, such as a graphic file or long text document. What Oracle datatype is best to store this kind of information? In Oracle7, a VARCHAR2 column could hold up to 2,000 bytes. Besides limiting the maximum size, a VARCHAR2 column can hold only character data, and not binary data. A LONG column could hold up to 2GB and can store character data. Together with the LONG RAW datatype, which can store binary data, LONG and LONG RAW were the best datatypes available in Oracle7 for storing LOB information. However, LONG and LONG RAW columns have many restrictions, including the fact that there can be only one LONG or LONG RAW column per database table. In addition, the only interfaces for manipulating LONG or LONG RAW data piecewise are the Oracle Call Interface and the piecewise fetch of LONG data through the DBMS_SQL package. Manipulating LONG or LONG DATA through other interfaces requires that the entire column be contained in one variable, which can be limiting. Because of these and other restrictions, none of the Oracle7 datatypes provide a satisfactory solution to storing true LOBs.

| Oracle **8** |
| and higher |

In Oracle8 and higher, LONG and LONG RAW columns are still available (with the same restrictions), and the VARCHAR2 datatype can now hold 4,000 characters. While this helps, these datatypes still are not useful for storing large objects. In order to do this effectively, Oracle8 introduced a new datatype family—the LOB family. There are four different kinds of LOBs, which are designed for different kinds of data: CLOB, NCLOB, BLOB, and BFILE. These datatypes are described in Table 12-1.

The data is stored within the database, so CLOBs, NCLOBs, and BLOBs are collectively known as *internal LOBs*. Likewise, because BFILEs store the data outside the database, they are known as *external LOBs*. LOBs have the following characteristics:

- The maximum size of a LOB is 4GB, rather than the Oracle7 (and Oracle8) limit of 2GB for LONG and LONG RAW data.

- LOBs can be manipulated using one of several interfaces, including the Oracle8 OCI and PL/SQL with the DBMS_LOB package. All of the LOB interfaces provide random access to a LOB for both reading and writing (except for BFILEs, which are read-only).

- Many of the restrictions on LONG or LONG RAW data do not apply to LOBs. For example, unlike LONG or LONG RAW columns, there can be an unlimited number of LOB columns (up to the maximum number of columns) in a given database table.

LOB Type	Description
CLOB	Similar to the Oracle7 LONG type, a CLOB can hold character data in the database character set.
NCLOB	An NCLOB stores fixed-width multibyte national character set data. In Oracle8i, an NCLOB can store variable-width multibyte data.
BLOB	Similar to the Oracle7 LONG RAW type, a BLOB can hold unstructured binary data that is not interpreted by the database.
BFILE	BFILEs allow read-only access to large binary files stored outside the Oracle database. Unlike the other three LOB types, BFILE data is stored in a separate file that is not maintained by Oracle. The database stores a pointer to the external file. Any modifications of BFILE data must be done outside the database, and thus do not participate in Oracle transactions.

TABLE 12-1. *LOB Types*

■ Objects can have LOB attributes, and methods can take LOBs as arguments. However, an object cannot have an NCLOB attribute, although a method can take an NCLOB argument.

■ LOBs can be used as bind variables.

Internal LOBs can be manipulated using either SQL DML statements or through one of the LOB interfaces. Either way, there is full transactional support and read consistency, just like non-LOB data.

Manipulating LOB Data

Unlike a LONG or LONG RAW column, the data in a LOB is not generally accessed directly. Instead, a LOB column in a database table actually stores a locator. This locator in turn points to the actual LOB data.

There are a variety of interfaces for manipulating LOB data, including the DBMS_LOB package, the Oracle Call Interfaces, the Pro*C/C++ and Pro*COBOL precompilers, Oracle Objects for OLE, and JDBC. LOB data can also be manipulated using direct SQL. We will see an example of the DBMS_LOB package in the

"Advanced Packages" section of this chapter, and the following example illustrates some LOB manipulations using SQL:

```
-- Available online as LOB_DML.sql
SQL> CREATE TABLE lobdemo (
  2      key NUMBER PRIMARY KEY,
  3      clob_col  CLOB,
  4      blob_col  BLOB,
  5      bfile_col BFILE
  6  );
Table created.
SQL> -- The following two INSERTs will add twp rows to the table.
SQL> INSERT INTO lobdemo (key, clob_col, blob_col, bfile_col)
  2      VALUES (50, 'This is a character literal',
  3                  HEXTORAW('FEFEFEFEFEFEFEFEFEFE'),
  4                  NULL);
1 row created.

SQL> INSERT INTO lobdemo (key, clob_col, blob_col, bfile_col)
  2      VALUES (51, 'This is another character literal',
  3                  HEXTORAW('ABABABABABABABABABAB'),
  4                  NULL);
1 row created.

SQL> -- We can also do INSERTs with the results of a query.    The
SQL> -- following will copy rows 50 and 51 to 60 and 61.
SQL> INSERT INTO lobdemo
  2      SELECT key + 10, clob_col, blob_col, NULL
  3        FROM lobdemo
  4        WHERE key IN (50, 51);
2 rows created.

SQL> -- This statement will update blob_col to a new value.
SQL> UPDATE lobdemo
  2      SET blob_col = HEXTORAW('CDCDCDCDCDCDCDCDCDCDCDCDCD')
  3      WHERE key IN (60, 61);

2 rows updated.

SQL> -- And finally, we can delete row 61.
SQL> DELETE FROM lobdemo
  2      WHERE key = 61;
1 row deleted.
```

As the above example illustrates, LOB data can be manipulated as if it were a VARCHAR2 or RAW column, as long as the data does exceed 4,000 bytes (the maximum length of a VARCHAR2 column). Above this length, you must use one of the other interfaces.

Pipelined Table Functions

Oracle**9i**
and higher

In order for a PL/SQL function to return more than one row of data, it must do so either by returning a REF CURSOR or a collection of data. The REF CURSOR case is limited to data that can be selected from a query, and an entire collection must be materialized before it can be returned. Oracle9i rectifies the latter situation by introducing pipelined table functions. A *table function* is a function that returns an entire set of rows (usually as a collection), and can be queried directly from within a SQL statement, as if it were a true database table. A *pipelined table function* is similar, but returns the data as it is constructed rather than all at once. Pipelined table functions are more efficient, because the data is returned as soon as possible. For example, the following function will return a collection of up to 20 records:

```
-- Available online as part of pipelined.sql
 CREATE TYPE MyType AS OBJECT (
   field1 NUMBER,
   field2 VARCHAR2(50));

CREATE TYPE MyTypeList AS TABLE OF MyType;

CREATE OR REPLACE FUNCTION PipelineMe
  RETURN MyTypeList PIPELINED AS
  v_MyType MyType;
BEGIN
  FOR v_Count IN 1..20 LOOP
    v_MyType := MyType(v_Count, 'Row ' || v_Count);
    PIPE ROW(v_MyType);
  END LOOP;
  RETURN;
END PipelineMe;
```

A pipelined table function must return a collection. Within the function the PIPE ROW statement is used to return an individual element of the collection, and the function must conclude with an empty RETURN statement to indicate that it is finished. Once we create the above function, we can call it from a SQL query using the TABLE operator:

```
-- Available online as part of  pipelined.sql
SQL> SELECT *
  2    FROM TABLE(PipelineMe);
   FIELD1 FIELD2
--------- ----------------------
        1 Row 1
        2 Row 2
        3 Row 3
```

```
 4 Row 4
 5 Row 5
 6 Row 6
 7 Row 7
 8 Row 8
 9 Row 9
10 Row 10
11 Row 11
12 Row 12
13 Row 13
14 Row 14
15 Row 15
16 Row 16
17 Row 17
18 Row 18
19 Row 19
20 Row 20
20 rows selected.
```

Although this is a trivial example, it shows how pipelined table functions can be used. They are often used to transform data from one type to another.

Advanced Packages

In addition to the language features that we saw in the previous sections, PL/SQL has many built-in packages. These packages add additional functionality to the language, such as communications protocols and access to the file system. Appendix A lists many of the packages that are supplied with the database. In the following sections, we will briefly describe some of the core packages.

DBMS_SQL

DBMS_SQL is used to execute dynamic SQL from within PL/SQL. Unlike native dynamic SQL (which is available with Oracle8*i* and higher), it is not built directly into the language, and thus is less efficient. The DBMS_SQL package allows you to directly control the processing of a statement within a cursor, with operations such as opening and closing a cursor, parsing a statement, binding input variables, and defining output variables. The following example illustrates some uses of the DBMS_SQL package:

```
-- Available online as dynamicDML.sql
CREATE OR REPLACE PROCEDURE UpdateClasses(
  /* Uses DBMS_SQL to update the classes table, setting the number of
   * credits for all classes in the specified department to the
   * specified number of credits.
   */
```

```
  p_Department  IN classes.department%TYPE,
  p_NewCredits  IN classes.num_credits%TYPE,
  p_RowsUpdated OUT INTEGER) AS

  v_CursorID   INTEGER;
  v_UpdateStmt VARCHAR2(100);
BEGIN
  -- Open the cursor for processing.
  v_CursorID := DBMS_SQL.OPEN_CURSOR;

  -- Determine the SQL string.
  v_UpdateStmt :=
    'UPDATE classes
       SET num_credits = :nc
       WHERE department = :dept';

  -- Parse the statement.
  DBMS_SQL.PARSE(v_CursorID, v_UpdateStmt, DBMS_SQL.NATIVE);

  -- Bind p_NewCredits to the placeholder :nc.  This overloaded
  -- version of BIND_VARIABLE will bind p_NewCredits as a NUMBER,
  -- since that is how it is declared.
  DBMS_SQL.BIND_VARIABLE(v_CursorID, ':nc', p_NewCredits);

  -- Bind p_Department to the placeholder :dept.  This overloaded
  -- version of BIND_VARIABLE will bind p_Department as a CHAR, since
  -- that is how it is declared.
  DBMS_SQL.BIND_VARIABLE_CHAR(v_CursorID, ':dept', p_Department);

  -- Execute the statement.
  p_RowsUpdated := DBMS_SQL.EXECUTE(v_CursorID);

  -- Close the cursor.
  DBMS_SQL.CLOSE_CURSOR(v_CursorID);
EXCEPTION
  WHEN OTHERS THEN
    -- Close the cursor, then raise the error again.
    DBMS_SQL.CLOSE_CURSOR(v_CursorID);
    RAISE;
END UpdateClasses;
```

DBMS_PIPE

DBMS_PIPE allows you to send messages between sessions that are connected to the same database. The sessions can be different client programs, or on different machines. As long as they can issue PL/SQL commands to the server, they can communicate. For example, you can use DBMS_PIPE to communicate between a stored procedure and a Pro*C program. This provides functionality similar to an external procedure.

Pipes are *asynchronous*—they operate independent of transactions. Once a message is sent along a pipe, there is no way of canceling it, even if the session that sent it issues a ROLLBACK. Thus, they can also be used to implement the functionality of autonomous transactions.

Messages are sent along a pipe by the writer by first packing them into a buffer, and then sending the buffer. The reader then receives the buffer and unpacks the message. For example, suppose we execute the following block from one SQL*Plus session:

```
-- Available online as PipeSend.sql
DECLARE
  v_PipeName VARCHAR2(30) := 'MyPipe';
  v_Status INTEGER;
BEGIN
  -- Pack some information into the pipe.  We will send the current
  -- date, along with a number and varchar2 value.
  DBMS_PIPE.PACK_MESSAGE(SYSDATE);
  DBMS_PIPE.PACK_MESSAGE(123456);
  DBMS_PIPE.PACK_MESSAGE('This is a message sent from the pipe!');

  -- Now we can send the message.
  v_Status := DBMS_PIPE.SEND_MESSAGE(v_PipeName);
  IF v_Status != 0 THEN
    DBMS_OUTPUT.PUT_LINE('Error ' || v_Status ||
                         ' while sending message');
  END IF;
END;
```

This will send a message consisting of a date, number, and string along the pipe MyPipe. Now, we can receive this message from another (or the same) SQL*Plus session connected to the same database, with the following:

```
-- Available online as PipeReceive.sql
DECLARE
  v_PipeName VARCHAR2(30) := 'MyPipe';
  v_Status INTEGER;
  v_DateVal DATE;
  v_NumberVal NUMBER;
  v_StringVal VARCHAR2(100);
BEGIN
  -- First receive the message.  This call will block until
  -- the message is actually sent.
  v_Status := DBMS_PIPE.RECEIVE_MESSAGE(v_PipeName);
  IF v_Status != 0 THEN
    DBMS_OUTPUT.PUT_LINE('Error ' || v_Status ||
                         ' while receiving message');
  END IF;

  -- Now we can unpack the parts of the message.  This is done
```

```
     -- in the same order in which they were sent.
     DBMS_PIPE.UNPACK_MESSAGE(v_DateVal);
     DBMS_PIPE.UNPACK_MESSAGE(v_NumberVal);
     DBMS_PIPE.UNPACK_MESSAGE(v_StringVal);

     -- And print them out.
     DBMS_OUTPUT.PUT_LINE('Unpacked ' || v_DateVal);
     DBMS_OUTPUT.PUT_LINE('Unpacked ' || v_NumberVal);
     DBMS_OUTPUT.PUT_LINE('Unpacked ' || v_StringVal);
END;
```

DBMS_PIPE can be used to send messages consisting of VARCHAR2, NUMBER, DATE, RAW, or ROWID data. User-defined object types and collections are not supported by DBMS_PIPE. Oracle Advanced Queuing can be used to send messages with these types.

DBMS_ALERT

DBMS_ALERT, similar to DBMS_PIPE, can also be used to communicate between sessions connected to the same database. However, there are several significant differences:

- Alerts are *synchronous*. An alert is not sent until the writing session issues a COMMIT. If it rolls back, the alert is not sent.

- A message sent along a pipe will be retrieved by only one reader. If there are multiple readers on a pipe, only one of them will get the message. Alerts, however, can be received by many readers simultaneously.

- Pipe messages consist of different packed portions, each of which can be a different datatype. Alerts, on the other hand, consist of a single text string.

- If two messages are sent along a pipe before they are read, a reader will receive both. If two alerts are sent, however, only the second alert will be received.

The following block illustrates how to send an alert, through the DBMS_ALERT.SIGNAL procedure:

```
-- Available online as AlertSend.sql
DECLARE
  v_AlertName VARCHAR2(30) := 'MyAlert';
BEGIN
  -- An alert is sent by the SIGNAL procedure.
  DBMS_ALERT.SIGNAL(v_AlertName, 'Alert!  Alert!  Alert!');

  -- It is not actually sent until we commit.
  COMMIT;
END;
```

Alerts are read with the WAITONE or WAITANY procedures. The following block illustrates WAITONE:

```
-- Available online as AlertReceive.sql
DECLARE
  v_AlertName VARCHAR2(30) := 'MyAlert';
  v_Message VARCHAR2(100);
  v_Status INTEGER;
BEGIN
  -- In order to receive an alert, we must first register interest
  -- in it.
  DBMS_ALERT.REGISTER(v_AlertName);

  -- Now that we have registered, we can wait.
  DBMS_ALERT.WAITONE(v_AlertName, v_Message, v_Status);

  IF v_Status = 0 THEN
    DBMS_OUTPUT.PUT_LINE('Received: ' || v_Message);
  ELSE
    DBMS_OUTPUT.PUT_LINE('WAITONE timed out');
  END IF;
END;
```

UTL_FILE

PL/SQL does not have any built-in capabilities to interact with the file system outside the database; it is designed to manipulate relational data within the database through SQL. Through the UTL_FILE package, however, a PL/SQL program can read from and write to a file on the file system. The file must either be physically located on the same machine as the server or accessible from it through a directory mapping (such as NFS).

UTL_FILE accesses files through a directory and filename. In order to access a file, the directory must be accessible to the database. There are two levels of security to accomplish this:

- The directory must be readable or writable by the operating system user that owns the Oracle processes.

- The directory must be specified by the UTL_FILE_DIR init.ora parameter. UTL_FILE_DIR can be a list of directories, or * to indicate that all directories are legal.

Once these have been satisfied, you can access files in the specified directory, as the following example illustrates:

```
-- Available online as UTL_FILE.sql
DECLARE
  v_FileHandle UTL_FILE.FILE_TYPE;
```

```
BEGIN
  -- Open the file /tmp/utl_file.txt for writing.  If the
  -- file does not exist, this will create it.  If the file
  -- does exist, this will overwrite it.
  v_FileHandle := UTL_FILE.FOPEN('/tmp/', 'utl_file.txt', 'w');

  -- Write some lines to the file.
  UTL_FILE.PUT_LINE(v_FileHandle, 'This is line 1!');
  FOR v_Counter IN 2..11 LOOP
    UTL_FILE.PUTF(v_FileHandle, 'This is line %s!\n', v_Counter);
  END LOOP;

  -- And close the file.
  UTL_FILE.FCLOSE(v_FileHandle);
END;
```

After running the above block, /tmp/utl_file.txt will look like the following:

```
This is line 1!
This is line 2!
This is line 3!
This is line 4!
This is line 5!
This is line 6!
This is line 7!
This is line 8!
This is line 9!
This is line 10!
This is line 11!
```

UTL_FILE can also be used for reading text files. Note that binary files cannot be accessed using UTL_FILE—only text files are supported.

UTL_TCP

Oracle**8i**
and higher

UTL_TCP, similar to UTL_FILE, provides PL/SQL with the ability to communicate outside the database. Instead of file access, however, UTL_TCP provides the ability to open a socket to a remote host, and read and write on it with the TCP protocol. The following example illustrates the use of UTL_TCP to get a single HTTP request from a host:

```
-- Available online as UTL_TCP.sql
DECLARE
   v_Connection UTL_TCP.CONNECTION;
   v_NumWritten PLS_INTEGER;
BEGIN
```

```
-- Open the connection at port 80, which is the standard HTTP port
v_Connection := UTL_TCP.OPEN_CONNECTION('www.oracle.com', 80);

-- Send HTTP request
v_NumWritten := UTL_TCP.WRITE_LINE(v_Connection, 'GET / HTTP/1.0');
v_NumWritten := UTL_TCP.WRITE_LINE(v_Connection);

-- Print out the first 10 lines returned
BEGIN
  FOR v_Count IN 1..10 LOOP
    DBMS_OUTPUT.PUT_LINE(UTL_TCP.GET_LINE(v_Connection, TRUE));
  END LOOP;
EXCEPTION
  WHEN UTL_TCP.END_OF_INPUT THEN
    NULL;
END;

UTL_TCP.CLOSE_CONNECTION(v_Connection);
END;
```

UTL_TCP can be used to implement any protocol that is built on top of TCP. In fact, UTL_SMTP, UTL_HTTP, and UTL_INADDR do exactly this, and use UTL_TCP internally.

UTL_SMTP

| Oracle**8i** and higher | UTL_SMTP is written on top of UTL_TCP and implements the SMTP protocol, used for sending email. It allows you to communicate with an SMTP server outside the database, as the following example illustrates:

```
-- Available online as UTL_SMTP.sql
DECLARE
  v_FromAddr VARCHAR2(50) := 'Oracle';
  v_ToAddr VARCHAR2(50) := 'YOUR_EMAIL_ADDRESS';
  v_Message VARCHAR2(200);

  -- Address of an SMTP server.  On Unix systems, 'localhost'
  -- will often work.
  v_MailHost VARCHAR2(50) := 'localhost';
  v_MailConnection UTL_SMTP.Connection;
BEGIN
  -- Message to be sent.  The message fields (from, subject, etc.)
  -- should be separated by carriage returns, which is CHR(10) on
  -- most systems.
  v_Message :=
    'From: ' || v_FromAddr || CHR(10) ||
    'Subject: Hello from PL/SQL!' || CHR(10) ||
```

```
         'This message sent to you courtesy of the UTL_SMTP package.';

      -- Open the connection to the server.
      v_MailConnection := UTL_SMTP.OPEN_CONNECTION(v_MailHost);

      -- Using SMTP messages, send the email.
      UTL_SMTP.HELO(v_MailConnection, v_MailHost);
      UTL_SMTP.MAIL(v_MailConnection, v_FromAddr);
      UTL_SMTP.RCPT(v_MailConnection, v_ToAddr);
      UTL_SMTP.DATA(v_MailConnection, v_Message);

      -- Close the connection.
      UTL_SMTP.QUIT(v_MailConnection);
END;
```

UTL_SMTP is designed for sending email through an existing SMTP server; it is
not designed to implement an SMTP server itself.

UTL_HTTP

UTL_HTTP implements the HTTP protocol, and allows a PL/SQL program to act as a
client communicating with an HTTP server (similar to a Web browser). UTL_HTTP
was first introduced in Oracle8 (and provided basic services in that release) essentially
just retrieving the results of a single HTTP request either on one piece (through
UTL_HTTP.REQUEST) or in smaller pieces (through UTL_HTTP.REQUEST_PIECES),
as the following example illustrates:

```
-- Available online as part of UTL_HTTP.sql
CREATE TABLE http_results (
  sequence_no NUMBER PRIMARY KEY,
  piece VARCHAR2(2000));

DECLARE
  v_Result UTL_HTTP.HTML_PIECES;
  v_URL VARCHAR2(100) := 'http://www.oracle.com';
  v_Proxy VARCHAR2(100) := 'YOUR_PROXY_SERVER';
BEGIN
  -- This call illustrates the functionality of UTL_HTTP
  -- as of 8.0.6.  It will retrieve up to 10 pieces of the
  -- response, each up to 2000 characters.
  v_Result := UTL_HTTP.REQUEST_PIECES(v_URL, 10, v_Proxy);
  FOR v_Count IN 1..10 LOOP
    INSERT INTO http_results VALUES (v_Count, v_Result(v_Count));
  END LOOP;
END;
/
```

Oracle8*i* extends UTL_HTTP to support the HTTPS protocol along with a client-side wallet. Oracle9*i* features a complete rewrite of UTL_HTTP, and includes support for HTTPS, cookies, redirects, persistent connections, and access to authenticated Web sites.

UTL_INADDR

| Oracle**8*i*** |
| and higher |

UTL_INADDR provides the ability to look up the IP address of a host based on its name with the GET_HOST_ADDRESS function. The GET_HOST_NAME function will return the name of the local host.

| Oracle**9*i*** |
| and higher |

In Oracle9*i*, GET_HOST_NAME can optionally take an IP address, in which case it will return the name of the host at the specified address. The following block illustrates how to use UTL_INADDR:

```
-- Available online as UTL_INADDR.sql
DECLARE
  v_HostName VARCHAR2(100) := 'www.oracle.com';
BEGIN
  DBMS_OUTPUT.PUT_LINE('Address of ' || v_HostName || ' is ' ||
    UTL_INADDR.GET_HOST_ADDRESS(v_HostName));
  DBMS_OUTPUT.PUT_LINE('Name of local host is ' ||
    UTL_INADDR.GET_HOST_NAME);
END;
```

DBMS_JOB

The DBMS_JOB package allows you to schedule a PL/SQL block to run automatically at specified times, similar to the UNIX cron utility. The block will be run by one of the Oracle background processes. To facilitate this, there are two `init.ora` parameters that need to be set:

- JOB_QUEUE_PROCESSES specifies the number of background processes to start. If this is 0 or not set, there will be no background processes for jobs and they will not run.

- JOB_QUEUE_INTERVAL specifies the amount of time, in seconds, that each process will wait before checking for a new job. A job cannot run more than once every JOB_QUEUE_INTERVAL seconds.

For example, suppose we create a procedure `TempInsert` with

```
-- Available online as part of DBMS_JOB.sql
CREATE SEQUENCE temp_seq
  START WITH 1
```

```
  INCREMENT BY 1;

CREATE OR REPLACE PROCEDURE TempInsert AS
BEGIN
  INSERT INTO temp_table (num_col, char_col)
    VALUES (temp_seq.NEXTVAL,
            TO_CHAR(SYSDATE, 'DD-MON-YYYY HH24:MI:SS'));
  COMMIT;
END TempInsert;
```

We can have `TempInsert` run every 90 seconds with the following SQL*Plus script:

```
-- Available online as part of DBMS_JOB.sql
SQL> VARIABLE v_JobNum NUMBER
SQL> BEGIN
  2      DBMS_JOB.SUBMIT(:v_JobNum, 'TempInsert;', SYSDATE,
  3                      'SYSDATE + (90/(24*60*60))');
  4    COMMIT;
  5  END;
  6  /
PL/SQL procedure successfully completed.

SQL>
SQL> PRINT v_JobNum

 V_JOBNUM
---------
        2
```

The SUBMIT procedure will submit the job for running. In the above example, the job will start running immediately, and will subsequently run at an interval of 90 seconds, based on the 'SYSDATE + (90 / (24 * 60 * 60))' expression, which indicates the next time the job is to be run.

Note the COMMIT calls in both the block that submits the job, and in the `TempInsert` procedure itself. Without the first, the job would not be submitted, and without the second, the changes made by the job would automatically be rolled back when the job completed.

As written, the preceding job will run indefinitely, until the database is shut down. It can be removed before this by calling DBMS_JOB.REMOVE, as the following block illustrates:

```
-- Available online as part of DBMS_JOB.sql
BEGIN
  DBMS_JOB.REMOVE(:v_JobNum);
  COMMIT;
END;
```

DBMS_LOB

Oracle**8**
and higher The PL/SQL interface to LOBs is the DBMS_LOB package. This package allows you to manipulate data stored in CLOB, NCLOB, BLOB, and BFILE columns. Among other things, DBMS_LOB allows you to compare two LOBs, append data to a LOB, copy data from one LOB to another, erase portions of a LOB, and perform INSTR or SUBSTR operations in addition to reading and writing LOB data with random access. DBMS_LOB also provides routines specific to BFILES, which enable you to open, close, and retrieve information about BFILEs. In Oracle8*i* and higher, DBMS_LOB also allows you to create and manipulate temporary LOBs.

Most of the DBMS_LOB subprograms take a LOB locator as an argument. This locator must be initialized and point to a valid LOB in the database. In order to create a new LOB locator, you can use the EMPTY_BLOB or EMPTY_CLOB functions.

The following example illustrates some of the DBMS_LOB subprograms:

```
-- Available online as part of DBMS_LOB.sql
/* Reverses the characters in the CLOB pointed to by p_InputLocator,
 * p_ChunkSize bytes at a time.  The result is returned in
 * p_OutputLocator.  For example, a call like
 *
 * ReverseLOB('abcdefghijklmnopqrstuvwxyz', output, 4)
 *
 * will set output to 'yzuvwxqrstmnopijklefghabcd'.  If p_ChunkSize
 * does not evenly divide the length of the input, the last chunk of
 * the input LOB, which will become the first chunk of the output
 * LOB, will be smaller than p_ChunkSize.  If p_ChunkSize is larger
 * than the length of the input LOB, then the output LOB will be
 * identical to the input LOB.
 */
CREATE OR REPLACE PROCEDURE ReverseLOB(
  p_InputLocator IN CLOB,
  p_OutputLocator IN OUT CLOB,
  p_ChunkSize IN NUMBER) AS

  v_InputOffset       BINARY_INTEGER;
  v_OutputOffset      BINARY_INTEGER;
  v_LOBLength         BINARY_INTEGER;
  v_CurrentChunkSize  BINARY_INTEGER;
  e_TrimLength        EXCEPTION;
  PRAGMA EXCEPTION_INIT(e_TrimLength, -22926);

BEGIN
  -- First determine the input LOB length.
  v_LOBLength := DBMS_LOB.GETLENGTH(p_InputLocator);

  -- Trim the output LOB to the input length.  Trap and ignore the
  -- ORA-22926 error if the output LOB is less than v_LOBLength
```

```
  -- already.
  BEGIN
    DBMS_LOB.TRIM(p_OutputLocator, v_LOBLength);
  EXCEPTION
    WHEN e_TrimLength THEN
      NULL;
  END;

  -- Set up the initial offsets.  The input offset starts at the
  -- beginning, the output offset at the end.
  v_InputOffset := 1;
  v_OutputOffset := v_LOBLength + 1;

  -- Loop through the input LOB, and write each chunk to the output
  -- LOB.
  LOOP
    -- Exit the loop when we've done all the chunks, indicated by
    -- v_InputOffset passing v_LOBLength.
    EXIT WHEN v_InputOffset > v_LOBLength;

    -- If at least p_ChunkSize remains in the input LOB, copy that
    -- much.  Otherwise, copy only however much remains.
    IF (v_LOBLength - v_InputOffset + 1) > p_ChunkSize THEN
      v_CurrentChunkSize := p_ChunkSize;
    ELSE
      v_CurrentChunkSize := v_LOBLength - v_InputOffset + 1;
    END IF;

    -- Decrement the output offset by the current chunk size.
    v_OutputOffset := v_OutputOffset - v_CurrentChunkSize;

    -- Copy the current chunk.
    DBMS_LOB.COPY(p_OutputLocator,
                  p_InputLocator,
                  v_CurrentChunkSize,
                  v_OutputOffset,
                  v_InputOffset);

    -- Increment the input offset by the current chunk size.
    v_InputOffset := v_InputOffset + v_CurrentChunkSize;
  END LOOP;
END ReverseLOB;
```

The following SQL*Plus session illustrates some calls to ReverseLOB:

```
-- Available online as part of DBMS_LOB.sql
SQL> CREATE TABLE lobdemo (
  2    key NUMBER,
```

```
  3     clob_col CLOB,
  4     blob_col BLOB);
Table created.

SQL> INSERT INTO lobdemo (key, clob_col)
  2     VALUES (1, 'abcdefghijklmnopqrstuvwxyz');
1 row created.
SQL> INSERT INTO lobdemo (key, clob_col)
  2     VALUES (2, EMPTY_CLOB());
1 row created.
SQL> INSERT INTO lobdemo (key, clob_col)
  2     VALUES (3, EMPTY_CLOB());
1 row created.
SQL> INSERT INTO lobdemo (key, clob_col)
  2     VALUES (4, EMPTY_CLOB());
1 row created.
SQL> INSERT INTO lobdemo (key, clob_col)
  2     VALUES (5, EMPTY_CLOB());
1 row created.
SQL> INSERT INTO lobdemo (key, clob_col)
  2     VALUES (6, EMPTY_CLOB());
1 row created.
SQL> COMMIT;
Commit complete.

SQL> SELECT key, clob_col
  2     FROM lobdemo
  3     WHERE key BETWEEN 1 AND 6
  4     ORDER BY key;
       KEY CLOB_COL
--------- -----------------------------------------------------------
         1 abcdefghijklmnopqrstuvwxyz
         2
         3
         4
         5
         6
6 rows selected.

SQL> DECLARE
  2     v_Source CLOB;
  3     v_Destination CLOB;
  4     v_Key NUMBER;
  5     CURSOR c_Destinations IS
  6       SELECT key, clob_col
  7       FROM lobdemo
  8       WHERE key BETWEEN 2 and 6
  9       FOR UPDATE;
```

```
10  BEGIN
11    SELECT clob_col
12      INTO v_Source
13      FROM lobdemo
14      WHERE key = 1;
15
16    -- Loop through rows 2-6, and reverse row 1 into them, in
17    -- varying ways.
18    OPEN c_Destinations;
19    LOOP
20      FETCH c_Destinations INTO v_Key, v_Destination;
21      EXIT WHEN c_Destinations%NOTFOUND;
22
23      IF (v_Key = 2) THEN
24        ReverseLOB(v_Source, v_Destination, 4);
25      ELSIF (v_Key = 3) THEN
26        ReverseLOB(v_Source, v_Destination, 2);
27      ELSIF (v_Key = 4) THEN
28        ReverseLOB(v_Source, v_Destination, 1);
29      ELSIF (v_Key = 5) THEN
30        ReverseLOB(v_Source, v_Destination, 10);
31      ELSIF (v_Key = 6) THEN
32        ReverseLOB(v_Source, v_Destination, 30);
33      END IF;
34    END LOOP;
35    CLOSE c_Destinations;
36    COMMIT;
37  END;
38  /
PL/SQL procedure successfully completed.

SQL> SELECT key, clob_col
  2    FROM lobdemo
  3    WHERE key BETWEEN 1 AND 6
  4    ORDER BY key;
     KEY CLOB_COL
--------- -----------------------------------------------------------
       1 abcdefghijklmnopqrstuvwxyz
       2 yzuvwxqrstmnopijklefghabcd
       3 yzwxuvstqropmnklijghefcdab
       4 zyxwvutsrqponmlkjihgfedcba
       5 uvwxyzklmnopqrstabcdefghij
       6 abcdefghijklmnopqrstuvwxyz
6 rows selected.
```

Summary

In this chapter, we have seen an overview of some of the more advanced features of PL/SQL, which come in two forms: language features and packages. These features provide PL/SQL with significantly more power and flexibility, and allow you to write much more useful programs. The features included external routines, native dynamic SQL, bulk binds, object types, and large objects. We also looked at the DBMS_SQL, DBMS_PIPE, DBMS_ALERT, UTL_FILE, UTL_TCP, UTL_SMTP, UTL_HTTP, UTL_INADDR, DBMS_JOB, and DBMS_LOB packages.

PART
IV

Appendixes

APPENDIX

A

Guide to Supplied Packages

his appendix catalogs many of the built-in packages that are available for use with PL/SQL.

Package Descriptions

PL/SQL has a lot of additional functionality that is available through supplied packages. These packages are owned by the database user sys. There are public synonyms for them as well, so they can be called without prefixing sys to the package name. EXECUTE permission on the package is necessary for users other than sys to call the procedures and functions within the packages. All of the packages are created by the catproc.sql script, which is generally found in the $ORACLE_HOME/rdbms/admin directory. You can look online in your Oracle system to find additional information—the individual packages are created in separate files. The location of the files is the same as catproc.sql. The files to create each package contain comments that provide further information about how to use them.

Each of the supplied packages is briefly described in the following sections, including the release in which they were introduced. For more information on these packages, see either *Oracle8i Advanced PL/SQL Programming* or the *Oracle Supplied Packages* manual.

DBMS_ALERT

Version Available   7.3

Description   The DBMS_ALERT package is used to send messages between sessions connected to the same database. Alerts are synchronous, meaning that they are sent when the transaction commits. Alerts are sent with the SIGNAL procedure, and received by the WAITONE and WAITANY procedures. In order to receive an alert, an interested session must register for it using the REGISTER procedure. Information about alerts can be found in the dbms_alert_info data dictionary table.

DBMS_APPLICATION_INFO

Version Available   7.3

Description   The DBMS_APPLICATION_INFO package is used to register information about a particular program in the v$session system table. This information can then be used in queries to determine what applications are running, and what they are doing. Specifically, DBMS_APPLICATION_INFO can be used to read and modify the `module`, `action`, and `client_info` columns of `v$session` for the current session.

The `module` column is meant to contain the name of the application. For example, SQL*Plus sets this column to the string "SQL*Plus." The `action` column is meant to contain the current part of the application that is running. For example, you could set `action` before entering a section of a Pro*C program. The `client_info` column can be set to an arbitrary string.

Oracle **8** and higher | DBMS_APPLICATION_INFO can also be used (through the SET_SESSION_LONGOPS procedure) to update the `v$session_longop` table, used to indicate the status of a long-running operation.

DBMS_AQ

Version Available   Oracle8

Description   DBMS_AQ implements the enqueue and dequeue operations for database queues, also known as Oracle/AQ. In Oracle8*i* and higher, there are also Java and C interfaces to Oracle/AQ. AQ can be used in conjunction with third-party messaging systems, or can be used alone.

DBMS_AQADM

Version Available   Oracle8

Description   DBMS_AQADM provides administrative functionality for AQ. It includes procedures to create and drop queues and queue tables, and to modify privileges for queues.

DBMS_AQELM

Version Available   Oracle9*i*

Description   DBMS_AQELM provides procedures to control AQ notification through email and HTTP. It allows you to configure details such as the mail host, port, sent-from email address, and HTTP proxy.

DBMS_BACKUP_RESTORE

Version Available   Oracle8*i* Release 8.1.6

Description   This package contains procedures to normalize the filenames used in the control file and recovery catalog on Windows NT systems. It is not designed to work on UNIX systems, or on releases earlier than 8.1.6.

DBMS_DDL

Version Available   7.3

Description   The DBMS_DDL package provides PL/SQL equivalents of some useful DDL commands that cannot be used directly in PL/SQL. Although dynamic SQL can be used to execute these commands as well, DBMS_DDL provides an alternative syntax. Among the procedures in DBMS_DDL are DBMS_DDL: ALTER_ COMPILE, used to compile packages, triggers, procedures, and functions; and ANALYZE_OBJECT, used to analyze tables, clusters, or indexes.

DBMS_DEBUG

Version Available   Oracle8i (although this package was present in earlier versions, it is not supported publicly until Oracle8i)

Description   The DBMS_DEBUG package provides a PL/SQL interface to the Probe debugger. It is intended primarily to implement server-side debuggers. Using DBMS_DEBUG involves interaction between two database sessions—one that is being debugged, and the other that controls the debugging process. In order to debug a procedure, it must have been compiled with the DEBUG option.

DBMS_DEFER

Version Available   Oracle8

Description   DBMS_DEFER provides an interface to automatically call procedures in other databases. It allows you to identify procedures to be called at a given set of remote nodes.

DBMS_DEFER_QUERY

Version Available   Oracle8

Description   DBMS_DEFER_QUERY is used to get information about calls set up using DBMS_DEFER. Some of this information is available through data dictionary views, but DBMS_DEFER_QUERY provides more details.

DBMS_DEFER_SYS

Version Available   Oracle8

Description   DBMS_DEFER_SYS is used to actually execute procedures queued up by DBMS_DEFER, and to set up the list of nodes that are available for distributed processing. It also provides a mechanism to re-execute procedures that have failed.

DBMS_DESCRIBE

Version Available   7.3

Description   The DBMS_DESCRIBE package has only one procedure—DESCRIBE_PROCEDURE. Given the name of a stored procedure or function, it will return information about the parameters that the subprogram takes. If the subprogram is overloaded as part of a package, information about all the overloaded versions is returned.

   In Oracle9*i*, the DBMS_METADATA package is available, which provides information about all database objects, not just procedures.

DBMS_DISTRUBUTED_TRUST_ADMIN

Version Available   Oracle8

Description   This package is used to maintain the trusted database list, which specifies the databases that are or are not to be trusted. Along with the central authority, it is used to determine which privileged database links can be accepted. In Oracle9*i*, the enterprise LDAP directory can also be used to manage the trusted database list.

DBMS_FGA

Version Available   Oracle9*i*

Description   DBMS_FGA maintains fine-grained security functions. It has four procedures: ADD_POLICY, which creates an audit policy; DROP_POLICY, which drops a policy; and ENABLE_POLICY and DISABLE_POLICY, which enable and disable policies, respectively.

DBMS_FLASHBACK

Version Available   Oracle9*i*

Description   DBMS_FLASHBACK is used to see data as of an earlier point in time. It is enabled on a session basis only. A given flashback can be specified in terms of wall clock time or a system change number (SCN). The GET_SYSTEM_ CHANGE_NUMBER procedure returns the current SCN, and the ENABLE_AT_TIME and ENABLE_AT_SYSTEM_CHANGE_NUMBER procedures enable a flashback for the specified point in time. DISABLE is used to return to normal processing.

DBMS_HS

Version Available   Oracle8

Description   The DBMS_HS package allows you to set and unset initialization parameters, capabilities, instance names, and class names for Oracle Heterogeneous Services (HS). Oracle HS allows you to execute SQL commands against a non-Oracle remote database, as if it were an Oracle database.

DBMS_HS_PASSTHROUGH

Version Available   Oracle8

Description   The DBMS_HS_PASSTHROUGH package provides an API to send a statement directly to the remote server, without it being interpreted by the local database. It provides procedures to open a cursor, bind input and output variables, execute, fetch results, and close the cursor, similar to the DBMS_SQL package. DBMS_HS_PASSTHROUGH must be called through a database link to the remote, non-Oracle system.

DBMS_IOT

Version Available   Oracle8

Description   The DBMS_IOT package creates tables that store results of the ANALYZE command on index organized tables. It has two procedures—BUILD_ CHAIN_ROWS_TABLE and BUILD_EXCEPTIONS_TABLE, which build a table used to store chained rows and rows that violate a constraint, respectively.

DBMS_JAVA

Version Available   Oracle8*i*

Description   The DBMS_JAVA package contains subprograms that control the behavior of the Java virtual machine contained in Oracle, which is used to run Java stored procedures. For example, DBMS_JAVA.SET_OUTPUT is used to route the output stream System.out to the same buffer used by DBMS_OUTPUT, which can then be viewed in SQL*Plus.

DBMS_JOB

Version Available   7.3

Description   The DBMS_JOB package is used to schedule PL/SQL jobs to run in the background. Jobs are scheduled to run at certain times by background processes. A job is just a PL/SQL block, often a call to a stored procedure. If a job fails, PL/SQL will try up to 16 times to run the job again until it succeeds. DBMS_JOB provides procedures to control the parameters to jobs and their execution behavior.

DBMS_LDAP

Version Available   Oracle8*i*

Description   DBMS_LDAP provides an API that allows access to LDAP servers located outside the database. Unlike the other packages, DBMS_LDAP is not installed by default. It can be installed using the catldap.sql script. SSL connections to an LDAP server can also be established.

DBMS_LIBCACHE

Version Available   Oracle9*i*

Description   DBMS_LIBCACHE has one procedure, COMPILE_CURSORS_FROM_ REMOTE. It is used to extract SQL and PL/SQL commands from a remote instance, and copy them to a local instance. Locally, they will be parsed and compiled, but not executed. This is useful in the event of instance failover, for example.

DBMS_LOB

Version Available   Oracle8

Description   DBMS_LOB is used to manage the four types of large objects— CLOBs, BLOBs, NCLOBS, and BFILEs. Through DBMS_LOB, you can access portions of a LOB for read or write. LOBs can also be accessed through the precompilers, OCI, and JDBC.

DBMS_LOCK

Version Available   7.3

Description   The DBMS_LOCK package is used to create your own user-defined locks. These locks are managed the same way as other Oracle locks. This means that they can be viewed in the fixed views in the data dictionary. User locks are prefixed with "UL" so they do not conflict with Oracle locks.

DBMS_LOGMNR

Version Available   Oracle8*i*

Description   DBMS_LOGMNR is used to populate the database views used by the Log Miner tool. This tool will analyze the database redo and undo logs for auditing information. In particular, the information in the redo log can be used to recover a corrupted database by determining the original values.

DBMS_LOGMNR_CDC_PUBLISH

Version Available   Oracle9*i*

Description   Oracle Change Data Capture is used to determine changes to database tables. DBMS_LOGMNR_CDC_PUBLISH is used to capture changes to given tables, and publish them to interested parties.

DBMS_LOGMNR_CDC_SUBSCRIBE

Version Available   Oracle9*i*

Description   Oracle Change Data Capture is used to determine changes to database tables. DBMS_LOGMNR_CDC_SUBSCRIBE is used to retrieve the information published through DBMS_LOGMNR_CDC_PUBLISH.

DBMS_LOGMNR_D

Version Available   Oracle8*i*

Description   DBMS_LOGMNR_D is used to create the Log Miner dictionary file. It contains one procedure, BUILD, which can extract the dictionary to either a flat file or the database redo logs.

DBMS_METADATA

Version Available   Oracle9*i*

Description   DBMS_METADATA is used to retrieve information about database objects, such as tables or procedures. The output is in XML by default. DBMS_ METADATA provides a superset of the functionality of DBMS_DESCRIBE.

DBMS_MVIEW (DBMS_SNAPSHOT)

Version Available   Oracle9*i*

Description   DBMS_MVIEW provides information about materialized views, including their rewrite capability. It can be used to refresh individual materialized views that are not part of the same refresh group. DBMS_SNAPSHOT is a synonym for DBMS_MVIEW, to reflect the fact that materialized views used to be known as snapshots.

DBMS_OBFUSCATION_TOOLKIT

Version Available   Oracle8*i*

Description   DBMS_OBFUSCATION_TOOLKIT contains two procedures: DESEncrypt and DESDecrypt. They encrypt and decrypt, respectively, string and raw values using DES encryption. By default, privileges are not granted to other users for this package.

DBMS_ODCI

Version Available   Oracle9*i*

Description   DBMS_ODCI contains one function, ESTIMATE_CPU_UNITS. It takes an input value in seconds, and returns the approximate number of CPU cycles that a function that takes that long to execute would use.

DBMS_OFFLINE_OG

Version Available   Oracle8*i*

Description   DBMS_OFFLINE_OG provides an interface to manage offline instantiation of master groups. Together with DBMS_OFFLINE_SNAPSHOT and DBMS_REPCAT_INSTANTIATE, the package allows you to manage a replicated environment.

DBMS_OFFLINE_SNAPSHOT

Version Available   Oracle8*i*

Description   DBMS_OFFLINE_SNAPSHOT provides an interface to manage offline instantiation of materialized views. Together with DBMS_OFFLINE_OG and DBMS_REPCAT_INSTANTIATE, the package allows you to manage a replicated environment.

DBMS_OLAP

Version Available   Oracle8*i*

Description   This package allows you to analyze materialized views and statistics generated by Oracle Trace. It can be used to plan the size and best usage of materialized views.

DBMS_ORACLE_TRACE_AGENT

Version Available   Oracle8

Description   DBMS_ORACLE_TRACE_AGENT provides one procedure, SET_ORACLE_TRACE_IN_SESSION. This allows you to turn the collection of information on or off in a particular session.

DBMS_ORACLE_TRACE_USER

Version Available   Oracle8

Description   DBMS_ORACLE_TRACE_USER provides one procedure, SET_ORACLE_TRACE. It allows you to turn the collection of information on or off in the current session only.

DBMS_OUTLN

Version Available   Oracle8*i*

Description   The DBMS_OUTLN package contains routines that allow you to manipulate stored outlines. A stored outline is the data pertaining to the execution plan for a given SQL statement. In Oracle8*i*, this package was known as OUTLN_PKG, and OUTLN_PKG is a synonym for this package in Oracle9*i*.

DBMS_OUTLN_EDIT

Version Available   Oracle9*i*

Description   DBMS_OUTLN_EDIT is an invoker's rights package that allows you to perform more operations on stored outlines, which are not available through DBMS_OUTLN.

DBMS_OUTPUT

Version Available   7.3

Description   The DBMS_OUTPUT package provides limited output capability for PL/SQL when used in conjunction with SQL*Plus or Server Manager. It is useful for debugging and testing your PL/SQL code. DBMS_OUTPUT is not meant to be used for writing reports—a tool such as Oracle Reports is generally better for this.

DBMS_PCLXUTIL

Version Available   Oracle8*i*

Description   This package provides intrapartition parallelism for creating partition-wise local indexes. Internally, it uses database jobs to create additional processes to do the work.

DBMS_PIPE

Version Available   7.3

Description   The DBMS_PIPE package is similar to DBMS_ALERT in that it allows communication between different sessions connected to the same database. Messages sent over pipes, however, are asynchronous. Once a message is sent, it will go through even if the transaction that sent it rolls back.

DBMS_PROFILER

Version Available   Oracle8*i*

Description   The DBMS_PROFILER package provides an API to the PL/SQL Profiler, which can be used for code coverage and/or performance analysis of PL/SQL applications. Many third-party development tools provide a graphical interface to the profiler.

DBMS_RANDOM

Version Available   Oracle8

Description   The DBMS_RANDOM package contains procedures to generate pseudorandom numbers. It is faster than a random number generator written purely in PL/SQL because it uses Oracle's native random number generator internally.

NOTE
In Oracle8, DBMS_RANDOM is not installed by default. It is installed as part of the PL/SQL Cryptographic Toolkit by running the `catoctk.sql` *script. This script creates the DBMS_CRYPTO_TOOLKIT package, which is used internally by DBMS_RANDOM.*

DBMS_RECITIFIER_DIFF

Version Available   Oracle8

Description   This package allows you to detect and resolve data inconsistencies between replicated sites, in conjunction with the DBMS_REPCAT_* packages.

DBMS_REDIFINITION

Version Available   Oracle9*i*

Description   DBMS_REDIFINITION allows you to reorganize tables online. It does this through incrementally maintainable materialized views.

DBMS_REFRESH

Version Available   7.3

Description   DBMS_REFRESH is used to create a group of materialized views (formerly called a snapshot group), which can be refreshed together as a group. It provides procedures to create, destroy, modify, and manually refresh these groups.

DBMS_REPAIR

Version Available   Oracle8*i*

Description   The DBMS_REPAIR package is used to detect and repair certain kinds of corruption in data and index blocks. As a general rule, it is meant to be used by administrators rather than developers.

DBMS_REPCAT, DBMS_REPCAT_ADMIN, DBMS_REPCAT_INSTANTIATE, DBMS_ REPCAT_RGT, and DBMS_REPUTIL

Version Available   Oracle8

Description   These packages are used to manage Oracle's symmetric replication facility, which requires the replication option. The following table summarizes the uses of each package. For more information, see the Oracle documentation.

Package	Description
DBMS_REPCAT	Allows you to administer and update the replication catalog and environment
DBMS_REPCAT_ADMIN	Allows you to create users with the necessary permissions

Package	Description
DBMS_REPCAT_INSTANTIATE	Allows you to instantiate deployment templates
DBMS_REPCAT_RGT	Allows you to create and maintain refresh group templates
DBMS_REPUTIL	Provides additional utilities used in Symmetric Replication

DBMS_RESOURCE_MANAGER and DBMS_RESOURCE_MANAGER_PRIVS

Version Available   Oracle8*i*

Description   These packages allow you to maintain resource plans, consumer groups, and plan directives, along with their associated privileges.

DBMS_RESUMABLE

Version Available   Oracle9*i*

Description   DBMS_RESUMABLE allows you to set limits on space or time for a given operation. When these limits are reached, the operation will be suspended until the problem is fixed, after which it can be resumed. Information about suspensions and resumptions is written to the database alert log and can be seen in database views.

DBMS_RLS

Version Available   Oracle8*i*

Description   The DBMS_RLS package allows you to specify fine-grained access control, based on individual rows. Through DBMS_RLS, you can create, drop, enable, and disable policies that control the access. It is available with the Enterprise Edition of Oracle8*i* and Oracle9*i* only.

DBMS_ROWID

Version Available   Oracle8

Description   The Oracle8 ROWID type is more complicated than the Oracle7 type, and the component portions of an Oracle8 ROWID are encoded. The DBMS_ROWID package allows you to convert between Oracle7 and Oracle8 ROWIDs, and obtain information about the component parts of a ROWID.

DBMS_SESSION

Version Available   7.3

Description   The ALTER SESSION command is not allowed directly in PL/SQL. The DBMS_SESSION package provides an interface to some of the options available with ALTER SESSION and is callable from a PL/SQL block. Dynamic SQL can be used as an alternative to DBMS_SESSION because it allows execution of arbitrary statements, including ALTER SESSION.

DBMS_SHARED_POOL

Version Available   7.3

Description   The DBMS_SHARED_POOL package is used to manage the shared pool. You can pin packages and procedures in the shared pool so they won't get aged out. This is a key component of a properly tuned PL/SQL environment.

DBMS_SPACE and DBMS_SPACE_ADMIN

Version Available   Oracle8

Description   The DBMS_SPACE package allows you to analyze segment growth and space requirements, while the DBMS_SPACE_ADMIN package provides for locally managed tablespaces.

DBMS_SQL

Version Available   7.3

Description   DBMS_SQL implements dynamic PL/SQL. Using this package, your program can construct SQL statements and PL/SQL blocks at runtime and execute them. DBMS_SQL can also be used to execute DDL statements from PL/SQL. Oracle8*i* introduced native dynamic SQL, which is generally faster and simpler than DBMS_SQL.

DBMS_STANDARD and STANDARD

Version Available   7.3

Description   Together, DBMS_STANDARD and STANDARD implement all of the built-in functions of PL/SQL. Unlike other packages, you do not have to prefix subprograms in these packages with the package name.

DBMS_STATS

Version Available   Oracle8*i*

Description   The DBMS_STATS package allows you to view and modify optimizer statistics, stored either in the data dictionary or a user-specified table. Only those statistics in the data dictionary will be used by the cost-based optimizer.

DBMS_TRACE

Version Available   Oracle8*i*

Description   The DBMS_TRACE package allows you to turn tracing of PL/SQL applications on or off and control the level of tracing. PL/SQL tracing can include information such as procedure entry or exit, exceptions raised, and SQL statements.

DBMS_TRANSACTION

Version Available   7.3

Description   The DBMS_TRANSACTION package provides procedures for transaction management. Many of the commands available here are also available in their SQL equivalents directly in PL/SQL. DBMS_TRANSACTION includes procedures to commit and roll back transactions, and issue the SET TRANSACTION command.

DBMS_TRANSFORM

Version Available   Oracle9*i*

Description   DBMS_TRANSFORM allows you to create, modify, and drop transformations. These transformations are used in the message formatting of Oracle Advanced Queuing.

DBMS_TTS

Version Available   Oracle8*i*

Description   The procedures in the DBMS_TTS package are used to determine information about transportable sets. They are meant to be used by database administrators. The TRANSPORT_SET_CHECK procedure verifies if a set of tablespaces is self-contained, and the DOWNGRADE procedure downgrades information relating to transportable tablespaces.

DBMS_TYPES

Version Available   Oracle9*i*

Description   DBMS_TYPES contains no procedures—it contains only constants that represent the types available in the database. It is used in interMedia applications.

DBMS_UTILITY

Version Available   7.3

Description   The DBMS_UTILITY package provides additional functionality for managing procedures, reporting errors, and other information. Included in DBMS_ UTILITY are FORMAT_CALL_STACK and FORMAT_ERROR_STACK, which can be used to determine the current PL/SQL call stack and error list.

DBMS_WM

Version Available   Oracle9*i*

Description   DBMS_WM provides an API to control the Workspace Manager. This manager allows you to work with long transactions in different workspaces, with each workspace having a different version of the records modified by the transaction.

DBMS_XMLQUERY, DBMS_XMLSAVE, and XMLGEN

Version Available   Oracle9*i*

Description These three packages provide an API to manipulate and convert XML data. XMLGEN converts a SQL query into XML output, and DBMS_XMLQUERY is similar to XMLGEN, except that it is written in C instead of PL/SQL. DBMS_XMLSAVE converts from XML into database data.

DEBUG_EXTPROC

Version Available Oracle8

Description DEBUG_EXTPROC is used to help debug an external routine. It provides one procedure, STARTUP_EXTPROC_AGENT, which starts the external procedure agent. Once this is done, you can attach to it in a debugger before executing your external routine.

SDO_CS, SDO_GEOM, SDE_LRS, SDO_MIGRATE, and SDO_TUNE

Version Available Oracle9i

Description These packages provide access to and control of various Oracle spatial features. Rather than sys, they are installed into the mdsys schema.

UTL_COLL

Version Available Oracle8i

Description The UTL_COLL package contains one function, IS_LOCATOR, which is used to determine if its argument is actually a collection locator or not.

UTL_ENCODE

Version Available Oracle9i

Description UTL_ENCODE is used to encode and decode RAW data into a standard format that can be transported between hosts. It provides three encodings: base 64, uuencode, and quoted printable. These formats are often used to encode the body of emails.

UTL_FILE

Version Available   7.3

Description   The UTL_FILE procedure implements file I/O in PL/SQL. Using this package, PL/SQL programs can read from and write to operating system files located on the server. The accessible files and directories are limited by parameters in the database initialization file for security. UTL_FILE can write text files only; it does not support binary files.

UTL_HTTP

Version Available   7.3

Description   The UTL_HTTP package is used to make HTTP callouts from PL/SQL or SQL. It is used to call cartridges in the Oracle Internet Application Server, as well as Web pages on the Internet. UTL_HTTP defines two functions: REQUEST and REQUEST_PIECES. REQUEST retrieves up to the first 2,000 bytes of a given Web page, and REQUEST_PIECES retrieves the entire page into a PL/SQL table. In Oracle8 and higher, proxies can be used for REQUEST and REQUEST_PIECES.

UTL_INADDR

Version Available   Oracle9*i*

Description   UTL_INADDR is used for Internet addressing. It provides two functions: GET_HOST_NAME, which returns the name of a host given its IP address; and GET_HOST_ADDRESS, which returns the IP address of a host given its name.

UTL_PG

Version Available   7.3

Description   The UTL_PG package provides conversion between COBOL numeric data and Oracle numbers. It is often used in conjunction with UTL_RAW.

UTL_RAW

Version Available   7.3

Description   The UTL_RAW package contains utility routines for working with RAW data, and for converting to and from RAW data. It supplements the built-in RAWTOHEX and HEXTORAW functions found in package STANDARD.

UTL_REF

Version Available   Oracle8

Description   The UTL_REF package allows you to navigate object references through PL/SQL. Unlike SQL, you do not need to know the object table name. UTL_REF provides procedures to select, lock, update, and delete objects based on their references.

UTL_SMTP

Version Available   Oracle8*i*

Description   UTL_SMTP provides an implementation of the SMTP protocol, which is used to send email messages. It allows you to communicate with an SMTP server located outside the database to send email.

UTL_TCP

Version Available   Oracle8*i*

Description   UTL_TCP provides an implementation of the TCP protocol, which is used for general Internet communications. For example, UTL_HTTP and UTL_SMTP are written to use UTL_TCP internally. UTL_TCP can be used to define your own protocol with a remote host.

UTL_URL

Version Available   Oracle9*i*

Description   UTL_URL is used to escape and unescape a given URL (universal resource locator). An escaped URL has illegal characters replaced with a numeric code prefixed by %.

APPENDIX B

PL/SQL Reserved Words

he words listed in this appendix are reserved by PL/SQL. Reserved words have special syntactic meaning in the language and thus can't be used as identifiers (for variable names, procedure names, and so on). Some of these words are reserved by SQL as well, and thus can't be used to name database objects such as tables, sequences, and views.

Table of Reserved Words

The following table lists the reserved words for PL/SQL, up to and including Oracle9*i*. In Oracle8*i* and Oracle9*i*, a number of reserved words were removed from the list, because they were not needed. They were considered to be reserved by earlier releases, however. Some new words (such as AUTHID and NULLIF) have been added for Oracle8*i* and Oracle9*i* as well. In the table, words that are reserved in Oracle9*i* and higher are in bold, and those that are reserved by SQL have an asterisk (*). Words not in bold are reserved by earlier releases. You should avoid using any of these words, however, to minimize potential conflicts.

You should also avoid creating a package with the same name as the Oracle predefined packages described in Appendix A, or a procedure with the same name as one defined in the STANDARD package.

ABORT	ACCEPT	ACCESS*	ADD*
ALL*	**ALTER***	**AND***	**ANY***
ARRAY	ARRAYLEN	**AS***	**ASC***
ASSERT	ASSIGN	**AT**	AUDIT*
AUTHID	AUTHORIZATION	**AVG**	BASE_TABLE
BEGIN	**BETWEEN***	**BINARY_INTEGER**	**BODY**
BOOLEAN	**BULK**	**BY***	**CASE**
CHAR*	**CHAR_BASE**	**CHECK***	**CLOSE**
CLUSTER*	**CLUSTERS**	**COALESCE**	**COLAUTH**
COLLECT	COLUMN*	**COMMENT***	**COMMIT**
COMPRESS*	**CONNECT***	**CONSTANT**	**CRASH**
CREATE*	**CURRENT***	**CURRVAL**	**CURSOR**
DATABASE	DATA_BASE	**DATE***	**DAY**
DBA	DEBUGOFF	DEBUGON	**DECIMAL***

DECLARE	**DEFAULT**[*]	DEFINITION	DELAY
DELETE[*]	**DESC**[*]	DIGITS	DISPOSE
DISTINCT[*]	**DO**	**DROP**[*]	**ELSE**[*]
ELSIF	**END**	ENTRY	**EXCEPTION**
EXCEPTION_ INIT	**EXCLUSIVE**[*]	**EXECUTE**	**EXISTS**[*]
EXIT	**EXTENDS**	**EXTRACT**	**FALSE**
FETCH	FILE[*]	**FLOAT**[*]	**FOR**[*]
FORALL	**FORM**[*]	**FROM**[*]	**FUNCTION**
GENERIC	**GOTO**	**GRANT**[*]	**GROUP**[*]
HAVING[*]	**HEAP**	**HOUR**	**IDENTIFIED**[*]
IF	**IMMEDIATE**[*]	**IN**[*]	INCREMENT[*]
INDEX[*]	**INDEXES**	**INDICATOR**	INITIAL[*]
INSERT[*]	**INTEGER**[*]	**INTERFACE**	**INTERSECT**[*]
INTERVAL	**INTO**[*]	**IS**[*]	**ISOLATION**
JAVA	**LEVEL**[*]	**LIKE**[*]	**LIMITED**
LOCK[*]	**LONG**[*]	**LOOP**	**MAX**
MAXEXTENTS[*]	**MIN**	**MINUS**[*]	**MINUTE**
MLSLABEL[*]	**MOD**	**MODE**[*]	**MONTH**
NATURAL	**NATURALN**	**NEW**	**NEXTVAL**
NOAUDIT[*]	**NOCOMPRESS**[*]	**NOCOPY**	**NOT**[*]
NOWAIT[*]	**NULL**[*]	NULLIF	**NUMBER**[*]
NUMBER_BASE	**OCIROWID**	**OF**[*]	OFFLINE[*]
ON[*]	ONLINE[*]	**OPAQUE**	**OPEN**
OPERATOR	**OPTION**[*]	**OR**[*]	**ORDER**[*]
ORGANIZATION	**OTHERS**	**OUT**	**PACKAGE**
PARTITION	**PCTFREE**[*]	**PLS_INTEGER**	**POSITIVE**
POSITIVEN	**PRAGMA**	**PRIOR**[*]	**PRIVATE**
PRIVILEGES[*]	**PROCEDURE**	**PUBLIC**[*]	**RAISE**

RANGE	RAW*	REAL	RECORD
REF	RELEASE	REMR	RENAME*
RESOURCE*	RETURN	REVERSE	REVOKE*
ROLLBACK	ROW*	ROWID*	ROWLABEL*
ROWNUM	ROWS*	ROWTYPE	RUN
SAVEPOINT	SCHEMA	SECOND	SELECT*
SEPARATE	SESSION*	SET*	SHARE*
SMALLINT*	SPACE	SQL	SQLCODE
SQLERRM	START*	STATEMENT	STDDEV
SUBTYPE	SUCCESSFUL*	SUM	SYNONYM*
SYSDATE*	TABAUTH	TABLE*	TABLES*
TASK	TERMINATE	THEN*	TIME
TIMESTAMP	TIMEZONE_ABBR	TIMEZONE_ HOUR	TIMEZONE_ MINUTE
TIMEZONE_ REGION	TO*	TRIGGER*	TRUE
TYPE	UI	UID*	UNION*
UNIQUE*	UPDATE*	USE	USER*
VALIDATE*	VALUES*	VARCHAR*	VARCHAR2*
VARIANCE	VIEW*	VIEWS	WHEN
WHENEVER*	WHERE*	WHILE	WITH*
WORK	WRITE	XOR	YEAR
ZONE			

If you want to use a reserved word, it must be enclosed in double quotation marks. For example, the following block is legal:

```
DECLARE
   "BEGIN" NUMBER;
BEGIN
   "BEGIN" := 7;
END;
```

Although this is legal, it is not recommended.

APPENDIX
C

The Data
Dictionary

his appendix describes some of the views in the data dictionary that are relevant to PL/SQL programmers. It does not include all of the views—just the more commonly used ones. A brief description of the data dictionary and how it works is also included.

What Is the Data Dictionary?

The data dictionary is where Oracle stores information about the structure of the database. The data itself is located in other areas—the data dictionary describes how the actual data is organized. The dictionary consists of tables and views that you can query, like any other database table or view. The views are owned by the Oracle user SYS.

The data dictionary is typically created when the database is created and installed for the first time. Without the dictionary, no PL/SQL work can be done. On most systems, there is a script called `catalog.sql` that creates the dictionary views, which is run as part of the database installation. `catalog.sql` can be found in `$ORACLE_HOME/rdbms/admin` on UNIX systems. This script should be run while connected as SYS, or connected with SYSDBA privileges in SQL*Plus.

For more information on the data dictionary views (including views not discussed here and the v$ performance views), see the *Oracle Server Reference*.

Naming Conventions

Many of the views have three different instantiations. These are known as `user_*`, `all_*`, and `dba_*`. For example, there are three instantiations of the information about the source for stored objects. The views that represent this are `user_source`, `all_source`, and `dba_source`. In general, the `user_*` views contain information about objects owned by the current user, the `all_*` views contain information about all objects accessible to the current user (not necessarily owned by them), and the `dba_*` views contain information about all objects in the database.

SQL and PL/SQL are not case sensitive. In order to implement this, all objects are converted into uppercase before they are stored (unless they are created with double quotes). Therefore, you should use uppercase when querying the data dictionary. For example, the `user_objects` view has a column `object_name` that contains the name of the object. These names are always stored in uppercase. The following SQL*Plus session shows a query against `user_objects`:

```
SQL> SELECT object_type, status
  2    FROM user_objects
  3   WHERE object_name = UPPER('ClassPackage');
```

```
OBJECT_TYPE      STATUS
-------------    -------
PACKAGE          VALID
PACKAGE BODY     VALID
```

Note the use of the UPPER function so that the query will return the desired rows. (ClassPackage is described in Chapter 9.)

Permissions

The data dictionary views are owned by SYS. By default, only SYS and users with the DBA system privilege can see all of the views. Users without the DBA privilege can see the user_* and all_* views, in addition to some others. They cannot see the dba_* views unless they have been granted specific SELECT privileges on them.

The data dictionary views should *never* be updated, even by SYS. They are updated automatically by the database as their relevant information changes. Oracle also provides scripts to modify the data dictionary tables when a database is upgraded or downgraded (such as u0801070.sql, which upgrades from an 8.1.7 database to the current release). These scripts can be found in the same directory as catproc.sql.

Types of Views

The various data dictionary views can be grouped into different categories, which are listed below. The data dictionary contains information about different types of database objects, as well as the relationship between them.

- Relational clusters, tables, and views
- Collections, LOBs, and objects
- Oracle8*i* and Oracle9*i* views
- Other database objects
- Partitions and subpartitions
- Indexes
- Materialized views, summaries, and snapshots
- Subprograms, methods, and triggers
- Source code and compile errors
- Dependencies and constraints
- Statistics and auditing
- Privileges and grants

The following sections list the views available in each category.

NOTE
Not all of the data dictionary views are described in this Appendix. For a complete listing of the available views, see the Oracle Server Reference. You can also query the `dictionary` *view, which contains the name and description of all the data dictionary views available.*

View Overviews

The following sections each contain a table that lists the data dictionary views for each category. All of the tables have four columns:

- **Type of Object**   Type of database object described by the view

- **View**   Name of the view

- **Contains Information About**   Which objects can be described by this view

- **Available in Release**   Which Oracle release first contained this view

Relational Clusters, Tables, and Views

The data dictionary views in this category describe the basic relational data storage objects in Oracle—clusters, tables, and views.

Type of Object	Data Dictionary View	Contains Information About	Available in Release
Clusters	all_clusters	Accessible database clusters	Oracle7
	dba_clusters	All database clusters	Oracle7
	user_clusters	Clusters owned by the current user	Oracle7
	all_cluster_hash_ expressions	Cluster hash functions for accessible clusters	Oracle7
	dba_cluster_hash_ expressions	Cluster hash functions for all clusters	Oracle7
	user_cluster_hash_ expressions	Cluster hash functions for clusters owned by the current user	Oracle7

Type of Object	Data Dictionary View	Contains Information About	Available in Release
	dba_clu_columns	Mappings of table columns to cluster columns for all tables	Oracle7
	user_clu_columns	Mappings of table columns to cluster columns for the current user's tables	Oracle7
Tables and views	all_all_tables	Accessible tables (relational and object)	Oracle8
	dba_all_tables	All tables (relational and object) in the database	Oracle8
	user_all_tables	The current user's tables (relational and object)	Oracle8
	all_col_comments	Comments on columns of accessible tables and views	Oracle7
	dba_col_comments	Comments on all table and view columns	Oracle7
	user_col_comments	Comments on table and view columns owned by the current user	Oracle7
	all_partial_ drop_tabs	Accessible tables that have been partially dropped	Oracle8*i*
	dba_partial_ drop_tabs	All tables that have been partially dropped	Oracle8*i*
	user_partial_ drop_tabs	Tables owned by the current user that have been partially dropped	Oracle8*i*
	all_refs	REF columns and attributes in accessible object type columns	Oracle8
	dba_refs	All REF columns and attributes in the database	Oracle8

Type of Object	Data Dictionary View	Contains Information About	Available in Release
	user_refs	REF columns and attributes of object type columns owned by the current user	Oracle8
	all_tab_columns	Accessible table columns	Oracle7
	dba_tab_columns	All table columns	Oracle7
	user_tab_columns	Columns of tables owned by the current user	Oracle7
	all_tab_comments	Comments on accessible tables	Oracle7
	dba_tab_comments	Comments on all database tables	Oracle7
	user_tab_comments	Comments on tables owned by the current user	Oracle7
	all_tables	Accessible relational tables	Oracle7
	dba_tables	All relational tables	Oracle7
	user_tables	Relational tables owned by the current user	Oracle7
	all_unused_col_tabs	Accessible tables that contain unused columns	Oracle8i
	dba_unused_col_tabs	All tables that contain unused columns	Oracle8i
	user_unused_col_tabs	Tables owned by the current user that contain unused columns	Oracle8i
	all_updatable_columns	Columns that are updatable in accessible join views	Oracle8

Type of Object	Data Dictionary View	Contains Information About	Available in Release
	`dba_updatable_ columns`	Columns that are updatable in all join views	Oracle8
	`user_updatable_ columns`	Columns that are updatable in join views owned by the current user	Oracle8
	`all_views`	Accessible views	Oracle7
	`dba_views`	All views in the database	Oracle7
	`user_views`	Views owned by the current user	Oracle7

Collections, LOBs, Object Types, and Tables

These data dictionary views describe the object types available in Oracle8 and higher—collections, LOBs, and object types:

Type of Object	Data Dictionary View	Contains Information About	Available in Release
Collections	`all_coll_types`	Accessible named collection types	Oracle8
	`dba_coll_types`	All collection types in the database	Oracle8
	`user_coll_types`	Collection types owned by the current user	Oracle8
	`all_varrays`	Accessible tables that contain varray columns varray types	Oracle8*i*
	`dba_varrays`	All tables that contain varray columns in the database	Oracle8*i*
	`user_varrays`	Tables owned by the current user that contain varray columns	Oracle8*i*

Type of Object	Data Dictionary View	Contains Information About	Available in Release
	all_nested_tables	Nested tables contained within accessible tables	Oracle8
	dba_nested_tables	Nested tables contained within all database tables	Oracle8
	user_nested_tables	Nested tables contained within tables owned by the current user	Oracle8
Large Objects	all_lobs	LOBs contained in accessible tables	Oracle8
	dba_lobs	All LOBs in the database	Oracle8
	user_lobs	LOBs contained in tables owned by the current user	Oracle8
Object Tables and Types	all_type_attrs	Attributes of accessible object types	Oracle8
	dba_type_attrs	Attributes of all object types	Oracle8
	user_type_attrs	Attributes of object types owned by the current user	Oracle8
	all_type_methods	Methods of accessible object types	Oracle8
	dba_type_methods	Methods of all object types	Oracle8
	user_type_methods	Methods of object types owned by the current user	Oracle8
	all_types	Accessible object types	Oracle8
	dba_types	All object types	Oracle8
	user_types	Object types owned by the current user	Oracle8

Type of Object	Data Dictionary View	Contains Information About	Available in Release
	`all_object_tables`	Accessible object tables	Oracle8
	`dba_object_tables`	All object tables	Oracle8
	`user_object_tables`	Object tables owned by the current user	Oracle8

Oracle8*i* and Oracle9*i* Views

The views in this section contain information about various types of database objects introduced in Oracle8*i* and Oracle9*i*, including the following:

- Contexts
- Dimensions
- External tables
- Operators
- Outlines
- Policies

For more information, see the Oracle documentation.

Type of Object	Data Dictionary View	Description	Available in Release
Contexts	`all_context`	Accessible contexts	Oracle8*i*
	`dba_context`	All contexts	Oracle8*i*
Dimensions	`all_dimensions`	Accessible dimensions	Oracle8*i*
	`dba_dimensions`	All dimensions in the database	Oracle8*i*
	`user_dimensions`	Dimensions owned by the current user	Oracle8*i*
	`all_dim_attributes`	Relationship between dimension levels and dependent columns for accessible dimensions	Oracle8*i*

Type of Object	Data Dictionary View	Description	Available in Release
	dba_dim_attributes	Relationship between dimension levels and dependent columns for all dimensions	Oracle8i
	user_dim_attributes	Relationship between dimension levels and dependent columns for the current user's dimensions	Oracle8i
	all_dim_child_of	Relationships between levels of accessible dimensions	Oracle8i
	dba_dim_child_of	Relationships between levels of all dimensions	Oracle8i
	user_dim_child_of	Relationships between levels of the current user's dimensions	Oracle8i
	all_dim_hierarchies	Accessible dimension hierarchies	Oracle8i
	dba_dim_hierarchies	All dimension hierarchies	Oracle8i
	user_dim_hierarchies	The current user's dimension hierarchies	Oracle8i
	all_dim_join_key	Joins between accessible dimensions	Oracle8i
	dba_dim_join_key	Joins between all dimensions	Oracle8i
	user_dim_join_key	Joins between the current user's dimensions	Oracle8i
	all_dim_levels	Levels of accessible dimensions	Oracle8i
	dba_dim_levels	Levels of all dimensions	Oracle8i
	user_dim_levels	Levels of the current user's dimensions	Oracle8i

Type of Object	Data Dictionary View	Description	Available in Release
	`all_dim_level_key`	Columns of accessible dimension levels	Oracle8*i*
	`dba_dim_level_key`	Columns of all dimension levels	Oracle8*i*
	`user_dim_level_key`	Columns of the current user's dimension levels	Oracle8*i*
External tables	`all_external_tables`	External tables accessible to the current user	Oracle9*i*
	`dba_external_tables`	All external tables in the database	Oracle9*i*
	`user_external_tables`	External tables owned by the current user	Oracle9*i*
Operators	`all_opancillary`	Ancillary information for accessible operators	Oracle8*i*
	`dba_opancillary`	Ancillary information for all operators	Oracle8*i*
	`user_opancillary`	Ancillary information for the current user's operators	Oracle8*i*
	`all_oparguments`	Arguments to accessible operators	Oracle8*i*
	`dba_oparguments`	Arguments to all operators	Oracle8*i*
	`user_oparguments`	Arguments to the current user's operators	Oracle8*i*
	`all_opbindings`	Binding functions for accessible operators	Oracle8*i*
	`dba_opbindings`	Binding functions for all operators	Oracle8*i*
	`user_opbindings`	Binding functions for the current user's operators	Oracle8*i*

Type of Object	Data Dictionary View	Description	Available in Release
	all_operators	Basic information for accessible operators	Oracle8*i*
	dba_operators	Basic information for all operators	Oracle8*i*
	user_operators	Basic information for the current user's operators	Oracle8*i*
Outlines	all_outline_hints	Hints that make up accessible outlines	Oracle8*i*
	dba_outline_hints	Hints that make up all outlines	Oracle8*i*
	user_outline_hints	Hints that make up the current user's outlines	Oracle8*i*
	all_outlines	Accessible outlines	Oracle8*i*
	dba_outlines	All outlines	Oracle8*i*
	user_outlines	Outlines owned by the current user	Oracle8*i*
Policies	all_policies	Policies on accessible tables and views	Oracle8*i*
	dba_policies	Policies on all tables and views	Oracle8*i*
	user_policies	Policies on the current user's tables and views	Oracle8*i*

Other Database Objects

The data dictionary views in the following table contain information about the remaining types of database objects, including the following:

- Database jobs
- Database links
- Directories
- Libraries

■ Sequences

■ Synonyms

Type of Object	Data Dictionary View	Description	Available in Release
Database jobs	`all_jobs`	Accessible database jobs	Oracle7
	`dba_jobs`	All database jobs	Oracle7
	`user_jobs`	Database jobs submitted by the current user	Oracle7
	`dba_jobs_running`	All database jobs currently running	Oracle7
Database links	`all_db_links`	Accessible database links	Oracle7
	`dba_db_links`	All database links	Oracle7
	`user_db_links`	Database links owned by the current user	Oracle7
Directories	`all_directories`	Accessible directories	Oracle8
	`dba_directories`	All directories in the database	Oracle8
Libraries	`all_libraries`	Accessible libraries	Oracle8
	`dba_libraries`	All libraries	Oracle8
	`user_libraries`	Libraries owned by the current user	Oracle8
Sequences	`all_sequences`	Accessible sequences	Oracle7
	`dba_sequences`	All sequences	Oracle7
	`user_sequences`	Sequences owned by the current user	Oracle7
Synonyms	`all_synonyms`	Accessible synonyms	Oracle7
	`dba_synonyms`	All synonyms in the database	Oracle7
	`user_synonyms`	Synonyms owned by the current user	Oracle7

Partitions and Subpartitions

Partitions, introduced in Oracle8, allow tables to be divided into different sections, each of which can have different storage. Oracle8*i* introduced subpartitions and also allowed LOBs to be stored in partitions. The data dictionary views in the following table contain information about the partitions and subpartitions of various database objects.

Data Dictionary View	Description	Available in Release
`all_part_col_statistics`	Statistics and other information about partitions in accessible tables	Oracle8
`dba_part_col_statistics`	Statistics and other information about partitions in all database tables	Oracle8
`user_part_col_statistics`	Statistics and other information about partitions in tables owned by the current user	Oracle8
`all_part_histograms`	Histograms on partitions of accessible tables	Oracle8
`dba_part_histograms`	Histograms on partitions of all database tables	Oracle8
`user_part_histograms`	Histograms on partitions of the current user's tables	Oracle8
`all_part_indexes`	Object-level partitioning of all accessible partitioned indexes	Oracle8
`dba_part_indexes`	Object-level partitioning of all partitioned indexes	Oracle8
`user_part_indexes`	Object-level partitioning of the current user's partitioned indexes	Oracle8
`all_part_key_columns`	Partitioning key columns for all accessible partitioned objects	Oracle8
`dba_part_key_columns`	Partitioning key columns for all partitioned objects	Oracle8
`user_part_key_columns`	Partitioning key columns for the current user's partitioned objects	Oracle8
`all_part_lobs`	LOB data partitions in accessible tables	Oracle8*i*

Data Dictionary View	Description	Available in Release
`dba_part_lobs`	LOB data partitions in all tables	Oracle8*i*
`user_part_lobs`	LOB data partitions in the current user's tables	Oracle8*i*
`all_part_tables`	Accessible partitioned tables	Oracle8
`dba_part_tables`	All partitioned tables	Oracle8
`user_part_tables`	Partitioned tables owned by the current user	Oracle8
`all_subpart_col_statistics`	Column statistics for accessible subpartitions	Oracle8*i*
`dba_subpart_col_statistics`	Column statistics for all subpartitions	Oracle8*i*
`user_subpart_col_statistics`	Column statistics for subpartitions of tables owned by the current user	Oracle8*i*
`all_subpart_histograms`	Histogram data for accessible subpartitions	Oracle8*i*
`dba_subpart_histograms`	Histogram data for all subpartitions	Oracle8*i*
`user_subpart_histograms`	Histogram data for subpartitions of tables owned by the current user	Oracle8*i*
`all_subpart_key_columns`	Key columns for accessible tables partitioned using the composite range/hash method	Oracle8*i*
`dba_subpart_key_columns`	Key columns for all tables partitioned using the composite range/hash method	Oracle8*i*
`user_subpart_key_columns`	Key columns for the current user's tables partitioned using the composite range/hash method	Oracle8*i*
`all_tab_partitions`	Partitions of accessible tables	Oracle8
`dba_tab_partitions`	All table partitions	Oracle8
`user_tab_partitions`	Partitions of the current user's tables	Oracle8
`all_tab_subpartitions`	Subpartitions of accessible tables	Oracle8*i*

Data Dictionary View	Description	Available in Release
dba_tab_subpartitions	All table subpartitions	Oracle8i
user_tab_ subpartitions	Subpartitions of the current user's tables	Oracle8i
all_lob_partitions	Partitions of LOBs contained in accessible tables	Oracle8i
dba_lob_partitions	Partitions of all LOBs	Oracle8i
user_lob_partitions	Partitions of LOBs contained in the current user's tables	Oracle8i
all_lob_subpartitions	Subpartitions of LOBs contained in accessible tables	Oracle8i
dba_lob_subpartitions	Subpartitions of all LOBs	Oracle8i
user_lob_ subpartitions	Subpartitions of LOBs contained in the current user's tables	Oracle8i
all_ind_partitions	Index partition information for indexes on accessible tables	Oracle8
dba_ind_partitions	Index partition information for indexes on all tables	Oracle8
user_ind_partitions	Index partition information for indexes on the current user's tables	Oracle8
all_ind_subpartitions	Index subpartition information for indexes on accessible tables	Oracle8i
dba_ind_subpartitions	Index subpartition information for indexes on all tables	Oracle8i
user_ind_ subpartitions	Index subpartition information for indexes on the current user's tables	Oracle8i

Indexes

The following table lists the data dictionary views that contain information about database indexes. For information on which views describe index partitions and subpartitions, see the previous section, "Partitions and Subpartitions." For more information on indexes in general, see the Oracle documentation.

Data Dictionary View	Description	Available in Release
all_ind_columns	Columns on indexes on accessible tables	Oracle7
dba_ind_columns	Columns on indexes on all tables	Oracle7
user_ind_columns	Columns on indexes on the current user's tables	Oracle7
all_ind_expressions	Functional index expressions for indexes on accessible tables	Oracle8*i*
dba_ind_expressions	Functional index expressions for indexes on all tables	Oracle8*i*
user_ind_expressions	Functional index expressions for indexes on tables owned by the current user	Oracle8*i*
all_indexes	Indexes on accessible tables	Oracle7
dba_indexes	Indexes on all tables	Oracle7
user_indexes	Indexes on the current user's tables	Oracle7
all_indextypes	Accessible indextypes	Oracle8*i*
dba_indextypes	All indextypes	Oracle8*i*
user_indextypes	The current user's indextypes	Oracle8*i*
all_indextype_operators	Operators supported by the accessible indextypes	Oracle8*i*
dba_indextype_operators	Operators supported by all indextypes	Oracle8*i*
user_indextype_operators	Operators supported by the current user's indextypes	Oracle8*i*

Materialized Views, Summaries, and Snapshots

Snapshots were first introduced in Oracle7. Oracle8i extended them to include materialized views and summaries. The data dictionary views that contain information about these types of objects are described in the following table:

Type of Object	Data Dictionary View	Description	Available in Release
Materialized views	all_base_table_ mviews	Materialized views using materialized view logs accessible to the current user	Oracle9i
	dba_base_table_ mviews	All materialized views using materialized view logs in the database	Oracle9i
	user_base_table_ mviews	Materialized views using materialized view logs owned by the current user	Oracle9i
	all_mview_ aggregates	Grouping functions in the select list of accessible materialized views	Oracle8i
	dba_mview_ aggregates	Grouping functions in the select list of all materialized views	Oracle8i
	user_mview_ aggregates	Grouping functions in the select list of the current user's materialized views	Oracle8i
	all_mview_ analysis	Additional information about accessible materialized views	Oracle8i
	dba_mview_ analysis	Additional information about all materialized views	Oracle8i
	user_mview_ analysis	Additional information about the current user's materialized views	Oracle8i

Type of Object	Data Dictionary View	Description	Available in Release
	`all_mview_detail_ relations`	Named detail relations in or referenced from the FROM list of accessible materialized views	Oracle8*i*
	`dba_mview_detail_ relations`	Named detail relations in or referenced from the FROM list of all materialized views	Oracle8*i*
	`user_mview_detail_ relations`	Named detail relations in or referenced from the FROM list of the current user's materialized views	Oracle8*i*
	`all_mview_joins`	Joins between columns in the WHERE clause of accessible materialized views	Oracle8*i*
	`dba_mview_joins`	Joins between columns in the WHERE clause of all materialized views	Oracle8*i*
	`user_mview_joins`	Joins between columns in the WHERE clause of the current user's materialized views	Oracle8*i*
	`all_mview_keys`	Columns in the GROUP BY clause of accessible materialized views	Oracle8*i*
	`dba_mview_keys`	Columns in the GROUP BY clause of all materialized views	Oracle8*i*
	`user_mview_keys`	Columns in the GROUP BY clause of the current user's materialized views	Oracle8*i*
	`all_mviews`	Accessible materialized views	Oracle8*i*

Type of Object	Data Dictionary View	Description	Available in Release
	`dba_mviews`	All materialized views in the database	Oracle8i
	`user_mviews`	Materialized views owned by the current user	Oracle8i
Snapshots	`all_refresh`	Accessible snapshot refresh groups	Oracle8
	`dba_refresh`	All snapshot refresh groups	Oracle8
	`user_refresh`	The current user's snapshot refresh groups	Oracle8
	`all_refresh_ children`	All objects in accessible refresh groups	Oracle8
	`dba_refresh_ children`	All objects in all refresh groups	Oracle8
	`user_refresh_ children`	All objects in the current user's refresh groups	Oracle8
	`all_refresh_ dependencies`	Dependent or container tables for accessible summaries or snapshots	Oracle8i
	`all_registered_ snapshots`	Accessible registered snapshots	Oracle8
	`dba_registered_ snapshots`	All registered snapshots	Oracle8
	`user_registered_ snapshots`	The current user's registered snapshots	Oracle8
	`all_snapshot_logs`	Accessible snapshot logs	Oracle8
	`dba_snapshot_logs`	All snapshot logs	Oracle8
	`user_snapshot_logs`	The current user's snapshot logs	Oracle8
	`all_snapshot_ refresh_times`	Refresh times for accessible snapshots	Oracle8

Type of Object	Data Dictionary View	Description	Available in Release
	`dba_snapshot_refresh_times`	Refresh times for all snapshots	Oracle8
	`user_snapshot_refresh_times`	Refresh times for the current user's snapshots	Oracle8
	`all_snapshots`	Accessible snapshots	Oracle7
	`dba_snapshots`	All snapshots in the database	Oracle7
	`user_snapshots`	Snapshots owned by the current user	Oracle7
Summaries	`all_summaries`	Accessible summaries	Oracle8*i*
	`dba_summaries`	All summaries	Oracle8*i*
	`user_summaries`	Summaries owned by the current user	Oracle8*i*

Subprograms, Methods, and Triggers

The data dictionary views that describe stored subprograms (packaged and schema-level), methods of object types, and triggers are discussed in the following table.

Type of Object	Data Dictionary View	Contains Information About	Available in Release
Subprogram	`all_arguments`	Parameters to accessible stored subprograms (packaged and schema level)	Oracle7
	`user_arguments`	Parameters to the current user's stored subprograms (packaged and schema level)	Oracle7
Method	`all_method_params`	Parameters to methods of accessible object types	Oracle8
	`dba_method_params`	Parameters to methods of all object types	Oracle8

Type of Object	Data Dictionary View	Contains Information About	Available in Release
	`user_method_params`	Parameters to methods of the current user's object types	Oracle8
	`all_method_results`	Return values of methods of accessible object types	Oracle8
	`dba_method_results`	Return values of methods of all object types	Oracle8
	`user_method_results`	Return values of methods of the current user's object types	Oracle8
Triggers	`all_internal_triggers`	Internal triggers on accessible tables	Oracle8i
	`dba_internal_triggers`	Internal triggers on all tables	Oracle8i
	`user_internal_triggers`	Internal triggers on tables owned by the current user	Oracle8i
	`all_triggers`	Accessible database triggers	Oracle7
	`dba_triggers`	All database triggers	Oracle7
	`user_triggers`	Database triggers owned by the current user	Oracle7
	`all_trigger_cols`	Columns used in accessible triggers	Oracle7
	`dba_trigger_cols`	Columns used in all triggers	Oracle7
	`user_trigger_cols`	Columns used in triggers owned by the current user	Oracle7

Source Code and Compile Errors

The views in this section describe the source code for various type of objects, as well as compile errors in that source code. The code for triggers can be found in the `*_triggers` views, described in the previous section.

Data Dictionary View	Description	Available in Release
all_errors	Compile errors for accessible views, packages, package bodies, functions, procedures, object types, object type bodies, and triggers	Oracle7
dba_errors	Compile errors for all views, packages, package bodies, functions, procedures, object types, object type bodies, and triggers	Oracle7
user_errors	Compile errors for the current user's views, packages, package bodies, functions, procedures, object types, object type bodies, and triggers	Oracle7
all_source	Source code for accessible packages, package bodies, object types, object type bodies, functions, and procedures	Oracle7
dba_source	Source code for all packages, package bodies, object types, object type bodies, functions, and procedures	Oracle7
user_source	Source code for the current user's packages, package bodies, object types, object type bodies, functions, and procedures	Oracle7

Dependencies and Constraints

Dependencies and constraints represent the relationships between types of database objects, and are documented by the following data dictionary views:

Category	Data Dictionary View	Contains Information About	Available in Release
Dependencies	all_dependencies	Dependencies between accessible objects	Oracle7
	dba_dependencies	Dependencies between all objects	Oracle7

Category	Data Dictionary View	Contains Information About	Available in Release
	`user_dependencies`	Dependencies between the current user's objects	Oracle7
Constraints	`all_cons_columns`	Columns in constraints on accessible tables	Oracle7
	`dba_cons_columns`	Columns in constraints on all tables	Oracle7
	`user_cons_columns`	Columns in constraints on the current user's tables	Oracle7
	`all_constraints`	Constraints on accessible tables	Oracle7
	`dba_constraints`	Constraints on all tables	Oracle7
	`user_constraints`	Constraints on the current user's tables	Oracle7

Statistics and Auditing

Database statistics and auditing allow you to collect information about, and log changes to, other types of database objects.

Category	Data Dictionary View	Contains Information About	Available in Release
Statistics	`all_associations`	User-defined statistics for all accessible objects	Oracle8*i*
	`dba_associations`	User-defined statistics for all database objects	Oracle8*i*
	`user_associations`	User-defined statistics for the current user's database objects	Oracle8*i*
	`all_ustats`	Statistics for accessible objects	Oracle8*i*
	`dba_ustats`	Statistics for all objects	Oracle8*i*
	`user_ustats`	Statistics for the current user's objects	Oracle8*i*

Category	Data Dictionary View	Contains Information About	Available in Release
	all_tab_col_ statistics	Statistics on accessible table columns	Oracle8
	dba_tab_col_ statistics	Statistics on all table columns	Oracle8
	user_tab_col_ statistics	Statistics on the current user's tables	Oracle8
	all_tab_histograms	Histograms on accessible tables and views	Oracle8
	dba_tab_histograms	Histograms on all database tables and views	Oracle8
	user_tab_ histograms	Histograms on the current user's tables and views	Oracle8
Database auditing	all_def_audit_opts	Default auditing options on accessible objects	Oracle7
	audit_actions	Descriptions of audit trail type codes	Oracle7

Privileges and Grants

The data dictionary views described in the following table document the column, table, and system privileges GRANTed to users and roles.

Type of Privilege or Grant	Data Dictionary View	Contains Information About	Available in Release
Column privileges	all_col_privs	Grants on table or view columns for which the user or PUBLIC is the grantee	Oracle7
	dba_col_privs	Grants on all table or view columns	Oracle7

Type of Privilege or Grant	Data Dictionary View	Contains Information About	Available in Release
	user_col_privs	Grants on accessible table or view columns for which the user is the owner, grantor, or grantee	Oracle7
	all_col_privs_made	Grants on table or view columns for which the user is the owner or grantor	Oracle7
	user_col_privs_made	Grants on the current user's table or view columns	Oracle7
	all_col_privs_recd	Grants on table or view columns for which the user or PUBLIC is the grantee	Oracle7
	user_col_privs_recd	Grants on table or view columns for which the user is the grantee	Oracle7
Table privileges	all_tab_privs	Grants on objects for which the user or PUBLIC is the grantee	Oracle7
	dba_tab_privs	Grants on all database objects	Oracle7
	user_tab_privs	Grants on objects for which the user is the owner, grantor, or grantee	Oracle7
	all_tab_privs_made	Grants on objects for which the user is the owner or grantor	Oracle7
	user_tab_privs_made	Grants on the current user's objects	Oracle7
	all_tab_privs_recd	Grants on objects for which the user or PUBLIC is the grantee	Oracle7

Type of Privilege or Grant	Data Dictionary View	Contains Information About	Available in Release
	`user_tab_privs_recd`	Grants on objects for which the user is the grantee	Oracle7
System privileges	`dba_sys_privs`	All system privileges granted in the database	Oracle7
	`user_sys_privs`	System privileges granted to the user	Oracle7

Index

D

INTERNATIONAL CONTACT INFORMATION

AUSTRALIA
McGraw-Hill Book Company Australia Pty. Ltd.
TEL +61-2-9417-9899
FAX +61-2-9417-5687
http://www.mcgraw-hill.com.au
books-it_sydney@mcgraw-hill.com

CANADA
McGraw-Hill Ryerson Ltd.
TEL +905-430-5000
FAX +905-430-5020
http://www.mcgrawhill.ca

GREECE, MIDDLE EAST,
NORTHERN AFRICA
McGraw-Hill Hellas
TEL +30-1-656-0990-3-4
FAX +30-1-654-5525

MEXICO (Also serving Latin America)
McGraw-Hill Interamericana Editores S.A. de C.V.
TEL +525-117-1583
FAX +525-117-1589
http://www.mcgraw-hill.com.mx
fernando_castellanos@mcgraw-hill.com

SINGAPORE (Serving Asia)
McGraw-Hill Book Company
TEL +65-863-1580
FAX +65-862-3354
http://www.mcgraw-hill.com.sg
mghasia@mcgraw-hill.com

SOUTH AFRICA
McGraw-Hill South Africa
TEL +27-11-622-7512
FAX +27-11-622-9045
robyn_swanepoel@mcgraw-hill.com

UNITED KINGDOM & EUROPE
(Excluding Southern Europe)
McGraw-Hill Education Europe
TEL +44-1-628-502500
FAX +44-1-628-770224
http://www.mcgraw-hill.co.uk
computing_neurope@mcgraw-hill.com

ALL OTHER INQUIRIES Contact:
Osborne/McGraw-Hill
TEL +1-510-549-6600
FAX +1-510-883-7600
http://www.osborne.com
omg_international@mcgraw-hill.com

Get Your **FREE** Subscription to *Oracle Magazine*

Oracle Magazine is essential gear for today's information technology professionals. Stay informed and increase your productivity with every issue of *Oracle Magazine*. Inside each **FREE,** bimonthly issue you'll get:

- Up-to-date information on Oracle Database Server, Oracle Applications, Internet Computing, and tools
- Third-party news and announcements
- Technical articles on Oracle products and operating environments
- Development and administration tips
- Real-world customer stories

Three easy ways to subscribe:

1. Web   **Visit our Web site at www.oracle.com/oramag/. You'll find a subscription form there, plus much more!**

2. Fax   Complete the questionnaire on the back of this card and fax the questionnaire side only to **+1.847.647.9735.**

3. Mail   Complete the questionnaire on the back of this card and mail it to P.O. Box 1263, Skokie, IL 60076-8263.

If there are other Oracle users at your location who would like to receive their own subscription to *Oracle Magazine*, please photocopy this form and pass it along.

☐ YES! Please send me a FREE subscription to *Oracle Magazine*. ☐ NO

To receive a free bimonthly subscription to *Oracle Magazine*, you must fill out the entire card, sign it, and date it (incomplete cards cannot be processed or acknowledged). You can also fax your application to +1.847.647.9735. Or subscribe at our Web site at www.oracle.com/oramag/

SIGNATURE (REQUIRED)	X	DATE	

NAME _____ TITLE _____

COMPANY _____ TELEPHONE _____

ADDRESS _____ FAX NUMBER _____

CITY _____ STATE _____ POSTAL CODE/ZIP CODE _____

COUNTRY _____ E-MAIL ADDRESS _____

☐ From time to time, Oracle Publishing allows our partners exclusive access to our e-mail addresses for special promotions and announcements. To be included in this program, please check this box.

You must answer all eight questions below.

1 What is the primary business activity of your firm at this location? *(check only one)*
- ☐ 03 Communications
- ☐ 04 Consulting, Training
- ☐ 06 Data Processing
- ☐ 07 Education
- ☐ 08 Engineering
- ☐ 09 Financial Services
- ☐ 10 Government—Federal, Local, State, Other
- ☐ 11 Government—Military
- ☐ 12 Health Care
- ☐ 13 Manufacturing—Aerospace, Defense
- ☐ 14 Manufacturing—Computer Hardware
- ☐ 15 Manufacturing—Noncomputer Products
- ☐ 17 Research & Development
- ☐ 19 Retailing, Wholesaling, Distribution
- ☐ 20 Software Development
- ☐ 21 Systems Integration, VAR, VAD, OEM
- ☐ 22 Transportation
- ☐ 23 Utilities (Electric, Gas, Sanitation)
- ☐ 98 Other Business and Services _____

2 Which of the following best describes your job function? *(check only one)*

CORPORATE MANAGEMENT/STAFF
- ☐ 01 Executive Management (President, Chair, CEO, CFO, Owner, Partner, Principal)
- ☐ 02 Finance/Administrative Management (VP/Director/ Manager/Controller, Purchasing, Administration)
- ☐ 03 Sales/Marketing Management (VP/Director/Manager)
- ☐ 04 Computer Systems/Operations Management (CIO/VP/Director/ Manager MIS, Operations)

IS/IT STAFF
- ☐ 07 Systems Development/ Programming Management
- ☐ 08 Systems Development/ Programming Staff
- ☐ 09 Consulting
- ☐ 10 DBA/Systems Administrator
- ☐ 11 Education/Training
- ☐ 14 Technical Support Director/ Manager
- ☐ 16 Other Technical Management/Staff
- ☐ 98 Other _____

3 What is your current primary operating platform? *(check all that apply)*
- ☐ 01 DEC UNIX
- ☐ 02 DEC VAX VMS
- ☐ 03 Java
- ☐ 04 HP UNIX
- ☐ 05 IBM AIX
- ☐ 06 IBM UNIX
- ☐ 07 Macintosh
- ☐ 09 MS-DOS
- ☐ 10 MVS
- ☐ 11 NetWare
- ☐ 12 Network Computing
- ☐ 13 OpenVMS
- ☐ 14 SCO UNIX
- ☐ 24 Sequent DYNIX/ptx
- ☐ 15 Sun Solaris/SunOS
- ☐ 16 SVR4
- ☐ 18 UnixWare
- ☐ 20 Windows
- ☐ 21 Windows NT
- ☐ 23 Other UNIX _____
- ☐ 98 Other _____
- 99 ☐ **None of the above**

4 Do you evaluate, specify, recommend, or authorize the purchase of any of the following? *(check all that apply)*
- ☐ 01 Hardware
- ☐ 02 Software
- ☐ 03 Application Development Tools
- ☐ 04 Database Products
- ☐ 05 Internet or Intranet Products
- 99 ☐ **None of the above**

5 In your job, do you use or plan to purchase any of the following products or services? *(check all that apply)*

SOFTWARE
- ☐ 01 Business Graphics
- ☐ 02 CAD/CAE/CAM
- ☐ 03 CASE
- ☐ 05 Communications
- ☐ 06 Database Management
- ☐ 07 File Management
- ☐ 08 Finance
- ☐ 09 Java
- ☐ 10 Materials Resource Planning
- ☐ 11 Multimedia Authoring
- ☐ 12 Networking
- ☐ 13 Office Automation
- ☐ 14 Order Entry/Inventory Control
- ☐ 15 Programming
- ☐ 16 Project Management
- ☐ 17 Scientific and Engineering
- ☐ 18 Spreadsheets
- ☐ 19 Systems Management
- ☐ 20 Workflow

HARDWARE
- ☐ 21 Macintosh
- ☐ 22 Mainframe
- ☐ 23 Massively Parallel Processing
- ☐ 24 Minicomputer
- ☐ 25 PC
- ☐ 26 Network Computer
- ☐ 28 Symmetric Multiprocessing
- ☐ 29 Workstation

PERIPHERALS
- ☐ 30 Bridges/Routers/Hubs/Gateways
- ☐ 31 CD-ROM Drives
- ☐ 32 Disk Drives/Subsystems
- ☐ 33 Modems
- ☐ 34 Tape Drives/Subsystems
- ☐ 35 Video Boards/Multimedia

SERVICES
- ☐ 37 Consulting
- ☐ 38 Education/Training
- ☐ 39 Maintenance
- ☐ 40 Online Database Services
- ☐ 41 Support
- ☐ 36 Technology-Based Training
- ☐ 98 Other _____
- 99 ☐ **None of the above**

6 What Oracle products are in use at your site? *(check all that apply)*

SERVER/SOFTWARE
- ☐ 01 Oracle8
- ☐ 30 Oracle8*i*
- ☐ 31 Oracle8*i* Lite
- ☐ 02 Oracle7
- ☐ 03 Oracle Application Server
- ☐ 04 Oracle Data Mart Suites
- ☐ 05 Oracle Internet Commerce Server
- ☐ 32 Oracle *inter*Media
- ☐ 33 Oracle JServer
- ☐ 07 Oracle Lite
- ☐ 08 Oracle Payment Server
- ☐ 11 Oracle Video Server

TOOLS
- ☐ 13 Oracle Designer
- ☐ 14 Oracle Developer
- ☐ 54 Oracle Discoverer
- ☐ 53 Oracle Express
- ☐ 51 Oracle JDeveloper
- ☐ 52 Oracle Reports
- ☐ 50 Oracle WebDB
- ☐ 55 Oracle Workflow

ORACLE APPLICATIONS
- ☐ 17 Oracle Automotive
- ☐ 35 Oracle Business Intelligence System
- ☐ 19 Oracle Consumer Packaged Goods
- ☐ 39 Oracle E-Commerce
- ☐ 18 Oracle Energy
- ☐ 20 Oracle Financials
- ☐ 28 Oracle Front Office
- ☐ 21 Oracle Human Resources
- ☐ 37 Oracle Internet Procurement
- ☐ 22 Oracle Manufacturing
- ☐ 40 Oracle Process Manufacturing
- ☐ 23 Oracle Projects
- ☐ 34 Oracle Retail
- ☐ 29 Oracle Self-Service Web Applications
- ☐ 38 Oracle Strategic Enterprise Management
- ☐ 25 Oracle Supply Chain Management
- ☐ 36 Oracle Tutor
- ☐ 41 Oracle Travel Management

ORACLE SERVICES
- ☐ 61 Oracle Consulting
- ☐ 62 Oracle Education
- ☐ 60 Oracle Support
- ☐ 98 Other _____
- 99 ☐ **None of the above**

7 What other database products are in use at your site? *(check all that apply)*
- ☐ 01 Access
- ☐ 02 Baan
- ☐ 03 dbase
- ☐ 04 Gupta
- ☐ 05 IBM DB2
- ☐ 06 Informix
- ☐ 07 Ingres
- ☐ 08 Microsoft Access
- ☐ 09 Microsoft SQL Server
- ☐ 10 PeopleSoft
- ☐ 11 Progress
- ☐ 12 SAP
- ☐ 13 Sybase
- ☐ 14 VSAM
- ☐ 98 Other _____
- 99 ☐ **None of the above**

8 During the next 12 months, how much do you anticipate your organization will spend on computer hardware, software, peripherals, and services for your location? *(check only one)*
- ☐ 01 Less than $10,000
- ☐ 02 $10,000 to $49,999
- ☐ 03 $50,000 to $99,999
- ☐ 04 $100,000 to $499,999
- ☐ 05 $500,000 to $999,999
- ☐ 06 $1,000,000 and over

If there are other Oracle users at your location who would like to receive a free subscription to *Oracle Magazine*, please photocopy this form and pass it along, or contact Customer Service at +1.847.647.9630

Form 5

OPRESS

Knowledge is power. To which we say,

crank up the power.

Are you ready for a power surge?

Accelerate your career—become an **Oracle Certified Professional (OCP)**. With Oracle's cutting-edge *Instructor-Led Training*, *Technology-Based Training*, and this *guide*, you can prepare for certification faster than ever. Set your own trajectory by logging your personal training plan with us. Go to **http://education.oracle.com/tpb**, where we'll help you pick a training path, select your courses, and track your progress. We'll even send you an email when your courses are offered in your area. If you don't have access to the Web, call us at 1-800-441-3541 (Outside the U.S. call +1-310-335-2403). **Power learning has never been easier.**

ORACLE
University

About the CD-ROM

nside the back cover of this book you will find the CD-ROM that accompanies *Oracle9i PL/SQL Programming*, by Scott Urman. The CD-ROM contains two types of information:

- Electronic versions of all of the examples used in this book. These can be found in the `code` directory. For information about these examples, see the `readme.html` file found in the `code` directory.

- Demo versions of six complete PL/SQL development environments from five different vendors. All of these tools are complete, and are licensed for a limited number of days. They are discussed in more detail in Chapter 2 of this book, and can be found in the `Development Tools` directory. The included tools are described here:

Tool	Version	Vendor
Rapid SQL	5.7.1	Embarcadero Technologies, **www.embarcadero.com**
DBPartner Debugger	4.0.1 (Build 83)	Compuware Corporation, **www.compuware.com**
SQL Navigator 3	3.2d11	Quest Software, **www.quest.com**
TOAD	7.1.7.21	Quest Software, **www.quest.com**
SQL-Programmer	11.01.0	BMC Software, **www.bmc.com**
PL/SQL Developer	4.0.3.415	Allround Automations, **www.allroundautomations.nl**

When you insert the CD-ROM on Windows systems, a small application will automatically start that contains more information about the CD-ROM, including details about how to install each of the tools and their license requirements. For more information, see `readme.html` in the root level of the CD-ROM.